Undoing Slavery

EARLY AMERICAN STUDIES

Series editors

Kathleen M. Brown
Roquinaldo Ferreira
Emma Hart
Daniel K. Richter

Exploring neglected aspects of our colonial, revolutionary, and early national history and culture, Early American Studies reinterprets familiar themes and events in fresh ways. Interdisciplinary in character, and with a special emphasis on the period from about 1600 to 1850, the series is published in partnership with the McNeil Center for Early American Studies.

A complete list of books in the series is available from the publisher.

UNDOING SLAVERY

Bodies, Race, and Rights in the Age of Abolition

Kathleen M. Brown

PENN

UNIVERSITY OF PENNSYLVANIA PRESS

PHILADELPHIA

Published by
University of Pennsylvania Press
Philadelphia, Pennsylvania 19104-4112
www.upenn.edu/pennpress

Printed in the United States of America on acid-free paper
10 9 8 7 6 5 4 3 2 1

Hardcover ISBN 9781512823271
Ebook ISBN 9781512823288
Library of Congress Cataloging-in-Publication Data
Names: Brown, Kathleen M., author.
Title: Undoing slavery : bodies, race, and rights in the age of abolition / Kathleen M. Brown.
Other titles: Early American studies.
Description: 1st edition. | Philadelphia : University of Pennsylvania Press, [2023] | Series: Early American studies | Includes bibliographical references and index.
Identifiers: LCCN 2022016201 |
ISBN 9781512823271 (hardcover)
Subjects: LCSH: Antislavery movements—North America—History. | Antislavery movements—Great Britain—History. | Human body—Political aspects—History. | Human body—Moral and ethical aspects—History.
Classification: LCC E441 .B748 2023 |
DDC 973.7/114—dc23/eng/20220609
LC record available at https://lccn.loc.gov/2022016201

For Angus,
and in memory of Robert David Corbett
(1931–2020)

Contents

Introduction: Abolitionist Body Politics 1

Chapter 1. Liberty of the Body 21

Chapter 2. Birthrights and Vindications 54

Chapter 3. One Blood 88

Chapter 4. Medical Materialism, Migration, and National Belonging 123

Chapter 5. In Search of Free Labor 164

Chapter 6. Maternal Blood and Tears 207

Chapter 7. Blood of the Fathers 252

Chapter 8. Liberating Bodies 292

Conclusion 335

List of Abbreviations 349

Notes 351

Index 427

Acknowledgments 443

Introduction

Abolitionist Body Politics

Veteran abolitionist and medical educator Sarah Mapps Douglass (1806–1882) had given this lecture on the circulation of the blood many times before. A human skull sat on the table next to her in the front of the hall. Behind her hung an anatomical drawing. Spectators craned their necks to see how she would use these props. Douglass usually drew audiences of several dozen women. Some attended out of curiosity, interested to witness an educated African American woman speak knowledgeably about the body's functions. Others hoped for a chance to tell her about the exhaustion they suffered from strenuous labor and long hours. A few women, eager to learn, had attended previous lectures or borrowed books that Douglass had recommended.[1]

On this Thursday evening in March 1861, however, the room was crowded with both "ladies and gentlemen." A member of Philadelphia's Mother Bethel African Methodist Episcopal Church reported for the *Christian Recorder* that Douglass held her audience "spell-bound" for over an hour with a lecture that ranged from the circulation of the blood in human beings to the physical lives of plants and animals. Although Douglass had delighted in the rigorous medical training she received from her teacher and fellow Quaker abolitionist, Ann Preston, at the Women's Medical College of Pennsylvania, she self-consciously omitted unwieldy scientific terms during her own lectures, choosing to impart information about anatomy and physiology in plain language. With this mixed audience of women and men, moreover, she delicately sidestepped female health problems and did not divulge her own suffering from a hernia and her resort to hydrotherapy to try to find relief.[2]

Speaking expertly and with a confidence that reflected nearly forty years of teaching, Douglass gracefully embodied the radical claim underpinning her lecture: human physiology, and with it, human intellect, knew no race. For Douglass, scientific knowledge about the circulation of blood "in creative beings" pointed to a universal foundation for sentient life. Acquiring knowledge about the common condition of flesh and blood was a first step to embracing fully the equality to which all were entitled and refuting the racist medical claims that African-descended bodies differed fundamentally from those of white people. For Douglass, it was also a matter of acknowledging "how marvelously has God fashioned these poor bodies" and honoring the duty to use them "to his glory."[3]

The scientific content of Douglass's lectures made her a trailblazer among African American women, but she was not the first African American to identify the body as key to the long fight against slavery and racism. Massachusetts-born Hosea Easton (1798–1837) intervened in scientific racism in 1837, at about the same time that Douglass concluded her career as an abolitionist poet and gave her full attention to activist teaching. Easton was a Congregational minister and the veteran of several protests against segregated church seating. In *A Treatise on the Intellectual Character and Civil and Political Condition of the Colored People of the U. States* (1837), Easton analyzed the plight of enslaved Africans and their descendants as one of stolen birthright, lineal rupture, and physiological as well as cultural adaptation. After being "lineally stolen from their native country, and detained for centuries in a strange land as hewers of wood and drawers of water," he observed, "their blood, habits, minds and bodies have undergone such a change, as to cause them to lose all legal or natural relations to their mother country." Having lost this connection to Africa, "they identified as belonging to no country—denied birthright in one, and had it stolen from them in another . . . they had lost title to both worlds." Easton's larger purpose was to analyze the damage slavery had inflicted on the intellectual and physical development of the enslaved, but he also denounced the racism that eroded beliefs in the unity of humankind. In a graphic and powerful section of his pamphlet, he recounted white people's quotidian denigrations of Black people's lips, noses, hair, feet, and skin with racial slurs. Many of the characteristics that white people ascribed to race, he argued, were in fact the consequence of slavery's brutalizing physiological impact on pregnant women and their offspring, a view that reflected his application of the widely accepted theory of maternal impressions to enslaved women.[4]

More typical of the abolitionist focus on bodies was Frederick Douglass's impassioned account of slavery's physical and moral violations. Speaking in the wake of the Fugitive Slave Act of 1850 and the consequent efforts of Vigilance Committees to protect enslaved refugees, Douglass (1818–1895, and no relation to Sarah Mapps Douglass) used the occasion of his July 4, 1852, address to indict slavery's pollution of its female victims and its leveraging of bodily pain to extract labor. Douglass was incredulous that this needed spelling out for his audience: "What, am I to argue that it is wrong to make men brutes, to rob them of their liberty, to work them without wages, to keep them ignorant of their relations to their fellow men, to beat them with sticks, to flay their flesh with the lash, to load their limbs with irons, to hunt them with dogs, to sell them at auction, to sunder their families, to knock out their teeth, to burn their flesh, to starve them into obedience and submission to their masters? Must I argue that a system thus marked with blood, and stained with pollution, is *wrong*?"[5]

Abolitionists like Easton, Frederick Douglass, and Sarah Mapps Douglass were at the center of a fight about Black bodies framed by the law of maternal inheritance and the growing commitments of science and medicine to concepts of biological race and racial hierarchy. They imagined and fought for liberty in embodied terms in the face of relentless judgments, threats, and material constraints. Their world was one in which most white people treated Black people as if their bodies were inherently out of place unless they were enslaved. Along with their fellow abolitionists, Easton, Douglass, and Douglass understood this treatment as a manifestation of the medical, legal, and economic colonization of African-descended people. For these activists, the condition of Black bodies provided the clearest evidence of their exploitation and set the terms for imagining both liberty and rights.

Taking a cue from these Black abolitionists and their most reliable white allies, this book chronicles the abolitionist pursuit of liberty for enslaved people in the body's own terms. By insisting that human rights were inseparable from relieving the bodily suffering of the enslaved, abolitionists challenged broader understandings of both human embodiment and legal personhood. My account departs from the popular view of a long humanitarian struggle to end slavery in which the legal recognition of universal rights, defined within an Enlightenment framework, opened the way for other crucial benefits centered on the citizen's need for protection from bodily harm. Rather, I argue, abolitionists advocated for the body's need for care and autonomy not as the hoped-for consequence of rights bearing, but as a necessary condition for achieving it. In taking this approach, they challenged the meaning of human rights for their own time to include the domestic, the intimate, and the bodily.

Undoing Slavery situates the abolitionist focus on bodies within a long history of debates about liberty, race, and motherhood. Abolitionists intervened crucially in the condition of millions of enslaved bodies as well as in the debates over the nature of race. It was an uphill battle. Over the course of two centuries, the scientific and popular understanding of race shifted from one in which bodies were understood to be imprinted by climate and experience to one in which race was believed to be innate. This shift was an outgrowth not only of scientific and medical racism but of the law—the federal and state protections of slave property that perpetuated slavery intergenerationally and obstructed people from claiming freedom for themselves and their children even if they escaped to so-called free states.

Abolitionists took aim at enslavers' power over the bodies of the enslaved, not simply as a matter of rights but of bodily violation. Numerous and staggering in their significance, the violations abolitionists condemned included the forcible removal of captives from African homelands, constraints on enslaved people's ability to move about at will, the colonization of women's bodies to produce children enslaved at birth, justifications of slavery with theories of unique Black anatomy, and the systemic separation of families. In addition to calling out these injuries, abolitionists engaged the bodies of consumers to try to undermine the coercive plantation regimes that depended on slave labor to produce cotton, sugar, rice, and tobacco. All of these forms of activism, I argue, constituted abolitionist body politics.

My decision to take the abolitionist focus on the body seriously, on its own terms, was prompted in part by several incongruities. Inheritable slavery, coercively perpetuated in the bodies of enslaved women and deeply embedded in the political economy of slavery, appeared to function as the cornerstone for biological race; yet, contests over the significance of the place of the child's birth and the status of the mother's womb revealed to contemporaries that this was instead a matter of jurisdictional authority. An enslaved woman's capacity (in theory) to give birth to a free child if she crossed into a free state clashed with both federal protections of enslavers' property and racist medical claims that insisted on African-descended people's innate and inherited suitability for slavery. In addition, I wondered why, beyond the obvious reason of his own interests in property, President Thomas Jefferson, the father of at least six children by an enslaved woman, all of whom he owned, looked to the Atlantic rather than to the domestic slave trade when he offered one of the first U.S. denunciations of violated "human rights." Finally, I also confronted activists' own experiences with slavery, illness, and bodily risk in tempering bold claims about the universal condition of the human body.

Viewing abolition from a perspective informed by abolitionists' engagement with enslaved bodies has yielded an interpretation at odds with both human rights history and critics of that history. Abolitionists gave human rights a pragmatic and domestic inflection that has not been acknowledged by most human rights scholars. Intimate family relationships and responsibilities became as important to abolitionists as the rights of unimpeded and uncoerced travel and the privileges of citizenship. The focus on the body brought family integrity, especially the mother-child relationship, care of the body, and the right to move at will into the frame of human rights. An individual's physical suffering, abolitionists believed, moreover, revealed the immorality of rights deprivations. Ahead of their time, abolitionists focused on bodily well-being, a concern eventually picked up by twentieth-century human rights advocates that also had the unfortunate result of creating normative standards for gender, family, and political economy.[6]

Examining the activist engagement with enslaved bodies requires a historical approach not only to medicine and law but to the human body itself. How did abolitionists comprehend the body, its capacities, and its vulnerabilities to harm? How did their views of the body vary according to their own social locations as free or enslaved, male or female, African-descended or white? How did they mobilize these understandings for political purposes and to what degree did this mobilization contribute to transforming popular understandings of the body? Informed by these questions, I approach the historical body through nineteenth-century assessments as encompassing the blood, the incarnation of will into action, and the sensory apparatus of lived experience that present-day advocates of social medicine, like their abolitionist forbears, believe may accumulate the harms of trauma, illness, and injury. All of these attributes of the material body reflected specific social, cultural, and epidemiological contexts, presenting a daunting task for the historian who hopes to extricate enslaved people's own bodily experiences from their subjection to enslavers' economies and epistemologies.[7]

The long history of attempts to use a biological notion of race to justify slavery and white supremacy has rightly made scholars of both slavery and diasporic Africa wary of a focus on the body. Approaching the fight to end slavery as a struggle over the control of Black bodies might seem to risk reiterating one of the main racist claims of slavery's defenders: that enslaved people were in their very essence merely exploitable laboring bodies who lacked intellectual capacity. Scholars who have documented African American legal, intellectual, religious, and political thought have intervened crucially in this racist assumption about Black historical subjects. Others have chronicled the rise of racist medicine and its pernicious legacies or recovered Black efforts to create scientific counterdiscourses. Rather than acquiesce to the notion that a focus on bodies unwittingly reinforces biological concepts of race, I examine nineteenth-century abolitionist beliefs in the body's impressionability on their own terms while keeping in mind twenty-first-century insights into the body's limited capacity to rebound from injurious conditions.[8]

As historians of the body have shown, the human body has its own stubborn logic. This was especially the case for slavery, which marked all in its wake. The Reverend Easton was eloquent on this point: whether suffering from the lash herself or witnessing another's suffering, an enslaved mother transmitted the injury to her unborn child. Even when emancipation lifted the formal constraints of slavery, former slaves could not shed bodies that had been beaten, disabled, malnourished, diseased, sexually abused, and traumatized by the loss of family connection. The abolitionist focus on the body, then, was important not just for the well-being of an immediate generation of enslaved people, but for the potential of subsequent generations to attain justice in the intimate terms of the body.[9]

Much like present-day practitioners of social medicine who warn against the negative impact of poverty, violence, pollution, and terror, abolitionist activists believed that the body's plasticity left it vulnerable to being physically imprinted by historical experiences. They argued that the mundane practices of both slavery and racism could get "under the skin," leaving those who would undo this harm with a problem deeply embedded in the bodies and psyches of its victims. Plasticity, however, had benefits; it meant that an injured or deprived body might heal or improve its capacities. In bringing body-centered legal, medical, and emotional-familial arguments about the humanity of the enslaved to bear on the larger issue of abolition, activists also contributed to shifting the meaning of key medical and legal terms, including "blood," "family," and "mother." In all of these endeavors, whether or not they intended to, abolitionists defined a normative human condition. Yet in their arguments about slavery's harmful impact and their development of practices of self and communal care, abolitionists acknowledged that distinct social locations turned universal truths into unique experiences and bodily conditions. The human condition might be universal, but there was not just one enslaved or one abolitionist body. Enslaved mothers, for example, had few buffers protecting them from bodily suffering but were nonetheless uniquely responsible for determining the status of their children. Sarah Mapps Douglass's mission to teach Black girls and women about their bodies recognized these as urgent needs for medical knowledge and care to counter racist medicine and exploitation.[10]

Bodies, of course, are never just flesh and blood but include functions like movement, thought, and emotions that are all components of "being." In the analysis that follows, I trace changes in several key beliefs about the body and its workings that framed the abolition movement: that the blood, in all of its many meanings, was the main source of the body's vitality and identity; that the body adapted to external circumstances like diet, labor, and climate; and that the mind, rather than being distinct from the body, could be best understood through the scientific mapping of the brain's structures. Of special interest is how nineteenth-century understandings of the body as "impressionable" to climate and circumstance gave way to a notion of inherited biological race.

Eighteenth- and nineteenth-century theologians, artists, poets, political theorists, and authors of legal treatises ranked matters of mind, spirit, and soul above those of the body, which was often depicted as base, animal, and a source of moral depravity. Colonized people, particularly women of African descent, were commonly depicted as lacking the spiritual and intellectual capacities that might have offset the determinism of their bodies. Some, like Phillis Wheatley, Mary Wollstonecraft, and Olaudah Equiano were at pains to prove that they could transcend what was understood as the constraints of their raced and sexed bodies. Yet even these pioneering rights advocates grounded their arguments against slavery in critiques of physical coercion. Within two generations of these late eighteenth-century radical voices, moreover, most abolitionists explicitly embraced a gender-conforming body as the foundation of natural rights universalism. Activists also witnessed a major departure from the Western and Judeo-Christian mind-body dichotomy that was to have a lasting impact on beliefs in biological foundations for race and sex difference: phrenology, the new science of the mind, which located physical, emotional, and intellectual capacities in the brain's structures. As we will see, phrenology theorized progressive possibilities for developing the brain's capacities; but its identification of a material basis for both individual and racial population traits undermined the potential universalism of human rights and liberties that had only recently emerged during the Atlantic revolutions in North America, France, and Saint Domingue.[11]

Changing medical views of the body took place against a backdrop of eighteenth- and nineteenth-century colonial geopolitical transformation, in which some populations gained significant freedoms to move at will while others lost either their mobility or their right to stay put. Representations of the body, its functions, and its suffering were powerful in part because they seemed to require little translation across regional and national boundaries, thus facilitating international networks and alliances. Taken collectively, the representational, documentary, and material record of bodies provides the historian with an archive that reveals changing patterns of labor, forced migration, escape, disease, reproduction, and state-sanctioned violence.[12]

A body-centered approach to abolition entails recognizing the movement's frequent invocation of the body as part of its first order of business: to unravel long-lived global practices of violence designed to extract labor from people whose entire persons were understood to be owned by others. These practices ranged from the threats of physical punishment to the engineered precariousness of intimate family relations used by enslavers to extract value from bound laborers. It means acknowledging that the violence inherent in slavery had immediate physical, although not only physical, consequences with long-lasting effects on victims. It means tracking activist methods that often required physical exertion and resistance, even when those methods were mundane and nonviolent. And it means recognizing abolitionist confrontations with new forms of bodily exploitation, constraint, and knowledge production that obstructed their undoing efforts. Abolitionists may have aspired to liberating enslaved bodies, but racist and regulatory reactions to escape, manumission, and emancipation, such as the laws curtailing free Black legal rights, effectively limited Black bodily freedoms. As they engaged in this long-term struggle, activists witnessed dramatic changes in their contemporaries' understandings of the body and the characteristics they attributed to race. In attempting to reconcile their own experiences with the conventional Western mind-body binary, some abolitionists recognized that there could be no meaningful exercise of rights separate from the well-being and integrity of the bodies of those who claimed these rights.[13]

* * *

Tracking the changing body politics of transatlantic slavery, settler colonialism, and slave maternity reveals a complex history of actual birth, medical racism, and abrogated legal personhood. Activists were inspired by religious beliefs in a universal human condition and the persistent struggles of African-descended people for liberation. Their efforts to counter racist legal and medical constraints on Black people required arguments about human bodies as well as direct intervention with their own bodies. The history I recount here begins with a critical intellectual genealogy of early modern articulations of human rights as being divinely wired in the human body but expressed through political relationships with sovereign rulers. Within this formulation, entitlements to liberty were narrowly understood to belong to Europeans. Early modern rights theorists described the embodied nature of rights variously as natural rights, birthright, rights of Englishmen, breathing the free or pure air of England, and claims to be of "one blood." Many of these concepts reflected Roman definitions of citizenship based on *jus sanguinis* (law of blood or ancestry) and *jus soli* (law of soil or birthplace) and pointed to the entangled meanings of "subject" and "human" within early modern European national spaces. Both definitions silently evoked the maternal connection to the newborn child.[14]

Historically, the body provided an important context and framework for the meanings of "liberty" and "slavery." At the heart of the relationship between sovereign and subject was the sovereign's pledge to protect the subject's body in exchange for the subject's loyalty and bodily sacrifice. From this embodied foundation for subjecthood, the concept of legal personhood emerged during the seventeenth and eighteenth centuries.[15] Abolitionists imagined "liberty" as the embodied realization of rights endowed by natural law. They based many of their claims on the premise that a person came by these rights at birth and could not be alienated from them any more than personhood could be asserted or sustained in the absence of a body. With birth, in other words, came physical existence in the world, and so began the individual's endowment with natural rights. Birthright, a concept rooted in medieval political theory about the subject's relation to the monarch, was the key to inalienable political rights. We might note here that, without motherhood, there could be no birthright, a requirement that natural rights theorists overlooked. But what could "birthright" mean in a system that, by the nineteenth century, relied on a law of maternal inheritance to reproduce the enslaved labor force? Birthright thus became a key concept in the effort to undo slavery's reproduction of itself by colonizing the bodies of enslaved women. It motivated the sentimental focus on enslaved mothers. It also played a role in the process through which self-emancipating refugees figured their successful escapes as a rebirth of new, liberated, selves.[16]

Enslaved people, originally defined as the property of enslavers rather than as subjects of the monarch and never conceived of as owning themselves, remained uniquely unprotected from violence resulting in damaged flesh and bone and appropriated blood, semen, milk, and sweat. Calling out these violations at the core of slavery, some abolitionists described the slave's cause as being driven by the need to comply with transcendent natural law, while others depicted it as removing the obstacles to self-ownership in Lockean terms. Still others presented their opposition to slavery as a critique of the excessive and abusive power of masters, a denunciation of enslavers' efforts to treat slaves like animals rather than humans. Among the most powerful blows to U.S. slavery came from the enslaved themselves when they escaped slave state jurisdictions, striking a blow not only for their own autonomy but against the financial networks that defined them as security for plantation debts.[17]

Building on these foundations, abolitionists across nearly three centuries asserted a standard of bodily justice rooted in divinely sanctioned natural law as both the foundation for human rights and the criteria for judging its violations. This standard for bodily integrity and well-being proved important for activists as varied as pacifist moral suasionists, political reformers, militants advocating violent resistance, and healers. The focus on the body also provided the foundation for other analyses of power and ultimately had implications for legal rights and medical approaches to all bodies. One such issue concerned the imprint left by slavery on the bodies of the enslaved. Although often it was not in their interest to calculate slavery's costs in permanent damage to Black people, the logic of abolitionist arguments pointed to these traumas as producing profound damage that continued to impair the body even after an enslaved person fled to a free jurisdiction or became emancipated. It was an uncomfortable truth: although emancipation represented a form of political birth, it could not yield new bodies unscarred by decades of coerced labor. Slavery's traces would remain on the bodies of those who survived it, etching memories of abuse and disability into the skin, flesh, and psyches even of those who managed to cross jurisdictional boundaries into freedom.[18]

Some medical men of the mid-nineteenth century aspiring to professional and cultural authority engaged in their own form of body politics to defend slavery. They rejected the plastic body of abolitionist discourse, damaged by the historical experience of slavery until it could be restored by emancipation, and argued instead for innate and permanent deficiency and disability of enslaved people. By the late eighteenth century, scientific racists had offered increasingly elaborate theories of racial difference. Backed by evidence of sketchy provenance, nineteenth-century doctors built on this intellectual foundation to claim that, in contrast to white people, people of African descent along with many other colonized populations had been endowed by both God and nature with bodies well-suited to enslavement, arduous plantation labor, and tropical climates, and given to precocious sexual maturity. Doctors eager for authority as medical professionals and expert legal witnesses offered testimony in disputes over inheritance, racial identity, homicide, and slave "soundness." For these medical men, race resided in specific body parts and could be detected in the shape of feet, leg bones, the female pelvis, cranial shape and capacity, hair, and skin. African descent had become a racial destiny akin to a disability, according to these physicians, and it justified perpetual slavery and legal incapacity.[19] Racist science and medicine became more entrenched in the medical profession during the nineteenth century and gathered new momentum after emancipation in 1865, as figures from across the political spectrum mobilized the concept of biological race to support white supremacy.[20]

Following nearly three centuries of efforts to liberate enslaved bodies reveals an undoing process with unexpected twists and turns rather than a straightforward campaign for expanding rights already defined under a U.S. rights-based legal system. To undo slavery was to become mired in the fleshy politics of transforming coerced agricultural labor and inherited slave status, countering medical theories about the biological basis of race, and challenging the enduring institutions of slavery's political economy. Escape, rebellion, family reclamations, the provision of care to refugees, dissenting public speech, and consumer boycotts were all crucial to this work. As abolitionists analyzed what it would mean to undo the mechanisms of coercion, they continually discovered pathways and practices complicit in slavery that limited freedom of movement, undermined the capacity of the newly emancipated to work for their own benefit, obstructed their ability to gain education, silenced activists, and slowly eroded or dramatically ruptured family ties.[21]

Many of the abolitionist projects analyzed here can be understood as the pursuit by both Black and white abolitionists of "embodied self-sovereignty," an analytical rubric of my own making rather than an actors' category, which had special resonance for enslaved women. Abolitionists' use of this pragmatic approach to embodied rights reflects efforts to define affirmative rights of self-protection for the disempowered. Embodied self-sovereignty was neither a license for mastery nor necessarily reducible to self-ownership, even though some abolitionists made claims for enslaved people using these terms. In communities like those in the United States in which sharp power inequities prevailed, embodied self-sovereignty was a protective rights claim with pragmatic, material meanings for those who pursued it. Understanding abolitionist activism as grounded in ideals of embodied self-sovereignty helps us to make sense of the central place of the body in abolitionist rights claims and the disproportionate number of abolitionists whose activism on behalf of the enslaved included healing and medicine as a means of countering slavery's disabling effects and scientific racism's toxic impact.[22]

Abolitionists imagined embodied self-sovereignty as a bundle of natural rights given meaning by exertions as laborers and membership in family, community, and nation. In its ideal state, this form of self-sovereignty incorporated a right to "belonging" based on physical proximity that arose from these human connections and precluded the coerced separations, sales, and migrations that turned enslaved people into property "belonging" to enslavers. It drew on a concept of birthright protections needed by all people if they were to enjoy uncoerced relationships in the world they shared with other rights bearers. Advancing embodied self-sovereignty was not a matter of physical assertion alone but required creativity and deep spiritual, political, and emotional resources. Embodied self-sovereignty derived from and fostered a sense of self, belonging, and value separate from the assessments of enslavers and markets.[23]

As part of the larger pursuit of embodied self-sovereignty, abolitionists raised critical questions about capitalism: Could capitalism be remade by leveraging the power of the consumer to create a new body politics, one that materialized the abstraction of commodification by connecting the bodies of enslaved producers with those of consumers? As participants in consumer boycotts of slave-produced goods, abolitionists revealed the connections between consumer habits and the continuing economic viability of slavery. They took aim at one of the central impediments to their vision of a world without slavery: the economic impact of human property on white wealth creation. Strategic silences in the U.S. Constitution created a relationship between federal and state governments that protected slave property. In addition to the value of slaves' productive and reproductive labor, enslavers used enslaved people as collateral for loans and to establish credit. Plantation productivity calculated on the basis of numbers of "hands," moreover, reduced whole persons to fragmented, commodified body parts. This subsuming of the slave's personhood under the legal definition of property manifested itself in mundane cruelties justified by enslavers as property rights. With each snap of the whip, restraining clamp of the manacles, and violent imposition of an enslaver's body to break the will of the enslaved, the property relation became material in the body's own terms.[24]

Approaching abolition through the history of the body opens new interpretive possibilities for the relationship between capitalism and slavery. It was no accident that the abolitionist project occurred at a particular moment in capitalism's reinvention and reevaluation of labor. Taking global approaches and expanding their definitions of capitalism, recent histories of capitalism have challenged the usefulness of U.S. regional distinctions and stressed instead the capitalist methods of plantation management and enslavers' participation in global economies. Yet these insights come at a cost: most global histories of capitalism emphasize supply-side and public narratives over domestic life and household economies, obscuring slavery's essential function of extracting labor from bodies and abolition's reliance on the household resources of female abolitionists.[25]

Missing from many of these recent studies of "slavery's capitalism" is the significance of extracting both *labor and laborers* from the bodies of enslaved women in the United States. In addition, much materialist analysis, from Marx to the new histories of capitalism, fails to account for the capital accumulation made possible by women's multiple labors and the consequences of capitalism's project of extracting and separating wage labor from the responsibilities for producing, nurturing, comforting, and healing laboring bodies. As several scholars have shown, these kinds of omissions are especially serious for how we understand the lives of enslaved women. A materialist analysis of the body reveals the combined impact of exploited reproductivity and domestic labor on enslaved women, making them crucial to slavery's profitability but also to historians' efforts to grapple with slavery's staggering toll on Black personhood. After the end of the transatlantic trade, British policymakers addressed concerns about the Caribbean labor supply by encouraging the reproductivity and nurturing work of enslaved women. This was also true in the United States, especially in Virginia, where enslaved populations grew at greater rates than elsewhere in the Americas, and after 1807 became a new source of slave labor for the Lower South. Any analysis of abolition's impact needs to address these intersectional blind spots and the central role of enslaved women forced to perpetuate slavery, a historically unique physical and psychic exploitation and a primary production of capital that secured the mortgage loans and other debts of enslavers.[26]

Recreating the bodily context for nineteenth-century activism also provides a fresh perspective on the contradictions between abolitionist and proslavery evaluations of enslaved people's bodies and capacities. It offers a new way to understand the crucial political battles over fugitive slaves as a high-stakes conflict over whether enslaved people would be allowed to contradict scientific racism and the principles of property law by demonstrating their capacity to survive as free people. Most important, it alters the view of the relationship between abolition and advocacy for free labor. Although the abolitionist focus on the enslaved body brought bodies centrally into the conversation about human rights, it sometimes made it appear that ending slavery would be sufficient to end physical exploitation and suffering.[27]

Pursuing justice for the enslaved, abolitionists turned to the body itself: its bones, sinews, and muscles, its sweat and tears, and its capacity to labor, reproduce, and survive. Most of all, abolitionists hearkened to the blood—a vital fluid endowed with spiritual meaning and commonly understood to express familial and ethno-national belonging—as the basis for a shared humanity. Conflicting interpretations of blood framed the nineteenth-century debates about bodies, race, and rights. Well into the nineteenth century, people across a broad educational and religious spectrum considered blood to be the essence of life itself. Significantly for this study, abolitionists, physicians, legal theorists, and laypeople viewed the shared blood of mother and child as creating the material condition of ancestry even if they differed in their assessments of the father's contribution. The claims to "one blood" had strong roots in Quaker theology and resonated with humanistic themes across much of the Judeo-Christian religious tradition. Much abolitionist fervor was sparked by actually seeing blood flow as a consequence of enslavers' efforts to crush the wills of people whose labor they were extracting. The act of witnessing or experiencing violent bloodshed featured prominently in early activists' accounts, making blood more than metaphor for abolitionists.[28]

There was nothing inherently egalitarian about blood. Historically, blood was fundamental to distinctions among families and populations and a means of naturalizing hierarchy. Spanish Catholics had invaded lands in the Americas with a genealogical framework that distinguished Christians from heathens and Indigenous peoples from Africans on the basis of blood. In Spanish parlance, African blackness might sometimes be expressed in legal and theological terms as "black blood."[29] Blood also became an important foundation of the reproducible chattel principle in 1662 with the codification in Virginia of what was already common Atlantic (and indeed, world historical) practice: the inheritance of slave status through the mother's blood connection to the child. Several decades after the 1662 law, this legal principle became known among Anglo lawmakers by its Latin expression, *partus sequitur ventrem*, a retrospective attribution of Atlantic slavery's systemic appropriation of the children of enslaved women to the Roman legal principle in which children of parents with different statuses inherited the condition of the mother in whose belly they grew.[30] The French subsequently codified maternal inheritance in the Code Noir (1685), a digest of colonial practices that reflected the Crown's effort to regulate and rationalize the exploitability of slaves but conceptualized race as akin to lineage. By the eighteenth century, references to race were regularly replacing an older focus on nations around the Atlantic basin.[31]

The "one blood" claims of early abolitionists drew upon blood's spiritual meanings to challenge exclusive concepts of blood as the basis for distinctions of family, nation, and race. Such claims also contradicted slavery's maternal inheritance principle and scientific efforts to locate race in the body. In addition, "one blood" provided abolitionists with a biblical path to natural rights arguments centered on birthright. In contrast, resistance to "one blood" arguments took many forms. The notion that blackness resided in specific structures of the skin, originally asserted in the seventeenth century, peaked during the eighteenth century accompanied by dubious evidence that skin color could be traced to blood pigments. These scientific claims about raced blood persisted into the nineteenth century but were supplanted by a new focus on specific body parts: the cranium, the fibula, the female pelvis, the hair, and the nose. Doctors as various in their theoretical positions as Benjamin Rush, Charles Caldwell, Samuel Cartwright, and E. M. Pendleton all contributed to a view of biological race that distinguished black and white susceptibility to disease and not coincidentally advanced the professional standing of doctors as experts. With each shift in the scientific classification of the blood—as a humor, a vital fluid, a non–racially specific bodily product, and a substance suspected of bearing a racial tincture—abolitionist insistence on "one blood" acquired different meanings, gradually fading in significance as other parts of the body became understood as "raced." With each new racialization of the body, "one blood" lost some of its power as a claim for a universal humanity. The racist medical claims about distinct racial anatomies and creations, moreover, underscored blood's narrower meanings. Out of different concerns, Black abolitionists adopted the ancestral meanings of blood to express connection to the enslaved on the basis of shared African descent and the common experience of racist persecution. Yet abolitionists like Sarah Mapps Douglass never abandoned the belief in blood unity. She saw opportunity in advancing a positivist medical view of circulating blood, one carefully curated to omit racist scientific claims about raced blood.[32]

In my focus on the human body at the center of abolitionist discourse and practice, I build on the work of scholars who have considered how depictions of the suffering body trigger the empathic response of a spectator or reader. For abolitionists, this was a medical and political as well as humanitarian issue, as it challenged the growing chorus of medical writers who contended that people of African descent lacked the same sensibility to pain as white people. As Elizabeth Clark has argued, sympathy, or the effort to cultivate identification between an audience and a suffering individual on the basis of the intelligibility of bodily pain, was one means of disputing this claim and bridging this gap to expand the "compass of humanity." Perceptions of pain were themselves at least partially historically contingent, triggered by specific fears of imprisonment, dismemberment, injuries to the flesh, and blood loss. Attitudes toward blood loss, to take one example, were highly dependent on context. Reducing the quantity of blood in the body through bloodletting, for example, was popularly accepted by both Black people and white people across the nearly three centuries of this study as a medical therapy for regaining health. What constituted medical care when administered by a doctor or lay healer in one context, however, became a powerful infliction of brutality, pain, and terror in others—and an actual risk to life and health for enslaved people. The rise of sympathy for suffering others, meanwhile, fueled humanitarian movements, a new emotional economy that the cultural historian Lynn Hunt has located in the rise of novel reading and the concomitant habits of imagination.[33]

Scholars have rightly criticized abolitionists for shortcomings ranging from creating self-aggrandizing taxonomies of feeling, displacing Black subjects with white empathy, analogizing slavery to other abuses of power, and relying problematically on universal claims. A critique of power featuring graphic depictions of suffering bodies could so easily become a voyeuristic spectacle; and the appropriation of "slavery" to describe the diminished sovereignty of other oppressed people, including disenfranchised white women, moreover, could undermine the focus on the enslaved. In creating a spectacle of the bodily suffering of African-descended people for white audiences, some white abolitionists reinforced difference rather than universal humanity. But as the historian Ana Stevenson observes, some white and most African American activists compared "women" to "slaves" as part of a "growing awareness of the connections between gender, race, and class," an incipient nineteenth-century version of intersectionality. The fact that many African American abolitionists persistently used the woman-slave analogy to call attention to the situations of enslaved women, moreover, points to the potential for even such flawed analogies to do important political and analytical work.[34]

As acute analysts of abolition have noted, sympathy could be a selfish and occasionally even a pornographic indulgence, offering little political traction. Ultimately, these critics argue, it provided only an impoverished emotional foundation for liberatory work, which, if focused on formal rights, represented an abstraction from the flesh-and-blood experiences of aspirants. Of particular concern to these critics was the practice of free, often white activists appropriating the experience of enslaved people. For some white abolitionists, such appropriations were indeed part of a harmful white fantasy of appropriated suffering. But for some dedicated free African American and white activists, including Elizabeth Chandler, Abby Kelley, and Sarah Mapps Douglass, striving for embodied empathy was also a process of emotional preparation for the dangerous work of activism.[35] Serious abolitionist activism did not stop with stirring words, moreover, but took root through the sustained practical work that followed. Abolitionists attempted to provoke the empathy of white audiences with graphic depictions of slavery's brutality to urge them to new political and social practices, including new habits of consumption. Even this empathic posture, so necessary to activating political work, seemed at times to tread dangerously on the pornographic transformation of suffering victims into titillating spectacle.[36] As several scholars have noted, the sensationalism of some misguided white attempts to recognize Black humanity instead produced new and more sinister racist oppressions. Hortense Spillers, Saidiya Hartman, Alexander Weheliye, Kyla Schuller, and others have argued persuasively that, by touting their own empathetic response to enslaved suffering, some white abolitionists reinscribed the racial subjugation of Black bodies. The embodied experiences of enslaved people, these critics contend, were swamped by white feelings and white testimony.[37]

Indebted to this crucial scholarly intervention but departing from it, I approach discourses of slave suffering within the larger activist project of liberating enslaved people that needs to be interpreted as one side of a historical argument. The movement's most staunchly committed activists were never in a position to control the legal and medical terms of debate, and they continually opposed the efforts of their proslavery opponents to interpret the enslavement of African-descended people as a consequence of race rather than of power. Although abolitionist depictions of suffering slave bodies unwittingly fed new racial formations, they originated out of the need to contest contemporary beliefs about and lived experiences of race, gender, birth, and labor to produce new meanings for human embodiment. Historical context is key in this analysis: the only nineteenth-century commentators who depicted enslaved people as happy and healthy were slave traders, enslavers, and their defenders.

The risks of white voyeurism obstructing the empathic road to meaningful political action were painfully obvious to Black abolitionists, who struggled to develop practices for visual media that would liberate rather than further constrain Black bodies. As Matthew Fox-Amato notes, abolitionist images such as *Branded Hand* (1845) and *Scourged Back* (1863) were the first "atrocity" photos, giving rise to "the capacity of the photograph to publicize violations of the body and to serve as a social witness." These images, aimed at stirring the empathy of the viewer by representing the injuries inflicted on enslaved people's bodies, also spread associations of Blackness with subjection that undermined other efforts, like those of Frederick Douglass, to circulate images of Black respectability and suitability for citizenship. As the scholar Ginger Hill notes, "Douglass celebrated photography because in viewing photographs, one had to grapple with the complexity of what it means to live an embodied existence."[38]

Even if one acknowledges the harmful potential of white voyeurism and self-aggrandizement, one cannot easily classify the foundational abolitionist claim to universal humanity, "God hath made of one blood all nations of men for to dwell on all the face of the earth," as an indulgence in pornographic spectacle. Abolitionists invoked "one blood" to claim a common humanity rooted in divine creation. The citation was to Acts 17:26, "God hath made of one blood all nations of men for to dwell on all the face of the earth, and hath determined the times before appointed, and the bounds of their habitation," part of a New Testament passage addressing concerns about the interactions among Jews and Gentiles.[39] Readers will see this phrase appear often in the history I recount here. Religiously inspired and justified, abolitionists reiterated this specific claim to universalism even as new spiritual, medical, and legal contexts challenged the political significance of blood to emphasize instead distinction and exclusion. Eventually, even abolitionists were compelled to create new political arguments from distinctions commonly drawn between "African" and "Anglo-Saxon."

Situating the abolitionist struggle in pragmatic issues of bodily sovereignty opens up a less teleological view of what human rights might have meant to its eighteenth- and nineteenth-century advocates and steers us away from the slippery slope of analogy. A truly historical understanding of human rights requires that we take the comments and actions of abolitionists seriously as expressive of a transforming rights landscape in which some people imagined "freedom" as a condition of safety from the disabling effects of physical coercion, even as others embraced a view of the liberal subject's agency and autonomy as necessary qualities in an emerging capitalist economy. Placing their advocacy of abolition in this context frees us from a history of human rights in which abolitionist investment in the language, integrity, and health of the body appears merely metaphorical and tangential to the main work rather than expressive of the body's necessary presence in rights bearing. This was the abolitionist contribution to the human rights landscape of their own time and their legacy for rights activists in the twentieth century.

* * *

In the chapters that follow, abolition appears as a series of overlapping yet continually transforming struggles, propelled by acts of slave resistance, rebellion, and free Black protest and framed by the application of English concepts of liberty to contexts distorted by racist medicine and the law of slavery. In North America, "freeborne Englishmen" encountered Indigenous spokesmen whose "one body" tropes aimed at creating bonds of amity between strangers. I follow these early exchanges across the eighteenth century's intensifying exploitation of female bodies to the nineteenth century's medical propositions about distinct races and human species. Inspired by African informants, personal experience, or their own acts of witness, abolitionists described slavery as theft and condemned the harsh physical toll it took on the enslaved. Advocates of gradual abolition and legalized manumission struggled with the reproductive math created by maternal inheritance: one enslaved woman's manumission might lead to an exponential growth in numbers of free people. In response to this potential problem, settler colonialism and plantation slavery reached an important accommodation during this period in the early United States, one that privileged birth and citizenship for white people but attenuated that connection for people of African descent, even if they were born in North America.

Abolitionists insisted on the bodily basis for human equality during a period in which the demands of a "second slavery" expanded slavery's geographic reach, intensifying the extraction of labor and shifting the entire burden of producing the enslaved labor force to enslaved women. Three persistent conditions foreshadowed that emancipation would do little to dismantle new racist formations centered on controlling Black bodies: the federal government's reaffirmation in 1850 through the Fugitive Slave Act of its protection of enslavers' property rights rather than the volition of the enslaved; the violent struggles over the status of slave refugees in states like Pennsylvania, where slavery had ended; and the intertwined legal and medical expertise mobilized to support white supremacy that echoed widespread white popular beliefs in Black inferiority and excluded free Black people from the benefits of full adult citizenship.[40]

For the scores of activists who were careful to forge and nurture interracial networks as they devoted their lives to the cause of ending slavery, the abolitionist body-centered critique of power offered a materialist analysis of injustice that had potentially broad application. Activists Lucretia Mott, Sarah Mapps Douglass, Frederick Douglass, Abby Kelley, Frances Ellen Watkins Harper, and Sojourner Truth figure prominently in this study because they did not lose sight of the crucial intersectional position of enslaved women amid the many analogies to slavery. By their own admission, and in their willingness to engage public audiences, they were "doers" of rights as much as they were advocates for rights.[41] Faced with the expanding reach of markets for plantation goods during the nineteenth century, transatlantic abolitionists challenged the market's effectual whitewashing of slave-produced commodities by connecting the bodies of consumers to those of enslaved producers. Meanwhile, the reliance on the enslaved mother's body to replenish the supply of slave laborers defined her intersectional role and spurred the medicalization of both race and reproduction. Sentimental depictions of enslaved mothers, which dated to the 1790s, acquired more potent meaning when these women shouldered the full burden of producing the plantation labor force in the post-transatlantic-trade United States.[42]

By the 1840s, wearied by the white radical abolitionist insistence on nonresistant techniques, Black abolitionists and a small number of their white allies called for militant responses, including escape, to challenge the jurisdictional boundaries and actual constraints on Black bodies. This call to militance was especially pointed for Black men, who were expected to demonstrate courageous leadership in legibly male ways, but it also mobilized Black women as defenders and caretakers of their communities. Legal measures, especially those designed to expedite the recapture of escaped slaves, were no better able to grapple with the reproductive math of an enslaved woman's crossing of jurisdictional lines (from slave state to free state) than were the eighteenth-century advocates of gradual abolition and legalized manumission. The convergence of legal exclusions and medical racism, which had been developing for centuries, came to a head in 1857 with the failure of Dred Scott's effort to claim some of the legal privileges of citizenship, including the recourse to writs of habeas corpus.

Several of the most important threads of this history wind through Philadelphia, the capital of North American Quaker communities and a center of early abolitionist activism, to Virginia, the first British colony to make slavery by birth a matter of law and home to an early Quaker emancipator. Both Philadelphia and Virginia figured importantly in abolition throughout the Atlantic. Philadelphia was the site of early Black freedom petitions and alliances with white abolitionists. It also boasted the first North American medical school and the center for the racist science of the American School of Ethnology, and became a hub for the nineteenth-century traffic in cadavers for medical dissection. For all of these reasons, it became a magnet for the medical education of the white southerners referred to colloquially in the city as "Virginia doctors." As the medical student Charles Bonner noted in 1842, "the atmosphere of Philadelphia is medical," and the city's medical schools offered abundant opportunities for hands-on learning. Philadelphia was also a center of national antislavery organization and the transatlantic "free labor produce" movement. Pennsylvania, moreover, was a crucial state for refugees on the Underground Railroad, many of whom had escaped from Virginia, and the slave catchers who pursued them. This study is not limited to Philadelphia and Virginia, but both places figure centrally in this history of abolitionist and racist body politics.[43]

For abolitionists, who sometimes referred to themselves as the "wide awakes," the body was the foundation of liberatory discourse, the subject of materialist analyses of power, and a practical focus for activism. Condemning the use of coercion to extract labor and reproductivity from enslaved people's bodies was a world-changing proposition. The novelty of abolitionism, in this view, lay in its assertion that freedom from physical coercion was the most basic of human rights; its radicalism lay in asserting those claims at a time when neither the U.S. federal government nor the majority of white Americans supported intervention into the nearly unrestricted power of enslavers over the bodies of the enslaved. In their effort to undo slavery, abolitionists provoked critical reimaginings not only of enslaved people's bodies but of all bodies. Their activist journey enabled them to see that slavery's legacy consisted not only in damage to the bodies and psyches of the enslaved, but also in support for the cultures of white racist aggression rooted in mundane habits, dramatic acts of violence, and beliefs in a biological basis for white supremacy.

Chapter 1

Liberty of the Body

The four German Quakers huddled around the small writing table in Thönes Kunders's home, waiting to affix their signatures to the petition they had laboriously written in English. All of them had made the transatlantic crossing from Krefeld, Germany, to Pennsylvania, and the terrors of the trip were still fresh in their minds in 1688. As they composed their missive to the Dublin (Abington, Pa.) Meeting, objecting to the ownership of enslaved Africans by Pennsylvania Quakers, their command of English sometimes faltered. But the unusual spellings and usages did not detract from their main point: slavery was a "traffic of men-body" that violated the major Christian tenet, "we shall doe to all men licke as we will be done ourselves, macking no difference of what generation, descent or Colour they are." Christians who stole or purchased Africans were as bad as the Turks, whose legendary slaving made every Christian "fearful and fainthearted" at the prospect of encountering their vessels at sea.[1]

The signatories to the petition, Garret Hendericks, Derick op den Graeff, Francis Daniel Pastorius, and Abraham op den Graeff, distinguished the slave trade from the European religious persecution that had sent men like them across the Atlantic. The traffic in men-body, they claimed, was essentially a violation of the human body based on a false perception of African blackness as a fundamental difference from European whiteness. Although Pennsylvania had provided refuge to Europeans "oppressed for Conscience sacke" by providing them with "liberty of conscience," it had failed to provide Africans with what the petitioners termed "liberty of the body." This oppression, based on their "Black Colour," led to a host of immoral behaviors by Quaker slave owners, including separating family members and inducing enslaved men and women to commit adultery. Noting the shamefulness of being known to Europeans as a people who "handel men licke they handel there [i.e. Europe] the Cattle," the petitioners concluded with a first-person identification with the wrongs suffered by enslaved people: "Pray, what thing in the world can be done worse towards us then if men should robb or steal us away, & sell us for slaves to strange Countries, separating Housband from their wife and children."[2]

The Germantown petitioners' Atlantic crossings came in the midst of the late seventeenth-century uptick in mercantilist activity, intensive slave trafficking, and appropriation of Indigenous lands. As Britain's stake in the plantation economies of the Americas grew, so, too, did its investments in the African slave trade. The signs of this commitment were already visible during the seventeenth century, with growing numbers of enslaved people in Barbados and the Chesapeake, the settlement of Carolina in 1670, and the incorporation of the Royal African Company in 1663. Yet this imperial countenancing of slavery did not go unchallenged. As early as 1685, Britons began raising objections to slavery as a violation of both humane principles and the laws of nature that determined health, arguing that it bred disease, material and emotional intemperance, and cosmic imbalance. The Germantown Quakers challenged slavery on narrower grounds as a sinful restriction on the bodily liberty of Africans. The claim that enslaved Africans had the innate capacity for full adult personhood was important to both of these arguments. Antislavery advocates took pains to depict the humanity of slaves in a variety of ways, broadcasting their bodily suffering and pain, their full emotional range, their innate "natural law" morality, and their intellectual capabilities.

Both the slave trade and its opponents' framing of arguments in terms of the body owed much to the novel way mercantilism moved people and goods around the world. Imperial sponsorship of conquest and commerce were remaking the Atlantic, spurring movements of people, commodities, and diseases that changed lived experiences and ways of knowing the body, the natural world, and the economy.[3] Atlantic mercantilism generated a distinctive sensory environment that left its mark on the human bodies it transported, marketed, injured, and displaced. These new patterns of bodily experience changed perceptions of seemingly universal truths about humanity. In this fast-changing environment, new legal concepts emerged and moved unevenly along imperial tracks, redefining what counted as the law of nature, the basis for an emerging law of nations. The human body persisted as a reference point throughout these transformations, even as it assumed different meanings in different contexts. In their diplomatic negotiations with Pennsylvania Quakers, for example, Indigenous peoples framed their concepts of alliance and amity in terms of a human body that was familiar, although not identical to how Quakers imagined it. Meanwhile, the personal experiences of witnesses to and victims of the slave trade, rendered in petitions, pamphlets, and poems, stirred antislavery sentiment throughout the Atlantic.[4]

Efforts to craft a law of nations to regulate wars and protect certain groups of people were at least in part a humanistic response to the essential violence of both mercantilism and slavery. But they also reflected the victory of a new state formation—the nation—and its power to define the criteria for full adult personhood in ways that excluded the enslaved and the Indigenous. Legal mechanisms to spring people from unjust detention and expressions of the subject's bodily liberty as natural right came out of the tumultuous seventeenth-century challenges to monarchical authority. Both the mechanisms as well as the expressions emerged during the period of European colonization and slave trafficking in ways that cemented the connection between bodily liberty and the condition of being a national subject. As early as 1662, exclusion and loss were at the heart of this new formation; even as English petitioners claimed "birthright," the children of enslaved women in England's colonies forfeited that right to the law of slavery.[5]

To believers in a universal humanity, the growing disparity between persons protected (at least theoretically) by the law of the nations and those whose wills could be legally subordinated by violence and commodification came to seem like an egregious double standard. This opposition between those graced with the privileges of national belonging and those who lacked such privileges played an important role in the emerging divides between Europeans, Africans, and Native Americans; the protected and the enslavable; those who needed advocacy and those who could advocate on behalf of others.[6]

Sovereignty and Birthright

Sovereignty and birthright, understood as political relationships rooted in the materiality of bodies, suffused early European theories of nations. The French natural and political philosopher and jurist Jean Bodin, ruminating on the state of a world rocked by colonial conquests of land and Indigenous populations, and by an increasing traffic in enslaved Africans, was especially concerned to address questions of proper governance and nationality in this new world. His *Six Bookes of the Commonweal* (1576), originally published in French and translated into Latin in 1586 and English in 1606, revealed blood and birth to be the main bases of inherited condition. But these were not the only factors. He also promoted a climatic analysis of national character that provided an influential model for understanding material bodies as the bedrock of political culture.[7]

Bodin imagined national belonging and just governance as leaving their mark on the bodies and blood of citizens. Just rulers distinguished themselves from tyrants through their relationship with their subjects' bodies. As Bodin saw it, "One of them accounteth his own goods to be the goods of his people; the other reckoneth not onely the goods, but even the bodies of his subjects also to be his own . . . the one chargeth his subjects as little as he can, neither exacteth any thing of them, but when the publike necessities so requireth; whereas the other drinketh his subjects blood, gnaweth their bones, and out of them also sucketh even the marrow, so by all meanes seeking to weaken them."[8] The just ruler's protection of the lives and bodies of subjects was the inspiration for the subject's loyalty: "Now the state of a royall Monarchie is quite contrare unto a tyrannie; for the king is so united with his subjects, that they are still willing to spend their goods, their blood, and lives for the defense of his estate, honour, and life."[9]

Bodin recognized that historically, most societies had distinguished between the status of slaves and freeborn men, but he worried about the consequences of slavery's brutalities on the health of the commonwealth. Freeborn status, as he defined it, was a birthright and could only be forfeited by the commission of a crime.[10] Noting that "the place maketh not the child of a straunger (man or woman) to be a citizen," a nod to *jus sanguinis* (law of blood or ancestry) over *jus soli* (law of soil or birthplace), Bodin explained the various pathways determining status: "wherefore as of slaves some are borne, some are made, so also of citizens some are made, some are borne." He defined "the natural Citizen" as "he that is free of that wherein he is borne, whether he be borne but of one of his parents a Citizen, or of both of them Citizens." In contrast to ancient times, in Bodin's own time the mother's citizenship might determine that of her child. Ultimately, Bodin feared the resurgence of slavery in the sixteenth-century Atlantic for the ways it aggrandized the private power of masters, turning it into domestic tyranny.[11]

Building on Bodin, the Dutch Calvinist jurist Hugo Grotius took on the questions of sovereignty and birthright in *Rights of War and Peace* (1625), an influential work of political theory and natural philosophy written while he was in exile in France. Grotius recognized God as the supreme authority who claimed rights to the lifeblood of all living things. Only God had the right to spill blood or to dictate that it be spilled on his behalf. Humans, in contrast, were instructed not to consume lifeblood. Yet Grotius acknowledged the customary power of enslavers over the life and death of captives, whose lives they might spare by enslaving them, only to continue to exercise unfettered command over their bodies.[12]

Grotius discussed relations among unequals as having a distinctive pattern of authority and right with diminishing degrees of self-sovereignty possible for those lower in the social hierarchy. The foundation of this inequality lay in the ability to exact one's will on the bodies of others or to avoid such an exaction on one's own body. "This is called Supreme," Grotius explained, "whose acts are not subject to another's Power, so that they cannot be made void by any other human being." Even though a king relied on the "Blood and Sweat" of his subjects to exert his will as a conqueror, the subjects doing the work of conquest could not claim to own that which they gained. Rather, the king owned the service of their blood and sweat, and thus the fruits of their conquests.[13] Grotius echoed Bodin on the importance of blood for lines of succession and affinities. He also justified slavery as a balanced exchange of labor for provisions, with "perpetual Obligation to Service . . . recompensed by the Certainty of being always provided for." The obligation of obedience by the enslaved stemmed from the symmetry of "their Labour and their Maintenance mutually answer[ing] one another."[14]

Yet Grotius hesitated at the thought that the state might exact a generational burden on those not yet born: "But for the Debt of a State, Children already born, as being Members of that State, may be obliged, no less than the Parents themselves," he argued, "but this Reason cannot hold for those that are yet unborn." Birth appeared as the beginning of a new political relationship that required intentional decisions. Poor parents retained the right over their unborn children, who could not be "rendered Slave forever" without "the express Consent of the Parents, joined to the Impossibility of having otherwise wherewithal to keep the children that are born to them." Thus, poverty or debt could make it possible for a parent to sell a child's birthright freedom even before birth.[15]

"Freeborn Englishmen"

Seventeenth-century English petitioners asserted a material interpretation of rights as capacities to move, perform, and practice bodily liberty in daily life. Early English articulations of the subject's rights came during two particular moments of contest over emerging state power. The first occurred in Calvin's Case (1608), a suit designed to test whether a Scottish subject's birth after Scottish King James VI's accession to the English throne as James I conferred on him the privileges of an English subject, particularly the right to possess land in freehold. Justices hearing the case defined the sovereign's relationship with Calvin as a matter of birthplace (within English territory), birth timing (*postnati*, meaning after James's accession), and allegiance derived from natural law and the relationship of the monarch's and subject's natural bodies. Speaking of his relationship to England, James I compared it to the legally conjoined marital body, positioning England as his lawful wife, and to the normative (nonmonstrous) singular human body ruled by a single head. Calvin was, indeed, entitled to the rights of an English subject.[16]

The second moment came as the conflict between Parliament and Charles I erupted in civil wars leading to the monarch's execution, parliamentary rule, and the Protectorate. Victims of state authority petitioned for their release and warned against tyranny. Complainants invoked the liberties of "freeborn Englishman" to refer to the privileges of being born (English and free) and of the rights they claimed attached to that condition. They drew on an intellectual lineage of English liberties crafted in large part by Sir Edward Coke. Coke linked the traditional liberties of the English subject, enshrined in the Magna Carta (1215, 1225) and reaffirmed in Calvin's Case (1608), with the emergent use of habeas corpus, a legal writ "fundamentally concerned with moving, holding, and releasing subjects' bodies" that empowered judges in the king's name to examine orders of detention made in other jurisdictions.[17]

Although their own words may not have been the trigger for writs of habeas corpus, prisoners revealed an evolving view of how notions of rights attached to bodies. Seventeenth-century petitioners invoked "English liberties" and described themselves as "freeborn Englishmen" to represent a bundle of rights belonging to the English subject naturally as a consequence of birth within the realm and the subject's embodied political relationship with the monarch. These articulations of rights came in direct response to authoritarian measures against the body—imprisonment, pillorying, corporal punishment, and transportation outside the bounds of the nation—as well as the loss of privilege, standing, and status. Unsurprisingly, as many of these authors wrote from prison or exile, an important iteration of these rights took the form of prisoners' efforts to activate a judge to issue a writ of habeas corpus to extract them from prison to appear before the court. Thus, "Liberty" could signify the body's occupation of a particular place. As the writ's most eminent revisionist historian has noted, habeas corpus was a prerogative writ first, and only indirectly a safeguard of the individual subject's liberty. As a result, the prisoner's own words, no matter how eloquent, were often less effective in securing a writ than the words of others.[18]

And yet prisoners wrote evocatively of their suffering while being detained. The earliest articulations of the rights of "freeborn Englishmen" came from the pens of persecuted religious dissenters who ran afoul of Archbishop Laud with their criticisms of the Church of England under Charles I. Along with William Bastwick and William Prynne, the dissenting Puritan minister Henry Burton was tried in 1637 by the Court of the Star Chamber (composed of the same justices who sat on the King's Privy Council), convicted, and sentenced to be defrocked and stripped of his academic degrees. In addition, lest there be any doubt about the state's power over his body, his ears were cut off and he was sent to the Isle of Guernsey for detention, out of reach of both his family and the judicial review provided by habeas corpus. Parliament responded to Charles I's punitive effort to silence his critics with the 1641 act abolishing the Star Chamber and underlining a provision for habeas corpus to be used as a remedy by anyone committed to prison contrary to the act. After several other twists and turns of fortune, Burton was restored to his ministry. In his 1646 *Conformitie's Deformity:*

In a Dialogue Between Conformity, and Conscience, Burton warned off the Lord Mayor of London, denouncing "tyranny over our Bodies, Estates, Freeholds, Liberties, Lawes, and Birth-rights of all English freeborn Subjects" as well as tyranny "over our Soules and Consciences."[19]

John Lilburne, a Puritan associate of Bastwick, Prynne, and Burton and an indefatigable writer, offered an idiosyncratic articulation of the rights of free-born Englishmen in the context of state-sponsored persecution. Lilburne spent three years in prison, from 1638 to 1641, before freedom and his involvement in the Leveller movement alienated him from Oliver Cromwell, his powerful supporter. Known to contemporaries as "Freeborn John," Lilburne authored *England's Birthright Justified* (1646), a summary of his many pamphlets and an emphatic declaration of the political liberties to which all men, born free and English, were naturally entitled as a matter both of English law and of the higher authority of natural law. Lilburne defended the several rights of Englishmen to know the crimes of which they were accused through a face-to-face process in court. He asserted the rights to remain silent in court and to be protected from unwarranted searches and seizures of property. "Oh *Englishmen*! Where are your freedoms?" he asked. "And what is become of your *Liberties and Priviledges* that you have been fighting for all this while, to the larger expence of your *Bloods* and *Estates*, which was hoped would have procured your *liberties* and *freedoms*?" He warned his contemporaries not to give "your Children yet unborne to curse you, for making them slaves by your covetousness, cowardly basenesse, and faint-heartednesse."[20] Two years later, having been imprisoned in the Tower of London by Cromwell, Lilburne asserted the court's authority to provide a remedy to detained individuals by reviewing the jailor's reasons for detaining them. In *The Prisoners Plea for Habeas Corpus* (1648), Lilburne presented recourse to the writ as a key natural rights entitlement that protected Englishmen from the arbitrary power of the state to oppress the body without demonstrating cause.[21]

As he looked back on the English Civil War from the perspective of opposing Cromwell, Lilburne directly confronted the state's capacity to enslave even freeborn English people in ways that had harsh physical manifestations. Conceding that "none are free, and that a true and perfect freedom cannot in this World be attained to," he insisted that the "prevention of being slaves may be attained to." Better to be a servant or subject who could "defend himself from the Will of him which governeth by the Laws; by which he that governeth is to govern" than to be a slave who "hath not a law to be a standard betwixt himself and his Lord." The King of Spain's relationship with his subjects provided an example to be avoided of a subject's degenerated status. The laws, Lilburne argued, should be "the Keys for opening the prison doors," and the "Writ of Habeas Corpus . . . the water of life, to revive a free English-man from the Death of imprisonment." No mere metaphor here: as a man imprisoned in an age when conditions in jails were often lethal, Lilburne's turn of phrase invoked a material freedom manifested in an ability to move to a safer and healthier space. "Are not the Laws of England grounded on the Laws of God," Lilburne asked, "in which every man ought to have a peculiar interest as his onely Freedom and Birth-right[?]"[22]

The legal assertion of the rights of "freeborn Englishmen" came up again in 1659 in a petition to Parliament protesting coerced transportation. Cromwell ordered the transportation of two gentlemen, Marcellus Rivers and Oxenbridge Foyle, accused of participating in a 1655 Royalist conspiracy. In *England's Slavery: or Barbados Merchandize* (1659), Rivers and Foyle protested the absence of legal process leading to their transportation to Barbados as well as the demeaning experience of being treated as common laborers.[23] The lack of legal process, they argued, violated the rights of "freeborn Englishmen." The phrase conjured an aspirational claim to a bundle of rights belonging to the English subject naturally, as a consequence of birth, rather than as privileges to be bestowed or earned. Without a formal legal process to strip a "freeborne Englishman" of his rights, coerced transportation could never be legal. Rivers and Foyle advocated for themselves, but their protest spoke to the condition of other prisoners sent by Cromwell to the Channel Islands and Isles of Scilly for detention.[24]

Parliamentary efforts to "better secur[e] the liberty of the subject" by limiting unchecked power to imprison accused criminals and to transport convicts "beyond the Seas" eventually resulted in the Habeas Corpus Act of 1679. Quakers, among other religious dissenters, resorted to writs of habeas corpus after being jailed, but the main political impetus for the act lay in the desire to subject all jurisdictional authority to the review provided by the writ. Parliament finally acted to pass the Habeas Corpus Act after a panic over a popish plot resulted in dozens of imprisonments of suspected Catholic agents. According to the legal historian Paul Halliday, the act addressed three problems: obstacles to issuing the writ, delays in making returns, and imprisonment in privileged places. The immediate beneficiaries of the 1679 Act were suspected Catholic activists imprisoned by Protestant watchdogs. Over time, the common law writ lost out to the writ supported by statutes. Most significant for our purposes, popular interpretations of the writ emphasized its capacity to safeguard the Englishman's body from wrongful imprisonment as a cornerstone of his liberties.[25]

When Henry Care compiled his *English Liberties, or the Freeborne Subject's Inheritance* (1680) during the rule of yet another Stuart king, Charles II, he defined the legal inheritance of the freeborn Englishman as including a bundle of legal rights. As a consequence of birth within a protected national population, an individual could claim the legacy of the Magna Carta, the Petition of Right, and habeas corpus. Care, like his Civil War era predecessors, had been a voluble critic of the Church of England's papist leanings and an energetic Whig opponent of James II's assumption to the throne. His pamphlet appeared a year after the passage of the Habeas Corpus Act normalized the court's authority to examine the grounds for an individual's imprisonment.[26]

The rights of "freeborn Englishmen" proved crucial for English colonial projects, including slavery. As Halliday observes, the notion of rights inhering in the subject's allegiance to the monarch, rather than arising from place of birth, made English liberties highly portable. Claimants on both sides of the Atlantic pushed back on Cromwell's failed Western Design, aimed at expanding English power into the Spanish Caribbean, as well as on the power of the state under parliamentary rule. "Freeborn Englishmen" also supported the growing exercise of English liberties by colonists seeking free trade and security of property, especially as it concerned the purchase of bound labor. These rights and liberties became all the more glorious and distinctive when articulated against the backdrop of the degradation of enslaved Africans, particularly those in Barbados.[27]

The logic of universal rights, evolving from the cries of prisoners to become claims that supported particular English, mercantile, and colonial projects, ran up against several thorny issues. Natural rights resided in physical bodies yet depended on political allegiance for their realization. They were conveniently portable but hinged on the event of birth, which entangled women in the process of producing English subjects in colonial spaces. They evoked the rights bearer's physical mobility and protection from painful punishments and purported to safeguard both the physical body and its privileges. Yet around the Atlantic basin, property rather than the universal protections of bodies was ascendant. English mercantile rivalries, the transatlantic slave trade, and metropolitan and colonial efforts to protect private property expanded the range of practices at odds with the universal application of rights and encouraged a concept of rights that attached to English rather than to all bodies. Natural rights, depicted as an abstract possession rather than an embodied birthright, would eventually become the freeborn Englishman's inheritance. During the final two decades of the eighteenth century, moreover, significant populations of people—including African captives, British convicts, impressed sailors, and Indigenous peoples dispossessed of their lands—were regularly deprived of what early antislavery petitioners termed "liberty of the body": the right to move at will, work for their own benefit, and maintain residence in the land of their birth. Even as the chorus of voices grew making universal claims to birthright liberties, so, too, did the gross abuses of impressment, forced transport, and slavery deriving from mercantilism and imperial expansion.[28]

One Blood, One Head, One Heart

Europeans may have reconfigured the meanings of the body to suit the demands of nation building and mercantilism, but they did not invent the body's significance. The language of a common humanity, rooted in both the body and a common interest in peace, was well established in Pennsylvania (known to Native inhabitants as Lenapehoking), even before North American Quakers appropriated it to argue against the slave trade. Blood imagery and references to the human body appeared in diplomatic speeches by both Europeans and Native peoples in early North America. Early European chroniclers observed that Native American communication included gestures as well as the spoken word. Upon meeting a European stranger, a Native headman might deliberately touch his guest's arm, chest, or head in greeting. The speaker might also self-referentially touch his own chest, arms, or head to signal a hospitable connection with his guest. This habit of connecting speech to the material body of the speaker anchored meaning in specific contexts and limited the possibilities of abstraction. It also grounded Native American speech and protocol in the common human bodies of Native and newcomer. In 1693, people from the Upper Delaware River declared to the Pennsylvania governor Fletcher that, if they proved false to their promise to be of "one Heart," the English could "cutt us all to pieces," a speech accompanied by "signes all over his body." Sincerity might be indicated by gesturing to the heart and contrasting it with the head, as in the 1701 agreement between William Penn and the Susquehannocks in which the headman struck his head three times to signal that the agreement was a sincere expression. Over time, references to gestures such as touching, embracing, and watching appeared more frequently in Native American speech as metaphors for protection, alliance, unity, and common interest.[29]

Even before William Penn arrived in Pennsylvania, parleys between the Lenne Lenape and both the Swedes and the Dutch featured references to the body as a way of communicating goodwill and a unified diplomatic vision. By the time Quaker migrants arrived in West Jersey and Pennsylvania, diplomatic protocol usually included mentions by both sides of brotherhood as being of one body. Although no transcript of the "Great Treaty" of 1682 between William Penn and the Lenape headman Tammanend survives, later Native American accounts of the words spoken suggest that Penn tapped the language of the body circulating among both Atlantic Quakers and Native Americans—one body, one blood, one heart, and one head—to emphasize the strong foundations for peace between the two peoples.[30]

In their meetings with Native Americans, British and French colonial officials used the language of embrace, blood, and a single heart to convey amity. Penn's itemized treaty with both the Susquehannocks and Potomacs in 1701 repeated the mythic language of the "Great Treaty," declaring that Indians and colonial settlers "shall forever hereafter be as one Head & One Heart, & live in true ffriendship & Amity as one People."[31] Governor William Keith addressed the Indians in attendance at the council in Philadelphia on May 11, 1722, with the observation, "You are the same flesh and blood with us, and we are all men, sometimes wise & sometimes weak."[32] Lt. Governor Patrick Gordon told the several chiefs of the Five Haudenosaunee Nations through his interpreter, Madame Montour, that Penn "took all the Indians of [the Province] by the hand; he embraced them as his Friends & Brethren," to which the Indians responded with their hope that both peoples and their children might continue as "one Body, one Heart & one Blood to all Generations."[33] Proprietor Thomas Penn, with the help of interpreter Conrad Weiser, gave a slightly different spin to the relationship in August 1732, when he told the assembled Indians that Penn had promised that the English "should be as Fathers to them, & that all his People should live in perfect Peace and Brotherhood with all the Indians, as if they were of one Blood and of one Body, without distinction."[34]

Native Americans were as likely as Europeans to use the language of sharing one flesh and one body to express alliance and diplomatic goodwill. The Susquehannocks expressed their close relationship and common understanding with William Penn in treaty negotiations in 1701, a relationship they recalled to Governor William Keith as more constant than that of siblings or parents and children. As a Susquehannock spokesperson recollected in 1720, Penn "would reckon them as one Body, one Blood, one Heart, and one Head," a bodily unity that made conflict impossible.[35] Speaking to the council in July 1712 through their interpreter Indian Harry, several Susquehannocks including Tagedrancey, Tanyahtickahungh, Knawonhut, and Soachkoat reminded the English that "the Proprietor, Govr. Penn, had at his first Coming amongst them made an agreement with them that they should always Live as friends & Brothers, and be as one Body, one heart, one mind, and as one Eye & Ear; that what the one saw the other should see, and what the one heard the other should hear, and that there should be nothing but Love & friendship between them & us forever."[36]

Over time, speakers in Pennsylvania embellished the language of a unified body to convey more nuanced meaning. In 1723 Whiwhinjac, the Conoy headman, instructed Governor Keith that "William Penn said, We must all be one half Indian & the other half English, being as one Flesh & one Body under one Head."[37] A Conoy translator used similar language in 1728, recounting that "they & all William Penns People are as one People, that Eat, as it were, with one Mouth, & are one Body & one Heart."[38] The Delaware chief Teedyuscung emphasized the British and Delaware inhabitation of one body as the basis for a common experience of sight, hearing, speaking, and action.[39] Haudenosaunee negotiators with the British invoked similar connections grounded on the common capacities of human bodies. Describing the New York colony's growth in strength and size, a Haudenosaunee speaker offered an account of a dependent infant nurtured to maturity by a solicitous Native mother until he reached equal standing as a sibling: "He came to us when he was but very little, and a Child, we suckled him at our Breasts; we have nursed him & taken Care of him till he is grown up to be a Man; he is our Brother & of the same Blood. He and We have but one Ear to hear with, One Eye to see with, and one Mouth to speak with."[40] The speaker invoked a maternal relationship, known cross-culturally to express both unity and asymmetry and to depict the evolution of the relationship between the Haudenosaunee and the British. Breast milk, child nurture, blood, and habitation within a single material body located the diplomatic alliance not just in the realm of a fictive and highly adaptive family but in the human body itself.[41]

Native American speakers continued to express diplomatic and commercial connection using bodily metaphors throughout the century, but occasionally the body served to articulate difference. At a council in Philadelphia in August 1732, Tyoninhongarao, the Mingo headman, applied the bond more selectively to the brewing conflict between the French and the English to distinguish Indians from Europeans: "the French and English were all from Europe, of the same kind of Flesh and Blood, & the Indians should leave them to fight it out among themselves."[42] In this moment of risk for the Mingos, the differences between Europeans and Indigenous peoples were apparent in their bodies.

The Native-Quaker diplomatic communication relied on the concept of a universal body that was unable to withstand the conflicts bred by settler colonial incursions. But it reinforced Quaker understandings of embodied politics, deeply rooted in the European theory of the law of nations, mercantilism, and their own experience of religious persecution.

Leviticus 17:11: "For the Life of a Creature Is in the Blood"

By the time the Germantown petitioners contended that Black people and white people were fundamentally alike, Quakers had distinguished themselves for their ambivalence as both merchants active in the slave trade and moralists uneasy about the traffic in human beings. Early Quaker testimonials against slavery often followed from witnessing the trade or the violence used against plantation laborers. Not surprisingly, Quaker opponents of slavery often invoked blood in their focus on the universal vulnerability of the human body. The commonly cited Acts of the Apostles 17:26, "he hath made all Nations of one blood," offered biblical instruction about a common humanity to those who witnessed bloodshed under slavery.

In his 1657 letter "To Friends beyond the sea that have African and Indian slaves," George Fox made the case against Quaker ownership of slaves, reasoning, "he hath made all Nations of one Blood to dwell upon the Face of the Earth." Fox subsequently traveled to Barbados in 1671, where he delivered a sermon on family order to slave-owning Quakers before traveling to North America. This sermon, which was later published in England and North America, advocated a Christian universalism in the face of emerging racial categories under West Indian slavery: "do not slight them, to wit, the Ethiopians, the Blacks now, neither any Man or Woman upon the Face of the Earth, in that Christ dyed for all, both Turks, Barbarians, Tartarians, and Ethiopians; he died for Tawnes and for the Blacks as well as for you that are called whites . . . being (as the Scriptures affirms) all of one Blood & of one mold, to dwell upon the Face of the Earth; for Christ (I say) shed his Blood for them, as well as for you."[43] Although opposed to slavery, Fox was no radical abolitionist. He suggested that to resolve the conflict between rights to liberty and rights to property, bound Africans should serve for an extended term of service.[44]

Fox's indeterminate views on slavery were followed by George Keith's more explicit antislavery declarations. A Scottish Presbyterian who became a Quaker in 1662 at the age of twenty-four, Keith traveled to East Jersey in 1685, eventually joining Pennsylvania's leading Quakers in that colony in 1688. By 1691, Keith's criticisms of Quakers for failing to make Christ the center of their faith generated a schism. In addition to their theological disputes with fellow Quakers, Keith's "Christian Quakers" stressed the physical as well as spiritual cruelties of slavery and encouraged Quakers to avoid becoming enslavers. Those who owned enslaved people were urged to emancipate them following a term of service to recoup the costs of raising a child to adulthood.[45]

Early antislavery activists in Pennsylvania picked up on the theme of blood as a source of human universalism and bloodshed as indicative of violent crime. Benjamin Lay, a British Quaker who lived in Barbados from 1710 to 1720 before migrating to Philadelphia, became notorious during the 1730s for the combined spectacle of his diminutive size and dramatic testimonies against slavery that included spilling fake blood. Lay wore clothes of his own manufacture and adhered closely to biblical injunctions to eat no flesh or blood. But it was his antislavery publication, *All Slave-Keepers that Keep the Innocent in Bondage,*

Apostates (1737), unauthorized by the Philadelphia Meeting, that caused the most drama among fellow Quakers, many of whom were slave owners.[46]

Lay's unsanctioned appeals had already disappeared from the Quaker testamentary memory of opposition to slavery when John Woolman wrote the first authorized Quaker antislavery pamphlet in Pennsylvania. *Some Considerations on the Keeping of Negroes* (1754) rocked North American Quakers out of any complacency they might have felt on the subject. Traveling through the plantation colonies of Maryland, Virginia, and North Carolina, Woolman witnessed slavery's inhumanity firsthand. He later denounced the institution in writing, referencing Fox's biblical citation and asking his fellow Quakers to "remember that all nations are of one blood." He eventually succeeded in convincing the Philadelphia Yearly Meeting to publish his essay. That same year, the Philadelphia Yearly Meeting published its own *Epistle of Caution and Advice* (1754), discouraging Quakers from buying and keeping slaves. The following year, the Philadelphia Yearly Meeting admonished members who purchased enslaved people.[47]

"One blood" and the bloody criminality of enslavers appeared prominently in other antislavery texts, including those by authors who refused to forswear beliefs in immutable difference. The Puritan clergyman Samuel Sewall quoted the same biblical verse in *The Selling of Joseph: A Memorial* (1700), the first antislavery pamphlet printed in Massachusetts. Staunch opponent of slavery he might have been, but throughout the pamphlet Sewall revealed his belief that people of African descent were racial others. He compared what he saw as their perpetual unassimilability into white New England society to blood that escaped its proper conduit within the body; "and there is such a disparity in their Conditions, Color & Hair, that they can never embody with us, and grow up into orderly Families, to the Peopling of the Land: but still remain in our Body Politick as a kind of extravasat Blood."[48]

Likened to a medical diagnosis of blood out of its proper place, African-descended people might persist in New England's body politic but would "never embody with us," an unusual caveat to the "one blood" maxim. In the hands of Anthony Benezet (1713–1784), a French Quaker residing in Philadelphia, who condemned spilling "the Blood of thousands of poor innocent creatures," "one blood" pointed to a shared human inheritance. He denounced Britain's participation in the "cursed Man-Trade" that resulted in the murder of Africans.[49]

The Universal Humoral Body

The appeal to "one blood" was certainly not the only way antislavery activists imagined universal humanity, but it was a striking refrain that conjured scientific as well as spiritual meanings. Long understood as an important element in early modern European humoral theory, blood was considered by most seventeenth-century practitioners to be the most "excellent" of the body's humors. Early modern theorists leaned heavily on Galen in their estimations that the quantity of blood in the body was equivalent to the amount of food and drink consumed and digested. Chyle, the milky product of the stomach's grinding and fermenting capacities, flowed to the stove-like liver, where it was heated, reddened, and turned into blood. Together with a mixture of the other three humors, blood then flowed into the veins and arteries, where, after being mixed with the air taken in by the lungs, it supplied the *spiritus vitalis*, or spirit of life.[50]

Medical authors of the time distinguished between blood as humor and blood as fountain of life, embedding the ancient humoral wisdom into a Christian framework, where it carried spiritual and symbolic meanings. Blood was also a key substance in early modern medicine's mode of argument by analogy; bodily fluids like blood and milk were compared and likened to each other. Medical theorists identified blood not only as resulting from the transformation of chyle but as the source of semen, fetal nourishment, and breast milk. Women's bodies, believed to be colder and moister than those of men, provided the prototype for how fluids moved around the body, changed form, produced new life, or were purged as excess.[51]

Blood retained a primacy of place in both scientific and popular thinking even as the humoral body of the sixteenth century gave way to the nervous and hydraulic bodies of the seventeenth and eighteenth centuries. These new models of the body's functions featured networks of sensitive nerves and the circulating action of the blood. Following William Harvey's 1617 use of vivisection to calculate the volume of blood as evidence of its circulation, analogies linking blood to milk lost some of their explanatory value. Yet blood's association with the heart as well as with the essential *spiritus vitalis* pulsing through the body continued to have medical and symbolic potency.[52]

Fifty years after Harvey, doctors in France and England experimented with transfusion, treating blood as a generic substance found in all mammals. In both countries, doctors attempted transfusions across the species divide, replacing human blood with the blood of dogs and sheep, usually with bad outcomes for both subjects. One of the obstacles to success was the coagulation of blood once it left the body. Those conducting the transfusions could never be sure that the blood flowed freely into the recipient's veins. Dr. Jean-Baptiste Denis, the French transfuser, was officially condemned in 1669 on both scientific and religious grounds (Deuteronomy 12:23 "Only be sure that you eat not the blood: for the blood is the life; and you may not eat the life with the flesh"). The fear of creating hybrid monsters, reflecting beliefs that transfused blood could transform human form, moreover, brought transfusion experiments to an inglorious end.[53]

Even as transfusion scientists treated blood as a universal fluid, natural historians and dissectionists posited racial disparities in bile, blood, and skin structures that explained differences in human complexions. Previous explanations based on the impact of climate on human bodies could not explain why the forced relocation of Africans and Native Americans to England did not result in whitening them. In 1665, the Italian pioneer of microscopic anatomy Marcello Malpighi found a gelatinous layer between cuticle and cutis, a feature of the skin subsequently dubbed the Malpighian layer, that he believed to be distinctly black in Africans. Malpighi's findings, later reported to London's Royal Society, were the first to attribute racial difference to an anatomical structure.[54] Malpighi's implication of the skin did not deter others from continuing to hypothesize a role for the blood in producing that difference. Dr. Thomas Towns writing from Barbados on March 26, 1675, to Dr. Martin Lister, secretary of the Royal Society, about the black blood of Africans, concluded that "the Blood of the *Negro's* is almost as black as their skin," and that blackness was "inhaerent in them," a finding that Lister duly submitted to the society.[55]

Early French theories about European and African difference owed much to François Bernier, a French physician whom some historians claim was the first to use "race" in 1684 to signify inheritable physical essence. In 1685, Bernier divided humankind into different biogeographic races, musing on blood's role in producing difference despite offering clear evidence of the identical color of African and European blood. Of African blackness, Bernier said, "the cause must be sought for in the peculiar texture of their bodies, or in the seed, or in the blood, which last are, however, of the same colour as everywhere else."[56] Bernier's views found support from L.P., the author of "Two Essays" (London, 1695), who interpreted Bernier's categories as even more innate than Bernier himself: "'Tis plain their colour and wool are innate, or seminal, from their first beginning," he declared; "their textures of their skins, and blood, differ from those of whites."[57]

During the 1690s, scientists in England's Royal Society, some of whom had invested in the Royal African Company, seriously considered the idea that the blood of Africans was different from the blood of Europeans. This notion was based in part on a mistaken interpretation of the microscopic studies of Antonie van Leeuwenhoek, who saw structural similarity in the skin of Africans and Europeans, and an overreading of Bernier.[58] Theories about race subsequently debated in England's Royal Society included discussions of polygenesis and blood as a source of difference. Although he had previously insisted that complexion was a superficial matter of tiny pigmented scales on the skin's surface, Leeuwenhoek eventually capitulated to the notion of black blood. In 1712, writing to the Royal Society, Leeuwenhoek wondered, on the basis of his studies of whale skin, whether the black skin of Guinea residents came from black blood.[59]

But it is not clear that the blood-based theory found much traction. As the English theologian Charles Leslie noted in his *New History of Jamaica* (1739), "whatever some credulous People may imagine, with relation to the Negroes Blood, I can assure you, it is equally fair with ours, and I'm surprised to find the contrary so strongly asserted in the *Philosophical Transactions*. I have seen Twenty of them let Blood in a Morning and have observed with as great Niceness as lay in my Power; yet never could discern the least Difference betwixt theirs and the *Europeans*."[60] Far from the metropolitan sites of European theory making about Africans, Leslie witnessed the medical bloodletting of enslaved people and saw nothing that made him doubt that humans shared one blood.

"We Are . . . Your Money"

Blood wrongly appropriated through enslavement figured in one of the earliest sustained condemnations of slavery by Thomas Tryon, a dissident English thinker whose commitments to universal humanity drew from Paracelsian medicine (the chemical approach to medicine and the body), alchemy, astronomy, natural history, and the experience of his own transatlantic crossings. Tryon spent six formative years in Barbados, where he worked as a hat manufacturer and merchant in Bridgetown. By the time of Tryon's arrival in 1663, Barbadian planters had already begun using slave labor to produce sugar. Half of the island's population in 1660 was enslaved African, with roughly twenty-seven thousand people working on plantations tending, harvesting, and processing cane. The rest of the island's inhabitants were white and included thousands of Irish Catholics who had survived being "barbadosed" during Cromwell's regime. By the mid-1660s, this white population had begun a steady process of decline owing to death or migration, even as numbers of enslaved laborers grew. Bridgetown had become a major port in the transatlantic trade, moreover, drawing more money and merchants to the city. A comprehensive slave code passed in 1661, the first in the British Empire, was already in place when Tryon arrived, formalizing the subordinated legal status of slave laborers.[61]

Tryon left Barbados in 1669 to return to England, where he pursued a career in London as a merchant engaged in the transatlantic sugar trade. Nearly twenty years passed before he attempted to market his hard-won Barbadian wisdom in the form of a guide to planters. During this time, England's active investment in the slave trade grew exponentially with the charter of the Royal African Company in 1672, resulting in a lucrative trade during the 1680s. Officially licensed British slave ships took captives from the Gold Coast, the Bight of Benin, and the Bight of Biafra and transported them to the Caribbean, the Chesapeake, and Carolina. Tryon may have been motivated by this intensification of the traffic during the 1680s to publish his guide, although the trend was already underway during the 1660s and would have been noticeable to him while he lived in Bridgetown. From his London mercantile vantage point, however, he would also have noticed the uptick in imports of sugar and exports of cloth and agricultural tools. It is almost certain that, given his scientific interests, he knew of the English experiments with blood transfusion as well as other recent scientific theories on race and health.[62]

Tryon hoped to reach a Quaker readership already alerted to the inherent sinfulness of a labor system built on violence. The procurement of slaves through warfare and the market in human beings was not easily reconciled with Quaker pacifism and beliefs in universal humanity. Although Tryon himself does not appear to have been a Quaker, he worked with the Quaker publishers Andrew and Tace Sowle, known for their list of works appealing to Quakers.[63]

Tryon's *Friendly Advice to the Gentlemen-Planters of the East and West Indies* (1684) was a work in three parts that aimed at what he saw as the linked goals of providing health advice to English planters in the tropics and awakening their consciences to the inhumane conditions suffered by enslaved people. His pen name, "Philotheos Physiologus" suggests the combination of natural history with religiosity but also hints at his acquaintance with a significant and widely known early Christian text by that name, available in translation in English as *Bestiaries. Bestiaries* provided a catalogue of animals and plants that overlaid mythical stories with Christian interpretations. Yet it is important to note that, despite the likely influence of *Bestiaries*, Tryon recognized a clear divide between brute creation (beasts) and human beings made in God's image.[64]

Beginning with a section on health for planters, Tryon emphasized immutable and universal rules drawn from humoral theory that governed "concoction," the process of digestion and metabolism of food that sustained human life. What differed among people, according to Tryon, was not their bodies, but the climate. Tryon did not see climate itself as the source of disease, however, but rather blamed human beings for adapting poorly to it. Taking issue with the proverb "Soon Ripe, Soon Rotten" that figured all tropical climates as essentially diseased, Tryon retorted, "this is all Mistake; they blame the Climate when themselves are only to blame: 'tis their own Intemperance, not that of the Heavens, which shortens their days." Habits of eating, exercise, and sleep (known in medical circles as the nonnaturals) that sustained good health in England would not necessarily keep a person healthy in Barbados. The smart planter would observe what Indigenous people consumed and adapt his eating habits accordingly. But he would also heed Tryon's advice about the impact of human behavior on celestial balance and aim to avoid the consequences of violence and anger.[65]

Tryon traced the divine logic behind tropical climates to a diminished need for human beings to toil hard to eat well in such climates. The sun's "nearer embraces," activated the "Earth's teeming womb," giving rise to tasty fruits that could not be found in colder climates. It followed logically that foods and drinks that stimulated the body's heat, like spices and alcohol, were dangerous to consume in Barbados because the combination of climatic and internal heat disturbed the body's natural processes of concoction. Similarly, dining at the hottest time of day was a foolish practice that prevented the stomach from doing its "kitchen-work." Disease that seemed to be a consequence of moving across the world was in fact a product of intemperance.[66]

Hints that Tryon incorporated information gathered directly from Africans in Barbados into his health advice are scattered throughout the book's first section. When recommending the native Barbadian root "Aguman," for example, alleged to have properties of clearing obstructions of the breast and stomach, he observed that Guinea natives made use of a similarly bitter root known as "Tantarobois" for similar purposes. Tryon likely referred here to the Hausa indigo variety *Indigofera diphylla* Vent., known as "tantaroba." Found today in the bush in Niger, it was used by the Hausa as a medicine to improve appetite and promote weight gain. Tryon also provided specific examples of long-lived Brahmins from the East Indies and "Ethiopians" from Guinea who remained vital past the age of one hundred, which he believed proved "that the fault [of early mortality] is neither in the Soil, nor the Climate, but it is Intemperance."[67]

Tryon's "Negro's Complaint of their Hard Servitude, and the Cruelties Practiced upon them" featured an enslaved speaker who denounced the slave trade for its systematic wickedness and violations of the law of nature. Acknowledging the fault of Africans who procured slaves for the European market, the commentator condemned the host of miseries European buyers inflicted on the bodies of captives, whom they sold "like Beasts" and "suffocated, stewed, and parboiled" in the holds of slave ships. As laborers on Barbadian sugar plantations, moreover, slaves were subject to other violations of natural law, including the body's need for regular rest. It seems possible that, as in his essay on health, Tryon may have drawn testimony from Africans themselves to make the case for slavery's inhumanity. Referring to the high mortality among enslaved people in Barbados, Tryon observed that any human being would suffer ill health or even death if forced to labor strenuously for such long hours in the hot sun without sufficient rest or food. Were those same slaves set to labor in England, with its cool climate, Tryon claimed, they would easily withstand the strain of the hard work and long hours. Tryon also found it unnatural that enslavers did not acknowledge enslaved women's maternal bodies and efforts at caring for their children, and that mistresses were no more compassionate than their husbands. Worse still was the unnatural practice of enslavers begetting children by enslaved women and subsequently enslaving their own "seed," a clear violation of the law of nature.[68]

Other violations derived from the widespread failure of planters to exercise reason. Worked to the point of exhaustion, enslaved people became caught in sugar-refining machinery, which resulted in crushed hands, arms, and other body parts, or suffered burns from molten juices in the cauldrons. Tryon's enslaved speaker, in contrast, possessed the wisdom and reason that the managers of sugar plantations lacked and articulated the specific violation of natural law by Barbadian planters: heavy workloads in the tropics, a climate in which God intended humans to work less hard.[69] Meanwhile, white planters in Barbados themselves violated the laws of health with gluttonous eating and drinking paid for with funds produced by slave labor. Barbadian planters were literally consuming their slaves and becoming "fat" and "drunk" with their "Blood and sweat." In this unnatural economy, cannibalistic plantations "drank up our innocent and unrevenged Blood."[70]

Such behaviors, both out of balance and extreme, not only violated the laws of nature but those of a common humanity. Christian beliefs in a common creation made human beings essentially equal and obligated Christians "to love us as your Brethren, descended from the same common Father, or at least [to] respect us as your Kinsmen, and of the same Lineage." Tryon's enslaved interlocutor noted that Barbadian slaveholders failed to abide by the grand principle of all religion, "to do as we would be done by," despite paying lip service to Christian values. The root of this evil, as the narrator explained, was the mistaken treatment of human beings as property: "For though we are, *O Great Creator*! the Work of thy Hands, and were made in thine Image, and endued with rational and immortal Souls, yet we are nothing more in many of our Masters esteem, than *their Money*." Tryon's slave narrator questioned the fundamental logic of slavery, doubting that justification could be found in descent or pedigree. He denied that mastery resulted from English people's having "some different Fabrick of your Bodies" or superiority of mind.[71]

Barbadian slavery, in short, had resulted in habits of life among the planter class that violated the divine laws of nature and bred cycles of suffering, destruction, and disaster, not only becoming a morbid force within the perpetrator's own body but bequeathing poor health to posterity and generating cosmic disasters, including pestilence, war, famine, and plague. Among the enslaved, meanwhile, it bred despair and wretchedness, prompting them to take their own lives in desperate attempts to end their pain and suffering. Planters remained unmoved, the slave narrator claimed, because the "Blood [of slaves] is of no value in the sight of our Masters," but he suggested that they should take note of enslaved people's desire for retribution and blood vengeance.[72]

Tryon tried to resolve the slave's critique of his master in a final essay that featured the restoration of hierarchy softened by humane treatment. The enslaved narrator condemned the planter drunkenness that resulted in hot, thick, and sharp blood, prone to disease and wrath.[73] Tryon's embrace of humane hierarchy, however, fell short of an abolitionist stance but positioned him to critique mercantilism for its commodification of human beings. Slaves were not beasts, the enslaved interlocutor insisted, but "humane rational souls," created in the image of God and possessed of innocent blood. He reiterated regretfully that, although white planters did not consider the enslaved to be worthy of being "your *Brethren*, we are however your *Money*."

This was the crux of the transformations occurring in the Atlantic basin during Tryon's lifetime: enslaved Africans had not been incorporated into a human hierarchy but commodified like beasts or things. Barbadian planters thus were no better than the Turks in their barbaric treatment of their bound laborers.[74] The essay ended with the slave's assurance that humane treatment would result in slaves willing to work for their masters as well as improved longevity and reproduction that would ultimately reap profits. Tryon's vision for restoring balance was thus to make slavery consistent with the hierarchical ideal of seventeenth-century English society.[75]

More intriguing, however, is the possibility that Tryon's main device for expressing the unnatural cruelty of Barbadian planters—their cannibalistic consumption of their laborers' flesh, blood, and sweat—might have reflected enslaved people's own views of their suffering as being consumed by gluttonous owners. Numerous European informants commented on the fears of captive Africans that slave ships transported people to gruesome deaths at the hands of white cannibals. Even the splotchy red color of many white people's skins seemed to Africans to betray their subsistence on human flesh and blood.[76] The possibility of an African source for the comments about Barbadian planters consuming their slaves seems less far-fetched when we place it in the context of Tryon's first section on health, where his mention of tantaroba, a botanical medicine locally known to the Hausa, likely reflected a conversation with an enslaved informant. In addition, Tryon's detailed description of the Middle Passage suggests at the very least a familiarity with captives who had survived their miserable journeys into slavery on vessels that docked in Bridgetown.

Protected People

The lure of profits from mercantilism and the transatlantic slave trade prompted small as well as powerful European states to assume the risks of violence on the high seas. Within this atmosphere of risk, Europeans created protections for mercantile players. In contrast, West African participants in the slave trade protected people by withholding them from the Atlantic traffic rather than trying to ensure their safe passage. Only with difficulty did European traders establish coherent trading relationships with West African leaders and merchants, a pattern that revealed African insistence on participating in the trade on their own terms. By entertaining interlopers, failing to provide captives, or simply refusing to do business with a particular European ship captain, West and West Central African societies engaged in Atlantic commerce selectively. This was especially true during the sixteenth and seventeenth centuries, but it continued to be a factor even by the early nineteenth century, a time when Africans had less discretion to refuse to trade owing to the demand for guns to protect their own populations from wars and slave raids. The transatlantic trade also provoked new coalitions, ethnic formations, and expressions of gender. As the historian Rebecca Shumway has shown for the Fante, coalitions of smaller states generated new polities and ethnic identities that offered protection from predatory neighbors as well as from European slave traders. Southern Ghana traded few slaves but large quantities of gold at a time when most West African regions were already fully engaged in supplying captives to the Atlantic trade. This initial delay in participation created political space for the formation of the Coastal Coalition, which protected southern Ghana from both the Asante and the transatlantic slave trade between 1700 and 1807.[77]

Selective participation was also the rule elsewhere on the African coast, with some West African societies departing from the general pattern of withholding women from the Atlantic trade for domestic uses and the sub-Saharan trade. The Bight of Biafra, for example, exhibited a distinctive pattern of supplying captives to the Atlantic market. Domestic economic factors in the region, including an alternative supply of kola nuts and male-dominated yam production, made African traders more willing to part with women. Elsewhere, the Atlantic slave trade gave new political and economic value to masculinity, an expressive form of power that was not necessarily restricted to men.[78]

Mercantilism created conditions of violence and risk that prompted European legal thinkers to imagine a rationalized international order with protections for oceangoing Europeans. Protocols for just wars and the treatment of prisoners carried the promise of mitigating the consequences of bitter rivalries among European nations. Such proposals could also lessen the risk to smaller states of being subsumed by their larger and more powerful neighbors. As mercantilist nations contested for the naval power to protect commercial shipping and the military strength to secure colonial markets, a new body of legal scholarship theorized regulations for national rivalries and conflicts.[79]

To take an example with lasting influence in the early United States, the influential work of Emer de Vattel, *The Law of Nations* (London, 1758), drew heavily from the concepts of natural law, Grotius, and the French physiocrats (economists who believed in natural economic laws and land as the source of national wealth) to define the nation through its relationships with other nations. As the nation came into focus for Vattel, so too did the individual subject, endowed with rights to protection from exploitation by unscrupulous rulers and predation by foreign enemies. These individual rights to protection resulted from the subject's relationship of belonging to a sovereign nation and loyalty to its monarch. Although such rights derived from the individual's relationship to a powerful state rather than from other sources of conceiving of "the human," the very fact of their articulation seeped into other depictions and imaginings of human nature and human rights. Imagining a category of human beings—subjects of a sovereign nation—who were in theory entitled to protection from violence and molestation at the hands of other sovereign nations ultimately spread the ideal of bodily protections as an essential feature of human entitlements.[80]

Both Vattel and the French physiocrats valued agricultural production as the nation's main source of wealth. But whereas for the French physiocrats, the toiling bodies of laborers disappeared in a thicket of calculations of profit from unregulated markets and soaring grain prices (the original laissez-faire economics), for Vattel the bodies of the nation's subjects remained crucial for its international strength. As soldiers and agricultural laborers, the nation's subjects created its wealth and strength.[81] Developing at the height of European mercantilism, this strand of international law vested rights in the bodies of individuals engaged in oceanic travel who could claim protections against the impositions of other mercantilist powers.[82]

Blood figured crucially in eighteenth-century international law as the vitality of the nation, much as it figured in medical literature as the *spiritus vitalis* of the human body. For Vattel, as for most eighteenth- and early nineteenth-century nationalists, the subject's blood was the fluid of patriotic love. Through heroic sacrifice, patriots "cheerfully" spilled their blood on "the field of honor." Valiant soldiers, draining their vital fluid as proof of their love of the nation, created a duty of protection on the part of the monarch. To avoid needless "effusions" of their subjects' blood, monarchs were to seek peaceful resolutions to conflicts whenever possible and to pursue only just wars. They also owed a duty of care to those men who returned from war. "It is repugnant, not only to humanity, but to the strictest justice," Vattel declared, that "generous citizens, heroes who have shed their blood for the safety of their country, should be left to perish with want, or unworthily forced to beg their bread."[83]

While Vattel argued that the monarch's judicious preservation of the blood of his subjects was a key to national well-being, he never questioned the need for subjects to sacrifice their bodies for the nation. In exchange, loyal subjects earned the right of protection from the predations of other nations. Thus the nation's protection of the individual subject was sealed in the blood of his military service. For Quakers, who would challenge this relationship of mutual obligation and protection, the loss of blood could never be interpreted as other than waste, occasioned by needless violence. Quaker love of nation, like the patriotic love of noncombatant women, children, and old people, would have to be demonstrated through some other sacrifice.

Vattel's *Law of Nations* proved to be a particularly influential text for mercantile powers as well as for the nations formed from colonies in the Americas. His definition of the nation as framed by mutual political obligations conveniently excluded Indigenous peoples' political formations; thus, they could be dispossessed without any violation of international law. Meanwhile Vattel articulated an international code for oceanic travel, warfare, and the treatment of captured European combatants that greased the wheels of both mercantilism and imperialism. The status of Europeans (and of their colonial settler populations) as subjects of recognized nations offered some basic protections that subsequently became part of foundational humanitarian definitions of full adult humanity as well as of natural rights.

In his attempt to regulate the interactions of sovereign nations, Vattel simultaneously defined both the nation and the protected adult person who resided within it. In theory, the person of a national subject was protected even when he left the shores of his homeland to travel across international waters. This privilege of protection derived from his subjection to a monarch and from his homeland's status as a nation among nations. The distinction between the unprotected Indigenous residents of the Americas (and later populations in Australia, Africa, and South Asia) and the protected European traveler, carrying with him the full complement of the privileges of humanity, left an important legacy for the meaning of adult personhood.[84]

European concepts of personhood under the law of nations crossed oceans into new lands where colonial settlers and administrators included concepts of property rights to justify the displacement of Indigenous residents. But Indigenous peoples countered with concepts of belonging drawn from principles of tenancy, residency, and tribal connection. As the headman Canassatego and the Haudenosaunee Gachadow observed during the Lancaster Treaty conference of 1744, Native people had a historic relationship with the land that gave them use rights. For the English, their rightful claim was to "ground in a country that lyes beyond Seas," where they lived before they came to the Americas; for Native

Americans, in contrast, it was an ancient relationship of many generations' duration dating back to "ancestors [who] came out of this very ground" (another interesting occlusion of actual birth). A person could not travel across an ocean and simply assume the same relationships and privileges as people who claimed enduring relationships with a place. Rights, according to these Native Americans, were not an abstract entitlement that arose out of imperium. The subject of a powerful distant monarch could not simply traverse the world expecting to impose the place-specific and relationship-specific rights he derived from his own subjecthood on people he planned to colonize. Rather, for Native claimants of the Americas, rights resided in a collective relationship to the land measured by habitation over the *longue durée* and counted in multiple generations.[85]

An Imperial Science of Embodied Race

Native American political interpretations of habitation and Vattel's effort to create a regulatory system for eighteenth-century imperial geopolitics that protected European travelers coincided with new scientific efforts to identify sources of difference rooted in place, climate, and bodies themselves. Eighteenth-century natural philosophers turned from blood to anatomy to postulate causes of human difference. Carl Linnaeus's *Systema Natura* (first edition 1735) created a taxonomy for all creatures, including humans. He divided human beings into four varieties based on geography. By the 1758 edition of the work, he identified each with a specific humor, color, characteristic temperament, and posture: American (red, choleric, upright), African (black, phlegmatic, relaxed), Asiatic (pale yellow, melancholy, stiff), and European (white, sanguine, muscular). Linnaeus's view of the world grew out of mercantilism and colonialism and helped to entrench it; one of his students would accompany the British naturalists Joseph Banks and Daniel Solander on their trip to Botany Bay (Australia) in 1769–1770.[86]

Colonial projects influenced medicine as well as science. Working to link humoral medicine with the knowledge derived from dissection, the French anatomist Pierre Barrère posited a link between black bile and black blood.[87] In his 1741 "Dissertation de la cause physique de la couleur des Negres," Barrère argued that dark bile tinted both the blood and skin of Africans. This conclusion was based not just on the appearance of the skin or on a theory of divine creation, he claimed, but on dissections of enslaved people he had "treated" on the island of Cayenne in the French colony of Guyane. His findings were discredited by Louis de Jaucourt, an independently wealthy French Huguenot and student of natural history who compiled an ill-fated medical dictionary lost at sea before it could be published. Jaucourt subsequently devoted his life to the French encyclopedia project, a massive compilation of Enlightenment era knowledge, coming to his own conclusions on the basis of dissections that revealed the color of Africans' bile to be the same as that of Europeans. Despite his errors, Barrère resisted the conclusion that different bodily composition meant distinct species, pointing to the evidence of fertility: couples composed of allegedly different races could produce children, and those offspring were themselves capable of reproducing. Clearly, despite their differences, human beings were all one species.[88] Just a few years later, the Edinburgh- and Leiden-educated Virginia physician John Mitchell interpreted color variation in human skin as a telltale mark of symmetry in nature rather than evidence of racial difference, and in no way undermining the unity of humankind.[89]

Further dissections led physicians to consider other organs and bodily structures as the source of racial difference. This was consistent with the general reorientation of medical theorists towards solid organ-based differences understood to be "deeper" than skin or blood. In 1755, Johann Frederick Meckel (the elder) concluded from his dissections that the skin of Africans was not the only part of the body that was dark. His dissection of an African man revealed a dark bluish rather than light greyish brain and dark pineal glands. Conducting simultaneous dissections of an African and a European as a way to test his impressions, Meckel reiterated the claim that the blood of Africans was black in contrast to the red blood of Europeans.[90] In *Traite de la couleur* (1765), Claude-Nicolas Le Cat denied the existence of black blood and bile, specifically Barrère's claims, but posited the existence of a fluid in African bodies he called *ethiops*, an ink-like substance that came from the brain and stained everything, including semen.[91] Thus blood continued to be marshalled as evidence for claims and counterclaims about the source of blackness.

Building on the conceptual insights of Barrère, Meckel, and Le Cat, the Dutch geographer Cornelius de Pauw used the emerging race science to contest the integrity of American flora, fauna, and Native inhabitants. He claimed in 1768 that black skin could be traced to a number of African bodily structures and conditions that had degenerated because of the climate: black pineal glands, dark tissues of the brain, noticeably darker blood, darker optic nerves, and the black seminal fluids of both African women and men. Skin color thus could be traced to the color of a father's seminal fluid.[92] Basically agreeing with Pauw that American species were inherently degraded, the Comte de Buffon, Georges-Louis Leclerc, insisted on monogenesis but offered a theory of human degeneration. His general focus was on reproductivity and the dynamic ability of species to change over time. Buffon's environmentalism provoked debates about the health and newness of the New World and the possibility of Native American racial degeneration. Several years later, in his *Notes on the State of Virginia* (1785, 1787)

Jefferson attempted to intervene in this debate to offer evidence that Africans rather than Native Americans were the degraded human type.[93]

"Snatch'd"

Enlightenment race scientists theorized about the significance of climate, physiology, and geography for human appearance in a world of mass migration, coerced transport, and slave trafficking. Indeed, Vattel's ideal rendering of full adult personhood as including privileges of protected movement was at odds with the actual circumstances of most Atlantic travelers during the eighteenth century. The African slave trade alone uprooted more than six million people during the eighteenth century and made European migrations look small in comparison. German redemptioners, transported British convicts, and impressed sailors, moreover, all contributed to the unfree character of eighteenth-century migration. Yet the ideal of free movement across the Atlantic persisted, leaving its mark on political theory, law, and culture during the century's final quarter.[94]

The ideal of unfettered mobility made its way into the poetry of the African-born and enslaved poet Phillis Wheatley. Wheatley's fame as a poet who exceeded dismal white expectations for African intellect can be traced in part to her embrace of spirituality in her poetry. Yet a closer examination of her poetry reveals Wheatley's politics of the body and its connections to her antislavery convictions. The dissonance between freedom of movement and the trafficking that moved the majority of those crossing the Atlantic also figured into the legal question raised in the 1772 case of James Somerset, decided just a year before Wheatley's trip to London: What impact did an enslaved person's movement across different jurisdictions have on his or her condition?

Wheatley arrived in Boston in July 1761 after being "snatch'd" from her family in Senegambia. A frail child whose missing front teeth provided the best clue of her age, she was part of a cargo of women and children deemed nearly unmarketable by the ship's captain. Although her new masters, John and Susannah Wheatley, assigned her domestic labor and nurtured her intellect, the seven-year-old's traumatic removal from Senegambia and transatlantic passage to New England left its mark on her. In her poetry, she articulated a sense of her own difference from the white New Englanders who surrounded her, embedding both subtle and occasionally bold references to her slave status and African identity. She also composed many poems intended to console bereaved parents, spouses, and other relatives, that simultaneously vented the formative experience of loss in her own childhood.[95]

The combination of a powerful imagination, Christian faith, and poetic sensibility could not help Wheatley escape the chill of a New England winter, just as it could not free her from slavery or heal her sick body. During her life in Boston, Wheatley never knew robust health. Respiratory distress contributed to her sense of debility. "I have been in a very poor state of health all the past winter and spring," she wrote to her friend Obour Tanner in July 1772. "[I] now reside in the country for the benefit of its more wholesome air. . . . Let me be interested in yr. Prayers that God would please to bless to me the means us'd for my recovery." In "On Imagination," Wheatley celebrated imagination's "imperial" power to enable a person to escape the bounds of the known world and transport her to paradisical destinations. Through flights of fancy her poetic voice described as "soaring through the air," even to "surpass the wind," the poet might "grasp the mighty whole / Or with new worlds amaze th'unbounded soul." Queen of the mind, imagination seemingly could defy the seasons of the natural world by "break[ing] . . . iron bands" of ice and provoking flowers to bloom despite winter's "frown." But the poem ends with Wheatley's acknowledgment that imagination had its limits:

> But I reluctant leave the pleasing views,
> Which Fancy dresses to delight the Muse;
> Winter austere forbids me to aspire,
> And northern tempests damp the rising fire;
> They chill the tides of Fancy's flowing sea,
> Cease then, my song, cease the unequal lay.

Wheatley's narrator remained in the cold, unable to move across "Fancy's flowing sea" and "unequal" to the task of writing poetry. In contrast to this disappointing limitation, many of Wheatley's poems celebrated the departure of a sick acquaintance on a journey of recuperation, a remedy she might have longed for during the first eleven years of her life as a slave in Boston. Her displays of sympathy for the afflicted through acts of imagination echoed those Adam Smith outlined in his *Theory of Moral Sentiments*—a description of the emotional economy that Smith believed accompanied the political economy of mercantilism—although she could not escape Boston's cold climate.[96]

Continued illness prompted Wheatley's doctor to recommend a change of climate, an extraordinary piece of advice to give to an enslaved person. The option of travel to improve her health signaled Wheatley's unique good fortune, setting her apart not only from other enslaved people but also from most free white people. For the world's bound laborers and itinerant poor, oceanic travel was generally a source of bodily suffering, not its cure. Africans usually crossed the ocean against their own wills, not voluntarily to improve the quality of their lives. Wheatley likely felt both the privilege and the fear of boarding a vessel to England, but as her poem lamenting her departure from her mistress Susannah Wheatley suggests, she also longed for better health and saw England's climate as a promising resource:

> Lo! *Health* appears! Celestial dame!
> Complacent and serene,
> With *Hebe's* mantle o'er her Frame,
> With soul-delighting mein.[97]

Crossing Atlantic jurisdictions with an enslaved person in tow presented legal risks that many enslavers did not want to assume. Could leaving a colonial jurisdiction where slavery was legal for England, which lacked positive law defining slave status, undermine an enslaver's claim to a man he had purchased to be his slave? This question prompted the suit of James Somerset, a man taken captive in Africa and purchased in 1749 by a Charles Steuart, a colonial customs official. Somerset had spent two formative years in Philadelphia, where he likely crossed paths with Olaudah Equiano (then going by the name Gustavus Vassa, who would later become a prominent abolitionist activist and author), Anthony Benezet, and John Woolman. Perhaps heartened by the city's climate of antislavery activism, Somerset decided to escape his master after Steuart transported him to England, prompting Steuart to recapture him with plans to ship him to Jamaica.[98]

Somerset contacted Granville Sharp, a young attorney and author of an influential abolitionist tract, who had already made a name for himself as a defender of the rights of the enslaved. The son of an archdeacon, Sharp had spent his early years apprenticed to a Quaker linen draper before embarking on a career as a civil servant and a writer. His first legal involvement in abolition occurred when a badly beaten enslaved man, James Strong, resisted being retaken by the master who had harmed him. The weakness of the legal argument against slavery in Strong's case prompted Sharp's own investigation, resulting in 1769 in *A Representation of the Injustice and Dangerous Tendency of Tolerating Slavery*. Sharp's treatise, the first abolitionist pamphlet by a British author, drew on historical and legal sources to argue that slavery had no legal ground in England. Citing the provisions of habeas corpus writs, the distinction between slavery and so-called consensual criminal transport, and humanitarian grounds, Sharp contended that no person could be removed from England against his will to be enslaved or subjected to slavery within the nation's boundaries.[99]

The Somerset case put Sharp's argument to a legal test by assessing the consequences of an enslaved person crossing jurisdictional lines when his master transported him from colony to metropole. For his part, Steuart received support from the powerful West Indian planter lobby that had an interest in sustaining the prevailing reasoning of Yorke-Talbot, the 1729 legal opinion of two Crown officers that an enslaved person would not be emancipated by virtue of either travel to England or Christian baptism.[100] The decision rendered in the Somerset case limited the power of masters to control the movements and determine the status of enslaved people they brought from the British colonies to England. The judge, Lord Mansfield, found that no positive law in England permitted Somerset's enslaver to ship him out of the country against his will. Mansfield himself believed he had refrained from a ruling with broader implications for the freedom of slaves in the British Empire. Yet broader interpretations of the Somerset ruling prevailed, suggesting that the nation's physical location—its "pure" air of freedom—as well as jurisdictional bounds might challenge the exclusiveness of the blood-based "rights of Englishmen." Edmund Burke took it to mean that "even a negro slave, who had been sold in the colonies and under an act of parliament, became as free as every other man who breathed the same air with him," when he set "his foot on English ground." A journalist describing the scene in Mansfield's courtroom the day of the decision, observed "Negroes . . . shaking each other by the hand, congratulated themselves upon the recovery of the rights of human nature, and their happy lot that permitted them to breathe the free air of England."[101]

Despite its limitations, the Somerset decision had important implications for Wheatley and others seeking spaces of liberty as well as for their white allies in Philadelphia. In the year after the Somerset decision, Dinah Nevil, a woman of Native American descent enslaved in New Jersey, declared her own freedom upon arriving in Philadelphia with her children. That same year, Anthony Benezet persuaded the Philadelphia physician and colonial assemblyman Benjamin Rush to advocate on behalf of a proposed Pennsylvania tariff to discourage the transatlantic traffic in African slaves. Rush drew from the Bible as well as from science, medicine, and theories of political economy to argue that African slavery had no special advantages over free labor, either on the grounds of African bodily constitution or of agricultural productivity, and represented a sinful mingling of English Christians with the "the Sweat and Blood of Negro Slaves." This indictment of West Indian sugar planters provoked Richard Nisbet, himself a West Indian planter, to defend slavery on the basis of biblical authority, which prompted Rush to issue a second, expanded pamphlet on the topic.[102]

In May 1773, Wheatley left Boston for London with plans to make the rounds of elite society in the metropolitan capital. A letter from Thomas Woolridge, an evangelical who had tested her authenticity by compelling her to compose a poem on the spot, had already prepared the way. As she later recounted to her friend and sometime patron David Wooster, there were meetings with Lord Dartmouth, Lord Lincoln, and "the Famous Dr. Solander, who accompany'd Mr. Banks in his late expedition round the world," as well as audiences with Lady Cavendish, Benjamin Franklin, and Granville Sharp. There were also visits to the Tower of London, with Sharp as her tour guide, and Westminster Abbey. Most important, that same year Wheatley secured a publisher for her poetry, which was issued as *Poems on Various Subjects, Religious and Moral.*[103]

Wheatley's volume of poetry contains hints of sorrows and desires, rooted in the unprotected body and carefully limned for commercial success with a white audience. In "To the Right Honorable William, Earl of Dartmouth," she briefly alluded to the violations of the transatlantic trade that resulted in her enslavement:

> I, young in life, by seeming cruel fate
> Was snatch'd from Afric's fancy'd happy seat:
> What pangs excruciating must molest,
> What sorrows labour in my parent's breast?
> Steel'd was that soul and by no misery mov'd
> That from a father seiz'd his babe belov'd:

Connecting surging colonial sentiment against imperial tyranny with her own experience as a saltwater slave, Wheatley bore witness to the tyranny of being violently removed from her father and her homeland. In contrast to her father, whose parental grief made him universally recognizable as a human actor, her unnamed captor was unnaturally "steel'd" against feeling. Wheatley kept the focus on her father's painful emotions, depicting herself only as a youthful victim of "cruel fate."

Wheatley's first version of this poem, composed under pressure in 1772 to prove her skills to the skeptical evangelical Woolridge, was less measured and reflected popular usages connecting climate to health and comparing the absence of compassion to a heart of stone. Contrasting the "Freedom" of the beaming sun under the promise of Dartmouth's governance with the colonial troubles that had gone before, she lamented that "From native Clime, when seeming cruel Fate / Me snatch'd from Afric's fancy'd happy Seat." New England's "northern clime" left her cold both physically, as a consequence of the cold weather, and emotionally, as a result of her the separation from her father. She chose "snatch'd," the same word Tryon had used to describe the involuntary transport of Africans to Barbados, to describe her kidnapping.

After six weeks of being treated like a celebrity, Wheatley returned to Boston, feeling healthier and having scored a major coup: her English friends could not reconcile what they saw as her astonishing cultural competency—to them a sure sign of her humanity—with her enslaved condition. They successfully pressured the Wheatleys to manumit her, and she wrote eagerly of her new freedom to Wooster, noting that she would now be entitled to keep "whatsoever should be given me as my Own."[104]

In other letters to her friends Wheatley was forthright about what else her trip to England had done for her well-being and self-confidence. "My voyage to England has conduced to the recovery (in great measure) of my health," she declared to Tanner in October 1773, although she admitted that she was once again indisposed with asthma and a cold. She expressed incredulity at the respect and kindness her English hosts had shown her. Their warm welcome was, for Wheatley, a sign of God's approbation of her steadfast religious faith, even as she hinted at the temptation to glory too much in earthly affirmations. Commenting on Tanner's discussion of Esau's sale of his birthright to his brother Jacob, Wheatley urged, "Dear Obour let us not sell our birthright for a thousand worlds."[105]

Traveling east across the Atlantic bore many fruits for the twenty-year-old Wheatley. Through it she temporarily escaped New England, a freedom of movement she could barely imagine in her poetry. She also gained a heady sense of her own ability to impress her English hosts. The respite from life in New England provided temporary liberation from both her enslaved condition and chronic illness. Although she mainly refrained in her poetry from references to her own ailing body and its susceptibility to the weather and the psychological burdens of being enslaved, glimpses of both appeared. Amid abundant disembodied commentary on the spiritual communion of Christians yearning for grace and on victims chafing under tyranny, her poem "To the Honorable William, Earl of Dartmouth" (1773) described being subjected to an "iron chain" and "lawless hand," as well as being "snatch'd," pierced by parental grief, and "tethered." In contrast to her poetry, her letters to friends and patrons referred to the trials of a frail body, racked with illness for months at a time, and the ambitions of a canny literary entrepreneur seeking sponsors to help her reach her target market: white evangelicals with antislavery leanings.

Wheatley's formative experiences provided a bodily counterpoint to the spiritual and literary modes of expression she aspired to in her poetry. Despite her atypical privilege and education, Wheatley was still a saltwater slave. She knew what it felt like to be taken forcibly from a family, transported across the Atlantic against her will, and sold to people who, however well-meaning, purchased her to embellish their own lives. She also knew what it felt like to be perpetually debilitated in her health.

Wheatley imagined and experienced freedom as the absence of "fetters." This was her bedrock understanding of what it would mean for her—for anyone—to experience fully the privileges of adult personhood. Her unusual status as an enslaved person with considerable material and intellectual privileges led her to emphasize the mind and spirit over the body, yet it was the body's condition, together with that of the spirit, that ultimately defined freedom. Her vision for her own life included the right to be an agent in her own destiny, publish her poetry, keep her earnings, and pursue literary acclaim. As she discovered, however, perhaps on the voyages to and from England, there was little freedom of mind and spirit possible when the body suffered or was coercively prevented from expressing the will.

Liberty of the body, as the Germantown petitioners and Thomas Tryon also understood it, included the freedom from being forcibly relocated, exploited for labor, and physically debilitated as a consequence of someone else's dominion. Both these denunciations of slavery's violations and the affirmative rights of national subjects to protection on the high seas influenced how Europeans were coming to imagine full adult humanity. Humanity consisted of protected people who could not be subjected to the coercions and violations of slavery; those lacking such protections were slaves. That the imagined circle of humanity resulted from a tautology did not diminish its power. The difficult task facing abolitionists was how to break into this circle to make universal claims for enslaved people that would enable them to exercise embodied liberty.

Chapter 2

Birthrights and Vindications

In the months following Phillis Wheatley's return to Boston from England in 1773, she capitalized on her newfound freedom with renewed confidence, reaching out to evangelical friends and allies to publicize her book and comment on politics. One of her supporters, the Mohegan minister Samson Occom, responded with his own views on slavery. A family friend of the Wheatleys', Occom had made a trip "over the great Water" to Britain in 1765, where he delivered over three hundred sermons to raise money for a Native American school. When his mentor, Eleazar Wheelock, diverted the money to found Dartmouth College in 1769, a school for Anglo-colonials, Occom felt betrayed. He became more outspoken throughout the 1770s on the topics of abolition and the need to protect Native Americans from the corruption of white Christians, whose mistreatment of him he increasingly attributed to their racism.[1]

Although Occom's letter to Wheatley does not survive, its contents clearly pleased her. Her response of February 11, 1774, reprinted one month later in the *Connecticut Gazette*, noted that she was "greatly satisfied with your Reasons respecting the Negroes, and think highly reasonable what you offer in Vindication of their natural Rights." Those who "invade[d]" the rights of Africans, she contended, could not help but be aware that Africa was being transformed through the "glorious Dispensation of civil and religious Liberty, which are so inseparably Limited, that there is little or no Enjoyment of one Without the other." The desire for these linked liberties, she claimed, stirred "in every human Breast," for "God has implanted a Principle, which we call Love of Freedom; it is impatient of Oppression, and pants for Deliverance; and by the Leave of our modern Egyptians I will assert, that the same Principle lives in us." Wheatley was unequivocal about the love of freedom as a divine gift bestowed on all human beings. Imbued with this desire, it was no wonder that enslaved people chafed against their enslavers' dominion. She called out white New Englanders for "the strange Absurdity of their Conduct whose Words and Actions are so diametrically, opposite," noting sardonically, "How well the Cry for Liberty, and the reverse

Disposition for the exercise of oppressive Power over others agree,—I humbly think it does not require the Penetration of a Philosopher to determine."[2]

Wheatley's pointed commentary on the hypocrisy of white colonials who railed against their own suffering under British tyrants while oppressing enslaved people shows her growing confidence in her own analytical powers upon returning from England. Identifying similarities between imperial dominion and the slave owner's exploitation of enslaved people, Wheatley castigated critics of empire who imagined natural rights as applying selectively only to members of their own group—in this case, fellow white colonials chafing under British mercantile regulations. This selective view of humanity—what one historian has described as the "circle of we"—reflected a vicious exclusion built into so-called universal rights claims; the enslaved were by definition outside of that circle on the basis of disabling laws, racial rationalizations, and the asymmetries of power separating them from the people who bought and sold them.[3]

The irony of this exclusion at a time of rising imperial tensions did not go unnoticed by Black people. On May 25, 1774, "a Grate Number of Blackes" submitted a petition to the newly appointed governor of Massachusetts, British general Thomas Gage. Responding to the replacement of Governor Thomas Hutchinson with a military governor as a political opportunity, the petitioners protested that they were being denied their natural rights and their children illegally deprived of liberty "within the bowels of a free and christian Country." "We have in common with all other men a naturel right to our freedoms," they declared, "without Being depriv'd of them by our fellow men." Drawing from the tenets of natural law, they insisted, "we are a freeborn Pepel and have never forfeited this Blessing by aney compact or agreement whatever." Their experience of family separation and alienation, moreover, testified to the injustices of being "dragged by the cruel hand of power from our dearest frinds and sum of us stolen from the bosoms of our tender Parents" to be "Brought hither to be made slaves for Life" in a Christian land: "Thus are we deprived of . . . the endearing ties of husband and wife we are strangers to for we are no longer man and wife then our masters or mestreses thinkes proper marred or on marred. Our children are also taken from us by force and sent maney miles from us wear we seldom or ever see them again there to be made slaves of for Life which sumtimes is vere short by Reson of Being dragged from their mothers Breest[.]"

Prevented by slavery, an individual could not fulfill divinely sanctioned family relationships and responsibilities that depended on intimate access and physical proximity: "[H]ow can a slave perform the duties of a husband to a wife or parent to his child [?] How can a husband leave master and work and cleave to his wife[?] How can the wife submit themselves to there husbands in all things[?] How can the child obey thear parents in all things[?]" The "chanes of slavery" not only subverted the wills of the enslaved, a clear violation of divine law, but also crossed earthly laws outlining social duties.

The forfeiture of birthright, the privileged recognition of one's humanity that came with birth, was one of the petitioners' main grievances. The petitioners averred that "if there had bin aney Law to hold us in Bondege we are Humbely of the Opinon ther never was aney to inslave our children for life when Born in a free Countrey." They concluded by requesting the governor to "cause an act of the legislative to be pessed that we may obtain our Natural right our freedoms and our children be set at lebety [liberty]." Their eloquence was to no avail; there were no changes to the law of slavery in Massachusetts until after the Revolutionary War.[4]

For three decades following the petition of the "grate number of Blackes," opponents of slavery argued that the privileges of full adult personhood applied universally. Most worked from the assumption that these privileges were the God-given "birthright" of all humans. As rights talk proliferated around the Atlantic during the American independence movement, the French Revolution, and the anti-imperial, emancipatory revolution in Saint Domingue, "natural rights" conferred by birth became inalienable "human rights." Advocates for ending slavery and widening the circle of humanity to include enslaved Africans had created a logic that was gaining a following. Yet, despite the participation of Black intellectuals who claimed rights and liberties as their own, many white Enlightenment figures rarely imagined human rights as extending beyond the rights of Englishmen.

As the Massachusetts petitioners noted, moreover, inheritable slavery could not easily be reconciled with the concept of "birthright." Birth signified the beginning of a separate material existence but one that was highly dependent on receiving care from others. What was the relationship between the physical event of a person's birth and the divine bestowal of rights? How did the rights of a parturient woman fit within this scenario? Was her connection to her child a matter of "natural rights" or a claim akin to possession, or something else entirely? And how should the abstraction of universal rights claims be reconciled with the specific local and physical conditions of suffering caused by family separations, imprisonment, beatings, and coerced labor?

Laws of Nature and of Nature's God

Just a few months before Wheatley's letter to Occom, Boston erupted in protest against Britain's mercantilist regulations, setting off a chain of events that sharpened the imperial crisis. The conflict escalated through the politics of bodies in the streets: acts of vandalism, physical resistance, and symbolically freighted disguise. But colonials also used the language of blood, filial bonds, and slavery to communicate the rupture of British sovereignty and the need to restore their liberty.

North Americans found the Tea Act (1773) particularly galling for the monopoly it gave to the East India Company and the small but unavoidable tax it attached to tea. The *Boston Post-Boy* reprinted a fiercely critical handbill that pointed to a larger conspiracy against colonial liberties that smacked of slavery: "The East-India Company, if once they get footing in this (once) happy country, will leave no stone unturned to become your masters. . . . They themselves are well versed in tyranny, plunder, oppression, and bloodshed . . . let your whole deportment prove to the world, 'that we will be free indeed.'" The writer warned of the fate of North American liberties if the East India company's oppressive governance of Indigenous peoples in India became the model for British imperial authority over its colonies.[5]

On December 16, 1773, Boston's Sons of Liberty dressed as Mohawk Indians and boarded British ships docked in Boston Harbor, seizing and destroying imported East India Company tea. This flagrant refusal to submit to the Tea Act became the defining moment in the imperial crisis. It was an act of vandalism that violated security of property, the rights claim with the greatest resonance for both Atlantic mercantilism and slavery. The Boston Tea Party's destruction of cargo cost the East India Company the equivalent of $4 million in modern currency. The Indigenous attire of the Tea Party vandals and the imperial nature of the destroyed property gave the act additional sting.

Why did the Sons of Liberty dress as Native Americans? Why not dress as African slaves or as the Anglo-American women who actually consumed most of the tea? Although centuries of English and European folk tradition included men dressing as women as a means of righting disturbances to the social order, the men so transformed were objects of ridicule, not principled individuals worthy of admiration. If dressing as women was clearly out, so was dressing as slaves. Despite the comparisons of their own oppression at the hands of British tyrants to the suffering of slaves, the Sons of Liberty protestors did not wish to appear slave-like in the eyes of the imperial officials they opposed. British imperialists sometimes figured all North American inhabitants to be "Indians," a reflection of the belief that residing in North America could have an uncivilizing effect on English people. Taking on the identity of Native Americans became the preferred form of protest against imperial rule and served as a pointed rebuke of the power engrossed by the East India Company over Indigenous South Asians.[6]

Britain's response to this vandalism was swift and harsh and inspired colonial defenders to compare it to a bodily violation. Parliament passed the Coercive

Acts, dubbed the "Intolerable Acts" by colonists, closing the Port of Boston, nullifying the colony's charter, restricting the colony's most enduring and democratic political institution—the town meeting—and permitting British troops to be quartered in privately owned buildings.[7] When the Coercive Acts arrived in Boston as parliamentary papers in the ship *Harmony* on May 10, 1774, the North American reaction was mixed. Many felt that the Tea Party radicals had gone too far with their destruction of property and had only reinforced British stereotypes of lawless colonial ruffians. Others saw the heavy-handed response of the Coercive Acts as a violation akin to rape. A London cartoonist depicted the measures as a sexual assault against America, figured as a helpless Indian princess being given a dose of bitter medicine by "Doctor" Lord North, while France and Spain looked on and Britannia covered her eyes in shame. Picked up by the engraver Paul Revere, the image became an iconic expression of imperial abuses of power (Figure 1).

Delegates to the First Continental Congress, which met in September 1774, discussed the need to coordinate colonial responses and build an Atlantic coalition, an ambition that pushed them toward articulations of English rights in more formal, legal, and less local and embodied terms. Looking to Quebec, which they hoped would join the continental movement, they authorized a letter

Figure 1. *The Able Doctor, or America Swallowing the Bitter Draught*, 1774. Library of Congress Reproduction #LC-DIG-ppmsca-19467.

written by the Pennsylvanian John Dickinson, a Quaker constitutionalist, explaining the British rights to which residents of Quebec were entitled (representative government, trial by jury, habeas corpus, landownership, and freedom of the press) and inviting them to form a representative assembly to send delegates to the next Continental Congress, to be held in Philadelphia in May 1775. British officials in Quebec quite predictably attempted to squelch publication of this and subsequent letters.[8]

The Continental Congress also endorsed a boycott of British goods and put a temporary stop to the importation of enslaved Africans. The boycott called for a cessation of nearly all trade between North America and its British and West Indian partners. It permitted South Carolina to continue exports of rice to Europe, a concession that reflected the influence of the colony's wealthy rice planters, but it suspended slave imports to the colony as it did for all colonies in the association. This Continental Association, as it was known, also denounced excessive consumption of luxuries and encouraged colonial manufactures. Congress called on every community to create its own governing and policing powers, known as Committees of Safety, to enforce the boycott. Instilling authority in their local committees empowered patriot insurgents to cajole, coerce, and even terrorize their neighbors into joining the cause.[9]

In late October 1774, Congress sent a petition to King George III seeking to resolve the conflict peacefully by appealing to time-honored concepts of the subject's bodily fealty to the sovereign. The petitioners adopted a conventionally deferential tone, appealing to George III's paternal authority and duty of care over his liberty-loving subjects. Their concerns focused on the range of injuries inflicted by the Coercive Acts, including the presence of a standing army, the violation of the sanctity of private households, and the fear of being transported to England for capital trials.[10]

The petitioners urged George III to take note of God's intentional location of British settlers in colonies with a legacy of liberty rather than in a land of slavery. "Had our Creator been pleased to give us existence in a land of slavery," they argued, "the sense of our condition might have been mitigated by ignorance and habit." This was walking a fine line, as British North America *was* a land of slavery, if not of enslaved Englishmen. But George III's petitioners carefully distinguished themselves from the "ignorance and habit" of men who could be treated as slaves.[11] They also urged George III to be mindful of the mutual constitution of his own royal authority, the reputation of the House of Brunswick, and the history of British liberty, declaring, "we were born the heirs of freedom, and ever enjoyed our right under the auspices of your Royal ancestors." Claiming that they anxiously guarded this "blessing they received from Divine Providence," the petitioners attested to their condition as feeling men and thinking subjects, and expressed fears for their posterity. They had only been stirred to petition by the "primary obligations of nature and society," in other words, the preservation of self and future generations. They expressed hope that George III would be unfazed by his subjects' zealous protection of their own liberties as inherent in their persons as freeborn, rights-bearing Englishmen and direct his indignation toward the true enemies of the colonists and their liberties, his conniving and manipulative ministers. The ministers were "daringly interposing themselves between your Royal person and your faithful subjects," disrupting the bonds of allegiance between the natural bodies of king and subject.[12]

In language reminiscent of Vattel's law of nations and his concept of sovereignty, the petitioners attested to the bodily and emotional basis for their loyalty: "these sentiments are extorted from hearts that much more willingly would bleed in your Majesty's service," they insisted, contrasting their steadfastness with the imperial violation of white colonial property rights. This violation and the larger imperial conflict exposed petitioners "to unexpected and unnatural scenes of distress," which they were as little prepared to cope with as a child who disobeyed a parent from whom he needed guidance and support. "We ask but for Peace, Liberty, and Safety," they declared, urging "that your Majesty, as the loving Father of your whole People, connected by the same bands of Law, Loyalty, Faith, and Blood, though dwelling in various countries, will not suffer the transcendent relation formed by these ties to be farther violated." Law, loyalty, faith, and blood—these characteristics of the British people, the colonial petitioners contended, connected George's subjects across time and space and should not be risked for the sake of engrossing power or wealth.[13]

The Continental Congress's resolves to cease trade with the British West Indies stirred wealthy sugar planters into action. Although unmoved by their North American counterparts' republican arguments, West Indian planters were provoked by the threat of famine and slave rebellion. Sugar plantations and the enslaved laborers who worked them simply could not be sustained without North American supplies, including wheat, meat, and timber. Planters' complaints and imperial fears about the security of its most valuable colonies compelled Britain to deploy some troops to the Caribbean rather than keep them on the North American continent to quell colonial unrest.[14]

Into this context of uncertainty about possible colonial allies and an imperial politics of fear around slave rebellion and the security of slave property, Thomas Paine arrived in Philadelphia in December 1774. Born to an English Quaker father and trained as a stay-maker, Paine's path to North America was paved by unsuccessful careers as a sailor, shopkeeper, and exciseman. Intellectually, Paine was heir to Enlightenment science and both Scottish common sense and moral philosophy. The science he imbibed directly through his wide-ranging reading as well as by attending lectures at the Royal Society by the astronomers James Ferguson, Benjamin Martin, and Dr. Bevis. Ferguson and Martin manufactured scientific instruments and worked within a Newtonian framework that stressed the precise movements of planets in an orderly and harmonious universe. Newtonian natural philosophy derived universal principles from the movement of bodies in space, offering a materialist model for politics, society, and ethical behavior. As one of Paine's eminent biographers noted, the "study of science lifted the soul of an islander" beyond the concerns of everyday life to questions of universality.[15]

In addition to Enlightenment natural philosophy, Paine embraced Scottish common sense philosophy, a close cousin to Scottish realism in its reasoning from the material world and transcendence of Locke's view of ideas as representations of material objects. Several strands of this philosophy fed Paine's emerging radical political views, grounding them in bodily sensation. The Scotsman James Beattie, author of *An Essay on the Nature and Immutability of Truth, in Opposition to Sophistry and Skepticism* (1770) started his ruminations on truth with what seemed to be a set of indisputable universals derived transparently from the sensate body's experience of a material world. These universals "went without saying" for Beattie and his fellow Scottish philosophers and seemed to require little specific cultural context to make their truth claims stand. Yet local material contexts mattered; for the Scottish philosophers and their North American followers, universal knowledge and meaning accrued through a sensate body that could only apprehend grand truths through direct and specific experiences.[16]

Assisted by his contact with Benjamin Franklin in London, Paine began his career in Philadelphia as editor of the *Pennsylvania Magazine*. Subscriptions soon rose in response to Paine's changes to its content. On March 8, 1775, perhaps as a consequence of Paine's first sustained contact with enslaved people, the magazine published a piece that many historians attribute to Paine in which the author condemned slavery as violating the principles of "Justice and Humanity." Using the legal principles of property rights, often at odds with abolition, the author made the case for the human rights of slaves. Slavery was "man-stealing," a variation on the wording used by the Germantown petitioners in 1688, made possible by the "unnatural" tactics used by Europeans to stir up conflict among Africans and strip kings of their subjects. No man, the author reasoned, except one convicted of desertion and treason could be so used. He denounced slave buyers for assuming that the market in slaves obviated any moral obligation to inquire into the circumstances of enslavement. Under these conditions, as in any other instance in which property was stolen, "the slave, who is the proper owner of his freedom, has a right to reclaim it, however often sold." Considering the fate of those already enslaved, the author took pity on the old and the infirm but held to a different view of the able-bodied. For the latter, the greater good of encouraging their agricultural industry justified placing them and their families on dangerous frontier lands as buffers to protect white society from Native Americans.[17]

After the conflict with Britain had become bloody, Paine published "A Serious Thought," his reflection on the global injustices committed by the British Empire. In it, he connected the push for independence with the need to free the colonies from the horrors of the transatlantic slave trade. He began with British cruelties to Indigenous peoples in India, which were harsh enough in Paine's view to provoke divine retribution. Adding insult to injury, Britain then failed to provide Christian examples to Native Americans. Even worse, Britain "hath employed herself in the most horrid of all traffics, that of human flesh, unknown to the most savage nations." Every year, Paine contended, British slave traders "ravaged the hapless shores of Africa, robbing it of its unoffending inhabitants to cultivate her stolen dominions in the West." This offense would surely be enough to trigger divine intervention, Paine predicted, leading God to "finally separate America from Britain. Call it Independence or what you will, if it is the cause of God and humanity it will go on."

Identifying the British Empire's implication in global wrongdoing as a step toward rejecting its authority allowed Paine to connect opposition to the slave trade with the process of independent state building. When America was able to eliminate George III as a divine intermediary and deal with God directly, its "first gratitude" could be shown with an act of "continental legislation, which shall put a stop to the importations of Negroes for sale, soften the hard fate of those already here, and in time procure their freedom." Independence and state building through political opposition to the slave trade would go hand in hand, Paine predicted, a logically necessary pairing of rights claims and state formation that relied on a cessation of human trafficking.[18]

Common Sense and Universal Rights Claims

Paine's argument about the moral wrong of the slave trade soon fell by the wayside to make room for a universal claim to rights based largely on property ownership. In his bestseller *Common Sense*, published in January 1776 and reissued with an addendum a month later, Paine presumed that his readers' basic knowledge of the human body, the geography of the continents, and the solar system would put this universal rights claim beyond debate. "The cause of America is, in a great measure, the cause of all mankind," Paine claimed. "Many circumstances have, and will arise, which are not local, but universal, and through which the principles of all lovers of mankind are affected, and in the event of which, their affections are interested." This modality of thinking and talking about rights abstracted them from the material lives of human beings and the specific conditions of local contexts, an important departure from Scottish common sense philosophy. The fact of Britain's having declared war on North American colonists was for Paine an act of war "against the natural rights of all mankind" and sufficient condition for American independence.

Paine laid out the human need for society and government as deriving from basic facts about human character and physical capacity. Society evolved from the limited physical strength of individual men to supply all their own needs for strenuous labor, a spontaneous cleaving to others that Paine likened to a "gravitating power." In contrast, government, which arose to provide security from the predations of others, was a sad consequence of man's fall from grace. Paine's standard for the necessary evil of good government stemmed from its adherence to natural principles favoring simple forms and to its limited purpose to support freedom and security, mainly of property. Complicated forms of government, such as the English constitution, he claimed, led only to misdiagnoses of political problems and erroneous prescriptions for their remedy, much as the complex workings of the human body led to a multitude of prescriptions for medicines of varying efficacy. Paine likened the king's dominance in the English constitution to the performance of a poorly aligned clockwork mechanism, "with all the wheels of a machine . . . put in motion by one" and unchecked by the other parts.

Paine's ethical framework rested on several "common sense" premises, including the original equality of all human beings, the "natural" destiny of America based on its geography, the unnaturalness of hereditary privilege, and the ability of corrupt systems and institutions to interfere with the processes of reason and virtue. Although Paine believed all human beings had been created as equals, he accepted that "male and female are the distinctions of nature, good and bad the distinctions of heaven." Virtue, which could not be inherited, depended on specific local contexts of society and government for its cultivation. He was especially concerned with generational relationships, particularly the obligations of North Americans to their posterity. If Americans failed to deal with the current crisis, they would unfairly saddle their descendants with an even larger problem.

Paine compared the situation of colonial politics to the seemingly "natural" consequences of men's sexual peccadilloes and misadventures. Like a man whose judgment in choosing a wife had been impaired by his attachment to a prostitute, Paine argued, those loyal to the English constitution no longer had the capacity to distinguish a good system of government (an honorable woman) from a corrupt one (a prostitute). The point of no return for the colonists—the bloodshed of April 19, 1775, at the Battle of Lexington—struck him, moreover, as being comparable to two sexual watersheds: the lost sexual innocence of a woman who has become a prostitute, and the outrage of a lover asked to reconcile with the rapist of his mistress. By either analogy, America the prostitute or America the dishonored male lover had been grievously wronged.

Paine's other strategic appeal to common sense was to present Turkey and Islam as foils for English democracy, but not in the usual way. It was not the virtue of the English constitution, he contended, but the English people who kept the Crown from being "as oppressive in England as in Turkey." The English people's acceptance of royal authority depended on the Crown's resort to mythic origin stories, "conveniently timed, Mahomet like," and crammed down the throats of the vulgar. Britain's "defense" of the American colonies during the Seven Years' War was no reason for colonial loyalty; the power around the throne would have done the same for Turkey if Britain's commercial interests had been at stake there as they were in North America.

Although Paine noted the ethnic diversity of the British mainland, his universal appeals for natural rights did not include Africans or Native Americans except to note their presence as threats encouraged by the Crown to torment white Americans. Natural rights, as he depicted them in *Common Sense*, applied to white colonists only, and their defense was the key "to mak[ing] the world new again," a rebirth he figured as being like Noah's repopulation of the world after the flood. What was needed was for America to shake off its timidity and awaken from its "fatal and unmanly slumbers."

Paine's *Common Sense* quickly became a colonial bestseller and paved the way for the Declaration of Independence six months later. Drafted by Thomas Jefferson and then amended by a committee that included John Adams and Benjamin Franklin, the Declaration based its claims on the right of North Americans to become a separate people. The Declaration built on Paine's argument by advancing a bold claim to universal human rights: "We hold these truths to be self-evident, that all men are created equal. That they are endowed by their creator with certain unalienable rights, that among these are life, liberty, and the pursuit of happiness."[19]

In making the logical leap from divine creation to "unalienable rights," the Declaration's authors skipped over the process of birth, an event that complicated the abstract linkage between the individual's existence and his actual life as a rights bearer. The necessity of being born of a woman's body and nurtured through youth to be able to claim one's endowed rights was nowhere mentioned. But elsewhere, abolitionist denunciations of slavery sometimes acknowledged birth and maternal nurture as creating quintessentially human bonds incompatible with the slave trade's foundation in commodification. The Declaration's implication that rights were a privilege of full adult humanity but were conferred at birth revealed a logical gap in the natural rights argument—the necessary labor of childbirth and child nurture that moved a person from birth to adulthood—with which subsequent abolitionists and human rights advocates would have to contend.

The authors of the Declaration concerned themselves with the violation by Britain of the fundamental rights of sui generis adult men. Most of the violations listed concerned tyrannical government practices (laws, legislative assemblies, taxes, corruption of judges), but a significant element dealt with tyranny in the form of proximate threats of coercion, either as violence, forced transport, or war. These included standing armies, troops quartered in private homes, violence committed against colonials, the incitement of Native Americans, captures of colonials on the high seas, and the transport of colonials to distant courts for trial. Jefferson's first draft of the Declaration included the slave trade as one of the inhumane practices the British Empire had foisted on colonials. Members of the Continental Congress from colonies reliant on slavery objected to this point, however, and so it was dropped, although the Second Continental Congress extended the boycott on importing enslaved people. In an earlier draft, then, the Declaration depicted exposure to the horrors of the slave trade as a violation of colonial settlers rather than of the enslaved. Such a narrow view of human rights, while inconsistent with Paine's earlier antislavery essays, built on the argument in *Common Sense* about the white colonial victims of imperial malfeasance. In both *Common Sense* and the Declaration, universal human rights looked a lot like the rights of freeborn Englishmen. Selectively recognized as the birthright of white North Americans and disconnected from their reliance on enslaved labor, universal human rights put the property rights of enslavers ahead of any protections of enslaved people.[20]

At the moment the Declaration of Independence raised the possibility of universal rights claims, moreover, a new racial geopolitics narrowed the populations to which they might apply. Across the Atlantic, a German anatomist and naturalist revamped the Linnaean system of four basic types of humans: Europeans (later Caucasians), Africans, Americans, and Asians. Johann Friedrich Blumenbach's *Varieties of Humankind* (1775), originally published in Latin, appeared in English translation in 1807. Caucasians, who Blumenbach first identified as a human type in 1795 in the book's third edition, were his prototypical and ideal Homo sapiens. In subsequent editions, they became the standard of beauty and perfection compared to other human types that Blumenbach described as degenerated by heat or climate. Blumenbach may have insisted on the unity of humankind and a single act of divine creation, but in his hierarchical schema of racial difference, beauty mirrored the geopolitics of settler colonialism and the slave trade and left a distinctly racist legacy.[21]

An African American Declaration

The Declaration of Independence's foundation for rights, which drew on antislavery sentiments like those expressed in Wheatley's poetry and Paine's critiques of the British Empire, encouraged several homegrown condemnations of slavery that expressed libertarian politics in terms of the body. The African American clergyman Lemuel Haynes (1753–1833) penned one of the first. Haynes's bold claim for African American liberty mobilized both political and religious arguments. The self-educated, Connecticut-born Haynes had been influenced by the writings of Anthony Benezet, a French Huguenot who spent his childhood in exile in London before moving to Philadelphia. After teaching school in Germantown, Pennsylvania, Benezet embarked on a forty-year career teaching free Black people and writing abolitionist tracts. Haynes, although never enslaved himself, was bound to service until age twenty-one as a consequence of being born out of wedlock to a white mother and enslaved father. He was already known as a veteran of the Battle of Lexington and a published poet when he penned "Liberty Further Extended: Or Free Thoughts on the Illegality of Slave Keeping" (1776). Quoting from the Declaration of Independence, Haynes contended that life, liberty, and the pursuit of happiness applied to Africans but with a particular emphasis: "I think it is not hyperbolic to affirm, that Even an affrican, has Equally as good a right to his Liberty in common with Englishmen."[22]

Haynes's argument drew from philosophy, natural history, the law of nations, and his own Congregational Protestantism. His starting point was the evidence "by ocular demonstration" of the abundant depravity and corruption of the slave trade. In other words, people could see with their own eyes that the slave trade was a pageant of horrors. The rest of the pamphlet built on the claim that slavery violated natural rights conferred by God upon all human beings, Black as well as white. Haynes played with the meanings of "nation" as both a political formation with special pertinence to the rights discourse of 1776, and an echo of biblical usage referring to a distinct people. His argument blended the law of nations—as articulated by Grotius and Vattel and appropriated by the authors of the Declaration—with the theology of a single divine creation. "I query," Haynes asked rhetorically "whether Liberty is so contracted a principle as to be Confin'd to any nation under Heaven." His answer was a resounding "nay." He noted that God was pleased to distinguish some men from others on the basis of natural ability, "but not as to Natural right as they came out of his hands."

Haynes's substitution of the Creator's hands for a mother's body reiterated the usual lacunae in natural rights expressions between the child's birth and the adult's assumption of rights, a formulation that made birth and child nurture disappear. Echoing the arguments of a long line of Quaker abolitionists, Haynes claimed "it hath pleased god to *make of one Blood all nations of men, for to dwell upon the face of the Earth,* Acts 17, 26."

All men had received the divine gift of natural rights, according to Haynes, and it instilled in them a natural desire to risk their lives to protect it. The conflict this presented for enslaved people reflected the immoral and illegal nature of the slave trade. Haynes chose his words carefully, hewing to revolutionary discourse: "That an African, or in other terms, *that a Negro, may justly Chalenge, and has an undeniable right to his* [freedom blotted out] *Liberty,*" he reasoned, "*Consequently, the practise of Slave-keeping, which so much abounds in this Land, is illicit.*" Haynes laid out the clear consequences of a single creation and the natural love of liberty God bestowed on all human beings: "And as all are of one Species, so there are the same Laws, and aspiring principles placed in all nations; and the Effect that these Laws will produce, are Similar to Each other. Consequently we may suppose that what is precious to one man, is precious to another, and what is irksom, or intolarable to one man is so to another, consider'd in a Law of Nature." It was no great leap, therefore, to conclude that "Liberty is Equally as pre[c]ious to a *Black man* as it is to a *white one,* and Bondage Equally as intollarable to the one as it is to the other . . . those privileges that are granted to us by the Divine Being, no one has the Least right to take them from us without our consen[t]." Nothing that Haynes had ever read in scripture justified enslaving a Black man any more than a white man. Indeed, he dismissed the entire idea of color as "the Decisive Criterion whereby to judg of his natural right." Haynes critiqued the logic of such color-based reasoning: "Because a man is not of the same color with his Neighbour, shall he be Deprived of those things that Distinguisheth him from the Beasts of the field?" There were also larger problems with the idea that Africans were the Atlantic world's natural slaves. Noting the legality of individuals forfeiting their rights only in instances of criminal wrongdoing, as in the transport of convicts, Haynes retorted, "But have the *affricans,* Ever as a Nation, forfited their Liberty in this manner[?]"

Haynes departed from his political and biblical reasoning to offer two sustained efforts to stir his reader's humanitarian feeling. The first concerned the inherent violence of separation and loss for the slave trade's victims, which Haynes found especially distressing for parents who suffered the loss of children. It appears to have been the most difficult section for him to write, as it was the passage in his essay with the greatest number of illegible and crossed-out words.

He voiced maternal grief in the first person, "O! my Child, why why was thy Destiny hung on so precarious a thread! Unhappy fate! O that I were a captive with thee or for thee!" Imagining the mother's despair as leading to suicide, Haynes then asked his presumptively white readers to put themselves in the broken-hearted African parent's place: "Let me ask them what would be their Distress. Should one of their Dearest *Children* Be snach'd from them, in a Clendestine manner, and carried to *Africa*, or some other foreign Land, to be under the most abject Slavery for Life, among a strang people? would it not imbitter all your Domestic Comforts? Would he not Be Ever upon your mind? Nay, Doth not nature Even recoil at the reflection?" Like Tryon and Wheatley before him, Haynes used "snach'd" to denounce the kidnapping at the heart of slavery.

Haynes condemned the slave trade's consumption of African blood and predicted, Tryon-like, that it would provoke revenge. "O!," he exclaimed, "what an Emens Deal of Affrican-Blood hath Been Shed by the inhuman Cruelty of Englishmen!" This bloodshed left a permanent record of violation that God would bring to account: "O ye that have made yourselves Drunk with human Blood! Altho' you may go with impunity here in this Life, yet God will hear the Crys of that innocent Blood, which crys from the Sea, and from the ground against you, Like the Blood of Abel, more pealfull than thunder, *vengeance! vengeance!*" Both the ocean and the land, which had absorbed the blood of the enslaved, would offer their testimony and there would be no escape for the guilty. "What will you do in that Day when God shall make inquisision for Blood?" Haynes asked rhetorically. Divine punishment was inevitable and awe-inspiring: "He will make you Drink the phials of his indignation which Like a potable Stream shall Be poured out without the Least mixture of mercy; Believe it, Sirs, their shall not a Drop of Blood, which you have Spilt unjustly, Be Lost in forgetfulness. But it Shall Bleed afresh, and testify against you, in the Day when God shall Deal with Sinners." Like the corpse in an early modern European inquest bleeding afresh when touched by the hand of the murderer, evidence of the slave traders' violations would be renewed and underscored on the Judgment Day so that God might bring them to justice.

Black and white, one species, all nations, consent, liberty, cries, blood: this was the language of a man steeped in the Bible and humanitarianism as well as in the political language of his day. Yet one suspects that Haynes was also reflecting on his own life as a bound servant, taken from his mother, who had, with great difficulty, begun to make his way into the ranks of educated white New Englanders. Ten years after his historic participation in the Battle of Lexington, Haynes received his license to preach as a Congregational minister. His 1776 essay on the natural rights of African Americans was not published during his lifetime—possibly out of a concern that the notoriety would damage his chances of leading a congregation.

Birthrights and Vindications

The success of the American Revolution transformed Atlantic and North American continental politics, forever changing the dynamic between ancien régime powers and their colonies and unleashing the United States as the newest imperial contender for territory in the Americas. Despite British general Cornwallis's surrender in October 1781 and Britain's formal recognition of American independence in the Treaty of Paris in 1783, Britain continued to behave as an imperial power in North America. It failed to acknowledge its Native American allies as sovereign nations when it ceded contested Indian territory to the United States. Britain also maintained its forts in the Great Lakes region, violating a condition of the peace that caused friction with the new nation. In addition, Britain took advantage of the fluidity of national identities caused by the mass exodus of loyalists across the northern border to Canada to continue impressing English-speaking seamen, regardless of nationality.[23]

Britain's loss of the North American colonies shifted the politics of abolition, giving the cause new adherents and political prominence. The watershed came in 1780 with Pennsylvania's gradual abolition act, the first such legal step toward emancipation in the Americas. The act carefully protected enslavers from incurring financial losses by requiring that those emancipated, children, would work for twenty-eight-year terms to compensate their owners. This reliance on the labor of children to offset the costs of their own birth and rearing became the pattern for other gradual emancipation measures throughout the Americas.[24]

From 1783 until the outbreak of revolution in France, abolition was no longer the hobbyhorse of religious dissidents and imperial critics but was aligned with the goals of redeeming nation and empire. A sensational legal case, a new empirical approach to exposing the slave trade's horrors, and the publication of firsthand accounts of slavery that testified to its inhumanity galvanized reformers and gave them new momentum. All of these occurred within a context of growing moral uncertainty and concern about the appearance of inhumanity in the British Empire.[25]

In 1781, word of the *Zong* massacre reached English newspapers. The *Zong* was a small slave ship owned by a Liverpool slaving family, the Gregsons, which ran into navigational and supply problems during its 1781 voyage from the Cape Coast of Africa (present-day Ghana) to Jamaica. The ship's captain, Luke Collingwood, a veteran slave trade surgeon who had never before captained a slave vessel, dealt with the shortage of drinking water by throwing 132 shackled Africans overboard to their deaths. Collingwood, who had been ill throughout much of the journey, subsequently died in Jamaica. The massacre would never have come to public attention if the ship's owners had not decided to pursue insurance reimbursement in court in March 1783. The initial jury decision in favor of the ship's owners led the insurers to appeal. The formerly enslaved Olaudah Equiano, also known as Gustavus Vassa, called the atrocity to the attention of Granville Sharp, who then joined with the insurers to prepare for the appeal.

The May 1783 trial came before Lord Mansfield, a judicial expert in marine insurance who had rendered the decision in the Somerset case. Mansfield was determined to limit the case to the question of the insurer's liability to reimburse the shipowners for loss of property. In contrast, Granville Sharp, who was advising the legal team for the insurers, wanted to expand the case to consider the bigger issue of human rights violations. The court was forced to rely on very limited testimony from a single surviving passenger, Robert Stubbes, who had a reputation as a drunk and a cheat. He had been in charge of the vessel briefly when it began to run low on water and Collingwood fell ill. The absence of any documentation of the killings, moreover, as a consequence of the loss of the ship's log, made Stubbes's testimony even more crucial. Although Judge Mansfield initially attempted to treat the massacre only as a loss of insured property, upon learning that it had occurred a day after a heavy rain, which would have replenished diminished water supplies, he acknowledged grounds for reexamining the evidence at a new trial. But there is no evidence that such a trial ever took place.[26]

The *Zong* trial occurred during the period of imperial soul-searching that followed the British loss of the North American colonies. British statesmen expressed concerns about the morality and efficacy of rule in the remaining portions of the empire. The conduct of the East India Company, which had long vexed Parliament, came under particular scrutiny. When first presented with the question of regulating the East India Company's political authority in India in 1773, the Irish statesman Edmund Burke defended the company's rights as a species of the individual's natural rights, authorized by its charter, and argued that infringement would only serve to engross the power of the Crown. Ten years later, following the loss of the North American colonies, Burke articulated the question of rights differently.[27]

In the East India Company bill he coauthored with Charles James Fox in December 1783 and in his speech before Parliament, Burke deprecated the gross abuses of power by the company's governor and the resulting destruction of lives in India. Burke was clear that such abuses in a far-off colonial territory were an evil that would come home to roost in England. He also defended the "natural rights of men" as "sacred things." The East India Company not only violated the spirit of the Magna Carta to restrain overweening power but aimed to establish monopoly and flex political muscle. "Political power and commercial monopoly are not the rights of men," he declared, adding, "it is fallacious and sophistical to call [the rights derived from charters] 'the chartered rights of men.'" The test for chartered rights, as Burke saw it, was whether they interfered with the natural rights of human beings to the detriment of those over whom they ruled. Burke proposed that the abuse of chartered rights by despotic and tyrannical powers like the East India Company should lead automatically to suspending the contract. This would provide "real chartered security for the *rights of men* cruelly violated under that [former] charter."[28]

The loss of the North American colonies also stimulated British Quakers to antislavery activism, an issue on which they lagged behind their North American peers. Despite the pushing and goading of their Atlantic counterparts, British Quakers did not take any concerted action until a younger generation advanced the agenda.[29] Under the leadership of William Dillwyn, student and protégé of Anthony Benezet, and the Briton John Lloyd, Quakers lobbied Parliament in 1783 to launch an investigation. A June 1783 petition signed by 273 Quakers and accompanied by the essay *The Case of Our Fellow Creatures, the Oppressed Africans* marked the beginning of this new British Quaker antislavery campaign.[30]

Taking notice of an opportunity for parliamentary movement on the issue, the petitioners identified the rights violations inherent in slavery. "Under the countenance of the laws of this country," they observed, "many thousands of these our fellow creatures, entitled to the natural rights of mankind, are held as personal property in cruel bondage" as a result of a traffic that featured "rapine, oppression, and bloodshed." No biblical precedent for slavery could be instructive in the present case, they argued, positing their own historical moment as one without precedent:

> the permission to hold slaves amongst the Jews, can in no wise be applied to the practice amongst us: for, blessed be the God and Father of all our mercies who hath made of one blood all nations of men, we now live under a dispensation essentially different from that of the law; in which many things were permitted to the Jews, because of the hardness of their hearts. All distinctions of name and country, so far as they relate to the social duties, are now abolished. We are taught by our blessed Redeemer to look upon all men, even our enemies, as neighbours and brethren, and to do unto them as we would they should do unto us.

The "one blood" dictum and the need to "do unto others" made the enslavement of any group of people impossible to reconcile with Christian principles.

The Case of Our Fellow Creatures also attempted to stir the fellow feeling of readers by appealing to the conditions and circumstances at the core of their concept of human rights. "This traffic is the principal source of the destructive wars which prevail among these unhappy people," and led to many other terrible "consequences, the mere recital of which is shocking to humanity." The list of violations included "the violent separation of the dearest relatives, the tears of conjugal and parental affection," and the "reluctance of the slaves to a voyage [*sic*] from which they can have no prospect of returning." Taken together, such a traffic "must present scenes of distress which would pierce the heart of any, in whom the principles of humanity are not wholly effaced."

The spectacle of cruelty presented by the Middle Passage and the fate of slaves in the West Indies resulted from the overweening power of slave traders and slave owners. Survivors of the inhumane traffic across the Atlantic faced new horrors upon arrival in the Caribbean: "by what is called the seasoning in the Islands, many are relieved by a premature death, from that series of accumulated sufferings which awaits their less happy survivors. . . . being sold to the highest bidder, and branded with a hot iron, they have yet to linger on, unpitied, the whole term of their miserable existence, in excessive labour, and too often under the merciless controul of unprincipled and unfeeling men, without proper food or cloathing . . . whilst every fault, real, or imaginary, is punished with a rigour which is but weakly restrained by the colony laws."[31]

Just a few months later, over five hundred Philadelphia-area Quaker men, alarmed by the prospect of North Americans returning to the slave trade under the authority of the new nation, formulated a petition to Congress asserting the just and natural right of enslaved people to their freedom and in the interest of the larger goals of piety and virtue. They addressed their petition to the Confederation Congress, "the Guardians of the common rights of Mankind and Advocates for Liberty," to record their sorrow at the "complicated evils" of a trade that reduced "thousands of the human species to the deplorable State of Slavery." Although the petitioners were relieved that the end of the war meant a stop to the terrible "effusion of human Blood," they worried that greed might propel some to renew the "iniquitous trade for slaves to the African Coasts," in clear contradiction of declarations of universal liberty.[32]

It wasn't the agitation of Quakers in either Britain or North America that finally stirred Caribbean planters to defend the institution that had built their fortunes, however, but the intervention of medical men. The historian Christopher Brown suggests they were provoked by the antislavery writing of a former naval surgeon and West Indian planter, James Ramsay. Ramsay authored a series of antislavery pamphlets that drew on his first-person experience of life in the West Indies as a slave owner. The fact that his pamphlet followed on the heels of American independence no doubt intensified its impact on West Indian planters, who had suffered the dual threats of slave rebellion and trade loss during the war.[33]

Until Ramsay's pamphlet appeared, the West Indian slave interest had mainly ignored antislavery publications out of England and North America, with the notable exception of Benjamin Rush's 1773 *Address to the Inhabitants of the British Settlement in America.* Significantly, like Ramsay's, Rush's was a pamphlet authored by a prominent medical doctor. Ramsay's *Essay on the Treatment and Conversion of African Slaves in the British Sugar Colonies* (1784), however, provoked West Indian slave owners to a detailed defense of the trade and their use of slave labor. They responded point by point to Ramsay and then to each of his subsequent responses to their publications. West Indian slave owners did not want to give up slavery, but they also did not want to be thought of as tyrants. Their defenses often included an effort to balance the moral scales by publicizing inhumane treatment of British workers and the sufferings of the British poor. This strategy echoed Benjamin Franklin's effort in 1771 to shift the blame for slavery from North Americans to the British and to pile on additional moral obloquy by pointing out Scottish abuses of coal miners and the evils of the British impressment system. Put on the defensive by West Indian defenders of slavery, Ramsay and his group of evangelicals at Barham Court, home to the evangelical Margaret, Lady Middleton, were forced to justify the conditions of British laborers. The editors of the *London Times* pointed out in 1788 that it wasn't just a question of the physical suffering of the slave that distinguished him from other laborers, but the fact of another person with power over him to reduce or increase that suffering.[34] Jamaican planters, meanwhile, responded to Ramsay's criticisms on medical grounds. At the Jamaican House Assembly Meeting later that year, the Committee of the House recruited medical opinion to explain the pattern of high mortality among the enslaved, pointing to the deaths from seasoning as a seemingly natural phenomenon for the newly captured Africans. At least one doctor attributed the staggering infant mortality to enslaved women's promiscuity and maternal deficiency, finding causes in the bodily practices of mothers rather than in the ordeals of being trafficked and forced to labor.[35]

The new activism of British evangelicals and the turn to evidence gathering were both aimed at forcing the British public to confront the horrors of the slave trade. As Brown has argued, the British evangelicals Hannah More, William Wilberforce, and John Newton saw the slave's cause as having the potential to "establish an appetite for moral reform without, first, requiring the sacrifice of familiar pleasures" by the British public. Thomas Clarkson, a fellow evangelical and the doggedly empirical author of *Essay on the Slavery and Commerce of the Human*

Species (1787), provided statistical evidence about the extent of British involvement in the trade and its costs, and estimated the profits that might be gained through legitimate commerce with Africa. This argument against slavery—that it incurred financial loss—was beginning to gain ground among British abolitionists who had formerly raised only moral objections to the traffic.[36]

As British momentum grew for abolition as a form of religious conviction, American political leaders carefully sidestepped the mention of slavery in framing their Constitution even as they leveraged it to support national unity. The ensuing compromise built national unity on the fractionated bodies of Black people and the deferred prohibition of the transatlantic trade. The Constitutional Convention of August 1787 featured roughly twenty-five enslavers among the fifty-five delegates, all of whom boasted greater wealth and education than the average white American. Antislavery northerners wanted enslaved people excluded completely from southern population totals used to determine state representation, while white southerners wanted slaves to be counted in full for representative purposes but without the attendant rights. The three-fifths compromise, as it came to be known, reflected the convention's placement of priority on white political agreement rather than abolition. The convention also agreed to a twenty-year restraint on congressional authority to end the transatlantic trade. The nationalism supported by the Constitution in these two measures made abolition a moral rather than political issue.[37]

Meanwhile, back in Britain, abolitionists continued to make political inroads. The mythos surrounding the British opposition to the slave trade figured it as a tale of Christian mission and apostolic following: twelve men, including Thomas Clarkson, Granville Sharp, and the publisher James Phillips, gathered in a London printing and bookshop to form the Society for Effecting the Abolition of the Slave Trade (SEAST) in May 1787. One of their primary purposes was to gather data and publicize the horrors of the slave trade. The group was composed primarily of Quakers but included the evangelicals Sharp and Clarkson. The organization commissioned Clarkson to produce an abbreviated summary of the data he presented in his *Essay* and began circulating this around England.[38]

At the request of Josiah Wedgwood, a wealthy pottery manufacturer, Protestant dissenter, and member of the newly formed SEAST, the employees Henry Webber and William Hackwood created an image inscribed, "Am I Not a Man and a Brother?" The design featured an enslaved man in shackles kneeling against a white backdrop. Although intended to have a radical impact on public sentiment, on the basis of scientific understandings of emotion, the depiction conformed to the informal rules of racial iconography in the seventeenth and eighteenth centuries. Artists never depicted adult enslaved men standing free as if unencumbered by bondage. Rather, when artists included enslaved men in European and North American portraits, they showed them in manacles, wearing the aristocratic house servant's livery, or in some other subordinate posture. More typically, images of male slaves featured children or clearly subordinated domestic servants. Wedgwood created cameo jewelry out of the image and sent a batch to Benjamin Franklin in 1788 with a note about how medallions like these worn by fashionable women would do more to spread the antislavery message than any tract or pamphlet could. The idea of wearing abolitionist principles would re-emerge during the nineteenth-century in the form of consumer boycotts of slave-produced cotton.[39]

That same year, Parliament easily passed the 1788 Slave Trade Act, also known as the Dolben Act, a measure intended to ameliorate the worst conditions of the Middle Passage: crowding, mortal disease, and the numbers of people transported against their wills. The act had but limited positive effect, however, and actually encouraged the trafficking of women and older children. Each slave vessel was required to carry a ship's surgeon to document deaths and causes of mortality. For vessels in which slave mortality was 2 percent or less, both the master and captain received a bonus. For slave mortality greater than 2 percent, the bounties paid for dead captives were reduced by half. Although the law represented the first time abolitionists had managed to influence policy about the slave trade, it was a crude intervention that failed to save many enslaved people's lives or reduce their commodification.[40]

In December 1788, the Plymouth chapter of SEAST commissioned a cross-section image of the slave ship *Brooks* to bring the physical and psychic horrors of the slave trade to the attention of the British public. The image, which was published by the Quaker James Phillips in London in spring 1789 as *Description of a Slave Ship*, circulated widely as evidence of the slave trade's violations of natural rights rooted in the most basic bodily needs. The rendering of Black people tightly packed on cargo decks conjured a treatment appropriate for animals or inanimate commodities rather than humans, a far cry from any acknowledgment of health needs, personal dignity, or bodily comfort. Yet one cannot help but wonder whether Britons interpreted the image as an indictment of slavery per se or of the cruelty of transport methods.[41]

As antislavery sentiment gained momentum in England, French abolitionists founded their own organization, the Société des Amis des Noirs, in February 1788. Spearheaded by Jacques Pierre Brissot, a journalist and supporter of the American Revolution, its cofounders included the Marquis de Lafayette and leading constitutional figures like the Comte de Mirabeau, and it soon gained other prominent adherents. The French group had been influenced by their English counterparts; Brissot lived in London during the period of SEAST's founding, and Clarkson put his muscle behind the French society and its lobbying efforts, attending all of its meetings between November 1789 and January 1790 and maintaining a close correspondence with Brissot. French abolitionists adopted an image similar but not identical to the one created by Wedgwood. In the French image, the enslaved man is more heavily and visibly manacled. Instead of looking heavenward like the figure in the Wedgwood image—perhaps a reflection of the more purposefully secular constitution of the Amis des Noirs—he looks straight ahead. The image of the *Brooks* slave ship, moreover, quickly found a following in France.[42]

Anglophone abolitionists soon found a powerful first-person spokesperson in Olaudah Equiano, the same man who had brought the *Zong* case to Granville Sharp's attention. Writing as Gustavus Vassa, Equiano produced a carefully crafted memoir of his experiences in Atlantic world slavery that featured the traumas of being kidnapped from Benin, separated from his family, and transported against his will in the stinking hold of a slave ship. Although scholars today remain divided about whether Equiano was born in West Africa or South Carolina, what is certain is the timeliness of his tale of forced transport. This form of coercion, even more than the sufferings of plantation slaves, had been at the heart of both the Somerset and *Zong* cases and pointed to a type of human rights violation that resonated with the growing coalescence of sentiment against the slave trade, impressment, and convict transportation.[43]

Equiano's *Interesting Narrative* (1789) demonstrated his own (and thus enslaved people's) capacity for refined feeling—evident in his bodily refinement, his sensibility, his morality, and his spirituality. Many English readers would have interpreted his life story as that of an inherently civilized man whose essential refinement had survived the brutalities of slavery. His was a Franklinesque portrait of a canny self-made man—perhaps literally if, as it seems, he had spent formative years in Franklin's home city of Philadelphia and his biography was partly fictionalized to present him as African by birth.[44] He chronicled his emergence as an intelligible man through his attainment of freedom, his accumulation of property, his conversion to Christianity, and his marriage to an English woman. But most of all, Equiano became intelligible as a man because of a refinement of spirit that refused to be extinguished, not because he outmuscled other men. His life story—and his ability both to survive and recount it—became the means of advocating for the enslaved.

At the behest of SEAST, Wilberforce, a member of the evangelical Clapham Sect, brought the issue of abolishing the trade before Parliament on May 12, 1789. He laid the groundwork for his speech by declaring that his aims transcended those of mere national or European interest to engage the whole world and its posterity. He also refused to lay the blame upon a particular party, arguing that the entire Parliament of Great Britain, rather than Liverpool merchants alone, were guilty. Wilberforce insisted that the trade had been carried on by men of humanity but that "the enormous magnitude and extent of the evil which distracts their attention from individual cases, and makes them think generally, and therefore less feelingly on the subject." The scale of the system of commodifying human beings, "more than the human imagination had ever before conceived," he argued, obstructed the empathy normally evoked by bearing witness to human misery. Rather than indict his fellow Britons for their moral failings, Wilberforce attributed their persistent evil course to an inability to bear witness as a result of the distance between merchants and the evil consequences of their investments. "If the wretchedness of any one of the many hundred Negroes stowed in each ship could be brought before their view, and remain within the sight of the African Merchant, that there is no one among them whose heart would bear it." The misery of Africans chained "two and two" and packed into the foul holds of slave ships was so great, Wilberforce claimed, it challenged the feeling witness to "bear to think of such a scene." But he also described the inability to see and feel the suffering wrought by the slave trade as a willful blindness, created by "interest draw[ing] a film across the eyes." It was the duty of all in Parliament "to trust not the reasonings of interested men" who made money from slave-produced goods.[45]

Revolution Again

What happened next provoked new iterations of rights declarations that were increasingly exclusive, even as they revived the body as the basis for universal rights. Just two months after Wilberforce's speech and across the English Channel, a spiral of poor harvests and rising bread prices crested in popular resistance. After several days of protests against King Louis XVI's decision to fire a popular minister and send Swiss mercenary troops to surround the city, on July 14, 1789, angry Parisians gathered at the Bastille, a much-hated prison that symbolized the arbitrary power of the monarch and the aristocracy. Rather than resist the angry crowd of artisans, journalists, lawyers, and women, the prison governor Launay surrendered, allowing the protesters to enter the fortress. After seizing the ammunition they came for, the rebels took Launay captive and decapitated him, mounting his head on a pike to parade around the city. The French Revolution's opening act had begun.[46]

Thomas Jefferson was living in Paris and serving as the United States minister to France when revolutionary fervor drove ordinary Parisians into the streets. Well known to the French as the author of the Declaration of Independence, Jefferson threw his support behind opponents of the old regime. He had enjoyed his time in Paris; French republicans treated him like a wise elder in matters of revolution and republican theory, and he was entranced by Parisian culture. Jefferson interpreted this dramatic moment in French history as further affirmation of the principles of liberty and equality that had inspired the American Revolution. When the Estates General—the French equivalent of Parliament—met in May 1789, Jefferson was among those who attended. Partisans of the revolution subsequently gathered at Jefferson's well-appointed house, where he lived with his two daughters and several enslaved men and women. Among them was Sally Hemings, with whom he subsequently fathered at least six children. Just days before the storming of the Bastille, his good friend the Marquis de Lafayette, a veteran commander of the American Revolution, asked for Jefferson's comments on the Bill of Rights he was drafting for presentation before the National Assembly.

While in Paris providing counsel on French human rights, Jefferson completed work on his *Notes on the State of Virginia* (1785, 1787), a history of sorts that he had begun during the American Revolution while he was governor of the state. His comments on racial physiques and mental capacities appeared as a strange and defensive digression in a chapter on the state's laws, a likely consequence of his attempt to reconcile Enlightenment principles with natural history justifications of North American slavery. His descriptions of people of African descent included derogatory comments about their sweat, smell, and imaginative capacity. His positive accounts of Native American cultures and physiques, in contrast, appeared as part of his effort to counter the Comte de Buffon's claims about New World degeneration. Published in Paris in 1785, *Notes on the State of Virginia* appeared in print for the first time in the United States in Philadelphia in 1788. Among his European peers, it reinforced Jefferson's reputation as an Enlightenment intellectual; among some African-descended and white people, it marked him as a racist betrayer of the universal values articulated in the Declaration.[47]

Following the fall of the Bastille, the deputies of the National Assembly, led by Lafayette, began the daunting task of listing the fundamental rights of human beings. Initially there was disagreement about the efficacy of such a document in France, which had a much larger population and longer history than the United States. As Lafayette explained to the assembly in July, the document should include only natural rights according to principles that articulated "what everyone knows, what everyone feels." There was also concern about a move to political abstraction as public order collapsed. Still, the deputies managed "in solemn declaration the natural, inalienable, and sacred rights of man." The essential rights included liberty, property (which was underscored separately as an "inviolable and sacred right"), security, and resistance to oppression. Sovereignty resided in the nation, and government existed to protect the liberties of citizens from encroachment, unfair punishment, and infringement of speech.[48]

When the French National Assembly presented its "Declaration of the Rights of Man and Citizen" on August 26, 1789, the reverberations crossed oceans. In England, Burke was stirred to write *Reflections on the Revolution in France* (1790), a long defense of social and political tradition as the sedimentation of ancient wisdom. Burke, who had championed the liberty of the American colonies and condemned the East India Company's atrocities, was distressed by the public support given to the French Revolution by English radicals. Burke took particular umbrage at dissenting minister Richard Price's sermon, "A Discourse On the Love of Our Country," celebrating the 101st anniversary of England's 1688 Glorious Revolution. In it, Price advanced radical definitions of country and citizenship. He also linked the "light" of the American Revolution to the "blaze" of events in France, claiming that the latter upheaval "lays despotism in ashes, and warms and illuminates Europe." This celebration of revolution raised Burke's ire and earned Price special mention in his *Reflections*.[49]

Seeing their beloved mentor Price attacked, both Mary Wollstonecraft, an emerging radical, dissenter, and feminist, and Thomas Paine, the celebrated author of *Common Sense*, issued rebuttals. Wollstonecraft, like so many other reform figures who thought against the grain of English political economy and imperial ambition, had connections to the textile industry. She was born in 1759 in East London's Spitalfields manufacturing district, the granddaughter of a master weaver. As Wollstonecraft described the motives behind her own hastily composed effort, "my indignation was roused by the sophistical arguments, that every moment crossed me, in the questionable shape of natural feelings and common sense." She was especially troubled by how the right to secure property and the insistence on submission to authority trumped the rights of the downtrodden, oppressed, and enslaved.[50]

Wollstonecraft's *A Vindication of the Rights of Men* (1790), the first response to Burke to appear in print, professed a Scottish common sense preference for plain spoken argument that was at odds with her convoluted, occasionally breathless, writing style. She was especially offended by what she saw as Burke's manipulation of his readers with complicated arguments and decorative prose. "What is truth?," she asked rhetorically, concluding, "a few fundamental truths meet the first enquiry of reason, and appear as clear to an unwarped mind, as that air and bread are necessary to enable the body to fulfill its vital functions." Highly contentious issues, Wollstonecraft argued, should be "brought back to first principles" so they could be determined through the application of reason rather than "the vagaries of the imagination, or scrupulosity of weakness."[51]

For Wollstonecraft, these fundamental truths included rights that were universal and natural. Liberty was at their core, trumping the right to security of property. "The birthright of man, to give you, Sir, a short definition of this disputed right, is such a degree of liberty, civil and religious, as is compatible with the liberty of every other individual with whom he is united in a social compact, and the continued existence of that compact." She argued against Burke's defense of tradition, asserting, "there are rights which men inherit at their birth, as rational creatures, who were raised above the brute creation by their improvable faculties; and that, in receiving these, not from their forefathers but, from God, prescription can never undermine natural rights." Yet despite this insistence on rights as unalienable, she made an exception in cases where a person's crimes "authorized society to deprive them of the blessing they had abused." Inalienable natural or "native" rights, as she defined them, derived from "birthright," yet the state might strip a person of these in cases of criminality.[52]

In a mercantile age, a person's right to move across oceans and different national jurisdictions quite predictably emerged as one of the central rights questions to be resolved. Naval impressment was one of the abuses most frequently cited by eighteenth-century rights advocates. Throughout the eighteenth century, Britain supplied its need for maritime labor by impressing skilled and experienced sailors who could otherwise make more money on private vessels. This was an essential labor strategy that made England into a naval superpower. Nearly 250,000 men were impressed between 1688 and 1815, a process that included being taken into custody and subjected to interrogation and physical examination to discover the telltale signs of seafaring experience: hard, calloused, and tar-stained hands. Although many North Americans fell victim to British press-gangs both before and after American independence, in theory press-gangs were limited to taking British subjects, a legal targeting of rights-bearing Englishmen that many English critics found hypocritical and unjust. The example of the French alternative, a bureaucratic division by skill of maritime workers who rotated into naval service at regular intervals, failed to dislodge the British press-gang.[53]

The transportation of criminals, in contrast, evoked equivocal responses from critics of the British Empire. Convict transport had changed over time, with the fiction of the transported convict's consent gradually replaced by the notion of transport as a mandatory penalty. Accompanying this shift, the transported convict gradually lost some of his or her potential for assimilability gained through serving terms of labor, and instead appeared to threaten contamination of the polity.[54] Having lost North America as a repository for its criminals, Britain briefly experimented with sending convicts to West Africa in the early 1780s. The disaster at the British forts on the Gold Coast ended these efforts and attention turned to the lands in the Pacific that Captain James Cook, Joseph Banks, and Daniel Solander had reconnoitered during Cook's first Pacific voyage in the *Endeavour* in 1769-1771. British imperial officials authorized Admiral Arthur Phillip to return in 1788 to the spot Banks and Solander dubbed Botany Bay with a new colonial vision for ridding England of its unwanted population. Phillip traveled with the First Fleet, a group of six ships contracted from the slave-trading company Camden, Calvert, and King, and loaded with nearly fifteen hundred convicts. Although representing several different ethnicities and national origins, all the convicts had been stripped of their national protections and rights. Together they left Portsmouth, England, in 1787 and arrived in New South Wales in January 1788. Convicts there belonged to the Crown but were not subject to a permanent loss of the rights of Englishmen, even though their penalty included long terms of servile bondage.[55]

Wollstonecraft's position on the rights of men appears to have been informed by both the emergent abolitionist movement and the practices of impressment and convict transport. In a 1788 review of Samuel Stanhope Smith's *Essay on the Causes of the Variety of Complexion and Figure in the Human Species* (1787), Wollstonecraft concurred with environmental explanations for apparent racial differences and with the fundamental unity of humankind.[56] Reviewing Equiano's autobiography two years later, she duly noted that Equiano had been wronged by being taken against his will from his African birthplace. But the real wrong, as Wollstonecraft saw it, was that learned people degraded Africans "below the common level of humanity" and claimed "that nature, by making them inferior to the rest of the human race, designed to stamp them with the mark of slavery." Although Wollstonecraft did not think Equiano evidenced superior intellectual powers—a coy evaluation in which she positioned herself as his judge—she speculated sardonically that Equiano would be the equal of the "mass" of people in a society more civilized than the Anglo Atlantic that had taken him captive as a child.[57]

A year after her review of Equiano and following on the heels of Wilberforce's speech in Parliament, Wollstonecraft's *A Vindication of the Rights of Men* revealed a more capacious view of divinely bestowed universal rights and of the violations represented by slavery and systemic poverty. She was at pains to privilege the mind over the body—an important claim for a young woman seeking to be taken seriously as a radical thinker—but she abandoned neither the body's materiality nor her deference to God. "I reverence the rights of men. Sacred rights for which I acquire a more profound respect, the more I look into my own mind; and professing these heterodox opinions, I still preserve my bowels; my heart is human, beats quick with human sympathies—and I fear God!" Indeed, the body was crucial to how Wollstonecraft imagined human equality. She lamented stark differences in power that led people to forget the physical basis for their common humanity. Oppression, poverty, and efforts to mimic the unhealthy habits of the wealthy left the poor "with a broken spirit, a worn-out body." Like a badly designed machine, "the clogged wheels of corruption" needed to be "continually oiled by the sweat of the laborious poor," an extraction of value "squeezed out of them by unceasing taxation."[58]

She framed her diatribe against Burke's *Reflections* within a familiar East-West opposition. Christianity and reason set the standard for civilization while the Muslim East stood for barbarism. By analogizing English tradition to the core features of Islam, Wollstonecraft indicted Burke's argument for too closely resembling the illogic and barbarism of Eastern practices.[59] In particular, she castigated him for his love of the aristocracy, challenging two of its most sacred supports, the transmission of landed property across generations according to the rules of primogeniture, and parental control over the marriage choices of children. Motivated by a concern for property and social capital, parents assumed unnatural control over their children's marriages, literally imprisoning them in some cases "to prevent their contaminating their noble blood by following the dictates of nature when they chose to marry."[60]

She considered the impressment of sailors to be one of the starkest examples of inconsistency in the English recognition of natural rights. In Burke's condemnation of the French Revolution, she noted sarcastically, he failed to acknowledge "that property in England is much more secure than liberty," and that "the liberty of an honest mechanic—his all—is often sacrificed to secure the property of the rich." She took Burke to task for "pretend[ing] that a man fights for his country, his hearth or his altars, when he has neither liberty nor property.—His property is in his nervous arms," a clear recognition that the lot of working people was tied to their bodies. She was especially struck by the contrast of harsh punishments for a workingman's act of theft while impressment, which took men "from their daily employments" and degraded them, went unchecked. Any government that acted in this manner, Wollstonecraft reasoned, could not be considered a good parent.[61]

Perhaps the worst of the English violations of natural rights supported by Burke's reverence for tradition was slavery, permitted "by law to fasten her fangs on human flesh, and the iron eat into the very soul." Indeed, slavery was hell on earth, as witnessed by "the lash resound[ing] on the slave's naked sides." As part of the slaveholding class, even women were corrupted by the perversion of slavery's immorality, Wollstonecraft noted, for "if the voice of rumour is to be credited, the captive negroes curse in all the agony of bodily pain, for the unheard of tortures they [the fair ladies] invent." The only expiation of English guilt Wollstonecraft could imagine was the counterfactual scenario of Parliament daring to cross the "planters and negro-drivers" by abolishing the slave trade so that the "natural feelings of humanity silenced the cold cautions of timidity, till this stigma on our nature was wiped off, and all men were allowed to enjoy their birth-right-liberty."[62]

In the two years following Wollstonecraft's *Vindication of the Rights of Men*, abolitionists gained some momentum but suffered from political reaction to events around the Atlantic. Clarkson's statistical evidence of the slave trade won them some allies, and they also made some headway against the West Indian lobby's stranglehold on parliamentary hearings. Yet the defeat of the Abolition Bill of 1791, the best hope of parliamentary action against the slave trade, dimmed the prospects for any further progress. Wilberforce brought it before Parliament in April 1791 amid a rising tide of post–French Revolution reaction and as news of the growing turmoil in Saint Domingue reached London. The bill was easily defeated 163 to 88. Granville Sharp publicly interpreted the vote as a delay rather than a defeat. His words on this occasion foreshadowed the shift in abolitionist tactics and emphasis from challenging the West Indian lobby's rights as slaveholders to mobilizing the power of British consumers. "We will never desist from appealing to the consciences of our countrymen," he declared, "till the commercial intercourse with Africa shall cease to be polluted with the blood of its inhabitants."[63]

Blood in the Sugar

Following the defeat of the Abolition Bill, British abolitionists regrouped to seek popular support. Activists gathered hundreds of petitions and opened new SEAST regional branches. They also began agitating for a national boycott of West Indian sugar.[64] Boycotts had proven their political effectiveness earlier in the eighteenth century. North American nonconsumption and nonimportation movements had helped to galvanize the colonial will to defy British imperial policy, even if they were never quite as damaging to British merchants as North Americans believed them to be. Consumer rejection of white sugar produced by enslaved laborers gave critical new energy to the antislavery movement, according to both contemporary leaders and historians of the movement. In both the North American and British boycotts, the fact that women regularly consumed the goods in question placed them at the center of boycott appeals and activity.[65]

British sugar boycotters connected the bodies of enslaved laborers and sugar with the bodies of consumers. They aimed at a new consumer-based moral economy based on critiques of both slavery and imperialism. In *An Address to the People of Great Britain*, published in 1791 by the Baptist dissident Martha Gurney, one of the few women printing and selling abolitionist pamphlets, William Fox attempted to stir the reader's disgust by associating the cruelty of the slavery used to produce sugar with the intimate act of consuming sugar through the mouth. Fox's evocation of the effluvia from enslaved bodies tainting the sugar on the table of British consumers resonated with early modern depictions of Indigenous cannibals and of the slave trader's traffic in humans as the equivalent of drinking their blood. In the context of advanced mercantilism, however, it was the British consumer who risked unwittingly committing acts of cannibalism by ingesting commodities flavored by the suffering bodies of the enslaved laborers who produced them.[66]

As the boycott gained momentum, news of the horrors of the Second Fleet to New South Wales reached London, adding new evidence of British imperial disregard for those understood to have forfeited the protections of subjects. The Second Fleet departed England in January 1790 and arrived in Botany Bay six months later with 26 percent of the convicts dead and many more debilitated from starvation and disease. The captains had decided to reserve stores of food to sell in New South Wales rather than distribute them to the convicts. This represented the radical failure of any moral economy, old or new, to restrain greed for profit. News of the deaths did not reach London until late fall 1791. Captains Traill and Ellerington were put on trial in spring 1792, but there were no convictions. Meanwhile, Camden, Calvert, and King, the company with the contract for the Second Fleet ships, secured another contract for the Third Fleet.[67]

Wollstonecraft's second manifesto on human rights, *A Vindication of the Rights of Woman* (1792), appeared in the midst of the sugar boycott, public knowledge of the Second Fleet disaster, and news of the slave rebellion in St. Domingue. Wollstonecraft's interest in the condition of women had been stirred by reading Catharine Macaulay's *Letters on Education* (1790), but popular support for the sugar boycott, with its explicit recognition of the political and economic clout of the English housewife, likely helped to refocus Wollstonecraft's attention on the connections between politics and domestic life. She insisted that her argument for a common humanity was rooted in a claim to soul equality and a capacity for reason. She also debunked the implicit right conferred by brute strength, acknowledging that "bodily strength seems to give man a natural superiority over woman; and this is the only solid basis on which the superiority of the sex can be built." But she stopped short of renouncing bodily difference, adding hastily, "let it not be concluded that I wish to invert the order of things."[68]

For Wollstonecraft, the soul was the birthright that grounded everyone's claims to humanity, but some individuals were also privileged to fully inhabit that humanity because of their capacity for reason. Motherhood, according to Wollstonecraft, was a woman's best opportunity for demonstrating her rational capacity and asserting her full humanity—but it was also the central relationship in families. By spurning the artifice of fashion and the distortions of aristocratic manners, women could realize their natural capacities for reason and moral sensibility in their role as mothers. Raised to live in their natural state, women would be prudent and responsible mothers—true adults—rather than vain, childish creatures, trained only to chase pleasure and to please men. Motherhood, Wollstonecraft argued, should define their relationship to the state and their value as citizens. This could happen, however, only if men also transformed and learned to value women in their natural state as morally dependable adult companions rather than childish playthings. It went without saying that female adulthood was incompatible with the Eastern harem.[69]

Wollstonecraft often compared women to slaves—most often Eastern slaves—to underscore her point about women's violated human rights and squandered human potential. In Wollstonecraft's analysis, if a woman remained too filled with passion, she risked being too gendered, like the women of the harem who appear in Wollstonecraft's text as the nameless "slaves" who were reduced to their sexual function as producers of male pleasure. Without the free will to act independently, there could be no true morality or adult responsibility. Lacking that freedom, a woman could not develop her reason, that key attribute of her humanity. "When, therefore, I call women slaves," Wollstonecraft explained, "I mean in a political and civil sense; for indirectly they obtain too much power and are debased by their exertions to obtain illicit sway." Her main point of reference was not Atlantic slavery but the bondage of the East, "the true style of Mahometanism," in which, she claimed, women were subordinate beings and not truly part of the human species. She found most of the thinkers and poets of her age, including Milton, Rousseau, and the Reverend James Fordyce, guilty of this dehumanizing proposition rooted in the "Mahometan" principle that "a girl should be educated for her husband with the same care as for an Eastern harem."[70]

Rationally performed duty rather than passion, moral autonomy rather than cloistered dependence, emerged in Wollstonecraft's comparison of the ideal middle-class woman to the woman of the harem. By offering this contrast, Wollstonecraft yoked her vision of the enlightened mother to the imperial ascendance of the West, making it a necessary component of the West's moral, economic, and political domination over the East. These deeply rooted tropes of motherhood and of Eastern barbarism would have a long life among British and American abolitionists.[71]

Why did the slaves Wollstonecraft referenced come mainly from the harems of the East when enslaved Africans would have offered the most salient and contested example of slavery in her own time? Indeed, as we have noted,

Wollstonecraft was one of the first to review Equiano's *Interesting Narrative* (1789), and in her review she quoted extensively from his account of slavery's impact on women. Why then, did she give the plight of enslaved African women short shrift in her *Vindication* devoted to defending the human rights of women?[72]

When Wollstonecraft invoked enslaved people of African descent, they were usually gender-neutral "slaves" and the logic was analogy, not intersection. After a lengthy discussion of the limited intellects of slaves, she compared (English) women to those "uncivilized beings who have not yet extended the dominion of the mind, or even learned to think with the energy necessary to concatenate the abstract train of thought which produces principles." On two other occasions Wollstonecraft referred specifically to enslaved Africans as analogous to women. In one instance, she compared the injunction to women to be sweet playthings for men to the demands on enslaved people to produce sugar, with language that evoked the sugar boycott. "Is sugar always to be produced by vital blood?" she asked rhetorically? "Is one half of the human species, like the poor African slaves, to be subject to prejudices that brutalize them, when principles would be a sure guard, only to sweeten the cup of man?"[73]

Wollstonecraft never revealed much specific concern for the plight of the enslaved mother whose painful agricultural labors in sugarcane fields and stolen reproductive capacity supported the Atlantic plantation complex.[74] She rarely acknowledged enslaved African or Native American women and appears to have found them distinctly unhelpful as foils for the "wrongs" of British women. Even when she focused on the case of African slaves, she took note of the deprivations of class—the want of a cultivated mind leading to a taste for bodily adornment—rather than the unique features of the enslaved woman's condition as chattel used to produce slave property for their masters.[75] It would little behoove her to dwell on the plight of enslaved women of African descent if her aim was to condemn middle-class women's foolish pursuit of indirect power through their sensuality rather than the injustice of backbreaking and heartbreaking labor. Generic slaves, slaves of the ancient world, and women of the harem and the seraglio—the Eastern slaves who so captured British and American imaginations—best exposed the perversity of middle-class women's aristocratic aspirations.[76]

Wollstonecraft's comparison of English women and slaves left many questions unresolved. What was the connection between "birthright" and natural rights? If natural rights were indeed a birthright, why didn't a mother play any part in passing these to her child? Wollstonecraft's suggestion that a woman's maternal capacity could be the basis for her citizenship helped to fill the lacunae between the mother's otherwise unrecognized status as the producer of a child, and the child's entitlement to natural rights at birth. If the mother herself was a rights bearer by dint of her motherhood, her production of a rights-bearing child appeared less mysterious even as it sharpened the critique of women's subordination to men. But for all its attention to the "rights of woman," Wollstonecraft's second *Vindication* confused matters even further. Her triangulation of women of the harem with English women's second-class citizenship and the enslaved mother's reproduction of the master's property failed to address slavery's fundamental violation of that maternal bond. This was not the disparity in rights that Wollstonecraft sought to illuminate in this publication. She found little use for the plight of enslaved African women to advance her claim for women's humanity in her second *Vindication.*

Ultimately, Wollstonecraft's approach to vindicating rights was not unlike that of Equiano, who indicted slavery for the wrongs it perpetrated by offering abundant evidence of his own capacity to transcend those wrongs to become a moral and feeling adult. Equiano's adult embodied an androgynous emotional and intellectual ideal for human achievement and refinement rather than male stoicism. In this, both he and Wollstonecraft evinced a shared concept of humanity and human rights that rejected extreme manifestations of gender as diminishing human potential. They shared with the Massachusetts petitioners of 1774 the use of the language of birthright to confer belonging to people often silently excluded from the revolutionary claims for equality and natural rights. This fraught relationship between enslaved women and the forfeited birthright of their children would continue to define slavery as well as activist efforts to undo it.

Chapter 3

One Blood

> Names & Ages of Negro Children born free of Mothers (late in the possession of Charles Logan) after attaining the ages of thirty years
> 35—Mourning of Beck Woodson 1784
> 36—Fanny of d[itt]o—1786
> 37—Sam of d[itt]o—1788
> 38—Joseph of d[itt]o—1790
>
> —Account of children born of enslaved mothers in the Pleasants estate ordered by the Virginia Court of Appeals, 1799

Using the language of "one blood" and birthright, eighteenth-century abolitionists around the Atlantic asserted a universal humanity. But what happened when claims to one blood conflicted with the more common perception of blood as the essence of family connection? This was the situation when two men appeared before Virginia's High Court of Chancery in 1797. One was a seventy-four-year-old Quaker and the executor of his father's vast estate; the other an enslaved man of about thirty years old reckoned by the state as part of the first family's wealth. In the lawsuit that brought them to court as allies rather than as adversaries, slavery's biopolitical calculations and natural rights contradictions appeared in high relief. Robert Pleasants, the Quaker (referred to hereafter as Robert), and Ned, the enslaved man, joined their suits in *Pleasants v. Pleasants* (1800) to challenge several Pleasants heirs who refused to comply with John Pleasants III's directives to emancipate slaves belonging to his estate. Their unlikely partnership reflected the tortuous path of abolitionism and slave law in Virginia during the age of Atlantic revolutions. At issue was how slavery's principle of maternal inheritance could be extricated from the bodies of women defined legally as the reproducers of slave labor.[1]

Ned's and Robert's belonging to families with distinct, yet intertwined fates reflected their different purchases on natural rights. The Pleasants family was large, wealthy, white, and well connected, with dozens of Pleasants men named John, Thomas, Samuel, and Robert appearing in hundreds of legal documents. In contrast, Ned and his family left only a sparse documentary trail; he appears to have been a young boy when his enslaver, John Pleasants III, died in 1771 (Figure 2). The only certainty in Ned's biography is his and his siblings' birth to an enslaved mother, a fact that made him part of a vast cohort of North American–born African-descended children whose lives testified to slavery's unprecedented growth in the plantation economies of the Chesapeake.

That these two men should appear in court on the same side of a legal challenge to slavery might seem surprising. The convergence of their legal interests in *Pleasants v. Pleasants* reveals how the terms of the legal debate—pitting "one blood," birthright, and natural rights against property rights—poorly captured the actual physical and material consequences of slavery for the enslaved. The circumstances leading to the suit reveal how mundane the racialization of the body could be. In Robert Pleasants's early experiment with free labor in a slave society, white neighbors interpreted any manifestation of Black bodily autonomy as threatening. The court's decision in *Pleasants v. Pleasants*, moreover, exposed the contradictions between body-centered natural rights assumptions and the biopolitical entanglements of classifying enslaved people as perpetually reproducing and inheritable property. The contested meaning of birthright for an enslaved child stood at the center of this conflict. Denials of the birthrights of children born to enslaved women became key to the persistent reproduction of slavery and would become the institution's mainstay after 1807. Conflicts over the value of slave labor, female reproductive potential, and child nurture became visible as lawyers for both sides advanced their claims within a legal context committed to protecting property rights.[2]

Examining Robert and Ned's efforts shifts our focus from the broad strokes of the history of blood and birthright, discussed in Chapters 1 and 2, to the habits of body, face-to-face interactions, and coercive relationships, defined and knitted together under slavery, that had to be unraveled for slavery to be undone. Dwelling at length on *Pleasants v. Pleasants* allows us to follow a white enslaver-turned abolitionist engaging with these problems in "real" time in Virginia, the first place in the colonial Atlantic in which maternal inheritance was codified into law as well as the first place in British North America where enslaved populations grew by birth rather than by capture. As a Quaker slave-trading and plantation interest that spanned Virginia's transformation from a society run by elite slaveholders to an economy broadly dependent on slave labor, the Pleasants family enables the historian to situate the family's abolitionist principles in the context

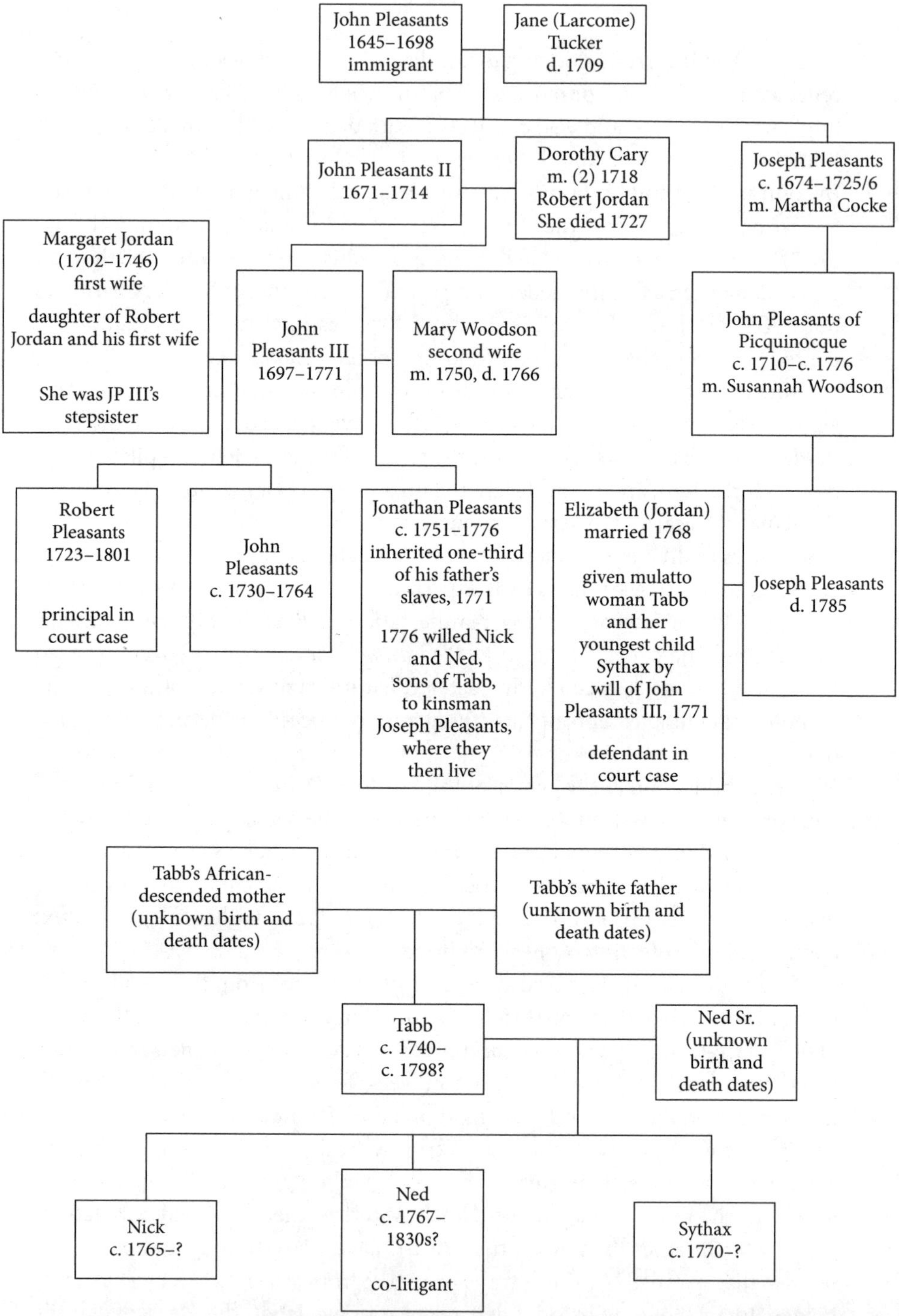

Figure 2. Pleasants family tree / Ned's family tree.

of embodied conditions on the ground: the crops grown, the hostility of white Virginians to Black people's liberties, and the central place of enslaved mothers in producing families reckoned as wealth by white planters.

The Way to Wealth

Children born Free of Mothers late in the Possession of Samuel Pleasants
14 Lucy of Judy—Jany. 1784
15 Delphia of d[itt]o Mar. 1786
16 Letty of d[itt]o Sepr. 1788
17 Mourning of d[itt]o Mar. 1790
18 Tabb of d[itt]o Novr. 1793

By the mid-eighteenth century, the Pleasants family was one of the largest tobacco-planting concerns in Virginia, boasting thousands of acres of land and holding hundreds of people in slavery. They were part of a vast network of wealthy and influential Quakers that extended from North Carolina to New England and across the Atlantic to Ireland and England. The family's success came from fortuitous intermarriages, Atlantic mercantile connections, and the early and steady acquisition of land and enslaved labor. The Pleasants family had been in the Virginia colony since the arrival in 1665 of John Pleasants (hereafter John I), son of a Norwich worsted weaver. Within four years, John I took out his first patent for land in Henrico County, claiming a property that became known as Curles. It boasted a prime location on a dramatic curve in the James River and was well situated for the water transport of people and goods. Like many white men in Virginia who rose above their ordinary beginnings, John I had the good fortune to marry a widow, Jane Larcome Tucker, who brought property and a daughter to the marriage. At some point before this union, perhaps under the influence of his wife-to-be, John I became a Quaker, a sect that was subject to legal harassment.[3]

Despite his Quaker affiliation, John I became one of Henrico County's leading men. In 1677, he and several other landowners in the county signed an account of their grievances submitted to the royal commissioners investigating the causes of Bacon's Rebellion (1676). By 1679, Pleasants was accountable for thirteen taxable laborers, a large number compared to his neighbors. He continued to accrue land in the vicinity of Curles as a consequence of debt collection and purchases. By 1687, Pleasants enslaved at least two boys, Dick and Joseph, whom he presented to the Henrico County court to have their ages judged—a process used to determine when they would become taxable adults.[4]

John I's financial success came not only through his use of enslaved people to produce tobacco but as a consequence of his role as a merchant and slave trader. Throughout the 1680s and 1690s, Pleasants worked as a consignee for the London mercantile house Paggen & Company, the third largest tobacco importer in England in 1686, a position that gave him an advantage in procuring his own slaves. This accounts, in part, for his significant investment in slave labor during the last two decades of his life. It also occasionally required some explaining. In 1684, Pleasants and his fellow Paggen & Company employee Richard Kennon, also of Henrico County, successfully avoided paying taxes owed to the county for owning adult enslaved laborers. Their claim, that the enslaved people in their possession were consigned by Paggen & Company for the purposes of resale and not actually employed producing tobacco, convinced the county justices to forgo the tax assessed on able-bodied adult male and female slaves.[5]

Importing slaves for resale also gave Pleasants an advantage in land acquisition. Under Virginia law, each individual brought into the colony, whether slave, servant, or free, earned the importer fifty acres of land. For much of the seventeenth century, the headright law encouraged settlers to transport both family members and servants and served as an impetus to land patents and land clearance—a dynamic that fed conflicts with Native Americans. During the 1690s, land claims for imported slaves spiked. This was the period when John I was acting on his own behalf and as an agent for other planters seeking to purchase newly trafficked Africans.[6]

By combining the roles of husband, father, and matchmaker with those of tobacco planter, merchant, and slave trader, John I amassed a significant fortune in land and slaves.[7] When he died in 1698, he entailed nine thousand acres of land and a dozen enslaved people to his four children. All of his children had married well, gaining land, slaves, and political connections of their own. To his son John II, John I gave nineteen hundred acres of land in Henrico, including the Curles Plantation. Ten years later, the widowed Jane divided her personal effects among her Tucker and Pleasants descendants and distributed several enslaved people she brought to the marriage as part of her jointure property; each of the children and grandchildren named in her will received a single woman or girl, a bequest that smacked of reproductive calculation. She also gave a boy named Neddy to her son Joseph, expressing the wish that he be trained to become a shoemaker. She reserved the gift of two enslaved people, "Ceaser" and Betty, to son John II.[8]

Investments in Enslaved People's Bodies

Children born Free of Mothers late in the Possession of Samuel Pleasants
11 Rose of Mariah & Will—Octr 1786
12 Kate of d[itt]o—Sept 1793
13 Jacob of d[itt]o—Feby 1797

Slavery was an important foundation for John I's way to wealth. Yet for him as well as for some of his descendants, the extraction of enslaved people's labor became abhorrent at some point just after midcentury. What was it about their relationship with enslaved people, their Atlantic mercantile networks, and their Quaker faith that turned some family members into abolitionists by the last quarter of the eighteenth century?

From the beginning of their tenure in Virginia, the Pleasants family boasted connections to influential Quaker merchants in Philadelphia and England. Over time, those Quaker contacts became more critical of the traffic in slaves. Scholars have debated the source of this growing revulsion toward the slave trade, highlighting Quaker spiritual principles, the rise of Enlightenment natural rights arguments, and the impact of mercantile activity. For some Quakers, they contend, abolition connected an emergent and capacious notion of "the human" to a concept of natural rights defined in opposition to slavery's systematic and brutal violations.[9] For other scholars, Quaker theology was less significant for Quaker humanitarian activism than the consequences of long-distance mercantile networks for moral and ethical imaginations. Engagement with distant markets stretched the imaginative capacities of mercantile players, according to the historian Thomas Haskell, increasing their receptiveness to and sympathy for the suffering of distant strangers.[10]

John II, however, seemed unmoved by the plight of the people he enslaved. He began his adult life with nearly two thousand acres and roughly half a dozen enslaved people, a substantial start in life for a young man at the end of the seventeenth century. His marriage to Dorothy Cary, daughter of a Warwick, Virginia, plantation owner, brought additional property to the estate. But perhaps more important for the growth of the family's wealth and power, John II assumed his father's relationship with Paggen & Company as well as with several other London merchants.[11] The inventory of John II's estate at his death lists fourteen enslaved people including Caesar and Betty, whom his mother had left to him out of her "jointure negroes." Five of the fourteen were children and three of the four were described as old, including Betty—likely the same woman his mother had given to him—and a woman named Pendah.[12]

The enslaved people on John II's plantations worked at a variety of tasks that reflected agricultural and artisanal diversification as well as a central dependence on tobacco production. Each enslaved person would likely have been given an allotment of the coarse blue linen listed in the inventory. Enumerated tools, including a range of specialized hoes (harrow hoes, broad hoes, weeding hoes, grubbing hoes, and hilling hoes), suggest that enslaved people spent most of their time cultivating tobacco. A well-worn plow and plowshare, moreover, pointed to the production of corn and wheat, as did a mill and grindstone. A substantial list of cattle (including cows, heifers, yearlings, bulls, cows, and calves), a brass skimmer and ladle, and earthen butter pots testified to the plantation's dairying activities. Equipment for land clearance and timber extraction reflected the estate's reliance on the purchase and "improvement" of new plantation lands. John II likely sold some lumber and used the rest for constructing buildings and fences or for fuel. The Pleasants estate also boasted smithing equipment and three guns, probably used to protect the estate's livestock from predators and to hunt for deer, pheasants, and turkey.[13]

When John II died in 1714 at the age of forty-two, his seventeen-year-old son John III received all of his "lands, mills and tenements on the south side of the James River." Under John III's long stewardship, the Pleasants family estate grew exponentially. The family's prosperity and calculations of future wealth depended on relationships with Atlantic merchants and shipping concerns that came directly to the James River, as well as those that did regular business in Philadelphia.[14] John III took goods on consignment from London and Philadelphia merchants for resale at stores in Virginia.[15] He formed a commercial partnership with his brother Thomas and his son Robert, placing imported cargos under Robert's management in 1747.[16] As the source of debt creation for smaller planters in the colony, John III and his partners turned their customers' debts into mortgaged lands and enslaved people that sometimes became part of the Pleasants estate.[17]

John III's long life contributed to the stability of his white family and encouraged capital accumulation, but it also created the conditions for family formation among the enslaved people of his estate. His original bequest of enslaved laborers not only survived with him but, along with several other enslaved people, produced families during the long life of their enslaver. Indeed, as the Pleasants estate grew, so did the proportional value of the people he claimed as enslaved property. At the time of his death in 1771, John III had an estate valued at 12,143 pounds sterling with 9,722 pounds—over 75 percent of the total value of the estate—represented by 215 enslaved people. This was a vastly different estate than that of his grandfather, who had claimed a dozen slaves and thousands of acres of land.[18]

A significant portion of the John III's wealth came from the bodies of enslaved women. Between the time of John I and John II, as we have seen, enslaved children became a more significant portion of the enslaved people listed on estate inventories, representing over a third of the enslaved cohort in 1713. Although no records reveal exactly how that population grew on John III's estate, whether by additional purchases of captive Africans, mortgages of enslaved people from other estates, or births to women already enslaved, births appear to have become a more important factor by the 1740s and 1750s, when John III had reached a prosperous middle age. The women born during these two decades were born in Virginia rather than West Africa.[19]

Twelve of these women, ranging in age from sixteen to twenty-nine and whose family formations left archival traces, had already borne twenty-one children by the time of John III's death in 1771. The oldest woman in this cohort, "Pindar," born in 1742 and perhaps a descendant of the woman named Pendah in John II's inventory, had five children ranging in age from four through twelve. The youngest woman, Sylvia, listed as the "daughter of Phillis," was only sixteen and not yet a mother. By the time Virginia's High Court of Chancery adjudicated John III's estate in 1799, these women and their daughters had given birth to another forty children. Recognizing a few individuals and their families in his will, John III acted within a thicket of enduring coerced relationships, many of which extended back generations to the enslaved people he had inherited upon his father's death.

Ned was just one of many enslaved children counted as part of this wealth when John III died. Sometime during the late 1740s, Ned's enslaved grandmother gave birth to a female child. This particular child, known archivally only by the name Tabb, was identified in the Pleasants family papers as a "mulatto." That the father of this particular enslaved child was likely white meant nothing to John III's calculation of her value; Tabb would remain enslaved. Virginia law legally distanced enslaved mothers and children from all fathers, but especially white fathers, thwarting publicly acknowledged family connections.[20]

Even if John III had been of a mind to free her, a 1748 recodification of the colony's 1723 law prohibited it. So Tabb grew to adulthood as part of the Pleasants estate. In 1771, when he wrote his will, John III bequeathed "Mulatto Tabb" and her youngest child, Sythax, to Elizabeth Pleasants, wife of his kinsman Joseph. Tabb had given birth to at least two other children by 1771, boys named Nick and Ned, who were at least four years old. Nick and Ned were legally, if not actually, separated from their mother and younger brother by the death of their aged enslaver and were given to John III's youngest son, Jonathan, a seventeen-year-old who received one-third of the estate's slaves.[21] When Jonathan died prematurely in 1776 at the age of twenty-two, he bequeathed Nick and Ned to his kinsman Joseph Pleasants, whose wife, Elizabeth, held their mother, Tabb, in slavery and with whom they already resided. Jonathan made no mention of Sythax, their younger brother, whose fate is unknown. Tabb's and Ned's relationship as enslaved mother and son placed them squarely in the portion of the estate's enslaved population that had grown rapidly in size and value between the 1740s and 1771.

Although the Pleasants men treated enslaved people as inheritable property that could be moved about at will, they acknowledged Ned's and Nick's family connection to their mother, Tabb. We are left to imagine the reasons for their specific arrangements for Tabb and her children. Perhaps Tabb's own insistence on their connection might have made her memorable to her enslavers. Or perhaps knowledge of Tabb's white father gave the Pleasants men some special reason for being mindful of her and her children. Could she have been the daughter of John III or one of his brothers or sons?[22]

Quaker Connections

> Names & Ages of Negro Children born free of Mothers (late in the possession of Charles Logan) after attaining the ages of thirty years
> 16—Tom—of Sukey decd Augt 1784

John III and his sons inhabited a small yet cosmopolitan and wealthy Quaker world. The same circuits of communication that carried spiritual guidance brought imported goods, commercial information, and eventually challenges to the moral foundation of prosperity built on slave ownership. John III's leadership of the Cedar Creek Virginia Meeting and his connections to prominent Quakers in West River, Maryland, and Philadelphia would have kept him current with the growing Quaker unease with slavery. When the Philadelphia Yearly Meeting reiterated its concerns about purchasing slaves in 1735, cautioning members against "encouraging the Importation of Negroes, by buying them after Imported," John III would have been one of the first Virginia Quakers to know.[23]

As a young man in his twenties, John III's eldest son Robert moved temporarily to Philadelphia, where he became acquainted with several prominent Quaker families and merchants, some of who subsequently became his relatives.[24] He formed important ties with the Pemberton family, who were wealthy merchants and enslavers like his father. During the 1740s, the decade when Robert first became acquainted with him, Israel Pemberton Jr. (1715–1779) was heavily invested in the commerce in British textiles and iron, but he also shipped flour, corn, barrel components, rum, and molasses. The Pembertons also supplied the Pleasants family with books for distribution further south. Israel remained

Robert's main correspondent until his death in 1779, at which point Robert turned to writing to his brother James Pemberton (1723–1809), a man his own age who shared his interest in books, commercial affairs, and eventually abolition. A prominent merchant and citizen, James was a member of Franklin's Library Company and the Board of the Pennsylvania Hospital.[25] Another of Robert's important early connections was John Smith, son-in-law of Quaker merchant James Logan and a successful Philadelphia merchant in his own right. Smith was a founding member of the American Philosophical Society. He had traveled to Barbados before returning to Philadelphia to run a successful store. After Robert returned to Virginia from Philadelphia, Smith offered to share his contact in Barbados. He also attempted to find a mutual business interest in the white cedar and cypress that grew in the swamps around Robert's tobacco plantations.[26]

Robert's marriages expanded his commercial and religious networks. His first marriage, to Mary Webster, brought him a connection to Josiah Webster, a Norfolk iron producer whose ironworks shipped pig iron to Bristol and Liverpool. In addition to supplying Robert with iron, Josiah carefully calculated Mary's marriage portion, selling off land he had reserved for her so that he could give the couple money instead of land or furniture.[27] When Mary died in 1757, Robert married Mary Thomas Hill, the widowed daughter of a West River, Maryland, Quaker planter.

Just as the Pleasants family was strengthening its ties with Philadelphia's Quaker merchant community, that region's Quaker leadership began to acknowledge the sinfulness of the traffic in slaves. In 1757, John Woolman, the author of *Some Considerations on the Keeping of Negroes* (1754) almost certainly met personally with Quakers at the Cedar Creek Meeting in Virginia and in North Carolina to try to persuade them of slavery's evils.[28] By 1758, the Philadelphia Yearly Meeting put teeth into the admonition against slave trafficking by banning all commerce in slaves and striking those who persisted from positions of authority. It also established a committee to visit and confront slave owners, a controversial practice that generated conflict.[29] A few Quakers went even further to distance themselves from slavery's evils. In 1761, Joshua Evans of the Haddonfield, New Jersey, Meeting decided to wear homespun, forswear animal meat, and avoid purchasing any goods made by slaves. As early as 1762, Woolman and others refused the products of slave labor, including having their bodies touch cloth dyed with slave-produced West Indian or South Carolinian indigo.[30]

It is not clear when John III and his son Robert began to apply the growing Quaker antislavery testimony to their own circumstances. Technically, their traffic in slaves had become indirect, through mortgages of other people's laborers rather than through purchases or sales, but the difference was a subtle one. Mortgaging slaves was a transaction based on the legal definition of enslaved people as a highly fungible and movable form of property. This means to gaining new slaves was marginal, however, compared to the childbearing capacity of the women enslaved by the estate.[31]

Quaker testimony about the humanity of enslaved people reached Virginia Quakers at the moment when native birth and family formation, rather than trafficking from West Africa, had come to characterize the colony's enslaved population. The people enslaved by the Pleasants family, many of whom likely had ancestors among Igbo and Gold Coast peoples trafficked between 1690 and 1730, were no longer newly commodified individuals but had their own family connections in Virginia. Like their enslavers, African-descended people in Virginia were increasingly likely to have been born in the colony in the midst of Virginia-born kin.[32]

Robert began openly discussing abolition with his correspondents during the 1760s. First Israel and then James Pemberton provided him with news and print materials recently arrived from London and updated him on the progress of Philadelphia Quakers. Robert also struck up his own correspondence with Anthony Benezet and other Quaker abolitionists. In 1762, Benezet sent Robert some pamphlets on the slave trade that had been recently published in Philadelphia; even at this early date, the Pleasants family was an important node in southern Quaker information networks.[33] Three years later, Robert, his son Robert Jr., his uncle Thomas, and several other Quakers were appointed by the Virginia Yearly Meeting to produce an epistle to the Quarterly and Monthly Meeting to consider a proposal "to put a stop to the further purchase of Negroes." In 1768, the Virginia Yearly Meeting denied members permission to "purchase a Negro or other slaves." The following year the Yearly Meeting agreed to try to persuade members of the assembly to pass a law ending the traffic in slaves.[34]

This stirring of North American Quaker antislavery sentiment, while significant for the Pleasants family, was not sufficient in and of itself to transform Robert's views of enslaved people and did little to nothing for the enslaved people themselves. Perhaps the succession of deaths and realignments within the family during the 1760s put him in mind of his own mortality and the state of his soul. The death of his second wife, Mary Thomas Hill, in 1762, following so quickly after their marriage in 1760, shocked and saddened him.[35] In an effort to articulate the beauty of his deceased wife's character, Robert praised her restraint with the household's "servants," whom he described as "people generally remarkable for carelessness & negligence."[36] These words, written in 1762, were certainly not those of a man convinced of the fundamental equality of humankind.

The death of Robert's younger brother and his father's namesake, John Pleasants Jr., in July 1764, however, seems to have shaken the family further. John Jr.

and Robert had served together as representatives to the Virginia Quarterly and Yearly Meetings. John distanced himself from the community of Cedar Creek Quakers after his decision to marry a non-Quaker. Robert wrote to his brother in 1759 to voice his disapproval of his choice of a wife. Robert's testimony to his brother's desire to reconcile with the Quaker meeting at his death—a longer and more intimate testimony than he provided for any of his wives—suggests the profound connection between the two.[37]

Other factors moving Virginia's planter class to distance itself from the institution that had made it rich included the self-interested appropriation of natural rights criticisms of British imperial rule. One of the signal contributors to this antislavery discussion, the Edinburgh-educated Dr. Arthur Lee of the wealthy Virginia planter family, published an "Address on Slavery" in the *Virginia Gazette* in 1767. Lee's address, directed at the assembly, appears to have expedited the passage of legislation just two weeks later to raise the duty on imported African slaves as a means of discouraging new importations and relieving planter indebtedness (the Crown later disallowed the law). Lee's essay also got picked up by Anthony Benezet, who bowdlerized it for republication in 1768, being careful to leave out Lee's warnings to white people about the dangers of slave insurrection.[38]

Lee had previously authored a defense of the colonies and a strongly worded indictment of Africans for being savage. By 1767, however, the year after his return to Virginia from England, his tone and his focus had shifted. He now insisted on the obligations of Christian masters to maintain a consistent commitment to natural rights both in their own colonial situation and in that of their slaves. Signing off as "Philanthropos" (loving and caring for mankind) on what was supposed to be the first installment of a two-part essay, Lee hewed to a natural rights argument that pointed to the contradictions between hereditary slavery and the law of nations.[39] "Now as freedom is unquestionably the birthright of all mankind, of Africans as well as Europeans," Lee reasoned, "to keep the former in a State of Slavery is a constant violation of that right, and therefore of Justice."[40]

Lee disputed the grounds used to defend slavery—consent, force, and birth—by arguing that a man could not consent to make himself an outlaw, a status he defined as slavery's essence. Outside the laws governing subjects, a slave was neither bound to obey them nor a beneficiary of their protections. Lee denied that any right could coexist with the use of force, which made slavery necessarily wrong, "since if the Parent cannot be justly made a Slave, neither can the Child be born in Slavery." He denounced both the legality and justice of enslaving Africans, noting the absence of the conditions of just war and British conquest. Ultimately, Lee turned to the wisdom common among abolitionists, "do unto others as you wou'd they shou'd do unto you," and asked whether it wasn't "the most outrageous violat[ion] of this & every other principle of right, Justice & humanity, who should make a slave of you and your Posterity forever." The linchpin of Lee's argument, complementing the connection he drew between the cost of slaves and the drain of specie from the colony, was the danger of slave rebellion. Lee saw this risk of violence as one of the fundamental evils of slavery, predicting "on us, or on our posterity, the inevitable blow, must, one day, fall; and probably with the most irresistible vengeance the longer it is protracted."[41]

In 1769, the Virginia House of Burgesses tried unsuccessfully to remedy the colony's shortage of specie and indebtedness to British merchants by discouraging slave importations.[42] Two measures to raise duties on imported slaves passed in the House of Burgesses in December of that year, but pressure from British merchants led the Crown to suspend the acts. A third measure to permit manumissions, supported by Robert and his fellow Quaker Edward Stabler, did not pass. The use of rights language nonetheless had made an impression on Robert. He copied into his letter book an undated article he attributed to the *Virginia Gazette* signed "A Virginian," which used the rights language he subsequently drew on to advocate for manumission.[43]

Conditional Manumission

> Names & Ages of Negro Children born free of Mothers (late in the possession of Charles Logan) after attaining the ages of thirty years
> 12 Biddy—of Grace Aug 1790
> Sold RC. Jack—of d[itt]o—March 1786
> 14 Milly—of d[itt]o—March 1788
> 15 Sally—of d[itt]o—March 1795

The story of Ned's and Robert's unlikely legal alliance began in 1771 when Robert's father, John Pleasants III, gave instructions in his will that addressed the tangle of blood, birthright, and maternal inheritance under slavery: "And my desire further is respecting my poor slaves all of them as I shall die possessed of shall be free (if they choose it) when they arrive at the age of thirty years and the laws of this land will admit them to be set free without their being transported out of the country. I say all my slaves now born or hereafter to be born whilst their mothers are in service of me or my heirs to be free at the age of thirty years as before mentioned to be adjudged of by my trustees their age."[44]

John acted boldly to create a manumission plan for the two hundred fifteen people he enslaved; they represented 75 percent of the wealth his heirs hoped to inherit, with the first state-sponsored gradual abolition plan in Pennsylvania still nine years away. The will's stipulation of thirty years of service reflected both George Fox's gradual emancipation scheme and the Virginia colony's mandate earlier in the eighteenth century for the mixed-race children of white servant women to serve extended terms. The will's provision created a complex maternal algorithm by which John III tried to balance the enslaved women's natural rights with his claim in perpetuity to their wombs and children. According to John III's plan, the legal classification of the women's wombs would change during the course of their lives. Women under the age of thirty who gave birth to children encumbered by thirty-year terms of service became capable after they turned thirty of birthing technically free children. By creating these thirty-year terms of service for some of the children, John III accounted for the costs of childbirth and child nurture and deducted these from the liberty "futures" he granted. We might note that no one acknowledged the value of enslaved women's labor in birthing and rearing children.[45]

John III personally arranged the bequests of certain of his enslaved people with whom he and his children shared a history. He bestowed special privileges on eight individuals, distinguished by a combination of age and occupation, listing them by name and allowing them to choose the Pleasants heir with whom to live. Joe Cooper, Old Sukey, Fanny, old Robin, Carpenter Will, old Nat, old "Cesar," and Aggy were "to be at their liberty to live with any of my children they shall choose and not to be controlled, and to enjoy the benefit of their labour as fully as if (they) were free, and if . . . any of them live to an age they cannot maintain themselves they shall have a maintenance from my estate, which is all the freedom I can give them consistent with the law of the land." But, John III noted, if they misbehaved, the trustees for his estate could return them to servitude.

Another person who John III described as "his man," Charles White, was to be allowed to take his two sons to work with him on the water, presumably as a boatman transporting cargoes, and to keep a third of what they earned. Phil, also described by John III as "his man," was to live with the Pleasants heir of his choice, who would supply him with "working apparel" and pay him 4 percent of his earnings. John III thought it "best" for Sharper and his wife, Biddy, not to "be at their liberty," as he deemed them "not capable of getting their livelihood."

There were still other dispositions of enslaved individuals, many of them children, whom John III bequeathed to his white Pleasants children and grandchildren. Gifts of enslaved children to white children became a signature of the elite Chesapeake planter class during the 1750s as the proportion of African-born slaves declined and native-born Afro-Virginians took their place. To his granddaughter Jane Pleasants, John III gave the enslaved girl Jenny. To his daughter

Mary, in addition to three hundred acres in Nansemond County, he gave the four children of Fanny, likely the same Fanny who was among the eight named individuals allowed de facto freedom. To his granddaughter Margaret Pleasants, he gave the enslaved woman "Pender" (previously spelled "Pindar") and her five children, with the caveat that Margaret pay Robert Langley ten pounds for each of the children raised at the expense of Langley's estate. This arrangement, which further tangled the lineage and costs of slaves mortgaged by Langley to John III, would come under scrutiny in *Pleasants v. Pleasants* in 1799 and again in 1811. John III also acted to thwart the wishes of his daughter Dorothy, paying her money in lieu of the enslaved girl Ciss, "which my daughter Dorothy took a fancy to . . . but without any foundation or gift from me to her."[46] John III directed his man Sam to "have liberty as a free man to hire himself & receive to his own proper use and disposal, any sum or sums of money he may Earn," on the condition he pay twelve pounds per year to the estate's executor "and not become chargeable therefore for Cloths[,] Taxes or any other matter." To his executor, Robert, John III gave the land he currently occupied (319 acres) plus two other tracts of land and eight enslaved people—Cufy, Gabe, Rachel and her child, and Patt's four children—five of whom Robert already had in his possession. All of these people qualified for freedom at the age of thirty.[47]

John III's sacrifice of family wealth for the sake of principle could not have been lost on expectant Pleasants heirs. Charged with carrying out the terms of his father's will and fearful of what an outbreak of hostilities with the British would mean for North American Quakers, Robert began a period of intense intellectual and political activity. At the same time, he was preoccupied with managing his own and his father's plantation lands, mills, stores, and mercantile business, knowing that these enterprises could not run indefinitely without the labor of enslaved people.

How exactly did Robert imagine a future without slave labor? The records of Robert's financial activities following his father's death present a picture of continuity with the family's long-term efforts at economic diversification and commercial networking. Robert generated income by renting out mills he or his father owned and hiring out enslaved laborers to other family members and neighbors.[48] He continued to trade with merchants across the Atlantic, including those in Liverpool, Bristol, and Barbados, as well as those in Philadelphia. His dealings with his brother, which featured large shipments of wheat produced on his plantations, were an important node in these commercial networks. In exchange for tobacco and flour, Robert imported a range of textiles, leather goods, salt and spices, iron goods, glassware, tableware, rum, wine, coffee, and sugar. The goods were insured and packaged in casks, barrels, and boxes marked with the Pleasants mark. Most of this merchandise was intended for resale at his stores and secured by debenture, often against expensive Irish linen or sugar. His overseas trade remained active from 1771 until 1775.[49]

Meanwhile, as the colony's planters faced mounting debts incurred through their trade with British merchants and growing tensions with imperial officials, even planters without moral scruples about slavery joined the chorus of those opposing the slave trade. Their motives ranged from a desire to hurt London merchants through nonimportation measures, to attracting more free white settlers, to protecting their own privileged access to the market, to reducing dependence on slave labor. A few, like Pleasants, objected to the slave trade on moral grounds and wished to go beyond prohibitions on the Atlantic trade to see even the domestic institution abolished.

After the Crown disallowed the legislation of 1769 to raise the import duties on slaves, the House of Burgesses tried again in 1772 to raise the duty as a nonimportation measure. Acting on behalf of the Virginia Yearly Meeting, Robert and Edward Stabler purchased two dozen copies of Benezet's writings for each Friends Meeting in Virginia for them to pass along to the powerful men of their communities. A committee of leading Anglican planters also drafted a petition asking the king to reduce the traffic in slaves to the colony. The argument condemned the inhumanity of the slave trade but framed the policy as a matter of the colony's prosperity and security. The Crown disallowed the duty, provoking further protests against the slave trade the following year. Even though Arthur Lee publicly presented moral reasons for denouncing the slave trade, claiming it was pernicious and inhumane, he continued to seek newly enslaved Africans. In response to county committees and other provincial calls for a prohibition on the trade, the House tried again to raise the duty on slave imports and to stop the flow of Africans into the colony in 1774 with a bill introduced by Richard Henry Lee, but Governor Dunmore's dissolution of the body left the matter unresolved.[50]

Meanwhile, Robert's correspondence with James Pemberton and Anthony Benezet kept him abreast of the progress of abolitionists in Pennsylvania. In 1773, Benezet wrote to Robert with reflections on Arthur Lee's 1767 address warning about the dangers of slave insurrection. Benezet, who had circulated an edited version of the address that omitted mention of rebellion, noted privately that rebellions in Brazil, Surinam, and Cayenne by enslaved people and Indigenous peoples had made Lee's warnings appear prescient. Benezet also enclosed a petition he had circulated with two hundred signatures calling for the end of the slave trade. The petition, Pennsylvania Quakers hoped, would bring North American Quaker antislavery testimony to the attention of Parliament.[51] In subsequent correspondence, Robert commented favorably on "Phisitian" Benjamin Rush's 1773 antislavery pamphlet, although he departed from Rush in believing that the universal emancipation of African-descended slaves followed by terms of service "like other foreigners" would be more effectual than levying prohibitive tariffs. He also introduced Benezet to the Virginia delegates of the Continental Congress, making special mention of Patrick Henry.[52] The Continental Congress moved on October 14, 1774, to include the slave trade in the nonimportation agreement, and Virginia made its own nonimportation resolution in 1774 to end the African trade. The following year, James Pemberton recounted to Robert proudly, Pennsylvania abolitionists formed a society "For the Relief of Negroes Unlawfully Held in Bondage," installing Pemberton as president.[53]

Robert saw opportunity in the public declarations of antislavery sentiments. He continued his own effort to achieve legal supports for both manumission and abolition by mobilizing his networks. When the wealthy and well-connected Virginia planter Robert Bolling asked for his help on November 1774 to import Portuguese clippings for his vineyard, citing the impediments to his wine production created by the Virginia Articles of Association, Robert agreed but exacted a quid pro quo. Robert segued smoothly from what he saw as the atrocious treatment of religious dissidents like himself to the treatment of enslaved people: "I would not be understood to mean, that the justice I speak of, is only due to dissenters in general, or to our society in particular. I wish it were extended to the poor slaves who have an equal right to freedom as ourselves." Although an Anglican, Bolling was sympathetic to abolition. After Robert's urging, he agreed to spread the word to his Anglican networks, noting sardonically, "should another Christ arise and call out to them to remove that evil from among them, the Land of Liberty [Britain] would never consent to it; you are well acquainted with the Profits Great Britain receives from her horrible commerce in human flesh."[54]

Revolutions

> Names & Ages of Negro Children born free of Mothers (late in the possession of Charles Logan) after attaining the ages of thirty years
> 29—Sally—of Rachel—1789
> 30—Gaby—of d[itt]o—1785
> 31—Winny—of d[itt]o—1798

The outbreak of hostilities with Britain in April 1775 and the Declaration of Independence in July 1776 represented turning points for North American Quakers, Virginia's enslavers, and enslaved people alike. Quakers along the eastern seaboard, many of whom were merchants, dreaded the coming of war and tried to configure themselves as neutrals. But the conflict, which featured violent insurgency and other forms of local pressure to choose sides, left very little space for Quaker neutrality. Robert initially viewed the escalating critique of Britain as encouraging colonial self-critique about slavery. He seems not to have shared the fears of the majority of Virginia's slave owners, who panicked when Governor Dunmore exploited their fears about the security of their slave labor force by proclaiming freedom in November 1775 to all slaves who joined the British. This was no empty threat; its potential impact was enormous. Enslaved people in Virginia numbered two hundred thousand or 40 percent of the population at the time of the Revolution. Without enslaved labor, there was no agricultural economy to speak of. With slaves emancipated, moreover, former enslavers feared the coming of a day of reckoning for their misdeeds.[55]

The unexpected death of Robert's twenty-two-year-old brother, Jonathan, in 1776 provided Robert with another opportunity to divest the Pleasants family from slavery. In 1776 it was still illegal to manumit enslaved people, so Jonathan adopted the strategy and nearly the same legal terminology used by his father. He directed that they be instructed to read, "as the most likely means to fit them for freedom," and be allowed to benefit from their own labor after reaching the age of thirty. As soon as the laws of Virginia permitted, he also directed that "the slaves I am now possessed of together with their increase" who wished to be free should enjoy "absolute freedom" conducive to "happiness which I desire they may enjoy in as full and ample a manner as if they had never been in bondage." Some of the enslaved people were singled out for immediate privileges, including Sharper and his wife, Biddy; Phillis, the wife of Caesar; Judy; and Stephen and his wife and child. Jonathan, as we have seen, bequeathed Ned and Nick to his kinsman Joseph Pleasants, with whom their mother, Tabb, and a man named Ned, likely their father, resided. Others, whom Jonathan identified as the progeny of Charles, Doll, and Matt, he distributed among various younger Pleasants heirs. Initially displeased with the bequest of slaves from his brother, Samuel acquiesced to his brother Robert's plan to free them in Philadelphia, where it was legal to do so.[56]

Although Robert's own antislavery convictions appear to have been biblically grounded, he perceived connections between "one blood" arguments and birthright that made him receptive to natural rights arguments for a manumission act. In the spring of 1776, as delegates met in Williamsburg to draft a state constitution, George Mason, who had previously articulated statist rather than moral arguments against slavery, drafted a bill of rights containing language that later inspired Jefferson's Declaration of Independence: "all Men are born equally free and independant, and have certain inherent natural Rights, of which they can not by any Compact deprive or divest their posterity."[57] Quaker antislavery activists, meanwhile, continued to make biblically based arguments. The New Jersey Quaker William Blakey wrote to Robert in December 1776 concerning the challenges of divesting from slavery. Blakey alluded to meeting Robert at his brother Samuel's house at the time of the Philadelphia Yearly meeting, "and understanding thou was possessed of Many Slaves, Thy Difficult situation came feelingly before the View of my Mind and my Desires are that thou may Dayly attend to the Dictates of Divine Wisdom which is able & willing to help out of every Difficulty & trying Dispensation (altho they may appear to flesh & Blood at times to be Insurmountable)." For Blakey, the cause of the enslaved came down to the fact that Christ spilled his precious blood for them as he did for all men, "in order to restore to a perfect state of freedom, Both body, soul & spirit." Racial prejudice could be explained as a matter of habit: the "long" custom of "ill treatment" made it hard for some to see enslaved people as brethren.[58]

What Blakey did not know was that Robert had already begun to transform the daily lives of the people enslaved on his estate. Bearing witness to the lives of enslaved people, he took action despite the continued illegality of manumission in Virginia. He informally emancipated his own slaves in 1777, supporting them for one year and allowing them to work for "the full benefit of their labor" on lands he owned in Henrico County a short distance from his plantation at Curles. In no time, irate white neighbors complained to the sheriff about unsupervised African Americans, although no one, as Robert later noted, ventured a specific complaint about vandalism, violence, or verbal abuse. According to Robert, the enslaved people "conduct themselves in an orderly inoffensive manner, not at large but in fixed habitations." In contrast, white neighbors "beat them without cause and killed & destroyed their Hogs and other property." As Robert explained to the local churchwarden tasked with fining him for allowing his slaves to be unsupervised, he believed that "all mankind, who are come to years of discretion, and have not forfeited it by their own misconduct, are by Nature equally intitled to freedom, that they are endowd with the same faculties (as being of the same Blood) and equally under the care & protection of the Supreme Being; who requires each to 'do unto others, as they would be done by,' and therefore I cannot look upon Negro's in the light which I fear too many do, as their Horse, or their Ox, destin'd to do their drudgery term of life, without fee or reward." Pleasants declared his desire "to do justly by them, and all men, without giving just occasion of offence to any," and to sacrifice "seeming present interest, in order to make the lives of that unhappy people more comfortable, by placing them on lands of my own in this Neighbourhood."[59] He noted that white landowners and tenants could not bear to see former slaves working for themselves, and he refused to pay the ten-pound fine, for to do otherwise seemed to him to be a false acknowledgement of evil.[60]

Robert spent the next five years working to galvanize support from Virginia's planter class for a legal end to slavery with special attention to the way slavery violated children. His Philadelphia Quaker allies supported his efforts, which they judged to be of tremendous value to the cause of abolition, even if they calculated their own interventions strategically.[61] As Robert informed Governor Patrick Henry in 1777, many slaveholders whose hands were tied by the prohibition on manumission were inspired by revolutionary rhetoric about human equality to engage in de facto emancipations, allowing enslaved people to work for themselves and live independently. For former slaves and those freed, this meant continuing to live "under the care and protection of their late masters either as tenants or servants on wages." As Robert knew only too well, such people remained vulnerable to harassment and subject to being picked up by churchwardens and "meddling people." Robert recommended to Henry a plan for gradual emancipation in which the children of all slaves would be freed "at the usual ages," eighteen for women and twenty-one for men, rather than at age thirty as stipulated by the wills of his father and brother. For Pleasants, such a plan simultaneously acknowledged the right of property (slave owners could free their human property if they wished) and struck at what he saw as the central injustice of inheritable slavery: "should Christians so far degenerated from the practice of Heathens, as not only with them enslave Captives, but *entail Bondage on their innocent offspring & then on their unhappy possessors forever?*" (my emphasis).[62] Together with Edward Stabler, Robert visited Henry to explain the motives of Quakers who had freed their slaves. Henry, Robert reported to Israel Pemberton, urged that freed slaves should remain on their master's lands to avoid trouble.[63]

As the war moved southward from New York to Philadelphia in 1777, Quakers hoping to remain neutral found themselves subject to exile by the revolutionary government for a host of offenses: the refusal to take up arms against the British, the nonpayment of taxes, and suspected Loyalist sympathies. Robert's brother Samuel, Henry Drinker, and Israel, John, and James Pemberton were exiled to Winchester, Virginia, in September 1777. They remained in detention until Robert and several other Quakers intervened to secure their return to British-occupied Philadelphia in early 1778. Israel Pemberton never recovered from the ordeal and died in 1779.[64]

Robert remained actively engaged in antislavery work throughout the war. He pursued a legal remedy to rescue people freed from slavery but wrongfully sold into "a second bondage" in North Carolina. He also continued his campaign to persuade Quaker slaveholders to manumit their slaves.[65] Meanwhile, in an effort to extricate themselves from a commerce that was draining the commonwealth of hard currency, Virginia's lawmakers prohibited the importation of slaves in 1778. Perhaps this policy made Virginia Quakers more willing to ally with and serve emergent state and national governments. Too, there was the landmark gradual abolition legislation in Pennsylvania in 1780, creating a plan not unlike John Pleasants's own. Robert and fellow Quakers petitioned the Virginia House of Delegates in 1780, citing natural rights, to repeal the 1723 statute banning private manumissions.[66]

Most Quaker enslavers did not emancipate slaves before the Revolution, leaving enslaved and newly freed people to seize their own opportunities to escape. The Henrico Meeting reported the "loss" of several manumitted slaves in 1782. Robert himself reported with some annoyance that eleven people "went away" with the British, including Carter Jack and his nephew London, whom Robert suspected had been coerced by his uncle to leave. They joined three others who left during the previous invasion, among them Charles White, the waterman, and his sons who had been manumitted by John III's will. In addition, twenty-one people died of a "fatal sickness," likely smallpox, spread by British troops. The British also seized Robert's household goods, clothing, and a horse and burned two valuable warehouses at Four Mile Creek after the tenant, who had not paid his rent, went over to the British side. Robert followed up on the disappearance of his people, writing to General William Phillips, commander of the British Army, to be sure that former slaves would remain free and not sold to the West Indies.[67]

The Virginia Assembly finally passed "An Act to Authorize the Manumission of Slaves" in May 1782. Robert had agitated vigorously for this measure, which permitted private manumissions under certain conditions. As soon as it passed, he freed the seventy-eight people in his possession. The measure's success owed to two strands of revolutionary thinking: anti-imperial sentiment that blamed the British for the slave trade, and radical support for a property owner's right to make decisions about his property. The act cautiously deferred to white fiscal concerns: it bound masters to provide support for emancipated slaves who were too old (defined as age forty-five and older), infirm, young, or in other ways potentially unable to support themselves through their own labor. This meant service for young people until the usual ages of eighteen and twenty-one rather than the lengthier term of thirty years laid out in John III's will. Aside from its obvious purpose to protect community coffers from the charge of impoverished or disabled free Black people, the measure kept newly manumitted people legally tethered to their masters. In the place of the families and communities that served as most poor people's first resort in case of dire need, free Black people were forever tied to their masters, the people the 1782 law held responsible for their economic support.[68]

Despite the seeming momentum of antislavery politics, however, petitions from Accomack, Henrico, and Hanover Counties following close on the heels of the Manumission Act's passage expressed white hostility in the face of African

American freedoms, especially independent residence, self-ownership of labor, and geographic mobility. Henrico County petitioners complained that owners, under pretense of "putting [slaves] free," "set them out to hire for themselves," which made it possible for "said Slaves [to] live in a very Idle and disorderly Manner." Such semifree slaves were allegedly motivated to steal in order to pay their masters the value of their hire, or, worse, they "encouraged the Neighbouring Slaves to steale from their Masters and others, and they become the receivers and traders of those Goods, having time to go at large." This, the petitioners claimed, "gives great discontent to other Slaves who are not allow'd such Indulgencies, it being generally believed that those Slaves don't labour sufficient to pay their masters their hire and clothe themselves in an Honest Manner."[69]

Robert's Henrico neighbors viewed unsupervised enslaved people as inherently troublesome in their most basic bodily dispositions. Note the specific practices and habits that white neighbors cited as offensive and destabilizing to their authority over their own slaves: idleness, the mobility to be "at large," the autonomy to labor and rest at will, and the opportunity to trade with enslaved people who had stolen goods. All of these reveal a measure of what I have called "embodied self-sovereignty," the most basic expression of liberty from slavery based on pragmatic expressions of bodily will and protections from violence. They interpreted the disparity between the condition of enslaved people and apparent Black freedoms as evidence of criminality. Any action reflective of their own wills—sitting at rest outside their cabins to catch a cooling breeze, walking alone on one of the county's dirt roads, moving swiftly by boat along one of its creeks, or congregating in a group for a celebration—testified to desires and capacities that were incompatible with the erasure of enslaved people's legal wills and personalities.

The successful passage of the 1782 manumission act enabled Robert formally to free the enslaved laborers still working for his estate and to turn his attention to the Pleasants slaves and their descendants still enslaved by his kin. He had persuaded several family members to free their slaves in 1781, including Mary, likely the widow of his brother Thomas, who manumitted five people ranging in age from fifty-five to sixty-six. Another kinsman, Thomas Pleasants, freed twenty-seven children ranging from six months to sixteen years old.[70] Robert's advocacy on behalf of enslaved people earned him the trust of people held in bondage by his family members. In 1784, an enslaved man belonging to his father's widow, Miriam Hunnicut Pleasants, requested Robert's intervention to end his abuse at the hands of her son John.[71]

In his correspondence, Robert took special aim at the inheritability of slavery. He wrote a long and spirited response to Francis Irby's defense of slavery, quoting the British advocate of American independence, John Cartwright, as saying

> Liberty is not derived from any one, but originally in every one; it is inherent and unalienable. The most antient inheritance cannot strengthen this right, the want of inheritance cannot impair it. The Child of a Slave is as freeborn, according the laws of Nature, as he who could trace a free ancestry up to the Creation. Slavery in all its forms in all its degrees, is an outrageous violation of the rights of Mankind; and odious degradation of human Nature. It is utterly impossible that any human being can be without a title to liberty, except he himself hath forfeited it by crime, which make him dangerous to Society. It is held imediately of God himself who gave it.[72]

The modest success of North American Quaker abolition efforts raised new questions for white Quakers keen for spiritual purity but less interested in intimacy with African-descended people. James Pemberton, who continued to be one of Robert's closest friends and political allies and a leader of Philadelphia's abolitionists, confessed to the London publisher James Phillips that his own embrace of the "one blood" maxim was less than full. For Pemberton, difficult questions arose with admitting African Americans to the Monthly Meeting, which he saw as inevitably opening the door to intermarriage: "while some friends are advocates for an unrestricted admission, others plead if no limitation is proscribed they must become entitled to the privilege of intermarriage, and I believe there are few who would freely consent to introduce such a union in their families which mixture some think would reverse the order of Divine Providence." Pemberton reasoned that God "in his wisdom inscrutable to us has been pleased to form distinction of Colour, for tho[ugh] of one blood he made all nations of men, yet it is also said he has fixed their habitation, which has been changed by avarice & ambition." The unnatural traffic in human beings had, in other words, led to the disruption of divinely assigned habitations, which had in turn led to what Pemberton deemed unwelcome opportunities for intimacy.[73]

Robert's letters from 1785 onward gave no indication that he shared Pemberton's discomfort. Pleasants was an avid letter writer who scrutinized the demeanor of his relatives for signs of worldliness. He had a keen sense of the importance of the body's disposition to lived religion and was quick to point out missteps. In his letters to friends and kin about slavery, Pleasants treated natural rights as a logical corollary of "one blood." His belief in "one blood" as the manifestation of a common divine creation put him at odds with scientific debates occurring in England, France, and Philadelphia about blood as a possible source of blackness. It also put him at odds with Jefferson, who in *Notes on the State of Virginia* would articulate a concept of blackness embedded in the bodies and brains of African Americans, implicating their sweat, their physical endurance, and their imaginative capacities. In contrast, Robert found equality in the unity of the blood as both a material entity and spiritually symbolic fluid.

Among Robert's boldest letters were missives to George Washington, Patrick Henry, and Thomas Jefferson. In 1785 Pleasants admonished Washington that, having enjoyed some success and fame during his life, it would be shame to be known to posterity as the man who had failed to free his slaves. Invoking the blood and treasure expended during the American Revolution, Robert reminded Washington of his providential duty of care over the enslaved. The logic of natural rights arguments and the Golden Rule supported emancipation, he noted, but he also pointed out the hypocrisy of risking lives to achieve liberty from the British while leaving slaves in bondage. He enclosed an antislavery pamphlet by John Dickinson, *Sentiments on What is Freedom and What is Slavery, by a Farmer*, for Washington's perusal.[74]

Robert carried on as if he were a one-man abolition society, maintaining correspondence with fellow abolitionists and following up on suits to extricate from slavery people who had already been freed.[75] James Pemberton updated him with newspaper copy on the Philadelphia Yearly Meeting's memorial to both houses of the U.S. Congress in New York, where Pemberton's brother John, Warner Mifflin, Samuel Emlen, and John Parrish were trying to keep the issue of abolition on the table despite the "violent" opposition of delegates from South Carolina and Georgia.[76] Optimistic about his progress at a time "when the rights of human nature are so well understood," and encouraged by Pemberton, Robert pressed ahead with his vision of a nondenominational state abolition society.[77] It seemed that a path for achieving their abolitionist ambitions was finally opening. Pemberton predicted that the abolition of the transatlantic trade had become a matter of "when" rather than if, although he remained cautious: "If success should attend the unabated endeavours which are using in GBritain & France, for abolishing the odious traffic to Africa, the evil root of slavery will be extirpated, and of course the poisonous branches [will?] gradually decay." Pemberton admitted, however, that "the opposition given to the assiduous efforts of our European Bretheren has been very great."[78] Meanwhile, there remained for Robert the practical details of running plantations and reengaging Atlantic markets for tobacco and wheat without the benefit of slave labor, an undertaking he managed by hiring the labor of freed people.[79]

Pleasants reached out widely to seek support for the newly established Virginia Abolition Society and his own gradual abolition plan, which was based on a more capacious vision of liberty for the formerly enslaved. Writing to the former Virginia governor Patrick Henry twice in 1790 to alert him to the society's plans, Robert urged him to join. But Henry was too savvy a politician to take a stand against slavery that would jeopardize his ability to win the vote of Southside tobacco planters—the part of Virginia that remained deeply invested in slavery.[80] Meanwhile, Robert submitted an essay for publication in Augustine Davis's *Virginia Independent Chronicle and General Advertiser* on July 7, 1790. The pseudonymous author "Humanity" justified his convictions with biblical scripture: "God hath made of one blood all nations of men for to dwell on all the face of the earth."[81] More pragmatically, Robert went to the source of Henry's problem, writing to Samuel Bailey, a Southside tobacco planter and Quaker, to persuade him and his fellow Quakers to join in the work of abolition. He also tried to recruit the wealthy planter Charles Carter.[82] He provided James Madison, then a representative to the U.S. Congress, with information about his gradual abolition plan in June 1791 in hopes of winning his support.[83] He also contacted Robert Carter of Nomini Hall, who had emancipated over five hundred slaves that year, to recruit his support for both a state plan for gradual abolition and the efforts of the Virginia Abolition Society.[84]

During the autumn of 1791, Robert engaged in a burst of abolitionist activity. An essay signed "Benevolence" took note of the "benign spirit of liberty . . . diffusing through the world" in its advocacy for disestablishment and abolition. That same month, he submitted a petition to the Virginia Assembly calling for the state to embrace gradual abolition and citing the violations of slavery against the enslaved "and their innocent offspring." A Quaker memorial to the U.S. Congress capped off a season that seemed filled with hope and progress on abolition.[85]

Rebellion and Revolution in Saint Domingue

> Names & Ages of Negro Children born free of Mothers (late in the possession of Charles Logan) after attaining the ages of thirty years
> 19—Jack—of Mary & Billy—1790
> 20—Mirtilla—of d[itt]o—1792
> 21—Jessie—of d[itt]o—1794
> 22—Kesiah—of d[itt]o—1796

What happened in Saint Domingue in 1791 shook the foundations of slave societies throughout the Atlantic world and upended Robert's abolitionist efforts. The prosperity of the sugar island—the jewel in the French imperial crown—depended on the brutal consumption of enslaved laborers' bodies. The body- and spirit-crushing plantation regime sparked traditions of African-based religious community, slave *marronage*, and violent resistance among the largely

African-born population. When the island's free people of color pressed for political equality with white planters and colonial administrators, citing The Declaration of the Rights of Man and the Citizen (1789), the French National Assembly failed to support them. More significantly for the growing conflict on Saint Domingue, the island's white planters refused to admit free people of color as their equals. Despite the efforts of the Société des Amis des Noirs, British abolitionists, and Atlantic Quakers, the majority of white Saint Dominguan planters and colonial officials believed that the racial subordination of free people of color was necessary to keep control over the enslaved. Throughout 1789, rumors of slave revolt and an actual revolt in Martinique raised the fears of white planters. In 1790, they responded swiftly and brutally to stop an uprising of free people of color.[86]

News of turmoil in Saint Domingue began to reach North American ports even before the revolts by enslaved people began in August 1791. Thomas Jefferson wrote of impending trouble to his daughter Martha in March 1791. The London Quaker publisher John Elliot informed Robert in June 1791 of the defeat of the measure before Parliament to abolish the slave trade. When the slaves of Saint Domingue revolted on August 22, 1791, word traveled quickly to Virginia. James Madison's letter to Robert Pleasants on October 30, 1791, informing him of his decision not to introduce a Quaker petition to abolish slavery to the U.S. Congress because the people he represented were interested in that "species of property," likely had already been influenced by the news from Saint Domingue.[87]

As word of the Saint Dominguan uprising spread throughout North America, Robert's Quaker networks continued to supply him with books, news, and encouragement. One of the pamphlets to reach him, *An Inquiry into the Cause of the Insurrection at St. Domingue*, was circulating among London Quakers as a form of damage control about the rebellion in Saint Domingue. The edition Robert received, however, had been reprinted by the Philadelphia Quaker publisher Joseph Cruikshank. The graphic examples of white planter violence committed against the bodies of enslaved people—particularly the brazen sexual violation of enslaved women and atrocities that included forcing slaves to consume their own flesh—could not have been lost on Quaker readers. Many Quakers believed that the undoing of slavery, a regime thoroughly suffused in violence, would naturally result in violence. In addition, the author of the pamphlet took pains to clarify that the advocacy of the Amis des Noirs on behalf of the slaves had not caused the revolt. Pleasants made sure to forward one of the copies to Patrick Henry along with the Virginia Abolition Society plan for gradual abolition "declaring the Children of slaves born after a certain time to be free."[88] Pemberton wrote with some resignation about the parliamentary stalemate, distilling what he had learned from Irish and French newspapers.[89]

Signs all around Robert suggested that the opportunities generated by the American Revolution were fast disappearing with the news of bloodshed in Saint Domingue. Zachariah Nixon wrote to break the news to Robert that, despite his best efforts with the powerful members of the Virginia Assembly, the abolition petition they had presented as a bill had been struck down by a large majority.[90] John Hough reported the difficulties of getting men of property to sign the petition, although he thought there might be some possibilities in Hopewell and Alexandria.[91] A new Virginia law in 1793 required the reexportation of slaves imported into Virginia illegally from Africa or the West Indies—a marked change from the 1778 law that had let them go free.[92] That same summer the first white refugees from Saint Domingue and their slaves arrived in Norfolk, an important port city in the West Indian trade. They were followed soon after by Moreau de Saint-Méry, who fled Paris to escape the guillotine and arrived in Norfolk to discover locals familiar with the French abolition debate.[93]

Robert's "Citizen of the World," an antislavery piece published in the *Richmond and Manchester Advertiser* on November 25, 1793, and almost certainly a reference to the French "citoyen," condemned slavery for its violation of innocent children: "How then can any professing to be disciples of Christ . . . reconcile the depriving our fellow Creatures of the common and acknowledged rights of men, and of Christians; and leave them and their innocent offspring as an inheritance from Generation to Generation? Or can it be consistant with sound policy to countenance so great a violation of justice in any Country?" Robert believed that there were "very few considerate people of any religious denomination, at this enlightened day, who can lay their hand on their heart and say that, they believe it to be wise and just to keep by coersive means any man (malefactors excepted) in a state of bondage, subject, like the brute Creation, to be bartered and sold, with the aggravated circumstance of being often separated forever from the most near and dear connections of life." He blamed custom and the "lust of power, supported by private convenience, or imaginary interest; thus to lay waste the tender feelings of humanity, and the moral obligations among men, children of the same Universal Father." Robert reiterated his own plan for "a law declaring the Children of Slaves to be born after the passing such Act free: and to be educated at the expence of the public: and bound out as other orphans generally are: or left under the care of those who hold their Parents, but removable at the discretion of the Courts, in case of improper treatment." The current manumission law did not go far enough, "considering the growing nature of the evil, and the fatal consequences that may ensue from the natural increase, and the length of time it may require to abolish it in that way." He opined that the legislature of a "free and enlightened people" should "devise some other mode for a gradual, but more effectual abolition" and recommended freedom at birth as being "more likely to answer every good purpose, without interfering with what is called private property, than what is above proposed (*for surely Children unborn are no mans property*)" (my emphasis).[94]

In addition to several other published pieces on the Christian faith behind his activism, Robert participated in abolitionist projects in his own and other states.[95] He forwarded to James Pemberton a list of Virginia vessels that engaged in the slave trade after the Revolution.[96] He secured an agreement to rent out his deceased son's plantation in Goochland County, Cedar Point, while protecting the houses of two enslaved people, Benjamin and Titus.[97] Legal affairs on behalf of freed people wrongly sold proceeded apace in North Carolina.[98] He offered congratulations to John Webster, kinsman of his first wife, on emancipating his slaves.[99] He received word from James Binford that neighbors in Northampton County were resisting the liberties that Binford had extended to his former slaves.[100] He also kept up a correspondence with the London Quaker abolitionist John Elliot throughout 1794 and 1795 and with the publisher James Phillips.[101]

Robert's sense of the fragility of freedom for former slaves was borne out by the fate of many of those who had been freed. When Thomas Pleasants of Goochland County, Robert's kinsman, freed his slaves in 1782, among them was a group of adults and children whose lives as free people were foreshortened by poverty, tragedy, legal trouble, and the provisions of the state's manumission law. This was the case with the Cooper family, whose members included blacksmith Roger Cooper, likely the Roger freed by Thomas at age thirty-three, and his young wife Clarissa, who was only fourteen in 1782 and in service for four more years. As Thomas made arrangements for minor children to serve until eighteen and twenty one, he once again became the master of bound laborers. By 1793, Clarissa was twenty-four and had born two children, Agnes and John, fathered by Roger, who emancipated all three of them in February of that year. Within less than a year, Clarissa was in court along with her mother, Chloe, with both women serving as a witnesses in the infanticide case of Bridget Cooper, aged twenty-two and identified as Clarissa's sister. Sister Nancy Cooper also served as a witness. By April 1795, the Overseers of the Poor bound Nancy's four children, Sally, Sam, Pegg, and Allen, ranging in age from one to seven, to Thomas Pleasants, an assignment they repeated the following year. Thomas Pleasants also assumed responsibility for Sylvia's children John and Joe; Daphne Cooper's children Nancy, Diana, and Becky; Averilla Cooper's children Sally and Catherine; Clarissa Cooper's children Royall and Benjamin; and Sal, the daughter of Aggy Cooper.[102]

Pleasants became more determined as his fellow planters grew more defensive and averse to risk, but his public rationale for abolition now included concerns about the possibility of slave rebellion. He had harsh criticism for the eminent Virginia legal scholar St. George Tucker, whose 1796 gradual emancipation scheme relied on a narrow reversal of the mechanisms that made slave status hereditary. Tucker's plan called for freeing only the female children of enslaved women. Pleasants acknowledged that "some regard ought to be had to the Public Mind," and conceded that a gradual abolition scheme might be best for Virginia, but "not as thou has proposed by an Act declaring the females only born after the passing thereof free, but all the Children of Slaves; that they aught to be placed in Situations to receive necessary Instruction in order to fit them for usefulness in Society, already too long withheld, and to invest them with sutable priviledges as an excitement to Industry." It seemed to Robert that Tucker's plan would emancipate too slowly and unjustly. Given present numbers and the "natural increase of that people" it was unlikely that enslaved people "should be continued very long in their present abject state without convulsions." Pleasants pondered the contradictions revealed by enslaved children's claims to birthright freedoms, asking "how can anything be deemed property not in existence?" He thought that Tucker's mandated twenty-eight years of service more than met the demands of enslavers for compensation, reasoning, "I presume no present holder of Slaves, or their Creditors, could have any just cause to complain of being deprived of any just right to property, were all the Children declared free, who might be born after the passing of such an Act." Robert's boldest rebuttal of Tucker, however, concerned the prospect of interracial marriage. Pleasants insisted that it was wrong for African-descended people "to be restrained by law from contracting marriages with whites."[103]

During this same period, Pleasants wrote twice to Thomas Jefferson, hoping to convince him of the importance of education for African American children, even as opportunities diminished for the newly freed. A short time later, he reported cryptically to St. George Tucker that Thomas Jefferson had "changed his mind" about race since writing *Notes on the State of Virginia.*[104] In a recodification of slave law in 1792, a new statute chipped away at the 1782 manumission law, allowing creditors of an estate to have first dibs on enslaved people who had been freed by the master.[105] That same code prohibited people of African descent from providing court testimony against white people.[106]

Setting the self-reproducing quality of chattel slaves against the legal principles protecting an owner's claim on other types of property, Pleasants rehearsed the arguments that his attorneys would eventually make in *Pleasants v. Pleasants.* "And He hath made of one blood all nations of men" was a bold declaration of equality, but it did not offer specific guidelines about how to undo the legal mechanisms of property and inherited status through which enslaved women produced enslaved children.

Ned

Children born Free of Mothers late in the Possession of Samuel Pleasants
21 Mourning of Sukey & Cuffee Augt 1792
22 Hampton of d[itt]o—Feby 1795
23 Jerry—of d[itt]o—Jany 1797
24 Aggy—of d[itt]o—Augt 1799

Even as Robert freed the seventy-eight people of his estate to work for themselves on portions of his land, other Pleasants family members balked at interpreting their Quaker faith as a mandate to part with their slave property. This was the reason why Robert's fellow litigant, Ned, had been kept waiting for the end to his enslavement. He was four years old when John III made his will; as a man nearing the age of 30, Ned, along with his brother Nick, his mother Tabb, and his likely father Ned, remained enslaved by Pleasants heir Elizabeth Pleasants.[107]

When Robert's repeated efforts to persuade and negotiate with family members failed, he brought suit on behalf of the Pleasants' slaves against his recalcitrant kin. He turned to Virginia's High Court of Chancery, over which the eminent law professor and antislavery sympathizer, Chancellor George Wythe, presided. Ned, probably in league with Robert, initiated his own suit against Elizabeth Pleasants, which was eventually joined to the action in *Pleasants v. Pleasants*. The Court of Chancery permitted Ned to sue as a pauper, that is, to disregard filing fees and court costs, and provided protections usually denied to the enslaved, stipulating that Ned's "said mistress do not presume to beat or misuses him upon this account, and that she suffer him to come to the clerk's office for commissions to take the depositions of his witnesses and to attend to their examinations and the trial."[108]

In addition to his freedom and that of the other Pleasants' slaves, Ned sought an "account of profits" remedy that claimed the value of labor performed by enslaved people and wrongly assigned to the Pleasants estate "during the time of detention." For at least fifteen years following the passage of the 1782 manumission law, during most of which time Ned appears to have been under the age of thirty, he continued to work unremunerated for Elizabeth Pleasants. He was the only enslaved person of the Pleasants estate, a cohort that by 1797 included nearly four hundred and forty slaves (the original two hundred-fifteen Pleasants slaves plus their children) to be named as a party to the suit, although the suit was understood to be on behalf of all those seeking freedom.

Chancellor George Wythe brought a capacious interpretation of liberty to his decision. He ruled that those born after the 1782 manumission act were entitled to freedom by birth, subject to the act's conditions of service. Those born before the act were subject to the lengthy thirty-year terms of service set out in John's will. Wythe's order also allowed those freed to seek an account of profits from their owners to compensate them for the loss they sustained during the period of their wrongful detainment in slavery.

Several members of the Pleasants family appealed to the Virginia Court of Appeals.[109] Composed of enslavers, the Appeals Court confirmed Robert's standing to bring suit and Ned's right to bring the action in forma pauperis because Robert had a "commendable reason" for bringing the suit.[110] The suit was one seeking "essential justice" (Justice Pendleton), that was founded on Ned's claim to "human liberty" (Justice Roane), and his "sacred" right to "liberty" (Justice Carrington). But despite their recognition of these lofty principles, the Appeals Court justices noted their concern over the financial burden emancipation would create for Pleasants' heirs.

The Appeals Court modified the Chancery Court's order to limit the number of people freed and the scope of their freedom. The complex legal reasoning invoked the law against perpetuities,[111] the right of property holders to alienate their property, and the legal personhood of enslaved people whose status was itself in question. The most significant difference between the two court's rulings concerned those individuals born **after** the state's manumission act in 1782—that is, children still well under age thirty in 1799 at the time of the ruling. Whereas the Chancery Court had declared them free, the Appeals Court encumbered a significant number of that cohort with an inheritable term of service.[112] Children who were more than thirty years old in 1782 were entitled to freedom immediately. Those who turned thirty between 1782 and the time of the order of the court, and those born after 1782 to mothers who were more than thirty years of age, were also immediately emancipated. But children who were not yet thirty in 1799, born to mothers who were not yet thirty at the time of their birth, were to serve until age thirty. This applied to all future generations.[113] The Appeals Court's order freed only one hundred eighty-five of the four hundred thirty-one people still enslaved in 1798. The remaining two hundred forty-six were to be emancipated only after they reached the age of thirty, as were any children born before their mothers reached the age of thirty.[114] In the effort to protect Pleasants' heirs from financial loss, the Appeals court placed hundreds of children and young adults in a condition of quasi-slavery that many of their children and grandchildren would inherit.

The Appeals court tasked the Chancery court with compiling family rosters for each enslaved woman, listing the children she bore after she turned thirty, a remit that resulted in documents remarkable for their clear display of how maternal inheritance normally created enslaver wealth (Figure 3). In this account of the children born to women over the age of thirty, enslaved by Charles Logan and Samuel Pleasants, twenty-six women are listed, seven of them with the fathers of their children, along with the names of sixty-five children. Families were subtly acknowledged by a hash mark under the name of a woman's youngest child to signify the end of one family list and the beginning of the next. This was only a partial account of these women's families, however, for the older children, born to the mothers before they turned thirty, were not listed. Children born to them before that age, a cohort that appears to have included Ned, were obligated to serve until they turned thirty. The changing legal status of a woman's womb thus created a divide within families, distinguishing the fate of siblings. The document also includes the names of twelve male children, ranging in age from eight to fifteen years old, who had been sold. Nine of twenty-six women, or roughly one-third, had lost sons to sale even after their former enslaver had made provisions for their future freedom.

The Court of Appeals unanimously rejected Ned's request for an account of profits, which had been allowed by the Chancery court.[115] To consider his legal reasoning was to open the door to suits from hundreds, perhaps thousands of people who had been wrongfully detained in slavery. It was also to question the entire foundation for evaluating enslaved people as commodities through assessments of physical condition, projected lifetime service, and reproductive potential rather than as laborers entitled to a share of the estate's profits.[116] Justice Roane could not find a "single instance" in which a jury had awarded an account of profits remedy, and Justice Carrington described it as "unprecedented."[117] An order affirming the account of profits remedy would have had important practical consequences for enslavers. It would have altered the "calculus of manumission" for those who could not establish "title" to their slaves by exposing them to an obligation to compensate former slaves for wrongful enslavement.[118]

In making this ruling, the Court of Appeals justices contended that the costs of rearing enslaved children and caring for the aged and infirm left no profits to be paid out to individuals wrongly detained. The implication of their decision was that the costs of raising and supporting an enslaved person equaled the profits generated by that person's labor over the course of his life. In other words, the Appeals justices concluded, in an enslaved population produced by births rather than by capture, enslaved laborers generated virtually no profit for their enslavers.[119] Missing from this reasoning was any acknowledgment of the value of the enslaved mother's physical and emotional labors in bearing and raising children—a crucial set of unpaid labors that produced planter wealth and would only grow in significance after the 1807 prohibition on the overseas slave trade made enslavers in the US wholly dependent on births as a source of new

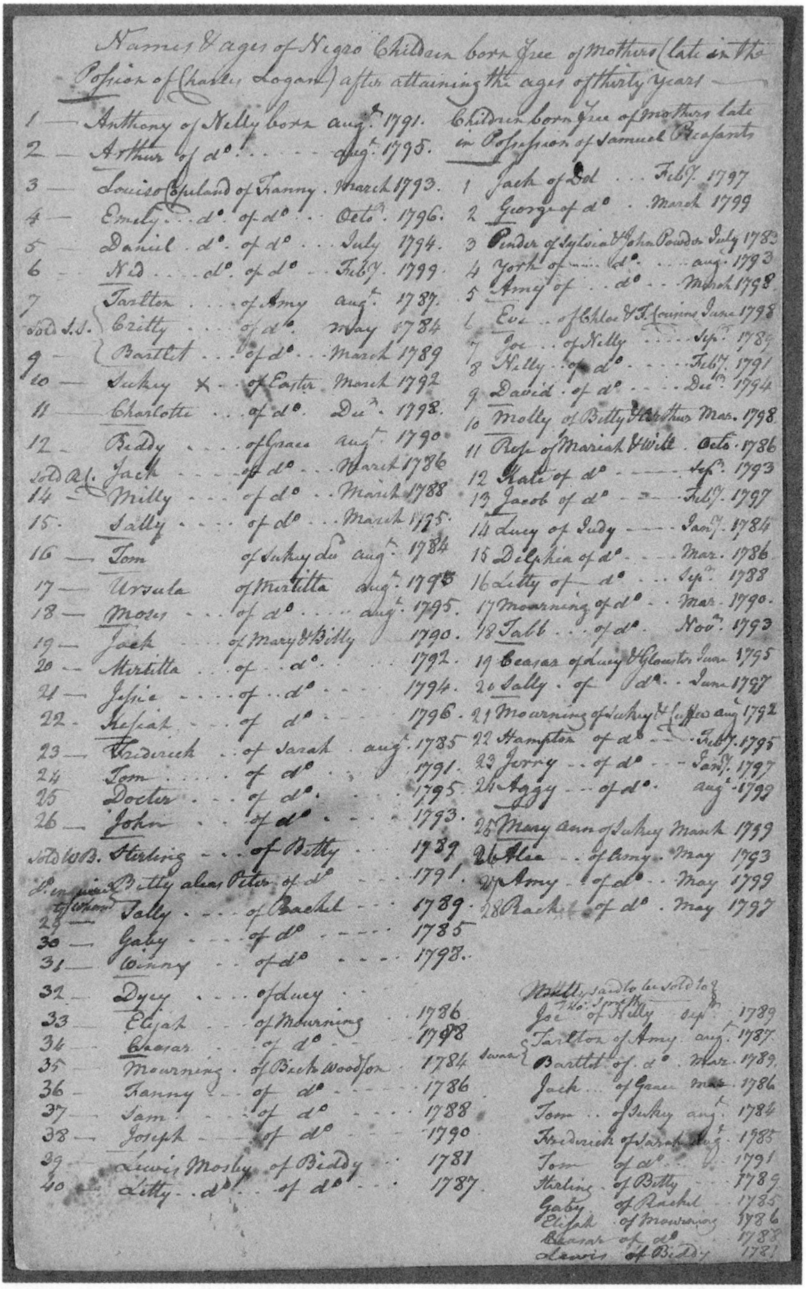

Names & ages of Negro Children born free of Mothers (late in the Possion of Charles Logan) after attaining the ages of thirty years

1 — Anthony of Nelly born augt. 1791.
2 — Arthur of do. ... Augt. 1795.
3 — Louiso Copeland of Franny . March 1793.
4 — Emely ... do. of do. .. Octo. 1796.
5 — Daniel do. of do ... July 1794.
6 — Ned ... do. of do .. Feby. 1799.
7 — Tarlton ... of Amy augt. 1787.
sold J.S. Critty ... of do. May 1784
9 — Bartlet ... of do. .. March 1789
10 — Sukey × of Easter March 1792
11 — Charlotte ... of do. Decr. 1798.
12 — Biddy ... of Grace augt. 1790
sold A.J. Jack ... of do ... March 1786
14 — Milly ... of do . March 1788
15. Sally ... of do .. March 1795.
16 — Tom of Sukey dec augt. 1784
17 — Ursula of Mertilla augt. 1795
18 — Moses ... of do ... augt. 1795.
19 — Jack of Mary & Billy 1790.
20 — Mertilla of do. 1792.
21 — Jessie of do 1794.
22 — Kesiah of do 1796.
23 — Frederick of Sarah augt. 1785
24 — Tom of do 1791.
25 — Docter of do. 1795.
26 — John of do. 1793.
sold W.B. Sterling of Betty 1789
[illegible] Betty alias Peter of do 1791.
[illegible] Sally of Rachel 1789
30 — Gaby of do 1785
31 — Winny of do 1798.
32 — Dycy ... of Lucy
33 — Elijah of Mourning 1786
34 — Ceasar of do 1798
35 — Mourning of Beck Woodson 1784
36 — Franny of do 1786
37 — Sam of do 1788
38 — Joseph of do 1790
39 — Lewis Mosby of Biddy 1781
40 — Letty do. of do 1787

Children born free of mothers late in Possession of Samuel Pleasants

1 Jack of Dol ... Feby. 1797
2 George of do . March 1799
3 Pinder of Sylvia & John Powder July 1783
4 York of ... do. ... augt. 1793
5 Amy of .. do ... March 1798
6 Eve .. of Chloe & T. Cousins June 1798
7 Joe .. of Nelly ... Sepr. 1789
8 Nelly . of do ... Feby. 1791
9 David . of do ... Decr. 1794
10 Molly of Betty & Arthur Mar. 1798
11 Rose of Mariah & Will . Octo. 1786
12 Kate of do — Sepr. 1793
13 Jacob of do — Feby. 1797
14 Lucy of Judy — Jany. 1784
15 Delphia of do .. Mar. 1786
16 Letty of — do .. Sepr. 1788
17 Mourning of do .. Mar. 1790.
18 Tabb .. of do. Novr. 1793
19 Ceasar of Lucy & Glouster June 1795
20 Sally . of do . June 1797
21 Mourning of Sukey & Cuffee augt. 1792
22 Hampton of do — Feby. 1795
23 Jerry .. of do .. Jany. 1797
24 Aggy .. of do. augt. 1799
25 Mary ann of Sukey March 1799
26 Alea .. of Amy . May 1793
27 Amy . of do .. May 1799
28 Rachel of do . May 1797

Milly said to be sold to Thos. Smith &
Joe of Nelly Sepr. 1789
Tarlton of Amy augt. 1787
sworn Bartlet of do. Mar. 1789
Jack of Grace Mar. 1786
Tom of Sukey augt. 1784
Frederick of Sarah augt. 1785
Tom of do 1791
Sterling of Betty 1789
Gaby of Rachel 1785
Elijah of Mourning 1786
Ceasar of do 1788
Lewis of Biddy 1781

Figure 3. Court-ordered accounting of children born to enslaved women in the Pleasants estate. The left-hand column lists the children numerically, the right-hand column lists the child's mother and birthdate. The family lists are incomplete, for they include only the children born after their mothers turned thirty. The Huntington Library, San Marino, California.

enslaved labor. Little surprise that all of the Appeals Court justices hearing *Pleasants v. Pleasants* balked at going down the legal path of an account of profits remedy; all would take a conservative turn in their own opinions on slavery cases in the decades after the Pleasants suit.[120]

This part of the decision of the court brings to light an essential feature of Robert Pleasants's efforts over nearly three decades to find a pathway to liberate formerly enslaved people. In his decision Justice Roane argued that "it seems to be a solecism, to award ordinary profits to recompense the privation of liberty; which, if it is to be recompensed, the power of money cannot accomplish."[121] Justice Roane's reference to Ned and other formerly enslaved people's liberty was entirely abstracted from their actual experience of exploitation. The justices' suggestion of a "set-off" "burthen" to support the "aged and infirm, and for the rearing of the children"[122] ignored both the value produced by the labor of enslaved people and the experience of being coerced into producing that value. Justice Roane's conception of "liberty" directed attention away from the coercion inherent in slavery and left those former slaves who were emancipated vulnerable to relationships with their former enslavers and with other white people in the communities in which they lived. Robert, in contrast, had learned to think about the entangled relationships that needed to be unraveled for formerly enslaved people to fully claim their liberty.

Coda

Robert died within a year of the Court of Appeals decision in *Pleasants v. Pleasants*. Hannah Twopence, a free African American neighbor, watched over him and supplied him with fresh linens on his deathbed. George Winston, a local carpenter, made his coffin. Robert's Henrico County taxes for 1802 listed him as being possessed of 1,063 acres. In keeping with his commitment to do right by his former slaves, Robert wrote a codicil to his will in February 1800 giving 350 acres of land and establishing a fund to build and sustain a school for free Black people. The same document designated friends to support elderly former slaves and intervened against Pleasants heirs who refused to provide schooling to people still in service. Robert called for bound people denied an education to complete their service a year early, at age twenty-nine instead of at age thirty, so that they might use the final year to attend school. His executors received a note of approbation from the London Yearly Meeting about his plan for the school, which was eventually built and used to educate free Black people.[123] For his part, Ned won his suit for freedom but lost his claim to be paid the value he had contributed to the Pleasants estate during his unjust detention after the passage of the 1782 manumission act. The justices' decision might reflect their surmise about Tabb's age when she gave birth to Ned, and their reasoning that, until he turned thirty himself, Ned was justly detained under the terms of John III's will. His life after emancipation is difficult to track with certainty. He might be the Ned Pleasants subsequently listed in the Henrico County tax lists as a "free negro." Or perhaps he is the Edward Pleasants, aged sixty, living free in Alexandria, Virginia, in 1827 with a wife and an enslaved girl. The fate of Tabb, Ned Sr., and Nick is unknown.[124]

Hundreds, perhaps thousands of white people descended from John Pleasants III. Their common surname and repeated use of certain Christian names did not mean that they shared a sense of loyalty to the family patriarch's abolitionist wishes. Several appear to have honored the family commitment to support aging slaves out of the funds of the Pleasants estate.[125] At least one, Samuel, freed his slaves when he died in 1816.[126] Another descendant, James Pleasants, became the governor of Virginia in 1822. Although an active opponent of corporeal punishment and an advocate of removing restrictions on free Black people, Governor Pleasants continued to enslave people and became a leading figure in the American Colonization Society.[127] Robert's executor, Micajah Crew, hired out former slaves and ensured that people promised their freedom by age thirty actually received it. The latter was the case with Phillis, the daughter of Mourning, a former slave of Charles and Mary Logan, and her children, who were still enslaved in 1809.[128] In addition, some of the children and grandchildren of the enslaved people caught up in the Langley mortgage of 1765 were still in bondage as of 1811.[129]

Robert Pleasants's insistence that he was of "one blood" with enslaved people spurred his efforts to emancipate them and allow them to benefit from their own labor. To accomplish this and to honor the blood bond of human creation, he sued his white kin—the people with whom most late eighteenth-century people believed he actually shared "one blood." As Pleasants's limited success reveals, undoing slavery required community support. It meant tracking down people illicitly sold when they should have been freed. It led to a court-ordered accounting of children born to women whose wombs changed status during their lives. Most important, it depended on people of color to survive white hostility and obstruction at every turn. Despite his efforts, many of the women conditionally "freed" by *Pleasants v. Pleasants* continued to have their bodies exploited to produce the next generation of bound mothers. This pattern, among others, contributed to the emerging concepts of race as innate to the body and determined at birth. It would fall to subsequent abolitionists to try to unravel the ties between race, slavery, and motherhood.

Chapter 4

Medical Materialism, Migration, and National Belonging

> Why would they send us into a far country to die? See the thousands, of foreigners, emigrating to America every year: and if there be ground sufficient for them to cultivate, and bread for them to eat, why would they wish to send the *first tillers* of the land away? Africans have made fortunes for thousands, who are yet unwilling to part with their services; but the free must be sent away, and those who remain, must be *slaves*. . . . This land which we have watered with *our tears* and *our blood*, is now our *mother country*, and we are well satisfied to stay where wisdom abounds, and the gospel is free.
>
> —Reverend Richard Allen, letter to *Freedom's Journal*, November 2, 1827

> And being in an agony he prayed more earnestly: and his sweat was as it were great drops of blood falling down to the ground.
>
> —Luke 22:44

Upon first considering emigration schemes for free Black people, the distinguished minister and civic leader Richard Allen saw their virtue. He was not alone in this sentiment. During the 1810s, the African American abolitionists Paul Cuffee, James Forten, and Daniel Coker all supported various plans for free African Americans to escape the racially hostile environment of the United States. It seemed an easier path to a better life than trying to achieve justice in white America. But as prominent white slaveholders flocked to the American Colonization Society (ACS) and encouraged free Black emigration to the West African colony of Liberia, without any reduction in their commitment to slavery,

Black Philadelphians balked. By 1817, Allen had been forced to reconsider his position. Chairing a meeting of free people of color in Philadelphia on July 6, 1824, Allen concurred with the condemnation of emigration to Liberia and helped to steer the gathering to its endorsement of emigration to the free Black republic of Haiti. Sponsored by Jean Pierre Boyer, Black emigrants to Haiti seemed likely to gain new opportunities for work, landownership, and full citizenship simply by stepping on Haitian soil, an intentional movement of the body into the national space of the Black republic.[1]

Three years later, when Allen penned a letter to *Freedom's Journal*, the first African American newspaper, he expressed his position with new emphasis. Reports of extraordinary mortality among African American migrants to Liberia beginning with the first ACS-sponsored voyage in 1820 had dampened his enthusiasm for emigration. He continued to disapprove of ACS-sponsored emigration; in addition, he no longer advocated that free Blacks leave the United States for Haiti. In place of emigration as a way to relieve the suffering of his people, Allen advanced a bold claim to national belonging that also located African-descended people religiously in the United States. "This land which we have watered with our tears and our blood is now our mother country," he declared, "and we are well satisfied to stay where wisdom abounds, and the gospel is free."[2]

Allen's revised assessment of Black migration in 1827 offers us a view of a distinguished African American's evolving thinking about the best path for both free and enslaved African Americans to achieve full adult personhood.[3] Drawing on his experiences as both a healer and a former victim of slavery, Allen considered the health impact of emigration as well as opportunities for African Americans to benefit from their own labor and enjoy the protections conferred by national belonging. He situated his advocacy of abolition within a diasporic politics in which the body's integrity and health were at stake in the main work of human rights. Not coincidentally, 1827 marked the year that Sarah Bass Allen, Allen's wife and a fellow healer during the yellow fever epidemic of 1793, organized African Methodist Episcopal women to provide domestic care for ministers who attended the church conference.[4]

It was only after Allen rejected colonization that he articulated an alternative to migration, claiming national belonging on the basis of African American labor. He identified African Americans as the "*first tillers*" of the soil during a period of accelerating federal acquiescence to the removals of Native Americans throughout U.S. territories. His reference to African and African American blood watering the soil tapped popular discourses about depleting bloodletting therapies and provided a principle of national belonging that paralleled the international legal principles developed by Grotius and Vattel. Like Grotius's and Vattel's warriors who sacrificed blood to support the nation in exchange for the sovereign's protection, African American laborers established their bond with the United States through bleeding and suffering. Allen represented Black bodies as intact and qualified for citizenship, moreover, rather than as the "hands," half hands," and quarter hands" of enslavers' accounting practices.[5]

Allen's anguish and anger over the disconnection between African American labor and national belonging points us to the fight over Black bodies in the aftermath of *Pleasants v. Pleasants*. Who would benefit from Black labor? Would African Americans be allowed to move at will? Would fixed habitation earn them the privileges of legal settlement? Between 1800 and 1830, rights landscapes for free Black people changed rapidly as the United States expanded and repurposed settler colonialism. As new forms of forced transport and refugee flight—both domestic and Atlantic—transformed population movements around the Atlantic basin, a thicket of different state policies ultimately gave rise to new strategies by and for free African Americans. Some, like Allen's original optimistic assessment of emigration, were in essence African American–initiated efforts to escape white racism by vacating slave states or even the nation itself. Others, like the planter-heavy ACS, attempted to disguise a purge of free Black people as a benign exodus. The involvement of Haiti's president Boyer briefly changed the international calculus of free Black migration by refiguring the migrants as invited refugees whose African lineage qualified them for citizenship.[6]

Allen's framing of national belonging in terms of the bodies and blood of laboring African Americans also represented an intervention into the scientific racism that was gaining a following during the nineteenth century as northern states turned from slavery to racial hierarchy. Allen offered a counterpoint to medical representations of African American bodies as racially distinct. During the 1820s, new technical language concerning blood shared little with popular understandings of blood and bloodletting. While not specifically challenging the universalism of "one blood" and blood's capacity to create citizenship by watering national soil, minute examinations of blood's material composition chipped away at its mystical significance and left specious claims about raced blood intact.[7]

A growing chorus of scientists trafficked in "evidence" drawn from collections of anatomical specimens and dissections to produce caricatures of racial difference. In this intellectual climate, phrenology—the study of the brain's material structures determining intellect and character—found a popular reception. Phrenology seemed to some to be compatible with reforms aimed at improving health and education. But scientific racists used phrenology and its offshoot, craniology—the study of skull shape and volume—to substantiate racial categories, with a few influential doctors going so far as to advance radical arguments about polygenesis, the theory of distinct creations of human species.

Supporters of polygenesis and scientific racism deployed what they interpreted as evidence of innate racial distinction to support conclusions that white people occupied the center of the human family while African-descended and Indigenous peoples inhabited the margins.[8]

Allen's concerns about the mortality of African Americans forced or persuaded to relocate to new climates, and his references to their blood evoked the medical education and debates over race occurring in Philadelphia. During the 1820s, medical students diagnosed the ills of colonial settler and plantation slave societies with detailed studies of local epidemics. European beliefs in the hazards of tropical environments dated to the sixteenth century, but by the nineteenth century, medical investigators in the United States had begun systematic studies of the impact of local climates, including specific conditions of rainfall, temperature, and changes to the worked landscape. These studies repeated long-standing popular beliefs about the fatal miasmatic consequences of rotting vegetation and the hazards of "seasoning," or acclimatizing to a new habitation, but several suggested that African-descended people had less susceptibility. Undertaken during a period of national economic and territorial expansion, these local studies supported claims about the South's distinctive disease environment. Objecting to African-descended people being sent to "far" countries to die, and rejecting the spurious claims of scientific racists, Allen and other African American intellectuals argued from the body to insist on the Americanness of Black people.[9]

Forced Migration, Transportation, and Exclusion

Allen's comment about the national belonging created by African American labor reveals the complex intersections of medical practice and theory, political economy, international law, and Indigenous dispossession. His objection to the coerced migration of free people of color took place during an era of several crucial human rights controversies: British naval impressment and convict transport; international reluctance to recognize the independent republic of Haiti in 1804; American enslavers' fears of free Black populations as enemies to slavery; and abolitionist agitation to end the transatlantic slave trade. In the United States, meanwhile, the removals of the continent's ancient inhabitants accelerated, reaching a crescendo during the 1830s. During these crucial years between 1790 and 1840, the global map of coerced movement shifted dramatically to take place mainly within national spaces where it was accompanied by new discourses touting freedom and warning of violent unrest.[10]

At the close of the eighteenth century, British needs for seafaring laborers had intensified. The wars with revolutionary and Napoleonic France led to an uptick in impressment. Between 1793 and the Battle of Waterloo (1815), press-gangs harvested tens of thousands of men, boosting the percentage of impressed laborers in the Royal Navy to an all-time high of between 50 and 75 percent of the men in service by the end of the wars.[11] Although all laboring men, whether privately employed British sailors, nonseafaring laborers, or foreign nationals, were vulnerable to British press-gangs, the impressment of American sailors, in particular, stirred American anger and inflamed tender national sensibilities. At least 12 percent of British naval laborers were foreign by 1805, a figure that included sailors from northern Europe, the Italian states, and Portugal. According to the estimate by impressment's most reliable historian, some ten thousand Americans were among those taken into service against their wills between 1793 and 1812, the date of the U.S. declaration of war against Britain. U.S. seafaring laborers were in an especially vulnerable position because U.S. ships often employed British seamen, making the vessels targets of press-gang raids. In addition, the genuine fluidity in U.S.-British identity along the northern border with Canada meant that some men had changed national affiliations several times during the 1790s and the early years of the nineteenth century. Finally, the shared Anglophone culture of Americans and Britons facilitated willful as well as accidental violations of American national sovereignty by press-gangs. During the War of 1812, American printers published poetry and other protests that favorably compared the freedom of the American sailor to the impressment of the British maritime "slave." Atlantic waters, according to this view, were intended to be a space for the citizens of sovereign nations to move freely without fear of detainment.[12]

Britain's continued practice of convict transport to South Africa and Australia further complicated the contrast between slave and free. British convicts, stripped of their national privileges as a consequence of their crimes, continued to be shipped with impunity to West Africa and Australia.[13] Outside this punitive national context, however, forced transport became a moral liability even if slavery itself did not. By 1806, as Christopher Brown has argued, British government officials saw virtue in abolishing the transatlantic trade even if their actual position was not so noble: Britain continued to rely on the products of slave labor but also gradually turned to contract coolie labor, described by its advocates as free but decried by many British abolitionists for the absence of a robust concept of consent.[14]

The successful bid for Haitian independence and the creation of a free Black republic in 1804 challenged the presumptive whiteness of the international vision of free oceanic access and movement for subjects of sovereign nations. In addition, the heavy losses of British and French troops to illness left British imperial and military officials staggered by the risks of tropical disease. Haiti's independence may also have had an influence on international law, hastening the abandonment of natural rights foundations. Although most nations refused formal recognition of Haiti, the fact that the island's African-descended population could now insist in theory on some of the international protections enjoyed by white nationals stirred unease. If Haiti's citizens were accorded the same protections for trade and travel extended to white sovereign nations, people of color would move about the world at will. White slaveholders throughout the Americas worried about the impact on white majority populations and slave economies if free (and recently freed) Haitians tried to relocate to the United States as their white Haitian refugee counterparts had done during the thirteen years of war and revolution in Haiti. This implicit challenge to white supremacy spurred the rise of international legal positivism with its distinction between civilized and uncivilized peoples as a means of excluding some nations from the international community.[15]

A racially pointed interpretation of events emerged from the pens of white Haitian refugees. They publicly blamed the British abolitionist William Wilberforce for radicalizing members of the French Amis des Noirs, arguing that the group's irresponsible rhetoric provoked the rebellion of Saint Domingue's slaves and led to the downfall of the planter class. Thomas Clarkson and other abolitionists responded to these charges in the spirit of the 1792 pamphlet British abolitionists had sent to Robert Pleasants; they insisted that the fundamental injustice of the slave trade rather than the tantalizing promise of freedom was the cause of the slave rebellion. Much as Thomas Tryon had figured the violations of Barbadian slavery as triggering a cosmic disturbance that would provoke vengeance and bloodshed, abolitionists observed that with the bloody rebellion in Saint Domingue, "Now's repaid the trade in blood."[16]

Virginia enslavers' fears of this repayment in blood for their own complicity in slavery prompted new restrictions and reprisals. Just six months after Robert Pleasants wrote the codicil to his will in 1800, Gabriel, an enslaved blacksmith belonging to Pleasants's neighbor Thomas Prosser in northern Henrico, organized a rebellion of enslaved and free black people. The conspiracy offered indisputable evidence of the violent repression of the bodies and wills of the enslaved. It also confirmed the worst fears of white enslavers that the rebellion in Saint Domingue was no anomaly but could occur in Virginia. The state responded swiftly, executing twenty-six suspected conspirators and transporting eight.[17] As the first plot uncovered in North America after the rebellion in Saint Domingue, Gabriel's conspiracy frightened Virginia's enslavers, including its political leaders.[18] Within months of the last executions, petitioners to the House of Delegates from King and Queen County blamed the 1782 manumission law for their present "Disturbed & Distressed Situation" and urged the law's repeal. They also expressed fear for their own security and the future of the state if free Black people were permitted to live on equal terms with white people. Voicing a white nationalist sentiment about land, they declared, "the Soil is our own & self preservation is the first Law in Nature and must be secured at all events." They were also clear that they cared little about the moral implications of their demand: "and if it cannot be done without doing what we would wish to avoid it must be submitted to as a Misfortune." Easy for the petitioners, who were white, literate, and landed, to make that choice. The petition ended with a line partially crossed out, expressing hope that the House "will devise ways & Means to clear the State of all Free Negroes as Fomenters of the late Disturbance."[19]

Under then governor James Monroe, the state of Virginia responded with stiffer laws restricting the movement of free African Americans. In 1801, county clerks were required to post lists of free African Americans living within their county in order to clamp down on escaped slaves passing as free. Any person of color subsequently entering the county would be treated as a vagrant, an application of the poor law to free African Americans, unless they could provide evidence of employment. The following year, the assembly required all free African Americans, whether they were property owners or unpropertied laborers, to register with their county clerks. The registry included evidence of lineage, identity, and appearance, even as the state took steps to exclude newly freed people.[20] State and county officials, along with Pleasants heirs, continued to treat the emancipated as contagious sources of unruliness. In 1809, Samuel Pleasants of Powhatan County offered a fifteen-dollar reward for apprehending Fanny, "a bright Mulatto Girl, about five feet, two inches high, seventeen years old, inclined to be fleshy . . ." Lest the connections to liberal manumission policies be unclear, he added, "she is one of those entitled to liberty—when she arrives at a certain age—under the will of the late John Pleasants of Henrico County, in consequence of which many of them are very ungovernable, many of her connections enjoy their liberty and live in the adjacent counties."[21]

In the midst of this potent brew of international and domestic motives to subordinate the freedoms of African-descended people, President Jefferson purchased the Louisiana Territory from Napoleon—an act of territorial expansion and planned Native dispossession that he justified as a way to expand the yeoman foundations of the nation, but which effectively prolonged the epoch of settler colonialism in North America. The Louisiana Purchase redrew the map of the United States and prompted slave owners to recalibrate their plans to seize opportunities in new western territories. It formed the keystone of the nation's sponsorship and expansion of colonial settler society, perpetuating a colonial biopolitics that supported white settler reproduction and the eventual clearance of Choctaws, Chickasaws, Cherokees, and Creeks from lands deemed suitable for producing cotton. The purchase also stimulated the movement of white slave owners and the sale of enslaved people into territories just coming into use as plantation lands.[22]

It was during this period that enslavers in the Upper South began moving enslaved people west and south in overland coffles and along coastal routes. The movement of Virginia-born slaves from the Upper South to the Lower South eventually substituted for the supply of African-born slaves brought into the United States through the transatlantic trade. Slaveholders in Virginia who were growing wheat rather than the more labor-intensive tobacco began during the 1790s to send redundant, but often skilled, enslaved laborers to New Orleans, where they were put up for sale in the port city's slave market. In Allen's terms, this was a rupture of the belonging generated by agricultural labor in a specific locale. The proportion of enslaved Virginians bound for New Orleans accelerated after 1800: one in twelve in the 1790s, one in ten between 1800 and 1810, and one in five in the 1810s. That defining trend of the internal slave trade would continue across the South as growing numbers of enslaved people were forced to cross state lines.[23]

Coffles created a public spectacle of suffering and subjection that left a literal trail of blood. The uptick in the coerced migration of enslaved people meant an increase in raw emotional and physical suffering as families were ripped apart and first- and second-generation North American–born slaves were forced to leave the only homes they had known. For those chained together in the coffle, the forced march subjected victims to coordinate their steps even as chains rubbed against chafed and bleeding flesh; missteps and stumbles could provoke painful punishments. But coffles also meant that more people, Black and white, enslaved and free, witnessed the coercion and commodification at the heart of slavery. The inexorable southern movement of enslaved people chained together provided irrefutable evidence of the vulnerability of the enslaved and the geography of enslavement. Charles Ball, who as a young man was sold by his enslaver and transported in a coffle, described the experience of being forced to leave his wife and children to join a coffle of fifty-one other enslaved people, recently purchased in Maryland:

> Thirty-two of these were men, and nineteen were women. The women were merely tied together with a rope, about the size of a bed cord, which was tied like a halter round the neck of each; but the men, of whom I was the stoutest and strongest, were very differently caparisoned. A strong iron collar was closely fitted by means of a padlock round each of our necks. A chain of iron, about a hundred feet in length, was passed through the hasp of each padlock, except at the two ends, where the hasps of the

> padlocks passed through a link of the chain. In addition to this, we were handcuffed in pairs, with iron staples and bolts, with a short chain, about a foot long, uniting the handcuffs and their wearers in pairs.[24]

The spectacle of enslaved people chained together in coffles shocked the abolitionist-leaning white people who witnessed them. Seven years old in 1805, Levi Coffin was from a North Carolina abolitionist family with roots in Nantucket. The family moved to New Garden, in Guilford County, North Carolina, where, following John Woolman's visit to the New Garden Meeting in 1767, members rejected slavery. The younger Coffin dated his own personal conversion to abolition to his witness of a coffle, in which the bound men responded poignantly to his father's questions: they were chained, they claimed, to keep them from running back to their wives and children. Coffin recalled being horrified at the thought of having his own father taken from him, and he claimed from that moment to grasp the violation of the embodied will of enslaved people that was the essence of slavery.[25]

In addition to the dynamic map of coerced movement produced by slave coffles after 1800, there was also the constricting map of escape, both through restrictive manumission laws and laws impeding migration to free states. This spoke to Reverend Allen's second objection: that the legal prohibitions on African American settlement, combined with the welcome extended to foreign "white" immigrants, was a deliberate effort to limit African American claims to available land. This pattern of legal restriction—after Gabriel's rebellion and the Louisiana Purchase—provided crucial context for the dynamic responses of enslaved and free people who sought refuge from white enslavers and hostile neighbors only to be met with new laws and restrictions on their freedom in so-called free states.[26]

States responded with new restrictions on newly freed Black people. When Ohio was admitted to the United States in 1803, it had a history of bloodshed and conflict with Shawnees, Delawares, Ottawas, Miamis, and Ojibwas dating back nearly a century and only recently concluded by the Treaty of Greenville. But having been formed out of the Northwest Territory, from which slavery had been excluded, Ohio was also technically a free state. Southern-born Jeffersonian republicans, transplanted New England Federalists, and southern antislavery evangelicals secured the state's decision to exclude slavery. But this did not protect smaller numbers of African Americans escaping from slavery in North Carolina and Tennessee. The geographically nearest northern sanctuary for escaping slaves from western Virginia, North Carolina, and Kentucky, Ohio was also a key territory for the riverine transport of enslaved people and goods heading south. Those on the move included slave drivers and their coffles, following the Ohio River southwest along the Ohio-Kentucky border to Cincinnati and across the southernmost border of Indiana Territory before it joined the Mississippi on the southern boundary of Illinois Territory.[27]

In the first two decades of its existence, Ohio's political compass pointed south. Southern interest in slave markets and slave labor informed the Ohio legislature's opposition to free Black migration and residency, its endorsement of the federal fugitive slave law passed in 1793, and its popular sentiment that free Black people should be discouraged from permanent settlement. When in November 1802 the Ohio constitutional convention produced the state's constitution, the first for a state carved out of the Northwest Ordinance territory, it prohibited slavery but embraced federal exclusions of free Black people from full citizenship. For example, it endorsed federal policy, set in 1792, excluding free Black men from militias. For the purposes of calculating county and congressional representation, Ohio counted only white males over the age of twenty-one. These same men were recognized as voters if they paid their taxes or contributed labor to build and maintain the state's roads. Soon after the U.S. Congress ratified the state constitution in 1803, the Ohio Assembly's first order of business was to consider banning free Black migration into the state. A year later, "An act to regulate black and mulatto persons" set residency requirements for free African Americans, mandating registration and an accompanying fee, possession of a county-issued certificate of freedom, and setting fines for anyone who provided assistance to runaway slaves in the state.[28]

Meanwhile, conditions in Virginia continued to deteriorate for free African Americans. Taking direct aim at the type of provision Robert Pleasants had included in the codicil of his will to support the education of the Pleasants freed people and their children, in 1805 the assembly prohibited the Overseers of the Poor from requiring free Black orphans to learn "reading, writing, and arithmetic" as it did for white orphans. This was not the same as making such learning illegal for free African American orphans, but it did remove a key legal support for education. The following year, the assembly expanded on earlier restrictions on free Black male access to firearms to make possession of any "firelock" illegal without the purchase of a license from the county court.[29]

In both Virginia and Ohio, moreover, laws regulating free and enslaved people attempted to parse race more precisely by making it hew to white impressions of physical appearance. Those whose appearances suggested Blackness and African descent shouldered a heavier burden of proving freedom. Although county officials in Virginia had been keeping registers of free Black people that included physical descriptions and genealogies, by 1802, when all free Black people were required to enlist, these registers became more comprehensive. Growing state interest in collecting information about the physical "evidence" of African descent among free Black people also appeared in judicial assessments of slavery. In *Hudgins v. Wrights* (1806), Virginia's Court of Appeals explicitly defined two different standards of proof in cases where an individual's enslaved condition was in question. If the alleged slave appeared to be white or Native American, then the burden lay with the party claiming ownership. If the alleged slave appeared to be of African descent, then he or she assumed the burden. Featuring the claims of the female descendants of Butterwood Nan, a Native American who might have been enslaved illegally, *Hudgins v. Wrights* evoked opposing fears: of wrongly enslaving people with white or Indian appearances, and of wrongly adding to the free population. Chancellor George Wythe's initial decision in favor of Nan's descendants placed the burden of proof on the claimant, on the grounds that "freedom is the birth-right of every human being, which sentiment is strongly inculcated by the first article of our 'political catechism,' the bill of rights."[30]

When the case went to Virginia's Supreme Court of Appeals, Judge St. George Tucker found that all Native Americans were presumed to be free in Virginia except those brought into the state as legal slaves between 1679 and 1691. In cases of Native American enslavement, the burden of proof lay with the alleged owner. Tucker also declared all white people to be always and forever free, with the implication that if an alleged slave appeared white, the burden of proof also lay with the party claiming enslavement. Tucker disagreed with his teacher Wythe that African Americans had a basic claim to freedom, reasoning that the Bill of Rights protected only free citizens or white aliens but did not abrogate the slave owner's rights of property or give freedom to people who had been slaves. He accepted Wythe's conclusions about birthright only as it concerned "white persons and native *American Indians*," but not "so far as the same relates to native *Africans* and their descendants, who have been and are now held as slaves by the citizens of this state."

His reasoning established that, in all other cases, appearance would determine the burden of proof in freedom suits. As Tucker saw it, physical appearance provided transparent clues about personal histories and racial lineage:

> Suppose three persons, a black or mulatto man or woman with a flat nose and woolly head; a copper-coloured person with long jetty black, straight hair; and one with a fair complexion, brown hair, not woolly nor inclining thereto, with a prominent Roman nose, were brought together before a Judge upon a writ of Habeas Corpus, on the ground of false imprisonment and detention in slavery: that the only evidence which the person detaining them in his custody could produce was an authenticated bill of sale from another person, and that the parties themselves

> were unable to produce any evidence concerning themselves, whence they came, &c. &c.

Tucker posed the question, "How must a Judge act in such a case? I answer he must judge from his own view. He must discharge the white person and the Indian out of custody . . . and he must redeliver the black or mulatto person, with the flat nose and woolly hair to the person claiming to hold him or her as a slave, unless the black person or mulatto could procure some person to be bound for him, to produce proof of his descent, in the maternal line, from a free female ancestor." Judge Roane agreed that a justice's assessment of appearance could frame an initial response to a complainant's claim on behalf of posterity but placed greater weight on the possible counterevidence of ancestry. Both justices believed that the law's assessment of blood reflected ancestry, which was itself determined by the blood connection of mother and child and usually manifested in appearance. Presumptive freedom and enslavement based on appearance, expressed in the opinions of *Hudgins v. Wrights*, continued to guide judicial decisions throughout the nineteenth century, making it nearly impossible for enslaved people of African descent to seek writs of habeas corpus to spark judicial review of their bound condition.[31]

With continued concerns about a growing free Black population, in 1806 the Virginia Assembly required all newly freed people to leave the state within one year or risk reenslavement. In at least two rural Virginia counties, free people continued to move about unencumbered, yet the threat of removal introduced new precarity to their lives, prompting Black petitioners to claim their right to remain.[32] Ohio followed suit in 1807 with the Supplementary Ohio Black Code. Although actual enforcement was lax, the law required newly arrived free Black settlers to post five hundred dollars bond for a guarantee of good behavior and self-support. It also banned any testimony in court by African Americans against white people. The following year, Virginia legislators cracked down on the mobility and autonomy that had for thirty years annoyed white neighbors of the people enslaved by the Pleasants estate and their descendants: no longer would masters be permitted to allow slaves to self-hire under penalty of a fine and the threat of the sale of the enslaved person in question.[33]

The same year that the state of Virginia took steps to minimize the size of the free Black population, Jefferson delivered his State of the Union message to Congress preparing the nation for the impending end to the transatlantic slave trade. His message reflected the rhetoric of the impressment protests, the ongoing British transport of "offending" criminals, the ideals of free trade and migration, and the backdrop of a new international calculus of race provoked by Haiti's independence. He explicitly condemned the transatlantic traffic in slaves as a violation of human rights: "I congratulate you, fellow citizens, on the approach of the period at which you may interpose your authority constitutionally, to withdraw the citizens of the United States from all further participation in those violations of human rights which have been so long continued on the unoffending inhabitants of Africa, and which the morality, the reputation, and the best interests of our country, have long been eager to proscribe."

Deciphering what "human rights" meant to Jefferson and his contemporaries and understanding why he found it easier to identify violations in a transoceanic context than in Virginia points us to the politics of slave labor, mobility, birthright, and belonging. Although he explicitly condemned the transatlantic traffic in slaves as a violation of human rights, Jefferson's main concern appears to have been the reputation of the United States rather than the suffering of Africans. Coming as it did in the midst of the conflict over British impressment of Americans, his message referred obliquely to the plight of violated American seamen. In Jefferson's human rights landscape, the blood and tears of African-descended laborers did not flow into tilled American soil; instead, Jefferson defined rights in contrast to oceanic trafficking. The rise of state-sponsored rights following the Constitution's Bill of Rights had left enslaved people lacking the most rudimentary of human rights. Not least of the consequences of this new rights context, the end to the transatlantic trade to the United States placed new importance on the reproductivity of enslaved women as the main source of enslaved labor for southern plantations.[34]

Restrictive domestic laws combined with the growing numbers of southern-bound slave coffles in Ohio and Virginia to inspire the dynamic geography of the Underground Railroad. Everywhere they looked, enslaved people in Virginia saw fellow slaves being transported south against their will. They also saw free Black people they knew being harassed, their freedom diminished, and their options to remain in the state of their birth being curtailed. After 1807, Ohio was no longer a safe destination for those aspiring to free lives. Illinois, Indiana, Michigan, Wisconsin, and Iowa rapidly followed suit with laws to curtail Black freedom.[35]

Exercising Personal Liberties

By the nineteenth century, government power assumed multiple and conflicting forms that pitted local communities, networks of free and enslaved Black people, state courts, and federal policies against each other. In the midst of constricting possibilities—to move one's body to safer ground, to take refuge, or to self-emancipate—enslaved people testified to their desire to remove themselves from slavery's cruelty and coercion. Their escapes from Virginia, Maryland, and Delaware began soon after the 1780 Pennsylvania Gradual Abolition Act. With the passage of a federal Fugitive Slave Act in 1793, Pennsylvania became an increasingly important haven for those seeking to escape both the threats and reality of family separations and sale into the Lower South. Under the terms of its Gradual Abolition Act, Pennsylvania slaveholders were required to register their enslaved laborers and forbidden from removing them out of state. In effect, such actions became subject to penalties much like those for kidnapping, which provided a modest protection for a newly created cohort of free people of African descent.[36] As the stream of refugees grew, Maryland enslavers agitated with their state's lawmakers to complain about Pennsylvania's resistance to enforcing federal protections for human property. In 1799, free Black people in Philadelphia petitioned unsuccessfully to Congress to roll back the Fugitive Slave Law, which made them vulnerable to being "seized, [and] fettered" by enslavers who used the law to perpetrate kidnappings. At the same time, southern efforts to pass stronger national legislation around reclaiming refugees failed in Congress.[37]

Interpreted from the perspective of liberty of the body, the issue of federal fugitive slave law enforcement takes on a different cast. As the legal historian H. Robert Baker has noted, the fundamental issue at the heart of the fugitive slave law—and indeed, one might argue of all slave law—was the "extent of government power over someone's body."[38] In many ways, state personal liberty laws codified the assertion of embodied self-sovereignty by free and enslaved Black people in a nation where slavery remained legal and slaves a protected form of property.

Pennsylvania's legal disposition to fugitives and to its free residents of color resulted from a threefold process initiated by Black people themselves: risky, individual acts of "self-emancipation," a term that fails to capture the physical exertion required for escape; the necessary creation of networks of white and free Black allies; and the practical and legal interventions of abolitionists. Two such interventions shaped the evolving legal landscape in the state. One was the consequence of the escape of a woman named Mary from the Maryland enslaver James Corse sometime in 1814. For two years, she resided in Philadelphia before giving birth to a daughter, Eliza. When a Philadelphia magistrate assisted Corse in apprehending Mary and her infant daughter, Corse had them imprisoned in the city jail. The warrant for their commitment to prison came from Samuel Badger, Esquire, an associate judge of the Court of Common Pleas, who had reasoned that "the daughter of Mary, a negro woman, the slave of James Corse, of Maryland," must also be "the slave of said James." A writ of habeas corpus brought Eliza before the Pennsylvania Supreme Court, where justices ruled that Eliza's conception and birth to a woman residing in a state in which slavery was illegal rendered her not a slave and therefore not subject to the Fugitive Slave Law of 1793. Chief Justice William Tilghman, already known as a judge sympathetic to the rights of enslavers, found Eliza to be free on the grounds that the Fugitive Slave Law applied only to persons held in service or labor in one state, who escape to another. As this did not apply to Eliza, he determined that, under the terms of the 1780 Pennsylvania Gradual Abolition Act, Eliza "was born free." In a concurring opinion, Justice Gibson tipped the scales to the "natural rights of [Mary's] child" over the positive and artificial rights of the master over the mother.[39]

If this ruling and a subsequent decision in an unreported case known as Kitty's case on behalf of an enslaved woman's children gave abolitionists hope that fugitives and free Black people would be protected within the state's borders, *Wright v. Deacon* (1819) dashed those hopes. The opinion by the same Justice Tilghman quashed a writ *de homine replegiando* (replevin by mainprise, the equivalent of bail for release during the trial) on behalf of a Maryland fugitive's challenge of his detainment. The African-descended plaintiff, known as Wright or Hall according to the case file, had first come before Justice of the Peace Richard Renshaw, who committed the plaintiff to prison to inquire into the claim of his alleged enslaver, the Maryland planter Rasin Gale. The plaintiff then sued for habeas corpus, returnable to Associate Judge Thomas Armstrong of the Court of Common Pleas. Armstrong heard the parties and issued a certificate for his removal by Gale. The fugitive's counsel argued that the matter was still being heard by Renshaw and that the plaintiff had a right to a jury trial. The decision pivoted on an alleged fugitive's lack of right to a jury trial or other process guaranteed to citizens of the state as such rights were inconsistent with the requirements of the 1793 Fugitive Slave Law. The fugitive's only remedy was to claim his freedom and to have the case tried in Maryland.[40]

The reaction from antislavery activists, which included petitions and lobbying, led to the passage of the nation's first personal liberty law in the same state that had issued the first abolition law in 1780. In 1820, Pennsylvania's new liberty law aimed to prevent the kidnapping of free Black people for the purposes of selling and enslaving them out of state. The "Act to prevent kidnapping" undermined the enforcement of the 1793 Fugitive Slave Law by prohibiting the removal of any person from the state with the design to sell or dispose of them "as a slave or servant for a year or years." Such a broad definition of illegal removal effectively collapsed the difference between recapture of an escaped slave and kidnapping of a free Black person. Unwarranted removal was classified as a felony and punished with a stiff fine and seven to twenty-one years hard labor. Under the terms of the 1820 law, aldermen and justices of the peace were prevented from issuing certificates of removal, which became a matter for judges, who had to file detailed reports before returning suspected fugitives. These provisions made the 1793 Fugitive Slave Law virtually unenforceable for this crucial border state.

Other states soon followed suit, with New York's 1828 law including the alleged fugitive's right to trial by jury.[41]

The piecemeal legal tests of the 1793 Fugitive Slave Law and state personal liberty laws created complex issues of competing state and federal jurisdictions. The 1820 Pennsylvania law did not detail the personal liberties to be enjoyed by free Black people as citizens of Pennsylvania but nonetheless created a buffer between the presumptions linking Blackness to slavery that emboldened enslaver claimants to pursue free African-descended people. In doing so, it also protected the precarious autonomy of free Black people living and working in the state. The jurisdictional issues became more complicated when, in 1825, the U.S. Supreme Court decided in the *Antelope* case that Africans trafficked under the flags of nations that continued to uphold the legality of the slave trade remained property even after being seized and brought to the United States. Africans who had been trafficked on a U.S. vessel, in contrast, were to be returned to Africa.[42]

Yet the 1820 personal liberty law did not end the illegal kidnapping of free people by slave catchers and procurers. The kidnapping of five free boys from the streets of Philadelphia in 1825 by a notorious gang of domestic enslavers, part of what the historian Richard Bell describes as the "Reverse Underground Railroad," stirred the city's Black community and their allies into action. In 1826, they successfully lobbied the state government for a new law to restrain slave catchers and stop kidnappers. The 1826 "Act to give effect to the provisions of the Constitution of the United States relative to fugitives from labour, for the protection of free people of colour, and to prevent kidnapping" altered the risk landscape for African-descended people in two main ways: first, the law established a legal procedure for removal that offered some protections to free Black people against kidnappers who operated under the cover of the 1793 Fugitive Slave Law.[43] The establishment of a summary hearing process, moreover, gave alleged fugitives time to prove their free status, which could not be denied on the basis of a slave owner's oath alone. Yet ultimately the law complied with the constitutional authority of the 1793 Fugitive Slave Law by creating mechanisms for the enslaver to procure a warrant for the alleged fugitive's arrest and for state peace officers to be obligated to serve it. The result was a compromise that neither fully accommodated the state's compliance with the Fugitive Slave Law nor delivered the security of rights to free Black people and alleged fugitive slaves that abolitionists had hoped for.[44]

Colonization and Emigration

The founding of the American Colonization Society (ACS) in 1816 and its subsequent effort to sponsor free Black emigration shifted the terms of debate about slavery and racial equality during this moment of competing jurisdictional authority over the bodies of alleged fugitives. It also spurred free African Americans to express their political solidarity with enslaved people in terms of blood ties. African Americans responded immediately and with growing urgency as the ACS drew influential followers like the Kentucky slave owner Henry Clay and the Virginia slave apologist John Randolph. In Philadelphia, three thousand people turned out for a protest meeting in response to the official debut of the ACS in January 1817. Contrary to the positions of Rev. Allen and James Forten, who initially supported colonization, the group opposed any plan to separate themselves from "the slave population of this country . . . they are our brethren by the *ties of consanguinity*, of suffering and of wrong" (emphasis mine). Noting the crucial role enslaved African laborers had played in taming the "wilds" of America, they also rejected colonization on the basis of their own embodied self-sovereignty: "we their descendents feel ourselves entitled to participate in the blessing of her luxuriant soil, which their blood and sweat manured."[45]

A few days later, free African Americans in Richmond gathered to discourage colonizationists from exiling free people to foreign countries. The petitioners requested that colonizationists consider relocating the exiles somewhere within the "land of our nativity," perhaps out of the concern for mortality and the conviction of their own birthright claims. They appealed to Congress for a grant "of a small portion of their territory, either on the Missouri River, or any place that may seem to them most conducive to the public good and our future welfare." Like their white counterparts, the Richmond petitioners considered land formerly in the possession of Native Americans as available for settlement by agriculturally minded Americans and saw little reason why Black people should be less eligible for the privilege than white people.[46]

By 1821, with the founding of Liberia, the ACS seemed poised to receive federal support. The ACS's version of colonization reassured white slaveholders by assuaging fears that slavery made race war inevitable. Slavery might continue safely, the ACS argument went, as long as colonization removed free African Americans, understood to be both innately deficient and injured by racism, from North America. The critic Levi Coffin expressed enslavers' interests more bluntly, claiming that the real purpose of the ACS was to expatriate the free Black threat to the security of enslavers' human property.[47]

The unprecedented mortality among migrants to Liberia appears to have shifted the views of African American leaders like Allen. Colonization, moreover, also had unexpected effects on its agents, changing their worldviews and politicizing those who crossed jurisdictional and cultural divides on fact-finding journeys. The journeys were often eye-opening for those who made them, and indeed, agents were likely to discover "facts" that were broadly unsettling as well as narrowly useful. As citizens of sovereign nations able to travel unmolested, some white colonization agents became aware of their own privilege while others unintentionally witnessed injustice where they expected to find a convenient place to send free African Americans.[48]

Haitian president Boyer's invitation to free African American migrants stimulated many of these fact-finding trips and opened fissures in the colonization movement. Upon becoming the sole leader of a unified Haiti in 1821, Boyer began reaching out to both white ACS members and free African American leaders to woo free Black laborers, who were much needed in his post–sugar plantation regime of small producers. The ACS had formally repudiated both Haiti and Boyer as early as 1818, however, and lost the support of many African Americans as a consequence, including James Forten, who became a vocal critic. The ACS's other prominent African American supporter, Paul Cuffee, died in 1817. The lone ACS agent to respond to Boyer's recruitment effort in 1821, the New Yorker Loring C. Dewey, was soon disavowed by the national organization. The ACS saw value in the emigration of free African Americans only if they relocated to West African colonies like Liberia. To sponsor their travel to Haiti, the hotbed of Black republicanism, was, in the view of white ACS leaders, only to fuel the simmering fires of an eventual race war in the United States.[49]

Free Black people, however, including those who had rightly begun to suspect the proslavery sentiments of the ACS and reject colonization, saw new opportunity in Boyer's invitation. Briefly, from 1824 to 1825, Boyer offered to pay transportation costs and provide high wages, tools, and education to qualified (i.e., "frugal" and "ambitious") African American migrants. His advocates, moreover, included prominent people of African descent including the Baptist minister Thomas Paul and the Haitian military officer Jonathan Granville, both of whom successfully recruited African American migrants, as well as the minister and activist William Watkins, the Reverend Richard Allen, and James Forten. Even when Boyer rescinded this offer after discovering corruption, the white Quaker abolitionist Benjamin Lundy, who traveled to Haiti to assess its possibilities in 1825 and again in 1829, painted a rosy picture of the situation and continued to support emigration to Haiti. A stalwart abolitionist publisher and early supporter of free labor produce, Lundy was at this point in his career involved in an independent scheme to subsidize the migration of free Blacks from Baltimore to Haiti, where they had been promised land in exchange for three years of agricultural labor. Unlike many other white supporters of Black emigration, moreover, Lundy accompanied migrants on their journeys.[50]

When white colonizationists analyzed the prospects of migrants to Haiti, they sometimes interpreted Boyer's incentives as operating as a form of natural selection that was unfavorable to U.S. interests. In an 1824 letter to his friend the Quaker shipping magnate Thomas Cope, the New York reformer and financier Thomas Eddy speculated about the type of African Americans who would be likely to leave the United States to take up President Boyer's offer, revealing the ease with which racism could be hitched to colonization schemes. Eddy supported the Boyer plan but believed that abolitionists needed to do more to assist and uplift the African Americans who remained in the United States, who he assumed would be "bad" characters rejected by Boyer.[51]

When agents actually witnessed the agricultural practices and living conditions of migrants in Haiti, their reviews were mixed. In 1825, on a fact-finding trip to Haiti at the behest of the Society of Pennsylvania for the Promotion of the Abolition of Slavery, J. H. Gibbon, a graduate of the University of Pennsylvania's medical school and the son of an Edinburgh-trained physician, cast some doubts on the condition of Haitian agricultural laborers and transplanted African Americans, contradicting reports of the government's preferential treatment of new immigrants from the United States. Writing to his friend Thomas Cope, who had corresponded with Eddy, he expressed concern about insufficient economic, political, and medical resources for immigrants. He also noted the military service required of men, a difficult condition for the pacifist Quaker sponsors of the plan to accede to and perhaps also worrying to them.[52]

Boyer's support for the voluntary migration project diminished, however, as a consequence of several factors. First, the French government's insistence on the payment of an indemnity to cover the costs of the loss of slave property buried the government of Haiti in debt. Second, as Boyer had discovered, too many migrants set foot on Haiti's shores to collect their bonuses and then promptly returned to the United States. And finally, despite the Haitian government's vaccination policy of 1810, the influx of African Americans provoked a deadly smallpox epidemic in the winter of 1824–1825, cooling popular enthusiasm for the migrants.[53] Boyer's Code Rural of May 1, 1826, subsequently made it difficult for abolitionists who touted Haiti's free labor economy; the code restricted the mobility of laborers in an effort to keep them on plantations.[54]

For some small number of African American emigrationists, like Cuffee, Allen, Forten, and Coker, African American- and Haitian-sponsored colonization had initially offered a welcome escape from white abuse and the increasing legal restrictions on free Black citizenship. News about the high mortality among the young and old from malaria, however, dampened the enthusiasm of prospective migrants to Liberia. African American opponents of the colonization scheme responded sharply in print to undermine the logic of the ACS and deter Black support. Samuel Cornish and John Russwurm commenced publication of *Freedom's Journal* in 1827 to coincide with the official end to slavery in New York and to rebut colonizationist arguments about African American racial inferiority and incompatibility with American political institutions. The editors also took pains to publicize the achievements of free African Americans. Russwurm's subsequent support for emigration led him to clash with Cornish and resign from the journal in 1829.[55]

Blood Science

Richard Allen evoked the blood and tears of African American laborers—people who in his view had more clearly earned the right to consider the United States their mother country than newly arrived white immigrants—to make a political argument about slavery. He expressed the relationship between a laborer's body and the land improved by his labor by evoking the bodily fluids actually expended in coerced agricultural labor. In 1827, Allen mentioned blood and tears, but in other contexts, as in his adoption of an anti-colonizationist posture in 1817, he also mentioned sweat, the physical currency of highly valued plantation labor. In all of these references, Allen conjured the physical exertions and functions of bodies that were increasingly being represented in anatomical specimen collections and assessed through dissection in medical research centers like London, Edinburgh, Paris, and his own city of Philadelphia.[56]

Allen's framing of the issue of national belonging in terms of the bodies of laboring African Americans represented an important intervention. With references to the blood and mortality of African-descended people, he harnessed several popular discourses about health, medicine, and agricultural productivity to make his case. For centuries, as we have seen, medical thinkers had speculated about African American bodies as racially distinct even in the face of contradictory evidence. Seventeenth- and eighteenth-century theories about black skin and blood pigment had elaborated medical language about blood that countered early abolitionist "one blood" claims. During the nineteenth century, as the bodies of enslaved and free Black people continued to be a topic of medical debate, the discussion of blood became even more insular. Connecting health to the issues of national belonging and forced exile, Allen summoned popular medical wisdom about seasoning and acclimatization. He depicted blood as generative of nation, not as a racially distinct fluid. His invocation of the Black laborer's blood watering the soil, moreover, was consistent with popular medical understandings of bloodletting as a therapy that "lowered" an overstimulated body. Much as Grotius and Vattel acknowledged the warrior's blood sacrifice for the nation, Allen's laborers expended blood that depleted their own bodies but enriched the national soil to produce wealth.

Allen's references to blood were increasingly at odds with the materialist and positivist trajectory of academic medicine. In his home city of Philadelphia, medical students and their professors collected anatomical specimens, dissected cadavers, and experimented with animal and human blood to determine blood's composition. Of these three research and teaching pathways, the work in blood science was the least racially inflected and yet the most distant from popular wisdom about blood. Most medical students appear to have assumed blood's universality, even across the animal-human divide, yet their minute examinations of blood's material composition and qualities were not easily reconciled with its popular mystical significance and symbolism. Their studies expanded the reach of medical materialism, potentially weakening the spiritual foundations of older abolitionist claims to "one blood." Indeed, detailed knowledge of common human blood chemistry and properties as the basis for all life could have created a new material foundation for blood's universalism, but the main consequence appears to have been to widen the gap between the emerging positivist scientific discourse about blood and popular spiritual, political, legal, and familial meanings of vitality, heredity, and belonging.

Philadelphia was home to North America's first medical school. Its "firstness" gave it strong transatlantic ties while its location in a booming mid-Atlantic port made it attractive to students from slaveholding colonies. Early in the eighteenth century, before its founding, aspiring physicians like John Redman began their medical training by apprenticing to local doctors before going abroad for intensive study and training in Europe: Edinburgh, London, Paris, and in Redman's case, Leiden, where he received a medical degree in 1748. Upon his return to Philadelphia, Redman began training his own students but sent them abroad to follow his path to a European medical degree. The Philadelphia native and physician John Morgan began his studies under Redman before completing a degree at Edinburgh. Morgan returned to Philadelphia in 1765 to join fellow Edinburgh graduate William Shippen Jr., who, along with his physician father, had been offering medical lectures in the city since 1762. Together they established the Philadelphia College of Medicine, which became the University of Pennsylvania Medical School in 1791. Benjamin Rush, who like Morgan had been mentored by Redman, took classes at the new medical college before embarking on his own circuit of European centers of medical knowledge: Edinburgh, a residency in London, and at the urging of Benjamin Franklin, consultations in Paris. By 1769 he, too, was back in Philadelphia treating patients and training students.[57]

Along with Morgan, Shippen, and Redman, Rush founded one of the first private medical societies in the United States, the College of Physicians, in 1787. Here, Philadelphia physicians learned about European race scientists like Johann Blumenbach, Comte de Buffon, Claude-Nicolas Le Cat, and François Bernier, as well as new North American theorists, like the Princeton president and minister

Samuel Stanhope Smith (1751–1819). Smith, a rural Pennsylvanian by birth who had worked as a tutor to a white slaveholding family in Virginia, produced one of the first North American treatises arguing for the original unity of humankind and emphasizing the environmental causes of racial difference. Trained in divinity rather than anatomy, Smith hewed to the purpose of reconciling human difference with biblical accounts of a single divine creation. He delivered "An Essay on the Causes of the Variety of Complexion and Figure in the Human Species" to the American Philosophical Society in 1785; it appeared in print two years later. According to Smith, the continuum of physical difference could be explained by climate, as could the state of a particular society and its manner of living; each of these factors left its imprint on the body. Yet Smith remained invested in human difference and was himself an enslaver committed to interpreting those differences as degenerations from a single creation. Among the differences he discussed were the allegedly curved legs of African-descended people; the superior manners, appearance, and intellects of domestic slaves over field slaves; and the changes observable in European-descended inhabitants of the southern region of North America.[58]

When yellow fever struck Philadelphia in 1793, the College of Physicians became the center of North American debates about race, disease etiology, and treatment. Rush's aggressive use of bleeding and purging to treat victims fueled some of the controversy, but Rush also erroneously assumed that people of African descent were less vulnerable to yellow fever than white people. Facing a critical shortage of attendants to care for the sick and dying, Rush and Mayor Clarkson appealed to city's African American residents to provide nurses. Rush specifically asked the Reverends Absalom Jones and Richard Allen for help, hoping to capitalize on their leadership and expertise in bleeding patients. When African Americans responded to Rush's call to serve and discovered as a consequence that African American (as opposed to African and Afro-Caribbean) immunity from yellow fever was a myth, they earned only the obloquy of white citizens for their civic-minded response. Jones and Allen defended their community's reputation in *Narrative of the Proceedings of the Black People*, where they detailed both African American vulnerability to yellow fever and their care for desperate and abandoned white patients. They also described their use of Rush's preferred technique, bleeding, to try to affect cures. In a document appended to the end of the essay, Jones and Allen thanked white abolitionists for their sympathy and support, noting "you are not ashamed to call the most abject of our race, brethren, children of one father, who made of one blood all the nations of the earth." In the potentially charged context of Black attendants taking the lancet to white arms, it was especially significant that Jones and Allen reiterated the principle of "one blood."[59]

Allen's remarks affirming "one blood" marked his debut as a public intellectual in circumstances that strengthened his subsequent leadership around Black resistance to colonization and objections to legal restrictions upon free Black people. A year after the epidemic, Allen founded the independent African Methodist Episcopal Church, Mother Bethel AME. He remained an active participant in the city's intellectual, political, and spiritual life during the years in which Philadelphia's medical establishment shifted its focus from blood to skeletons and organs. It is likely, in light of his own skills in bleeding patients and providing care, that he would have known something of the developments in medical science occurring in his city, especially since the growing reliance on dissection and anatomical specimen collection put the bodies of his own community at risk for body snatching. But it is also probable that his political and spiritual responsibilities kept him firmly grounded in the languages of blood and health that reflected popular and practical understandings.[60]

Across the city from Allen's Mother Bethel Church, the College of Physicians served as a forum for ambitious men to launch their careers. The North Carolina native, Penn Medical School graduate, and leading scientific racist Charles Caldwell was one such doctor. Although he eventually parted company with the College of Physicians, his mentor Benjamin Rush, and the University of Pennsylvania, his training and his membership at the College of Physicians provided the platform he needed to make his professional mark. Caldwell's scientific racism derived from three sometimes contradictory sources: extensive reading in French and German race theory, a postcolonial conviction that American medical thinkers needed to assert their intellectual autonomy from their European peers, and an empirical reliance on physical appearance similar to the reasoning in *Hudgins v. Wrights* (1806). In 1795, the year he became a member of the College of Physicians, Caldwell translated Blumenbach's *Elements of Physiology* from the original Latin for the Philadelphia publisher Thomas Dobson.[61] He was, therefore, well grounded in hierarchical schemes of racial classification circulating around the Atlantic. Yet Caldwell's disagreements with Rush kept him from an appointment on Penn's medical faculty. He remained active in medicine from his perch as a natural science professor in the college, however, delivering a sarcastic rebuke to an English doctor, John Haygarth, who had proposed an alternative model of imported disease to Caldwell's own proposition that specific local climatic disturbances and insect proliferation—grasshoppers, flies, and mosquitoes—had caused yellow fever. Caldwell's was a controversial stance at the College of Physicians, which had in 1798 endorsed the view that yellow fever was a foreign importation. That same year, after completing his own experiments demonstrating blood's vitality, Caldwell decided to forfeit his College of Physicians membership.[62]

Despite being outside both the College of Physicians and the Penn Medical School, Caldwell established himself as North America's leading medical race theorist with the publication of two rebuttals to Samuel Stanhope Smith's enlarged and expanded *Essay on the Causes of the Variety of Complexion and Figure in the Human Species* (1810). Smith's second edition had come in response to critics in London, Edinburgh, and New York who cited anatomical evidence, reflecting the field's emergence as a key part of the eighteenth-century medical curriculum in Europe and the British Isles. Anatomists privileged their experience as dissectionists over textual mastery and competence in materia medica. Lacking medical training, Smith made claims based on history and climate in ways that made him vulnerable to critics who pounced on his lack of historical documentation and ignorance of anatomy.[63]

In two essays, published in 1811 and 1814, Caldwell presented his own authority as superior to Smith's not only on the basis of anatomical expertise but as a consequence of his insider status as a native of the U.S. South. Caldwell asserted his own objectivity, technical anatomical knowledge, and historical evidence of "blood" (i.e., race) mixing that Smith had failed to acknowledge. In a prefatory note, the editor of the 1814 version of Caldwell's essay denied that Caldwell was merely gathering facts to defend the institution of slavery. Rather, the editor observed, "our intention is neither to degrade one race of men nor to elevate another, but, as far as we may be able, to develop the truth. We endeavor to speak of the Africans precisely as we find them." Caldwell fronted his professional expertise, emphasizing empirical information about appearance but suggesting that some observations might be more accurate than others. Anatomists, he claimed, understood the human body in ways that escaped their lay counterparts.[64]

Using the language of raced blood, Caldwell insisted that Smith's examples and explanations of human difference were flawed. The Hungarian, Laplander, Portuguese, and Hottentot cases, he argued, could be better explained as the consequence of blood mixture rather than the impact of the environment. He offered a similar rebuttal to Smith's attribution of darker southern European complexions to climate. Smith had not considered the mixing of southern Europeans with Moors, according to Caldwell, failing to acknowledge that they "left behind them, in the provinces they had overrun, a portion of their blood, which still flows in the veins, and contributes to darken the complexions of their descendants. So incontestable is our evidence in support of this, that in many families in the south of Spain, the Moorish features are not yet effaced." Jews presented a somewhat different case, according to Caldwell. He dismissed Smith's contention that Jews had adopted the national "countenance" wherever they lived, instead asserting that they were "*a brown people* . . . we mean that their complexion is never lighter than a brown, *when their veins are free from christian blood*."[65]

As for Smith's argument that the white inhabitants of the United States manifested a degenerated physique, Caldwell rebutted the claim on the basis of his own familiarity with the South. People of European ancestry in the United States were "certainly not, as some would have it, *semi-Indianized*," he retorted, and asserted that the era of climatic darkening of white complexions in the South had already come to an end. He also disputed Smith's positive comparison of domestic to field slaves, insisting that what Smith was actually observing in house servants was "individuals partaking of a twofold race—the European ingrafted on the African stock. Nor ought a mistake of the latter kind to be considered as extraordinary. It is well known that there are mulattoes, the descendants of a white father and a Black mother, who inherit, but with little alloy, their maternal complexion, with much of the regularity and symmetry of the paternal features."

As he explained more emphatically in 1814, rather than adapting to the climate, southerners who appeared to be darker than their white counterparts did "not contain in their veins the unadulterated blood of European ancestors. They are the offspring of that licentious intercourse of sexes and colours, which so disgracefully prevails in every country where slavery is tolerated." Caldwell's final nail in the coffin of the argument for environmental causes of human degradation was Smith's failure to account for the uniformity of complexion among Indigenous peoples in the Americas regardless of the latitude of their residence.[66]

Caldwell mobilized "truths" about differences in African and European appearance to build an argument that he described as "incontestabl[e]" for having been derived from his own expert observation as an anatomist. He took aim at Smith's argument about the environmental causes of difference but coyly insisted that he was not making an affirmative argument about separate creations or distinct races. Focusing on Smith's example of the allegedly distinct form of African-descended people's legs and feet, Caldwell denied that divergent skeletal shapes could have resulted as an adaptation to the environment. Rather, the anatomist claimed to know what Smith did not: that the form of African limbs was a function of a straighter fibula and the distinctive shape of the foot a reflection of a distinct alignment of the os calcis and astragalus. Accepting much, although not all, of what the environmentalist noted as key features of African and European disparity, Caldwell affirmed the evidence of difference without having to expend his own intellectual capital by making risky arguments about separate creations.[67]

By 1814, Caldwell's argument had become more elaborate and more technical. He noted matter-of-factly that black skin color was derived from pigment secreted in the *rete mucosum*, a claim that followed Le Cat and had appeared in the comprehensive *Encyclopédie ou Dictionnaire raisonné* (1751–1772): "That the complexion of the negro is the result of secretion and therefore immutable, is a truth which seems obvious from a variety of considerations." Among Smith's many problems, according to Caldwell, was that he was unable to distinguish between general and local causes, a weakness that was especially obvious in his discussion of Henry Moss, an African-descended person who exhibited a loss of skin pigment that fascinated white doctors. Caldwell dismissed Smith's claim that Moss was in good health. Rather, in Caldwell's analysis, Moss's pigment loss reflected the action of a skin disease, a local cause rather than a general ailment that impeded the operation of black pigment in the *rete mucosum*. Caldwell also debunked Smith's argument that African blackness reflected a higher proportion of black bile. Quite the opposite, Caldwell contended, offering personal testimony about the discrepant health of African- and European-descended peoples from Delaware Bay to St. Mary's River, Florida, and reasoning that greater bile would have resulted in higher, not lower, rates of Black illness.

Caldwell's essays led the trends in medical science. As a consequence of comparative anatomy's ascendency, medical students between 1790 and 1820 were required to take courses in anatomy and urged to produce dissertations based on experimental results.[68] This methodology led to revised accounts of the relationships among the body's fluids, including chyle, thoracic duct "milk," blood, breast milk, tears, and urine. No longer did these substances appear as interchangeable components of the body's fluid economy. Blood, in particular, following the pathbreaking work of the British surgeon John Hunter, transformed from a potentially corruptible source of disease to a resilient fluid that retained its vitality as long as it circulated within a living organism. Early nineteenth-century medical students were fascinated by blood's capacity to assimilate substances without altering its own basic composition, and the reemergence of what appeared to be chyle or thoracic milk in coagulated samples.

Penn's young medical degree recipients tried to identify the chemical components and functions that made blood uniquely vital and resilient. Most of their experiments worked from evidence of the color and texture of bodily fluids to theories about circulation. Experiments on animal subjects focused on testing blood's resilience following injections of poisons and putrid substances.[69] In 1793, the year that yellow fever struck Philadelphia, for example, Adam Seybert completed his dissertation "Being an Attempt to Disprove the Doctrine of the Putrefaction of the Blood of Living Animals," an important standard for subsequent studies of blood and disease etiology. Seybert subjected dogs to starvation, a diet of putrid food, and the injection of a variety of substances directly into the blood vessels. Although the dogs died in the vast majority of the experiments, none showed any evidence of putrid blood when autopsied. Seybert concluded that the blood of a living creature had the capacity to assimilate foreign matter. Diseased blood injected into the blood vessels of another creature might adhere to that blood like contagion did to a piece of cloth or an old building, but it did not change the substance of the host's blood.[70]

In the decade following Seybert's work, several students completed landmark studies of the blood. Nathaniel Chapman, born in Virginia and later an influential professor and founder of the American Medical Association, conducted a study built on Seybert's findings. He injected a range of substances into dogs and cats to demonstrate that digestion, respiration, and blood circulation changed the essential forms of foreign matter introduced to the stomach or the veins. "Though the blood be alive to impressions, and perhaps even more exquisitely than the solids," he observed, "it being designed that all matters should be excluded the circulation, they lose their specific mode of action when introduced." He conceded, however, that, despite the protective function of the blood, some medicines did appear to have specific effects on specific parts of the body.[71]

Dr. James Hutchinson Jr.'s "An Experimental Essay on the Conversion of Chyle into Blood" disputed theories about chyle's transformation into blood.[72] Hutchinson's empirical studies of dog blood included a postscript from his case notes that featured a lone human subject over whose blood products he assumed proprietary control. The case was of a "mulatto" woman, aged forty-five, identified only as A.B., who complained of headache, pain in her bowels, and an absence of menstruation for three months. Hutchinson ordered her to be bled twelve ounces, keeping her blood for observation. A white serum soon separated out of the blood. On the next visit she was bled ten ounces, and Hutchinson observed the same change in the sample. A.B. claimed to feel better—or did she just want to avoid a return visit?—even though she still had a headache. The white serum's continued purity convinced Hutchinson that it was the fluid of the thoracic duct. At no point did he draw any conclusions about racial difference based on his observations of her blood, which served as a generic sample.[73]

Blood science in the early nineteenth century dismantled the body's fluid economy but affirmed the vitality of blood. It yielded no new insights about race, leaving the medically orthodox to repeat the conclusions of eighteenth-century French researchers about black blood, and the curious to engage in their own ruminations, sometimes based on scripture.[74] When blood transfusions resumed in the early nineteenth century in England, there was no discussion of racially distinct blood, perhaps because the common English identity of the experimental subjects rendered the issue moot. James Blundell, a young British obstetrician, attempted to use human-to-human transfusions to save the lives of women who had suffered significant blood loss during childbirth. The subjects of his interventions were parturient women whose bodies had been central to early modern understandings of the body's humoral ebbs and flows. Blundell observed that, without his intervention, the cold, pale, clammy, and weak patients eventually succumbed within a few short hours. Although the results were mixed—Blundell's patients had only a 50 percent chance of surviving his operations—this was 50 percent greater than if no transfusion had been attempted.[75] One of Blundell's successful transfusions, reported in the *Philadelphia Journal of Medical and Physical Sciences* (*PJMPS*) in 1825, featured the injection of four ounces of a robust husband's blood into the veins of a drooping postpartum wife. According to Blundell, this was enough to restore her vitality and save her life. None of Blundell's transfusions crossed the lines of what doctors on both sides of the Atlantic were contending were biologically distinct races, leaving the issue of "raced" blood unchallenged.[76]

Within four years of Blundell's experiments (but before they were reported in the *PJMPS*), the French physicians J. L. Prevost and J. A. Dumas provided experimental data pointing to the importance of respecting species boundaries when transfusing blood. In their "Examination of the Blood and Its Action," a study based on microscopic observation and reported to Philadelphia's Academy of Natural Sciences, they warned that, although red blood cells from different animals might look alike, transfusion could only be successful if it occurred within the "same species." It is unclear what impact this conclusion had on transfusion practice among humans except to rule out the animal to human transfusions that had been so disastrous during the seventeenth century. For the purposes of their experiment, "species" did not fragment the category human but lent credence to the claim that all people were of "one blood."[77]

Meanwhile, the debate continued about blood's role in disease. Chapman, now editor of the *PJMPS*, privileged the actions of disease-causing agents on organs rather than on fluids. He based his position on Seybert's and his own work in contradistinction to the claims of a young New York medical student, Jacob Dyckman, whose "Pathology of the Fluids" (1814) still emphasized blood as a source of disease. Critical of Dyckman, Chapman urged American physicians to adopt a postcolonial stance in relation to European blood science, concluding, on the basis of observation and experimentation, that blood could not be a primary vector of disease. Certain foods and substances changed the appearance, smell, and taste of bodily fluids like breast milk and urine, he acknowledged, but those same substances resulted in no changes in the blood. Adding noxious substances to the blood, moreover, while compromising the vital function of the organs, resulted in no perceptible change in the blood. Chapman joined the medical chorus that disputed the finding that contagion made its way into the blood from the outside.[78]

Chapman's identification with solidism as the path forward for training reflected and directed the movement of the medical field in Philadelphia. The growing demand for medical training that included dissection pushed universities and unaffiliated physicians to change their offerings. In the years 1820–1822, more than 40 percent of University of Pennsylvania Medical School graduates attended extracurricular dissection courses, had private instruction, or voluntarily took the mandatory course a second time. A report to the Penn School of Medicine in 1824 noted that private dissection rooms had multiplied to an "injudicious extent." The next year, Penn made plans to expand its own anatomical facilities. Meanwhile, Charles Caldwell worried about the impact of the rising number of students on the quality of the profession. As professor of medicine at the newly founded Transylvania University, in Kentucky, Caldwell denounced the medical school "mania" for producing the lowest rank of doctors.[79]

The demand for hands-on training in which students were not simply observing but doing their own dissections, created a spike in the demand for cadavers during the 1820s. As the Penn Medical School founder William Shippen had learned in 1765, sourcing cadavers locally provoked angry protests. Yet body snatching became a cottage industry in cities with ambitious medical schools, leaving vulnerable the bodies of the poor, especially those who died in almshouses and hospitals, and African Americans buried in segregated cemeteries. As the dean of medicine at the University of Pennsylvania (1822–1851) and author of a widely used textbook, William E. Horner received numerous requests from out-of-town colleagues seeking bodies for their medical schools. As he explained to his fellow doctor, Harvard professor John Collins Warren, in 1824, supplies were short in Philadelphia because "the town has been so uncommonly healthy." Despite Philadelphia's liberal policy toward "harvesting" corpses from public cemeteries and the almshouse, Horner claimed to be unable to supply even one-fourth of the cadavers demanded. In 1828, representatives of the city's anatomical science communities signed what was in essence a noncompete agreement in which they committed themselves to distributing cadavers fairly "to sustain the medical interests of Philadelphia, and to prevent the public scandal and excitement incident to the cultivation of anatomy."[80]

The rise in dissections had a direct and immediate impact on people of color and other poor people. Penn medical students dissected deceased almshouse and hospital patients, many of them of African descent, who had succumbed during their treatment. But even those who left the almshouse or hospital intact might end up under the dissector's knife. The editors of *Freedom's Journal* addressed the problem of grave robbing in one of their first issues. In a short column offering "An easy way to secure dead bodies in their graves," the editors provided instructions about interspersing thick layers of straw in the dirt to prevent body snatchers from digging up their prize. The enthusiasm for anatomical training created a genuine threat to the ability of poor people generally and free Black people in particular to ensure that their departed family and friends received the respectful treatment in death that they had not received in life.[81]

After 1818, Penn medical students writing about blood turned from experiments to synthetic field essays that offered descriptions of the body's hydraulics and changes in blood color as a consequence of oxygenation. In 1829, John Josiah White's "Inaugural Essay on the Circulation of the Blood" offered a comparison of the heart to a water hydrant, a technology invented in the city of Philadelphia by Water Works chief engineer Frederick Graff in 1802.[82] More often medical students described the heart as a pump. As Samuel Stones observed in 1828, "the Blood is a peculiar fluid, circulating throughout the vessels of all classes of animated beings" and deserving of attention from experts in all fields of medical knowledge.[83]

As late as 1860, even students from slaveholding states continued to embrace blood's vitality even if, as we will see, some medical scientists continued to cast doubt on its universality. The Tennessean Isaac Jones began his essay "The Blood" with the state of the field but adopted a materialist approach to the brain's need of blood nourishment to support intellect, vigor of mind, and reason, concluding, "we see from this that all of our psychical and mental powers and forces, and actions as well as the physical are indirectly dependent on the blood."[84] A year later, the Delawarean John Crawford Spear concluded his essay "The Blood" by declaring enthusiastically, "blood is the sine qua non of animal existence, gives us physical and mental capacity—life!"[85] Spear's comment reflected the general acceptance of blood's vitality and universality, even as contradictory claims about raced blood persisted. The Philadelphian Blencove Fryer stood out for his contention, based on chemical and microscopic analysis, that men's and women's blood differed in color and specific gravity.[86]

Indeed, the nineteenth-century medical students and transfusionists examined here viewed all human blood as essentially the same—a continuity that flew in the face of emergent scientific racism. As the Penn medical student Melson Rowland explained in 1859 following his review of the history of transfusion and his critique of seventeenth-century animal-to-human blood transfers, "how a human being could live by the blood of an animal of a different species, whose assimilative powers are not alike, and whose blood is peculiarly adapted to itself, or answer for one that lives differently, and of a higher order in creative beings, appears to me to be the result of gross ignorance on the part of the prosectors of transfusion."[87]

Yet, off the grid of academic medicine, contradictions persisted; laypeople continued to interpret a person's external appearance as indicating deeper dissimilarities, while some practitioners stubbornly continued to use blood from humans interchangeably with that of animals as well as other substances to increase the volume of fluid in the veins of depleted patients. For reckless transfusionists, blood was blood was blood, whether it came from animals or humans, and its character as a vital fluid that circulated throughout the body trumped its particular qualities. This allowed blood to retain some of its humoral universalism, captured in nineteenth-century descriptions of temperament and complexion as "sanguine."[88] Drawing on many different languages of belonging, white abolitionists continued to insist that the blood of enslaved people was "human," "orthodox," indistinguishable from their own, and its spilling indicative of a painful violation of the enslaved person's body and self-sovereignty.[89]

Brains and Skulls

Stripped of some of its mystical and symbolic meaning, blood's universality remained an open question for many medical theorists. The same could not be said for the skull, which increasingly served as the main evidence for theories of biological race. Yet even for advocates of scientific racism, the human body did not consistently offer evidence of race difference. In the hands of these ambitious race scientists, skeletons and organs had the dual capacity to illustrate both generically human and race-specific phenomena, a flexibility that made it possible to exploit African American cadavers for use in anatomical collections and selectively marshal evidence that allegedly proved that African Americans did not belong fully to the (white) human family.

Penn's Medical School provided institutional support for the work of some of the period's most prolific and influential voices in scientific racism. The school's vast collection of anatomical specimens represented one of the institution's greatest investments and most valuable resources. As the major draw of the university for southern and foreign medical students, the specimen collection reiterated this medical appropriation and exclusion: the bodies of people of African descent and Native Americans could be possessed in life and death without being fully admitted to the human race—or even to the medical school.[90]

The southernmost of the elite medical schools in the early United States, Penn had historically attracted large numbers of southern students. Indeed, under the deanship of the Virginian William Horner, students from slaveholding states always outnumbered those originating north of the Mason-Dixon Line. Horner was a major figure in the field of anatomy and in Penn's regional appeal for white southern students. Beginning in the 1810s and building on the vast collection of his colleague Caspar Wistar, Horner amassed an enormous specimen collection that included the remains of people of African descent. Horner collected these human remains through networks with his brother doctors and access to almshouse and hospital patients. Within the collection, these specimens served as models both of Black anomaly and human typicality. They also provided Horner with the data for his successful publications. His *Special Anatomy and Histology*, first published in 1823 as *Lessons in Practical Anatomy for the Use of Dissectors*, went into six editions in its first twenty years. Horner's subsequent *Treatise on Special and General Anatomy* (1826) became the standard text for medical students for decades. Through the success of his textbooks, Horner's methods and instructions guided anatomy and dissection practices in the United States.[91]

Horner used African American bodies as medical fodder for both normative and comparative anatomy, creating a community of white knowledge producers among Philadelphia's medically trained anatomists. In the first edition of his first textbook, weighing in at 548 pages, Horner provided seemingly dispassionate and encyclopedic "how-to" dissection instructions; yet a few details revealed the gruesome and chilling relationship between the prestigious medical school and the city's poorest residents, especially African Americans. Horner referenced a case of an "old African woman" whose gall bladder had filled with fluid and another patient with a fractured patella "now in the Philadelphia Almshouse." He repeated medical orthodoxy about skin pigment being lodged in the *rete mucosum*, the second layer of skin, noting that this location became especially obvious to the dissector when cutting the soles of African American feet. In a note designated with an asterisk, Horner mentioned that "an opinion prevails among anatomists of Philadelphia that the prostate is larger in the African than in whites. Indeed this much may be said of all the organs of generation in both sexes." Comparative anatomy thus formed the bonds of community among the city's dissectionists, who learned their trade and advanced their skills by using the bodies of African Americans and poor white people.

Most shocking, it appears that anatomists in the Penn Medical School may have been deliberately seeking out African American cadavers for dissection. In his widely used 1823 textbook on anatomy and dissection, Horner noted, "a muscular subject without much fat answers sufficiently well for this [femoral hernia] dissection; the male black is therefore most frequently resorted to in our school." Simply put, Dean Horner explicitly recommended in a widely circulating textbook that Black men made the best cadavers for certain dissections.[92]

The robust southern enrollment at Penn was not simply a consequence of Horner's Virginia networks, then, but resulted from his creation of an intellectual climate hospitable to scientific racism. This would not have been a difficult task because popular racism in the nation as a whole was compatible with the conclusions of racist science. Horner would eventually fall into line with a host of French theorists, especially Georges Cuvier, maintaining the unity of the human race but locating hereditary features of race in the body: black pigment in skin cells; the formative influence of culture, economy, and eating habits upon the structures of teeth, jaws, and face; the inverse relation between facial angle (more pronounced in "Mongolians" and "negroes") and cranial capacity; and his own claim, based on his analysis of human remains of a "coal black" African man, that people of African descent had more pronounced and developed "odoriferous" glands in their armpits than white people.[93]

As Horner's own work attests, the seeds of racist science were being sown not in the blood but in the body's solid structures, an approach that provided the foundation for phrenology, the materialist science of the mind. Phrenology emerged from the work of the Viennese brain scientist Franz Joseph Gall and his collaborator Johann Gaspar Spurzheim. While Gall contended that the shape of the skull and the size of the brain correlated with intellectual capacity, Spurzheim, in contrast, saw in the study of brain structure the possibility of improvement in the human race through self-knowledge of strengths and weaknesses and directed cultivation of the brain's positive qualities. Together, the two men mapped the brain's material structures and posited connection to different mental faculties.[94]

Upon hearing Spurzheim lecture in England in 1814, the English lawyer George Combe became a convert to phrenology. At times Combe appears to have adapted Spurzheim's version of the emergent science to support his antislavery views and philosophy of self-improvement. Combe published several popular books on the subject, including *Essays on Phrenology* (1819) and *A System of Phrenology* (1825). Yet, despite these progressive leanings and networks with key American abolitionists like Lucretia Mott, Combe's ambition to establish phrenology as a legitimate science made him willing to ally opportunistically with racist theorists like Charles Caldwell and craniologist Samuel George Morton. Combe conducted a correspondence with Caldwell, even visiting him at his plantation in Kentucky, where Caldwell enslaved people. Although his private responses to Caldwell's letters suggest that he never embraced Caldwell's polygenetic position, Combe nonetheless provided an intellectual scaffolding readily appropriated by scientific racists.[95]

Not surprisingly, Philadelphia became the site of the first North American Phrenological Society in 1822. One of its founders, John Bell, born in Ireland in 1796 and raised by his uncle in Petersburg, Virginia, had trained in medicine at the University of Pennsylvania. The other two founders, Philip Syng Physick and

Benjamin Coates, were also respected physicians and Penn Medical School faculty. A Philadelphia publisher produced editions of Spurzheim's and Gall's studies, moreover, as well as the first American edition of Combe's *Elements of Phrenology*.[96] Bell was part of the movement of physicians who criticized natural philosophy for its unscientific and vague claims about sympathies, essences, and influences. He and his colleagues called for a new brain science—a materialist approach to the study of the mind. "The brain is the material instrument of the mind, and the essential organ of animal life," he claimed, identifying it as the seat of instinct in animals and reason in human beings. He mapped out different regions of the brain, claiming that each had a capacity as distinct as those of the body's organs. Differential development of these regions of the brain explained the differences between men and women, the range of abilities within a particular national population, and the "varieties of the human race." Bell predicted correlations between cranial "development" and the characters of the "Negro," the "Caucasian," the "Malay," the "Chinese," the "Tartar," and others. Boasting of the field's practical applications, he anticipated ascertaining how far certain "stocks" might be able to improve and the degree to which they might benefit from education and good government. As for the practitioners of the emerging field, he declared phrenology to be not mere skull-gazing, but the study of the mind that embraced knowledge of the various races.[97]

Meanwhile Caldwell, by this time a faculty member at the medical school at Transylvania University, ramped up his own commitments to scientific racism with a work on phrenology in 1827 and one disputing monogenesis in 1830.[98] Caldwell opened his dissent by repeating the claim of Stanhope Smith's critics that the scriptures held no authority in physical science. Much of his *Thoughts on the Original Unity of the Human Race* consisted of an extended rebuttal of Buffon, Smith, and the more recent monogenetic argument of Dr. James Cowles Prichard, a Quaker physician who had advanced a theory about the unity of the human race. Caldwell reiterated several of his earlier claims about racial difference, most of which hinged on his central assessment of "Caucasian superiority" based on intellect, complexion, and figure. In this he relied on European race theorists Blumenbach, Le Cat, and Bernier, applying their evidence for distinct races to support an argument many of them did not make—that human difference reflected the existence of different species.[99]

Caldwell perpetrated claims about black blood and provided extensive evidence of the resilience and persistence of distinct species in the plant and animal worlds. Although his experiments had shown him that blood and chyle did not vary with diet, he repeated his claim that Africans had a black pigment "formed from the blood" and compared it to animal musk or the castor of the beaver.[100] He was likely reinforced in his conviction that blackness came from black blood, not black bile as some thought, by the work of the French natural historian Julien-Joseph Virey, the revised edition of whose *Histoire naturelle du genre humain*, published in 1824, followed Meckel in insisting that racial blackness originated within rather than outside the body. Virey, whose compendium appeared in English translation in 1837 and would later inform the racist science of Louis Agassiz, took a hard line about black blood, linking it to other allegedly racial characteristics like the diminished action of the lungs and a lesser need for pure air. Dissections of Africans, according to Virey, conclusively revealed this interior blackness as well as contracted cranial capacity.[101]

Caldwell also debunked fertility as an indicator of intraspecies reproduction, an argument the craniologist Samuel George Morton would later embrace. God must have created distinct human species, he reasoned, considering the suitability of different races to thrive in different climates and the persistence of racial traits over time (especially obvious to him for Jews and Gypsies). "We are inclined to a belief in the original plurality of races, which bear to each other the relation of species," he concluded at the end of his tome.[102]

Caldwell carefully gerrymandered his categories to fit the geopolitics of the nineteenth-century world. He ranked aboriginals in New South Wales as "in all respects, inferior to the Negroes of Africa," while defining "Caucasian" expansively to include dark complected Europeans: "the swarthy Spaniard and the olive-colored Italian are as real Caucasians as the fair German and the high complexioned Swede."[103] Caldwell's work subsequently proved influential for his student Samuel Cartwright and Morton, who cited Caldwell's reasoning in *Crania Americana* (1839).[104]

Phrenology's serious reception by medical thinkers and its subsequent lay popularity would have a lasting impact on abolitionist body politics. Several abolitionists saw opportunity in phrenology's acknowledgement of environmental influences on intellectual capacity, and many incorporated its terms and principles into their discussions of character and hopes for Black progress. But a few took note of its white supremacist intellectual bedfellows and its foundational importance for craniology, and debunked it. The Philadelphia abolitionist Lucretia Mott wrote to Combe in 1839, hoping to steer him away from the American Colonization Society and to probe the politics of his phrenological theory. Combe reassured her of his continued abolitionist views. The Edinburgh-trained African American physician James McCune Smith, however, publicly attacked phrenology's claims to be a science in 1837 and pointed out flaws in the data and the reasoning about the shape of the skull and the brain's capacities. Although his lectures are no longer extant, the coverage they received and his subsequent critiques of phrenology suggest his argument: in light of Smith's own medical training, Combe's claims simply didn't add up.[105]

With the growing medical interest in the body's solid structures and the popularity of phrenology as a study linking brain form and function, U.S. medical scientists fatally embraced the notion of raced bodies. Caldwell, Cartwright, and Morton, who asserted these racial claims most radically, were not outliers but enjoyed institutional privileges at the nation's elite and newly established medical schools. Claims of "one blood" had not been definitively refuted, but influential doctors asserted the existence of black blood to great acclaim. Their publications were warmly received, especially by southern readers opposed to abolition and inclined to believe, using the example of Saint Domingue, that African-descended people were physically disqualified from living in conditions of republican liberty because "it is not in the blood—they were never made for it!" This linkage of blood to politics, along with emergent frameworks for finding racial differences in the body, were beginning to make "one blood" claims appear quaint.[106]

Contagious Climates

Even as Penn's antebellum medical students continued to affirm blood's universal vitality, their medical theses reflected new attention to the discrepant susceptibility of different populations and specific local disease patterns. Beliefs in the hazards of tropical environments for Europeans dated to the sixteenth century, but by the nineteenth century, medical investigators had begun systematic studies of the impact of climate, including local conditions of rainfall, temperature, and changes to the worked landscape. This broad diagnosis of the ills of colonial settler and plantation societies was of particular significance for the political economy of slavery, where claims to "peculiar" subtropical climates bolstered the white South's claim to need the "peculiar" institution because of the alleged disease resistance of Black bodies.[107]

In increasing numbers after 1818, dozens of Penn medical students, many from slaveholding states, provided accounts of environmental disturbances causing disease in case studies of local outbreaks. It is helpful to interpret these studies as part of the medical response to the expansion of settler colonialism in the early United States. This large-scale expansion was composed of thousands of settler households, doing what we saw the Pleasants family do in Virginia: deploying labor to bring new land into cultivation by clearing timber and brush, draining marshes, diverting streams, and plowing, fertilizing, and seeding fields. Prevailing medical theories listed all of these activities as potential sources of disease, especially when they resulted in rotting vegetation.

During the 1820s the numbers of local studies spiked. In 1822, the year of Denmark Vesey's failed conspiracy in Charleston, South Carolina, one Penn medical student saw political lessons in his study of local climate. The South Carolinian William McCaa's "The Manner of Living and Disease of the Slaves on the Wateree River" sidestepped racial arguments about disease immunity to trace discrepancies in survival to the individual's own adaptations to specific climates. Although he took as fact that enslaved people survived in conditions that killed white men—one of central justifications for the use of slave labor throughout the Atlantic basin—he disagreed with the flatness of the racial analysis. Enslaved people recently transported from Virginia to South Carolina often died during their first year, he noted, an observation that resonated with both the emerging pathways of the internal slave trade and the high mortality that subsequently provoked Richard Allen's denunciation of coerced colonization. Those who survived their second summer, he argued, had as good a chance of being healthy as a South Carolina native—although he noted that native-born children (did he mean enslaved or white or both?) were particularly susceptible before the age of five. Following this discussion of climate and seasoning, however, McCaa endorsed other observations of differences that he connected to both race and condition. Enslaved rural laborers did not feel the health effects of emotional disappointments, he contended. When afflicted by pain and illness, moreover, they resorted to remedies steeped in superstition and credulity, like horseshoes over the door and ligatures on bewitched limbs. McCaa specifically addressed the Vesey conspiracy, noting that no plantation laborer appears to have allowed the desire for liberty to unhinge his reason as had happened for the urban-dwelling Vesey and his conspirators. He concluded his essay with examples to prove the "facility" with which enslaved women "bring forth their young."[108]

Many of the theses about local climatic causes of disease traced the source to specific instances of rotting vegetation or standing water. James Gregory's 1827 "Inaugural Essay on Bilious Fever, as It Prevailed in Mecklenberg County, Virginia" pinpointed the fermentation of green timber as the cause of a "pestiferous halitus" that produced a "most violent form of bilious fever" in "all who were within its reach." In general, however, Gregory observed "blacks" to be "excepted though some suffered," a racial claim riven with contradictions that echoed Rush's earlier ambivalent claims about Black sufferers of yellow fever.[109] In his 1824 "Inaugural Dissertation on the Autumnal Fever of Greensville County, Virginia," John Parham identified the seasonal flooding of the Meherrin River as a health hazard. Standing water in the late summer caused miasmatic exhalations so toxic that those who breathed them immediately vomited. His own apprenticeship as a young doctor included assisting a veteran physician in his work attending to stricken "servants" and free people of color who worked on nearby plantations.[110]

Although focused on an urban port rather than a rural hinterland, Samuel Jones's study of endemic fever in the city of Philadelphia in 1820 reflected similar assumptions about disease causation and offered case studies based on the treatment of African Americans. In a thesis of epic length and ambition, Jones attempted to identify different diseases within an enteric fever epidemic on the basis of the outbreak's location, symptoms, and responsiveness to specific therapies. He described the conditions in the city's "southern section," "where negroes lived in hovels, in filth, overcrowded," and lacked a change of clothes. Of the three hundred almshouse patients afflicted with endemic fever who had some connection to these "negro alleys," either through work, social contacts, or habitation, a full 25 percent would die. Jones oversaw the treatment of several African American victims, including a "maniacal" woman confined in the cells with an ulcer on her thigh, a middle-aged "mulatto" whose gastritis responded to the consumption of draughts of cold water, and a female almshouse patient recently released from the obstetric department who died after a period of "idiotic gaiety." When his remedies failed, Jones benefited from the opportunity to dissect the unclaimed body. In one of the thesis's many tangents, he defended the practice of bloodletting, comparing the relief it provided to the patient's pulse to the relief experienced by an enslaved laborer when his physical burden was lightened: "Thus the oppressed slave, sinks beneath the burthen to which his strength is unequal, and strives in vain to rise until a portion of it is removed." Even the physical demands of slavery might offer analogies to explain the mysterious workings of the afflicted human body.[111]

This attribution of illness to small changes in the local environment reflected the continued salience of climatic theories of disease and of human difference more broadly. Medical students who mastered the literature about tropical climates and comparative disease environments subscribed to theories of local causes. Peter H. Anderson, writing about an outbreak of typhoid fever in Amelia City, Virginia, in 1827–1828, offered a cosmopolitan and comparative view of climate but ultimately identified a microlocal source of disease: a farmer's "family" fell sick when he failed to drain a stream on his plantation completely, leaving rotting vegetation and mud to breed unhealthy gases. Stream drainage, like so many other acts of bringing land into cultivation, was a key process in expanding the reach of settler colonialism.[112]

For some, diseases caused by local miasmas could be traced to larger changes in agricultural methods and economy. John D. Porter's 1829 "Inaugural Essay on the Bilious Diseases Which Prevailed on the Rappahannock River" traced the disease pattern in Virginia to recent shifts from pasturage to planting. Enslaved laborers bore the brunt of declines in healthfulness; as he noted, "the endemics of this climate bear with a greater degree of violence upon the African population, and those of the whites whose necessities compel them to labour in the marshy lands, and who are necessarily exposed to the alternate action of the oppressive sun and heavy dews of autumn." Expanding the plantation economy to new lands not only produced unhealthy conditions but inspired new remedies. Porter took special note of an enslaver who substituted the bark of a local tree, *Cornus florida*, or the flowering dogwood, for cinchona—the Peruvian tree bark that had become a key element in the materia medica.[113]

Several southern students carefully referred to "laborers" or "servants" rather than "slaves" and, like Porter, identified occupation rather than race as the cause of disease. The Georgian William W. Waddell, who self-consciously categorized his intervention into disease theory as that of a southerner, referred to afflicted enslaved people as "laborers."[114] Jeremiah McCredy of Pennsylvania, who offered advice drawn from his mentor Nathaniel Chapman on planting trees to reduce the unhealthfulness of miasmata, observed that people who cleared the land were most susceptible to disease.[115] Twenty years later, James E. Gayley of Henrico County, Virginia, drew on differences in the disease susceptibility of house and field "laborers" to point to the significance of microenvironments in disease etiology. Enslaved laborers working the fields were more likely to fall ill.[116]

These students were not just echoing medical theory about the causes of local epidemics or pointing to climate and habit as explanations for difference in disease susceptibility but producing something new: diagnoses of diseases incubated by colonial projects, in particular, plantation slavery and settler colonialism, and new medical expertise gained through access to Black people's bodies. Their case studies focused on places with specific colonial histories but had broad purchase for national and international medical communities. Threaded through their discussions of disease were allusions to Indigenous dispossession, forced transports of enslaved people, influxes of white settlers, land clearance, planting of new lands and new crops, and the creation of legal impediments to exclude free Black people from the expanding sphere of settler society.[117]

Refutations

In 1832, the young Sarah Mapps Douglass, daughter of the hairdresser Robert Douglass Sr., from St. Kitts, and the activist Grace Bustill Douglass, offered her own thoughts about national belonging and the wrongheadedness of forced Black emigration by means of an analogy to the maternal-infant bond. Aiming her comments at fellow free African Americans, she argued for the strength of emotional ties to homeland, personified as a maternal Columbia. Dismissing as specious the claims of emigrationists that Black people would receive better treatment and opportunity in Haiti, Mexico, or British territory, Douglass presented her own patriotism as that of an infant with enduring love for its mother: "And though she unkindly strives to throw me from her bosom, I will but embrace her the closer, determining never to part with her." When forced to defend her position in a subsequent issue of the *Liberator*, Douglass concluded, "This is my own, my native land."[118]

Five years after Douglass, the Reverend Hosea Easton laid out similar arguments but in the medical language of bodies and with reference to the influence of climate and diet on blood and health. For Easton, differences in skin color and hair texture were normal variations found in nature and reason for celebration rather than evidence of distinct racial categories. Once on North American soil, he argued, Africans became "seasoned" to become Americans "by birth and blood":

> Complexion has never been made the legal test of citizenship in any age of the world. It has been established generally by birth and blood. . . . If blood has anything to do with it, then we are able to prove that there is not a drop of African blood, according to the general acceptation of the term, flowing in the veins of an American born child, though black as jet. . . . The blood of the parents in seasoning to this climate becomes changed—also, the food of the mother being the product of this country, and congenial to the climate—the atmosphere she breathes—the surrounding objects which strike her senses—all are principles which establish and give character to the constitutional principles of the child, among which the blood is an essential constituent.

Easton conceded that "racial prejudice" exuded a "pestiferous breath" that poisoned the atmosphere and, along with slavery's violence, left strong negative impressions on pregnant women and their unborn children. Slavery might leave its mark on physiognomy, posture, and demeanor but, he insisted, the imprint of manners, diet, climate, and government meant that "every child born in America, even if it be as black as jet, is American by birth and blood." Under the dissector's knife, he claimed, all bodies were the same.[119]

African Americans figured national belonging in the intimate terms of the body. For Allen, it was a consequence of physical habitation and strenuous labor, whereas for Douglass, it grew from a love of country akin to mother love. For Easton, it grew out of his environmental materialism and the changes in African bodies through exposure to American conditions. Long-term residence in a particular place led to acclimatization, which in turn encouraged health and longevity. Ruptures caused by coerced transportation might make a person ill, perhaps morbidly. This lay understanding both drew on and departed from the language of eighteenth-century international law with its focus on military sacrifice and theories of sovereignty underpinning rights to free maritime movement. Using similar analogies to encourage free African American migrants, Haitian president Jean Pierre Boyer proposed a form of pan-African citizenship that implied a notion of shared blood; the act of African-descended persons stepping onto Haitian soil conferred national belonging. Although Allen and Boyer shared with other abolitionists the rhetorical tactic of substituting bodily fluids for the actual laboring bodies of enslaved people, the fluids they imagined were neither contaminating nor disgusting but generative.[120]

As Allen and other abolitionists would elaborate in subsequent decades, violations of human rights occurred not simply in the context of forced transport across the Atlantic, as Jefferson had noted in 1806, but in the multiple sources of domestic coercion and restriction on African American geographic movement, the lack of security from bodily violation even after death and burial, and the overt racism of comparative anatomy. Allen evoked blood's universality and vitality during an age of forced migration and violent territorial expansion that produced illnesses and trauma. These outbreaks, in turn, created opportunities for aspiring white medical practitioners, eager to make their professional mark as healers of white enslavers and their human property. Blood, sweat, and tears were not mere rhetorical flourishes but essential features of African American experience that African Americans themselves repurposed as evidence of their belonging in the United States.

Chapter 5

In Search of Free Labor

Give ev'ry man his own just due.
And take not what belongs to him,
For theft and stripes all slaves might sue
The men who rob his fettered limb . . .

How nice to eat candy not tinctured with blood!
And help on free labor by eating my food
If I think of the millions in bondage still groaning!
It is some consolation, that the crime, I'm disowning.

—George Washington Taylor, Philadelphia Free Labor Produce Association Board member, no date

What if the key to undoing slavery could be found in domestic spaces with women's production of the intimate bodily comforts of household members—their provision of the cotton bedsheets, undergarments, and printed calicos that touched the skin, and their choices of beverages and foods on the table? If female consumers were willing to forgo slave-produced cotton, rice, sugar, coffee, and tobacco, could their sacrifice of comfort, convenience, and cost be harnessed to undermine markets for slave-produced goods and bring an end to the slave's suffering? As part of their campaign to end slavery, nineteenth-century abolitionists tried to leverage the power of consumers to unravel the labor practices, technologies, and markets for slave-produced goods. They staked their claim on two moral issues with consequences for bodies: that female consumers, whose domestic labors required such intimate connection with slave-produced commodities like cotton and sugar, would choose "free" over slave produce; and that "free" labor provided a viable economic alternative to slave labor and would alleviate its physical and psychic harms. By some accounts, free labor improved the health, fertility, morality, and longevity of former slaves even as it made their labor more productive. But free labor's naysayers contended that labor contracts and wages could not match slavery's coercive means of extracting agricultural productivity from Black bodies. As they worked to spread the practice of ethical consumption to bring an end to slavery, advocates for free labor created a transnational network for consumer boycotts and imagined new markets for free produce goods. Along the way, they confronted unexpected problems with sourcing goods and vexing questions about what it meant for labor and produce to be "free." This, in turn, raised the third of free produce's claim on bodies: the need for extensive investigatory travel to learn about the local circumstances and mechanics of commodity production and to identify producers of free goods. Dealing with conditions on the ground as they tried to source and supply goods, free produce activists struggled to figure out what made labor and produce "free."[1]

Activists imagined several different scenarios for the free labor they hoped would replace slave labor. In its ideal form for newly emancipated populations, a "free" woman's domestic labor supported a "free" male agricultural laborer. But free labor could also take the form of small-producer households, as in the white yeoman South, in which entire families engaged in agricultural labor. However they imagined it, activists assumed that family relationships, constrained and degraded under slavery, would be naturally remade in supporting free labor households. Advocates pointed to free labor's economic, environmental, and demographic as well as moral benefits. They saw a crucial role for consumer behaviors, which were themselves an increasingly important feature of male wage-earning households, in remaking the lives of former slaves.[2]

Following the story of free labor produce activism, we get a different view of the connections among laboring bodies, the commercial circuits moving raw cotton to manufacturers, and the bodies of consumers. The physical burdens of labor, the material contingencies of agricultural products as they were cultivated, harvested, and processed, and the sensuous experiences of consumption all appear in the same frame. Free produce abolitionists linked the intimate experiences of the consumer's body to the slave labor that produced consumer goods: the planting, picking, ginning, and baling cotton and the harvesting, milling, and refining of sugar. Their efforts to locate free cotton anticipated many of the problems of locating, purchasing, and guaranteeing the quality of cotton after slavery ended in the U.S. South, while the search for free sugar took them far from the United States. The free produce movement made ethical consumption a form of activism and linked it to the consumer's bodily experiences of a commodity—the texture, colorfastness, and durability of cotton or the taste and texture of sugar. Seen from this perspective of intersecting material analyses, undoing slavery was as much a matter of remaking slavery's agricultural infrastructure and the habits of consumers as it was of liberating enslaved bodies.[3]

The nineteenth-century free labor produce movement took place in two overlapping phases, one profoundly local and the other expansively global. In the first, beginning in the 1820s and continuing through the 1850s, African American men and women, male and female shopkeepers, consumers, and antislavery fair organizers sourced free produce goods from small producers, often Quakers from North Carolina, and encouraged ethical consumption locally; in the second, emerging during the 1840s and 1850s, a transnational white male Quaker leadership struggled to source free labor produce goods globally as well as nationally, and to create international markets. Although prominent African American abolitionists, British Quakers, and local networks of American Quaker activists continued to support the later iteration of the free produce movement, by the 1840s the American abolitionist leaders William Lloyd Garrison and Wendell Phillips were denigrating it as futile. The global nature of the efforts to source and market free cotton, moreover, opened up a divide between the white male leadership of the movement, its African American and white female supporters, and the intensely local networks of the movement's most dedicated adherents.[4]

In their search for sources of free cotton, activists stumbled on several troubling obstacles that revealed how profoundly slavery had shaped the economic infrastructure: unfamiliar credit instruments, shortages of capital and technology, and fundamental wealth inequalities among producers. The task of sourcing free cotton provoked investigations of previously unimaginable possibilities and the formation of new global networks. During trips to source "free" goods, activists witnessed unfamiliar labor systems and saw firsthand the compromised nature of some free labor endeavors. Researching the possibilities of "free" commodities transformed the politics of some activists and challenged them to develop more rigorous definitions and sophisticated analyses.

Consumers as Activists

The free produce movement prescribed a pathway to ending slavery that was personal, domestic, moral, and peaceful. At issue was how, in an age of intersecting markets and the global circulation of people and money, a person might still be implicated in the sins of slave production even if she disavowed slavery. The movement's ethical accounting led inevitably to the conclusion that the consumer of slave-produced goods was as guilty of physical cruelty and robbery as the enslaver. Free produce advocates linked the sinfulness of enjoying sugar, rice, and cigars with the bloodstained profits of slave owners. The innocence of the non-slaveholder was possible only if a person severed financial connections with slaveholders and the markets for slave-produced goods. But innocence also included a more intimate and embodied meaning—the refusal to have one's body nourished, clothed, or comforted by morally tainted commodities. It required acknowledging that commodification could not remove the taint of slavery, leaving as the only remedy the avoidance of the physical connection between slave-produced goods and the consumer's body.

Antislavery activists used boycotts to instill a visceral awareness of slavery's horrors among potential allies as well as to undermine slavery's power over enslaved bodies. Previous Atlantic basin consumer boycotts had proven the power of consumers to further the goals of political movements. North American nonconsumption and nonimportation movements during the 1760s and 1770s had helped to galvanize the colonial will to defy British imperial policy, even if they were never quite as damaging to British merchants as North Americans believed them to be. Britons, too, used the boycott effectively during the antislavery movement of the early 1790s. The British consumer rejection of slave-produced sugar bolstered the antislavery movement and sparked the ban on the international slave trade. It also inspired North American entrepreneurs and investors to join the boycott by attempting to substitute maple sugar for West Indian slave-produced cane sugar. Maple sugar appealed to consumers because of its seemingly nonviolent extraction and processing methods, the tree's status as a native species, and its sourcing by yeoman farmers in the woods of New England rather than by slave laborers in the British sugar colonies. In both the North American and British boycotts, women's importance as the regular consumers of the goods in question placed them at the center of boycott appeals and activity. Free produce activists hoped that boycotts of slave-produced goods would heighten consumers' market awareness and bring antislavery politics home to the consumer's own body while simultaneously forming bonds of moral community.[5]

A small cohort of American abolitionists had, from the 1810s, drawn connections between relieving the bodily suffering of the slave and consumers' refusal of the bodily pleasures provided by the products of slave exploitation. As in the two previous boycotts, the process of researching the origins of goods, evaluating the labor involved, and purchasing only ethical produce permanently changed an individual's orientation toward slavery and membership in an activist community. An antislavery consumer who diligently participated in the free produce movement was engaged in a politics of the body as well as an exercise of political and economic will. The process of becoming a free produce consumer politicized men and women—but especially women—to engage in other antislavery work requiring bodily commitments. Public speaking, standing up to angry crowds, and withstanding the trials of the abolitionist speakers' circuit—ridicule, barrages of eggs and rotten produce, and violence—required a commitment of the body as well as the spirit. Such commitments gave white people some inkling of the way racism impinged on African American bodily expressions of political, economic, and social will, including freedom of movement and property ownership.[6]

The Quaker Elias Hicks helped to connect the British antislavery boycotts of the 1790s to North American antislavery when he began calling out fellow Quakers at the 1811 Jericho, New York, Monthly Meeting for their hypocrisy in consuming slave-produced goods. Focusing on the sensitive issue that the Virginia Quaker Robert Pleasants had raised during the 1790s—that Quakers with long-tail gowns and brightly colored cloaks often found it impossible to renounce their material wealth in slaves—Hicks hammered home the connection between benefiting from the exploited labor of slaves and the consumption habits of wealthy Quakers. He gave his appeal particular resonance for pacifist Quakers by connecting the products and profits of slave labor to the acts of war that produced slaves. His radical (and to his opponents, aggressive) message shook Quakers from Philadelphia to New England, splitting meetings into Hicksite and Orthodox factions in 1827–1828.[7]

Across the Atlantic, the British Quaker Elizabeth Heyrick connected consumer boycotts with abolitionist "immediatism" and reignited the British antislavery movement. Heyrick was a wide-ranging reformer and author of didactic children's literature spelling out dire consequences of bodily filth and cruelty to animals. She built her reform agenda on the bodily manifestations of morality. In *Immediate, Not Gradual Abolition*, first published in London in 1824 and then in Philadelphia, she called for renewing the boycott of West Indian sugar until slavery was ended.[8] Heyrick's intervention came during the post-transatlantic trade period known as amelioration, in which British public debate centered on curbing the excesses of cruelty as part of the effort to improve the demographic sustainability of the enslaved population. Before Heyrick, most abolitionists took a cautious approach to ending slavery. In 1823, Thomas Fowell Buxton had joined forces with William Wilberforce to denounce slavery in a speech to Parliament and form a society calling for gradual abolition. The Quaker John Joseph Gurney, Buxton's brother-in-law, focused on the need to end the flogging of women, noting that properly observed distinctions between the sexes enabled societies to rise out of barbarism into civilization. For Gurney, Black laborers would be as motivated to work as white laborers only if they possessed that "gift from God," the right to property in their own persons.[9]

The British Quaker Joseph Sturge, later to become one of the main organizers of British antislavery, credited Heyrick with jolting his family's reform priorities and domestic practices and reigniting the strategy of consumer boycotts to defeat slavery by connecting it to immediatism. But he also should have credited his sister, a social justice activist in her own right. In response to Heyrick's publication, Sophia Sturge organized the household she shared with her brother to boycott sugar. The move was consistent with Joseph's views on morality as being manifested in embodied practices with economic consequences.[10]

Sturge and other members of his family embraced free labor as a political economy expressive of the values of the modern West. Sturge's brother John spelled out free labor principles as part of a progressive imperial philosophy in *Short Review of the Slave Trade and Slavery, with Considerations on the Benefits That Would Arise from Cultivating Tropical Productions with Free Labour* (1827). John approached free labor as both a substantive "undoing" of the physical and moral evils of slavery and an imperial strategy with promising global consequences. As John explained, slave labor violated divine laws for both the moral treatment of fellow human beings and land use. Such violations spawned negative consequences for all parties, manifested in declining populations of laborers, exhausted soil, decreasing land values, and the degradation of West Africans, Irish peasants, and enslaved people themselves. Turning enslaved people in the British West Indies into free producers of sugar and replacing Indian cotton manufactures with English and Irish manufactures would create the rising tide that would lift all boats, as John imagined it. The free labor at the core of his vision, moreover, was defined broadly to encompass a semifeudal form of tenancy.[11] At roughly the same time, as we have seen, in response to the efforts of the American Colonization Society to sponsor the exile of free people, African Americans argued that the slave's laboring body already satisfied the conditions for citizenship. Intellectuals like Richard Allen were focused not on how free labor conformed with natural law, but on the laboring body's fluid sacrifices as sufficient to earn the benefits of national belonging.[12]

By the late 1820s, several American Quakers had established societies and stores dedicated to promoting free labor produce even as others continued to investigate the possibilities for free Black emigration. Charles Collins opened the first store in New York City in 1817, followed by Jane Webb's store in Wilmington, Delaware, in 1825. The following year Benjamin Lundy, editor of the *Genius of Universal Emancipation* (1821–1839), opened a store in Baltimore. Lundy, who would later employ the young William Lloyd Garrison as an editor, also supported some limited voluntary colonization schemes in Haiti and Texas (not yet part of the United States), a position that many of his abolitionist contemporaries, white and Black, would eventually reject. Lundy's African American associate, the entrepreneur Robert Purvis, influenced the editor's views on the use of free produce tactics but ultimately disagreed with him on colonization.[13]

Antislavery Quakers in Philadelphia came together to form the Free Produce Society (FPS) in 1827, the same year that Samuel Cornish and John Russwurm brought *Freedom's Journal* to press. James Mott, a young cotton and wool merchant whose business connections with slaveholders distressed his wife, Lucretia Coffin Mott, was a prominent member. As Mott noted to her parents-in-law in 1826, "I confess I should be much better satisfied, if they could do business that was in no wise dependent on slavery, and perhaps some will appear after a while." Soon after joining the new FPS, Mott quit the cotton business and focused instead on the wool trade. The Motts may have become politicized to boycott slave produce after meeting Purvis, who started the Colored Free Produce Society (CFPS) in 1830, as well as hearing the views of other prominent African American activists. Among them were the Philadelphia businessman James Forten and Richard Allen, who offered Mother Bethel Church for the inaugural meeting of the CFPS and became a staunch advocate of the movement.[14]

Quaker women formed their own organization, the Female Association for Promoting the Manufacture and Use of Free Cotton, in 1829, reflecting their beliefs in white women's special moral sensibility and the fact that so much of women's domestic labor involved cotton. The mouthpiece proclaiming their distinctive qualifications for such work was Elizabeth Margaret Chandler, a young Quaker from rural Chester County, Pennsylvania, who had begun to write editorials for Lundy's newspaper. Chandler argued for the urgent moral necessity of women's consumption of goods made only by free labor. Known for her savvy condemnation of the consumer-driven market for slave-produced cotton—"without the consumers of slave produce there would be no slaves"—Chandler put white female consumers who were "too sensitively refined to bear a description of the horrors of slavery" squarely in the frame. "Now we assert, that they *all* are implicated, who are consumers of the produce obtained through the medium of slave labour; and that therefore all, though not perhaps in an equal degree, must be sharers of the guilt." The solution, as Chandler saw it, was for such women to "avoid lending your support to the slave system, by refusing to be benefited by its advantages; and you can aid its extinction, by giving on every occasion the preference to the products of free labour." As "Civis" noted in Lundy's *Genius of Universal Emancipation* in 1830, cotton fabrics "were more necessary for the convenience of the female part of the community," making women's cooperation with boycotts essential.[15]

By the early 1830s, consumers dedicated to free produce could find goods in several Philadelphia area stores. Lydia White, a white Hicksite Quaker, opened a free produce store in Philadelphia in 1830 (Figure 4). It was patronized by several

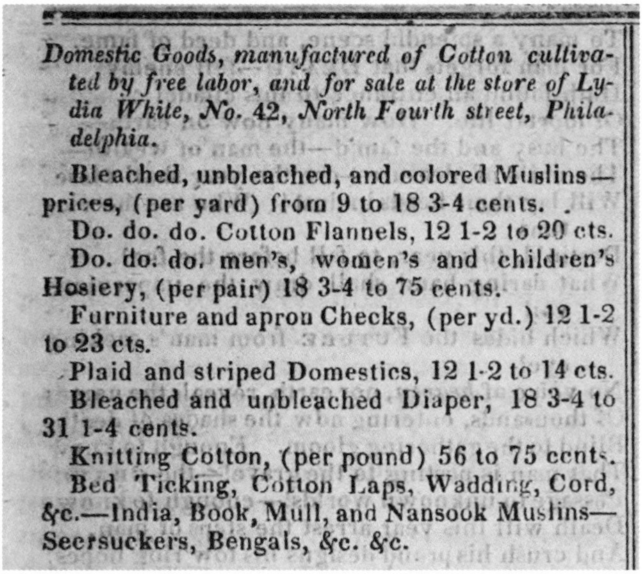

Domestic Goods, manufactured of Cotton cultivated by free labor, and for sale at the store of Lydia White, No. 42, North Fourth street, Philadelphia.

Bleached, unbleached, and colored Muslins—prices, (per yard) from 9 to 18 3-4 cents.

Do. do. do. Cotton Flannels, 12 1-2 to 20 cts.

Do. do. do. men's, women's and children's Hosiery, (per pair) 18 3-4 to 75 cents.

Furniture and apron Checks, (per yd.) 12 1-2 to 23 cts.

Plaid and striped Domestics, 12 1-2 to 14 cts.

Bleached and unbleached Diaper, 18 3-4 to 31 1-4 cents.

Knitting Cotton, (per pound) 56 to 75 cents.

Bed Ticking, Cotton Laps, Wadding, Cord, &c.—India, Book, Mull, and Nansook Muslins—Seersuckers, Bengals, &c. &c.

Figure 4. Advertisement for Lydia White's store. From Benjamin Lundy, *Genius of Universal Emancipation*, vol. 13 (1832–1833).

prominent Philadelphia area abolitionists as well as ethical consumers from as far as North Carolina. It thrived for sixteen years, making it the longest lived free produce store in the region. In addition, Sidney Ann Lewis's store in Philadelphia provided free labor goods.[16] White, Mott, and Lewis were all founding members of the Philadelphia Female Anti-Slavery Society (PFAS) in 1833.

African American activists embraced free produce and the white activists who pursued it. Purvis brought the storekeeper Lydia White to the attention of the National Negro Convention of 1833, the third such gathering, where the convention recognized her for her persistent efforts on behalf of the slave. Crucially for his own dedication to free produce consumption, Purvis had the support of his wife, Harriet Davy Forten, daughter of James Forten, who maintained a free produce household from the time of their marriage in 1831. African American women at Mother Bethel Church established their own Colored Female Free Produce Society in 1833 with its own store. The free African American lumber merchant and Underground Railroad conductor William Whipper followed suit in 1834 with his own temperance and free produce store.[17]

The interracial PFAS, founded in 1833 under the leadership of Lucretia Mott, Lydia White, Sarah McCrummell, and Margaretta Forten, made free produce a founding principle: members, the constitution declared, should "at all times and on all occasions . . . give the preference to free produce over that of slaves." The society often pursued new opportunities to source free produce goods, as in 1837, when they initiated a correspondence with a newly formed antislavery society in Port-au-Prince, Haiti, seeking information about free labor commodities, and passed along information to a Buckingham County, Pennsylvania, antislavery society with similar goals.[18]

During the first decade of organized consumer efforts to avoid slave-produced goods, the supply of free cotton goods was limited and came from either North Carolina Quakers or local Quaker experiments. In Chester County, for example, a hotbed of Underground Railroad and free produce activism, several Quakers began growing their own cotton. Joseph Preston, brother to the abolitionist and future medical educator Ann Preston, later reminisced that he wore a shirt made from cotton grown in Chester County, "and a very good and substantial garment it was, though the muslin was not smoothly finished. It was spun and woven by Jacob Pusey, at Hockessin, Delaware." Around 1831, his father, Amos Preston, and his neighbor Ezra Mitchner, who "wished to clothe their children without slave-labor," "procured some cotton seed from North Carolina. My father planted a small plot in his garden; the cotton came up, grew luxuriously, and made a beautiful appearance. In due season, the balls opened, displaying the natural white cotton, new balls appeared each morning, until, as I remember, a frost after the middle of September wilted down the plants." In contrast to his father's small plot, Mitchner, "a man of ingenuity and enterprise," grew a large crop. He "made a small gin to clean the seed out of the cotton. Both crops made a small bale, which was sent to the factory, and my father's share was about five and a half yards. After bleaching this on the sod, my mother made one for my father and one for me, and I doubt whether either of us ever wore shirts that would stand as much wear as these."[19]

Free produce activist networks were often coextensive with the Underground Railroad. In 1838, the American Free Produce Association (AFPA) (1838–1847) established its operations at a depository at 31 North Fifth Street, under the management of J. Miller McKim (1810–1864), an Underground Railroad operative and contributor to the *Anti-Slavery Standard*. The AFPA and the Philadelphia Free Produce Society of Friends that succeeded it sourced free labor cotton from producers in North Carolina. McKim's depository remained important to the distribution of free produce goods to stores in the Quaker hinterland for nearly a decade. In Penn's Grove, a Chester County community some forty-five miles outside of Philadelphia with its own Quaker meeting, Quakers ran a free produce store beginning in 1839 under the management of Elizabeth Kent, a member of an Underground Railroad family that included the textile mill owner Joseph Kent. After her death in 1848, two Quaker sisters from nearby Sadsbury

Township, Mary and Catherine Scarlett, took over this task. They were themselves members of a family that had provided decades of service to the Underground Railroad.[20]

No matter who organized them and whom they targeted, all free produce associations of the 1830s and early 1840s faced at least three major dilemmas. First, there was the problem of sourcing goods that could be reliably authenticated as containing only the products of free labor. Nearly all slave-produced commodities came to the consumer through two phases of labor that included cultivation and processing. Creating a market for "free" goods required identifying reliable producers and educating consumers so they could grasp the geopolitics of free labor economies. But even if free labor advocates could locate cotton, sugar, rice, or coffee grown without slave muscle and know-how, they often could not surmount the challenges of certifying a "free labor" refining process. As the Quaker Levi Coffin, a North Carolina native and Underground Railroad operative, explained to the Philadelphia Quaker Samuel Rhoads, free labor goods generated suspicion even among antislavery Quakers. He recounted an exchange with an Indiana Quaker who expressed "an opinion that it was all a deception practiced on the people[;] a money making scheme," although he was "willing to admit that I [Coffin] thought they were free labor goods he would not call in question my varasity but he believed I was deceived by you that were engaged in it at Philadelphia."[21]

In addition to consumer suspicions of fraud, the reliance on slave labor for processing plantation commodities worked against the promise of purity. Cotton gins, sugar mills, and rice mortars, pestles, and baskets required muscle to process raw materials. The technology was not designed to protect distinctions between materials processed by different producers. The challenge of achieving pure processing was exacerbated, moreover, by the small quantities of raw "free" cotton producers were seeking to have ginned, spun, or woven. In contrast to consumers of slave-produced goods, who experienced only the whiteness and refined texture of the finished cloth, free produce consumers reanimated the connections between the brutal physicality of slavery and cotton fabric. By insisting that the purity of the free produce commodity was necessary to sustain the moral purity of the consumer, they created their own form of commodity fetishism. An entire bolt of cloth, barrel of sugar, cask of coffee, or bag of rice could lose its standing as free produce if it could not be certified as "free" of slave-produced cloth, sugar, coffee, or rice.

Second, there was the problem of the quality of produce: free cotton garments tended to be coarse, and many people complained that free sugar candy was disgusting. Even the hyperbolic Chandler was forced to acknowledge that "the texture of your garments will perhaps be coarser than that of your accustomed wear, but they will cling less heavily around your forms, for the sighs of the broken-hearted will not linger among their folds."[22] As Mott's granddaughter later recalled, "free calicoes could seldom be called handsome, even by the most enthusiastic; free umbrellas were hideous to look upon, and free candies, an abomination." Indeed, for an earlier generation of Quakers who wore unbleached free produce fabric, the failure of the cloth to meet market standards became a brand of sorts. The telltale signs of free produce manufacture broadcast the wearer's decision not to purchase the goods made by slaves.[23]

Finally, there was the problem of competitive pricing of free produce goods. Often sourced in small quantities from places distant and unfamiliar to North American consumers and incurring additional costs because of the compensated nature of the labor, free labor produce goods came with a higher price tag. Even though consumers could not be certain that free labor goods were pure of any slave-produced vestiges, the higher cost and inferior quality marked their authenticity. If the goal was to supply free labor goods widely to nineteenth-century consumers to bring about the collapse of slavery, however, higher costs obstructed wide distribution by pricing free labor goods out of reach for most working-class people.[24]

Despite these challenges, the early free produce societies enjoyed modest success, perhaps because of their gender and racial politics and their relationship to the emergent abolitionist movement: they included men and women, Quakers and non-Quakers, African Americans, and white allies. Indeed, women's active participation seems to have been key, although the embeddedness of these societies in interracial antislavery networks also seems to have been crucial. Ideas passed among African American and white activists (the links between Lundy and Purvis and White, Sarah Mapps Douglass and Elizabeth Chandler, and Lucretia Mott and W. L. Garrison are but some of the most prominent examples), although it is not clear that all participants engaged this issue for the same reasons. White activists appear to have been as hopeful as their African American peers that a vigorous market for free labor produce would undermine slavery. But as Mott's comment on her husband's early cotton business suggests, white abolitionists were perhaps even more concerned with distancing themselves from the theft that was at the heart of slave labor.[25]

Like many abolition projects, the goal of consuming only free produce engaged people in a process that often politicized them by changing their own bodily and economic awareness. Thinking about the sources of food and clothing compelled abolitionists to acknowledge their own location in the circulating profits of slavery. This new mindfulness gripped not just the consumer but the aspiring supplier. The need to travel to investigate labor arrangements and the conditions of commodity production honed business savvy, knowledge of commodity chains, and cosmopolitan sensibilities.

Political Economy

American free produce advocates adopted the language of physical health from British anti-saccharites and the graphic references to the body from African American activists. Chandler equated eating candies made with slave-grown sugar with the disgusting specter of cannibalism, a common theme of the earlier British antislavery sugar boycotts of the 1790s that she brought to a new audience around 1830:

> Oh press me not to taste again
> Of those luxurious banquet sweets!
> Or hide from view the dark red stain
> That still my shuddering vision meets
>
> Away! 'tis loathsome! Bear me hence!
> I cannot feed on human sighs,
> Or feast with sweets my palate's sense,
> While blood is 'neath the fair disguise.[26]

Chandler was interested not just in eliciting disgust for consuming the blood and sweat of slaves but in connecting that disgust to the intimate contact of the consumer's body with slave-produced cotton cloth. A moral and sensible woman would be horrified by candy containing "the red life-drops of his human slave" or the sight of an agonized enslaved woman weeping "scalding tears" from her "bloodshot eye." So should she be repelled by the prospect of the cruel context for, if not actual physical traces of blood and sweat on, the cotton fibers produced by enslaved women:

> Look! they are robes from a foreign loom,
> Delicate, light, as the rose leaf's bloom;
> Stainless and pure in their snowy tint,
> As the drift unmarked by a footstep's print.
> Surely such garment should fitting be,
> For woman's softness and purity.
> Yet fling them off from thy shrinking limb,
> For sighs have render'd their brightness dim;

And many a mother's shriek and groan,
And many a daughter's burning moan,
And many a sob of wild despair,
From woman's heart, is lingering there.[27]

Yet disgust over blood was a tricky posture for female consumers. Chandler and most other abolitionist women carefully situated the blood on the imagined slave-produced cloth to avoid any allusion to menstruation. Images of blood on a careless woman's skirts came too close to evoking the contamination of menstrual blood and conjured a female foulness that would work at cross purposes with the message to women to aspire to moral purity in their consumer decisions.

Attempts to source and market free labor goods raised new questions about the connectedness of all participants in national and regional economies, whether as planters, slave laborers, processors of agricultural goods, manufacturers, shopkeepers, or consumers. Diligent free produce advocates needed accurate geopolitical information. Writing in 1832 from Michigan, where she had moved with her aunt, Chandler inquired of her friend Hannah Townsend "whether Java coffee is the production of free labor." Chandler's usual coffee likely came from Brazil, the source of most coffee for the U.S. market by the 1840s, and was a product of slave labor. Townsend, who later achieved renown as the creator of *The Anti-slavery Alphabet* (1846), responded with pamphlets and reassurance that Java coffee was "of free produce as it comes from the East Indies." Her answer reflected the as-yet-uncomplicated opposition in the minds of free produce disciples between slave and "free" labor and their naive assumptions about plantation slavery as exclusively located in the western hemisphere.[28]

Abolitionists around the Atlantic basin were still seeking basic facts about the conditions of tropical commodity production. As the British government began the process of emancipation in 1834 with a recommended period of apprenticeship for former slaves and compensation for enslavers, abolitionists wondered whether apprentices were really free. Hearing reports of the continuing cruelties under apprenticeship, Joseph Sturge undertook a tour of the British West Indies in 1837 to determine whether apprenticeship had effectively reinstated slavery. Sturge was already convinced of the virtues—moral and economic—of free labor. His account of his journey targeted the British reader and does not appear to have been published elsewhere, although it was circulating in Philadelphia in 1838.[29] Accompanied by fellow abolitionist John Scoble, a Congregational minister; Thomas Harvey, a Quaker abolitionist and reformer; and the physician William Lloyd, Sturge toured the islands, recording detailed observations of climate, landscape, foliage, crops and markets, labor practices, and the condition and manners of former slaves. He noted his first experience of being a racial minority, registering "deep interest" at being in the midst of a "dark" population. Gradually, Sturge's perceptions of blackness shifted; as he attended a Moravian church in Antigua filled with nearly eight hundred people of color and only one other white person, he observed, "In looking over a congregation of blacks, it is not difficult to lose the impression of their color. There is among them the same diversity of countenance and complexion as among Europeans; and it is doing violence to one's own feelings, to suppose for a moment that they are not made of the same blood as ourselves."[30]

Sturge seized opportunities to ask apprentices and free Black people about how their present lives compared to those under slavery.[31] Most of Sturge's interviewees claimed that they were better off under apprenticeship, mainly because they could no longer be flogged at will. Yet most also qualified this simple comparison with information about the harsh laws that permitted employers to penalize them for lateness to work, bilk them of their labor on provision grounds, or, in the worst case of being fired, separate them from family members still employed on estates. Some unfortunates ended up at the workhouse, where they were forced to labor on the treadmill, a gruesome ordeal that Sturge witnessed on several occasions.[32]

Sturge also embarked on a biopolitical investigation of the well-being of former slaves that took stock of the condition of individual bodies and population health. He recorded information about punishments for alleged crimes, births, infant mortality, and population size as part of the effort to measure the impact of apprenticeship and emancipation. Montserrat caught Sturge's fancy because it appeared healthier for former slaves than the other islands.[33] In Barbados, in contrast, he noted that, after 1834, child mortality rose and mothers strongly resisted having their children bound as apprentices. He assessed the moral health of Black people, as evidenced by rates of marriage and church attendance, and linked it to physical well-being, as evidenced by reproductivity. This latter measure reflected both a genuine humanitarian concern based on the belief that population increase indicated overall well-being, and a challenge to claims by slavery's defenders that emancipation would lead to a labor shortage. Sturge scrutinized various local laws that constrained the mobility, family formation, sustenance, and morals of former slaves. Generally, he found that fully emancipated laborers, like those in Antigua, had more money and better-quality food and clothing, and that former enslavers had no desire to go back to the old system of bondage. He cheerfully concluded that "the Abolition Act [had] emancipated both planters and negros."[34]

In Sturge's analysis, true freedom resulted in tangible domestic and moral practices that had a direct impact on bodily habits and in turn spawned new bodily capacities. "Freedom is 'an ever-germinating principle,'" he explained, "not a fixed entity of good." Its benefits could be measured objectively in the frequency of marriage, the improvement of domestic habits, the proportion of husbands and wives living together, and the numbers of mothers "withdraw[ing] from field labor to their household affairs."[35] Compared to a system of free labor, apprenticeship was as bad as slavery for people who might still be legally coerced, punished, and unjustly treated when they tried to care for their families. Implicit in his analysis, as in most arguments for the benefits of free labor, was that the bodily exigencies of working for one's own benefit would result in the industry and self-discipline needed for social order and a prosperous economy.

Sturge saw no evidence that impending freedom would devastate the economies of the West Indies. All signs pointed to free labor, compensated with money rather than in kind, being more efficient than slave or coerced labor. He assessed the shortcomings of apprenticeship as including the island's production and price of export crops. Antigua, for example, now exported sugar, molasses, rum, and arrowroot raised by free Black laborers, whereas before emancipation, cotton, indigo, and tobacco had been the only crops. "Free labor" had increased profits for proprietors as a consequence of plow agriculture, task work, and the diversification of crops.[36]

While Sturge traveled the Caribbean from late 1836 until mid-1837, his sister Sophia dealt with his correspondence and seized opportunities to advance her own antislavery work. In July 1837 she wrote to an unidentified correspondent requesting copies of "Address to the Queen," most likely the petition eventually signed by nearly four hundred thousand English women urging the end to the apprenticeship system. She also asked for copies of an engraving of the notorious West Indian Tread Mill, used to punish enslaved people for alleged infractions, and fifty copies of the anti-apprenticeship *Statement of Facts*.[37] Prompted by these and other efforts of the Sturge family and their allies, Parliament brought the British experiment with apprenticeship to an end in 1838.

A National Convention and a Fire

Free labor activism surged in the United States as abolitionists greeted the end to British apprenticeship as a victory for their cause. Eager to counter assertions that emancipation would lead to spikes in crime and violence, the American Anti-Slavery Society commissioned James Thome and J. Horace Kimball to conduct their own fact-finding trip to the Caribbean in 1837. The resulting study, *Emancipation in the West Indies: A Six Months' Tour of Antigua, Barbados, and Jamaica in the Year 1837* (1838), largely supported the findings of Sturge and Harvey by showing that emancipation had resulted in greater Christianity, literacy, and school attendance among freed people, who also demonstrated a willingness to work for wages.[38]

In Philadelphia that same year, free labor produce activists from around the northeastern United States joined forces to hold a national conference in conjunction with the Anti-Slavery Convention of American Women. The event coincided with the grand opening of a new meeting space, Pennsylvania Hall, constructed for the express purpose of making large meeting rooms available for antislavery activists. The name they gave to their conference, "Requited Labor," expressed their reservations about defining labor as "free." PFAS, which had purchased four hundred dollars' worth of shares in the new building, publicized the meetings and sent eighteen delegates to the national convention, including five African Americans.[39] Delegates from throughout the Northeast attended the meeting to address the question of consumer complicity by establishing clear connections between the physical violence used against enslaved people and the products of their labor.

But the optimism and lofty goals of convention attendees were crushed; within twenty-four hours of their first session, an anti-abolition crowd that likely included southern medical students set fire to the hall. With the blessing of the Whig anti-abolitionist mayor John Swift, firefighting crews allowed it to burn. Lucretia Mott reflected on the violence stoically, noting, "though they were assailed by & driven from place to place by a furious mob yet they were enabled through God's help to finish their business satisfactorily." The group's second session took place at the still smoking "ruins of Pennsylvania Hall."[40]

Regrouping several months later, the group created a new free produce association, the American Free Produce Association (AFPA). Delegate and publisher Lewis Gunn denounced the purchase of slave-produced goods as "the grand stimulus of the abominable system of oppression." Letters from free produce supporters recalled the refusal of North American women to drink tea or to purchase British goods during the 1770s. Others testified against coerced labor in Dutch Java and the "piratical" slave trade in the Caribbean. In just six years, the answer to Chandler's question about coffee from Dutch Java reflected more sophisticated activist knowledge of a complex world of coerced labor.[41]

David Lee Child, the husband of Lydia Maria Child, provided grisly details of the link between laborers' brutalized bodies and the commodities they produced. He reminded delegates of Benjamin Lundy's depiction of a finger found in a cup of coffee and a whip found in a hogshead of molasses. Purchasing slave-produced goods, he claimed, was the equivalent of drinking the blood of slaves who had been beaten or killed on southern plantations, a charge that resonated with the British sugar boycotters' equation of sugar consumption with cannibalism. For Child, the barbarity of northern consumers purchasing and enjoying these slave-produced commodities was equivalent to the outrages committed by the uncivilized Eastern slaveholders who preoccupied Anglo-American reformers. "Are we the children of Penn and the Pilgrims," he asked rhetorically, "or are we in some dark corner of heathendom, with rapacious and pitiless Arabs and Algerines; cutthroat Khoords and Thugs, Juggernants, burners of widows, feeders of crocodiles with living virgins; regular child-killers and murderers of decrepid fathers and mothers?" Questions like these not only exposed American reformers' views of essential differences between East and West but also complicated subsequent global efforts to seek ethically produced tropical commodities outside of the plantation economies of the Americas.[42]

Gunn concluded the publication with a lengthy essay assessing the criminal and sinful elements of consuming slave-produced goods. Avoiding the purchase of slave produce, he claimed, changed the consumer's worldview and stimulated discussion about her responsibility in a global marketplace stocked with ill-gotten goods. He debunked the objection that boycotting unrequited labor produce falsely substituted a "physical exertion" for a moral action. For Gunn, this objection was the pedant's attempt to sidestep the hard work of abstaining from slave-produced goods.[43]

Among the attendees of this convention was young Abby Kelley, a delegate from the Lynn, Massachusetts, Female Anti-Slavery Society, who was just beginning her thirty-year career as an intensely engaged activist. Lydia White, proprietor since 1830 of the longest running free produce store in Philadelphia and PFAS founder, was also present along with two of her prominent patrons, Lucretia Mott and Sarah Grimké After the conference ended, White changed the name of her store to the Requited Labor Store to reflect the group's increasingly sophisticated analysis of "free" labor. Also in attendance was a group of Pennsylvania Quakers, most of them involved in PFAS and the Underground Railroad, who would later form the core of the politically engaged Progressive Friends.

This was one of the peaks in the free produce movement in the United States. According to Gunn's optimistic estimates for the movement, the AFPA might persuade half a million consumers to join its ranks if it successfully recruited all abolitionists, all Quaker antislavery society members, and all free African Americans. Gunn's location in Philadelphia, home to the largest urban free Black population in the country, likely fueled his optimism. Success on this scale might also have seemed possible to Gunn, who believed the free produce movement had the potential to change the heart of the consumer by transforming both her bodily habits and her purchasing behavior. A consumer who diligently avoided proscribed foods—sugar, rice, and coffee—and allowed only requited-labor cotton to touch her skin was newly oriented to the connections linking her own body to the profits reaped by the slave owner and the brutalities of coerced labor. Establishing this link between the bodies of consumers and slave laborers to undermine the whitewashing effects of commodification was one of the AFPA's signal accomplishments.

The burning of Pennsylvania Hall, culminating a decade of white racial attacks on the community institutions of Philadelphia's African Americans and abolitionists, however, took its toll on activists. Philadelphia's antislavery women, who had contributed generously to financing Pennsylvania Hall, organized a third Anti-Slavery Convention of American Women in 1839 but had difficulty finding a secure venue. They settled on meeting at a little-used riding school. This was the last Anti-Slavery Convention of American Women. Members of PFAS continued to petition the Pennsylvania state legislature and Congress, but their meeting minutes often reflected the officers' unhappiness with the half-hearted efforts of members. Thereafter, PFAS devoted greater energy to the domestic labor of the sewing circle, where members produced antislavery-themed objects for sale at the annual fair, a move that might itself have seemed to mimic the conservative gender assumptions underpinning nineteenth-century visions of free labor: the withdrawal of women from remunerated labor and their focus on supporting male laborers with domestic comforts.

Yet this perhaps underestimates PFAS's resilience, the persistence of its African American members, and its keen engagement with U.S. politics. It may also reflect an overly narrow definition of what constitutes political work. Take, for example, the labor of supplying crafted articles and foods for the annual fair, the organization's main fundraiser. As the PFAS minutes revealed in 1859, after two decades of hosting the annual fair, the outsourcing of the labor of doorkeepers, carters, porters, and waiters did not mean that PFAS members were simply managers. Members continued to sew, paint, compile anthologies of poems and stories, and supply cakes, candies, and beverages, all made from free produce goods. Members also staffed the tables at which these items were displayed and sold. Crafting and selling items to raise much-needed funds continued to be the labor of women and was part of the endless political work of abolition, not separate from it. The fair enabled PFAS to support the city's Vigilance Committee during the 1840s and 1850s, allowing the society to sustain a strong antislavery presence in the city.[44]

Transatlantic Connections

Meanwhile, back in Britain, the defeat of apprenticeship in the Caribbean brought new attention to the causes of free labor and free produce. Sturge founded the British and Foreign Anti-Slavery Society (BFAS) in 1839, but his advocacy of free labor was capacious enough to include condemnations of Britain's effort to substitute notionally free "coolie" labor for slaves. That same year, Sturge launched his campaign against exploited South Asian labor by condemning the transport of slaves from Madagascar to Mauritius.[45] His sister-in-law Lydia Albright Sturge, married to his brother Edmund, was also involved in this effort, writing to an unknown correspondent to get a copy of John Scoble's 1840 address on so-called "hill coolies," a population known as the most socially marginal and easily exploited of South Asian migrant laborers.[46] Sturge also supported the Irish Catholic nationalist Daniel O'Connell's condemnation of the U.S. ambassador Alexander Stevenson, a Virginia plantation owner, for his alleged "traffic in blood," a phrase Sturge subsequently adopted.[47]

Sturge began to hatch ambitious plans for his family's commitment to free labor produce. In July 1839, Sturge wrote to the American Gerrit Smith, himself an abstainer from slave produce, about how Sturge could avoid slave-produced cotton. Sturge claimed his main difficulty in turning his principles into practice was finding a supply of free cotton. The following year, he supported a petition titled "The Equalization of the Duties on the Tropical Productions by Free Labourers," a measure intended to undermine slavery, increase the comforts of the poor, develop British colonial resources, and open new markets for British manufactures.[48] He retained a view of capital's vitalism, telling a correspondent in 1840 that he did not want his money to be "idle." This conflation of capital with the workers Sturge also hoped to spur to productivity reflected his continued investment, along with his brothers, in British industries.[49]

Sturge's next major effort on behalf of abolition was a coup of global organization. The 1840 London World's Anti-Slavery Convention drew delegates from throughout Europe, the Caribbean, South America, the United States, and Australia. Just a month before the convention, the American Anti-Slavery Society split into two factions over the appropriate place of women in the abolition movement. The immediate catalyst for the split was William Lloyd Garrison's nomination of the organizational dynamo and firebrand lecturer Abby Kelley to the business committee. The Garrisonian wing supported Kelley and women's active participation in the movement, while Lewis and Arthur Tappan and their fellow evangelicals, including eight African American men, argued that the question of women's equality was a distraction from the focus on enslaved people. They withdrew to form their own organization, the American and Foreign Anti-Slavery Society.[50]

Sturge agreed with Tappan and his allies. Anticipating that the Americans would bring the controversy with them to the convention, he attempted to stave off conflict by urging Mott and the other female delegates, several of whom represented the American Free Produce Association, to skip the meeting on the grounds that their presence would hurt rather than help the cause of abolition. When the American women appeared at the convention anyway, the convention leadership voted on June 12, 1840, to exclude all eight of the American women delegates, leaving them to attend the meeting from behind a curtain that blocked them from the view of male delegates.[51] Following the convention, Lucretia Mott wrote to the Boston abolitionist Maria Weston Chapman of her disappointment not only that they were not seated as delegates but that their efforts to call a public meeting for women came to naught despite support from the British abolitionists Anne Knight and Elizabeth Pease.[52] Mott doubted the reason given for their exclusion, that the departure from the usual British practice of excluding women from public meetings would "prejudice the cause of human freedom."[53] "In Birmingham," she reported to Chapman, "my appearance on the platform, in a large meeting at the Town-Hall was as heartily cheered as if I had been worth hearing." She also received "cheers loud & long" after her speech at a temperance meeting in Dublin. Her conflict with Sturge notwithstanding, Mott and her husband met with him socially while they were in Britain, and Henry Stanton and his new bride, Elizabeth Cady, maintained contact with Sophia Sturge during their tour of the British Isles.[54]

Mirroring this official rift with the Garrisonians, the convention failed to fully endorse free labor produce. Joseph's brother John presented an updated report on free labor principles that differed significantly from his 1827 essay in omitting condemnations of the immorality of European involvement in the slave trade. It also included an account of the successes of free labor production in the Americas and a bibliography of works extolling the many virtues of free labor (environmental, moral, demographic, and economic). Ultimately, however, the convention failed to back a proposed declaration supported by the American Free Produce Association delegates condemning the use of slave-produced goods and settled instead for creating a list of slave-produced commodities to avoid.[55]

Sturge's stubborn alliance with the American men who opposed women's participation in the convention, despite personal knowledge of his sister's active involvement in antislavery, protected the gender politics of free labor ideology from challenge and left an unfortunate legacy for the larger free produce and abolition movements. By silencing the dedicated female consumers of free produce goods, Sturge and his network privileged both free labor political theory and the global networks needed to promote it. No female voices challenged the "bourgeois-imperial" assumption that the free wage-earning male laborer was the natural partner of a domestically employed woman. By keeping the female delegates behind a curtain, Sturge encouraged abstraction in the place of the local, material commitments of female free labor activists. Following the convention's close, Lucretia Mott seized opportunities to explain the importance of the free produce movement at a meeting held at London's Exeter Hall, where both she and Garrison were invited to speak.[56] Sturge, however, did reconsider some of his own thinking about race. By November 4, 1840, in a letter to his close ally John Soul, Sturge acknowledged that he had decided to adopt the phrase "emancipated population" rather than "negroes" for all future correspondence and publication.[57]

Sturge's meetings with American abolitionists sparked his curiosity about the politics of slavery in the United States, the new target for global activism following the end to the British experiment with apprenticeship. During the winter of 1840–1841, Sturge prepared for an extended U.S. trip, ostensibly motivated by his interest in pursuing both the universal abolition of slavery and international peace. Early in his journey, he arranged to meet with the captives taken from the slaving vessel the *Amistad*, and bore witness to the inhumanity of the slave market in Alexandria, Virginia.[58] In New York City, he renewed an acquaintance with the physician James McCune Smith, whom he had met previously in England, where Smith was studying medicine. In Philadelphia, Sturge met with Quakers who had strong commitments to both the Underground Railroad and free produce activism, including Abraham Pennock, Enoch Lewis, James and Lucretia Mott, and James Forten. Robert Purvis recalled for Sturge his testimony to a Philadelphia jury that the anti-abolitionist mob that burned Pennsylvania Hall had not been triggered by actual "amalgamation" but by the sight of Purvis helping his darker-complected wife Harriet Forten out of their carriage.[59]

As he traveled, Sturge repeatedly compared the United States with Britain and remarked on the hypocrisy and illogic of British trade policy. Despite protestations against slavery, Britain's main commercial connection to the United States was through the southern cotton trade. Sturge found it ironic that British trade restrictions in the form of the protectionist Corn Laws blocked the importation of American wheat, the product of free labor, a regulation that hurt Britain's working class and unintentionally stimulated American manufacturing. While in New England, Sturge visited two textile factories where the female workers enjoyed better conditions than those of both enslaved women in the British Caribbean and wageworkers in Manchester. To bring wageworkers in England up to the standards of American factory workers, he argued, reformers would need to lift them out of the poverty and degradation of their domestic lives. In this, Sturge tacitly acknowledged that wage work alone could not transform the conditions of laborers.[60]

Sturge's free labor produce advocacy disrupted a neat taking of sides against Garrisonian abolitionists and may have helped bridge the divide between the two groups. Although the poet John Greenleaf Whittier, Sturge's American escort, had sided with the American and Foreign Anti-Slavery Society, Sturge still met with the Garrisonians. During his meeting with Garrison, who at this point still supported the free produce cause, they agreed to disagree on the woman question. He also met with Angelina Grimké, her husband, Theodore Weld, and her sister Sarah. The Grimkés and Weld were in retirement in New Jersey following Weld's vocal cord impairment and Angelina's obstetric injury. There they maintained a free produce household and followed Sylvester Graham's low stimulation diet of vegetables, cold food, and water. The New Yorkers Gerrit Smith and Charles Collins also provided Sturge with models of abstinence from slave labor produce. Smith had been abstinent for seven years, whereas Collins was both an activist and supplier of free produce goods at his Cherry Street grocery store.[61] After meeting with Whittier and Sturge, Lucretia Mott lamented, "Truly he [Whittier] is almost lost to us . . . he seemed to enjoy going place to place with Joseph Sturge, and we were glad of their little calls on us." She reflected on the rift, admitting, "I can't help loving Whittier & J. Sturge too, even tho' they have wronged us, in the course they have pursued. So long as they retain any sympathy for the suffering bondsman, I shall feel a tender regard for them, even tho' in other respects they go halting."[62]

The upshot of Sturge's visit to the United States was that he became more interested in the possibility of boycotting slave-produced goods through a combination of personal abstention and state regulation. But it may be that his sister Sophia had more to do with this growing interest than we have considered heretofore.[63] During his absence, Sophia maintained his network of correspondents and filled her own letters with extracts from his accounts.[64] Free labor was very much on her mind. She wrote with directness to the British Quaker Richard Allen in April 1841: "Hast thou entered into further calculation respecting the establishment of a manufactury for free-grown produce—some of our friends feel very much interest in the subject." She also followed up on Daniel O'Connell's promise to James Birney to send an address on slavery that could be read to the Irish in America by continuing to press O'Connell to produce the address.[65]

When Sturge returned from the United States to Birmingham, he rejoined a family circle committed to opposing state-sanctioned violence against the bodies of the laboring poor. The Sturges actively opposed the Opium War, the arming of police in his home city, and the transport of exploited South Asian labor. They also advocated for government restriction of slave-produced imports.[66] While Sophia Sturge remained active as an officer of the Ladies Negro's Friends Society, her sister-in-law Lydia Albright Sturge also became involved in the Anti-Slavery Society.[67] Free trade, abolitionist disavowal of slave-produced goods, and opposition to the recruitment of indentured laborers came up again at the second World Anti-Slavery Convention, held in London in June 1843.[68] In 1844, Sturge entered the debate over whether to prohibit importation of slave-produced sugar from Cuba and Brazil into England. He produced a testimonial in opposition to British protections of the West Indian sugar monopoly and condemned Thomas Blair, G. W. Anstie & Company's importation of slave-produced Brazilian sugar. He took the occasion to reiterate the resolution of the 1840 World Anti-Slavery Convention to support free produce.[69] With the successful reduction of the protective duties supporting West Indian sugar in 1844, Sturge shifted to a more dedicated effort at making personal boycotts feasible and assumed leadership in the transatlantic free produce movement.[70]

Sourcing Free Produce

Meanwhile, a group of Quaker abolitionists in Philadelphia hatched their own plans to turn the desire for free produce into an international consumer movement. Seven years after the burning of Pennsylvania Hall, they hoped to capitalize on the potential of slave produce boycotts to create a sustainable business. They worked largely independently of the women of PFAS, who continued to push for abstention from slave-produced goods and to patronize free produce stores, making both actions a matter of moral integrity. PFAS sent a dozen women to serve as delegates to a Free Produce Society meeting in 1842. The following year, a PFAS committee visited the city's bakeries to evaluate their claims to make sweets with "free" sugar. Several of the bakers reported purchasing free sugar from the shopkeeper Lydia White, a stalwart member of PFAS. Compared to these free produce women, the new Quaker free produce advocates were more market oriented and global in their aspirations. They were also no longer in step with the most zealous wing of the American abolition movement. After initially supporting the free produce movement, Garrison, Gerrit Smith, and Lewis Tappan had grown disenchanted with its potential to deal a blow to slavery.[71]

In 1845, Philadelphia Quakers formed the Philadelphia Free Produce Association of Friends of the Philadelphia Yearly Meeting (PFPAF). Rather than ask for advice from veteran American abolitionists, many of whom boasted nearly two decades of experience with free produce, Samuel Rhoads and George Washington Taylor turned to England and the heyday of sugar boycotts under the leadership of Thomas Clarkson for inspiration and guidance. Rhoads (1806–1868), married to fellow Quaker Anne Gibbons, imagined a transatlantic cotton boycott, centered on Britain and powerful enough to bring down slavery. He authored *Considerations on the Use of the Productions of Slavery* (1844) in which he urged members of the Philadelphia Yearly Meeting to boycott slave-produced goods. The following year, Rhoads wrote for advice to his Belfast correspondent, the antislavery activist Francis Anderson Calder, who reminded the Philadelphia abolitionist of God's unknowable plan.[72]

Calder's spiritual counsel came in response to Rhoads's questions about encouraging the British substitution of linen for slave-produced cotton. "You rather mistake when you state linen is so much used here," he explained to Rhoads. "It is cotton that is used almost universally, but I am sure that in innumerable instances *linen could be substituted*." Umbrellas, bedding, handkerchiefs, even women's dresses, if the colors were bright and fast, might all be made of "free" linen rather than slave cotton. But he doubted the efficacy of a boycott. The effort would be much more complicated than the 1790s boycott of the single commodity of slave-produced sugar:

> In fact, the cotton &c &c seems to [be?] like as it were an immense net thrown over the nation by the Evil Spirits from which the [most?], sincere abolitionist cannot entirely extricate himself, as—almost every movement he comes in contact with *this slave produce net*. I may instance a very few. The silver in circulation, the wicks of our candles, & as our paper is made from rags of all sorts, our newspapers & our very *Bibles* are impregnated with some of its abominations,—may not this very sheet of paper which I now write on, could its history be traced might be found, that is substance was reared by injustice & cruelty.

Calder sympathized with the difficulty of Rhoads's scheme to reduce the consumption of slave-produced cotton in its most valuable markets—Britain and the United States—but his own heart lay with efforts to inculcate Irish children with a new sensitivity toward the suffering of animals. He concluded sadly, "I wish there were half as much feeling in behalf of the unfortunate slaves in the Southern States as there is in Gt Britain in behalf of Animals."[73]

Rhoads's colleague George Washington Taylor, a native of Chester County, Pennsylvania, was no radical by the standards of his day. He had turned to free produce after a decade of searching for a livelihood that would allow him to remain close to both his family and a robust Quaker meeting. Chester County in the nineteenth century was a region of fertile fields, creeks, prosperous farms, and mills. Agriculture and its associated industries—dairying, saw mills, tanneries, grist mills, and cotton mills—supported a large population of white wage laborers and a growing number of free African American laborers, many of whom had recently escaped slavery. Farmers in the county had long been connected to regional and Atlantic markets. Chester County also had a long history of edgy abolitionism, led by white Quakers and African Americans, and was home to several Underground Railroad stations. Taylor's teacher, the mathematician Enoch Lewis, was one of the leading Quaker abolitionists in the county.[74]

Although his father had been a small-time merchant, Taylor found it difficult to find a store that could turn a profit without the sale of alcohol. He began exploring the possibilities of free produce in 1845, the same year that a group of Quakers, including his former teacher Lewis, formed PFPAF.[75] After corresponding with Calder, Taylor's fellow organizer Rhoads wrote to Thomas Clarkson, by then an elderly man, for guidance about the feasibility of a British cotton boycott. Clarkson responded by recounting the success of the sugar boycott of the 1790s in which hundreds of thousands of consumers refused to purchase West Indian sugar. He also offered information about South Asian cotton, but ultimately referred Rhoads to Joseph Sturge, who was himself supplying Lewis Tappan with free cotton manufactures shipped from Liverpool.[76]

Sturge offered Rhoads several pieces of advice. First, he warned him of the limits of English free cotton manufactures, acknowledging that "it will be a long time before we still are able to supply you with the fine goods you want." He also noted the difficulties of marketing free produce: "I shall be glad to know how you are getting on with your Cotton manufactory & what precautions you take to satisfy the concerns that they have the genuine article—In addition to a stamp upon each of the pieces of Cotton we send a ticket with each saying where the Cotton grows, who bought it, who spun & wove it (if printed) who printed it."[77]

With the blessing of the PFPAF Board, Taylor opened a free produce warehouse in Philadelphia in 1846. Together with Rhoads, he worked for nearly twenty years to develop supply chains across the United States and abroad for raw materials and establish factories for manufacturing finished goods. They were not alone in this endeavor but, as they discovered, some of their confederates were poorly prepared to join the effort. Although several correspondents expressed a desire for free produce, "uncontaminated with the guilt of slavery," they were quickly frustrated by problems with quality and supply.[78] With only limited capital to devote to purchasing free cotton directly from white southern producers, Rhoads and Taylor discovered that their enterprise was subject to the vagaries of communication networks, seasonal markets, and unfamiliar credit and transport mechanisms. To Taylor's surprise, a letter from Philadelphia sometimes took nearly as long to reach rural Mississippi as it did to cross the Atlantic to England. In addition to being newcomers to the southern cotton market, the Philadelphians were disadvantaged by the cumbersome nature of their communications.[79]

Rhoads and Taylor hired two field agents, Nathan Thomas of Indiana and Levi Coffin of Ohio, who worked diligently during the fall of 1845, traveling on foot throughout Mississippi to source raw cotton from small producers who used no slave labor. Thomas was the son of two North Carolina Quakers and reputed to be the first white child born in New Garden, Indiana. He and his father had led the antislavery Friends who separated from the Indiana Yearly Meeting in 1843 after the Orthodox Friends condemned them for their political support of the Liberty Party and the free produce movement. The year he began his work for PFPAF, Thomas was thirty-two years old, the father of a large family, and newly widowed. He would marry again in 1846. Coffin, born in North Carolina before relocating to the same Indiana county as the Thomases in 1824, was an active agent on the Underground Railroad and ran a store in Newport, Indiana. His wife, Catherine White Coffin, was also active in the Underground Railroad and free produce movements. Coffin, who had also separated from the Indiana Yearly Meeting, began his work as a field agent for PFPAF at the age of forty-seven. Both men put their own bodies on the line during their investigations. Coffin observed that months of travel on foot throughout the South led to a dramatic weight loss that left his clothes hanging on his diminished frame, while Thomas recounted malaise, depression, and a fear of violence.[80]

Thomas began his search for free produce cotton in Holly Springs, Mississippi, where his deceased first wife (Diggs) had relatives. But the clumsiness of Taylor's arrangements for sending bank drafts first to Coffin, who would then forward them to Thomas, meant that Thomas couldn't act expeditiously to buy up free cotton when he found it. Thomas also believed it fanciful of Coffin to think that cotton could be shipped first and paid for on receipt. In his experience, payment needed to be made up front. In addition, Thomas and Coffin found that several small producers were not yet done picking cotton as late as mid-November. As they later learned, late pickings were usually lower in quality.[81] In at least one instance, Coffin reported, he made up for the shortness of hands by helping to pick, making "quite a figure in a cotton field." In another instance, Thomas found enslaved people who had been released from work for the Christmas holidays and paid them to gin the cotton. He tried this tactic during the regular work season but needed to secure permission from the slaves' "claimints [*sic*]" to pay them and to use the planter's gin. Although enslaved people performed the labor, Thomas believed that providing compensation technically made the cotton a product of "free" labor.[82]

Taylor and Rhoads ran into some of the long-standing problems that faced previous aspiring suppliers of free produce. First, as he explained to the PFPAF Board of Managers, it was difficult to keep free cotton from mixture with slave cotton, a problem that made authentication challenging.[83] Searching for free cotton far and wide exacerbated the issue of authenticating the conditions of its production, as Sturge observed in his letter to Rhoads.[84] Second, quality, price, and supply were almost impossible to control. Taylor's enterprise required fine cotton for shirting but there was also a need for coarse cotton for caps and candlewicks. Two retailers urged the board to consider finding a new manufacturer to supply customers with finer-quality calico and shirting.[85] Turnover among producers was also frustrating. Upon identifying a free labor cotton producer on one trip, Thomas and Coffin would return the following season to discover that the planter (on more than one occasion, a widow), had moved, died, or decided to hire slaves to accomplish the ginning. By 1848, Taylor, Rhoads, and their Memphis agent were urging Thomas to focus more on identifying suppliers of free cotton than trying to make purchases at the gins.[86] Third, the global context of PFPAF's search for free labor products also worked against them. British merchants of U.S. slave-produced cotton were beginning to seek sources elsewhere in the world by the 1850s, opening up new possibilities but also heightening the competition for cotton produced outside the American South. Through his correspondence with Clarkson, Rhoads learned of the possibilities of sourcing East India cotton.[87]

Perhaps most important, Taylor had limited ability to tap into the network of zealous abolitionists, male and female, white and Black, who had sustained the boycott movement during the 1830s. In part this weakness stemmed from the fact that Taylor's main relationship with his supporters was as retailer-consumer rather than as a fellow member of a moral community, making it difficult for him to win over consumers on the basis of enthusiasm for the free produce goods themselves. Seeking to provide Rhoads with detailed information about the Cincinnati market, where he claimed people were constantly requesting free labor goods, Coffin explained that Philadelphia suppliers simply were not providing enough appealing, attractive, and affordable choices for pragmatic Midwestern consumers:

> Cheap goods are most sailable here, particularly cheap prints, calicoes that would cost in Phil from eight to 12 or 14 cents per yd good colours, fast, would be much the most sailable in the West . . . the colors have not generally been durable of the F.L. [free labor] Prints, and they have generally been high priced for the quality of the good, which has made it hard business to sell them while others goods handsomer and better colours were sold nearly 50 per cent lower—Brown Muslin sheets be 4/4 wide heavy good article, I think there should be a large proportion of Calicoes & Brown Muslins, some fine Bleached Muslins, Bed Ticking,

> Duelling, Apron check, Ginghams, Colored Muslins, chints, Pantiloon stuff &c Satinetts and lanes are often enquired.[88]

Rhoads, Thomas, and Taylor began a correspondence with Memphis cotton broker John Krafft who tutored them in some basic principles of cotton production and markets. Originally from Pennsylvania, Krafft had experience dealing with Philadelphia merchants and banks.[89] At least initially, he accepted the men's desire for "free" cotton on its face and wrote confidently of his ability to procure it. He would have no trouble getting hold of free cotton, he explained, as one-fifth of the cotton brought to market from northern Mississippi was of that kind and good quality. Indeed, free cotton, produced and processed by white farmers, was likely to be of higher than ordinary quality: "white people who plant seldom make more than from five to 20 bales and handle it with more care than the larger planters (who trust to their slaves) and generally get it out of the fields earlier: and it is a fact perhaps not known by you that the bulk of the cotton shipped from here to New Orleans fetches a higher price in the average than from any other point in the cotton region. We pay no more for free labor cotton than any other." If Rhoads and Taylor's British friends wanted a constant supply of cotton, they could rely on Krafft's honor that it would be the product of free labor.[90]

Krafft offered to charge $1.25 per bale to source free cotton and provided the men with a tutorial on the "Liverpool Standard," a scale created by the Liverpool Cotton Brokers' Association to grade variations in quality that corresponded to pricing. "Free labor" cotton was likely to be sold in parcels of fewer than five bales at a time. Writing late in the 1845 season, he informed them that "choice" cotton was fetching 7¾ to 8 cents, "good fair" from 7¼ to 7½ cents, "fair" was 6¾ to 7 cents, and "midds to m. fair" from 6¼ to 6⅝ cents per pound. His fee covered the costs of purchasing, weighing, labor, mending, cartage, and storage. He also provided rates for shipping to New York and New Orleans along with interest calculations. Freight on cotton shipped to New Orleans was $1 per bale, with insurance ½ percent. Rhoads and Taylor discovered that insurance would be more expensive than Krafft had estimated when PFPAF purchased a policy from the Insurance Company of the State of Pennsylvania at the rate of $19 per $1,200 worth of cotton shipped from New Orleans to Philadelphia, or roughly 1.6 percent.[91]

Krafft urged them to buy larger lots of cotton to get better prices and suggested that they find "a proper person engaged to go around amoung them in August just before they begin to pick & make the contracts." He described the seasonal rhythms of production and sale, recommending contracts laying claim to "all cotton picked within a certain period of the fall & afterwards for all cotton delivered before the end of the year & afterwards for their last pickings which is the most inferior." This recommendation proved difficult for Thomas, who was juggling his own farm and family life in Indiana. As Krafft imagined it, the agent hired by the association "would be able to attend to the supply of at least 10 gins of 50 saws each which would be about the number required to carry out a profitable growth of cotton[.] this person would be able to attend to all these gins by constantly going from one to the other appointing stated & regular persons to be at each gin to settle & carry them on & forward the cotton to market for shipment."[92] Krafft also encouraged Rhoads and Taylor to create a predictable supply network. The trick would be "to employ only such persons in it as can be trusted—the ginning and preparing for market is no experiment all these things are reduced to a system as easy to calculate as the spinning of the articles with yarn."[93]

Several times, Krafft walked the men through the process of buying on credit, a lesson they were slow to learn. Writing in October 1846, he noted that the cotton crop was good at that very moment and scolded them for the inefficient way they had made their purchases the previous year. In the future, he recommended, they should send funds by letter of credit from some well-known house or bank in Philadelphia rather than attempt their previous patchwork methods.[94] When Rhoads failed to follow the instructions, sending a letter of reference from his creditor, Thomas P. Cope, Kraft admonished him, noting that his failure to comply prevented the cotton from being sent directly.[95] Yet when Krafft finally sent 25 bales, he had to admit that 4 of them were not of the quality he had promised. He insisted, however, that the best of them was as good as another large and expensive shipment of 225 bales sold at New Orleans on his account and purchased by a Philadelphia spinner.[96] Duly noting the dirty bales a couple of months later, Rhoads supplied Krafft with the corresponding numbers so he could trace them to the suppliers. Rhoads and Taylor subsequently sent 10 bales to England but were not pleased with the shipment. Rhoads put in an order for 20 more bales to go to Liverpool via New Orleans for shipment to Joseph Sturge marked "JS/B c/o/ Hodgson and Ryley, Liverpool."[97]

As the work of sourcing free cotton proceeded, the pragmatic Memphis agent raised questions about fundamentals. What made cotton "free"? Krafft asked. Was it the type of laborer who did the planting? The picking? The ginning? Or the baling? Did all steps of production need to be performed by nonslave (i.e., white) labor for the cotton to be accounted "free"? Krafft was doubtful that this was possible and urged Rhoads to be practical. "The only way to get the cotton you want is to dispense with ginning by white people," he insisted, arguing that if all the other processes were "free," ginning by enslaved people should not render it "slave" cotton.[98] As the agents in the field struggled with sourcing, Krafft urged Rhoads and Taylor to keep their desire for free labor cotton secret from planters and sellers, for fear that, if known, it would drive up the price. He dismissed the possibility that India cotton would ever compete with the southern commodity on the grounds that the shipping costs would make it too expensive.[99]

It complicated matters that a substantial portion of the raw cotton that PFPAF purchased needed to be shipped to England to be manufactured. Rhoads placed an order with Krafft for two thousand dollars' worth of free cotton in October 1846, drawn on the account of fellow PFPAF member Abraham Pennock.[100] Krafft enlisted his merchant friend J. H. Irwin of Philadelphia to act as a go-between for PFPAF, receiving free cotton shipments and sending money to Krafft, but this did not always work as planned. As Krafft reported to Rhoads on two occasions in early 1847, he had not received any money from Irwin so he was unable to purchase cotton.[101] There were still other problems, including once charging Rhoads an inflated price based on the weight of wet cotton that was much lighter once it dried. Ultimately, Krafft reported sending 141 bales to Liverpool and certified it with AEB & Company with instructions to sell it to Rhoads's friends. He suggested a new route for the cotton, via Pittsburgh, to avoid high freight costs, and he reported sending 50–100 bales of the best free labor cotton to the Philadelphia merchants Carson and Newbold.[102] He also reported sending some high-quality cotton to an English spinner, and 200 bales to Andrew E. Byrne in Liverpool. Unfortunately, however, the English shipment of free cotton got mixed up with slave labor cotton, so Krafft had to scramble to provide the numbers and barrel marks to sort out the shipment.[103] Several Liverpool merchants began doing business directly with Rhoads and Taylor. Krafft indicated to Rhoads in early 1848 that he was happy to give Francis Thompson, a Liverpool merchant, a regular supply of free cotton if he established a line of credit in either New York or Philadelphia, which he eventually did.[104]

Taylor and his associates believed that free labor merchandise would generate enough profits to make it a sustainable business. After Taylor opened his own store in Philadelphia, Coffin wrote with questions and instructions and proposed selling Taylor's goods on commission in his own Cincinnati store. He inquired about Taylor's costs for hogsheads of free sugar and molasses. He also reminded him of the need for a greater supply of brown or bleached muslin, noting that the brown variety was more in demand than any other item of free goods but at a greater price differential, making it impossible to sell for profit. Coffin noted that he himself would need a number of raw cotton bales, adding, "a capitalist would take hold of this business if they were shure they could make money at it."[105]

Complaints about Taylor's merchandise came from all quarters. W. R. Wheeler, the postmaster of West Elkton, Preble County, Ohio, a "true Anti-Slavery Methodist" and the new owner of Coffin's store, complained that, although the goods he purchased from Coffin in 1845 were comparable to slave labor cotton goods, the printed cloth from 1846 was "inferior in quality, figure, and color." Why were "free labor calicos coarser, less durable, and more pricy than other prints," and why were they not more like the Merrimack prints manufactured in Lowell, Massachusetts, Wheeler wondered. Struggling to suit Quaker consumers who were "not so plain" as well as those who were downright fashionable, Wheeler could not move the calicoes Coffin supplied off the shelves. If Taylor could not provide better-quality prints, Wheeler's Ohio business could not survive. His customers were willing to make reasonable sacrifices to avoid slave labor cotton, he explained, but pricing, quality, and durability needed to be comparable. Some of his customers had even begun to give themselves a calico "loophole," so they could purchase slave labor calicoes while still boycotting other fabrics made from slave-produced cotton.[106]

Convinced that their commercial viability depended on cultivating a strong British market, PFPAF sent Rhoads and his wife, Anne, to investigate potential markets and allies in Britain in 1847. There they encountered Joseph Sturge, who had entered a new phase of activism around free produce consumption. With the removal of the protective duties supporting West Indian sugar in 1844, Sturge hoped to make personal boycotts feasible.[107] Identifying a source of free cotton that year, perhaps through his Philadelphia contacts, Sturge began advertising free produce goods to the public.[108] The American peace activist, abolitionist, and reformer Elihu Burritt (1810–1879) joined Sturge's reform circles in Britain, where Sturge convinced him of the potential for free produce efforts to undermine markets for slave-produced goods.[109] Meanwhile, Sturge's American ally Tappan wrote to Sturge's fellow BFAS officer Scoble in search of information about the status of emancipated slaves and staple crop production in the British West Indies, a potential source of free produce goods.[110]

Upon arriving in England, the Rhoadses stopped first in Birmingham, where they enjoyed the hospitality and "kindness" of Sturge and his wife, Hannah, and gained introductions to the family's reform network. Together they met some of Britain's most prominent Quaker activists, including Anna Richardson, Mary Lloyd, Elizabeth Allen, Elizabeth Backhouse, Maria Candler, Isabel Casson, and Sarah Dymond.[111] This represented a departure for Rhoads, who rarely collaborated with American Quaker women even though they made up the main body of Philadelphia-area free produce consumers. Anne Rhoads became indispensable to his efforts in England, where she formed close friendships with many of the women PFPAF hoped to recruit, including Dymond, Allen, and Hannah Sturge.[112] As Hannah Sturge noted in a letter to Anne in September 1847, "increased attention is turning to the use of Free grown in preference to Slave grown produce—but we need some far greater demonstration to stir the manufacturers *to seek* for Free grown cotton."[113]

Anna Richardson proved to be an important spokesperson for the movement and a key link between British consumers and American activists.[114] In 1848 she rallied British Quakers with a call to purchase only free labor cotton. As she explained to her readers in the *British Friend*, the main impediment was the will of the British consumer. Quoting Samuel Rhoads on the potential of a British consumer boycott to introduce "the discussion of the slavery question . . . upon every plantation in the South," she detailed possible sources of free cotton from India, the British West Indies, and the American South. She also extracted a testimonial from Henry Bibb, formerly enslaved, about the usefulness of a consumer boycott for dealing a blow to slavery. The following year, she wrote to PFAS offering to donate valuable items to their annual fundraising fair on the condition that the proceeds go to the free produce efforts of Rhoads and Taylor. PFAS agreed to donate half of the proceeds, and the transatlantic fundraising partnership commenced.[115]

During their travels, the Rhoadses encountered J. D. Lang "of America," actually a Presbyterian clergyman from Australia, who had a big scheme for producing free cotton. Lang was in Britain pitching his plan to Manchester and Glasgow capitalists and traveling the country seeking investors. His plan, in a nutshell, was to recruit both British peasant labor and southern planter expertise to cultivate cotton in Cooksland (Queensland). In addition to his aim to deal a blow to American slavery, Lang acknowledged that he wanted to prevent Queensland from being "overrun" by "coolie" labor. Ultimately, he claimed, using "European free labour, cotton and other products could be grown in Australia for the home market" and would easily undersell the slaveholders of America and Brazil "through the magical influence of free labour alone."[116]

Samuel and Anne Rhoads also met Sturge's frenetic associate Burritt. Abolition ran in the Connecticut Burritt family; his brother Elijah enjoyed a brief stint as a newspaper editor in Georgia before rumors of his distribution of David Walker's *Appeal* led to his hasty departure. The younger Burritt ended up in England, where he successfully published on a number of reform topics and organized thousands to join the League of Universal Brotherhood, an international peace organization. Burritt had plans to open his own free produce store in London as well as to establish several free cotton manufactories. As part of his research on cotton supplies, Burritt wrote to Taylor in September 1846 in the hopes of introducing the movement to England and France: "I want to know a short history of the cotton you have already received from the South—from what State—who were the producers—the number of a similar class that might be encouraged to grow cotton in the same way—how you were able to put yourselves in communication with them—your means of informing the poor non-slaveholder through the South that their free labour cotton will be bought at a premium." He inquired about plans for transport and manufacture of free cotton, "so that it shall not be confounded with the slave stained article." He suggested erecting a factory in the country "that shall confine itself to the manufacture of Free Labour cotton through the establishment in every larger town of stores or shops which . . . shall keep free labour cotton, sugar, rice, coffee, molasses, tobacco, &c, and no other articles." He signed off with reassurances to Taylor that Joseph Sturge was with him, heart and hand, as were many other influential British reformers.[117]

In the following months, Burritt wrote incessantly to Taylor, demanding immediate attention.[118] He was a man big on vision but with limited agricultural knowledge. Several months into his correspondence, he admitted that he had no idea whether cotton was sown in the fall or the spring. As Burritt flailed around trying to locate free cotton for his English store, he decided to sponsor a naive young Englishman, Charles Downman, to travel to Georgia to grow free cotton. Downman had been considering a move to Australia, but Burritt convinced him it would be no more dangerous to go to Georgia. He envisioned Downman as but the first in a succession of migrants who would form the nucleus of a free labor colony in the American South.[119]

There were several problems with Burritt's plan, and through them Taylor learned more about the difficulties of providing authenticated free cotton to consumers. Downman had not the slightest idea how to grow cotton. He also knew nobody in Georgia, had very little money, and kept raising suspicions as he traveled the state asking for advice. Just when it seemed that he might be able to access a plow, some land, and some cotton seed, however, the need to contract out the ginning to a large planter appeared daunting. Most large planters were using their gins full time, and sharing a gin run by enslaved people jeopardized the authenticity of the desired free product. Unless one could find an owner using free labor to run the gin, efforts to produce a pure product might founder.[120]

Southern Sourcing

Over the course of several years as Taylor's southern agent, Nathan Thomas traveled widely across the South through Mississippi, Tennessee, Alabama, Arkansas, and Texas. Normally these trips took place in the autumn, after his own agricultural season had ended. As Thomas explained to Rhoads about his travel plans in the spring of 1850, his absence from his own affairs was only possible because of his wife's willingness to take on additional responsibilities as part of her contribution to the cause. It was difficult to travel during the spring months, "it being in our seeding and planting time."[121] Thomas's work on behalf of the

Free Produce Association compelled his wife to add agricultural management to her own domestic labor.[122]

Thomas recorded for his Philadelphia correspondents scenes of southern rural communities with devastated landscapes, limited infrastructure, poverty, and brutality in a region dependent on slave labor and cotton. Everywhere he traveled during harvest time, Thomas witnessed cotton on the move. North and west of Holly Springs, Mississippi, the markets of Memphis were the big draw. In December 1849 Thomas described meeting "many wagons loaded with cotton" as he left Marshall County, Mississippi. Pulled by mules or oxen along muddy roads, the wagons hauling cotton bales made their way to Memphis traveling ten to fifteen miles per day. At day's end, wagoners arranged a "universal camp out even in Memphis," where Thomas witnessed as many as one hundred wagons camping together. Wagoners brought their own provisions to sustain them on the journey and purchased groceries upon reaching Memphis. The Memphis markets offered barrels of whiskey, cheese, butter, eggs, dried and fresh apples, candles, brooms, shoes, cigars, household furniture, wagons, carriages, and boats, but the small producers Thomas followed usually limited their purchases to flour, bacon, and pork.[123]

Thomas learned to identify free cotton producers by the appearance of the people accompanying the wagon to market. Those producing cotton without slave labor usually sent wagons driven by two white men, the white landowner and his son or neighbor, whereas slave-produced cotton farmers sent an enslaved man to accompany the wagon. The problem, Thomas discovered, as he followed up on these visual cues, was that most free producers had to rely on gins owned by larger planters and run on slave labor. It seemed impossible for a small producer to avoid contracting with a large planter for the ginning.[124]

As Thomas traveled between Holly Springs and Fulton, he found the countryside unforgiving; "no one who lives there and has not traveled is aware of the Miasmatick atmosphere and the consequent depression of spirits and almost ready at times to dispair yet in the darkness sometimes rises a gleam of home and lights appear." But it was the "bad" moral atmosphere as much as the unhealthy climate that affected him. Part of Thomas's distress came from witnessing the violence of slavery, as on the occasion when he went outside to wash himself and saw a tall man whipping an enslaved woman, unmoved by her "piteous cryes begging for mercy" and seemingly unfazed by Thomas's presence.[125] The greed at the heart of slavery also left its imprint on the landscape, where the lack of stewardship resulted in plundered stands of oak, with damaged trees left to fall to the ground, and badly eroded soil. After traveling through Tippah and Itawamba Counties, Thomas reached the town of Cotton Gin, an old Chickasaw trading post where the steamboats stopped. From there, he journeyed through hilly country with settlements abandoned and grown over with young pine. He quoted the county clerk, who described the mass movement of white farmers to new lands, leaving depleted fields in their wake, as resembling a flock of blackbirds.[126]

When he reached Itawamba County in eastern Mississippi, Thomas witnessed cotton production and transport for the more distant market of Mobile, Alabama. In Itawamba, planters sent their cotton on flat boats from the headwaters of the Tombigbee River on a two-hundred-mile journey to Mobile. He found a few planters engaged in free labor cotton production and using free labor gins, but generally, as elsewhere, the cotton produced without slave labor was ginned by enslaved people. As was his practice, he kept samples of the cotton from each plantation where there was hope for procuring free produce. In the midst of discussing the security of his correspondence, he reported to Rhoads sardonically, the only way a letter addressed to a stranger would attract any attention in the South was if it was addressed to "NIGERS and COTON." He misspelled both deliberately and scrawled them in upper case block letters to illustrate white southern ignorance, illiteracy, and preoccupation with profit.[127] The "whole of go of this country is cotton and Niggers for as more cotton to buy more Niggers," he noted bitterly. White yeoman farmers, Thomas believed, failed to recognize that slavery was also the source of their own oppression.[128]

Sobered by the reports from Thomas and Coffin, Taylor searched for new ways to source free cotton. His agents' experience suggested that the farmers producing the cotton he wanted were too poor to invest in their own gins. As the Memphis agent Krafft explained to Taylor, "I can get any quantity of cotton grown and handled by white people & brought to market by them but they are generally poor people and are obliged to employ slave labour on the ginning of it—therefore the only way to get it *pure in every particular*, is to get the gins & have them set up at different points convenient as possible to a larger neighbourhood of poor white people who are always willing & indeed prefer delivering their cotton at a fair price *in the seed* payable in cash at the gin."[129] Most small producers were willing to sell cotton to free labor produce agents, but unless they were part of Thomas's and Coffin's Quaker networks, they were without slaves by necessity, not on principle. This fact, in and of itself, added to the unpredictability of sourcing; commitments to produce "free" cotton could be disrupted by a householder's death, his decision to hire an enslaved laborer, or a move to new land.

In a letter to Rhoads in January 1846, Thomas mentioned the idea of providing poor farmers with gins. Thomas recommended that the free produce agents "seeke such settlements as ware mostly of the poorer class and have gins erected to be managed entirely by free labour." He had already taken matters into his own hands by ordering a gin to be put up in Lafayette County at the head of navigation on the Tallahatchie River, where there was a "large settlement of people who farm on a small scale." Coffin, meanwhile, constructed two gins in Cincinnati for use in the South. One of the potential buyers, William McRay in Oak Ridge, Mississippi, a son-in-law of the Quaker Pleasant Diggs, had been approved for a loan from PFPAF to buy a gin but decided not to accept because he couldn't get his outbuildings ready quickly enough for the coming season. The other went to the Hunt family of Lafayette County, Mississippi, based on their promise to supply one hundred bales of cotton. The Memphis agent Krafft reported receipt of the gin and castings in October 1846. Within just a few years, he boasted, Hunt's gin, regarded as one of the best in the country, was already supplying very fine, high-quality cotton.[130] As Thomas and Coffin learned, however, a gin's power and speed did not always guarantee high-quality cotton lint. Hunt subsequently occasionally hired enslaved people to do the ginning, but to Thomas's relief, he did not try to pass off his cotton as "free labor."[131]

Once Krafft overcame his own reluctance to get involved in providing gins to poor white producers, Taylor turned his attention to making contact with cotton gin manufacturers in New England.[132] In 1848, Krafft had notified Rhoads of a gin manufactured in Boston that was powerful enough to process eight bales a day.[133] During his correspondence with the Boston Sugar Refining Company, Taylor vouchsafed his desire to purchase cotton gins for the use of poor white families who relied on the labor of family members. Such a model of household manufacture would have been familiar to him from his own childhood in the mill country of Chester County. A gin could be purchased and set up for three hundred dollars, and several households could share it. Investing in gins for the use of poor white families would make the supply of free cotton more predictable. In another day and age, such a plan might have been labeled "development" and been part of a policy to stabilize the fortunes of poor white families in the South. It promised to connect them directly with markets for their agricultural products and reduce their dependence on the gins owned by larger planters.[134] Eventually, in response to Thomas's suggestion, Taylor ordered him an English cottage gin, which he had some success at selling in the South.[135] But during the 1850s, funds could not be raised to provide cotton gins in sufficient number to produce an adequate supply of free cotton to English and northern factories.

Turning Points and Free Produce Loyalists

The years 1849–1850 proved to be a turning point for many members of Taylor's networks. Back in England, Sturge and his family continued their abolitionist activism. Sturge's sister-in-law, Lydia Albright Sturge, wrote to Queen Victoria in 1849 on behalf of the Ladies Society of Birmingham asking Her Majesty to abstain from slave-produced goods in her household as an example to every household in the realm.[136] Sturge, who hosted Frederick Douglass during his exile in Britain in 1846, met William Wells Brown, the African American novelist and activist, at the Paris Peace Congress in 1849. A year later he hosted Henry Highland Garnet, the militant ex-slave and free labor produce activist, during his British speaking tour.[137]

In an effort to improve the quality of his calico goods, Taylor inquired about several U.S. manufacturing possibilities. The New England calico printer Job Eddy had plans to take possession of a bigger mill, making his old mill available for Taylor.[138] Taylor also corresponded with Andrew Robeson Jr. in March 1849, whose Fall River print works had gone bankrupt in 1848.[139] By 1850, however, conditions were worsening for the agents tasked with sourcing free cotton in the South. In December 1849, Thomas reported that he was treated with suspicion simply by virtue of being from the North and that he had been threatened with being shot.[140] The general cry, he observed, was that slaves were better off than laborers in the North.[141] In the aftermath of the crisis in Congress in January 1850 leading to Henry Clay's introduction of the Compromise of 1850, Thomas disclosed that white southerners suspected he might be trying to steal slaves and that he feared for his safety. Writing from Franklin County, Alabama, on January 22, 1850, Thomas described the entire county in an uproar over the events in Congress. Although he had identified free cotton in Shelby County and in the Free State of Walker, he was afraid to continue on his journey to Georgia and South Carolina.[142] Back in New Garden, Indiana, in February, Thomas reported being depressed in spirits, citing feelings of "distress," "degradation," and "misery." He was saddened by the arrest of two neighbors, a white man and an African American man, as they traveled south on business. He also warned Rhoads that Krafft was alienating poor white people—the very people they needed to cultivate free cotton—with his haughtiness, secrecy, and purchasing methods.[143]

Taylor responded to national events by intensifying his search for free sugar outside the United States and continuing his search for a textile factory. In 1847, Rhoads had corresponded with Margaret Collins, the widow of free produce store owner Charles Collins, wondering how he could authenticate the sample of Puerto Rican free sugar she had sent him.[144] Taylor wrote to the Boston Refining Company about their source of sugar, discovering that, although they were currently working with Cuban sugar produced by enslaved people, they would soon be working with sugar from Manila, understood by activists to be "free."[145] The following year he made inquiries about free produce in Bassa Cove, Liberia, and began a lengthy correspondence with the Liberian president, Stephen Benson.[146] He also worked through the Baptist missionary W. L. Judd to make direct contact with the Haitian emperor. Deciding to investigate sources for himself, in 1850 Taylor spent several months traveling to Puerto Rico, Barbados, Jamaica, Demerara, and Saint Croix. The condition of "free" Black labor in Bermuda seemed compromised to him, and Puerto Rico proved to be as much in the grip of plantation slavery as ever. Saint Croix had the greatest potential for sourcing free sugar, and soon Taylor was importing sugar and molasses to Philadelphia.[147] In the meantime, he corresponded with David White of South Carolina about sourcing free produce rice but without success.[148] Another contact wrote to Taylor to introduce the Englishman Frederick Tuckett, who wanted to discuss cotton gins.[149]

In 1854, Taylor purchased a Chester County water-powered textile mill from Henry Webster, whom he employed as a manager. Webster had married Rest Elizabeth Lamborn, a member of a prominent Chester County abolitionist family whose female members included free produce advocates, Underground Railroad operatives, and Progressive Friends. Webster had previous experience farming and running a woolen mill. Taylor's new mill was located in Doe Run, a creek in the heart of Chester County and the site of numerous textile, grist, and clover seed mills.[150] All seemed to be going well for Taylor until the Depression of 1857 made it impossible for him to pay his workers in cash. In desperation, he began paying them in cloth. He struggled to keep the factory running by investing his own funds until the Civil War's emancipations of enslaved people made free produce an unsustainable business. In 1864, his Chester County mill was offered for public sale. Eight years later Taylor was still trying to settle accounts with the widow Elizabeth Webster over the value of mill machinery.[151]

Taylor's experiment with sourcing free labor goods revealed the difficulty of creating a business model from a moral community. Well into the 1840s, Quaker women in both Britain and the United States supported the effort locally by running stores and purchasing "free labor" goods. Taylor's failure to incorporate these zealous supporters of free produce into his organization appears to have been a structural weakness. There no women on the board of the Philadelphia Free Labor Produce Association of Friends, despite an explicit invitation to female Friends to come to one of the first meetings in Philadelphia in June 1845.[152] This was perhaps because of the organization's reliance on a transatlantic business model rather than on local activists, and its roots in a self-consciously conservative cohort of Quaker society. Most of the women in Taylor's life were devoted wives and mothers who looked after large families and instilled Quaker values in children.

The abolition movement had changed by the 1850s, moreover, in ways that rendered free produce consumption a seemingly less radical commitment compared to other branches of the movement. By the early 1840s, Garrison denounced the free produce effort, advising abolitionists that it was better to subject the body to the trials of traveling, lecturing, writing, publishing, and fundraising than go to the trouble of procuring a free cotton garment with the assumption that one had discharged one's moral obligation to oppose slavery. "Let us beware," he warned, "that at straining at a gnat, we swallow a camel." Wendell Phillips, who had previously supported the free produce effort, likewise dismissed the movement as one of self-indulgent moralism. When he arrived at the Judgment Day wearing his suit made of slave-produced cotton, Phillips predicted sardonically in 1847, his actions on behalf of the slave would more than outweigh his failure to remain uncontaminated by slave-produced goods. Although the abolitionist lecturers Abby Kelley and her husband Stephen Foster attempted to avoid consumer complicity in slavery by buying a farm in Worcester, Massachusetts, from which they raised crops and ran an Underground Railroad station, even they stopped endorsing the free produce movement. By the 1850s, Foster was ridiculing free produce advocates, thus falling into line with Garrison.[153]

The most economically sophisticated analysis of the free produce movement came in 1853 in the pages of the *National Era*, an antislavery paper associated with the Liberty Party and edited by Gamaliel Bailey and John Greenleaf Whittier. In "Free Cotton vs. Chattel Slavery," the author disowned the economic analysis of Calvin Ellis Stowe, the biblical scholar and husband to Harriet Beecher Stowe, on the grounds of its "degradation of free labor." Calvin's analysis came as the Stowes were touring England in 1853 following the publication of Harriet's *Uncle Tom's Cabin*. During their travels they met Joseph Sturge and discussed the moral and economic significance of consuming only free labor produce. Calvin subsequently addressed antislavery crowds at Congregational Hall and Exeter Hall, where he touted the virtues of cheap Chinese labor as a substitute for slavery. Deriding Stowe's analysis of the desirability of Chinese labor underselling slave labor, the author of the *National Era* article also denounced Henry Clay for suggesting China as a source of "free" labor. Stowe's analysis, while not shared by all white abolitionists, built on a common abolitionist trope of U.S. slavery as a throwback to the tyranny of Eastern despotism. Seen through this lens, the conditions of Chinese labor seemed to pose little threat to the consciences of white Americans, who viewed the degradations of labor as endemic to Eastern barbarism. As the author of the *National Era* piece noted, however, in a global labor market the exploitation of South Asian and Chinese labor degraded all labor. Ridiculing the notion that the slaveholder could be starved out of his use of human chattel, the author suggested that, on the contrary, what was needed was a rise in the value of the slave such that no man could afford to own him.[154]

Sturge wrote to Rhoads about some of these dilemmas in 1859. Over a decade earlier, Sturge had donated five hundred dollars to the Philadelphia Association to hire an agent to source southern cotton. Sturge was appalled that the British trade in South Asian labor went under the guise of "free" labor. He thought the South Asians laboring in Jamaica were little better than slaves, and he reported with outrage that "2 British steamers with large cargoes of human beings [are] destined for slavery in Cuba under the name of free labourers." Sturge was sorry to hear that Taylor's Chester County factory was not producing more, but he reported optimistically on his own enterprise: an estate in Montserrat that he was running on free labor principles.[155]

Several prominent African American abolitionists continued to endorse the boycotts of slave-produced goods as a morally consistent means of achieving the larger goals of ending slavery. As Rhoads pointed out in a letter to the *Liberator* in February 1850, even as Garrison and his followers had abandoned the path of consumer boycotts, former slaves like Henry R. Marshall and William Wells Brown considered it the duty of antislavery activists to refuse to purchase slave-produced goods. Henry Highland Garnet toured England in 1850 advocating for free produce, although Douglass took him to task for his failure to provide more support to the effort in the United States. In 1852, Jacob C. White Jr. (1837–1902), namesake of the prominent leader, healer, and owner of Philadelphia's Lebanon cemetery and graduate of the Institute for Colored Youth, urged other free Black people to avoid slave-produced goods as a matter of moral consistency. Refugees in Canada like Henry Bibb, and free Black people in Philadelphia and Ohio, moreover, saw potential in a Brazilian-invented flax machine to replace slave-grown cotton with the cheaper flax substitute, thereby undermining the value of slave labor.[156]

Frederick Douglass persisted in urging people to avoid slave produce as a means of weakening the economic power of the slave owner. Echoing an older generation of female free produce advocates, Douglass translated the consumer wrong of buying slave-produced sugar into the intimate female realm of fashion. Using language reminiscent of medical treatises that described disease clinging to fabric, he noted, "we enter the wardrobe, and the sighs and groans of the slave are lingering around the seams of our clothes, and floating amid the folds of our garments." The pain and suffering of the enslaved producers of the cotton in the garments worn by white northerners gave the clothing a tainted, almost diseased, history and an association with violence and cruelty—quite opposite to the effect female consumers aimed for.[157]

Douglass challenged his readers to see the products of slave labor in their full historical and economic context rather than simply as alluring commodities: "But who will say, when Carolina's rice, with snowy whiteness, tempts the taste, perhaps the hands that gathered this were severed from some loved and lost embrace? Who will gaze upon the manufactured cotton, and see the stain, the stain of blood and tears upon its warp and woof? Who will look beneath the delicate proportions [*sic*] of the sugar cane, and see the stinging and clotted lash, and on their surface trace the agony of tears?" Seeking a transformation in the consumer's desire for the "snowy whiteness" of Carolina rice, southern cotton, and refined white sugar, Douglass brought into view the blood and tears of the slave who produced them.[158]

In fact, Douglass was paraphrasing fellow African American activist and poet Frances Ellen Watkins Harper, a free woman born and raised in Baltimore and mentored by her uncle, the minister, teacher, and anti-colonizationist William Watkins. As Harper put it in a letter to the Underground Railroad operative William Still in October 1854, "Oh friend, beneath the most delicate preparations of the cane can you not see the stinging lash and clotted whip?" Harper had become a free produce convert after reading Solomon Northup's *Twelve Years a Slave* (1853). Writing to Still, she explained: "I have reason to be thankful that I am able to give a little more for a Free Labor dress, if it is a little coarser. I can thank God that upon its warp and woof I see no stain of blood and tears; that to procure a little finer muslin for my limbs no crushed and broken heart went out in sighs, and that from the field where it was raised went up no wild and startling cry unto the throne of God to witness there in language deep and strong, that in demanding that cotton I was nerving oppression's hand for deeds of guilt and crime."[159]

Coming from Douglass's and Harper's pens, the bodily purity rhetoric refuted the magical whitewashing effect of commodification. For Harper, however, it went further. As she explained to Still, "if the liberation of the slave demanded it, I could consent to part with a portion of the blood from my own veins if that would do him any good." As she saw it, the consumption of slave-produced commodities was akin to consuming the body of a family member, much as the "Hindoo" character in a story she had heard was "loth to cut a tree because being a believer in the transmigration of souls, he thought the soul of his father had passed into it." She imagined and honored a family relationship between the body of the enslaved laborer who produced the commodity and her own consuming body, and she was willing to seal it in blood.[160]

As late as the mid-1850s, Douglass passionately denounced the northern consumption of southern slave-produced goods as hypocritical to antislavery politics and "an aggression upon the very citadel of life, robbing a human heart of its liberty and rights, its energies and manhood." The crime was in the continual consumer demand for rice, cotton, and sugar, despite all that was known about the harm inflicted on the enslaved. Douglass concluded, "we may hail the free-labour movement as a harbinger of hope, and ensign of progress, and a means of proving the consistency of our principles, and the earnestness of our zeal. By so doing we may prove to the South that we not only denounce Slavery as robbery and piracy, but we are endeavouring to shake our hands from sharing in its spoils and participating in its crimes."[161]

* * *

The free produce movement invoked the impurity of slave-produced goods by linking the slave's blood, sweat, tears, and suffering with the materiality of cotton, rice, sugar, and tobacco. The point was to link the commodity with the spectacle of the suffering slave's body such that it became physically uncomfortable, perhaps even sickening, for the consumer to consider intimate use of the good. Using visceral language about bleeding bodies, activists hoped to provoke consumers into engaging their bodies in abolition through selective acts of consumption. But free produce activists also engaged their bodies in sourcing free produce. Their success depended on the efforts of agents on the ground who tangled with the material realities of the South's cotton economy and the initiative of activists like Sturge and Taylor, who traveled to investigate labor conditions.

Despite Douglass's significant support, the latter-day free produce effort was built on transatlantic ties and commercial networks and did not reflect the priorities of local producers or consumers. It had confused politics around the labor and activism of women, whose support it needed, and it suffered from the fact that it was composed mainly of white, male, middle-class Quakers. This homogeneity set them apart from their predecessors and seems to have hampered their ability to sustain a consumer movement. Rather than ask for advice from veteran female activists, many of whom continued to embrace radical positions on abolition and human rights, Sturge, Taylor, Rhoads, Burritt, Thomas, and Coffin chased a grand vision of a British boycott built on consumer volition.

There were other unintended negative effects of the free produce movement, including the depiction of the physical residue of slave production as capable of "infecting" the consumer, and the highlighting of the dissonance between the slave's body and blood and the snowy white appearance of so many of the commodities free produce advocates tried to source. Free produce agents who traveled the South to try to find free labor cotton, moreover, ended up seeking a commodity produced by white people rather than by enslaved laborers. Yet none of these possible distortions of the free produce principle were enough to put off African American abolitionists like Brown, Douglass, Watkins, White, and Garnet, or PFAS loyalists like Mott, Grimké Weld, and Lewis, all of whom continued to find it both disgusting and hypocritical to consume the products of slave labor,

For all its blind spots, the effort to source free goods had profound effects on its advocates. Free labor produce societies engaged people in a process that politicized them. This proved true not just for the consumer but for the aspiring supplier. The need to travel to investigate the conditions of commodity production forced parochial Quakers into a wider world of supply chains. It opened their eyes to a complex range of labor practices, including the use of family labor by southern white yeoman farmers and wage labor to finish raw cotton in the Chester textile factory. It also widened the divide between the work of men like Taylor, who would find it necessary to travel in search of free sugar and cotton, and the untapped local wisdom of female storekeepers and consumers whose choices were supposed to provide the movement with its moral energy. Ultimately, for all participants in the free produce movement, viewing cotton in relation to the bodies of both consumers and enslaved laborers revealed the reach of slavery into all aspects of antebellum life and raised questions about what it meant for labor to be "free."

Chapter 6

Maternal Blood and Tears

There was a shocked silence in the Indiana antislavery meeting after the white physician and known Democratic Party mouthpiece Theodore W. Strain shouted out his challenge to Sojourner Truth, calling on her to prove that she really was a woman. Then more shouting, the brandishing of a gun, chaos. As the conflict veered toward violence, Truth asked Strain why he doubted her. Strain retorted with what seemed to him an obvious "tell," Truth's deep voice. "Your voice is not the voice of a woman," he declared, "it is the voice of a man." He requested that she show her breasts to the women in the audience as proof of her female sex. More than a physical attribute of sex, a woman's breast signified her capacity to mother. An enslaved woman's breast made her vulnerable to exploitation as a producer of enslaved children and wet nurse to white children. Deciding not to meet the challenge with a half measure, Truth insisted on displaying the evidence to the entire audience. Unfastening the clasps of her white blouse to reveal a breast, she put to rest the rumors, circulated by Strain and others, that she was really a man in woman's clothing. She also took the opportunity to impugn the manliness of her hecklers, offering them the breast with which she claimed to have nursed many a white child to the exclusion of her own children. Lobbing a hateful rejoinder about her breast resembling a sow's "teat," Dr. Strain lost his forty-dollar wager on the truth about Truth's sex, leading the *Liberator*'s contributor to comment sardonically on the "physiological acumen" of a "western" physician.[1]

Truth's bold self-assertion in displaying her body in public affirmed and legitimized her humanity even as it limited its imagined scope. Tall, slim, middle-aged, dark-complected, and wearing plain dress, Truth exuded neither the buxom vitality of a woman in her childbearing prime nor the embellished femininity of a fashionable lady. She was, most importantly, not white. Dr. Strain's challenge reflected antebellum racial exclusions that denied African Americans the privileges of legal personhood, but it also revealed the narrow gendered channels within which humanity could be claimed. What if Sojourner Truth had not been a woman? Would that have made her testimony against slavery any less compelling? For the white doctor, a Southern Democrat, casting doubt on Truth's femaleness was a means of debunking her life story as a former slave and its use to advance the cause of abolition.[2]

For Truth, her self-assertion on this occasion, as on several others, required that she reveal her womanhood as fully embodied. Exposing her breasts was both poignant and transgressive, for it brought into public view a part of the female body kept private by respectable white women but regularly displayed as a sign of the exploitability and commodification of enslaved women's maternity. As Truth well knew, the breast of an enslaved woman was not only not fully her own, as was the case with all breastfeeding women, but also not fully in her power to give to her child. An enslaved woman's breast might be exposed and palpated in the slave market to reveal childbearing history and potential future fertility. Privileged fantasies about that breast stirred the lust of the men who enslaved her. That breast, proffered, fed the children whom enslavers so crudely calculated as "increase," and withheld, initiated the process of weaning that marked the opportunity for enslavers to sell a mother's child.[3]

Truth's confrontation helps us identify several abolitionist strategies to depict enslaved people as familiars deserving of white empathy rather than as strangers. In doing so, abolitionists brought the intimate and domestic to bear on nineteenth-century concepts of human rights. First, abolitionists represented the enslaved as normatively gendered and sexed to anchor claims that enslaved people occupied a universal and sympathetic category of humanity. This strategic use of gender conformity in the nineteenth century would leave a stubborn legacy for subsequent human rights and social justice campaigns. Second, abolitionists exposed slavery's fundamental cruelty and systematic violation of the essential elements of the human condition. A focus on violated slave motherhood answered all of these strategic needs, but it also appealed to abolitionists for the reason that, as the site for producing new slaves, an enslaved woman's body was crucial to slavery's perpetuation in the United States after the closing of the transatlantic trade in 1808. Third, motherhood was already a politically activated and sentimentally rich category that expanded its emotional carrying capacity during the antebellum period. Nineteenth-century print and visual culture sources depicted white middle-class mothers as engaged in ethereal acts of love, erasing the backbreaking physical labor of mothering or relegating it to those deemed less refined: working-class or enslaved women. It was within this context that abolitionists offered an alternative view of enslaved women's maternal bodies and made a strategic decision to represent them as bleeding from grief and loss rather than from rape, miscarriage, and childbirth.[4]

It mattered who your mother was in the enslaving states of the U.S. South as in so many slave societies around the world. The experience of being a mother, moreover, challenged abstract ideals of self-sovereignty. Motherhood's embodied math—one person became two people—fit uncomfortably with liberal political concepts of individualism. An enslaved mother, connected to the child who had been born of her body, moreover, was at her most vulnerable physically and emotionally. Slave motherhood also raised other issues about race and jurisdiction that we will consider in Chapters 7 and 8: Was the inheritability of slave status somehow intrinsic to the enslaved mother's body, as slaveholders would have it, even if she escaped to a free state? If escape gained her the capacity to bequeath natural rights to a child born of her body, what did this mean for scientific racism's notions of inheritable race as a key criteria for enslavement?

Even as abolitionists seized on the plight of the enslaved mother as emblematic of all that was immoral and unnatural about slavery, motherhood was in the process of being medicalized as a "condition" of white womanhood and a source of economic value for enslavers. Young medical students eagerly pursued the mysteries of conception, menstruation, and childbirth, with white women as their implied subject. While some dismissed the reproductive travails of African American women as physically insignificant, others drew conclusions about all women from the Black female bodies they had treated or dissected. That medical students also demonstrated interest in male reproductive organs, including studies of venereal disease and strictures of the urethra, reminds us of the larger context of nineteenth-century biopolitics and political economy. Prolific reproduction for both white and enslaved populations remained a priority in territories where white people aspired to statehood and enslavers desired to expand slavery. The medicalization of motherhood kept pace with its sentimentalization and reflected its crucial importance for the demography and political economy of the South. To appropriate and reinvent the iconography of motherhood, then, struck at the heart of the culture of slaveholding and territorial expansion.[5]

The Slave Mother

Although Richard Allen did not mention them in his 1827 letter arguing for African American claims to national citizenship, enslaved women's bodies could have generated an even more basic form of belonging than nationality. Birth created a specific connection between two people, a mother and a child, that began at a specific historical moment with an intimate physical bond, and in a precise location. Outside slavery, the circumstances of birth normally established two crucial features of the child's identity: kinship and homeland. In the U.S. context, however, there were limits to a white mother's determination of a child's status when she gave birth on foreign soil. According to the 1790 Naturalization

Act, reiterated in 1795, 1798, and 1802, a white mother alone could not determine the status of her foreign-born child; that child's citizenship required a father who had at some point resided in the United States. Under the law of slavery, in contrast, a mother's enslavement had long been sufficient to enslave her child. An enslaver's claim to mother and child even before the child drew her first breath vitiated birth's potential to create fundamental relationships to people and place. To be an enslaved child meant having the identity and belonging conferred by birth appropriated by slavery's principle of maternal inheritance. To be an enslaved mother meant being forced to surrender control over the living product of one's own body. When free state jurisdictions threatened to disrupt the maternal inheritance of slavery by providing a "free" homeland, and slavery's defenders embraced a model of inherited race that strengthened the determining force of maternity, the mother-child relationship became hotly contested once again by abolitionists and their opponents.[6]

The grief of the enslaved mother—in particular, the link between the physicality and emotion of sundered maternal ties—became one of the most important abolitionist tropes of slavery's violation of nature, and with it, the human rights of enslaved people. The trope was, in its essence, a rebuttal of arguments by some of slavery's defenders that enslaved women were bad mothers. Abolitionists on both sides of the Atlantic produced soaring rhetoric about children torn from the arms of tearful mothers, nursing infants stripped from the maternal breast, and the connected bodies of mother and child ripped apart by sale. Compared to Robert Pleasants's condemnations of slavery's fundamental injustice to the innocent children who inherited their condition, nineteenth-century American abolitionists focused more on slavery's systematic violation of motherhood. This shift coincided with the change in the meaning of "breeding" from a description of any woman, white or Black, in the midst of her childbearing years, to the deliberate cultivation of her reproductive potential to increase the property in slaves.[7]

Historians have interpreted this evocation of distressed motherhood in a number of critical ways: as a sentimental appeal to white sympathy, as pornographic indulgence in another's pain, or as a means of articulating white bourgeois women's own legal and familial constraints by speaking for—and sometimes as—broken-hearted enslaved mothers. While these arguments have productively exposed self-interest and self-affirmation as crucial motives in the white politics of empathy, abolitionists' use of the figure of the suffering slave mother was more than mere wallowing in the sentimental culture of motherhood. Depictions of enslaved mothers weeping accomplished several other goals. They invested slave mothers with the qualities of a fully legible womanhood (as distinct from the supposedly coarse and stunted emotions of poor women and the licentious enslaved mistresses of the West Indies), thus making the case for enslaved women's full adult humanity. Abolitionists reminded their audiences that the ability to shed tears was a distinctly human attribute. Put somewhat differently, it became possible to imagine the human through the figure of the weeping mother and to think about human rights as encompassing intimate family connections.

Depictions of enslaved mothers also celebrated the qualities and emotional sensibilities to which bourgeois women, both white and African American, aspired. Encouraging public empathy for the plight of enslaved women unable to provide the physical and emotional nurture to the children they had borne, white middle-class reformers did not simply affirm themselves and attempt to universalize bourgeois maternal values—although they did do this. Along with African American activists, they also reinterpreted motherhood through the lens of both their own experiences and their recollections of their own mothers, glorifying it and infusing it with sentiment. The abolitionist focus on enslaved mothers thus potentially revalued the emotional baggage of motherhood for all women, framing it as a right and a need and making maternal emotions fleshy in ways that exposed the tensions between maternity's materiality and highly idealized depictions of white mothers.[8]

As the opinions delivered in *Pleasants v. Pleasants* made clear, motherhood was slavery's institutional Gordian knot, binding future generations to their condition as chattel and linking the status of slaves past, present, and future. As the British abolitionist Thomas Fowell Buxton argued before Parliament in 1823, citing the policies in New York, Ceylon, Bencoolen (Sumatra), St. Helena, and Colombia, severing the child's inheritance of enslaved status from an enslaved mother would mean "that slavery would burn itself down into its socket and go out."[9] The enslaver's view of the function of slave motherhood stood in especially stark contrast to white motherhood in an era of capitalist expansion and middle-class formation. The significance of motherhood grew tremendously between the second half of the eighteenth century and the first three decades of the nineteenth century as Enlightenment theories about education, refinement, and intelligence emphasized the human capacity for learning and civilization. White mothers played a key role in building their children's cultural capital, according to these theories, by teaching them basic reading skills and instilling morality and manners. In fulfilling the roles of educated, moral, and tender-hearted mothers and wives, white women were depicted as crucial resources for the middle-class household, if no longer manifestly as important to the household economy. Added to this, religious revivals owed much to women's participation and to their reputations for being better able to open their hearts, if not their minds, to God's grace.[10]

Even as this happened, however, medical and classificatory science stressed hierarchies, embedded in human bodies and evident in brains, that determined certain outcomes—occupational, moral, and intellectual—based on sex and race. This reinterpretation of motherhood within a framework that served colonialism hinged on certain well-worn tropes of Indigenous and enslaved women. Women's rights advocates on both sides of the Atlantic placed their own situations along an historical arc of changing manners and mores in which Western Christian societies had achieved an unprecedented standard of male and female companionship. "In the beginning, and among tribes which are still in a primitive condition," the British intellectual Harriet Taylor Mill observed in an 1852, "women were and are the slaves of men for the purposes of toil. All the hard bodily labor devolves on them."[11]

In Britain, where antislavery sentiment, galvanized by the sugar boycott, developed into a popular movement by the 1790s, concern over the condition of African slaves in the Atlantic followed in the wake of an earlier concern with Eastern slavery. We saw this in Chapter 2 with Mary Wollstonecraft's evocation of the condition of women of the harem to underscore her point about violated human rights and squandered human potential. Building on the belief in their own capacity as moral stewards whose performance of duties was necessary to human (and humane) progress, Wollstonecraft's abolitionist peers focused on sentimental depictions of enslaved mothers, a genre within abolitionist print culture that reached its first peak during the 1790s. Hannah More's 1788 poem "Slavery," which detailed the violation of the basic tenets of humanity inherent in the slave trade and held sacred by slave traders themselves, helped to create the genre. More was a member of London's intelligentsia before joining William Wilberforce's evangelical and abolitionist Clapham circle. Her graphic poem about a captured African woman, separated from her child, figured them as one flesh rent by sale:

> I see, by more than Fancy's mirror shewn,
> The burning village, and the blazing town:
> See the dire victim torn from social life,
> The shrieking babe, the agonizing wife!
> She, wretch forlorn! is dragg'd by hostile hands,
> To distant tyrants sold, in distant lands!
> Transmitted miseries, and successive chains,
> The sole sad heritage her child obtains!
> Ev'n this last wretched boon their foes deny,
> To weep together, or together die.
> By felon hands, by one relentless stroke,

See the fond links of feeling nature broke!
The fibres twisting round a parent's heart,
Torn from their grasp, and bleeding as they part.
Hold, murderers, hold! not aggravate distress;
Respect the passions you yourselves possess.

Extricating the child from the mother's grasp, the slave trader ripped apart the fibers connecting their hearts. More represented the desire of mother and child to remain connected as so fundamentally human that it would be recognizable even to the most hardened slave trader. Most important, she insisted that the violence she depicted was not simply by "Fancy's mirror shewn," that is to say, not simply the product of her imagination, but based on documentable fact.[12]

Much of this poetry remained in circulation during the 1820s and 1830s, but it took on new urgency as abolitionists reported eyewitness accounts and real-time legal cases of enslaved mothers and children forcibly separated and desperate women killing their infants to protect them from lifetimes of suffering. This was part of the effort, endorsed by the American Anti-Slavery Society, of putting the "peculiar and revolting" features of slavery before the public to argue on behalf of the slave's equality with the "freeborn subject." Poetry, as one scholar has noted, was an effort aimed at both consciousness-raising and activist community building.[13]

By the 1820s, building on the legacy of women's literary contributions and boycott activity, female abolitionists expressed an acute gender consciousness of their special moral and political obligations as Christian women to act on behalf of their enslaved sisters. The most obvious example of this was the emergence of "his and hers" antislavery medallions, both of which originated in England, that aimed to stir the empathy of the white viewer in gender-specific ways. In 1787, as we have seen, the Society for Effecting the Abolition of the Slave Trade (SEAST) produced an image of a kneeling, manacled enslaved man who asks, "Am I not a man and a brother?" As long as this was the main image of the enslaved, the message was not necessarily gender specific. A viewer of the image during the Age of Revolution could easily see in it both the suffering of a particular enslaved man and the generic suffering of enslaved people as a violation of humanity. But when, in 1826, the Birmingham, England, Ladies Society for the Relief of Negro Slaves put the figure of a kneeling woman on the cover of their first report with the caption, "Remember those in bonds, as bound with them; and them that suffer adversity, as being yourselves also in the body" (Heb. 13:3), both images assumed a gender particularism. Both images appealed to the gendered empathy of the white viewer to overcome the perceived differences of color and condition to sympathize with a brother or sister. The path to recognizing the humanity of the slave was first to recognize him or her as a fellow man or woman.[14]

Left unsaid was the implication that the abolitionist's embrace of the slave as brother or sister was a key proof of civilization and a foil to barbarism, either of the historic variety or in what abolitionists understood to be its contemporary stronghold in the East. To maintain the moral upper hand, as Joseph Gurney and other British critics of amelioration had noted, Western humanitarians needed to respect the sex distinction that separated barbaric peoples from civilized ones. Enslaved women needed to enjoy some of the privileges of white women, especially in respect of their bodies; at the very least, states claiming moral authority needed to be on the side of condemning the brutal treatment of enslaved mothers and their children.

"No Stranger May Intermeddle"

Yet for most abolitionists in the United States, slave mothers were not a particular focus of concern until the middle of the 1830s. During that decade, the special horrors of enslaved motherhood and the ability of white female abolitionists to empathize with and broadcast the pain of their "sisters" in bondage became the dominant refrain of abolitionist activism in the northern United States. Abolitionist women of both races emphasized slavery's violation of the intimate bond between mother and child and underscored in language reminiscent of legal and theological discussions of marriage that they were of one flesh and should not be torn asunder. To separate mother and child was to transgress against nature. This was but one of the particular violations of slavery upon women. In contrast, the separation of enslaved husbands and wives tended to be depicted as an injury against the natural rights of enslaved men.[15]

As abolitionists elaborated the exquisite suffering caused by slavery's disregard of maternal love and connection, they depicted the bond between mother and child as sacred. Depending on the poet's personal history, these literary depictions drew on experiences of constrained freedom or maternal loss or both. A slave mother's grief at her inability to protect her child became the suffering of a martyr, the trial that gave her struggle eschatological significance. Such depictions also sanctified motherhood, creating an ideal for all women rooted in the intense love and connection of mother and child, and with it the vulnerability of being undone by grief and loss. For free African American women, moreover, as Erica Dunbar has noted, mother-work extended to kin and community through mutual aid societies like the Daughters of Africa and included spiritual mentorship in church congregations.[16]

Elizabeth Margaret Chandler was the first American poet to address the subject of the physical violation of the slave mother's bond with her child. In addition to her Quaker sensibilities, Chandler brought her own experience with loss: her mother died when she was just one year old and her father, a New Jersey farmer turned Philadelphia physician, died when she was nine. In an 1831 essay, she coined the term "mental metempsychosis," an exercise in empathy she urged on readers to prompt them to action.[17] Using the first person in "The Slave Mother's Farewell," Chandler strove to "capture" the bodily manifestations of emotion much as More had done:

May God have mercy on thee, son, for man's stern heart hath none!
My gentle boy, my beautiful, my loved and only one!
I would the bitter tears that steep thy young and grief-doom'd head,
Were springing from a broken heart, that mourn'd thee with the dead.
And yet how often have I watch'd above thine infant sleep,
With love whose gushing tenderness strove vainly not to weep,
When starting through my timid heart, the thought that thou
couldst die,
Shot, even amidst a mother's bliss, a pang of agony.
My boy! my boy! Oh cling not thus around me in thy grief,
Thy mother's arm, thy mother's love, can yield thee no relief;
The tiger's bloody jaw hath not a gripe more fierce and fell
Than that which tears thee from my arms—thou who wert loved so well!
Farewell! farewell!—They tear thee hence!—and yet my heart beats on;
How can it bear the weight of life, when thou art from me gone?
Mine own! mine own! Yet cruel hands have barter'd thee for gold,
And torn thee, with a ruthless grasp, forever from my hold!

In Chandler's poem, the mother is unable to protect or keep the child she describes as "mine own" from the slave trader's cruel grasp. Ultimately, what abolitionists viewed as the Eastern genealogy of the slaveholder's barbarity ("the tiger's bloody jaw") and the commodification of her beautiful son ("barter'd . . . for gold") left her helpless to hold onto him.[18]

From her earliest writings, Chandler made use of "blood and tears" references, revealing both her familiarity with the language of the African American activist Richard Allen and perhaps, too, her father's medical profession. In an 1827 poem written to observe the July Fourth holiday, she described among the horrors of slavery the enslaved's shedding of "tears of blood," perhaps an allusion to Christ's sweating of blood at Gethsemane, the olive grove identified as the site of his agony before his betrayal. It was not a question of watering the land with the fluids of their laboring bodies but of an unnatural spectacle with divine overtones that testified to the great wrong of slavery and demanded the nation's atonement.[19]

Chandler was perhaps best known for poems that insisted on the moral imperative of abolitionism for white women, whose claims to a higher moral nature rested on the belief in the intrinsic virtue of their maternal duties. Her 1830 poem "The Kneeling Slave," inspired by an Englishwoman's gift of a seal bearing the image "Am I Not a Woman and a Sister," popularized the parallel gender construction of humanity captured in the Wedgwood medallions.[20] Her often-repeated mantra in "Think of Our Country's Glory" urged white American women to identify with the sufferings of the enslaved mother:

Think of the frantic mother
Lamenting for her child,
Till falling lashes smother
Her cries of anguish wild!
Shall we behold, unheeding,
Life's holiest feelings crushed?
When woman's heart is bleeding,
Shall woman's voice be hushed?[21]

One of the first African American poets to work in this emotional vein was Sarah Louisa Forten, the daughter of Philadelphia's influential free African American merchant and civil rights activist James Forten. Although neither motherless nor enslaved, Forten brought firsthand knowledge to her critique of American rhetoric about liberty. She consciously protected herself from harmful exposure to racism by secluding herself from casual interaction with white people, and she respectfully maintained the distance between her own experience as a free woman of color and that of her poetic subject.[22]

In "The Slave Girl's Address to Her Mother," Forten approached the slave mother's suffering as a daughter hoping to comfort her grieving parent. Although she urged her mother not to weep, the daughter-narrator seemingly lost sight of this goal as she recounted the sorrows and suffering of her people: "torn from our home, our kindred and our friends, / And in a stranger's land, our days to end." Friendless, and exiled from her homeland, the enslaved daughter was abandoned: "no heart feels for the poor, the bleeding slave; / No arm is stretched to rescue and to save." The hypocrisy of slavery in a land that boasted "all are free" left a "cruel stain" and provoked the daughter to remark cynically, "Freedom, what art thou?—nothing but a name." Contrasting the tangible and embodied injuries inflicted on enslaved people with the soaring rhetoric of liberty, Forten found the words to ring hollow.[23]

Forten questioned the presumption of Western Christian exceptionalism in "An Appeal to Women," published in the *Liberator* in 1834. In her "Appeal," Forten reminded white women that Christianity's reputation for moral goodness rested on divine assertions of "one blood." Did the white women of Forten's generation really embody the purported nobility of their Christianity? Did the United States?

> We are thy sisters,—God has truly said,
> That of one blood, the nations he has made.
> Oh, christian woman, in a christian land,
> Canst thou unblushing read this great command?[24]

One of the most popular white female poets of the 1830s, Hannah Flagg Gould, expressed what she imagined to be the enslaved mother's ambivalence about sustaining the life of a child doomed to slavery. In many of her poems, Gould unabashedly appropriated her enslaved subject's sufferings into the first person.[25] Herself motherless at an early age, Gould was also the author of a poem opposing Cherokee removal that featured a noble Cherokee chief protesting federal policy with righteous but dignified anger. Gould framed "The Slave Mother's Prayer" (1832) in the context of grueling field labor and tears "that wet the soil."

> I bend a form with ceaseless toil
> Consuming all the day;
> And raise an eye that wets the soil,
> As wears my life away.
>
> . . . How wretched must that mother be,
> (And I'm the hapless one,)
> Who begs an early grave of thee,
> To shield her only son!
> I would not that my boy were spared
> To curse his natal hour;
> To drag the chains his birth prepared
> Beneath unfeeling power.
> Then, ere the nursling at my breast
> Shall feel the tyrant's rod,
> O lay his little form at rest
> Beneath the quiet sod!

Gould's saintly enslaved mother prayed not only for the son whose suffering she hoped might be relieved by death, but for the sinful master who would eventually meet his maker. While Gould's sanctification of the enslaved mother smacked of a toxic white fantasy of the all-forgiving African American, it also claimed for her a moral and spiritual generosity and bigness of character that revealed the enslaved, rather than the enslaver, to be the true Christian.

By the time antislavery activists gathered in Philadelphia in 1833 to form the American Anti-Slavery Society (AAS), African American and white female poets had already clearly established the violations of enslaved mothers as one of the key wrongs against enslaved people. Convention leaders articulated their opposition to slavery as a violation of the universalism of "one blood" and anathema to "principles of natural justice," "our republican forms of government," "the Christian religion," and the "prosperity of the country." One hundred and fifty years after the Germantown petitioners denounced manstealing, Philadelphia activists denied that there was a difference between capturing Africans and enslaving Americans. "Every man has the right to his own body—to the products of his own labor—to the protection of law," they insisted, detailing the gross wrongs of "being treated by their fellow beings as marketable commodities—as goods and chattels—brute beasts; are plundered daily of the fruits of their toil without redress; really enjoying no constitutional nor legal protections from licentious or murderous outrages upon their persons; are ruthlessly torn asunder—the tender babe from the arms of its frantic mother—the heart-broken wife from her weeping husband—at the caprice or pleasure of irresponsible tyrants." They also offered warm, if condescending, encouragement to antislavery women on the grounds that "one million of their Colored Sisters were pining in abject servitude," holding out the example of British women's successful sugar boycott as a model of female activism.[26]

Three days after the founding of the AAS, a group of white and Black abolitionist women gathered in the Philadelphia schoolroom of one of their members to constitute a new organization for women to end slavery and restore to people of color "their inalienable rights." The Philadelphia Female Anti-Slavery Society (PFAS) included women who endorsed the purchase of free labor produce as the "surest means of abolishing slavery." Along with their role as consumers, the women highlighted their duty as Christians, a conjunction that would eventually evolve into concern for the special responsibility of female activists and the plight of female slaves.[27]

The protections owed to mothers soon became an important unifying principle for antislavery women. During the New York Anti-Slavery Convention of American Women held on May 9–12, 1837, support for motherhood emerged as a political strategy—a compromise among abolitionist women who differed on how best to claim their activism—rather than simply as an emotionally irresistible subject. Nearly two hundred abolitionist women, Black and white, from the Northeast and mid-Atlantic, gathered for four days in New York City. The emphasis on motherhood as a political tactic appeared in the motion of Abby Ann Newbold Cox, known to her colleagues as Mrs. A. L. Cox. The Philadelphia-born Cox was one of the vice presidents of the convention and was married to a founder of the AAS, the physician Abraham Liddon Cox. She had offered a conservative dissent the previous day against the resolutions of Angelina Grimké and Lydia Maria Child that stressed a woman's undisputed moral right to speak publicly and act politically. Boston abolitionists knew her as a racist who tried to prevent women of color from joining the New York Female Anti-Slavery Society.[28] Cox was a clear example of the broad continuum of nineteenth-century racism in which a woman harboring anti-Black sentiments might nonetheless engage in serious antislavery activism.

Hoping to unify conference factions, Cox emphasized women's key role as mothers as the foundation for their political activism. This move hearkened back to the conservative legacy of Wollstonecraft's maternal framework. Cox underscored the importance of inviolable motherhood for claims on behalf of the humanity of enslaved women that could overcome divisions of race and class among women as a group: "That there is no class of women to whom the anti-slavery cause makes so direct and powerful an appeal as to mothers; and that they are solemnly urged by all the blessings of their own and their children's freedom, and by all the contrasted bitterness of the slave-mother's condition, to lift up their hearts to God on behalf of the captive, as often as they pour them out over their own children in a joy with which 'no stranger may intermeddle.'"[29]

Cox drew from Proverbs 14:10: "The heart knoweth his own bitterness; and a stranger doth not intermeddle with his joy," which spoke of intimate experiences so subjective that no stranger could truly comprehend them. In addition to her knowledge of scripture as a source for this passage, Cox may also have been familiar with Ann Mason Freeman's spiritual memoir, *A Memoir of the Life and Ministry of Ann Freeman*, published in London in 1826 and republished in Exeter, New Hampshire, in 1831. Freeman had come to prominence as a Bible Christian preacher in England before being drawn to Quakerism and relocating with her husband to Dublin. Freeman used this phrase to describe the private joys of domestic and familial connection, a meaning Cox clearly applied to enslaved women. For Freeman, a woman's intimate knowledge of the people under her care in her household gave her religious authority over them.[30]

Yet it would be incorrect to conclude that the focus on motherhood was simply a gambit to bring conservative reformers into the antislavery tent. In fact, its inclusion among the human rights violated by slavery supplied actual common ground. Female abolitionists as diverse in their views as Abby Cox, Abby Kelley, Angelina Grimké, Sarah Mapps Douglass, Frances Watkins (Harper), and Sojourner Truth all focused on motherhood as the essential case illustrating slavery's violation of humanity. The maternal tears of the enslaved woman could mobilize women and men across race, class, and political lines. Lamenting the sorrows of the enslaved mother in this way became an important unifying feature of abolitionist activism.

The blood and tears of enslaved women did more than dramatically embellish the spectacle of motherhood, however; they broadcast the claim that the wombs of enslaved women should be spaces of liberty, and they testified to the materiality of familial belonging, comparable to the laborer's blood and tears in Allen's claim to national belonging. An enslaved woman did not simply produce the fluids—blood, tears, and milk—that testified to her humanity; she also produced the children who represented biopolitical and economic value for enslavers. The poetic rendering of the slave mother's bodily fluids and clinging infant pointed to motherhood as a physical as well as emotional state, generative of belonging, much like Allen's claims about laborers "watering" the land.[31]

The focusing of white women's empathy on enslaved mothers, while self-serving, occurred within a context of circumscribed possibilities for expressing emotional connection more broadly across the color line. Some of this constraint reflected common European views of white people's embodiment of civilization as including space for civilized Christian women to express virtuous empathy for the downtrodden. But empathy expressed across the divide of gender as well as race raised uncomfortable questions for nineteenth-century would-be reformers about the moral integrity of white women's humanitarian appeal. The only appropriate focus for white women's empathy, some of these critics might have argued, was on enslaved women and children. For a white woman to express too much compassion for Black men, especially those who were physically in their prime, threatened to undermine her claim to speak from a perch of virtuous respectability. The connection between African American men and white women was virtually unrepresentable and nearly inadmissible in Anglo-American public life. The burning of Pennsylvania Hall in Philadelphia in 1838 by a white anti-abolitionist mob, discussed in Chapter 5, spoke to the power of this taboo. The mob, which pelted the hall with rocks and threatened the multiracial gathering of abolitionists with additional violence, prompted white and Black abolitionists to flee the hall together. The sight of white women and African American men leaving the hall arm in arm was enough to drive the crowd to arson.[32]

The assertion of white women's bond with enslaved women on the basis of their common womanhood and motherhood, in contrast, was a conservative appeal on behalf of the slave that stayed carefully within the bounds of white female propriety and left undisturbed the repressed possibilities of relationships between Black men and white women. White women simply could not claim to feel too much on behalf of enslaved men—it violated too many taboos, touched too closely on white fears about slavery and abolition generally and about African American men specifically. To declare oneself to be a passionate advocate of an enslaved man's rights would have been to diminish one's moral clout as a respectable white woman. Indeed, despite this deeply internalized discretion by abolitionist women, anti-abolitionist propagandists condemned their opponents as "amalgamationists" depicting white women in cartoons as the partners of outlandishly dressed and outrageously comported African American men (Figure 5).

A month after Cox unified the women at the New York convention using the framework of motherhood, a small group of female abolitionists, strongly influenced by Hicksite Quakerism, reprised the claim of humanity as a single standard for men and women alike. Reacting to the Boston Pastoral Letter of June 28, 1837, in which a gathering of ministers denounced female abolitionists

Figure 5. Edward Williams Clay, *An Amalgamation Waltz*, 1839. Smithsonian National Museum of American History, https://americanhistory.si.edu/collections/search/object/nmah_325555.

who addressed mixed-sex audiences (revealing that, in addition to taboos around their connection to Black men, white women's public proximity to white men was also problematic), abolitionist women vigorously asserted their moral equality as the basis for a yet unrealized political and legal equality. As Angelina Grimké put it: "All moral beings have essentially the same rights and the same duties, whether they be male or female." Somewhat more pithily, she observed "what ever it is morally right for man to do is morally right for a woman to do."[33]

But there were even more sharply pointed declarations of political and participatory equality by Sarah Grimké in *Letters on the Equality of the Sexes* (1837) about the way marriage enshrined the legal disabilities of women in custom and practice, giving them an appearance of having been determined by nature. When Catharine Beecher condemned the sisters' public speaking as undermining the domestic foundation of woman's moral authority, Angelina Grimké's response left little room for the second-class citizenship of wives. She declared that human rights were not founded on sex: "I recognize no rights but human rights—I know nothing of men's rights and women's rights; for in Jesus Christ there is neither male nor female." The desire for a single standard of moral conduct—a position Grimké shared with Enlightenment feminists such as Wollstonecraft who grounded their universalism in dissenting Protestantism—led her in this instance to de-emphasize any special gendered axis of connection with the enslaved woman.[34]

God might have been the source of universal humanity, but motherhood became the sine qua non of gendered humanity and an important political focus of abolitionist claims. Even those activists like Angelina Grimké who insisted on a single standard of morality still made the case for abolition by pointing to the unique vulnerability and suffering of enslaved women, especially acute for those who were mothers. For Grimké, the argument about the special circumstances of enslaved mothers followed the biopolitics of American slavery: the reproduction of the slave labor force occurred through birth rather than through the transatlantic traffic in Africans. It struck her as ludicrous that, with the 1808 ban, protections for African-descended mothers and their children applied only to those born in Africa rather than to those born in North America. "It will be, and that very soon, clearly perceived and fully acknowledged by all the virtuous and the candid," she declared, "that in *principle* it is as sinful to hold a human being in bondage who has been born in Carolina, as one who has been born in Africa." The universality of birthright, for Grimké, trumped the national jurisdictions and birthplace that had circumscribed Jefferson's 1806 human rights declaration.

Grimké also saw the uses of the abolitionist appeal to white mothers. In her closely argued *Appeal to the Christian Women of the South*, which stated that

American slavery was in no way justified by the Mosaic law regulating servitude among the Jews, she provided southern white women with a test of their adherence to the Golden Rule. "I appeal to you, my friends, as mothers; Are you willing to enslave your children?" She chastised her imagined white southern reader with the hypocrisy of her position: "why, if as has often been said, slaves are happier than their masters, freed of the cares and perplexities of providing for themselves and their families? why not place *your children* in the way of being supported without your having the trouble to provide for them, or they for themselves?"[35] Grimké exhorted her female readers to think of themselves as capable of political influence and action on behalf of the enslaved rather than as powerless and less culpable than their menfolk. She cited the bravery of women from the Bible and throughout history to inspire her southern white readers, making special note of the Quaker poet and reformer Elizabeth Heyrick and the British female sugar boycotters whose actions brought an end to the transatlantic slave trade.

Grimké retired from the abolitionist speakers' circuit in 1838 after marrying fellow abolitionist Theodore Weld, who had himself withdrawn from lecturing after suffering permanent damage to his voice. Together with her sister Sarah, they set up a farm household in New Jersey run on Grahamite principles of a low-stimulation diet and abstinence from slave labor produce. Enduring a difficult pregnancy, she gave birth to her first child, a son, in 1839, a second son in 1841, and a daughter in 1844. In 1848, at age forty-three, she suffered a miscarriage. The years following the children's births were dominated by physical pain caused by a prolapsed uterus and a hernia. Relief came in the form of a belt rigged to hold her body in place so that she could do her household work and walk for short distances. She later turned to the sitz baths prescribed by a hydropathic doctor. The intimate nature of her bodily affliction kept her out of the public eye and limited her activism for the rest of her life. Her disability was known to her sister and to friends like the physician Harriot Hunt and Sarah Mapps Douglass, herself a hernia sufferer, but was hidden from public view, leaving some to conclude that she had abandoned the cause of abolition.[36]

Grimké Weld handed off her spot on the abolitionist lecture circuit to fellow Quaker Abby Kelley, a teacher from Lynn, Massachusetts, who had grown up on a farm in Worcester, Massachusetts. Kelley had become part of Lynn's reform community, known for its dedication to Grahamite health principles, peace, and temperance. Lynn was also home to Mary Gove, who was just emerging during the early 1830s as an important health reformer who focused on women's health. After joining the Lynn Female Anti-Slavery Society and becoming its secretary, Kelley collected signatures for antislavery petitions. At Kelley's invitation, Angelina Grimké addressed her first "promiscuous" audience in Lynn, riling the Boston ministers into denouncing public speaking by women. Kelley also attended the Anti-Slavery Convention of American Women in New York in 1837 and the Grimké-Weld wedding in Philadelphia just nights before the ill-fated Pennsylvania Hall was destroyed by angry anti-abolitionist mobs in 1838.

After spending a week with the Grimké-Welds in New Jersey, Kelley began her own speaking career in 1839, traveling to conservative towns throughout rural Connecticut. With the support of her sister Olive and the Connecticut surgeon and abolitionist Erasmus Darwin Hudson, Kelley began speaking to small audiences, passionately denouncing the hypocrisy of Americans who had fought for freedom during the Revolutionary War only to use it to "snatch the babe from the arms of its father or mother," or "tear husband and wife asunder." She condemned those who would weep for the helpless victims of barbaric Eastern practices that brought infants and widows to early graves but failed to recognize the tragic fate of enslaved infants and widows in their own country.[37]

During this tour, Kelley faced animosity from two sources: conservative ministers who opposed giving women public platforms, and those hostile to her advocacy for enslaved African Americans. When she shared the podium with James Lindsay Smith, a refugee from slavery in Virginia who had escaped to Philadelphia, an angry group of proslavery protesters disfigured the carriage horse belonging to their traveling companion. Some of the anger may have been triggered by Kelley's pitch: she combined a gendered appeal to white empathy for enslaved mothers with an insistence upon a divinely ordained moral universalism, noting in an 1840 editorial in the *Anti-slavery Standard* that the human mind was identical "whether enveloped in a black or white, a male or female exterior."[38]

As we have seen in Chapter 5, the AAS divided over several differences in philosophy and strategy in May 1840, with the question of women's public role in the movement, provoked by Kelley's nomination to the business committee, as the proximate cause of the split. After Kelley's supporters won the vote to retain her on the business committee, Lewis Tappan led a walkout of delegates opposed to her presence. The protestors formed the alternative American and Foreign Anti-Slavery Society, convinced that effective advocacy for the slave meant avoiding what they saw as the ancillary issue of women's right to speak in public.

Upon leaving New York for a convention in New Haven, Kelley quickly learned that some abolitionist men deemed her physical presence to be a distraction of biblical proportions. Henry G. Ludlow, a minister who had led the Spring Street, New York, congregation to endorse immediate abolition, had himself been the victim of angry anti-abolition mobs in 1834. He had also supported the Grimké sisters, but after the AAS split he became hysterical as he tried to describe the threat that Kelley posed. After the meeting over which he presided voted to hear Kelley speak, Ludlow argued that women had no business leaving the nursery to "lord it over men" by speaking in public. The danger, as he saw it, evoked Adam's fall from Garden of Eden: "She beguiles and blinds men by her smiles and her bland, winning voice," making them incapable of "right and efficient action." He decried "the magic influence of Miss Kelley's voice and beauty," insisting that "men had not the strength to resist woman's appeal." After stomping out of the meeting, Ludlow returned to make a heated denunciation of the "sorcery of a woman's tongue" thrown around his heart and a defiant refusal to submit to "PETTICOAT GOVERNMENT." Ludlow succeeded in convincing the assembly to deny Kelley and every other woman at the convention the right to speak.[39]

Ironically, as Ludlow's hyperbolic language revealed, the woman he wished to silence was a powerful speaker—one of the most commanding white abolitionist speakers of either sex to take the stage. Her voice could be heard over the rumble of men's voices without losing its pleasant tone, and she had charismatic appeal. Ludlow's argument, that he found her impossible to resist, was one of the reasons she enjoyed such success on the speaker's circuit. Despite Kelley's insistence that her right to speak derived from an egalitarian universalism of rights and duties, her ability to draw audiences depended in part on the spectacle of her white femaleness in public.

Disgruntled abolitionist men were the least of Kelley's problems, however. As she discovered in Cornwall Bridge, Connecticut, in 1840, drunken anti-abolitionist agitators were potentially life threatening. At one lecture, she reported to her colleague Dr. Hudson, a protestor hurled a full bottle of rum that shattered just below her. On a subsequent evening, as she prepared to speak to a small assembly, she was taken aback when a drunken man entered the room with a club, shouting "Where's the damn nigger bitch that's going to lecture here?" He proceeded to smash his way through the audience to Kelley's oil lamp, plunging the room into darkness and forcing the assembly to flee. A near repeat performance by the same agitator the following night, this time with a rifle, forced the group to seek safety in the home of an ally.[40]

Kelley's participation in the successful 1842 Rhode Island campaign to prevent the new state constitution from expanding suffrage only to white men provoked the most violent response to her still emergent career on the speaker's tour. Although not her first experience sharing the podium with an African American man, it was her first time working closely with Frederick Douglass, and it was his inaugural speaking tour. Hostile crowds shouted "Nigger" and pelted Kelley and her entourage with stones and rotten eggs. The scene after the 1842 anniversary convention in New York City was much the same, with an angry crowd throwing oranges and eggs at the departing abolitionists, telling them to take the projectiles back to their Black wives, and labeling them "White niggers."[41]

Kelley gave special emphasis to the suffering of enslaved women in her public presentations. Her networks with other abolitionists, including the women of PFAS involved in caring for refugees, makes it likely that this was less the work of her own imagination than of information passed from refugees themselves. Summoning the passion for which she was known and withstanding the near daily insults and threats of violence, Kelley developed new techniques. Borrowing heavily from Chandler's methods of "metempsychosis," of mentally transporting herself into the material circumstances of an enslaved person, she explained to the New Hampshire abolitionist Nathaniel Rogers how she steeled herself to face a hostile public by imagining herself within the body of the suffering slave:

> I sit down in the cool of the day, alone with none but God to hold communion with, and in the exercise of love to him, become myself the slave—when at such a moment I feel the fetters wearing away the flesh and grating on my bare ankle bone, when I feel the naked cords of my neck shrinking away from the rough edge of the iron collar, when my flesh quivers beneath the lash, till, in anguish, I feel portions of it cut from my back; or when I see my aged and feeble mother driven away and scourged, and then the brutish and drunken overseer lay his ferocious grasp upon the person of my sister and drag her to his den of pollutions—ah!

Following this train of thought, she witnessed in the imagined, violated enslaved woman "the fires of liberty going out in her bosom and the light of intellect gradually giving place to the blank of idiocy, and she becoming a mere plantation brute." Kelley likened slavery's degradation of Black intellect to the impact of the corrupt authority of "Doctors of Divinity" over their white northern congregations. Instead of inspiring moral courage, ministers discouraged their congregants from taking a stand against slavery. Their moral obstruction not only compounded the slave's victimization but served to exploit northern churchgoers, which Kelley compared to picking away at their flesh and bones and imprisoning their immortal souls.[42]

Privately ruminating on this spiral of wrongdoing as preparation for public appearances, Kelley claimed, moved her to the strongest possible representations of slave suffering and condemnations of southern slave owning and northern antipathy. The pain and trauma of enslavement, she acknowledged, could not easily be represented in the spoken word. For Kelley, this meant "we must resort to the expedients of barbarous nations and express ourselves by significant signs, speaking through eloquent gesticulations . . . we must do this until we can invent a language that is equal to the subject."[43] Passionate arguments on behalf of enslaved women did not protect Kelley from violent protests by people offended by her very presence in public meetings. At one Connecticut lecture in September 1840, a local minister condemned her publicly as a "jezebel" for traveling with male companions, ending her chances of drawing sympathetic audiences.[44]

Having survived the early ordeals in Connecticut and Rhode Island, and the movement's split into exclusionary and open factions, Kelley began traveling more widely, organizing districts and preparing the way for other speakers. She became known as an excellent front woman because she could enter a neutral district and warm it up. During 1842–1843, she traveled and spoke with Douglass in upstate New York, but as he became more acclaimed as a speaker, she often traveled alone. Kelley's usual routine in a small city was to spend a few days paying personal visits to the homes of likely patrons. It was for this reason that she despised campaigning in New York City, where a day of trekking around on foot across the vast expanse of the city might yield nothing if potential sponsors were not home. Once she had generated a sufficient network to book a hall (often a church) and attract a decent-sized audience, overcoming or circumventing the objections of conservative ministers whose antislavery politics she had denounced, she began a series of abolitionist meetings. She was especially successful in rural districts and small towns, where she carefully coordinated her meetings to respect the rhythms of seasonal agricultural labor. No sensible antebellum activist would have tried to gather an assembly on an evening during the fall harvest or spring planting.

When Kelley took the stage, her goal was to stir her audience to convert to abolitionism, much as a revival preacher might attempt to move his audience to choose the path to salvation. She offered passionate denunciations of the southern slave power, the complicity of churches, and the immorality of maintaining a political union with slaveholders. On at least one occasion, she interrupted a religious service with an uninvited lecture on church corruption. Her speeches included excerpts from letters written by fellow abolitionists and the singing of hymns to stir the crowd.[45]

Kelley also pursued the twin goals of raising money and strengthening abolitionist networks. She used meetings as opportunities to sell subscriptions to abolitionist publications like the *Anti-slavery Bugle*, the *Liberator*, or one of fellow activist Stephen Foster's pamphlets. She moved easily among white and Black abolitionists, consolidating her friendship with Sarah Mapps Douglass and Douglass's photographer brother Robert Jr. by having him take a daguerreotype for a lithograph that could be distributed in activist circles. If all went well and Kelley gained political and financial momentum in a particular county, she might call in one of the movement's big draws: the freeborn African American Charles Remond, or the former slaves William Wells Brown or Frederick Douglass.[46]

After secretly marrying Stephen Foster in 1845 and becoming pregnant, Kelley took a break from the speaker's circuit. For ten months after her daughter's birth in May 1847, she remained at their farm in Worcester, Massachusetts, while Foster continued to travel. As she reported to Foster, she developed a bond with her infant that she suspected was unique to her role as mother and that she expressed with language that echoed her descriptions of the connections between enslaved mothers and their children:

> She has so thoroughly entwined herself about me that I fear it would rend me in pieces to take her away—It is not to be expected you can feel as I do—you have not been with her constantly for nearly four months and watched her every look and heard her every breath; some intelligence dawning upon her and expanding every hour—she does not look up to you as to me, so imploringly for her food and the supplying of all her wants, reminding me constantly of her entire dependence, and of her incapacity to defend herself from whatever wrongs she might suffer, and that I am her natural guardian and under the most sacred obligations to make her happy.

In response to Foster's urging that she leave the baby to come visit him on the road, she demurred, perhaps out of the fear of another pregnancy, justifying her decision using the language of maternal love: "there must always be a vacuum where our little one is not—The love I bear her is trifling compared with that which I bear for her father, but I should feel her absence much."[47]

Yet, unlike Angelina Grimké, Kelley did return to the speaker's circuit. She was one of the only female abolitionists on the road who had a very young child. Jane Elizabeth Hitchcock Jones of Oneida, an abolitionist speaker assigned to the western districts and expecting a baby herself, thought less of Kelley for leaving her infant daughter behind. Indeed, despite her professed awareness of her special bond with her daughter, Kelley could hardly be accused of being a sentimental mother herself, even though sentimental motherhood was essential to her ability to connect with audiences. Throughout her leave from the circuit, Kelley remained deeply invested in abolitionist politics, using her daughter Alla's nap time to catch up on reading and correspondence. In May 1848, when Alla was barely a year old, she plunged back into her work with gusto. Her husband and a coterie of family, friends, and hired people cared for her daughter in Worcester while Kelley traveled to upstate New York, New York City, Philadelphia, rural Pennsylvania, and Ohio. She sent regular letters home inquiring after her daughter's well-being and periodically visited, as in August 1848, when she stayed with Alla while Stephen joined Lucy Stone and William Wells Brown at a series of meetings. Although her letters did not reveal that the separations left her bereft, her pale and sickly appearance at one particular event in 1849 provoked Stone to ask about her health. Kelley responded that "when I left my little daughter I [felt] as though I should die. But I have done it for the sake of the mothers whose babies are sold away from them."[48]

When Alla came of age to write her own letters and expressed longing for her absent mother, Kelley's responses were brisk and matter-of-fact. In many ways, she exceeded Wollstonecraft's vision of an ideal rational mother: Wollstonecraft imagined a woman suffused with delicate and feminine emotions whose commitment to motherhood had overlaid these with a calm, dutiful, and rational exterior. Kelley, in contrast, was rational to the core and went about her abolitionist business with a laser-like focus. Communicating to her young daughter that she would be longer from home than she originally planned, she told Alla that she would "preach to these wicked men, and make them good, so that they would let the poor slave mothers go home to their children." Anticipating the lonely girl's complaint, she added, "do you often think of the little slave girls who can never see their dear mothers again?" Alla was not yet five years old when she received this message from her mother.[49]

Abolitionists and allied women's rights advocates continued to focus strategically on the special embodied and emotional suffering of enslaved women during the 1840s and 1850s. The Providence Anti-Slavery Society collected the essays of several prominent writers and activists around the theme of expanding liberty, dubbing the publication *Liberty Chimes* (Providence, 1845). Frances H. Green, a prominent writer of fiction and of domestic how-to literature, was one of the contributors. Green's essay "The Slave-Wife" retold a story she claimed to have been told by a male informant about a heartbroken man named Laco, a former slave who had reached safety in Canada after burying his saintly, light-skinned wife, Clusy, a victim of her master's sexual abuse. Green's notional male informant commented on Laco's "noble intellect," but dwelled on the enslaved man's physical and phrenological attributes in ways that were both racist and out of bounds for a female reporter: "he was, I think, as fine a specimen of the physical man, as I ever knew. Tall, muscular, and every way well-proportioned, he had the large expansion of chest and shoulders that are seen in the best representations of Hercules. He was quite black, the skin soft and glossy; but the features had none of the revolting characteristics which are supposed by some to be inseparable from the African visage. On the contrary they were remarkably fine—the nose aquiline—the mouth even handsome—the forehead singularly high and broad."[50] Proving himself the equal of his favorable phrenology, Laco recounted the story of his dead wife, Clusy, describing her as appearing white: "At least no one would suspect that she had any African blood in her veins, Some have said that the only trace of it was in her eyes; and they were large, and soft, and brilliant, although very black." Clusy retained her purity despite the pressures of her abusive circumstances, shedding torrents of blood from repeated whippings severe enough to prompt the stillbirth of her child, fathered by Laco. Among the many morals of the tale was slavery's failure to respect marriage bonds, represented by Laco's sad disbelief that Clusy's master had failed to acknowledge her as Laco's lawful wife.[51]

Several white male poets, including one of the era's most famous, addressed issues of alienation, sexual exploitation, and the impossible contradictions of enslaved motherhood. In Quaker abolitionist John Greenleaf Whittier's "Farewell of a Virginia Slave Mother" (1843), a mother mourns her stolen daughters' transport to southern rice plantations, where the labor regime is enforced by the whip, insects torment, and the sun burns through the sickly moist air to scorch laborers. With her children beyond the comfort of their mother's arms, the mother grieves that "no mother's eye is near them, there no mother's ear can hear them," and tries to take comfort in the thought of God's love for them. In Whittier's dirge, the bereft mother laments their separation not only from family but also from their childhood home. In an allusion to sexual exploitation that would have been unusual in a poem by a woman, Whittier's enslaved mother noted that her daughters would toil "through the weary day," only to become "the spoiler's prey" at night. The Philadelphian John Collins, a fellow Quaker and the lithographer for Samuel Morton's racist account of divergent cranial capacities, *Crania Americana* (1839), based his "The Slave Mother" on an account reported in the abolitionist press of a fugitive woman's successful effort to save her infant by denying it. Only the recourse to abandonment enabled this mother to escape to freedom and reunite with her baby.[52]

Like their white allies, free African American women in the North focused on violated motherhood as one of the main evils of slavery, and in doing so revealed the constraints of their own position as activists. In communities of northern free Blacks, the "woman question" turned more on the issue of respectability, a condition of class rooted in bodily refinement and self-regard that nonetheless required some acknowledgment from white people. This recognition eluded many aspiring free Black people despite educational attainment, multiple generations of freedom, and public reputations for commercial and intellectual integrity.[53] As an outgrowth of the pursuit of this elusive respectability, African American women faced constraints on their public leadership and speech, albeit differently from their white counterparts. At least two problems emerged for female speakers. First, to speak candidly about sexual politics among

African Americans was to risk the larger campaign for racial respectability, already beleaguered in most states as white male suffrage advanced at the cost of free Black political and civic rights. For some African American male activists, women's public activism and the discussion of the sexual nature of enslaved women's exploitation jeopardized the appearance of female propriety and delicacy in ways that reflected badly on Black people. Such was the hostile outcry from African American men about Maria Stewart's candid assessment of African American gender politics that she retired in 1833 after only a brief speaking career to take a behind-the-scenes role in the antislavery movement. Second, if a woman's integrity, dignity, and even survival were under constant assault, it was nearly impossible to translate her strategies into a white middle-class idiom. The challenge to conventions of polite respectability appeared less egregious if a reported ordeal of violated chastity (rape) was also one of distressed motherhood.[54]

If gender conformity provided evidence for universal humanity, what happened when enslaved people failed to conform to white gender norms? The gender-bending escape of Ellen Craft and her husband, William, provides an example of the problems with claims to universal humanity based on the alleged universality and legibility of gender norms. The wealthy British Quaker abolitionist Sarah Jane Dymond found it hard to imagine the exigency of survival for enslaved people like William Craft. Craft was on tour in England with Ellen, speaking about the couple's use of "deception" to escape slavery. Dressed in men's clothes, Ellen passed as a white man, making it possible for the couple to travel north undetected. Their ruse struck Dymond not as a brilliant play on gendered expectations but a potential source of moral corruption. She disapproved of the couple's flaunting of their tactics while on the road, as "by the constant repetition of the tales of the deception & artifice they used in making their escape not only be the means of propagating the arts of deceiving, but so habituate themselves ["themselves" crossed out] to them, that they will lose the perception of what is truth." Dymond righteously shared her concern with the Crafts, but "they were very full of excusing themselves by stating that the system of Slavery was in itself one of deception, & that they had been brought up in it," she reported to her correspondent Anne Rhoads. "It is a horrible and startling idea, but too true!"[55]

African American activists found it frustrating to ally with white women, who so often disappointed with their timidity, racism, and capricious decisions to push for the rights of "their sex," by which they often meant the issues that most concerned white women. As Sarah Mapps Douglass later recalled, her mother, the abolitionist Grace Bustill Douglass, endured racist treatment even from Philadelphia Quakers who professed to be abolitionists. The senior Douglass, who attended the Arch Street Weekly Meeting, found herself sitting alone in a pew as a consequence of the meeting rule forbidding Blacks and whites to sit together. When they learned of this policy at the Arch Street Meeting, Sarah and Angelina Grimké were appalled and sat with Douglass and her daughter Sarah in protest.

Sarah Mapps Douglass later described her own coming to consciousness about racism and slavery as a shift from an intermittent perception of slavery's brutality to a newfound awareness of shared vulnerability. One part of that journey was her acquaintance with Elizabeth Chandler's poetry, which she admired and appreciated. Douglass's April 1832 "Moonlight," published in the *Liberator* under the name "Zillah," alluded to her sorrow over the deaths of a beloved mentor and beloved friends, as well as to the loss of those who had emigrated to a "foreign land." That same year, as she sparred publicly with supporters of colonization, Douglass quoted from the English travel writer Anna Brownell Jameson, "we must feel deeply before we can act rightly; from that absorbing, heart-rendering compassion for ourselves springs a deeper sympathy for others, and from a sense of our weakness and our own upbraidings arises a disposition to be indulgent, to forbear, to forgive." Douglass acknowledged how slow she had been to embrace an obligation to fight for the slave, comparing her insufficient response to a failure to imagine the slave's vulnerability as her own:

> One short year ago, how different were my feelings on the subject of slavery! It is true, the wail of the captive sometimes came to my ear in the midst of my happiness, and caused my heart to bleed for his wrongs; but, alas! the impression was as evanescent as the early cloud and morning dew. I had formed a little world of my own, and cared not to move beyond its precincts. But how was the scene changed when I beheld the oppressor lurking on the border of my own peaceful home! I saw his iron hand stretched forth to seize me as his prey, and the cause of the slave became my own. I started up, and with one mighty effort threw from me the lethargy which had covered me as a mantle for years; and determined, by the help of the Almighty, to use every exertion in my power to elevate the character of my wronged and neglected race.[56]

The historian Gay Cima interprets this passage as Douglass performing her own act of metempsychosis, the work of attempting to inhabit the condition of the slave for the purpose of enabling effective abolitionist activism.[57] It seems likely, however, that Douglass's decision to make the slave's cause her own might have been triggered by a particular traumatic incident—perhaps the violent reprisals in the aftermath of the Nat Turner Rebellion, discussed in Chapter 7, or a kidnapping.[58]

What Douglass did not say, but which appears in other correspondence, is that she had thoroughly internalized her mother's experience with racism at the Arch Street Meeting, as well as her mother's activist engagement and aspirations for her daughter to become a teacher. Grace Douglass was a founding member of PFAS, which Sarah subsequently joined in 1836. After initially running a school with the financial backing of PFAS, Sarah asserted her own competence and independence in 1840 and shook off their management. The relationship with the organization subsequently endured several ups and downs, with PFAS pledging one thousand dollars in 1847 to purchase a stove for her schoolroom (where the members often held meetings) but retracting their payments of the room's rent in 1849 when enrollments declined. Douglass's mission as a teacher of Black children and public lecturer for lay audiences was central to her sense of self-worth.[59]

Douglass's suffering from a hernia and her later unhappy marriage to the Reverend William Douglass spurred her conviction that anatomical and physiological knowledge was a path to Black female self-sovereignty. Her subsequent career as a medical student, teacher of science to African American women, and public lecturer on health, hygiene, and anatomy suggests that she had connected the particular traumas of enslaved and free women to a lack of knowledge and a lack of access to care. The remedy she offered was to educate young women about their bodies as a source of self-protection and a disavowal of the scientific racism that demeaned them.[60]

As the historian April Haynes has noted, Douglass's public embrace of anatomical knowledge by Black women flew in the face of the emerging racial politics of purity. By the 1850s white women were becoming more conservative in their advocacy of rigid standards focused on purity as a white possession rather than as an active virtue. In this context of constraint, it became more difficult for Black women to speak about slavery and retain a claim to respectability, particularly if they sought to testify firsthand to its evils.[61] Harriet Jacobs epitomized this challenge when she decided to tell the story of her own sexual exploitation while enslaved—a public acknowledgment of a loss of chastity—without relinquishing her claim to virtue. Others skirted the issue or avoided U.S. audiences. During her successful speaking tour in England in 1859, the free African American Sarah Remond boldly exposed southern "concubinage" in ways that would have been more difficult for her in the United States.[62]

Yet there were other ways that African American women could focus on the violation of enslaved women's personhood without stirring controversy among antebellum audiences. Poems about their suffering provided indisputable evidence of the physical manifestations of an enslaved mother's grief and hinted at other traumas. Consider some stanzas from Frances Ellen Watkins Harper's "The Slave Mother," part of a collection of her original poems published in 1854. The poem was likely inspired by her encounters with female refugees from slavery, but perhaps was also inflected by her orphan's grief at the loss of her own mother:

Heard you that shriek? It rose
So wildly on the air,
It seemed as if a burden'd heart
Was breaking in despair.

Saw you those hands so sadly clasped—
The bowed and feeble head—
The shuddering of that fragile form—
That look of grief and dread?

Saw you the sad, imploring eye?
Its every glance was pain,
As if a storm of agony
Were sweeping through the brain.

She is a mother pale with fear,
Her boy clings to her side,
And in her kirtle vainly tries
His trembling form to hide.

He is not hers, although she bore
For him a mother's pains;
He is not hers, although her blood
Is coursing through his veins!

He is not hers, for cruel hands
May rudely tear apart
The only wreath of household love
That binds her breaking heart.

His lightest word has been a tone
Of music round her heart,
Their lives a streamlet blent in one—
Oh, Father! must they part?

No marvel, then, these bitter shrieks
Disturb the listening air:

She is a mother, and her heart
Is breaking in despair.

Watkins compelled her readers to bear virtual witness with their eyes and ears to the condition of the enslaved mother's entire body: her shrieks, her clasped hands, her bowed head, her "shuddering fragile form," her eye, and her brain. In this, as in most abolitionist poems and hymns about enslaved mothers, the mother's grief has dramatic physical manifestations. Her tears, her broken heart, the sundering of her blood connection to her child (with "her blood . . . coursing through his veins") all testify to emotional violation, but also hint at systemic sexual violence. Despite the mother's birth pains, that coursing blood, and their blended lives, the narrator's voice three times declares "he is not hers."[63]

Whether white or African American, poets generally sidestepped the issue of the enslaved child's paternity, although some did portray enslaved fathers as frustrated and heartbroken. With the exception of a handful of bold abolitionist women (Sarah Remond, Harriet Jacobs, and Angelina Grimké) who broke with conventions of respectability to speak of slavery's systemic sexual exploitation of women as "pollution," "ruin," and "concubinage," most women focused instead on the bodily expressions of the enslaved mother's grief. Depictions of enslaved women's physical expressions of sorrow pointed to slavery as a throwback to Eastern barbarism—the white slavery of the Turks and the Barbary pirates—rather than as an institution that belonged in a Christian nation. The enslaved woman's pain and suffering transcended words as the noise of her grief broke through the readerly soundscape. Tears, broken hearts, and pale, shaking women, bereft of the children in whom their blood flowed, evoked their violation. This focus on embodied motherhood highlighted women's right not to be separated from their children—a right that had yet to be affirmed in the courts that adjudicated divorce for white people. No one mentioned the blood and semen of coerced sex or asserted the enslaved woman's right not to be impregnated to produce the children counted as slave property.[64]

Medicalizing Motherhood

Even as antebellum poets and fiction writers depicted enslaved women as emotionally and physically racked by the grief of separation from their children, just as all mothers would be, antebellum physicians pursued the time-honored project of medicalizing female bodies—a complex task in a nation committed to slavery. Dr. Strain's 1851 challenge to Sojourner Truth, while shocking in the context of nineteenth-century political theater, was in keeping with academically trained doctors' increasing reliance on physical examinations as the best means of discovering the truth about a woman's condition. Yet no antebellum doctor would have asked of a refined white woman what Strain had asked of Truth. Indeed, professors of medicine and aspiring doctors stressed the need to proceed with delicacy when dealing with white female patients. They developed cautious protocols for intimate medical examinations that were designed to discover objective truths about fertility, menstrual irregularity, sexual history, pregnancy, and the resort to abortion, but suspended such protocols when treating almshouse patients, white and Black, and enslaved women, who could marshal fewer protections against invasive examinations.[65]

The reliance on gathering objective information through physical examinations stemmed in part from the larger project of nineteenth-century medical jurisprudence. Antebellum doctors sought to solidify their professional standing as experts in a range of legal cases including insanity claims, poisoning, questions about gestational age, alleged infanticide and abortion, racial identity, and warranties for the health of newly purchased slaves. The prominence in medical jurisprudence of questions about women's bodies presented a tantalizing opportunity for regular physicians who aspired to medical and legal authority. European doctors had been asserting claims to special knowledge about female reproduction since at least the sixteenth century. By the nineteenth century, these historic claims had been repurposed in the United States to serve national interests in perpetuating the patterns of settler colonialism—the spread of a white settler population into former Native American territory—through the encouragement of white female fertility and interest in white maternal and child health. Medical claims to expertise over the management of enslaved people's health, driven by a similar quest for professional authority, played to enslavers' interests in laborers as property. As several scholars have shown, enslaved women became experimental subjects for new surgical techniques that eventually became the standard treatment for all women suffering from gynecological ailments.[66]

One consequence of this repurposing was the replacement in medical textbooks of the person of the refined white woman with her organs, a trend that both reflected and contributed to American class formation. As Nora Doyle has shown, white women's persons disappeared from the prying eyes of medical students, even as the uterus, an organ long viewed as troublesome and inherently diseased, took its place and became a generic marker of femaleness. A second consequence flowed from the first: the contradictory use of Black women's bodies as exemplars of both racial specificity and generic femaleness. "Woman" as an unqualified term in the medical literature usually meant "white female," but during the nineteenth century, as medical schools sourced cadavers from vulnerable and marginalized populations, the data supporting generalizations about sexed bodies often came from Native American and African-descended people.[67]

Medical dissertations and publications reveal the stakes of knowledge about antebellum women's childbearing capacities. Following the University of Pennsylvania Medical School professor William Dewees's inaugural course on obstetrics in 1806, medical theses about menstrual disorders, gynecological afflictions, and the risks of childbirth increased in number. Student authors parroted medical wisdom about treating menstrual disorders and identifying the signs and symptoms of pregnancy. How could a doctor know for sure that a woman was pregnant? How could doctors effectively manage a woman's reproductive capacity? Aspiring doctors answered these questions with an eye to their own role as reproductive experts, weighing in at the level of individual diagnosis and treatment. Medical thesis writers cited case histories involving enslaved, free Black, and white women, revealing their efforts to establish knowledge of a woman's reproductive status independent of the patient's subjective accounts. In most of these studies, the childbearing capacity and presumed delicacy of genteel white women were the dominant professional and biopolitical concerns. This was one facet of the production of racist medical knowledge that featured some doctors claiming expertise as managers of enslaved people's health.[68]

Students attending the University of Pennsylvania Medical School reflected professional medicine's interest in women's reproduction and the broad embrace of the racialization of medical knowledge. Graduates from slaveholding states outnumbered those from non-slaveholding states during most of the first six decades of the nineteenth century; residents from the slaveholding states appear to have been as likely as their northern peers to write about women's reproductive health and maternal and child health.[69] This robust representation of the slaveholding states in Philadelphia's medical schools was known to contemporaries like the Quaker abolitionist Lucretia Mott, who lectured to a group of Philadelphia medical students in 1849. She beseeched them not only to avoid the temptations of the city but to take a stand against slavery, "a system which degrades and brutalizes three millions of our fellow beings." Her allusion to the presence of southern slaveholders in the audience who "may be more immediately connected to this system," provoked some to leave the room abruptly while others "halted at the door & remained to the close." Impressed by their attention, Mott exhorted them, "I believe there is a work for you to do when you return home, if you would be faithful to yourselves."[70] The implication was that even diligent medical care for enslaved people, such as that provided by men such as James Green Carson, a 1839 Penn Medical School graduate who returned to his plantation in Mississippi, could not substitute for the actual emancipation of bound people.[71]

Nineteenth-century medical students depicted adult womanhood as a condition that required professional care. Many repeated the prevailing wisdom of Dr. Thomas Denman (1733–1815), the British naval physician turned obstetrician who had published extensively on midwifery and the reproductive ailments of women. Denman's early career included a nine-month tour on a British ship that patrolled the West Coast of Africa during the final year of the Seven Years' War, an experience that likely familiarized him with emergent theories about race and tropical climates. When his naval career failed to advance, he turned to obstetrics and gynecology, a booming field that reflected Britain's new biopolitical interests in the growth of its national population. Denman's proficiency in this professional role, crucial to the transformation of male midwives into professional male obstetricians, included his invention of a forceps that bore his name.[72]

Denman had three major influences on late eighteenth- and early nineteenth-century medical students, all of which contributed to the medicalization of motherhood. First, he established guidelines for conducting intimate gynecological examinations, which set the standard for the respectful treatment of fee-paying white middle- and upper-class women; second, he insisted on a relationship between climate and menstrual onset; and third, he theorized, implicitly about white women only, that menstruation's signal role in female maturation coincided with women's attainment of physical beauty, intellect, and appeal for men.

Denman's *Introduction to the Practice of Midwifery*, first published in London in 1788 as a compendium of previously published essays, was widely reprinted for five decades by publishers in New York; Philadelphia; Brattleboro, Vermont; and Paris. In this canonical text, Denman laid out a protocol for intimate examinations that appears to have persisted for decades as the standard for treating white patients. Acknowledging that women disliked internal examinations in which male doctors inserted fingers into their vaginas, Denman nonetheless cautiously recommended such examinations for doctors seeking reliable information about women far advanced in pregnancy or about to begin labor. Examinations done earlier in gestation, he admitted, offered little reliable information about fetal age or disposition. For this reason, and in consideration of the risk to the refinement and decency of white female patients, Denman advised doctors not to resort to intimate internal examinations unless absolutely necessary.[73]

The position Denman recommended for women undergoing these examinations reflected the race, class, and condition of patients. Denman reported that in England, women were required to lie on their sides with their knees drawn up to enable the doctor's access to their vaginas. To avoid charges of indecency or suspicion of lascivious intent, Denman stipulated that such examinations never be conducted without an attendant present. The contrast between Denman's recommendations and the protocols developed during the 1850s by J. Marion Sims and other American gynecological surgeons, that female patients assume a position on hands and knees subsequently known as the Sims position, is striking, as is the doctors' arrival at this standard by operating repeatedly on the bodies of enslaved and poor white women.[74]

Denman's claims about the relationship between menstruation and disease reflected colonially derived wisdom about the impact of tropical climates on health; in particular, on how heat accelerated the onset of puberty in women. This was an issue of particular interest for doctors in the subtropical climates of Virginia, the Carolinas, Georgia, Tennessee, Mississippi, and Alabama, who puzzled about whether there were differences among white, African-descended, and Native American women inhabiting the same climate, and how to account for them. Elias Willis Napier of Nashville, Tennessee, wrote in his "Dissertation on the Causes, Symptoms, and Treatment of Amenorrhea" (1811) that normal menstruation began "in our climate" during the fourteenth year and ceased by the age of forty-eight or fifty. In his 1816 "Essay on Menstruation," Richard Mason of Virginia concurred with Denman's estimates of onset and duration, while his fellow Virginian Robert Mosely observed that amenorrhea was caused by luxury and not found among "savages that inhabit our own country; here we find the female leading an active life, indulging in none of the luxuries of art, but their food consisting of nature's bounty." Mosely's focus on luxury rather than on strenuous field labor as a cause of female infertility reveals his focus on privileged white women and his sidestepping of an earlier debate in the Britain Caribbean about the impact of enslaved women's labor on birth rates and infant mortality. H. O. McCall of Kentucky (1818) reasoned that normal menstrual flow accompanied women's sexual desire for men. Celibate Shaker women, unsurprisingly, suffered from poor menstrual health.[75] J. M. Hill of Gainesville, Alabama, noted in 1855 that all human females menstruated, no matter how "primitive" their lives, but acknowledged the impact of climate and urban habits.[76]

Several students observed that menstrual health could be influenced by luxury, diet, leisure, emotions, and the resort to abortifacients. Napier cited strong emotions, severe colds, and the effects of being confined in ballrooms or other crowded assemblies as leading to its suppression. Napier also warned that women's resort to the herb sabine, a popular folk remedy to bring on menstruation, could provoke abortion, and he recommended bloodletting in its place. Mosely noted additionally that menstruation, the equivalent of a seminal secretion, indicated a woman's arrival at adulthood and her readiness to discharge her duty, which was the "propagation of the species." He touted his own success treating an emaciated nineteen-year-old "servant" girl whose menstruation had been suppressed for nine months (!) with a fortifying diet and doses of the known abortifacient *Polygala senega*. He also boasted of success in curing two other female patients in the Philadelphia almshouse.[77]

The South Carolinian William McCaa, whose dissertation denied that race accounted for the differential disease survival rates of Black and white people, contended that enslaved people never suffered from diseases that afflicted wealthy people who led luxurious, sedentary lives. But McCaa's observation of racial differences in childbirth required greater intellectual gymnastics. "It is known that the inhabitants of warm climates menstruate comparatively at an early period of life," he declared, "and that labour with them is a less serious operation than with those of a colder region." McCaa found the warm climate's easing of childbirth to apply even to "the wealthy and dissipated portion of society who enjoy the genial sun of South Carolina," but the effect was magnified in enslaved women "who unites with the advantages of climate extreme simplicity of life, and who are strangers to deformity," making a difficult labor a "rare occurrence." He offered as examples two illustrative cases. The first concerned an eighteen-year-old enslaved woman, "surprised by nature," who had her first baby under a tree by herself while in the middle of her field work. The second was of a doctor called to the bedside of an enslaved woman, only to discover that she had already delivered herself of a dead child whom she concealed before retreating to bed, allegedly to avoid work.[78] Subsequent student theses expanded on McCaa's framework for racial difference to contend that, along with cousin marriages, interracial unions resulted in progeny that lacked the capacity to reproduce.[79]

Scores of McCaa's fellow medical students dutifully churned out essays on menstruation, amenorrhea, uterine hemorrhage, symptoms and signs of pregnancy, abortion, childbirth, and cesarean section. They offered remedies that included the use of blisters to the skin of the thighs and groin, heat on the abdomen and pudenda, and electricity applied directly to the uterus.[80] As J. M. Hill explained in 1855, menstruation was "extremely liable to become deranged and come under his [the physician's] care for restoration to health." Isaac Jones of Fayette, Tennessee, noted the connection between a woman's emotional condition and her reproductive organs, observing in 1860 that surprising or sad news could throw the nervous female "into hysterical convulsions, perhaps she may be the subject of menorrhagia, amenorrhea, or dysmenorrhea."[81]

Confirming Denman's claims, nineteenth-century medical students distinguished "pure" circulatory blood from the fluids produced during menstruation, uterine hemorrhage, birth, or abortion. According to this framework, menstruation was a secretion rather than "pure" blood and not the regular offloading of excess, as depicted in humoral models of previous centuries.[82] This formulation was consistent with the way bloodletting had fallen into disfavor as a remedy for diseases caused by inflammation and overstimulation. Several students, including William G. Freeman of Norfolk, Virginia, went even further to debunk the value of bloodletting as a therapeutic approach to treating illness. Writing in 1861, Freeman argued that human bodies had undergone historical changes in their constitutions, making bleeding an ineffective treatment.[83]

The cause as well as the source of blood flow mattered. Writing in 1869, Daniel C. Malone of Pennsylvania observed that in women of "our" (presumptively white) race, uterine hemorrhages should not be confused with either normal menses or the discharge of the blood from gestation and delivery.[84] As part of the growing complexity of classification and analysis, some medical doctors elaborated new distinctions between male and female blood. Blencove Fryer, for example, claimed in his 1859 dissertation that men enjoyed redder blood with more red corpuscles than women, although women's blood changed color when they were pregnant.[85] Writing that same year about transfusion, Melson L. Rowland reported the belief that transfused blood could change a recipient's fundamental qualities and noted that "animals cannot live by the blood of others of different species." For this reason, transfusion should only occur within species.[86]

Asserting expertise over women's bodies through the medicalization of their reproductivity, physicians vigorously resisted women's efforts to diagnose or treat female conditions without professional intervention. This professional assertion was especially pronounced around interventions into menstrual irregularity and pregnancy. Who was to say when a woman who ceased to menstruate had amenorrhea and when she was actually pregnant? Who should be able to regulate a woman's recourse to the medicines that might be equally effective in restoring the menses or ending a pregnancy? Was restoring the menses the same as abortion?

Along with essays about menstrual function and dysfunction, aspiring doctors summarized their ability to detect pregnancy by using intimate examination techniques. Robert Woodhull Clark's 1860 "Signs of Pregnancy" provided a detailed analysis of the unreliability of women's self-reported symptoms. Spontaneous bleeding during pregnancy, Clark warned, was not to be confused with menstruation but might point to an impending spontaneous abortion. The physician should find out whether the patient was married or not, and whether she had recently had sexual intercourse. In contrast to this reliance on women's provision of information, Clark identified two symptoms, morning sickness and breast tenderness, that offered objective evidence of pregnancy. Clark commented on the changed appearance and shape of breasts in pregnant women, especially the darkening of nipples in "brunettes." He debunked the presence of milk in the breasts of pregnant women as a reliable symptom because it could occur in women who were not pregnant (and even in men), caused by other factors like uterine tumors or stimulation of the mammary glands.

Most important, Clark dismissed women's reports of quickening, which typically occurred at 4–4.5 months, as a reliable legal or biological milestone. "The period technically called quickening is not to be taken as that at which the foetus becomes first endowed with life; taken in that sense, quickening takes place at the time of fecundation, for the child is really and truly alive at all stages of intrauterine existence, and indeed from the moment of conception in the ovary." In some women, Clark averred, quickening was never observed at all, while others, not actually pregnant, claimed to experience it. Gas and spasmodic twitching, moreover, could be mistaken for quickening. Clark concluded, "It is almost valueless as a sign of pregnancy, taken singly, there being so many sources of fallacy."[87]

Reliable data could be collected from a woman's body without her subjective contribution, but only after the third month. The problem was not simply that women's knowledge of their own bodies was unreliable, but that women often intentionally tried to disguise the truth.[88] "Women, by their carriage and dress," Clark noted, "can often conceal their condition from outward and superficial observers, but if a direct and thorough examination be made, the diagnosis can rarely be difficult."[89] He nonetheless provided a list of "objective" symptoms: the presence of "kiestine" in the urine, detectable by the cheesy smell, but not completely reliable unless the doctor had complete control over a woman's consumption of food and drink (Clark noted that this symptom might occur also in men who ate too much cheese or drank lager beer); the "violet appearance of the living membrane of the vagina and labia," which might also occur because of tumors; the enlargement of the abdomen (which Clark noted, at great length, could be quantified through measurement); and ballottement, the doctor's insertion of a finger into the vagina to press against the uterine wall to diagnose pregnancy through touch. Only the latter manipulation could provide definitive proof of pregnancy and only when it was performed after the fourth month. In addition, there was the auditory evidence of a developing fetus. Clark reported, almost poetically, that a fetal heartbeat detected in the middle of the fourth month resembled "the muffled tick of a watch." He compared the placental noise known as uterine souffle to the cooing of a dove, the sound heard when putting a seashell up to the ear, or that made by blowing on the mouth of a bottle.[90]

This issue of physician authority over what had been formerly a woman's own account and regulation of her menstruation became especially pointed in relation to new medical jurisprudence around abortion. Following the 1803 British law criminalizing post-quickening abortions by poison and making pre-quickening terminations a transportable offense, medical students in the United States took up the cause of what they described as the protection of the life of the mother and the fetus. The issue pitted fragile professional authority and expertise against traditional folk and lay medicine practiced by women. John Putnam Batchelder, a young physician who had received some medical instruction at Harvard, identified the unregulated (i.e., not under the supervision of an academically trained physician) practice of abortion as one of the threats to the medical profession in his 1818 oration to the western district of the New Hampshire Medical Society. Batchelder later taught one of the nation's first courses on medical jurisprudence. Within three years, Connecticut passed the first law criminalizing abortion by poison, with Missouri (1827) and Illinois (1827) following soon thereafter.[91]

Medical students anticipated entering a transformed landscape of medical jurisprudence in which physicians often felt besieged by attorneys' interrogations in court. Beginning during the 1810s, Penn medical students writing about amenorrhea warned of the possibilities of women using emmenagogues to restore delayed or suppressed menses and ending a pregnancy. In 1827, John W. Reese summarized contemporary medical wisdom about causes of amenorrhea and detailed several remedies that needed to be used with caution. A year later, in his "Inaugural Dissertation on Amenorrhoea," Jehu Peters cautioned that the use of emmenagogues to restore menstruation could actually provoke abortion.[92] In "Signs of Pregnancy and Delivery" (1846), William A. McClure of Clarksville, Tennessee identified evidence of pregnancy and recent birth that would meet legal standards.[93]

Within ten years of its founding in 1847 by the Penn medical professor Nathaniel Chapman, the American Medical Association took a strong stand on the criminality and moral evil of abortion. Ostensibly the motives were humane desires to protect women and fetuses from harmful medical practices, but the long history of rivalry with midwives and traditional folk and lay medicine reveal the professional stakes. Using language that reflected their view of the outmoded nature of humoral medicine, which had always included women's need to restore blocked menses, the American Medical Association in 1857 blurred distinctions between emmenagogues, abortifacients, and the destruction of the fetus using instruments.[94] The impact on student medical theses was immediate. Charles McCall of Philadelphia, writing of criminal abortion in 1858 and noting the British transport in 1803 of abortionists to Botany Bay, was explicit that a physician's opposition to unregulated abortion was a matter of defending the rights of the unborn infant. In 1861, William Savery of Philadelphia explained in his medical thesis "On Abortion," that the medical position against abortion was based on the "preservation of human life" even before quickening and observed that only recently had the "rights of the embryonic being" been considered. It went without saying that the rights to which Savery referred were the rights of notionally "white" fetuses.[95]

No such lofty sentiments about the rights of either mother or fetus graced the medical debate about enslaved women's bodies. Southern planters found innumerable ways both to encourage and coerce enslaved women to bear children and to sell those who remained childless. It was a foundation of plantation medicine that, like other women in the torrid zones, women of African descent were naturally prolific mothers, allegedly giving birth with ease and providing infants with breasts full of milk. Belief in this latter capacity provided the rationale for the use of Black wet nurses. Yet planters had been claiming for decades that enslaved women foiled their calculations of profitable "increase" by deliberately preventing or terminating pregnancies, an allegation that dated to the British debates about abolishing the transatlantic slave trade. Indeed, some historians have argued that enslaved women likely made use of cotton root as an emmenagogue to bring on the menses.[96]

When the South Carolina–educated E. M. Pendleton (1815–1884) weighed in on the issue of enslaved women's fertility as part of his larger interest in plantation profitability and agricultural productivity, he admitted that women's assignment to agricultural labor every bit as grueling as that assigned to men diminished their fertility, but he suggested that vicious habits, especially promiscuity, were the greater culprit. Both conditions made enslaved women more likely to have need of medical attention than white women. These negative factors aside, Pendleton contended, enslaved women remained better suited to strenuous labor than their white counterparts, whose constitutional frailty would not permit the combination of strenuous physical labor and pregnancy. He dismissed the possibility that women of African descent might know how to manage fertility better than academically trained doctors, a contention with which the physician John H. Morgan disagreed. Testimony from Underground Railroad refugees reveals that women did indeed resent and resist their enslaver's pressure on them to bear children.[97]

At roughly the same time as the opposition to abortion was gaining momentum, medical doctors debated the need and moral imperative to supply anesthesia to women in childbirth. The humanitarian argument for its use pointed to its ability to reduce genteel white women's fear and suffering. There was no such concern expressed about the enslaved women Anarcha, Betsy, and Lucy, subjected to multiple gynecological surgeries by J. Marion Sims, and others who suffered through similar experimental treatments. Anesthesia was not being used in 1845, when Sims began his experiments, but within two years, a doctor in Scotland and one in the United States had provided it to their parturient patients. In his "Essay on Anaesthesia in Parturation" (1861), Thomas Reid of Fayette, Tennessee, opposed the use of anesthesia for all women on the grounds that labor pains were natural, not pathological; but he was not reflective of the dominant trend for attending to well-to-do white women.[98]

The move to treat the female body as one that a woman could manipulate to create deceptive appearances, especially around the state of pregnancy, motivated doctors to find empirical forms of assessment that bypassed the subjective reporting of female patients. White male medical students in their early twenties recounted the myriad ways a woman's own reporting might be erroneous or deliberately false. The medical practitioner sought to extract trustworthy evidence from the female body, especially when he was contributing to medical jurisprudence.

This effort at collecting objective data was consistent with medical approaches to race as a material condition of the body that could be assessed through the appearance of the skull, feet, facial features, hair, and skin. Nineteenth-century courts relied on both lay and so-called expert assessments of appearance more than on an individual's own testimony about ancestry and identity. Increasingly the condition of the female body was depicted as similarly unsubjective. These were not parallel or analogous tracks, however, but derived from a common source: the exploited bodies of African American women.[99]

An Enslaved Mother's Song

For most of her career as an abolitionist speaker and itinerant minister, Sojourner Truth made motherhood a key feature of how slavery robbed her of her personhood. Not without reason. Alone among abolitionists, Truth was both the child of an enslaved woman and herself an enslaved mother. We can see both risk and calculation in Truth's carefully cultivated public image as a respectable and virtuous woman. Contemplating Truth's scrupulous grooming of that image, her reputation for speaking candidly is even more amazing, even if, with Nell Painter, we conclude that the speech in which she repeated a rhetorical question, "Ain't I a woman?," was possibly apocryphal.[100]

Not all of Truth's public performances were as subject to appropriation and repackaging as her "Ain't I a Woman" speech. One well-documented occasion, her attendance at the inaugural meeting of the Pennsylvania Progressive Friends on May 22, 1853, offers a glimpse of Truth's own carefully chosen performance of motherhood. The Progressive Friends had split off from the main body of Quakers in Philadelphia over continued activism against slavery, including their participation in the Underground Railroad. Truth had been in Philadelphia in the months before the meeting, spending time with William Still, Lucretia Mott, and other abolitionists. She had spoken to a PFAS meeting twice, in January and May, with the second appearance coming just days before the Progressive Friends gathered at the Old Kennett Meetinghouse. Addressing PFAS in the ethnoracial language of the day, she appealed to the Anglo-Saxon race to work on behalf of the oppressed African, a necessary capitulation to the contemporary usage that reflected the overlapping meanings of race, nation, and lineage.[101]

The hymn Truth chose for the Progressive Friends Meeting was in many ways typical of the repertoire of abolitionist music. "O Pity the Slave Mother" was a well-known song published in the Oberlin Social and Sabbath School hymnbook in 1846. William Wells Brown included it two years later in his compendium of abolitionist hymns, *The Anti-slavery Harp*.[102] The enslaved mother Truth invoked in song had a flesh and blood presence in her child's life despite describing herself as kinless:

I Pity the slave-mother, careworn and weary,
Who sighs as she presses her babe to her breast;
I lament her sad fate, all so hopeless and weary,
I lament for her woes and her wrongs unredressed:
O who can imagine her heart's deep emotion,
As she thinks of her children about to be sold;
You may picture the bounds of the rock-girdled ocean
But the grief of that mother can never be known!

The mildew of slavery has blighted each blossom,
That ever has bloomed in her path-way below;
It has froze every fountain that gushed in her bosom,
And chilled her heart's verdure with pitiless woe;
Her parents, her kindred, all crushed by oppression;
Her husband still doomed in its desert to stay;
No arm to protect from the tyrants aggression—
She must weep as she treads on her desolate way.

O, slave mother, hope! see—the nation is shaking!
The arm of the Lord is awake to thy wrong!
The slave-holder's heart now with terror is quaking,
Salvation and Mercy to Heaven belong!
Rejoice, O rejoice! for the child thou art rearing,
May one day lift up its unmanacled form,
While hope, to thy heart, like the rain-bow so cheering,
Is born, like the rain-bow, 'mid tempest and storm.

Unlike the other enslaved mothers of abolitionist poems and images, the mother in Truth's hymn had not yet lost her child. But the soul-crushing conditions of slavery had, like a blight on plants, mildewed and frozen within her what should have been verdant, warm, and flowing. Slavery destroyed nurturing emotion as well as physical vitality.

As with most of the hymns in this collection, the title line was followed by the word "Air" and a simple reference to the popular melody to which it should be sung. The singer of "The Slave Mother" was to follow the tune of "Araby's Daughter," a song that the performer presumably already knew and needed no musical notation to sing. Other abolitionist hymns were also set to the melodies of songs well known to American audiences. "The Blind Slave Boy" was to be sung to the tune of "Sweet Afton," "Ye Sons of Freemen" was set to the "Marseilles Hymn," and "The Slave's Lamentation" was to follow the melody of "Long, Long Ago."

The pattern reveals an antebellum cultural competency exploited by activists; most Americans, no matter what their musical literacy, had familiarity with a canon of popular music that they knew well enough to sing. Creating abolitionist lyrics for these popular tunes enabled activists both to perform for audiences and to elicit their participation. Poignant lyrics about the suffering of violated slaves and their longing for freedom were more effective if they could be sung. It was a powerful technique for stirring audience participation and creating a moment of collectivity. One can imagine a large audience singing the hymns a cappella, generating a spiritually intense, even electric, unity that might have a lasting impact on those who witnessed it. Collective singing was also a physical experience of breathing, phrasing, and vocalizing. Once exposed to an abolitionist hymn, it is possible that an individual returning to that well-known tune might recall the abolitionist content—or at the very least the profound feelings those words evoked when sung collectively in a large hall.

But for some of those singing or hearing a performance of the melody of "Araby's Daughter" set to the lyrics of "The Slave Mother," there may have been other layers of meaning. "Araby's Daughter" first appeared in 1817 as a poem written by the Irish Catholic songwriter and poet Thomas Moore (1779–1852), a member of Lord Byron's and Percy Bysshe Shelley's circle of romantic poets. At the urging of Byron, and like many of his contemporaries, Moore, who had traveled to Virginia, Bermuda, and Philadelphia as a young man, turned to the East for poetic inspiration, exploiting the British interest in the Orient. The original poem was ten stanzas long and part of the epic poem "Lalla Rookh," which chronicled the tragic fate of two star-crossed lovers in Persia and alluded to Irish colonial struggles with Britain. In the final section of "Araby's Daughter," the poet laments the suicide by drowning of the female protagonist, who is mourning her lover who died in a failed effort to defend Iran from tyrants. Its final stanza proclaims,

> Farewell!—Farewell! until pity's sweet fountain
> Is lost in the hearts of the fair and the brave,
> They'll weep for the Chieftan who died on that mountain,
> They'll weep for the Maiden who sleeps in the wave.[103]

After publication in England, "Araby's Daughter" enjoyed enormous popularity, not only in England and the United States, but around the world. It was the most widely translated and monetarily rewarded English-language poem (Moore took home three thousand pounds) of its time. Like many popular poems of the period, it offered an attractive opportunity for composers and the purveyors of sheet music to profit. The British composer George Kiallmark (1781–1835) created a melody for "Araby's Daughter" that soon became wildly popular: sixteen editions of sheet music were published between 1820 and 1831, making it Kiallmark's best-selling composition. The Philadelphia publisher G. E. Blake produced sheet music for the piece as early as 1824. Such popular airs were perfect fodder for abolitionist hymn writers seeking well-known melodies already connected to deeply sentimental, and in this case, oriental, themes, to pair with new lyrics.[104]

That Sojourner Truth included a hymn in her appearance before the Progressive Friends in 1853 was not unusual. She was in the habit of singing before abolitionist audiences during her long career as a preacher and activist. When she felt afraid, as she did in Northampton, Massachusetts, in 1844, she sang (loudly),

> It was early in the morning
> Just at the break of day
> When he rose—he rose—he rose
> and went to heaven on a cloud.

In the spring of 1852 in Ohio, she chose to sing Garrison's "I am an Abolitionist" (to the tune of "Auld Lang Syne"). Her choice of "The Slave Mother" appears to have been singular, however, although the venue—the first meeting of the Progressive Friends of Longwood, Pennsylvania—offers some clues.[105]

After the Hicksite split, many Hicksite Quakers became less engaged with abolition and attempted to silence the speech of their fellow Hicksites on this topic. By the early 1850s, Quaker abolitionists around the United States were beginning to withdraw from their meetings to form cadres of Progressive

Friends. At Longwood, the group included Mary Pennock, Sarah and Ruth Dugdale, Ann Coates, Alice Eliza Hambleton, Robert and Harriet Purvis, Cyrus Burleigh, Hannah Cox, and Rebecca and Bartholomew Fussell. Many of the women were members of PFAS, all of them were involved in the Underground Railroad, and several of them, including Ann Preston, subsequently became involved in women's medical education.

The Progressive Friends combined intense political commitments to abolition and opposition to the Fugitive Slave Law of 1850 with the basic tenets of Quakerism. But they also turned to Spiritualism, a movement defined by insistence on the spirit's transcendence of the body—perhaps appealing for a group dedicated to ending a labor system rooted in coercion and bodily suffering. Sarah Grimké wrote to her friend Harriot Hunt, a practicing physician to whom she turned for advice about her own and her sister's physical ailments, to recount one of her first experiences with a spiritualist medium: "My precious mother has come back to me; she tells me to be patient, to fulfill daily duty, & all will be well . . . Whilst we were sitting silent, some one enquired if the spirit of my mother was present, an affirmative rap came—the person then asked if I wished to ask any questions or rather if I wished to communicate with my mother; I replied, 'nothing occurs to me at present, I have constant communication with my mother'—distinct & continued rappings followed this observation." As Grimké explained to Hunt, she had no reason to mistrust the medium, who appeared to be a "gentle, unpretending, artless youth, and I cannot but believe he is a telegraphic wire between this sphere and the next—Some deeply instructive remarks came from the spirit world, & one revelation That was entirely new to me." Grimké hastened to add that contact with the dead should not be mistaken for spirituality, which required a connection with God. As she noted for her own case, she hardly needed spiritualism to make contact with her mother, for her mother's spirit was always with her.[106]

What did this particular hymn mean to Truth? Having been an itinerant preacher since 1843, it is likely that Truth was familiar with "Araby's Daughter" before she learned the abolitionist lyrics to the song. Was there any emotional connection for Truth between the song's lament for the death of the despondent maiden and the abolitionist lament for the enslaved mother? The romanticized and exoticized Persian location of the original lyrics—evoking an oriental form of slavery similar to the one that captured Wollstonecraft's attention—lends additional meaning to the antislavery content of the lyrics Truth sang. The Persian maiden's watery grave, tended by mythical sea creatures, mirrored the grief of the slave mother, as deep as the "rock-girdled" ocean.

Sojourner Truth's performance of "The Slave Mother" at the meeting of Progressive Friends reminds us of the political effectiveness of motherhood as a rallying cry for abolitionists, and its pointed rebuttal of the ways North American slavery appropriated motherhood to increase the human property of enslavers. Truth's decision to sing this particular hymn is a vivid example of how abolitionists mobilized their own bodies to take aim at the institutionalized bodily exploitation of enslaved people. In this instance, both the performer and her performance trained the audience to consider the plight of enslaved women. There was little imaginative gap between Truth's own biography as an enslaved mother, her physical presence singing this particular hymn, and her effort to stir her audience to political action. As the recorder of the meeting noted, "Sojourner Truth, an emancipated slave mother, after uttering a few impressive sentences, expressed herself as being deeply moved to sing."[107] To witness such a performance was to be reminded that the ordeal of slavery was not an abstract injustice captured by the image and slogan "Am I Not a Woman and a Sister," but a regular pattern of coerced sex, pregnancy, birth, caretaking, and separation experienced by particular women—represented in this case by the aged woman standing before them singing "The Slave Mother."

Considering the spiritualist leanings of the assembly at Longwood, we must also recall Truth's relationship with her own enslaved mother and her tragic relationship with her son Peter, who disappeared while on a whaling voyage in 1843. The suicide theme of "Araby's Daughter" left a ghostly trace in a song about enslaved mothers who, as many poets observed, might be longing for death, both for themselves and for the children they could not protect from slavery. This theme also foreshadowed the tragic experience of Margaret Garner, who in 1856 killed her infant to spare her a life of slavery, and the refugee Rebecca Jones, who declared to the Underground Railroad conductor William Still that she refused to bring more enslaved children into the world. Spiritualism offered women like Truth the possibility of communion with her own mother and son, so she would not be kinless like the enslaved woman of her song.[108]

Spiritualism also offered Truth and other abolitionists an opportunity to imagine an escape from the confines of the bodies, including their own, that they confronted every day in their activism. This might have been welcome respite from a fight that pitted egalitarian understandings of the human body against demeaning racist depictions. White hecklers like T. W. Strain attempted to discredit Truth's arguments on behalf of abolition and women's rights by questioning her identity as a woman. His comparison of her breast to an animal "teat" revealed the way that racist medicine and popular racism were actually two sides of the same coin. Truth, in turn, attempted to use the evidence of her maternal body not just to expand the circle of "the human" but to center it on Black women like herself. This was an important move, as it transformed Black maternity from its place at the center of slavery's economic calculations and physical exploitations to being a key trope of humanity. It was important to insist that the bodies and family longings of the enslaved were familiar to white Americans rather than exceptional or deviant, but such normative depictions also had their limits; the depiction of Black women as suffering mothers did little to challenge gender conformity or redefine power relations in families of free laborers. It was also not clear that the focus on enslaved mothers could effectively counter the racist medicalization of Black women's bodies.

Chapter 7

Blood of the Fathers

> In the name of God, we ask you, are you men? Where is the blood of your fathers? Has it all run out of your veins? Awake, awake; millions of voices are calling you! Your dead fathers speak to you from their graves. Heaven, as with a voice of thunder, calls on you to arise from the dust.
>
> —Henry Highland Garnet (1815–1882), August 21, 1843

Henry Highland Garnet's impassioned speech, now known as his "Call to Rebellion," unnerved the crowd gathered at the National Convention of Colored Citizens in Buffalo on August 17, 1843. Moral suasion had been the dominant philosophy of abolitionist activism since Nat Turner's rebellion in 1831. In the context of a movement with significant Quaker and female participation, Garrisonian abolitionists urged a model of patient restraint for African American men rather than vengeful fury. But Garnet had had enough with patience. "Years have rolled on," he cried, "and tens of thousands have been borne on streams of blood and tears, to the shores of eternity." He identified the original wrong—the theft of people from the coast of Africa and their transport across the Atlantic without their consent—and traced the perpetuation of that wrong to men professing to be Christians but with "corrupt and sordid hearts." Their own hearts "broken" at being taken from their beloved homeland, Africans were doomed to "unrequited toil and deep degradation." Their children, native-born Americans, were burdened with memories of the lashes their fathers bore and the violation of their wives, children, mothers, and sisters. "Think how many tears you have poured out upon the soil which you have cultivated with unrequited toil and enriched with your blood," Garnet urged. He made the case for bondsmen to "act for themselves" with the familiar rallying cry, "LIBERTY OR DEATH," which hearkened back to revolutionary rhetoric.

If the slave mother was the iconic image of suffering humanity under slavery, what options did that leave for enslaved men to make their own claims to embodied humanity? How were they to undo slavery's denial of paternity? The disapprobation of Garnet's message by Frederick Douglass and others at the 1843 National Negro Convention reflected this dilemma of activist men: how to express manhood in a manner legible to the white men who must agree to embrace them as fellow citizens but remain consistent with the abolition movement's effort to cultivate empathy for enslaved people, especially women and children. The questions for Black men ranged widely from the issues of dignity and self-government of the body, to identifying historical, political, ancestral, and filial legacies, to challenging racist scientific theories about Black men's physical capacities. Many men appeared to be seeking answers to the question of what paternity could mean for African-descended men across centuries of slavery.

There was also the vexed question of militance as a core quality of manhood. If African American men followed Garnet's call to use their bodies to throw off their shackles and shed the blood of their oppressors, they risked inevitably violent reprisals, not only against themselves but also their loved ones. Women and children would pay the price for militant male resistance. Slavery, like a state of perpetual military conquest, relied on violence to instill terrified compliance among the enslaved; but unlike war, southern slavery was fully integrated in supporting the domestic lives of white women and children. This white domestic presence, which communicated innocence to white antebellum audiences, created scenes of domestic intimacy that provided crucial camouflage for slavery's mechanics of terror. The same mechanisms of sympathy for enslaved mothers that abolitionists mobilized for their cause worked against undoing slavery through violent uprisings in which white "innocents" were part of the human toll.[1]

As men like Douglass, James McCune Smith, William Whipper, William Still, and William Wells Brown worked to forge communities of abolitionist resistance through their intellectual and political leadership, their choices were circumscribed by their ties to white abolitionists and their need for funds. When enslaved people resisted their circumstances with violence, as they did in the Southampton (Nat Turner's) Rebellion of 1831, white abolitionists recoiled from advocating militancy and searched for other means. Enslaved rebels as well as others deemed suspicious suffered death or banishment as a consequence of white reprisals. Moral suasion, the chief tactic of Garrisonian abolitionists, dominated the campaign against slavery throughout the 1830s and early 1840s. As Garnet's "Call to Rebellion" reminded his listeners, however, being on the path of patient endurance meant living with the knowledge that millions of African American men, women, and children continued to be exploited. What was the acceptable cost for ending their suffering? No one, not even the militant writer David Walker or Garnet, wanted white audiences to imagine that cost in terms of the bloodshed of white women and children, yet the conclusion, after the Southampton Rebellion, seemed inescapable.

As long as slavery's regime of terror infiltrated domestic as well as agricultural and public spaces, white slave owners knowingly risked the lives of white women and children. The security of these "innocents," as southern slaveholding interests saw them, required that the punishment of slave transgressions be swift and sure. As the aftermath of the Southampton Rebellion demonstrated, it was the white victims of slave rebellion, rather than enslaved women and children, whose suffering captured the imaginations of white readers. It was no easy task to embody a standard for Black manhood in a world in which the well-being of white "innocents" would always trump that of enslaved women and children. Given the impossible choice, few Black men would immediately follow the path of militant confrontation recommended by Garnet, but growing numbers took heed of abolitionist calls for the enslaved to escape.

Legacies of Slavery

The dilemmas of finding an appropriate model for African American manhood in white-dominated society were rooted in slavery's history as an exploitative system that preyed on family relationships, particularly that between father and child. Robbed of their chance to have intimate ties to their children or to live in sustained, close proximity to family members, enslaved men were more likely than women to be commodified as individual laborers. Shortages of labor in colonial North America precipitated some of this focus on male bodies; the great demand for male labor in a colonial setting where land was plentiful and labor scarce increased the value placed on male strength and stamina. Such qualities were especially important for those of the laboring classes whose livelihoods depended on them. But impediments to landownership—legal prohibitions for slaves, economic barriers in the case of working-class white men—made the value of the robust, laboring, male body even more important for those without landed property. The propertyless free laborer made his way in the world by virtue of his strength and his wits, but at least he owned his labor. His enslaved counterparts were not so lucky. Although the only value others might confer on the enslaved was calculated with reference to their bodies, even this most personal of resources was owned by another. Stealing oneself—known to the master class as "running away"—was one of the fundamental ways of refuting the basic assumptions of slavery's chattel principle. Significantly, it was also a refutation undertaken more often by men than by women.

For men in slavery, the performative, mobile body became an important resource for personhood. The bitter irony of slavery, however, was that this precious and most personal of resources also bore the brunt of exhausting labor, discipline, brutal punishment, and sexual violation. The bodies of enslaved men might express manhood, but they were also likely to be damaged and disfigured by the brutalities of life in bondage.[2] Enslaved men reclaimed their own bodies in seemingly mundane ways through clothing, speech, dance, song, fighting, courtship, fatherhood, and travel to see family. When men traveled long distances on foot to visit wives and children, even at the cost of their own need for sleep and physical healing from the demands of slave labor, they testified to the importance of being connected to family. Many men persisted in these relationships even after they were ruptured by sale, sexual violence, or escape. Some worked with Underground Railroad activists to help bring wives and children across state lines into freedom, while others submitted themselves to bondage once again to remain with family.[3]

Examining masculinity for enslaved men as well as for free men of color forces us to confront yet another fundamental issue: the conflation of manhood (as opposed to some fictive, gender-neutral personhood) with human dignity. Historically, those excluded from the benefits of propertied manhood have had to stake their claim by critiquing the exclusiveness of male privilege and arguing that the rights of citizens should be accessible to their own group, if not to all people. Subjected to a labor system and a legal context that attempted to strip them of their humanity, enslaved men struggled to find space to be men. Was an enslaved man's assertion of manhood just an insistence on his own humanity? Was it even possible in the nineteenth century for a person to assert his or her humanity in a nongendered idiom—to be recognized by others as fully human without having a specific gender?[4]

The creative responses of Black men to the constraints placed on their manhood were key developments in the history of masculinity—ones that uniquely expose how contemporaries came to understand the intertwined relationships of manhood, humanity, and property. During the many decades of Atlantic slavery, enslaved men's and women's struggles against their exploitation triggered changes in conceptions of what it meant to be human that challenged slavery's chattel principle. In the space between these transformations in the meanings of manhood and the denial of humanity at the core of slavery, male slaves enacted manhood with their bodies stubbornly, defiantly, and sometimes militantly. They created a culture of male performance that offered them some protections from violence but also occasionally led to them to dominate fellow slaves, particularly women. Expressions of slave manhood also fueled the fears of white people whose narrow tolerance for enslaved people's self-assertion left little possibility for male self-determination and expression—except in those cases in which a man's sexual and reproductive claims on Black women promised to increase the master's profit. The masculinity of the enslaved took root and flourished in physical performances and familial and community relationships even as white masculinity was developing alternative foundations for male authority derived from landed property, literacy, political participation, military service, emotional refinement, and evangelical religion.[5]

Perhaps the most obvious visual evidence of how white contemporaries sought to deny the physical presence of Black manhood was its inadmissibility in white portrait art. From the sixteenth century on, Europeans often depicted the enslaved attending the white male or female subject of a portrait or hovering in the background shadows, barely visible in the chiaroscuro, a counterpoint to white skin. Surveying these depictions of the enslaved, one is struck by the predominance of women and children. No portrait of a European woman, to my knowledge, included a depiction of an undemeaned Black man in his prime. Most often, the white female subjects of portraits were accompanied by children, female attendants, or men whose manhood had been domesticated and contained by the wearing of livery or manacles to symbolize subordination to an enslaver's will. By the late eighteenth century, however, when they were depicted as the lone subjects of portraits or sculptures, Black men appeared as eroticized, aestheticized, and powerful bodies. The work of these representations was fetishistic and erotic, reflecting the commodification of enslaved men's reproductive capacities following the end of the transatlantic slave trade.[6]

Depictions of sexualized Black male bodies occurred in the context of the eighteenth century's new emotional calibrations of white manhood, expanding both the options for and the seeming deficiencies of Black men. Yet the obstacles to achieving propertied manhood continued to limit enslaved men's self-expressions. Sensibility—the emerging value of emotional refinement—which had counterpoints in the cultures of intellectual and physical refinement, encouraged literate men to demonstrate that they were also men of feeling. By this standard it was no longer sufficient simply to be a rake, a wit, or a man who ruled with an iron fist. Such men's anachronistic emotional styles revealed them to be but superficially civilized; to be truly civilized, a man had to be capable of sympathy, intense feeling, and measured but authentic emotional expression.[7]

Black men's performances of manhood during the antebellum period built on these antecedents and bore many similarities to the expressions of manhood by white men who lacked property and counted on their muscle to get through the world. With their path to property blocked by law and custom, free Black men viewed the high-risk conditions of the maritime trades as an opportunity for advancement and a steady living. Older, more likely to be married, and invested in longer maritime careers compared to their white counterparts, free Black sailors in the early decades of the nineteenth century explicitly described their lives at sea as fulfilling male ideals of hard work and provision for families. It gave many men an opportunity to experience firsthand the opportunities of free labor and to witness the subordination of enslaved laborers throughout the Atlantic. Yet long absences took their toll on Black families and left sailors without the roots of established households or the benefits of property ownership. Sailors in port with money in their pockets filled city streets and patronized local businesses. Brothels and taverns became substitute households, a space where men could enjoy social and sexual intimacy, store personal belongings, and rest and care for their bodies.[8]

On shipboard, and at work on the wharves and docks of North America's port cities, Black men became cosmopolitan in their knowledge of the world and their connections to news, commerce, and politics. No surprise that some of the most enterprising enslaved and free men could claim some experience on shipboard or working on the waterfront: Olaudah Equiano; Denmark Vesey, an ex-sailor who recruited followers from Charleston for an ill-fated rebellion in 1822; Frederick Douglass, who made his escape from slavery by knowing the ways of the Black maritime world; and Robert Smalls, a boat pilot who became famous for his exploits during the Civil War. Compared to white sailors, who were denigrated as crude, unpolished men on the margins of society, Black men in the maritime trades were central to Black leadership in the nineteenth century. The political potential for networking among Black maritime workers was recognized backhandedly by the Negro Seamen Acts of 1822 in South Carolina, a set of restrictions on the freedoms of ostensibly free Black sailors based on the principle of quarantine from contagion; the state later issued a prohibition on the use of habeas corpus for imprisoned Black sailors. Within two decades, several other states as well as Cuba passed similar laws. An estimated ten thousand to twenty thousand Black seamen were incarcerated under these acts, a significant curtailment of Black mobility that appears to have done little to prevent Black men from turning the experience of maritime labor into political networking, communication, and leadership.[9]

For rural men, in contrast to their urban counterparts, roads connecting plantations, paths through the woods, and plantation quarters provided opportunities for limited male self-assertion. Geographic literacy—knowing how to get from plantation to plantation and to navigate local rivers, creeks, and shortcuts through the woods, or how to escape for a few days' respite as well as run errands to the next plantation—distinguished enslaved men from their female counterparts, whose assigned labor and care for children resulted in more circumscribed lives. This was, in part, what made Harriet Tubman's accomplishments so miraculous. She embodied the geographic literacy and mobility typical of Black men within a petite female frame, turning herself into an expert guide for refugees from slavery.[10]

In addition to city streets, taverns, and rural spaces, enslaved and free people of color also claimed sacred space as their own during the antebellum period. There were very few separate Black churches before 1865 in the South, but in the North, Black churches became the anchors of free Black populations early in the century, supporting African American aspirations to property ownership and education and fostering community. Philadelphia's Mother Bethel Church (1794) and African Episcopal Church of St. Thomas (1792); in New York City, Mother African Methodist Episcopal Zion Church (1800) and Abyssinian Baptist Church (1808); and Boston's African Baptist Church (1806) all supported African American communities and became key institutions in resisting slavery, racism, and the shrinking civil rights of free African Americans. In these sacred spaces, preaching, song, music, food, and clothing nurtured a sense of soul equality for both men and women. Men provided much of the intellectual and publicly recognized leadership for these institutions while women created spiritual networks, provided moral discipline, and supported the material comforts of church celebrations. In addition to bolstering an ethos of stoic endurance and the promise of a heavenly reward, African American church communities gave rise to mutual aid societies and other forms of organizational life that improved the conditions of Black lives in the here and now.[11]

Personal demeanor could also communicate resistance to white supremacy. With their voices, gestures, postures, physical cultures, and clothing, Black people expressed what the historian Stephanie Camp has described as "the pleasures of resistance," which included bodily comportment as well as quite deliberate efforts to refuse the soul-crushing realities of slavery. White observers were especially likely to comment on men's fluid bodily movement, song leadership that elicited communal responses, and edgy combinations of clothing pattern and color. Descendants of enslaved men were also likely to recall acts of generosity, hard work, or singing and storytelling. All suggested a man's insistence on kinship, community and belonging as the most basic responses to slavery's destructive force.[12]

Fathers and Homelands

In their speeches and writings, men with politics as different as John Brown Russwurm (1799–1851) and Henry Highland Garnet turned to the history of bravery and leadership in the diasporic Atlantic to legitimate their political choices and inspire Black audiences.[13] Russwurm was born in Jamaica in 1799 to a white planter father, originally from Virginia, and an enslaved mother. As a young man, he attended school in Quebec and then moved with his father to Portland, Maine. Soon after his father's unexpected death, young Russwurm left for Boston, where he taught in schools for "colored youth" and became acquainted with a small coterie of educated free Black men in the city. In 1824, with the support of his stepmother and while enrolled at Bowdoin College, he wrote an essay detailing Toussaint L'Ouverture's key role in the rebellion in Haiti. In "Toussaint L'Overture [*sic*]: The Principal Chief of the Rebellion in St. Domingo," Russwurm celebrated the former slave's character and leadership in bringing the French colony through slave rebellion and emancipation to independence and nationhood. He described L'Ouverture with a warm admiration, even adulation, that was especially poignant coming from a young Black man with a deceased white father. His reverence for the Haitian hero also appeared in his commencement address, "The Condition and Prospects of Hayti," delivered in 1826.[14]

After receiving his degree, Russwurm teamed up with Samuel Cornish in 1827 to launch the first African American newspaper, *Freedom's Journal*. The response to the journal was initially enthusiastic but waned as Russwurm went public with his support of colonization. Russwurm's vision of a future beyond the United States reflected his skepticism about the possibility of full citizenship for African Americans. He saw the problem of race prejudice as intractable and intrinsic to the white body itself: "So easily are these prejudices imbibed, that we have often noticed the effects on young children, who could hardly speak plainly, and were we a believer in dreams, charms, &c., we should believe that they imbibed them with their mother's milk."[15] Although Russwurm was clear that he was no believer in dreams and charms, he imagined the freedom of men of African descent as fully expressed in their bodies, even affecting the way they walked. He considered "some other portion of the globe where all these inconveniencies are removed where the Man of Colour freed from the fetters and prejudice, and degradation, under which he labour in this land, may walk forth in all the majesty of his creation—a new born creature—a Free Man!" He repeated a remark attributed to Sir James Yeo, "while on the African coast, that the natives whom he saw were a fine athletic race, walking fearlessly, as if sensible of their important station as men, and quite different from the thousands of their brethren whom he had seen in the West Indies and the United States."[16] With L'Ouverture as his standard for Black manhood and his hopes pinned on Liberia, Russwurm traded his tenuous connection to the United States—he had lived in the country for little more than half his life and was a U.S. citizen through his white father—for a pan-African diasporic identity born out of his Jamaican mother and his homeland.[17]

Russwurm's embrace of colonization, which most African American abolitionists were rejecting during the later 1820s, put him at odds with his contemporary David Walker (1796/7?–1830). Walker, a used clothing dealer in Boston, tried to take the case for violent resistance directly to enslaved African Americans. Technically, Walker enjoyed freedom as a birthright; his mother was a free woman of color and his father enslaved. But violent attacks against the free Black residents of Cincinnati, Ohio, in 1829 made clear the vulnerability of all African-descended people, free as well as enslaved. His *Appeal to the Colored Citizens of the United States* (1829) called on the simmering anger of all African Americans, but especially men, and their desire to resist violently, if necessary, against white people who perpetually denied them liberty, livelihoods, and justice:[18]

> Will any of us leave our homes and go to Africa? I hope not. Let them commence their attack upon us as they did on our brethren in Ohio, driving and beating us from our country. . . . Let no man of us budge one step, and let slave-holders come to beat us from our country. America is more our country, than it is the whites—we have enriched it with our *blood and tears*. The greatest riches in all America have arisen from our blood and tears:—and will they drive us from our property and homes, which we have earned with our *blood*? They must look sharp or this very thing will bring swift destruction upon them. The Americans have got so fat on our blood and groans, that they have almost forgotten the God of armies.

Walker's raw call to arms echoed Richard Allen's language of embodied citizenship as well as centuries of language comparing slavery to cannibalism. But he also tried to stir his peers to collective militant resistance against white oppressors. The prospect of a collective defense of the Black community was appealing for a man whose enslaved father had been unable to protect him.

The *Appeal* mortified white abolitionists; such militancy made it difficult to assuage white fears that emancipated slaves would incite a vengeful race war. Walker distributed his pamphlet up and down the eastern seaboard using the networks of the Black maritime world that connected his Boston business to other Atlantic ports. His success was the specific spark for laws restricting Black sailors' contact with urban slaves in South Carolina, Georgia, North Carolina, and Florida.[19] Authorities in Milledgeville, Georgia, finding twenty copies of Walker's *Appeal* in newspaper editor Elijah Burritt's office in early 1830, used

Burritt's unproven connection to Walker to settle a political score and run him out of town.[20]

Manhood

The disadvantages of asserting African American manhood in such an embodied way were obvious to many nineteenth-century reformers, who brought aspirations to a more genteel manhood to bear on their observations of all that was wrong with slavery. Evangelical Protestantism also contributed to this trend. After Methodists won a following on both sides of the Atlantic, to be followed soon after by Baptists, manhood appeared to be as much a matter of restraint as of display. An evangelical man distinguished himself by reining in his baser passions. This cut him off from many of his male peers, who enacted male identity in ways that flaunted these passions through alcohol consumption, fights, gambling, tests of physical prowess and skill, and the sexual exploitation of women. Evangelical men disavowed such rowdy, potentially explosive scenes of male rivalry and sociability. As an alternative, they sought out their male evangelical peers to create a pious community of brothers. Itinerant preachers also cultivated manly reputations for their endurance of hardship on the circuit, steadfastness in the face of temptation, and aloofness from popular cultural forms that required self-assertion and physical display. Disparate eighteenth-century popular cultures of manhood gave way to nineteenth-century electoral politics, white mob violence directed against both African Americans and immigrants, and party platforms with positions on American expansion.[21]

If an enslaved man could feel the degradation and the humiliations of slavery as much as any white man would—if he could aspire to the refined experiences of learning, cognizance of eternal life, and love of his fellow human beings—what could be the justification for keeping him a slave? Christian piety, however, especially in the way the Society for the Propagation of the Gospel presented it to the enslaved, created a dilemma for Black manhood. It celebrated the combination of deference, duty, and humility that was supposed to mark the character of the ideal slave but made the pious man less able to succeed in the hardscrabble world of white men. As a tool of the master class, this type of piety smacked of subordination and submission rather than male assertion. It was a poor resource for a man seeking license to resist slavery physically. Its call to its followers to resist the temptations of the world, moreover, especially the vices of popularly enacted masculinity, was in many ways irrelevant for enslaved men, who had been systematically prohibited from indulging in these pleasures.[22]

But piety could be interpreted differently. It could license a man to insist on the equality of his soul, his right to be seated in the main body of the congregation, or time off to observe the Sabbath. It could also provide him with a speaking role at a time when there were few legitimate ways for a Black man to be heard in public: he might voice an opinion about the Christian upbringing of his child or become a mouthpiece for the Lord through preaching. Efforts to save other souls and to testify to his own salvation became justifications for an African American man's public speech. Black evangelicals, male and female, reached across the racial divide to white as well as Black souls in turmoil. Listeners described African American preachers as having a particular charismatic presence that enabled them to stir the hearts and spirits of their listeners. Such a gift was not the exclusive prerogative of men—African American women's claims to mystical piety and ecstatic experience were taken seriously by white and Black alike. Even if male preachers struggled to make their voices heard in a crowded field, however, enslaved men on nineteenth-century plantations carved out lives defined by spiritual and community leadership. Accounts of plantation life include descriptions of men initiating songs, leading dances and ring shouts, and guiding ecstatic religious experiences. From this attendance to the spirits of those within their communities, African American men began to combine spiritual with political authority. Both Denmark Vesey and Nat Turner, to take two prominent examples, drew on their spiritual authority to forge militant political leadership.[23]

To depend so much on one's body to assert manhood was to risk reinforcing racist depictions of Black men as brawn rather than brain, whose physicality appeared to white defenders of slavery to be a potential threat to the livelihoods of white working men, the lives of slaveholders, and the virtue of white women. The fact that so much white effort went into twisting the vitality of African American men into racist depictions of danger revealed its potential appeal for many—not simply other African American men and women, but white men and women as well. In white men, after all, such vigor was celebrated. White supremacy could not brook rivals for white men's dominance, however, necessitating that Black manhood be demeaned, exoticized, or violently suppressed until it posed no competition.

The response of Black men to this dilemma is instructive. The Massachusetts butler and successful author Robert Roberts urged Black men to leave the noisy attractions of male display on the streets for the quiet and orderly world of domestic labor in the parlors of the wealthy. Roberts provided explicit instructions in *The House Servant's Directory* (1828) for Black men to attain professional dignity and secure employment by taming their physicality. He tried to teach his readers to become aware of the way they walked, of how they looked after their clothing, and the jarring presence of their own laboring bodies in domestic spaces whose alchemy depended on effacing the traces of the labor needed to produce them. The manhood he recommended—a model of quiet endurance and professional competence that some of his readers might have interpreted as feminized—was at odds with the ways white people described Black men inhabiting city streets. But Roberts hearkened back to evangelical Christianity's potential to provide a resource for Black men, with a passage in his introduction that enjoined those of the servant class to recall but not to respond to the injuries that more powerful people inflicted on them.[24]

Roberts's message of professional advice and emotional and physical restraint flew in the face of Walker's call to arms. The promotion of domestic service for African Americans, moreover, irked Black abolitionists through the antebellum period and beyond.[25] Roberts's vision of Black professional demeanor also stood in stark contrast to the visceral expressions of enslavers' power coming from the southern states, where a landmark court case, *North Carolina v. Mann* (1829) underlined the master's right to commit physical violence on the bodies of enslaved people. When Lydia, a young woman hired out to an aging and indebted mariner, John Mann, attempted to escape his punishment, Mann retaliated by shooting her, wounding her seriously. Her mistress's guardian, Josiah Small, hired an attorney who succeeded in getting a local grand jury to indict Mann. The lower court disputed Mann's right to inflict serious injury on an enslaved person owned by someone else, but on appeal to the state supreme court, Judge Thomas Ruffin issued a now-infamous statement on the master's absolute right to physically punish, restrain, or even kill the people he enslaved:

> A submissive and entire obedience to the will of the Master can alone be expected to produce that subordination and those efforts of labor exacted from the slave. That submission of will can only follow from the power of the Master over the Body—a power which the Slave must be made sensible is not usurped, but conferred at least by the law of man, if not of God. Restraint, therefore, constant, vigilant, not unfrequently severe and exemplary and painful punishments of the slave is the unwelcome, and the necessary task of the Master. This discipline belongs to the state of slavery. They cannot be disunited without abrogating all the rights of the master and annuling the duties of the slave. It makes a curse of slavery both to the bond and the free portion of our population. But in the actual condition of things, there is no remedy. The power of the master must be unconditional and implicit. It is inherent in the relation of Master and Slave.

Ruffin acknowledged the institution's dependence on raw physical power and its backing by the state. Enslaved people, by this account, were always about to break their bonds unless restrained by constant white domination.[26]

Shedding Blood

Public depictions of Black manhood, and with them, the latitude for self-definition, changed dramatically with the Southampton Rebellion led by Nat Turner in 1831. Little is known about Turner's family ties, and that fact alone suggests some of slavery's toll on him. Speaking to Thomas Gray, the white man who interrogated him while he awaited execution, Turner described his father as an enslaved man who managed to escape slavery. No historian has been able to provide a clearer picture of Turner's father, and the information about his mother is sketchy at best. Turner allegedly told Gray that his parents had raised him to believe he was extraordinary on account of his religious and intellectual sensibility.[27]

Turner made no mention of David Walker's pamphlet, Ruffin's opinion, or of abolitionist agitation among Quakers across the state line in North Carolina. Divinely sanctioned natural rather than political signs—an eclipse in February 1831 followed by a strange greenish halo around the sun in mid-August—allegedly convinced Turner that the time was right to strike a blow against the owners of Virginia's Southside tobacco plantations and cornfields. In this interpretation of natural signs, he was a messianic prophet whose relationship with God resulted not in submission but in becoming a Christian soldier.[28]

In taking on the role of freedom fighter, Turner relied on his physical as well as spiritual leadership. His scarred body testified to the rigors of field work and the risks of injury for fatigued laborers working long years in sun-baked fields. Beginning at the household of his young master, the stepson of Joseph Travis, Turner and roughly seventy men set off across the dirt roads ringing the tobacco and cornfields of St. Luke's Parish, stopping at each house to kill the white inhabitants. In all, he and his men killed fifty-five men, women, and children, with Turner having a direct hand in several of the deaths. Following Turner's capture, trial, and execution, the Penn Medical School alumnus Dr. Orris A. Browne, Southampton County's coroner who also served as a judge in Turner's trial, dissected Turner's body and allegedly kept his skull as a souvenir, which he engraved with his initials. Other white souvenir seekers took pieces of the enslaved rebel's cadaver to demean the rebellion's threat to white supremacy.[29]

From the night of the violence in Southampton to the present day, Turner's decision to shed the "innocent" blood of white women and children has polarized opinion about his legacy. The focus on white innocence in a society in which enslaved women were coerced into providing domestic services—including cooking, cleaning, sewing, childcare, and sex with white men—is a curious one. To be innocent of slavery's violations of the human rights of enslaved people, a white woman would have had to renounce the benefits of an enslaved woman's substitution for her in the fields, in the kitchen, and in the sexual act or the birth that resulted. Even if she did not belong to a household with slaves, a white woman benefited from the privileges of whiteness, which included the recognition of marital ties, kinship, the connection to legitimate children, and an aspiration to the ideal, if not lived experience, of release from arduous field labor.

But what of the twenty-five white children Turner and his men dispatched during the night of killing? Surely, even if no white adult in a slave society can be counted as innocent, a white child should not be held accountable for the world his grown-ups made. Yet this is perhaps the wrong question if it is the only question we raise. The deaths of Turner's young victims should inspire us to consider a different issue: that white children's "innocence" derived in part from the protections they enjoyed from the predations and exploitations regularly suffered by enslaved children. Enslaved children endured traumas triggered by unbuffered white domination over their parents, their kin, and themselves. This included separation through sale of parents and siblings, witnessing corporal punishments and rapes, and daily deficiencies of food, material comforts, and security. As Robert Pleasants and many nineteenth-century abolitionists noted, enslaved children were the true innocents because they had done nothing except to be born to enslaved mothers. With slavery taking the place of a birthright and the protections that rendered white childhood innocent, enslaved children suffered and died without any accounting like that provided for Turner's young white victims.[30]

In the aftermath of the Southampton Rebellion, authors, engravers, and journalists rushed to capitalize on the sensational murders of white women and children by enslaved men. Graphic images of white women in distress—a magnet for white readers already drawn to the seemingly exotic alchemy of race and sex in the slave South—emphasized Black predation on fragile white innocence. The images were a striking departure from the time-honored visual culture prohibitions on depicting powerful adult African-descended men in the same frame as white women. The representation of enslaved men as savage, moreover, troubled abolitionist efforts to equate U.S. slavery with the barbarism of the East. In abolitionist comparisons of southern slavery to Eastern barbarism, it was enslavers rather than the enslaved who were the true barbarians. Popularly circulated images of ferocious enslaved men undermined the strategies of abolitionists, who were keen to depict enslaved people as conforming to legible human types—men and women with sentiments, family connections, and motives familiar to white men and women (Figure 6). But the engravings generated by the Southampton Rebellion also undermined white southern efforts to depict slavery as a paternalistic institution, consistent with the ideals of white domestic life.[31]

Following the Southampton Rebellion, the Virginia State Assembly debated the risks of continuing to be a slave society and abolitionists everywhere strategized and regrouped. In 1831 Virginia's governor John Floyd gained possession of a letter signed by "Nero" that connected the spate of recent incidents that frightened white slave owners. Nero claimed that both he and Nat Turner were following orders of a chief who knew of both David Walker's *Appeal* and of the absconding Georgia editor Elijah Burritt, alleged to possess a cache of copies. Nero also promised more violence. Although there was no evidence that Nero's persona or claims were authentic, they spoke to a collective white southern fear of a widespread violent conspiracy to end slavery.[32]

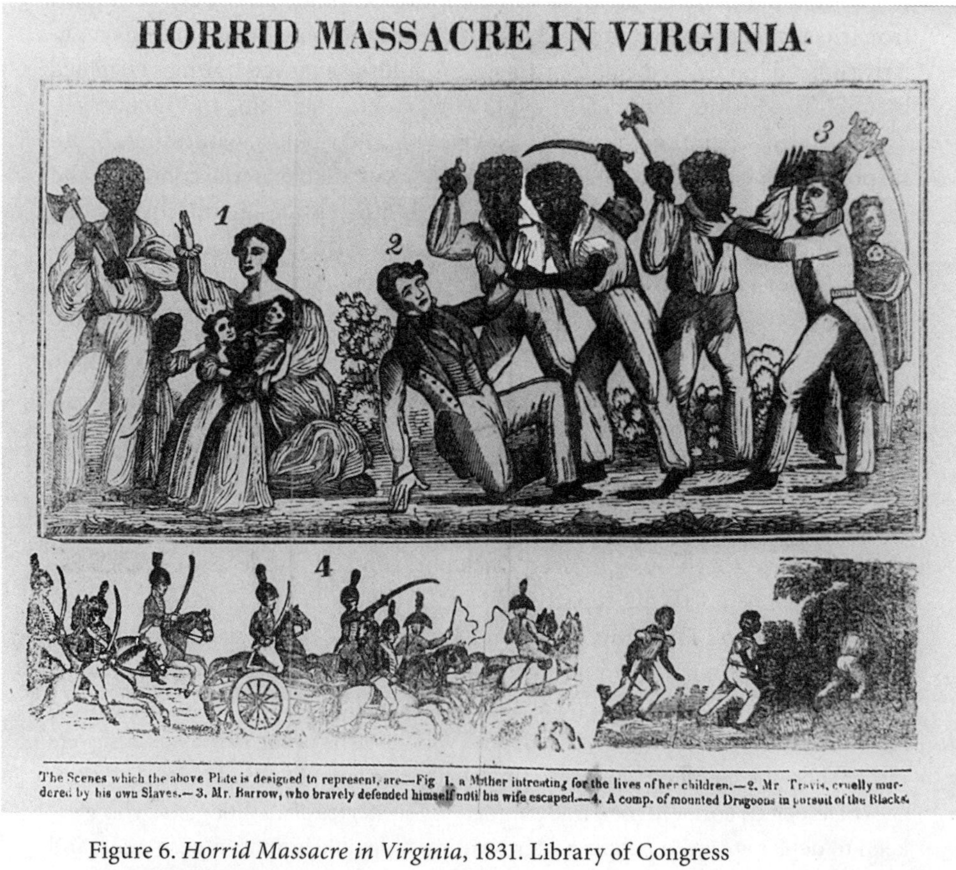

Figure 6. *Horrid Massacre in Virginia*, 1831. Library of Congress LC-USZ62-38902.

Garrisonian abolitionists' commitments to nonresistant methods came in response to the Southampton Rebellion in Virginia, and signaled that they would seek means other than armed conflict to liberate enslaved people from the bondage that constrained them. In Philadelphia, however, white mobs went on the rampage, aiming less to murder Black people than to raze their civic and religious institutions and destroy their private property so that they would be forced to leave their neighborhoods. Throughout the 1830s, white arsonists targeted free Black residences, churches, schools, and orphanages. Excluded from the brotherhood of firefighting gangs that included Irish Catholics, who also fell prey to white Protestant mob violence, African Americans had little recourse when white mobs set their buildings alight. When Black men stole the firefighting equipment of the Fairmount Engine Company in August 1834, over four hundred white men took their revenge on the neighborhood surrounding the Flying Horse carousel amusement hall in Moyamensing, south of the city. Black homes, churches, and orphanages were reduced to ashes over the course of three nights of rioting, forcing Black residents to relocate to New Jersey or to the city proper. The destruction of this neighborhood was followed by attacks on African Americans and their civic institutions in 1835 and 1837.[33]

Elsewhere during the 1830s, abolitionists committed to moral suasion fell victim to violent attacks. News of the abolitionist newspaper editor Elijah Lovejoy's murder in 1837 sent shock waves through the American Anti-Slavery Society. Lovejoy had for several years faced down hostile proslavery crowds in Indiana who vandalized his newspaper offices and printing press. He persisted in defending the freedom of the press even when faced with a mob threatening his life. More shocking to white abolitionists, even his wife's physical intervention to protect him could not deter his enemies. Antislavery societies around the nation declared Lovejoy a martyr for the cause—perhaps the first white martyr—even as they murmured against his decision to defend himself with a gun. PFAS members vowed "that our brother's blood shall not in vain cry to us from the ground" and warned that speed would be important if abolition was to be accomplished peacefully.[34]

Slavery's defenders again found themselves on shaky ground in 1839 when a group of West African men aboard the schooner *Amistad* claimed their natural right to defend their liberty. Captured by the Portuguese in Sierra Leone and sold in Havana, Cuba, to Spanish planters, the men rose up against the crew of the schooner transporting them against their wills, killing the captain and the cook. Led by Joseph Cinque (Sengbe Pieh), the men demanded that the two Spanish enslavers return them to Africa. Instead, the Spaniards navigated the schooner north where it was intercepted by the U.S. brig *Washington* off the coast of Long Island. The brig's captain, Thomas Gedney, who would later seek compensation by right of salvage in the form of a share of the value of the enslaved men, brought them to a New London jail where they were charged with murder and detained. When the case was referred to the federal district court, abolitionists provided the men with legal counsel and produced a statement asserting their rights as free men to resist being taken into slavery. "They are severally natives of Africa and were born free," they asserted, "and ever since have been, and still of right are and ought to be free, and not slaves, as in said several libels pretended, or surmised." Nor could they be enslaved as a consequence of the laws of Cuba or of Spain, but rather needed to be understood as victims: "each of them were, in the land of their nativity, unlawfully kidnapped & forcibly and wrongfully carried on board of a certain vessel, near the coast of Africa then & there unlawfully engaged in the slave trade, by certain persons to them unknown." Their actions in killing the captain and cook who were transporting them against their wills, moreover, "were incited by the love of liberty natural to all men, and by the desire of returning to their families and kindred . . . or to seek an asylum in some free State where Slavery did not exist, in order that they might enjoy their liberty under the protection of its government."[35]

The Connecticut district court justice ruled that Cinque and his men could not be treated as salvage property to compensate the planters, the Spanish government, or Captain Gedney (who, they argued, could find his remedy from the rest of the *Amistad*'s cargo), and dismissed the murder charges against them. The U.S. government, in an effort to appease both Spain and white southerners, appealed the case to the Supreme Court, where Justice Taney issued a writ of habeas corpus to bring the detained men before the court in *U.S. v. Cinque*. John Quincy Adams came out of retirement to defend the men, arguing that, as free men, Cinque and his fellows had a natural right to fight to regain their freedom.[36] Commentary by the phrenologist Lorenzo Fowler and a portrait of Cinque commissioned by Robert Purvis, completed just weeks before the Supreme Court's expected verdict, supported the interpretation of Cinque's leadership as motivated by virtue—justice and liberty—rather than barbaric rage. Justice Story wrote the opinion in favor of the *Amistad* captives—that the Africans were not slaves and so could exercise self-defense and kill their captors—but did so narrowly. Abolitionists throughout the nation celebrated the decision as a victory, and at the PFAS meeting on March 11, 1841, members proclaimed the "triumph of Justice." At this same meeting, PFAS gave its first donation to the City's Vigilance Committee.[37]

Searching the Past

Nat Turner's leadership provoked white southerners to clamp down on enslaved people with unbearable new restrictions and prompted abolitionists' soul-searching about the path out of slavery. In response, African American abolitionists grappled with the circumstances of their own birth families and searched the past for models of male leadership in an effort to honor diasporic African lineages. James McCune Smith (1813–1865), to take one prominent example, was born in New York City in 1813 to Lavinia, a self-emancipated slave from Charleston, South Carolina. His father, Samuel Smith, was likely his mother's enslaver. The younger Smith listed his father as a New York City merchant on his enrollment forms for medical school in Glasgow, but it is not clear that they ever had a relationship as father and son. As a child attending New York City's African Free School, Smith was acknowledged by his teachers as bright and promising. There he became lifelong friends with Henry Highland Garnet and Alexander Crummell. After being rejected from U.S. medical schools because of his race, Smith traveled to Scotland in 1832, where he received an M.D. from Glasgow University in 1837, the first African American to earn such a degree. His training in Glasgow included anatomy and dissection classes taught by Dr. James Jeffray and work with patients at the Lock Hospital for the treatment of venereal disease. He topped off his medical training with a stint in Paris to gain additional clinical experience. Such an education would have been the envy of any aspiring physician.[38]

While in Glasgow, Smith joined the Abolition Society, an association that prepared him for antislavery politics back in the United States. Returning to New York in 1837, Smith established his surgical and medical practice at 93 West Broadway. There he gave a public lecture, "The Fallacy of Phrenology," disputing the claims of phrenologists based on the dubious correlation of skull morphology with that of the brain. He debunked the notion that the outer shape and dimensions of the human skull revealed an individual's traits, character, and intellect. According to an account of the lecture published in the *Colored American*, Smith presented skulls and notations on a blackboard to challenge phrenological conclusions about the superior intellects of Europeans, refuting the notion that the brain's materiality could be mapped precisely for the qualities of an individual's mind.[39]

The following year, Smith's "Abolition of Slavery and the Slave Trade in the French and British Colonies" appeared in the *Colored American*, a journal that Smith would later edit. Initially delivered as a speech, Smith's essay celebrated the French and British for providing successful models of abolition in the Americas. Although he made clear his love of his country, echoing Sarah Mapps Douglass in referring to it as "my own, my native land," he drew on the religious practice of fraternal instruction to justify British abolitionist interventions in the United States.[40]

Like his friend Henry Highland Garnet and fellow activist John Brown Russwurm, Smith turned to African diasporic history to find examples of inspirational male leadership. As was the case for Russwurm, his search led him to Toussaint L'Ouverture. In 1841, Smith gave a speech to benefit the New York City Colored Orphans Asylum, "A Lecture on the Haytien Revolutions: With a Sketch of the Character of Toussaint L'Ouverture," in which he offered a brief analysis of the revolutions and L'Ouverture's heroic role. Smith used population statistics to calculate an annual loss of five thousand African lives in prerevolutionary Saint Domingue, a violation of the conservative principle of the "law of nature" that paved the way for rebellion. Smith also argued for the impact of caste—the distinction between white landowners and free creoles—that came to a head with the murder of Vincent Ogé.[41]

In comparison to the often-condemned "orgies" of the French Revolution that produced rivers of blood and a tyrant, Smith depicted the revolutions in Haiti as ultimately producing a peacemaker, Toussaint L'Ouverture. Smith portrayed L'Ouverture as a Christian man of character who had maintained his virtue and integrity uncontaminated by the degradations of slavery that surrounded him. In the prime of his manhood at age forty-seven, L'Ouverture remained honest and faithful in his marriage to one wife and in his service to his master. Once freed, however, Toussaint proved his genius as a military and political leader who, according to Smith, put newly freed people back to work as paid laborers on the island's plantations to sustain the new nation's prosperity. Under this new labor regime, which resulted in "more moderate labors of the men, and the rest enjoyed (when required) by women," the flagging African population "CONSIDERABLY INCREASED." As Smith noted, "here is undeniable evidence, that the SLAVERY of the time was more disruptive of human life than the wars, insurrections, and massacres to which it gave birth." Population gains and losses became for Smith, as they had for Sturge and other free labor advocates, a way to assess the morality and sustainability of different forms of political economy.[42]

Under L'Ouverture's leadership, Saint Domingue "enforced the duties of religion" but severed the ties of church and state. This made it possible for a moral order to take hold that condemned indecency and extolled modesty, the best "defence of women." By Smith's account, however, Napoleon's dark and tyrannical spirit ultimately doomed L'Ouverture's tenure and brought about more war and bloodshed as well as L'Ouverture's arrest and deportation to a lethal French prison. That L'Ouverture's literacy enabled him to become "the patriot, the father, the benefactor of mankind" provided an example of the importance of Black education.[43]

The same year as his lecture on Haiti to benefit the New York City Colored Orphans' Asylum, Smith spoke before the city's Phoenix Society, a forum for Black learning and community improvement, on the "Circulation of the Blood."

Smith offered a scientific lecture on the human body's inner mechanisms to an African American audience interested in learning. Although the text of the lecture no longer exists, for Smith, the common condition of the human body was key to his vision of human equality. Two years later, in 1843, Smith presented his views to the New York City Philomathean Society and Hamilton Lyceum on the substance and meaning of race in "The Destiny of the People of Color." Laws barring free African Americans from voting and participating fully in civic life ironically testified to their common intellect and humanity, he argued. If they were actually inferior, no laws would have been necessary.[44]

Passengers and Conductors

In addition to identifying heroes from the African diasporic past, African American abolitionists encouraged enslaved people to physically remove themselves from bondage by "stealing" themselves from their enslavers. This was a direct invitation to the enslaved to avail themselves of the networks of the Underground Railroad. Building on nearly two centuries of enslaved people's successful escapes from bondage, the Underground Railroad emerged as a network of allies, safe houses, and recommended routes north. It became a clandestine form of community migration that countered the internal slave trade's forced transport of thousands of enslaved people from the Upper South to the Lower South. Numerous contemporaries testified to the participation by white Quakers, especially those in the border states and the upper Midwest, as crucial to this migration. Quaker involvement appears to have begun quite early, even in the slaveholding South. According to several Quaker accounts, North Carolina–born Levi Coffin, along with his cousin Vestal Coffin and an enslaved man, Saul, became involved in the work of the Underground Railroad in North Carolina in 1819 when they helped a refugee, John Dimery, reach Richmond, Indiana.[45]

Yet such a large-scale secret movement of people could have occurred only with the active support of free Black people and their institutions, including communities, churches, and risk-taking activists. Beginning in the 1830s, as the historian Cheryl LaRoche has shown, communities in Rocky Fork and Miller Grove, Illinois, Lick Creek, Indiana, and Poke Patch, Ohio, as well as countless other smaller settlements welcomed and sheltered fugitives and enabled them to pass secretly to their next safe haven. Moving along opportunistic and makeshift routes, thousands of enslaved people evaded slave patrols and headed north, with many eventually reaching safety in Canada. Their efforts gave the lie to white southern depictions of slavery as a benign institution.[46]

Philadelphia became the eastern gateway of the Underground Railroad by the early nineteenth century, and many Pennsylvania activists provided leadership and support. Despite his own recommendations of patient endurance, William Whipper (1804–1876) encouraged action in the form of escape. His free birth, education, and commitment to universal brotherhood may have made it more difficult for him to embrace the militancy of Walker, although he had no qualms about active participation in the Underground Railroad. Whipper was born in Lancaster, Pennsylvania, in 1804 to a manumitted North Carolina woman and her former enslaver, with whom she lived openly. His father ensured that Whipper benefited from the same education as his white half siblings. Whipper left Lancaster to work in Philadelphia during his twenties. In 1832, he joined James Forten and Robert Purvis in a successful protest against the proposed ban on the migration of free Black people into the state. At age thirty, Whipper established a temperance and free labor grocery store next to Mother Bethel Church in Philadelphia. He witnessed firsthand the violent backlash against Black civic assertion, including the mob violence against Black schools, churches, and orphan asylums in the city between 1834 and 1837. Later in life, Whipper founded the American Moral Reform Association to try to reform Black manners, in particular, to end alcohol consumption and urge African Americans to industriousness.[47]

Under Whipper's stewardship, the Underground Railroad corresponded with the actual railroad in Pennsylvania. During the mid-1830s, after relocating to the Susquehanna River community of Columbia, Pennsylvania, Whipper began a lucrative partnership with Steven Smith, an African American businessman who had purchased his own freedom and begun a prospering lumber business. Their investments in coal, lumber, and eventually railcars and rail lines allowed them to become active operators on the Underground Railroad. Hundreds of fugitives hid in Whipper's Columbia warehouses until he could transport them to safety in railcars with false bottoms. Refugees took clandestine routes to Pittsburgh, Philadelphia, and points north.[48]

Throughout his antislavery activism, Whipper remained committed to a peaceful path out of slavery. In 1837, Whipper made the case for the virtues of nonviolent resistance in an essay, "Non Resistance to Offensive Aggression." In it, he observed that "the love of power is one of the greatest human infirmities, and with it comes the usurping influence of despotism, the mother of slavery." Although he conceded that self-defense was consistent with the laws of nature, he urged free Black people to adopt reason rather than follow passion. Inflamed with a "demon-like spirit of passion," "professedly civilized nations, as well as the more barbarous tribes" succumbed to baser feelings. Whipper found it tragic that "the very bones, sinews, muscles, and immortal mind, that God, in his infinite mercy has bestowed on man" to pursue the principles of "righteousness, justice, peace on earth, and good-will to their fellow men" were employed instead to "[protract] the period when the glorious millennium shall illumine our world." He urged his readers to ask themselves "is it reasonable, that for the real or supposed injuries that have been inflicted on mankind from the beginning to the present day, that the attempted redress of the same should have cost so much misery, pain, sweat, blood, and tears, and treasure?" Whipper's answer was an emphatic no, and he equated vengeful violence with sinking below the standard of humanity. "If man's superiority over the brute creation consists only in his reasoning powers and rationality of mind," he argued, "his various methods of practicing violence towards his fellow creatures, has in many cases placed him on a level with, and sometimes below many species of the quadruped race." It was a clear indictment of the slaveholding class.

As Whipper surveyed recent history, he concluded that no one had "ever given a more powerful impetus to the cause of peace, than the modern abolitionists. They have been beaten and stoned, mobbed and persecuted from city to city, and never returned evil for evil, but submissively, as a sheep brought before the shearer have they endured scoffings and scourges for the cause's sake, while they prayed for their prosecutors." Prescient about the triggers for violence, he interpreted it as miraculous that "not the life of a single individual has been sacrificed on the altar of popular fury. Had they have set out in this glorious undertaking of freeing 2,500,000 human beings, with the war-cry of 'liberty or death,' they would have been long since demolished, or a civil war would have ensued; thus would have dyed the national soil with human blood." The success of the abolitionist cause was, in Whipper's view, based in its restraint and reliance upon the "weapons" of "reason and moral truth." He would rethink this conviction later in life, concluding that racism rather than slavery appeared to be the catalyst for white supremacy.[49]

Smith and Whipper moved in the same circles as the Underground Railroad conductor David Ruggles (1810–1849), born in Norwich, Connecticut, to two free parents. After relocating to New York City, Ruggles worked as a grocer and free labor produce retailer before taking up printing, bookselling, and journalism. He also became an agent for the *Emancipator* and the *Journal of Public Morals* and an editor of the *Mirror of Liberty*, the first magazine owned and produced by an African American. His location in New York City, his travels, and his vast network made him a vital force in the Underground Railroad.

In 1835, Ruggles published the *Abrogation of the Seventh Commandment*, the first abolitionist text to deal explicitly with rape as a violation of God's laws, identify it as intrinsic to slavery, and hold the white women of the North and South accountable for its perpetuation against enslaved women. That same year, he helped to found New York City's Vigilance Committee, organized to protect refugees from slave catchers. He remained active as its secretary but he also brought an engaged physical presence to pursuing the city's slave catchers, resulting in his own serious injury on more than one occasion. He personally sheltered and mentored Frederick Douglass, newly escaped from slavery, sending him to New Bedford for work. In 1839, after being accused by Samuel Cornish of the New York City Vigilance Committee of mishandling funds, he published a pamphlet in his own defense. He issued his own call for militant action in 1841 in a notice in the *Liberator* calling for enslaved people to rise up. He continued to edit the *Mirror of Liberty* until 1842, when ill health and blindness forced him once again to seek a cure.[50]

By the 1840s, white abolitionists who had forsworn violence called for escape from slavery's "prison" as part of a larger plan to bring slavery down. Gerrit Smith, a political abolitionist who had not hewed to the Garrisonian nonresistance line, publicly called for enslaved people to run away in a speech in January 1842 at the Anti-Slavery Convention of New York. In May 1843 at the New England Anti-Slavery Convention, Garrison similarly urged the enslaved to "assert your manhood" and "transform yourselves from things into men" by leaving enslavement through flight. Both activists knew that escape contributed to an enslaved person's "depreciation" and so represented a loss of value for the enslaver. Yet both men stopped short of urging militant confrontation with white enslavers, counseling instead patient endurance that was in some ways inconsistent with their recommendation of escape.[51]

The persistent pattern of enslaved people escaping across boundaries like the Mason-Dixon Line demarcating slave and free states revealed both the weakness of federal enforcement of the Fugitive Slave Law of 1793 and the South's complete dependence on it to protect slavery. If that state line should become a national border, as some Garrisonians threatened, slavery would be severely undermined. This was exactly what worried white southerners. Gerrit Smith's 1842 statement encouraging enslaved people to escape coincided with John Quincy Adams's reading of an antislavery petition in Congress that called for the dissolution of the United States—a dramatic ultimatum that Garrisonians would echo in the April 1842 *Liberator*, concluding that the only alternative was "dissolution of the Union or the Abolition of Slavery." The PFAS echoed the sentiment in September 1844, declaring, "our influence shall be exerted in support of the doctrine that abolitionists can consistently have no union with slaveholders," but carefully stipulated that PFAS officeholders must swear to uphold the United States Constitution.[52]

White southerners reacted with alarm at the possible loss of federal authority over border states like Pennsylvania that were receiving fugitives. If a state boundary became a national border, Joseph Underwood of Kentucky predicted, slavery would be undone in Kentucky, Maryland, and large portions of Virginia.

Calls for enslaved people to escape coincided with the call for disunion, as in the *Liberator*'s "Disunion Pledge" of June 27, 1845, which made use of the language of blood. Noting how the Constitution failed to provide fugitives from slavery with any protection from their pursuers, the pledge's signatories declared their hope to "clear their skirts from innocent blood." Within three years, even the prudent members of PFAS had backpedaled on their support for the Constitution by calling for "the immediate peaceful dissolution of the American Union."[53]

For Whipper, Smith, Ruggles, and numerous others, living one's abolitionist convictions meant putting one's own body on the line to take risks daily to assist in life-or-death escapes for slavery's refugees. Being an Underground Railroad conductor meant expanding the role of protector and risk-taker to its full political and activist potential. It also meant combatting the legacy of forced migration with a system of clandestine escape that chipped away, one escape at a time, at the property relationship of slavery.

Resistance and Moral Suasion

Into the midst of the abolitionist chorus urging moral suasion came Henry Highland Garnet's "Call to Rebellion," an incitement to action delivered in a public forum. Garnet, the son of enslaved refugees from Kent County, Maryland, escaped from slavery with the help of the legendary Underground Railroad conductor Thomas Garrett, who brought Garnet's parents and their seven children to safety in Wilmington, Delaware, and Bucks County, Pennsylvania. Garnet grew up in New York City, where he became acquainted with the Reverend Theodore Sedgewick Wright, the pastor of the city's First Colored Presbyterian Church. He attended the African Free School with James McCune Smith and Alexander Crummell. In 1828 he took a job as a cabin hand on a ship headed to Cuba and returned to New York one year and several voyages later to find his family threatened by the prospect of reenslavement. In the years following this trauma, he suffered an injury to his leg that later required it to be amputated.

While a student at the Noyes Academy in Canaan, New Hampshire, Garnet met his future wife, Julia Williams, an alumna of Prudence Crandall's Canterbury (Connecticut) Female Boarding School. White mob violence on September 9, 1834, closed Crandall's school permanently, sending Williams to the Noyes Academy, which suffered its own attack at the hands of an angry white mob the following year. Garnet and two other male students, including Crummel, briefly attempted to defend themselves with a shotgun. Upon returning to New York City, Garnet and several friends successfully organized a club for radical abolitionists that drew over a hundred and fifty young African Americans. Garnet subsequently received additional schooling at the radical abolitionist college at Oneida Institute, where the president and Evangelical Congregationalist minister Beriah Green trained two dozen African American ministers. Following his four years at Oneida, Garnet had a stint as a teacher at the Troy Academy, where he received additional theological tutoring from Nathan S. S. Beman, a New School Presbyterian and local pastor. In 1840, Garnet became a force in the national abolitionist movement when he gave the first speech by a former slave to the American Anti-Slavery Society just days before white and Black members opposed to women's leadership and public activism left the organization to form the American and Foreign Anti-Slavery Society.[54]

Garnet's 1843 "Call to Rebellion" was one of several post–Nat Turner articulations of militant abolitionism. It followed that of Peter Paul Simons, a porter from New York City, who in 1839 delivered a workingman's call to action. Simons denounced educated people of African descent for their elitist refusal to work at jobs they considered beneath them and condemned their focus on moral elevation, warning them, "remain inactive, and you but raise another generation of slaves, and your children's children to the last posterity will spend their lives in as bitter oppression as ye do now today. Remain inactive and your children will curse the day of their birth. . . . Remain inactive, and the almighty himself will spurn you for lack of courage, and not properly using your agency . . . physical and political efforts are the only methods left for us to adopt. We must show ACTION! ACTION! ACTION! and our will to be, or not to be; this we must study, this we must physically practice."[55] Simons, who was not highly book-learned, was a member of the New York City African Clarkson Association, a mutual aid society for working-class people like himself. He equated nonresistance and moral elevation with a diminished and inappropriately whitened masculinity. Rather than lofty principles, Simons urged action and hard work. Overcoming poverty with material gain was at the center of his ideal for Black masculinity. When Samuel Cornish refused to publish Simons's speech in the *Colored American*, Simons purchased advertising space and published it himself, demonstrating that a Black man with money, no matter how rudimentary his education, could be a man with a voice.[56]

Two years after Simons's call to action, the *Liberator* published David Ruggles's letter to "Colored Americans," in which he urged, "Rise, brethren, rise! Strike for freedom or die slaves! . . . in our cause, mere words are nothing—action is everything. Buckle on your armor . . . remembering that our cause demands of us union and agitation." Ruggles's inspirational call emerged from his commitment to a broad scope of abolitionist activism: publishing, subscription sales, support of free labor produce markets, and participation in the Underground Railroad.[57]

Building on both of his predecessors and drawing on his training as a Presbyterian minister, Garnet admonished his listeners in his controversial 1843 speech to take a stand for freedom. In doing so, he recognized the risk to enslaved people: "however much you and all of us may desire it, there is not much hope of redemption without the shedding of blood. If you must bleed, let it all come at once—rather *die freemen, than live to be slaves*." Although he did not cite David Walker's 1829 *Appeal,* which made a similar pitch to enslaved people to end slavery through militant action, Garnet followed a similar logic based on the fact of Black majorities in southern slaveholding states. "Strike for your lives and liberties," he declared, and "remember that you are FOUR MILLIONS!"[58]

When he gave his speech in Buffalo in 1843, Garnet's militancy had crested. He had survived the terrors of slavery, being a refugee, and stealthy movement along the Underground Railroad. He had developed an awareness of a larger African diaspora during his maritime employment. And he had also experienced the fear of having his family dispersed by slave catchers, the physical toll of manual labor on his body, and the rage of the white mob, angered at the thought of education for Black students. Little wonder that his pantheon of African-descended heroes included Denmark Vesey, "a martyr to freedom," whose liberation plan Garnet described as the most "complicated and tremendous plan" ever formed in "the whole history of human efforts to overthrow slavery." Garnet claimed that Vesey's "tremendous movement shook the whole empire of slavery. The guilty soulthieves were overwhelmed with fear. It is a matter of fact, that at that time, and in consequence of the threatened revolution, the slave States talked strongly of emancipation."

Citing a violation of souls as well as bodies, Garnet believed Vesey's name belonged with those of Moses, Toussaint L'Ouverture, and Lafayette. Garnet also extolled "the patriotic Nathaniel Turner," who "was goaded to desperation by wrong and injustice." Despots recorded his name "on the list of infamy," but "future generations will remember him among the noble and brave." Garnet added "the immortal Joseph Cinque, the hero of the Amistad," and Madison Washington, "a slave on board the brig Creole, of Richmond," headed for New Orleans with over four hundred fellow slaves when "nineteen struck for liberty or death." As a result, the whole number was emancipated.

For Garnet, the lessons of history were clear: "Noble men! Those who have fallen in freedom's conflict, their memories will be cherished by the true-hearted and the God-fearing in all future generations; those who are living, their names are surrounded by a halo of glory." He exhorted enslaved men, "Brethren, arise, arise! Strike for your lives and liberties. Now is the day and the hour. Let every slave throughout the land do this and the days of slavery are numbered. You cannot be more oppressed than you have been—you cannot suffer greater cruelties than you have already. *Rather die freemen than live to be slaves*."

Yet as several scholars have noted, Garnet's speech was less a call to rebellion than to make collective face-to-face demands on masters for liberty, no matter the consequences. He urged an end to patient endurance, such as that recommended by Whipper, advocating instead for the power of a collective refusal to labor. Garnet laid out an argument for the moral responsibility of enslaved people to resist slavery, the evil system that obstructed their ability to receive God's grace. His dramatic language, heightened emotion, and references to blood and death, however, alarmed some of the Garrisonian attendees of the convention. Even if his aim was a work stoppage, Douglass chastised him, confrontational methods would lead to ill-fated insurrections. In response, Garnet clarified his main message: that enslaved people should make a nonviolent demand for their liberty, taking steps to seize it or die only if refused. This did not assuage Maria Weston Chapman, who offered a condescending criticism of Garnet in which she questioned his bona fides as an abolitionist. Garnet responded sharply in a letter to Chapman, published in the *Liberator*, noting that, as he was no longer a slave, he was free to "think on the subject of human rights without 'counsel.'"[59] Following public disapproval of his speech by the Garrisonians (with the exception of James McCune Smith, who admired his moxie), and praise for his manhood by abolitionists in the Liberty Party, Garnet began to take the possibility of African American emigration more seriously. But he also pursued other means of undoing slavery, moving to England in 1850, becoming a missionary to Jamaica in 1852, and promoting the cause of free labor produce.[60]

Martin Delany (1812–1885), like Garnet, Smith, and Douglass, was an intellectual who struggled with the question of how to identify a path out of slavery. He shared Garnet's militant perspective, Smith's commitment to providing medical care to free Black people, and Douglass's turn to the printed word to stir Black readers. Delany was born in 1812 in Charles Town, Virginia, to an enslaved father and a free mother, Pati, who taught her children to read. Threatened with punishment for violating the law prohibiting such education, Pati removed the children to Chambersburg, Pennsylvania, where their father, a skilled carpenter able to purchase his own freedom, subsequently joined them. Delany seized opportunities for formal education in 1831 in Pittsburgh, studying classics and apprenticing to an abolitionist doctor, who taught him medicine. By 1836, he was skilled enough in bleeding and cupping to open his own office as a medical practitioner.[61]

Beginning in 1839, Delany experimented with a number of different forms of activism. He traveled throughout the South and Southwest, observing the effects of removal on the lives of Indigenous peoples and the systematic coercion of enslaved people by slave owners, local communities, and state and federal governments. During the 1840s, he founded a Black newspaper, *Mystery*, and co-edited the *North Star* with Frederick Douglass. Even as he engaged in journalism as a form of activism, Delany never forgot that medicine offered him a means to provide much-needed care for African Americans. His previous training in Pittsburgh enabled Delany to apply successfully to Harvard University Medical School, where he enrolled in 1850. His medical education was cut short, however, when white student protests forced him and the two other African American students in his class to withdraw. Like so many abolitionists, by the 1850s Delany would adopt an increasingly radical position, putting him at odds with many of his fellow African American activists. His serialized publication *Blake: Huts of America* (1859, 1860–1861), featured an African American hero who led a Pan-American insurrection.[62]

William Wells Brown's path to militancy was less direct. Born in Lexington, Kentucky, in 1814 to an enslaved mother, Elizabeth, and a white relative of her enslaver, Brown (1814–1884) spent twenty years as a slave before escaping to freedom. He was just beginning to become active in antislavery circles in 1843, when Henry Highland Garnet gave his controversial speech at the Buffalo convention. Rejecting Garnet's call to arms, Brown allied himself with the moral suasion school of abolition. During the 1840s, he assumed greater responsibilities, first as a member and then as a paid agent of the American Anti-Slavery Society. From 1849 to 1854, he traveled to England and Europe on an extended speaking tour where he met British abolitionists and peace activists. At the Paris Peace Congress of 1849, for example, he met Joseph Sturge, the English activist Richard Cobden, and the French novelist Victor Hugo, and stirred his audience with his account of the horrors of slavery.[63] By the time he returned to the United States in 1854, Brown had completed *Clotel* (1853), the first novel by an African American, a tragic account of Thomas Jefferson's mixed-race daughters. Like so many of his fellow activists, Brown had also adopted a more militant approach to undoing slavery, inspired in part by the example of Toussaint L'Ouverture and fed by the potential of enslaved men, who Thomas Jefferson warned would "vindicate [their] right to freedom by physical force."[64]

Vigilant Men and Women

African American men pursued other forms of militant action with assistance from Black communities and white allies. Of these, escaping slavery was arguably the most politically significant. Enslaved people who fled to the care and protection of a "free" jurisdiction claimed the right to geographic movement that slavery had denied them. Under the auspices of personal liberty laws, Black activists formed Vigilance Committees to protect people suspected to be fugitives and to provide aid to African Americans in distress. As the work of the Philadelphia Vigilance Committee (PVC) revealed, protecting fugitives was less a matter of pure legal maneuvering than of gathering a critical mass of community members who could prevent slave catchers from carrying out their business.

Male activists appeared in the most public roles of Vigilance Committees. In Pennsylvania, activists worked within the provisions of the 1826 law, which created a legal process for slave owners to remove enslaved people from the state but which also included some protections from kidnapping. Two of the founding members of the PVC, Jacob C. White, Sr. (1806–1872) and James J. G. Bias (1807–1860), were well-regarded medical practitioners. White, born free in neighboring Kensington, was a dentist, bleeder, barber, and free produce store operator. He relocated his family to the Mother Bethel Church neighborhood, which was home to other prosperous free Black families, including the Fortens and Bustills, and several schools for Black students. Bias, born enslaved in Maryland, had worked closely with a physician before arriving in Philadelphia. For both men, community activism included providing medical care.[65]

The model for the PVC came from David Ruggles, who organized the New York Vigilance Committee around three main goals: disrupting kidnapping plots, exposing kidnappers to publicity and prosecution, and offering protection and aid to fugitives.[66] Within two years, Robert Purvis had summoned a similar committee in Philadelphia. Purvis had significant experience and networks in abolitionist circles. He had been involved in the founding of the American Anti-Slavery Society in 1833, serving on its Board of Managers from that date. He had also attended the first, second, and third annual Colored Conventions held in 1831–1833 in Philadelphia. In addition, Purvis and Harriet Forten Purvis, whom he married in 1831, mobilized their wealth and connections on behalf of refugees from slavery, often sheltering them in their home.[67]

Upon returning to Philadelphia in the fall of 1834 after a trip to Britain, Purvis became a central figure in the city's interracial antislavery activist networks.[68] On April 19, 1835, he gave an address to PFAS, of which his wife and sisters-in-law were members. By 1836 he had become directly involved with the escape of four enslaved brothers (renamed Dorsey for their own protection) who were the sons of their enslaver, the Frederick, Maryland, plantation owner Sobrick Sollers. The brothers arrived at Purvis's home on Ninth and Lombard Streets, which often served as a safe house for fugitives. Fearing that they would not be safe there, Purvis transported three of the four to his farm in Bucks County on the Neshaminy River, where he arranged employment for them (the fourth brother remained in Philadelphia). When slave catchers caught up with them, Purvis managed to get two of the three brothers on their way to Canada, but one of the men was captured. With the assistance of a lawyer and support from the community, Purvis helped the detained brother to make a successful jailbreak. It was the plight of the Dorsey brothers that convinced Purvis of the need for a Vigilance Committee to provide the physical and financial support for refugees newly arrived from neighboring slave states.[69]

In addition to his work with the PVC, Purvis undertook to defend the civil rights of free African American men in 1838 when the state of Pennsylvania threatened to strip them of voting privileges by inserting the word "white" into the new state constitution. Threatened with disenfranchisement, Purvis wrote *Appeal of Forty Thousand Citizens* (1838), a compilation of African American historical contributions as soldiers, caretakers of yellow fever victims, and civic-minded citizens. He also provided evidence of free Black economic independence with figures that demonstrated free Black industry and their disproportionately small presence on the poor rolls. Loss of the vote, Purvis contended, meant loss "of the panoply of manhood," and he declared that free citizens of color would not give up their "birthright" without a struggle. To leave free Black men without a political voice was to subordinate entire Black communities, the equivalent of being "transferred to the dominions of the Russian Autocrat, or of the Grand Turk." He challenged his readers to find historical evidence that Pennsylvania had ever intended free Black taxpayers to be excluded from citizenship. He rejected the suffrage exclusion as the retrograde embrace of slavery unjustly perpetrated on law-abiding Pennsylvania taxpayers. It revealed to Purvis how ambitious political men in Pennsylvania were willing to cater to the South to get ahead. Himself of mixed ancestry, Purvis lampooned white fears that "the purity of white blood should be sullied by intermixture with ours."[70]

When the state legislature ratified a new constitution that curtailed free Black voting, Purvis became more involved in Vigilance Committee work and the Underground Railroad, becoming the president of the PVC in 1839 and providing key leadership in other capacities. The Vigilance Committees of the 1830s were underfunded organizations, separate from antislavery societies. Work during that decade in Philadelphia included saving a boy from being sold out of state in violation of the 1826 personal liberty law and attending the Court of Common Pleas to support a man named James, claimed by Mr. William Maxwell of Kent County, Maryland, in 1839. The PVC often worked closely with attorneys to initiate legal actions. One of the most frequent was the request for a writ of habeas corpus, which required detainees to be brought before the court as a means of preventing slave catchers from simply removing them out of state. In the case of a Woodbury, New Jersey, detainee on June 5, 1839, this latter tactic failed when the prison guard refused to serve the writ obtained by the PVC.[71]

David Paul Brown, a stalwart attorney for the PVC who began his studies as a medical student of Benjamin Rush before reading law, frequently defended fugitives whose liberty was threatened by former masters. Brown defended Mary Gilmore, an Irish girl being raised by respected free Black owners of a bakery, Jacob and Elizabeth Gilmore, but claimed as a slave by Robert Atkins (Aitkin) of Baltimore. He also defended a pregnant mother of a three-year-old, Mary Sheppard, from the claims of Virginia enslaver John Walke in 1837. Brown's service to the free Black and fugitive communities was memorialized in 1841 when members of Mother Bethel Church gave him a silver pitcher featuring a kneeling enslaved woman on the front panel.[72]

From the outset, the PVC depended upon women's networking and direct provision of care to refugees. As agents in the field, Underground Railroad operatives, or activists living in the city, African American and white women provided news of safe havens and information about free status within the state of Pennsylvania. They also performed the basic "body work" of providing food, clothing, medical care, and shelter. White's wife, the seamstress Eliza Bustill Miller White, a descendant of one of the city's most prominent free Black families, founded the female PVC and served as its president. PFAS also supported the PVC, making its first formal donation to the group in the spring of 1841. The PFAS member Hetty Reckless served on Philadelphia's Vigilance Committee from at least 1841 and stood on the Committee of Fifteen as its only female member by 1842. In addition, women active on Philadelphia's Female Vigilance Committee raised funds to pay the women whose labor supported refugees. They were actively involved in fundraising and providing practical material assistance—food, clothing, shelter, transport, and medical care to refugees.[73]

The turning point for the PVC came in 1842 with *Prigg v. Pennsylvania* (1842). The case began, like so many interstate conflicts over enslaved people, with an enslaved woman deciding to move with her family from her former habitation in Maryland to a free home in Pennsylvania. But in ways that did not come under dispute directly in the court records but remained a central implication of the events, it also exemplified the utter disregard for the well-being and security of free Black people, in this case, of a free Black man struggling to protect his wife and children, including a child born on free soil, from abduction and trial as slaves in Maryland.

The woman in question, Margaret Morgan, escaped from Maryland to Pennsylvania in 1837. Margaret had been born to two enslaved people who had enjoyed de facto freedom on the estate of their master, John Ashmore. When Ashmore died intestate in 1824, he freed or sold most of the people he had enslaved. Neither Margaret nor her parents were listed in the estate inventory taken in that year. Sometime before 1832, Margaret appears to have married a free

Black man from Pennsylvania named Jerry Morgan. They lived together with their children in Harford, Maryland, the same community where Margaret had grown up with her parents. When her parents died, the couple relocated to York, Pennsylvania. For a few years, Margaret and Jerry lived unmolested in York County, where they had another child. Then Margaret Ashmore, Ashmore's widow, sent the Harford County constable Edward Prigg and her son-in-law to Pennsylvania to claim Margaret Morgan and her children as her slaves and to bring them back to Maryland. At issue were Margaret's status, that of her children, and the state that would have jurisdiction. Technically, Margaret might still have been defined as a slave under Maryland law, but her child born in Pennsylvania was a different story. Could an enslaved woman residing in a free state during her pregnancy and the birth of her child give birth to a free child? Previous courts had said yes.[74]

After Prigg and the other slave catchers sent by Ashmore crossed the state line into Pennsylvania in February 1837, they went before York County Justice of the Peace Thomas Henderson for an arrest warrant. Upon receiving it, and with assistance from Constable William McCleary, they rounded up Margaret and her children over the protests of her husband, Jerry. At this point, the Prigg party departed from the requirements of the 1826 Pennsylvania liberty law that a judge of a court of record approve the evidence before issuing a certificate of removal. Despite not having that crucial document and promising Jerry Morgan that they would reconvene in court the next day, Prigg took Margaret and her children back across state lines into Maryland that night. This prevented Jerry from gathering allies to prevent her removal and ultimately determined that Margaret's case would be heard in Maryland, where she had a weaker presumption of freedom. Margaret and her children lost their case; the family, including the child born in Pennsylvania who had the strongest claim to freedom, were reported by abolitionists to have been sold further south by Ashmore. Jerry Morgan took his protests to the governor of Pennsylvania, Joseph Ritner, but when he was found on a Susquehanna River canalboat not to have papers to prove his free status, he was seized as a suspected fugitive. Morgan's effort to escape by leaping off the canalboat ended with his tragic drowning. Not only had he lost his bid to protect his wife and children and have them returned to him, but he lost his life as a consequence of presumptions based on his race.[75]

Morgan's effort on behalf of his wife and children was not without effect, however. Governor Ritner directed the York County sheriff to deliver warrants for the arrest of Prigg and the other slave catchers. Maryland's governor Thomas Veazey delayed, and when the Maryland legislature finally responded in the spring of 1838, they argued that Pennsylvania's personal liberty laws abridged the Constitution's confirmation of the rights of enslavers to reclaim escaped slaves. Governer Veazey sent a message to the new Pennsylvania governor Porter requesting dismissal or referral to the U.S. Supreme Court.[76] Following the 1839 indictment of Edward Prigg for kidnapping Margaret Morgan and children, the PVC reorganized with Purvis as president. This is when the organization's hands-on work of supporting fugitive bodies really began.

In 1841, *Prigg v. Pennsylvania* was the first fugitive slave case to reach the Supreme Court; previously the court had followed the doctrine that slave status was a matter for states to decide.[77] During the 1820s, the nationalism of the Marshall court began to wane in favor of more robust state's rights rulings, but after 1835, under Chief Justice Roger Taney, the court embraced nationalism once again. In the *Prigg* decision, the Supreme Court struck down Pennsylvania's personal liberty law as unconstitutional. Justice Joseph Story's constitutional nationalism guided his interpretation that the Constitution had provided a prior guarantee of security of property to slave owners as a condition of the union of states.[78]

The 1842 *Prigg v. Pennsylvania* decision was not only a setback to the work of the men and women of the PVC; it was also a blow to a free Black man's rights to protect his family as any white man would have done. That same year, the celebration of West Indian Emancipation Day on August 1 with a Black temperance parade sponsored by the city's white and Black abolitionists and several churches sparked an angry Irish Catholic mob to lash out at African American people, homes, and institutions. The mob attacked the Black celebrants at Lombard and Fourth, and when Black men fought back, the violence spread to Fifth and Eighth Streets, dangerously close to Robert Purvis's home on Ninth and Lombard. Armed and prepared to defend his young family, Purvis decided thereafter to take a less prominent role in the PVC. The terror and trauma provoked him to move to rural Byberry. The PVC revived in 1843 under the leadership of Alexander Crummell, Hetty Reckless, and J. Miller McKim and operated in a lower public register. Emancipation Day celebrations continued, however, including the one held in neighboring Bucks County, Pennsylvania, in 1844.[79]

Also in 1842, Harriet Jacobs came through Philadelphia during her escape from slavery and told her story to the PVC and Philadelphia's abolitionist women. Many of these women had recently stepped up to provide hands-on support for slavery's refugees following the 1839 indictment of Margaret Morgan.[80] Jacobs's account revealed the cost of slavery for women but also the limits of militant male resistance. There was no man to protect Harriet Jacobs; she could only maneuver around men to try to protect herself and her child. Ultimately, she saved herself by going into hiding for seven years and then by fleeing, but her flight did not damage slavery as much as her decision to tell her story and publish it in 1860.[81]

The PVC of the 1840s continued to have interracial male leadership, with a four-person acting committee composed of Jacob C. White (by 1849 the proprietor of the city's African American Lebanon Cemetery), Nathaniel W. Deepee, William Still, and the white Quaker Passmore Williamson.[82] Its nineteen other members included J. Miller McKim, the free produce activist, Presbyterian minister, and newspaper editor; Purvis, who had organized the city's original Vigilance Committee; Charles Reason, born in Haiti; John P. Burr; Jeremiah Asher; Henry Gordon; Morris Hall; and Isaiah Wears, a veteran of the resistance to the 1838 disenfranchisement campaign.[83]

The greatest success of the Pennsylvania abolitionists during that decade came in 1847 with the passage of a reframed personal liberty law that offered some protections to free Black people claimed by enslavers under the 1793 Fugitive Slave Act. Under the provisions of the 1847 law, which limited judges, justices of the peace, and aldermen from issuing certificates of removal to enslavers, state judges retained the right to issue a writ of habeas corpus to an individual detained by a claim of ownership. Such a protection slowed down but did not stop slave catchers from kidnapping free people. The 1847 law also provided that the state would not detain alleged fugitives in jails except in instances where a judge had jurisdiction over the case, which allowed free Black and abolitionist communities to continue to use their numbers and presence to protect individuals from being removed summarily. Finally, the 1847 law closed the 1780 "sojourner" loophole that permitted enslavers to bring enslaved people into the state for six months without risk. These protections, carefully formulated to avoid the provisions of the 1826 personal liberty law that had been struck down, nonetheless reactivated the anger of Delaware, Maryland, and Virginia slave owners who feared for the security of their human property. Their dislike for the 1847 law and the continued successes of enslaved people escaping across state lines into Pennsylvania would set up the political tinderbox of the 1850 Fugitive Slave Act.[84]

Public Testimonies

The Vigilance Committee work of the 1830s and 1840s was risky and often physically demanding, especially for women providing care for fugitives. But even formal male leadership roles drained the bodies of activists. Providing testimony against slavery in public was one of the most frequent public forms of African American male abolitionist activity—requiring men to brave the public stage and withstand hecklers, threats of violence, and the rigors of exhausting travel and speech giving. These were the trials of public speaking that made female public speech so controversial and fueled arguments against them. But in all likelihood it was not the act of speech giving that raised the bar for women, as challenging as that was, but the potentially violent behavior of male audiences that gathered to hear activists.

Frederick Douglass was renowned among male abolitionists for his powerful presence at the public lectern. He did this in numerous ways, including communicating bodily empowerment to his white audiences in ways that impressed but did not threaten. Speaking before the Massachusetts Anti-Slavery Society early in his career in 1842, he commented, "I appear before the immense assembly this evening as a thief and a robber. I stole these limbs, this body from my master, and ran off with them." But if he was the quintessential Black abolitionist speaker, self-referentially summoning a resistant male body, he was also among the most generous and supportive to his female peers, white and Black.[85] Douglass endured numerous threats to his person, including an attempted murder by an angry white mob in Pendleton, Indiana, in September 1843 that left him seriously injured. The violence directed at Douglass seemed to some onlookers to be at odds with the presence of white women and their infants in the crowd of Douglass's supporters. But, in truth, it differed little from the proximity of white domestic life to the daily violence of slavery.[86]

Facing his former enslaver's threat to reenslave him, Douglass left the United States for England to protect his hard-won freedom. Douglass's "Reception Speech" in May 1846 came during this extended exile. Douglass lectured in Belfast in December 1845 and in early January 1846. He also attended the Birmingham Temperance Society meeting on December 15, 1845, with Sturge, who greeted him warmly and invited him to dine at his home.[87] The reformist crowd at the "Reception Speech" was likely more ebullient than usual because of recent victories under Prime Minister Robert Peel to repeal the long-despised Corn Laws. Like most nineteenth-century political meetings, it took place before an entirely male audience. The sympathetic assembly responded to Douglass with boisterous affirmations and shared condemnations, including "hear, hear," hisses, and shouted questions. Their dynamic participation shaped the content of his speech, compelling him to respond to the crowd with additional examples. This was typical of the heady atmosphere of nineteenth-century political meetings on both sides of the Atlantic and part of the attraction for the men who attended. Shoulder to shoulder in a crowded hall with men whose political commitments had drawn them to the meeting on short notice—in Douglass's case, just three days—audience members claimed speaking roles for themselves.[88]

Douglass spoke at length about slavery, not as a southern but an American institution, "a system that derives its support from the non-slave-holding states, as they are called, as from the slave-holding states." Aside from the immediate uses of physical coercion—whippings, scourging, branding—to terrify enslaved people into submission, Douglass argued, "the physical power needed to keep the slaves in bondage lies north of the line. The southern states admit their inability to hold their slaves, except through protection afforded by the northern states." For Douglass, the illogic of the demographic math—three hundred thousand men capable of holding three million in slavery—exposed the truth: "It cannot be. The slaves could by their own power crush their masters if they would, and take their freedom, or they could run away and defy their masters to bring them back. Why do they not do this? It is because the people of the United States are all pledged, bound by their oaths, bound by their citizenship in that country, to bring their whole physical power to bear against the slave if such an event should arise." The audience erupted with cries of "Shame!"[89]

Douglass also took pains to distinguish the American institution built on coercion and terror from the British habit of describing "every bad thing by the name of slavery." He listed the uses that he believed diminished the power of the word to evoke the horrors of the American context: in common parlance, intemperance, disenfranchisement, and having to work hard, might be described as "slavery." Indeed, these were several of Sturge's dearest reform causes. But Douglass insisted that "the term slavery is sometimes abused by identifying it with that which it is not. Slavery in the United States is the granting of that power by which one man exercises and enforces a right of property in the body and soul of another."

Douglass went on to detail the treatment of enslaved people as if they were brutes and property, noting the denial of the right of marriage to three million people in the United States. Those who did manage to find virtuous companionship lived with the constant threat of having their loved ones "torn asunder" by "man-stealers." This obstacle to Christian virtue, combined with the lethal punishments exercised against those who tried to gain education, resulted in a train of predictable evils that Douglass intimated need not be spelled out for his audience of Christian reformers: "I need not lift up the veil by giving you any experience of my own. Every one that can put two ideas together, must then see the most fearful results from such a state of things as I have just mentioned."[90]

The audience cheered loudly as Douglass described his exposition on the "physical evils of slavery" as an effort not to change the minds of his British listeners with an account of physical suffering, but to put slaveholders on notice that "the curtain which conceals their crimes is being lifted abroad." They responded with loud applause when he declared, "We want them to know that a knowledge of their whippings, their scourgings, their brandings, their chainings, is not confined to their plantations, but that some negro of theirs has broken loose from his chains." He then briefly listed the forms of torture, well known to his British audience from reports exposing such practices in the West Indies, that he claimed were even more intrinsic to American slavery. Quoting John Greenleaf Whittier, Sturge's close friend, he observed,

> What ho! Our countryman in chains,
> The whip on woman's shrinking flesh,
> Our soil yet reddening with the stains,
> Caught from her scourgings warm and fresh.[91]

The whip, the thumbscrews, the bloodhound, and the stocks were necessary to keep the slave in subordination. Without them, an enslaved person would immediately "walk out from the house of bondage and assert his freedom as a man." Still more horrifying to the sensibilities of the Christian reformer—and in a sharp rebuttal of the demographic arguments used by slavery's defenders during the British period of amelioration—Douglass decried the practices of the slave-breeding states, including his home state of Maryland, to produce new slave property for sale throughout the rest of the South.[92]

As Douglass continued his account of terror and bloodshed, audience members interrupted him with questions: What book was he quoting from? (The answer, Theodore Weld's *American Slavery as It Is*.)[93] When another person tried to ask a question, Sturge sought to protect Douglass, insisting, "I must beg that there may be no interruptions." But Douglass welcomed the audience's questions and responded to a query about the value of a "good slave" (the answer to which the audience hissed), observing critically that the British demand for cotton raised the value of slave property (the audience erupted in loud cheers at this condemnation of the British support of the American cotton market). Douglass then turned to the blood money that supported churches in the American South. When Douglass claimed "we have men sold to build churches, women sold to support missionaries, and babies sold to buy bibles and communion services for the churches," an audience member objected in horror, "it is not true!"

Douglass contrasted the situation in the United States, where the pulpit took a mainly proslavery stance, with Britain, where dissenting ministers supported abolition. At this point in his career Douglass still identified with the Garrisonians and insisted that slavery was a sin that needed to be purged from churches, even to the exclusion of slaveholders from communion. He recounted the efforts of the "come outers" (abolitionists who left their churches to protest clerical refusal to condemn slavery), claiming "now we have succeeded in making it unpopular and discreditable to hold Christian fellowship with slaveholders." This church-focused protest must have interested Sturge, given his own efforts to protest mandatory support of the Anglican church.[94]

Sturge reminded the audience that Douglass's own freedom was precarious. He urged them to purchase his "little book," *The Narrative of the Life of Frederick Douglass*, the proceeds of which Douglass used to support himself and his wife and children. Douglass then explained that his purpose in coming to England was to mobilize British influence over the United States, an influence he claimed was greater than that of any other country. "The slaveholders felt that when slavery was denounced among themselves, it was not so bad, but let one of the slaves get loose, let him summon the people of Britain, and make known to them the conduct of the slave holders towards their slaves, and it cuts them to the quick, and produces a sensation such as would be produced by nothing else."[95]

Condemnations in Britain would go further to shame and expose the evils of slavery, Douglass explained: "I expose slavery in this country, because to expose slavery is to kill it." The slaveholder wanted his silence, because the heat and light of truth would kill the institution, a not-so-subtle comparison of slavery to the rotten-smelling miasmas understood to cause deadly disease. He urged his audience to pledge to have "no Christian fellowship with slaveholders." The audience erupted in loud cheers at this, and at the suggestion that the Evangelical Alliance stiffen its policy to refuse to admit slaveholders. Douglass also urged his audience to inundate the press with condemnations of southern slaveholders. "Let the atmosphere of Britain be such that a slave holder many not be able to breathe it," he urged his audience. "Let him feel his lungs oppressed from the moment he steps on British soil." In this, Douglass inverted the usual analogy comparing liberty to breathing the pure air of England and gestured to the poetry of Sarah Forten, who had compared the sickly effects of racism to heavy, oppressive air.[96]

Douglass raised the example of the Free Church of Scotland, condemning it for accepting contributions from American slaveholders. "I charge them, in the first place, with having struck hands in Christian fellowship with men-stealers. I charge them, in the next place, with having taken the produce of human blood to build free churches, and to pay free church ministers in Scotland." "Christians of England! We want you to say to the Free Church of Scotland, the words you have just heard: '*Send back the money.*' (Cheers) I believe that the sending back of that money to the United States, will do more to unrivet the fetters, to break the chains of the bondsman, and to hasten the day of emancipation, than years of lecturing by the most eloquent abolitionists." He then urged the crowd to forgo the cheers and to chant instead "send back the money." As the crowd erupted, "the effect produced was indescribable."[97]

As Douglass returned to his seat amid a groundswell of applause, Dr. Reverend Campbell testified to Douglass's manhood, representing it as having undergone a dramatic transformation that would result in a distinguished lineage.

From his early life as a species of property and "our representative of three millions of men," Campbell declared that Douglass "has been raised up! Shall I say the *man*, (cheers), if there is a man on earth, he is a man." A key component of Douglass's manhood, according to Campbell, was that, as a former slave, his tolerance for fear was greater than that of an ordinary man. Escaping slavery, in Campbell's translation of Douglass's character, had forged his peerless manhood. Campbell stirred the crowd, "We must see more of this man (cheers), we must have more of this man. One would have taken a voyage round the globe some 40 years back—especially since the introduction of steam—to have heard such an exposure of slavery from the lips of a slave." He urged Douglass on with his mission: "Let the ministers meet him; let them hear him; let them grasp his hand." "He must send for his wife (immense cheers). He must send for his children. (renewed cheers). I want to see the sons and daughters of such a sire. (loud cheers)."[98]

Creating Heroes

As first moral suasion and then formal politics failed to bring slavery to an end, Douglass and his brother abolitionists embraced an embodied militance born out of the identities of the male protectors and heroes they had summoned and whom they had determined to emulate.[99] Douglass's self-making project included carefully curating his own public image as a respectable man. Well dressed, composed, and serious, his daguerreotype images communicated a steady and dependable presence: that of a man whose refined appearance embodied citizenship even if his nation failed to acknowledge him. The "habitual display" of embodied citizenship, as the scholar Ginger Hall notes, entered a contested field of representations of Black people dominated by racist imagery and scenes of enslaved people's suffering.[100]

Perhaps nothing spoke as poignantly to the dilemmas of Black masculinity as Douglass's efforts to create an enslaved hero in his 1852 novel *The Heroic Slave*. He based his hero on the real life of Madison Washington, the self-emancipated slave from Virginia who became the leader of the rebellion on board the *Creole*. Washington was one of the men who earned the praise of Henry Highland Garnet in 1843; he himself appears to have been inspired by the African Joseph Cinque, who led the rebellion on the illegal slave ship *Amistad* in 1839. Washington reportedly had learned of Cinque's bravery when, at the home of Robert Purvis, he viewed a painting commemorating the uprising.[101]

Upon glimpsing Madison alone in the woods—a space of temporary liberty in which Madison could utter his thoughts out loud—Douglass's white narrator, Mr. Listwell, described him as being "of manly form, tall, symmetrical, round, and strong. In his movements he seemed to combine, with the strength of the lion, a lion's elasticity. His torn sleeves disclosed arms like polished iron." Listwell's depiction of Madison hearkened to the allegedly primitive physical endowments of the African by likening him to the king of the African savannahs, the lion. But Douglass salvaged and tamed this primitive power to present it as valuable to the industrializing economy. With arms like polished iron, the substance that stood for technological superiority as well as the achievements of the rapidly changing economy, Madison could not be mistaken for a savage. Rather, his body reflected the potential of Black men, as Douglass saw it, for free labor in the burgeoning industries of the North. The physical being and potential value of the labor of Black men suffused Douglass's portrait of this hero. In his own well-known account of achieving manhood, recorded in *Narrative of the Life of Frederick Douglass* (1845), the necessary rite of passage was violent conflict with a white man. Douglass, like Madison, represented his youthful self-assertion as a matter of the will's expression through the body.

As the struggles to undo slavery and protect free Black people continued into the 1850s, the measures to control Black bodies intensified. Activists continued to argue that the universality of the human body was the foundation for equality, but Black men recast the history of African-descended people in ways that claimed and ennobled their lineages and emphasized their capacity as a people to resist slavery. The physical demands of activism, meanwhile, had begun to shift in response to a new focus on the militant body as a body in flight. Refusing to relinquish their mobility, enslaved people seized opportunities to escape. Their persistence in attempting to reach spaces of liberty fueled the conflict among abolitionist activists, white enslavers, and the federal government.

Chapter 8

Liberating Bodies

Frederick Douglass stood before the graduates of Western Reserve College in Hudson, Ohio, on July 12, 1854, prepared to intervene in a conversation among highly educated men of science about the fundamental nature of humankind. Theories about separate creations and distinct human species had been circulating around the Atlantic basin for over a century, but since the 1820s medical theorists had been advancing a stubborn argument for racial difference. Douglass's first line of defense for a common humanity came from a not unexpected source. He reminded his audience of the Bible's clear message on the unity of the human species, the brotherhood of man, and the reciprocal duties of human beings to each other. "God has made of one blood all nations of men for to dwell upon all the face of the earth" was a truth for Douglass, but he warned his audience of the threat to this scriptural wisdom posed by theories about the diversity of human origins. Even if one ultimately conceded the notion of separate human creations, which Douglass did not, the debate revealed a central and unanswered question still dogging the United States: "whether the rights, privileges, and immunities enjoyed by some ought not to be shared and enjoyed by all." Douglass's presence at the podium as a keynote speaker to the 1854 graduates offered the most compelling evidence for his rights claim, demonstrating a refined cultural competence all the more remarkable for having been nearly squandered by slavery.[1]

Douglass's speech came in the midst of a serious setback for the abolition movement. The passage in 1850 of the Fugitive Slave Act plunged free Black communities across the country into crisis. The act, part of the Compromise of 1850, empowered federal commissioners to support slave catchers in returning fugitives to their enslavers. The expedited legal process, moreover, created new dangers for free Black people who became more vulnerable to kidnapping and abduction. Douglass had been personally involved in some of the most dramatic rescues since the act's passage, including that of the Christiana, Pennsylvania, fugitive William Parker, who sought refuge at Douglass's home in Rochester, New York, before Douglass provided him with safe passage to Canada.[2]

Despite the crisis, Douglass accepted the invitation to speak at the commencement of a college known for its collaboration with Underground Railroad activists. He used the opportunity to reiterate some of the fundamental principles of the abolitionist movement and to push back on the growing chorus of racist scientific "truths" recently consolidated in the publication of Josiah Nott and George Gliddon's *Types of Mankind* (1854) and mobilized to justify slavery. His defense of the unity of the human race echoed the claims of abolitionists that rights needed to be understood as materially embodied, but some of his language had changed. Like several of his abolitionist counterparts, Douglass occasionally spoke of Anglo-Saxon and "negro" blood, although he insisted on their equality. Differences among human beings, moreover, did not signal to Douglass that humankind lacked unity. Rather, he found adequate scientific explanation for difference, including what appeared to be higher and lower forms of humanity, in the physical imprint of conditions and environments on people's bodies: "I think it will ever be found, that the *well* or *ill* condition of any part of mankind, will leave its mark on the physical as well as on the intellectual part of man. A hundred instances might be cited, of whole families who have degenerated, and others who have improved in personal appearance, by a change of circumstances. A man is worked upon by what *he* works on. He may carve out his circumstances, but his circumstances will carve him out as well."[3]

The circumstances that Douglass described as "carv[ing] out" people had become grimmer over the course of the antebellum abolition movement. At the time of his speech, abolitionists faced three escalating challenges: a transformed codified rights landscape for free Black Americans, the persistent claims of scientific racists, and the wear and tear of activism on their own bodies. The passage of the Fugitive Slave Act had heightened the risk of violence in the free states that bordered slavery, putting the lives of free Black people in jeopardy and leaving Douglass and his fellow abolitionists newly subject to the dangers of mob violence and legal persecution. Abolitionists, including those who had been active in the cause for nearly two decades, dug in to oppose the law. With the risks of their activist work amplified, those who had withstood decades of public speaking, draining travel, violence, and, in the case of African Americans, incessant racist disrespect, began to show signs of the strain on their bodies and their psyches.

Scientific racists advanced claims that directly contradicted the abolitionist focus on humankind's unity. Making reductive arguments about how skulls and facial characteristics determined human potential, influential doctors from medical schools throughout the United States contended that African Americans represented a species of human beings separate from white people, described in these texts as Anglo-Saxon or Caucasian. Gathering comparative data from skulls, bones, and external appearances, these medical men provided support for slavery by arguing for polygenesis—the theory of more than one human creation—and insisting that their analyses of human cranial shape and capacity proved that white people possessed superior intellectual powers. References to blood as reflecting ancestry, moreover, crept into the language even of committed abolitionists as they struggled to sustain the egalitarian promise of "one blood."

This would have been a dangerous argument for African Americans at any time, but it was especially potent during the 1850s as new ways of imagining the rights-bearing person presented stark contrasts to depictions of the enslaved as bodies suited for grueling plantation labor. Disembodied representations were on the rise: capitalists promoted the fictions of contract, consent, and the ability of an individual to sell his or her labor as if it could be separated somehow from the body; spiritualists made contact with the restless, rapping spirits of the dead; and white middle-class women described their domestic work and maternal labors as emotional and rooted in love rather than bodily exertion.

There was nothing abstract about the Fugitive Slave Law, however. It licensed the physical seizure of African-descended people right under the noses of free Black people and their white allies—and in the name of a concept of human property that many northerners viewed with distaste, if not outright hostility. Policies that permitted the sale and transport of enslaved people and supported enslavers to recover them if they escaped reduced enslaved people to essential laboring bodies, unaffected by changes in habitation or jurisdiction, and unable to move toward any self-defined attainment of human potential.[4]

By escaping across state lines, enslaved people denied the fictive ownership of their persons that prohibited them from moving without the permission of enslavers. They also circumvented their enslaver's absolute right to move or sell them. They gave the lie to slavery as an intrinsic condition of a person's being and pointed to its contingency on the reach of the enslaver's power; a successful escape could end the imposition of will and make a body free. In this sense, fugitive slaves bestowed birthright liberties on themselves, substituting escape for a birth that should have endowed them with rights.

As the author of the 1846 "Remedy for Slavery" pointed out, however, escapes by individuals could not be the mechanism that freed all enslaved people; such an outcome would require all slaves to take flight and reach the North at once. Yet individual escape might still have a larger systemic effect by making it too complex, costly, or risky for people to invest in slave labor in the border states of Maryland and Virginia, thus undermining slavery and making it less profitable. Perhaps escape's most important impact, however, was the blow it struck against the paternalistic and racist argument supporting slavery: that enslaved people were physically and intellectually unsuited for liberty.[5]

Proslavery ideologues, meanwhile, had a vested interest in denying the facts of coercion and exploitation so that the condition of enslaved bodies did not appear to be the result of damaging treatment, but rather their natural state. Slavery's defenders issued a camouflaging flurry of rhetoric about the cruelty of northern wage slavery and pointed to the alienation and exploitation inherent in separating a person's labor from the material condition of his or her body. Wage labor, they contended, made a fractured mosaic out of the interconnected lives of master and slaves within a paternalistic order. The cost for white women of a "free" labor economy, these defenders of slavery argued, was poverty and sexual vulnerability. Here was the trope of innocent white womanhood, trotted out in a new guise—in the persons of northern wage slaves rather than the victims of the rebellious slave's vengeance—a sleight of hand that once again obstructed the view of enslaved women and children as victims. It was an attempt to make the injured and exploited bodies of enslaved people disappear in the pathos of the suffering bodies of white northern women.[6]

Douglass, like most other abolitionists, was provoked less by southern critiques of northern labor than by the racist theories of men with medical degrees and faculty positions at medical schools. The proslavery interpretation of wage labor had limited purchase, not just because abolitionists' pecuniary investments in industrial capitalism blinded them to the fate of "wage slaves"—although for some this was certainly true—but because many, including Douglass, had witnessed slavery's brutality firsthand. Compared to slavery in the United States in the 1840s and 1850s, wage labor, particularly in the U.S. factories that aimed to distance themselves from the horrifying specter of industry in Manchester, England, seemed benign. This was especially the case for those American textile companies that employed white women. Abolitionists who toured these factories did not see within them the horrors of slavery. Rather, they saw what seemed to be a regulated space in which labor was carried out without the threat of physical pain. For others, plantation labor remained a problem to be solved by replacing slave and other bound labor not by waged factory labor but with "free" agricultural wage labor, a form of compensated labor connected to the land and defined and secured by contract.[7]

During the decisive decade of the 1850s, as white southerners pressed successfully for increased federal power to recapture and reenslave refugees, the United States Supreme Court stripped enslaved people of standing in courts of law and insisted on the embeddedness of their enslaved status in their very persons. The

Supreme Court's decision in the Dred Scott case in 1857 represented a political rendition of the theory of polygenesis, an opinion that reiterated enslaved people's stateless condition as a natural manifestation of race, allegedly materialized in the body. Abolitionist success did not simply require that they persuade skeptics of an abstract universal principle of human equality; rather, it had to overcome white people's perceptions that the physical consequences of poverty, hard labor, and coercion represented innate rather than acquired bodily differences. There was also the question of caring for those harmed by poverty, grueling labor, and the trauma of escape as they sought refuge from slavery.

Alternative Medicine as Movement Culture

It was 1842, and David Ruggles could not remember the last time he felt healthy. He had left New York City, headed for the home of his friends Lydia and David Lee Child in Northampton, Massachusetts, in hopes that a change of climate might save his life. Ruggles had been ill for the last five of his thirty-one years. His dimming eyesight had finally given way to blindness, and chronic pain and illness reduced his once active body to invalidism. Many of his symptoms, including dyspepsia, chronic bowel inflammation, nervousness, and mental debility, likely bore some relation to the high-stakes life of a man who had regularly risked his personal safety to rescue refugees from slave catchers. In desperation, Ruggles began experimenting with water treatments for his sightless eyes and racked body. Through correspondence with Robert Wesselhoeft, a student of the Water Cure founder, Austrian Vincenz Priessnitz, Ruggles self-treated until he regained some rudimentary vision and felt restored to health. The miraculous improvement convinced him that others, too, might benefit from the regime of bathing, drinking, and wet wraps. Through his vast network, he knew of plenty of people whose health had suffered as a result of stress and overwork during the never-ending campaign to undo slavery.[8]

The intrepid New York City activist was not alone in his efforts to restore his own health. Abolitionist activists had been self-diagnosing, sharing remedies, and offering health advice to each other since the late 1830s. Preparing for hostility and violence at every stop on the circuit, abolitionist speakers suffered from ailments with long-term emotional as well as physical consequences. As they took their message about the material deprivations and suffering inflicted by slavery on enslaved people to an often hostile public, they expended their own bodies and suffered illness and debility. Their message—that liberty meant little in practical terms if did not translate into physical, economic, and sexual self-sovereignty—emphasized the practical exercise of rights over their technical possession. The stresses were especially acute for Black activists who often presented their own bodies as evidence of their right to have rights. Henry C. Wright did not exaggerate when he described the Grimké sisters' speaking tour as their "Labors," but that term was even more apt for the efforts of Black activists like Frederick Douglass, Frances Ellen Watkins Harper, Sojourner Truth, and Charles Remond.[9]

Ruggles turned his self-cure into a center for restoring the health of people who had failed to find relief from other treatments. Situated in Florence, Massachusetts, just outside of Northampton, his water cure establishment attracted activists and welcomed Black as well as white patients, making it unusual among spas. Literally unable to see his patients, Ruggles relied on his sense of touch, which he claimed had been sensitized as a consequence of his blindness. He held patients' hands and touched their skin to get readings of electricity, which he called "vitality" or "power." This sensory information enabled him to diagnose ailments and prescribe treatments.[10]

One of Ruggles's first patients, the itinerant preacher Sojourner Truth, came to him in 1845 with stomach and bowel problems, leg sores, and joint and muscle pain. Ruggles put her through a water cure treatment of wet packs and baths to produce a physical crisis designed to provoke her will to be healed. Truth did not like the treatment, but she admitted that it cured her many ailments. William Lloyd Garrison, who had been suffering from ill health since his speaking tour with Frederick Douglass in 1847, likewise gave up his busy schedule of lecturing, editing, and letter writing to visit Ruggles's clinic. In the summer of 1848, he began four months of treatment with cold water baths, wraps, and plunges, which he claimed improved his cough and side pain. His cure and his effective mobilization of his network gained Ruggles other patients, including the historian and activist William Cooper Nell and Mary Ann Day Brown, wife of the radical abolitionist John Brown.[11]

Although Ruggles's establishment of a water cure facility was a unique response to his own poor health, there was nothing unique about debilitated health among abolitionists. The health problems they faced were important not just because they threatened to limit the number of people with the energy and capacity to maintain the grueling schedule of public speaking on the circuit, but because illness also threatened to curb the performative "proofs" of a common humanity. Claiming that such a common humanity included enslaved people, Douglass asked his audience to imagine a world of "changed circumstances" in which the bodies of enslaved and working-class laborers, freed from the coercion that had left its mark on them, would be able to reach their full human potential. But the invitation to engage in this imaginative process depended on the capacity of speakers like Douglass to exude recognizable and admirable universal qualities. In the physical acts of speaking and engaging with their audiences, abolitionist speakers connected their own physical presence—especially their endurance of hardship—with the claim that all people qualified for this common humanity.

It was with good reason that the topic of health preoccupied many activists. One of the most talented early speakers on the circuit, Theodore Weld, permanently damaged his vocal chords in the early years of his public speaking career and was forced to retire in 1836. Frederick Douglass and William Lloyd Garrison each fell ill after their brief tour together in Pennsylvania in 1847. Nathan Thomas, the intrepid southern agent for the Philadelphia Friends Free Labor Produce Association who attested to the debilitating impact of his southern trips on his health, returned home to his family exhausted and soon after succumbed to cholera. Activists passed news of their illnesses and remedies to each other, offering tips about methods that had proven successful in their own cases.[12]

Hydropathy was often the preferred therapy, combining the virtues of self-care, simplicity, and efficacy that were especially appealing to women. Angelina and Sarah Grimké, Harriot Hunt, and Sarah Mapps Douglass reported to each other on their uses of cold water bathing and sitz baths to treat a variety of ailments. Sarah Grimké was pleased to hear from Douglass in February 1845 that she intended to try bathing once the weather warmed. Douglass appears to have been quickly persuaded of the benefits of hydropathy: by spring 1846 she was treating her ailing father with cold water bandages, to good effect, and owned a water cure handbook, which she lent to Angelina. Hydropathic methods had worked so well for both Sarah Grimké and the family's hired woman, Bridget, that Angelina decided to use them on herself. Weld, meanwhile, escorted his mother to a water cure center in Brattleboro, Vermont, where he also received treatment for his ailing throat. When Angelina updated Douglass in 1849 about her own progress with her hernia, distressed bowels, and an unexplained lump, she inquired about Douglass's use of the water cure at home and expressed relief that the closing of Douglass's school would provide her with "a suspension of bodily labor." Hunt, both Grimké sisters, and Douglass continued to share news of successes and failures in treating their various afflictions, although Douglass and her father never availed themselves of a water cure treatment center, a privilege that appears to have been reserved mainly for white invalids.[13]

Diagnosing and treating their own bodies was crucial self-care for activists seeking to maintain the strength of a movement that relied on individuals reaching as many northerners as possible through public lectures. Abby Kelley's frequent correspondence about health offers a glimpse of the ways abolitionists on the speakers' circuit developed their own culture of self-care. Kelley, like many other activists, had been influenced by the health reformers Sylvester Graham and George and Andrew Combe. Graham's low-stimulation diet substituted water for alcohol and caffeinated beverages, and prescribed light meals of crackers rather than heavy cooked dishes with meat and sauces.[14] George Combe's revisionist medical guide *The Constitution of Man Considered in Relation to External Objects* (1828) became both influential and controversial for what critics denounced as his materialist and atheist message. The Combe brothers recommended alternatives to the regimens of regular physicians, urging readers to follow natural laws, which they identified as access to fresh air, moderate diets, and exercise.[15]

Kelley appears to have adapted these alternative medical approaches along with some water cure techniques to manage her own health on the speaker's circuit. She adopted the routine of daily washing to maintain her health, and bed rest and sweating to recover from sickness. Throughout her decades as an abolitionist speaker and organizer, she reported illnesses that began with a sore throat before becoming more serious ailments, with the inflamed throat often lingering. This pattern of illness was familiar to nineteenth-century public speakers.[16] As Kelley explained to her future husband Stephen Foster in early January 1844 as she recovered from a "head-ackey, feverish condition," an unexpected closing of the meeting house near Utica in which she was supposed to lecture meant that her "sore throat is not taxed to night—Was pretty sick I can assure you all day Saturday and Sunday—had a raging fever—but fasting threw it off so that on Monday I was up all day and have now entirely recovered, except my throat, which, however, is on the gain, and I think will be well in a day or two."[17]

Kelley's success in keeping herself well enough to lecture continuously gave her great confidence in both her judgement and the strength of her own constitution. She believed Foster to be less strong and resilient than herself. After urging him to travel to Utica to receive care from their friend Paulina Wright, who she claimed would be able to "do as much as any one to cure you up when you are sick," she advised him to travel less and "move slowly—your health demands it, My constitution is rigorous, else it would not have risen so quickly from under such a cold."[18] Upon hearing in January 1843 that he had attended an antislavery convention despite being ill, she demanded, "Do you intend to commit suicide?" She sympathized with his impatient desire to defer bodily rest until slavery was ended, but she doubted that this was a smart strategy. Even after slavery ended, she reminded him, there would be "thick clouds" and "days of blackness." Leave off writing, lecturing, and attending conventions, she urged, until fully restored to health.[19]

After marrying Foster just before her thirty-fifth birthday and becoming pregnant at age thirty-six, Kelley arranged for alternative medical care for the birth. Writing to Foster from the road in April 1847 in her eighth month of pregnancy, she asked, "Shall I write Paulina to be with me in May? . . . I don't want a doctor." Indeed, Kelley might have been correct in her belief that Paulina Wright could provide her with better care than a regular physician.[20] Paulina had joined Kelley on the abolitionist lecture circuit in 1845 before deciding to study medicine. Despite formal obstacles to her training in New York City, Wright completed her studies and began to give lectures to female audiences in 1846 with the help of an anatomically correct imported French mannequin.[21] Having safely given birth to a child in May 1847, Kelley acknowledged to Foster three months later how physically trying the ordeal and the subsequent recovery had been. "I never told you how much I suffered. . . . But I am getting to feel more like myself, now—am almost well of the piles having taken a sitz bath nearly every day—My other weaknesses too, seem to be gradually passing away."[22]

As Kelley and Foster reached their forties and slavery was no closer to ending, Kelley experimented with other methods. She supported a young relative to gain training in midwifery and the water cure, while she herself consulted a clairvoyant about Foster's health.[23] She trusted the clairvoyant in part because she recommended treatments, including instructions to Foster, similar to Kelley's own medical regimen. The clairvoyant advised Foster to talk less, take warmer baths, and follow a water cure regimen of wet bandages and an external cold water douche in the morning. She also urged Foster to take long walks in the open air.[24]

Kelley's world was filled with abolitionists moving between antislavery and health reform and finding receptive female audiences—a testimony to the desire for embodied self-sovereignty underpinning both reforms. Paulina Wright's interest in medicine, for example, built on Grahamite principles of self-government and a quest for liberty from external forces causing the body to suffer.[25] Wright subsequently experimented with the water cure for her own health, as Kelley reported to Foster, stopping in New York to "put herself under Mary Gove's care" at her water cure establishment.[26] Kelley's lecture circuit protégé Elizabeth Hitchcock Jones, who traveled with the veteran abolitionist to learn the art of public speaking, also recognized the intersections between rights and health. Speaking to the Ohio Women's Convention in 1850, Jones urged her audience to think not in narrow terms of the rights of the slave or the woman, but in terms of human rights for all. She subsequently turned to children's literature to provide an unvarnished account of American slavery for young readers. Jones also began giving public lectures on physiology, which she found to be a lucrative pursuit, provoking Kelley to wonder why Lizzie was able to make more money lecturing on physiology than on antislavery; "Is it because physiology is to the popular mind a more agreeable theme, or is her soul more in her subject. I hope she will be particularly careful with her health—for the work has none of such women to spare."[27]

The health of female activists was serious business among abolitionists. Many activist women had been influenced by Mary Gove Nichols, whose innovative methods and candid teaching about female health had gained a following. Harriot Hunt, Ann Preston, Paulina Wright Davis, Sarah Grimké, and Sarah Mapps Douglass had all benefited from Nichols's teachings. Grimké and Hunt agreed with Nichols that sexual overuse and involuntary motherhood—two of the main violations of enslaved women but something even free women suffered—were the source of women's ill health. Douglass and Grimké corresponded with each other about female health, with Grimke sharing advice she had received from Hunt. A growing network of women with knowledge of anatomy and health turned from moral reform to sexual citizenship, embracing the ideal that self-knowledge about the body and sexuality was the path to better health. This was in part the motive of the Philadelphia Female Anti-Slavery Society (PFAS) members who welcomed the lectures of Dr. Frederick Hollick, a self-styled promulgator of scientific information to women about female anatomy and desire. Hollick gave several public lectures in Philadelphia between 1844 and 1846 before being tried for obscenity. Mary Grew and her fellow PFAS member Elizabeth Bunting defended Hollick publicly in 1846 by offering testimonials to the female audience's approbation of the learning experience.[28]

Out of these abolitionist circles of self-diagnosis, self-treatment, and information sharing came a new institutional resource: a medical school to train female doctors. Founded in 1850 by the Quaker abolitionists Dr. Bartholomew Fussell and Dr. Joseph Longshore and the businessman William J. Mullen, the Women's Medical College of Pennsylvania (WMCP), located in Philadelphia, emphasized a curriculum in physiology. After graduating in the first class of students in 1851, the abolitionist and Progressive Friend Ann Preston, child of Chester, Pennsylvania, free produce activists, accepted a professor's chair and began offering courses at the WMCP. One of her first classes included Sarah Mapps Douglass, who attended the school between 1852 and 1853. Douglass delighted in Preston's lectures, which broadcast a female teacher's commitment to providing women with clearly communicated knowledge about the female body. Under Preston, who became the school's dean, WMCP subsequently trained many of the nation's first female doctors, African American as well as white.[29]

The medical training Douglass received at WMCP not only enriched her capacity as a science teacher but also enabled her to expand her profile as a public lecturer. Following her formal medical education at WMCP in 1852–1853, Douglass revamped the science content of her classes at the Institute for Colored Youth (ICY), where she taught for twenty-four years, and began public lectures on the body's anatomical structures and functions. Using a specially designed French mannequin, perhaps similar to the one Pauline Wright featured in her lectures, as well as anatomical drawings and a skull, Douglass provided scientific information to lay audiences composed of Institute parents, women, and the general public. Writing to her friend Rebecca White, Douglass noted, "I gave my third lecture on the circulation of the blood. . . . I had what I consider a good company, 38 deeply interested women." Douglass earned money from these efforts—in this instance, $3.50—but she also gained acclaim that led to additional lecture opportunities. She participated in the Banneker Institute, an intellectual forum that eventually became Cheyney University, and she also belonged to the Gilbert Lyceum, a literary society cofounded by Jacob White Sr. that welcomed men and women, Black and white. Douglass took pains to communicate clearly and simply, as she noted to White, so that the women in her audience would not complain of her use of big words. As in other public lectures by Black activists and intellectuals, in Douglass's case the messenger was the message: an educated Black woman, speaking candidly about intimate topics ranging from the circulation of the blood to female anatomy, providing scientific information aided by props but without the toxic residue of the racist science being disseminated by the city's medical schools.[30]

Abolitionist efforts to battle illness and sustain their own physical strength also appears to have kept them mindful of the physical suffering of enslaved people. The strong will needed to overcome illness and pain or even to imagine alternative remedies connected abolitionist activism with activism for health. As Sarah Grimké counseled a suffering Sarah Mapps Douglass in 1845, using language reminiscent of abolitionist rhetoric and the water cure, the ocean of Jesus's love was "measureless, it is in this ocean he let us sometimes bathe our weary souls and rejoice in him." Yet, she acknowledged, "at other times have we not to go to Gethsemane & according to our measure sweat great drops of blood & agonize under the suffering which is laid upon us."[31] That language would certainly have resonated not only for Sarah Douglass, but also for Nathan Thomas, David Ruggles, Stephen Foster, Frances Watkins Harper, and Grimké's own sister Angelina, as well as the innumerable enslaved people for whom they agitated.

Phrenology, Craniology, Polygenesis

The commonsense medical regimen recommended by Dr. Andrew Combe and his more famous older brother George—fresh air, bathing, and diet reform—became popular among abolitionists and other reformers seeking new ways to sustain bodies worn down by the labors of activism. So they were understandably shaken by George Combe's seeming endorsement of Samuel George Morton's project to prove that white cranial capacity and intellect exceeded that of African Americans and Native Americans. By 1847, Morton's studies had led him to follow earlier race scientists, including Charles Caldwell, in abandoning reproductive capacity as a criteria for species and tentatively embracing polygenesis: "Since various different species are capable of producing together prolific hybrid offspring," he claimed, "hybridity ceases to be a test of specific affiliation" and "constitutes in itself, no proof of the unity of the human species."[32]

In fact, although Combe contributed an appendix to Morton's *Crania Americana* (1839), he disagreed with several of Morton's findings, particularly that people of African descent had smaller intellectual capacity than Native Americans. Lucretia Mott diligently took on the task of explaining to Combe why the "Colonizationists and Abolitionists cannot harmonize" and encouraging his antislavery views. He reassured her of his unwavering support for abolition, yet his public support of Morton's work and his collegiality with Caldwell helped to make phrenology available to slavery's defenders and tainted it with a racist agenda. Mott and Combe remained friends, however, allied over their commitments to secular public education, nonheroic medicine, and antislavery.[33]

As outlined by Combe and performed by lay practitioners, phrenology read a living person's character and potential from the shape of the head. This was in keeping with nineteenth-century medicine's fractional approach to seeing the body in parts. When appropriated by craniologists and proslavery apologists as a static criterion for racial hierarchy rather than as a measure of individual adaptation, however, the study of the skull provided an essentialist rationale for the different fates of enslavers and the people they enslaved. Based on measurements of the skulls of dead people, craniology, in contrast to phrenology, left little possibility for progressive environmentalism.[34]

For those committed to the notion of innate racial difference and hierarchy, it was but a short step from attempting to locate racial essences in the size and shape of skulls to capturing those essences in photographic images. Racist scientists seized on the new technology of the daguerreotype to represent in visually dramatic ways the theories of racial difference. Yet exactly how an image was supposed to demonstrate racial difference transparently was not clear. In 1850, the Harvard scientist Louis Agassiz commissioned the photographer Joseph T. Zealy to take images of African-born people enslaved in Columbia, South Carolina, as a way to exhibit ethnic, racial, and familial characteristics. The poses themselves marked the bodies of the photographic subjects as different from white subjects. Rather than center portraits on shoulders and heads, as they might have done with white subjects, Agassiz and Zealy posed the enslaved people with bare torsos so that heads, shoulders, chests, upper arms, stomachs, buttocks, and genitals were on display. The men were positioned to reveal full frontal and rear nudity, which one perceptive scholar has suggested was revealing of Agassiz's own homoerotic desires. Delia, the lone female subject, was compelled to pose with her breasts bared while the camera captured her obvious reluctance to be so exposed. Although Agassiz put the images on display at only one limited exhibition, his collection of daguerreotypes communicated that the white scientist's right to gaze negated the bodily privacy of the enslaved person.[35]

African Americans pushed back vigorously on the various manifestations of scientific racism and racist medicine. Following his 1837 public lecture "The Fallacy of Phrenology," in which he disputed the claims of phrenologists that the outer shape and dimensions of the human skull revealed an individual's character and intellect, James McCune Smith engaged in both scholarly and pragmatic care work to meld his careers as abolitionist and physician. Most notable among the published works was his "Dissertation on the Influence of Climate on Longevity" (1846). As his medical biographer notes, with this essay Smith "pioneered the use of medically based statistics as evidence against notions of racial inferiority."[36] Smith used population data from the 1840 census to dispute the claims of racist science that enslaved Africans could withstand the hot climate of the southern states but sickened and died as free people in the cooler North. Smith's analysis of census data critiqued population studies that ignored longevity. He concluded that people of African descent lived slightly longer than their white counterparts in the South despite the hardships of slavery. In New England however, where climate theorists did not expect people of African descent to live as long or reproduce as prolifically, their population grew at a greater rate than that of the white population. Stressing environmentalism and adaptation, Smith contended that African American bodies had successfully transformed in the face of new climates, habits, and circumstances, a claim ventured but not substantiated by the Reverend Hosea Easton nine years earlier.[37]

Smith's provision of medical care, especially to children, was part of his rebuttal of the racist medicine that flourished during the 1840s. Getting medical treatment to underserved populations was both a humanitarian act and a specific intervention in the medical statistics being used to justify slavery. In 1846, Smith became the attending physician for New York City's Colored Orphan Asylum, dedicating his practice to sustaining the health of Black children by providing inoculation and treatment for serious illnesses. Professionally identified with regular physicians, he condemned the use of homeopathy to treat sick children in the city's orphanages by presenting statistics that showed an unchecked high death rate.[38]

Smith debunked the entire concept of distinct races. There was more diversity within any racial category, he argued, than between categories. Categories themselves were socially constructed and varied regionally and individually. Ever the environmentalist, Smith also produced a series of portraits, "Heads of the Colored People: Done with a Whitewash Brush" (1852), which situated the physiognomy, labor, and posture of a few individuals within the context of their labor. The title was a none-too-subtle dig at phrenology and a reminder of the laboring lives of ordinary free Black people. His subjects included a news vendor, a bootblack, a washerwoman, a schoolmaster, and a gravedigger.[39] In "On the Fourteenth Query of Thomas Jefferson's Notes on Virginia" (1859), Smith disputed the very terms of the debate (what is to be done with the colored populations and can they be elevated) to raise questions about what counted as elevated.[40]

Yet several Black activists and intellectuals found uses for phrenology and mobilized it for abolitionist projects or their own purposes. The African American physicians Henry E. Lewis of Michigan, who also lectured on mesmerism, and H. Jerome Brown argued for phrenology's progressive possibilities. James Bias, the Philadelphia bleeder, physician, and Philadelphia Vigilance Committee (PVC) member who saw potential for Black people in phrenology's environmentalism, published a pamphlet, *Synopsis of Phrenology*, in 1852. Jacob White Jr., son of PVC member Jacob White Sr. and a graduate of the ICY who later became a teacher, delivered a lecture during the 1850s at the Banneker Institute on the possibilities of phrenology, along with lectures on the meaning for Black people of abstaining from slave produce and alcohol. Of these phrenology enthusiasts, it must be said, at least one, White, argued before a Banneker Institute audience, perhaps for the purposes of debate, that slavery had been beneficial to the African.[41]

Frederick Douglass appropriated phrenological discourses but mainly agreed with his friend James McCune Smith when he weighed in on the debated links between bodies and rights in 1854 with his "Claims of the Negro Ethnologically Considered," the commencement address he delivered at Western Reserve College with which this chapter begins. For Douglass, the larger debate boiled down to one question: Is the Negro a man? Douglass pointed to the denial of African American manhood as the essence of the defense of slavery. He found it especially unfair that phrenologists and craniologists compared a (white) man who had enjoyed all the privileges of wealth and education to individuals who had experienced none of these advantages (usually African American, uneducated, and unimproved, in Douglass's view). This principle, that inequality left its marks on the body, was at the heart of abolitionist arguments about human rights as embodied self-sovereignty, and it also supported Douglass's rebuttal of racist science.[42]

The exclusion of African Americans from the human family seemed incredible to Douglass. "Man is distinguished from all other animals, by the possession of certain definite faculties and powers, as well as by physical organization and proportions," he observed. "He is the only two-handed animal on the earth—the only one that laughs, and nearly the only one that weeps." Douglass appealed to what seemed to him a principle of humankind that was beyond dispute: "Common sense itself is scarcely needed to detect the absence of manhood in a monkey, or to recognize its presence in a negro." "His speech, his reason, his power to acquire and to retain knowledge, his heaven-erected face, his habitudes, his hopes, his fears, his aspirations, his prophesies," Douglass contended, "plant between him and the brute creation, a distinction as eternal as it is palpable."[43]

Douglass circled back to his conflict with polygenists over first principles. "Tried by all the usual, and all the unusual tests, whether mental, moral, physical, or psycological [*sic*]," he argued, "the negro is a MAN—considering him as possessing knowledge, or needing knowledge, his elevation or his degradation, his virtues, or his vices—whichever road you take, you reach the same conclusion, the negro is a MAN." The emergence of racist science in support of slavery and polygenesis created a shocking contradiction of beliefs drawn from the Bible. "I say it is remarkable—nay, it is strange," Douglass declared, "that here should arise a phalanx of learned men—speaking in the name of science—to forbid the magnificent reunion of mankind in one brotherhood." Despite his shocked dismay, Douglass presented his rebuttal using two key argumentative strategies: the exposure of economic and political interests advanced by polygenists, and alternative explanations of evidence. "The proposition to which I allude, and which I mean next to assert, is this, that what are technically called the negro race, are a part of the human family, and are descended from a common ancestry, with the rest of mankind. . . . It involves the question of the unity of the human race."[44]

It was one thing for the lowly to cast doubt on the concept of human unity, Douglass noted, but another for elite people to couch their own interests in claims to separate creations. He urged his listeners to consider that 99 percent of those insisting on polygenesis were Anglo-Saxon slave owners. This "may account somewhat for the repeated attempts on the part of Southern pretenders to science, to cast a doubt over the Scriptural account of the origin of mankind." In a not-so-veiled allusion to southern slavery's systematic patterns of rape and enslavement of the mixed-race children of white slaveholders, Douglass slyly shared his doubts that southern theories of polygenesis had "an honest parentage." The core problem, as he saw it, was that "the very crimes of slavery," meaning its degradation and destruction of African American people, "became slavery's best defense." There was no doubt in Douglass's mind that the racist scientists Josiah Nott, George Gliddon, Samuel Morton, Charles Hamilton Smith, and Louis Agassiz were duly consulted by proslavery men.[45]

Douglass raised other important objections to the cluster of arguments implicated in polygenesis. He objected to so-called historians, especially Morton, who turned Egyptians white so as to glorify their civilization while effacing any connection with African people. For Douglass, this was but one part of the larger insult to people of African descent, in which "to be intelligent is to have one's negro blood ignored." Using the language of blood as lineage, Douglass intervened in the racist "mulatto exception" theory—the theory that individuals with one Black and one white parent exhibited intellect superior to those with two Black parents—to debunk it with reference to maternal inheritance. In an interesting inversion of the law of maternal inheritance, Douglass pointed out that "there is, however, a very important physiological fact, contradicting this last assumption; and that fact is, that intellect is uniformly derived from the maternal side. Mulattoes, in this country, may almost wholly boast of Anglo-Saxon male ancestry."[46]

Ultimately, Douglass decided strategically to acknowledge white, well-to-do, and educated people's perceptions of physical difference in the bodies of the poor and the enslaved and then to dispute the notion of innate disability. In Douglass's view, poverty and oppression left an imprint on the body regardless of race. He wrote at length about his experience of seeing the sad specimens of the Irish poor: "these people lacked only a black skin and woolly hair, to complete their likeness to the plantation negro. The open, uneducated mouth—the long gaunt arm—the badly formed foot and ankle—the shuffling gait—the retreating forehead and vacant expression—and, their petty quarrels and fights—all reminded me of the plantation, and my own cruelly abused people." Variations in the human condition around the globe suggested to Douglass that circumstances had something to do with modifying various phases of humanity; a new creation would not be necessary to explain each instance. Most important for Douglass, "a diverse origin does not disprove a common nature, nor does it disprove a united destiny."[47]

Douglass concluded with a ringing endorsement of the universality of both human beings and human rights. "Human rights stand upon a common basis; and by all the reason that they are supported, maintained and defended, for one variety of the human family, they are supported, maintained, and defended for *all* the human family; because all mankind have the same wants, arising out of a common nature." "His title deed to freedom, his claim to life and liberty" are the same, he reminded his audience before warning them prophetically, "God has no children whose rights may be safely trampled upon."[48]

Fugitive Slave Law

By the time Douglass spoke to the Western Reserve audience in 1854, abolitionists had passed a crucial tipping point. Douglass combatted an iteration of race science newly dangerous because of its possible political application: a static, inherently enslaveable, African-descended body, which state and federal laws codified legally and politically. As we have seen, these codifications became more dangerous to African-descended people with the Supreme Court ruling in *Prigg v. Pennsylvania* (1842) that the state's personal liberty law was unconstitutional. *Prigg* set the stage for escalating conflicts among local, state, and federal lawmakers over the fate of refugees from slavery and the security of free Black citizens.[49] This setback was followed by the passage of a strengthened federal Fugitive Slave Act in 1850, plunging free Black communities into crisis and creating new risks for Underground Railroad refugees and their Vigilance Committee allies.

The Fugitive Slave Act's new strictures pushed Douglass and his allies to adopt a more militant position, akin to Henry Highland Garnet's declaration of 1843. Bracing for the act's passage, abolitionists gathered in Cazenovia, New York, on August 21, 1850, for a protest meeting that resulted in an iconic image (Figure 7). The overflow crowd of over two thousand women and men forced the organizers to relocate from the Free Congregational Church to an apple orchard belonging to the abolitionist Grace Wilson. Flanked by Emily and Mary Edmondson, two sisters recently escaped from slavery in Washington, D.C., Frederick Douglass, Theodosia Gilbert, and Gerrit Smith appear in front of a large, bonneted crowd in the daguerreotype taken by Theodore Weld's brother Ezra Greenleaf Weld. Gilbert was the fiancée of William L. Chaplin, the activist imprisoned for his part in the attempted escape of enslaved people from Washington that had largely failed but resulted in the Edmondsons' safe passage to New York. Led by the sisters, the crowd sang a song in honor of the slain activist Elijah Lovejoy (d. 1837). Smith circulated his "Letter to the American Slaves from those who have fled from American Slavery," to gather the signatures of the nearly fifty formerly enslaved people in attendance before publishing the document in the September 5, 1850 issue of Douglass's newspaper the *North Star*. The letter called openly for enslaved people to engage in militant resistance, justified by the fact that slavery was a "state of war." Therefore, enslaved people became morally justified to "plunder, burn, and kill" as well as to pursue all means to effect their escapes. Three months later, the white abolitionist William Elder conceded that pacifism was a privilege of whiteness that African Americans could afford little more than their African ancestors who had been taken captive. "The world has been cultivated by blood," Elder concluded. "Without the shedding of blood there is not remission of sins. There must be death for sin."[50]

Part of the Compromise of 1850, the Fugitive Slave Act had been designed by James Mason of Virginia to assuage white southern mistrust of the North by

Figure 7. Fugitive Slave Law Convention, Cazenovia, New York, August 22, 1850. After Ezra Greenleaf Weld (American, 1801–1874). Daguerreotype 6.7 × 5.4 cm (2 5/8 × 2 1/8 in.), 84.XT.1582.5. The J. Paul Getty Museum, Los Angeles.

expediting the claims of enslavers and stripping state and local authorities of the duty of enforcement. As opponents of the law predicted, kidnappings of free Black people rose. At the same time, the law gave federal officers the power to compel ordinary citizens, in the form of posses, to support the physical police work of enforcement. This latter provision appears to have had an effect opposite that which lawmakers intended. Raids by slave catchers and the summary judgements of federal commissioners provoked formerly neutral bystanders to become involved, activated by the blatant intrusion and aggression of agents of slavery into free states and free Black communities. State Senator James P. Milliken of Indiana, part of a cohort of Maine transplants to Dearborn County, denounced the law as "tyrannical," a violation of human rights, and a disgrace in the "eyes of the whole civilized and Christian world."[51]

Within a few months of the Fugitive Slave Law, Dr. Samuel Cartwright's 1851 "Report on the Diseases and Physical Peculiarities of the Negro Race" revealed that slave law and racist medicine shared an underlying logic. Both aimed at controlling the bodies of laborers by defining them as innately deficient and restraining their mobility and their wills. While legal codes defined enslaved people as lacking rights to bodily integrity—a legal incapacity making embodied self-sovereignty impossible—medical racism depicted the enslaved as physiologically and temperamentally incapable of self-government and self-support. As the leading American school ethnologist Josiah Nott explained in a speech in 1850 before the Southern Rights Association in Mobile, Alabama, African-descended people, unlike their racially superior white counterparts, lacked the physical and mental capacities needed to flourish under conditions of liberty; he would develop this theme more fully in *Types of Mankind* (1854).[52]

Building on the ethnological work of Nott and his mentor Samuel Morton, as well as on his own experience as an enslaver and southern doctor, Cartwright transformed issues of plantation management—the loss of labor consequent upon the escape or diminished performance of enslaved people—into medical problems. Cartwright coined the term "drapetomania," which he defined as the repeated running away of enslaved people. Efforts to escape slavery's terrors became for Cartwright and his followers a disease rather than a defiant act of self-emancipation. For Cartwright, the recalcitrant and resistant bodies of enslaved people were by definition diseased; if they resisted slave labor, they were not suitably pliable to the enslaver's will and so they must be ill. Although Cartwright enjoyed continued professional success and respect, he was not without his critics, including a contributor to two issues of the 1851 *Charleston Medical Journal and Review* who disputed Cartwright's claims about racial differences manifested in blood and anatomy. Although the author harbored no doubts that enslaved Africans were suited to strenuous plantation labor, he mused that

Cartwright's polygenetic views were as capricious as classifying black sheep and white sheep as separate species.[53]

With the passage of the Fugitive Slave Act in 1850, the bodies of enslaved people—particularly their mobility—took on new legal, political, and medical significance. Each African-descended person who successfully left slavery and embarked on a new life refuted the principles of slave law and racist medicine that aimed to constrain them. Escapes across state lines, moreover, provoked questions about jurisdictional boundaries that fueled the sectional crisis. In instances in which an enslaver lodged a claim with a federal marshal, that marshal initiated a process to capture and detain the suspected fugitive. The fugitive (refugee) had to be physically taken in to federal custody and locked up, an imposition that created a demand in Philadelphia for sturdy locks "of the better class."[54]

In addition to these issues, the legal status of alleged fugitives turned on questions of identity that vexed jurisdictions in an age before fingerprint technology. White people's racism made them poor witnesses and compounded the confusion about individual identity. Enslaved people were especially vulnerable in these instances because of the absence of formal birth certificates, baptismal records, or other supporting legal documents. Resolving questions about an alleged fugitive's status required that federal commissioners establish the identities of refugees, making their physical characteristics newly important to all stakeholders. When writs of habeas corpus brought individuals alleged to be fugitives before local courts, those assembled heard testimony from claimants about the physical appearance, including scars, height, and complexion, of people alleged to be slaves. This attention to appearance differed from cases in which the individual's racial identity was itself in question. In those latter cases, courts encouraged juries to draw their own conclusions about appearance but allowed testimony from medical and other "experts" about bodily characteristics believed to be reflect race rather than personal histories.[55]

One of the first Pennsylvania cases following the passage of the new federal law came in February 6, 1851, when Philadelphia resident Euphemia (Tamor) Williams, aged forty, was arrested in her home and brought before U.S. commissioner Edward Ingraham, a Philadelphia lawyer. Under the terms of the 1850 law, Ingraham, rather than a state or local official, was to handle instances of alleged fugitivity. The case turned on the Maryland enslaver William T. J. Purnell's claim that Williams had been his slave some twenty-two years earlier. Complicating the case, Williams was the mother of six children, ranging from infancy to seventeen years, all of whom had been born in Pennsylvania. J. M. McKim and Passmore Williamson of the PVC obtained a writ of habeas corpus so that Williams could be reunited with her children while she waited for her hearing. Members of the Female Vigilance Committee prepared to attend court with Williams, where she expected to come face-to-face with her former enslaver.[56]

The lawyer for Purnell claimed that Williams, as a young enslaved woman known as Mahala, had run off with a young man enslaved by the neighbor who had hired her labor.[57] The administrator of the estate of George Purnell called several witnesses who attempted to align their declared memories of Mahala with the flesh and blood Euphemia Williams sitting before them in the court. One by one, they stumbled under the interrogations of PVC lawyer, David Paul Brown. Zachariah Bowen, who described having known Mahala in 1827 and claimed to be able to identify her as Williams in 1851, said "she was about sixteen or seventeen; she was about an ordinary size, not the smallest size, nor the largest; she was neither thick nor thin; there was nothing remarkable in her more than is common; nothing in her speech; she was about the same color as the woman here; I never saw a great deal of change in a nigger, from sixteen to thirty-five or forty, sometimes they grow fatter, sometimes leaner." Under intense questioning, Bowen added, "I know her by her general favor, and have no particular mark." When pressed, another witness Robert Bowen revealed that he could recall very little about her master or any relevant details about her situation. In contrast, a witness for Williams, the Chester County shoemaker Henry Cornish, swore that he had known her in Pennsylvania during the same time that her claimant alleged her to be enslaved in Maryland. Cornish declared that he came to court because "he is a vigilant man, and my principle is to save any person whose liberty is in danger."[58]

Sarah Gayley's testimony about the physical being of Williams, a girl she had known as Fanny Coates, demolished the claimant's case. Gayley revealed that both she and Williams had similar scars on their foreheads. Judge John K. Kane, who was not sympathetic to alleged fugitives, called both women to the bench to examine their scars. Williams had kept her forehead covered by a turban to prevent her accusers from incorporating the scar into their descriptions of her. Brown won the case when he pointed out that the witnesses for Purnell did not know about the scar, unlike those acquainted with Williams during her youth in Chester County.[59]

If the Williams case tested the legal process for enforcement of the Fugitive Slave Law, the bloodshed in rural Christiana, Pennsylvania, revealed the intensity of enslavers' desires to control the bodies of enslaved people and their willingness to use the Fugitive Slave Law to do so. The violence occurred on September 11, 1851, when free Black people and their white allies tried to defend four Maryland refugees from being taken back into slavery. Noah Buley, Nelson Ford, George Hammond, and Joshua Hammond had fled from Edward Gorsuch's Baltimore wheat plantation. The fugitives were hiding at the home of the African American William Parker, who had organized a militia to protect the community's free Black members from the slave catchers who threatened their freedom. Gorsuch, who had been deputized as a federal marshal for the action, obtained a warrant in Philadelphia for the removal of the fugitives before heading for Christiana. Members of the Underground Railroad warned Parker that Gorsuch and his posse were coming. As Gorsuch and his men approached, Parker's wife Eliza blew a horn to mobilize the militia. There is some evidence that Black women as well as men answered Eliza's call. Caster Hanway, the local miller, showed up at Parker's with Elijah Lewis, a local shoemaker, to warn Gorsuch and his men to desist before there was violence. But Parker's men fired defensive shots, killing Gorsuch and wounding his son Dickinson. After Vigilance Committee members hustled Parker and the fugitives off to Canada with help from Frederick Douglass, Hanway ended up being charged with treason for allegedly masterminding the "riot," but was acquitted.[60]

As the rate of kidnappings of alleged fugitives accelerated, free Black communities and their white abolitionist allies across the nation responded to the emerging crisis by revitalizing their Vigilance Committees.[61] The PVC had lost some of its vigor after the attacks of 1842 drove Robert Purvis from the city, but members took steps to revive it in December 1852.[62] One of Purvis's close associates, William Still, saw this second incarnation of the PVC as an extension of the Underground Railroad and a crucial defense against the state's southern sympathies. Still was born free in New Jersey in 1821 to parents who were refugees from slavery. First Still's father, then his mother, escaped from their enslaver in Maryland, but two of his brothers remained enslaved. At the age of twenty-two, Still moved to Philadelphia, where he joined the Pennsylvania Society for the Abolition of Slavery. Almost immediately, he began sheltering and caring for refugees who came to Philadelphia. Meanwhile, Still built his own life, one of the privileges of freedom, by marrying, fathering children, and purchasing a home.[63]

As was the case with most African American activists, the stakes of Still's labor would only increase after the passage in 1850 of the Fugitive Slave Act. But Still's stakes in the Underground Railroad were also personal. Men such as Still and Jacob White appeared publicly as the defenders of free communities even as they themselves remained vulnerable to racist violence and hostile litigation. In 1851, the white abolitionist Seth Concklin was killed during an unsuccessful attempt to help Still's brother Peter and his family escape from slavery. Although Peter managed to reach Philadelphia, where he was reunited with his brother, Peter's wife, Vina, and their children were captured and reenslaved. Peter began the arduous process of raising funds to purchase his wife and children, finally succeeding in 1854.[64]

Still's engagement in Vigilance Committee and Underground Railroad work reflected a genealogical response to family loss, a trauma with which he was familiar, and a journalistic, detail-oriented approach to bearing witness. Compiling fine-grained accounts of the lives of people whose enslavement left gaps in their life stories, Still documented slavery's relentless production of victims, refugees, and exiles.[65] His work with the Underground Railroad during the 1850s included assisting 649 refugees, many of whom stayed in his home and received care from his wife, Letitia. He recorded information about refugee family connections with an eye to future efforts to put families back together that had been separated by slavery and refugee flight. He took careful notes about their physical appearances and their ordeals—including a description of their demeanor, the proximate cause for fleeing slavery, the circumstances of their escape, and their eventual fate. In these accounts, Still demolished any notion that "good" masters satisfied enslaved people's desires for autonomy and self-determination.

Still's commentary on refugee appearance, intelligence, and character reflected a complex combination of nineteenth-century concepts of racial heritage as a matter of "blood," phrenological evidence of intellect and ability, and a mindfulness of the politics of complexion. Interpreting the will to escape slavery's prison as evidence of strength of character, Still assessed Underground Railroad passengers as physically and intellectually superior to the average slave. In his accounts, "bright mulattos" and people with "white blood" in their veins appear frequently as heroic refugees highly motivated to attain liberty; yet he also offered testimony to those with "brown" or "dark" complexions being similarly motivated and exhibiting similar initiative and intellect. He commented on the high and large foreheads of two female refugees, Jane Johnson and Caroline Gassway, a trait that signaled intellect according to the phrenological standards of the time. He carefully sidestepped tenets of scientific racism, however, and offered testimony to the success of refugees in finding employment to support themselves. In this way, Still refused to give race a determinative power over other attributes of personhood even as he used the terms and concepts of ancestry common in his own time. Indeed, Still's implicit theories of personhood gave primacy to personal experience rather than any biological notion of race. In his notes about Julia, the wife of Sheridan Ford, for example, Still noted, "as a woman she had known something of the 'barbarism of slavery' from every day experience, which the large scars about her head indicated according to Sheridan's testimony." Slavery rather than race, Still concluded, had left the most significant marks on this woman's body.[66]

Still delayed any publication of his case notes to protect the refugees and field agents who made escape possible, but fundraising required the sharing of stories of successful escapes. The veteran free produce advocate and Underground

Railroad operative J. Miller McKim went public with several of these stories, taking care to protect individual identities. McKim traveled to England in the fall of 1853 to testify to the work of the Underground Railroad and the Vigilance Committee to raise funds from a more sympathetic British public.[67]

The strength of the PVC lay in its support from the community, including the often invisible labor of its female allies. As in the 1840s, the PVC of the post–Fugitive Slave Law era relied on networks of women, Black and white, to take responsibility for the committee's dangerous "hands-on" work. These labors took many forms. Women as well as men took on the risky physical labor—the body work—of facilitating enslaved people's journeys across state lines and caring for them once they became refugees. Harriet Tubman led this high-stakes work in collaboration with Thomas Garrett, another legendary Underground Railroad conductor. Black and white Vigilance Committee members contacted potential refugees in slaveholding states, provided passes to enable their safe travel, made clothes, identified safe shelter, prepared beds, transported fugitives, cooked for them, and provided medical aid. Graceanna Lewis and Abigail Goodwin, two white members of the Female Vigilance Committee, operated safe houses.[68] On one occasion, Lewis wrote from Kimberton, Pennsylvania, to report the arrival of fugitives from New Chestertown to Thomas Garrett's Longwood Meeting House. She was concerned about the fugitives being revealed by a Black woman who had been left behind and knew of their plan. Lewis sought advice about how best to get them to Canada and provide them with financial support.[69]

Although Still recorded the refugee's stories, many of his subjects received intimate care from his wife, Letitia. She welcomed them into the Still home, fed them, provided medical attention, and gave them clean clothes and bedding. For many refugees, this was their first night in a safe house.[70] One of Still's correspondents chided him for letting this burden fall so heavily on Letitia, who regularly washed and ironed late into the night. The medical practitioner James J. G. Bias and his wife, Elizabeth, shared in this work, as did other Black women, anonymous to us, who sewed, took in boarders at the last minute, or passed along messages and funds for travel. These networks of female agents and care providers supported the everyday struggles and pragmatic work of individual escape.[71]

In addition to hands-on physical labors, women provided administrative and fundraising labor. The Philadelphia Female Vigilance Committee, like its brother organization, was fully integrated from the start. The African American activists Esther Moore and Hetty Reckless led the white activists Lucretia Mott and Mary Grew in supporting its efforts. They participated in committee meetings, served in leadership positions, and coordinated public activities to raise money.

Reckless pushed her male counterparts to secure and send aid to escaped slaves as the most pragmatic form of support for refugees seeking to launch new lives. Several ladies' antislavery societies and sewing circles in Philadelphia and elsewhere sent the PVC clothing and bedding, including socks, chemises, pants, sunbonnets, aprons, capes, shawls, bed quilts, and pillowcases. PFAS members raised funds to pay for clothes, food, transport, and court fees. They, too, depended on work by Black women auxiliaries who knitted and held concerts, soirees, and public lectures, but also by Black working-class women in the field of action who provided information, transport, and aid to refugees.[72]

On at least one occasion, the staunch Vigilance Committee supporter Lucretia Mott voiced doubts about the huge investment of energy and funds into individual escapes as a way of undoing a labor system continually replenished by births. Wouldn't it be better to strike a fatal systemic blow to destroy slavery "root and branch"? Mary Grew responded by reminding her that escapes, although limited in number compared to the growing enslaved population, ultimately undermined the security and value of slave "property." Mott appears to have been satisfied with this answer and continued her fundraising and advocacy for refugees in court as part of the Female Vigilance Committee.[73]

The PVC's provision of care for refugees was nothing short of a transfiguration of the enslaved person's body and identity. Occasionally using the term "resurrection" to describe the safe emergence of refugees from boxes or chests where they hid during their escapes, PVC members facilitated a former slave's rebirth into a new life as a free person. In addition to releasing refugees from these physical confines, PVC agents offered a therapeutic cleansing of trauma through the recounting of life stories and the details of escape. PVC members listened attentively, asked questions, and provided affirmation for the refugee's heroic survival of their ordeals. They also cared for the refugee's body by providing access to bathing, medical care, new clothing, food, and temporary shelter. Most important, PVC members urged refugees to shed slave names and take on new names that would mark the transition to freedom and offer protection for new identities and new lives. The process was complete when the PVC sent refugees to new homes, often across national borders to Canada, and received reports from successfully transplanted free men and women earning wages for their labor. Reading between the lines of Still's record, one can detect the PVC guiding these transfigurations, encouraging the escapees to lay down the burdens of traumas experienced as slaves for the expanded possibilities and liberties of new lives.[74]

Refugees often endured dangerous conditions to make their escape from slavery. Still recounted numerous cases of fugitives whose harrowing escapes put their lives at risk. Abraham Galloway and Richard Eden of Wilmington,

North Carolina, were forced to stow away in a ship carrying turpentine and tried to protect themselves from the toxic fumes by swaddling themselves in silk oil cloth shrouds. The turpentine drew blood from their pores, leaving them near death, but as Still reported, "The invigorating northern air and the kind treatment of the Vigilance Committee acted like a charm upon them, and they improved very rapidly from their exhaustive and heavy loss of blood."[75]

It was not unusual for fugitives to suffer serious injuries and to require extensive medical care upon arrival in Philadelphia. Robert Jackson fled from Martinsburg, Virginia, in November 1853 after learning that he would be sold. His escape appeared to have been foiled when he was misled by someone pretending to be an Underground Railroad operative and shot during the ensuing skirmish. When he finally arrived in Philadelphia, "The Vigilance Committee procured good medical attention and afforded the fugitive time for recuperation, furnished him with clothing and a free ticket."[76]

Romulus Hall (alias George Weems) was not so lucky. In March 1857, he traveled overland from Charles County, Maryland, for nine days and nights, suffering from frostbite. Upon reaching Philadelphia, he lost his toes but seemed to be recovering before lockjaw and mortification set in. The only Philadelphia refugee to lose his life, according to Still, Hall was buried in Lebanon Cemetery, founded in 1849 by the PVC member Jacob White. In his commentary, Still thanked Drs. J. L. Griscom and H. T. Childs for providing medical services and Mrs. H. S. Duterte and Mrs. Williams for preparing the body for burial.[77]

One of the common elements of fugitive accounts were descriptions of escapes along waterways. Water travel proved a less hazardous means of escape than overland routes because of the speed of the journey (hours rather than days or weeks) and the ability to avoid trackers and witnesses. Most of the 285 Virginia refugees whose escapes Still recorded in his notes traveled by water. Anthony Blow (alias Henry Levison) from Norfolk, Virginia, escaped on the steamship *City of Richmond* in 1854 with help from the ship employee John Minkins. Blow had been shot three times during his life for his refusal to be whipped. Minkins was also involved in the rescue of Isaac Forman on the same steamship.[78]

Henry "Box" Brown was perhaps the most famous fugitive to use the strategy of mailing himself across state lines to reach freedom in Pennsylvania. During his twenty-one-hour ordeal, he doused himself in water and fanned himself with his hat to keep the air circulating. When his box arrived in Philadelphia 1849, PVC members gathered for his "resurrection." After christening him Henry Brown, the PVC sent him first to McKim's house for breakfast and a bath, and then to Lucretia Mott's household, where "clothing and creature comforts were furnished in abundance." Brown also spent some time at William and Letitia Still's house. Several others used the same tactic with success. William "Box"

Peel Jones arrived by steamer in a box in April 1859. He had spent seventeen hours in a box, but upon his release, he was "well cared for by the Vigilance Committee." He, too, received care from Letitia Still.[79]

Several women also hid themselves in boxes and luggage to make their escapes on steamships. One woman mailed herself to Mrs. Rachel Myers, an elderly African American shopkeeper and member of the Female Vigilance Committee. The fugitive emerged from her container speechless and seemingly near death. Members of the PVC cared for her and gradually revived her.[80] Lear Green of Baltimore endured a similar "resurrection" after spending eighteen hours on a steamship inside the luggage of a free Black friend.[81]

A few refugee women found it necessary to disguise their gender, something that no men were recorded by Still to have done to make their escapes. This pattern of enslaved women passing as men flies in the face of the accusation aimed at Sojourner Truth for passing as a woman and makes it appear even more outlandish. Clarissa Davis, 1854, from Portsmouth Virginia, hid in a confined space for seventy-five days until she could make her escape on the same *City of Richmond* steamship that transported so many refugees. She then shifted to male attire to avoid detection. Maria Weems, an enslaved girl of fifteen, successfully escaped from Washington, D.C., disguised as a male carriage driver. Mary Millburn, alias Louisa F. Jones, similarly donned male clothing to facilitate her escape on a steamship in 1858.[82]

As the historian Jesse Olsavsky has argued, face-to-face work with refugee women became the basis for the exchange of information and learning that led to the development of more sophisticated feminist analyses of slavery. PFAS and PVC members came into direct contact with female refugees, whose stories they solicited, listened to, and learned from. Still, for example, talked to nearly two hundred women, many of whom reported verbal abuse, beatings, and whippings. Harriet Jacobs, who passed through Philadelphia in 1842, not only shared her story with the men and women of the PVC but learned from them about the conditions other enslaved women had faced.[83] Mary Ann Shadd Cary, Frances Ellen Watkins Harper, Abby Kelley, and Lucretia Mott all incorporated information from fugitives into speeches, poetry, news articles, and novels. Throughout the 1850s, the PFAS welcomed a series of formerly enslaved women as well as abolitionist activists to address their meetings.[84]

Still's decision to record the testimonies of refugees in 1851, after being reunited with his brother, provides a glimpse of the systemic damage that slavery inflicted on the bodies and psyches of enslaved people. Using the abolitionist language of the body, one fugitive woman told Still that she would wade through blood and tears for her freedom.[85] Barnaby Grigby, alias John Boyer, reported that he wanted to "live by the sweat of his own brow."[86] Sale and separation from family members loomed large among refugees' explanations of why they decided to run. Still often noted that, for enslaved people residing in the border states of Maryland and Virginia, the threat of being sold farther south prompted flight. This fate came to pass more often for men than for women, but it was enough to launch women like Matilda Mahoney of Baltimore on a desperate attempt at escape.[87]

The conditions under which women remained in the Upper South posed clear harm. Still heard accounts of women threatened with sale if they did not accede to the sexual demands of enslavers and enslavers' kin. The wife of Robert Brown alias Thomas Jones resisted her enslaver's sexual advances and suffered the fate of being sold farther south as a consequence.[88] Others were provoked to run because their enslavers' bankruptcy made sale to the Lower South more likely. Some women reported endless childbearing that resulted in heartbreaking separations when children were sold like merchandise. A few spoke candidly about being broken by the combination of domestic, agricultural, and reproductive labors.[89]

Vigilance Committees regularly attempted to obtain writs of habeas corpus to extract fugitives from detention so that they would not be returned to slavery. This served the purpose of removing the detained refugee from the jurisdiction of the federal marshal and into the courtroom. It also introduced a delay that could allow communities to assemble to prevent by their massed presence what slave catchers tried to accomplish by stealth and force. Abolitionist Henry B. Blackwell requested a writ of habeas corpus in 1855 to stop a group of accused fugitives from being hustled by their slave owner out of town and beyond the reach of free Black supporters in Cincinnati, Ohio. Without recourse to habeas corpus, critics of the Fugitive Slave Law noted, there was little to stop kidnappings.[90]

Yet as many refugees discovered, writs of habeas corpus or of replevin (bail) were no panacea for the plight of the fugitive or kidnap victim. Calculations about the possible failure of legal measures were evident in an escape recorded by Still. Cordelia Loney, fifty-seven years old, enslaved by Mrs. Joseph Cahell of Fredericksburg, Virginia, was brought into Philadelphia by her widowed mistress after several of her children, including a sick daughter, had been sold. The PVC offered her the choice of leaving the city quietly or swearing out a writ of habeas corpus. Loney decided to take her chance with the Underground Railroad rather than risk a Philadelphia court appearance, making her escape at the same time that a fellow fugitive, Daniel Webster, went to trial in the city.[91]

The kidnapping of John Freeman in 1853 revealed the weaknesses of protections for free Black citizens from the claims of enslavers and the contested legality of bodily searches of alleged fugitives. It also pitted the jurisdiction of state courts against federal authority over the bodies of fugitives. Freeman had been born free in Georgia and had lived in Indiana since 1844. Indianapolis authorities tricked Freeman into appearing before the federal commissioner, who detained him, claiming he was a fugitive named Sam. Freeman's lawyers succeeded in obtaining a writ of habeas corpus and in delaying Freeman's hearing until witnesses could be gathered, but the judge insisted on holding him. The U.S. Marshall Robinson permitted Ellington, the man who claimed Freeman as his slave, access to Freeman's body while in detention, where he forced Freeman to strip so he could search his body for scars and other identifying marks ahead of the hearing. In the meantime, lawyers for Freeman made contact with the real "Sam," who had escaped to Canada, and managed to refute Ellington's claims when Ellington's son was unable to identify Freeman.[92]

Subsequent cases of alleged fugitives turned on evidence of the accused's record of physical labor or physical identification. In 1859, Daniel Webster, alleged to have escaped from a Virginia enslaver, succeeded in defending his freedom with assistance from PVC counsel. Although Webster had been residing in Harrisburg when he was captured, the case went before the federal commissioner in Philadelphia. Lucretia Mott and several other white women once again packed the courtroom, but in addition there were many Black women in attendance. Witnesses traveled from Harrisburg to testify to Webster's free life there, with key testimony coming from an elderly African American doctor who presented a work log showing that Webster had labored for him during the year before he was alleged to have escaped from slavery. Webster asked the court to measure his height in an effort to invalidate the enslaver's claim, although the result was not conclusive.[93] Webster was released but took the precaution of making his way to Canada. Just a year later, the case of Moses Horner turned against him when his enslaver's witnesses testified to a physical characteristic that Philadelphia commissioner John Cadwalader could see with his own eyes: Horner was what was commonly known as "pigeon-toed." His decision to return Horner to his enslaver provoked a crowd of Horner's African American supporters to attempt to stop the carriage from taking him away and resulted in the arrests of ten men.[94]

The case of Jane Johnson in 1855 brought PVC and Underground Railroad operatives into the middle of the conflict between federal and state jurisdictions. Johnson and her two sons were being transported by her enslaver, John Hill Wheeler of North Carolina, who was on his way from Washington, D.C., to New York to catch a boat to Nicaragua, where he was assigned to serve as the U.S. minister. PVC members Passmore Williamson and William Still confronted Johnson's enslaver on the departing ship and asked Johnson directly if she wanted to be free. When she responded "yes," they removed her with the help of African American allies. The PVC took her to Still's house for safety before sending her to New York. In this case the enslaver, Wheeler, obtained a writ of habeas corpus from District Court Judge Kane, who ordered Williamson to produce the fugitives. Williamson refused to comply on the grounds that he did not have them in his possession. As the only white person involved and so the only one with fully recognized and protected political rights, including an expectation that he should know the Constitution, Williamson was held in contempt by Judge Kane, who confined him in Moyamensing Prison. In addition, the enslaver Wheeler complained against six African Americans, including William Still, for assisting in Johnson's "abduction."

In the midst of the Court of Quarter Sessions, Johnson appeared in the courtroom flanked by the PFAS and Female Vigilance Committee stalwarts Lucretia Mott, Sarah Pugh, Mary Grew, Rebecca Plumly, and Sarah McKim. Johnson affirmed in court that she had left her master willingly. Mott positioned her body strategically during Johnson's exit from the court to block her from the federal marshals who were prepared to arrest her. The southern-sympathizing *New York Herald* reported that the Vigilance Committee were the real kidnappers who stole Johnson and her children away from their family, while abolitionists condemned Kane for using habeas corpus as an instrument of slave catching.[95]

Several of the fugitive cases involving the PVC contributed to questions about the innate capacity of the enslaved mother's body. Was an enslaved woman's body intrinsically an incubator for new slaves, as enslavers and proponents of racist medicine would have it? Or did a woman's involuntary reproduction of slavery end when she moved across state lines into Pennsylvania? The Maryland court's initial ruling as well as the subsequent Supreme Court decision in *Prigg v. Pennsylvania* glossed over the question of her child's birth in Pennsylvania; Margaret Morgan and all of her children appear to have been returned to slavery following *Prigg*. By 1851, the complicating factor of a freeborn infant might save the child from enslavement but did not provide any protection for his family. Daniel, enslaved by Dr. Robert Franklin of Anne Arundel County, Maryland, and Daniel's wife, Abby, and child Caroline, enslaved by Barbara Wailes of Baltimore, had escaped to Columbia, Pennsylvania, before the baby's birth. Despite the child's obvious dependence, the presiding commissioner Richard McAllister (Dickinson College class of 1840) who had been appointed commissioner by Robert C. Grier (Dickinson College class of 1812 and associate justice of the U.S. Supreme Court) sent the family back into slavery in Maryland minus its youngest member.[96]

A second case in 1853 raised similar issues. Samuel Halzell, a leading slave catcher, took into custody Helen Dellam, aged forty, and her son Dick, aged ten.

Helen was pregnant at the time, and Dick's father was a free Black man. They had escaped with a group of enslaved people from Baltimore County, Maryland, and settled in Columbia, Pennsylvania. Helen and her son were claimed by John Purdue. Federal commissioner Ingraham of Philadelphia issued a warrant for their removal. Helen's husband was away at the time working on a canalboat. Before Ingraham could hear the case, a writ of habeas corpus brought it before Judge Kane. The hearing began with Passmore Williamson and McKim in attendance and Kane's son Robert as part of the legal team for Dellam, along with David Paul Brown. "A large number of ladies," including Lucretia Mott, who had been following the case for years, were present in court. Black witnesses claimed that they had met Helen in Columbia prior to the date of her alleged escape. Purdue noted that his father-in-law had given him Helen as a wedding gift. Kane wanted to know why Helen's white employer or pastor had not testified, and clearly gave more weight to white witnesses. As a consequence of the racial weighting of testimony, Helen and Dick Dellam were remanded to be transported back into slavery.[97]

Physical acts of escape, including the work of caring for, transporting, and "rebirthing" fugitives, had significant political impact. With every successful act of escape, with every christening of an enslaved person with a new name and a new life, members of the VC offered evidence that countered the scientific racism of the day. If state lines and birth were the determination rather than biology, then there was nothing intrinsic to an African-descended body that made a person suited to slavery and slavery had no biological justification.

Free Labor and the Laborer's Body

As the debate over slavery intensified during the 1850s, a singular southern voice denounced abolitionism, along with other northern "isms," for its tacit acknowledgement of the failures of societies built on free labor, liberty, and equality. The Virginian George Fitzhugh, descendant of the seventeenth-century Virginia lawyer William Fitzhugh, advanced a radical critique of the social vision of abolitionists and all of their other commitments. Following a series of articles and a book, *Sociology for the South* (1854), Fitzhugh published *Cannibals All! or, Slaves without Masters* (1857), a sustained, multifaceted critique of abolition and its consequences. According to Fitzhugh, abolitionists and their fellow travelers had erroneously latched onto "liberty" and "equality" in historically inaccurate ways as representing the legacy of the American Revolution. In their wrongheaded pursuit of expanding liberty and equality, they were in fact dissolving the social bonds of property, family, and dependence—a trend that ran against the true needs and nature of human beings. In Fitzhugh's own agenda for these social bonds, however, the hierarchical southern social order that supported white supremacy clearly trumped any consideration of the needs of African-descended families. Slavery, Fitzhugh contended, was one of the time-honored and biblically sanctioned relations of dependence that brought out the best in both enslaved people and their "masters."[98]

Fitzhugh's defense of slavery notably avoided any grappling with the condition of African-descended people's bodies. He offered no details about the physical circumstances of people enslaved in the American South. He avoided the issue of enslaved people's bodies entirely except to insist that their basic needs for food, shelter, and security were provided for by benevolent masters. He also did not reference the arguments of race scientists to try to justify slavery, but simply asserted without much elaboration that African-descended people were enslaved because they were naturally suited to slavery. He provided no evidence from scientific racism about anatomy, intellect, or proclivity to disease to make his argument. Tellingly, he also provided no detailed descriptions of enslaved people's daily labors other than to claim that they were happy, without worry, and among the least exploited and most well-cared-for laborers on the earth. Fitzhugh lifted the conclusions of scientific racists from the context of bodily comparison and analysis in a fashion consistent with his posture of looking away from the scenes of violence and injury all around him in the antebellum South.[99]

Yet even if Fitzhugh carefully avoided the subject of enslaved people's suffering, there were plenty of suffering bodies in his account: the bodies of exploited white women and children working in Britain's satanic mills, robbed of their childhoods, their health, and their liberty. In many ways, we can see that Fitzhugh followed the argumentative structure of abolitionist claims with his denunciation of free labor punctuated by the evidence of suffering bodies as barometers of unethical labor practices. Providing detailed accounts of their suffering, Fitzhugh argued that wage-earning women and children were the true slaves. Their broken, injured, and debilitated bodies pointed to the moral iniquity of capitalism. This was yet another version of summoning the suffering of innocent white dependents to defend slavery.

The economic punch line of *Cannibals All* was a claim with which all free labor produce advocates would have agreed: slavery's economic tentacles, especially the market for its agricultural commodities, permeated every aspect of daily life in the North. To do away with slavery, then, was to cut off the North from the goods—necessities as well as luxuries—that sustained the lives of free laborers. As Fitzhugh admitted, however, his home state of Virginia was especially vulnerable to abolitionist calls for disunion. He linked his state's fate to that of Pennsylvania, citing Horace: "Besides, Virginia loves her nearest sister,

Pennsylvania, and cannot bear the thought of parting company with her. Tecum vivere amem! Tecum obeam lubens!" (With thee I fain would live, with thee I'd gladly die.)[100]

Fitzhugh raised issues that many abolitionists preferred to avoid. Unlike Jamaican treadmills, textile machinery appeared as the crowning glory of Western progress. Lacking slavery's overt coercion and what abolitionists continued to identify as Eastern-style barbarism—a form of power displayed through the literal maiming and disintegration of subordinated human bodies—industrial wage labor appeared clean, modern, and humane. Embracing industrial manufacturing and advancing its interests in the poor rural districts of Ireland and England, moreover, appeared to some abolitionists to be humanitarian work, a boost to failing local agricultural economies where peasants lived in abject poverty.

Abolitionist associations of American slavery with Eastern barbarism blunted their response to the atrocities of wage labor. Even if they saw "free labor" in factories as similarly shocking and revolting, they interpreted it as being of a different order of labor exploitation than slavery. Although many abolitionists would have agreed that some British factories clearly were satanic mills that injured the health and safety of the women and children who worked there, American factories, in contrast, seem to have avoided the worst excesses of Manchester and Birmingham. To those who toured them, they appeared instead as temples of rationality, order, and progress. In addition, free labor was remunerated, placing it in a different category from the labor stolen from enslaved people. But were the bodies of the "free" laborers actually free of the debilitating physical consequences of labor that overtaxed the enslaved person's body and subverted the individual's will? Absent the whips, chains, and other visible violations of the laborer's will that left marks on the body, the violation of the free laborer was more difficulty to detect.

In part because of their own long-standing commitments to interpreting slavery's brutality as a throwback to Eastern tyranny, and in part owing to their resistance to proslavery arguments about "wage slavery" in England and the U.S. North, many abolitionists interpreted both factory and rural free labor as positive alternatives to slavery. Model factories, such as those that abolitionists visited, appeared as pinnacles of Western technology where workers consented rationally, by way of contract, rather than as a consequence of physical coercion. The labor contract, as Amy Dru Stanley has argued, replaced bondage through the addition of the marriage contract that engaged women to provide care for the male laborer's body. Under free labor, the laborer retained self-ownership but sold his labor, an alienation that was possible only if he, his wife, or the individual he paid to provide domestic services assumed responsibility for his bodily maintenance. Compared to slavery, which extracted labor by using the direct threat of harm to body and psyche, contracts seemed to extract labor from the body through an exchange and without observable violence. Abolitionists believed they were witnessing the purifying power of consent when they saw labor extracted seemingly without the physical subordination of the laborer's body.[101]

This was Angelina Grimké Weld's interpretation of factory labor in 1846, when she toured a New Jersey textile factory. On one of her rare excursions out of her own home, where she had been confined with a debilitating gynecological condition, Grimké Weld reported to her sister Sarah and her husband that she took a steamboat to Gloucester Point to see an "emmence Cotton Manufactory . . . were highly gratified with seeing all the different processes from the raw cotton just taken from the bat to the finished muslin—the machinery most beautiful—400 hands employed."[102] This was part of the mill village created by David S. Brown, a New Jersey Quaker who had purchased land across the river from Philadelphia. When Grimké Weld visited them, the mills were only in their second year of operation. Advertisements for the mills depicted them as a hub of manufacturing, with ships traversing a picturesque waterway and smoke billowing out of the factory stacks. Walking through a model factory, Grimké Weld did not see wage labor leaving its mark on the bodies of the laborers, although her reference to laborers as "hands" might have tipped her off.

Anne Rhoads was similarly impressed by her visit to a Leeds flax mill during her trip to England in 1847. Accompanied by the free produce activist Elihu Burritt, Rhoads observed the manufacture of flax thread in a factory where they prepared "yarn for the finest cambrics." Rhoads was especially impressed by the employees, "1000 men women and children who looked well and in good heart," although she noted that they ran "10,000 spindles in one room." Free labor drove the entire production process from extracted plant fiber to spun yarn to cambric fabric.[103]

Fitzhugh occasionally criticized abolitionists for being socialists and communists, when he wasn't claiming that societies based on slavery incorporated the benefits of both systems. Some abolitionists, like Frederick Douglass, clearly saw similarities between the situation of the Irish peasant and the slave in the American South. Others astutely noted that the labor of coolies was itself a form of bound labor dressed up with a contract to make it appear free. But as Stanley notes, at the center of most abolitionist critiques of slavery was the assumption that free labor's advantage came in part because of its reliance on marriage, understood as a contract of its own that conveyed status as well as an exchange of labor for maintenance. Free labor's deference to marriage provided capitalism with a vital connection to an allegedly natural order and a necessary moral bulwark against a variety of evils that would have weakened the bond between husband and wife.[104]

For many abolitionists, the free labor of men supported by marriage continued to appear as an ideal worth pursuing as an alternative to slavery. The diehard British abolitionist and free labor advocate Joseph Sturge decided to purchase a plantation in Montserrat in 1857, motivated in part by a desire to meet the demand for free labor produce from within the British Empire. But he likely also wanted to intervene in the argument that West Indian economies were declining because former slaves could not be transformed into free laborers. Montserrat, which Sturge had taken note of in 1837 as an island with potential for the health and prosperity of laborers, became the headquarters of Sturge's new business. He started with an estate of eleven thousand acres and subsequently joined forces with his brother to purchase two additional estates. Initially, at least, he tried to produce sugar cane with hired labor. As he wrote to his free labor produce associate Samuel Rhoads in 1859, "I am about sending out a Steam Engine to grind the Sugar cane & export by next winter."[105] Sturge also launched plans to build schools, churches, and a hospital, reflecting both a desire for paternalistic control and his refusal to embrace a free labor concept in which the welfare of the laborer's body became separated from the work he performed.[106] Until his death, Sturge remained a believer in the benefits to individual, family, population, and economy of a system of agricultural production based on compensated labor.

A few Black abolitionists, convinced by the late 1850s of the need for emigration, saw new potential in schemes for the free labor production of cotton. Garnet's African Civilization Society, formed in 1858, focused less on the physical and moral benefits of free cotton for laborers and consumers and more on the geopolitical potential of free cotton production for the African continent. Substituting the export of free cotton for captives, Garnet believed, would benefit not only Africans but the African Americans who participated in the projects as they prepared themselves for full citizenship in the United States. Martin Delany, meanwhile, committed himself to free cotton projects in Liberia and Nigeria, the culmination of years of advocating emigration for free African Americans.[107]

American abolitionists assumed that the suffering of Black bodies within the national boundaries of the United States was not only relevant to the argument over slavery but definitive for condemning the institution. Fitzhugh's response was to look away, not only to the North but also outside of the United States to try to contextualize northern abolition within what he viewed as a dangerous global-historical trend toward atomized individualism. According to Fitzhugh, that individualism led to white pauperism by dissolving the Filmerian hierarchies and bonds of dependence that constituted human nature, society, and slavery.

Dred Scott

> [African Americans] had for more than a century before been regarded as beings of an inferior order, and altogether unfit to associate with the white race, either in social or political relations; and so far inferior, that they had no rights which the white man was bound to respect; and that the negro might justly and lawfully be reduced to slavery for his benefit. He was bought and sold, and treated as an ordinary article of merchandise and traffic, whenever a profit could be made by it.
>
> —Justice Taney, March 5, 1857

Douglass's words to the Western Reserve audience of 1854—"God has no children whose rights may be safely trampled upon"—were prescient. The 1857 *Dred Scott v. Sandford* Supreme Court decision was the culmination of a decade of court action taken by the litigating parties. The Court's dismissal of Scott's case represented the legal expression of craniology. As Dred Scott and his lawyers argued, embodied self-sovereignty was an ideal for freedom incompatible with coercion, constraint, and inflicted terror. Above all, it was an ideal for human rights incompatible with having one's body treated as someone else's property.

Chief Justice Roger Taney, who had himself been an enslaver in Maryland but had manumitted his slaves some thirty years earlier, set the case aside on the basis of his opinion that Scott, an enslaved man who had moved in and out of free and slave states, had no standing as a U.S. citizen to bring his suit. Scott's lawyers had made use of a writ of habeas corpus to get his case before a U.S. federal court, but now the Supreme Court declared that he had no such right. The comparison to Ned's success in petitioning the eighteenth-century Virginia Supreme Court for standing in *Pleasants v. Pleasants* is difficult to avoid. In the instance of Scott, the high bar of national citizenship appears to have disabled an enslaved petitioner, but there was also the new potence of biological concepts of race in the intervening sixty years.

In his explanation of why Scott had no standing, Taney hewed to a strict construction of the Constitution that implicitly invoked the theory of polygenesis. The Constitution, Taney claimed, merely reflected the will of the founders, themselves slave owners, who excluded people of African descent from their concept of "the people." Taney's assertion, however, did not reflect what we have seen to be the contested notion of "the people" during the 1780s and the 1790s and the convictions of men like Robert Pleasants that humankind was of "one blood." Hearkening to his own version of history, Taney insisted that all people of African descent were burdened by a status informed by the condition of slavery, a contention that carefully sidestepped the deliberate legal mechanism created to tie children to the status of their enslaved mothers.

Offering a political rendition of the theory of polygenesis, Taney concluded that African Americans were neither part of "the people" referenced in the Constitution, nor part of the family of nations or the family of man. As such, they could claim no rights, privileges, or immunities of citizens. Were they to be treated as citizens, Taney warned, they would be able "to go where they please at every hour of the day or night without molestation." Their exercise of the citizen's rights, in other words, would include freedom of movement and arms bearing, two outcomes that would (apparently) jeopardize the security of white people. In addition, Taney found that the Missouri Compromise's exclusion of slavery from territories yet to be admitted to the union exceeded the federal government's authority as defined under the Constitution.[108]

Abolitionists were disappointed and angered by Taney's decision. But Frederick Douglass found hope that Taney's articulation of Black exclusion, an extreme provocation, might energize slavery's foes. Taney's harmful rationale for the decision, Douglass observed philosophically, was "a means of keeping the nation awake on the subject. It is another proof that God does not mean that we shall go to sleep, and forget that we are a slaveholding nation."[109] In many ways, Douglass was correct. Under conditions of increased numbers of refugees and greater Black legal jeopardy and vulnerability to kidnapping, abolitionists were pushed to positions of greater exertion and militance. By June 1857, J. Miller McKim reported to PFAS, two fugitives were passing through Philadelphia every day.

Already throughout the decade and increasingly after Taney's decision, PFAS became more active and outspoken in its condemnation of state and federal laws and the men who enforced them. The indefatigable Lucretia Mott, who had been an activist since the 1820s, was attending not just monthly PFAS meetings but emergency meetings for free Black people in Harrisburg and Columbia. Together with Thomas Whitson, she also attended "large meetings" in the lower part of Chester County along the Maryland border. At the PFAS meeting during which she reported her activities, she confessed the need for younger activists, as "some of the old and faithful laborers feel their strength failing." Yet the sixty-five-year-old Mott was hardly defeated. She stirred her PFAS colleagues with a paraphrase of William Cullen Bryant's "The Battlefield" (1837):

Truth struck to earth revives again
The eternal years of God are hers;
But error wounded writhest in pain
And dies amid her worshipers.

Later that year, Mott reported on a trip to Baltimore in which she met with free Black people and spoke freely against slavery.[110]

PFAS continued to use petitions to condemn state and federal laws, as they had done in their protests against the Kansas-Nebraska Act in 1854 and their condemnation of the South Carolinian Preston Brooks's beating of Charles Sumner on the Senate floor. In 1858, they petitioned to make Pennsylvania free soil so that no alleged slaves could be tried there. That same year, upon the death of the infamous Judge Kane, PFAS publicly celebrated the end of his abuse of power, denigration of state's rights, and violations of habeas corpus. Four years earlier PFAS had refused to engage in any eulogies for Edward Ingraham, the notorious federal commissioner who had inflicted so much cruelty on fugitives. They similarly condemned Judge Cadwalader, although he was still very much alive, for returning a Black man to slavery in 1860. In both 1859 and 1860, PFAS again petitioned the Pennsylvania House and Senate to end the enforcement of the Fugitive Slave Law and to guarantee personal liberty in the state.[111]

In the aftermath of *Dred Scott v. Sandford*, PFAS intensified its efforts around its main fundraising vehicle, the annual fair held every December. As Mott noted, far from being a mere ladies auxiliary fundraiser, the annual fair was the "main instrumentality" of PFAS abolitionist activism and also funded many of the state's abolitionist organizations. To ensure its success, the fair managers began planning early in the year to secure a venue and to solicit free labor goods to be sold. Expenses were significant and included the rent for the hall and the hire of doorkeepers, carters, porters, and waiters. In addition, fixtures, advertisements, shipping costs for goods arriving from overseas, and the purchase of books, toys, ice cream, cake, and candy all required PFAS labor and investment. Proceeds from the fair had for over three decades supported the state antislavery society, paid for the society's abolitionist subscriptions, and financed the care of refugees. To add to the draw of free labor goods and refreshments, PFAS managers secured prestigious speakers drawn from the national abolition speaker's circuit. In 1856 William Lloyd Garrison addressed attendees; in 1857 it was Charles Remond and Sarah Remond; and in 1858 William Wells Brown conducted a reading of his work. By January 1859, PFAS members resolved to make the fair national. That year's fair, however, held at the Concert Hall, was disrupted when the venue's trustees ordered them to take down the flag with the Liberty Bell, the

"'76" insignia, and the bell's inscription, "Proclaim Liberty throughout all the land, unto all inhabitants thereof." Undaunted, the PFAS Fair Committee gathered up their goods and refreshments and moved to the more hospitable Assembly Building.[112]

Black abolitionists were, as Douglass predicted, fired up by the Taney opinion. The already disillusioned Delany, who had published *The Condition, Elevation, Emigration, and Destiny of the Colored People of the United States, Politically Considered* (1852) calling for the emigration from the United States to Central America, turned to fiction after 1857 to make his case for action. Delany's serialized novel *Blake: or the Huts of America*, which began to appear in installments in 1859, provided an account of a fugitive slave who revived African American militancy by invoking the inspiring leadership of Gabriel Prosser, Denmark Vesey, and Nat Turner.[113]

The activism of John Stewart Rock, born free in Salem, New Jersey, in 1825, also reached a crescendo after *Dred Scott*. As a child, Rock had been protected from agricultural labor by his parents so he could receive an education. After teaching for several years in his hometown in New Jersey, he attempted unsuccessfully to overcome racial bars to medical school. Dentistry proved an easier professional path, which he pursued in New Jersey before moving to Philadelphia to practice. When the opportunity arose to enroll in medical school, he seized it, graduating from the American Medical College in Philadelphia in 1852. The following year, he moved with his family to Boston, where he began a medical practice and provided care for sick refugees. He also became more politically prominent in abolitionist circles, participating in the 1855 Colored National Convention in Philadelphia where, along with Charles Remond and Robert Purvis, he visited the jailed Underground Railroad conductor Passmore Williamson. His abolitionist philosophy combined militancy (that same year he urged enslaved people to engage in a dramatic strike for freedom) and anti-racist science (a speech titled "The Unity of the Human Races"). In 1858, at Boston's Faneuil Hall celebration of Crispus Attucks Day, Rock urged his audience to celebrate the beauty of Blackness, making the case for the aesthetic superiority of African over white features, and extolling Black acts of bravery. He had no sympathy for Martin Delany's call for African American emigration, however, even though his own effort to secure a national passport failed in the aftermath of the *Dred Scott* decision's denial of Black citizenship. He also took issue publicly with white abolitionist allies who impugned Black men's will to fight slavery with both "physical and moral courage."[114]

As the national and local political stakes intensified, putting free as well as enslaved Black people at greater risk, Black women redoubled their efforts as speakers and activists. Sojourner Truth gave speeches in Silver Lake,

Indiana, in 1858. Lydia Bustill and Letitia Still became members of PFAS, where they joined Harriet Purvis, who had already stepped up to a more active role.[115] In the context of diminished attendance at monthly meetings, the presence of Bustill, Still, Purvis, and Sarah Mapps Douglass was significant, making the PFAS of the late 1850s a fully integrated association.

Frances Ellen Watkins Harper was perhaps the most celebrated and accomplished speaker of the group of inspirational African American women who intensified their efforts during the 1850s. Beginning in 1854, Harper lectured at a furious pace, working as an agent for the Maine Anti-Slavery Society until 1857, for the Pennsylvania Anti-Slavery Society until mid-1858, and then on the lecture circuit in Michigan, Ohio, New Jersey, New York, and Pennsylvania. Witnesses to her public lectures described her as a stirring and passionate speaker with a "soft musical voice" and "slender and graceful" body, although Harper reported on other occasions being mistaken for a man or a white woman "painted brown."[116]

Stung by the exclusion from citizenship manifest in Taney's pronouncement that Black people "had no rights that white people were bound to respect," Harper provided an eloquent rebuke that spoke to the hypocrisy of white Christians, the biopolitics and political economy linking Maryland and Virginia with the Deep South, and the national shame of slavery. In "Liberty for Slaves," delivered before the New York Anti-Slavery Society in 1857 and reprinted in the *Anti-Slavery Standard*, Harper reflected on the alchemical transformation of enslaved people's bodies into profits: "A hundred thousand new-born babes are annually added to the victims of slavery; twenty thousand lives are annually sacrificed on the plantations of the South. Such a sight should send a thrill of horror through the nerves of civilization and impel the heart of humanity to lofty deeds. So it might, if men had not found out a fearful alchemy by which this blood can be transformed into gold. Instead of listening to the cry of agony, they listen to the ring of dollars and stoop down to pick up the coin. (applause)."

In a condemnation reminiscent of Thomas Tryon's Paracelsian critique of the cosmic consequences of greed, Harper decried enslavers who ignored the claims of "one blood" and turned the blood of their captives into gold. Her listeners would have understood "stooping down to pick up the coin" as a reference to Judas's betrayal of Jesus or as an anti-Semitic trope that equated enslavers with Jews. She articulated the bitter irony that the Constitution had turned out to be but poor protection for enslaved people and people of color: "Had it been my lot to have lived beneath the Crescent instead of the Cross, had injustice and violence been heaped upon my head as a Mohammedan woman, as a member of a common faith, I might have demanded justice and been listened to by the

Pasha, the Bey or the Vizier; but when I come here to ask for justice, they tell me, 'We have no higher law than the Constitution' (applause)."[117]

Harper's contemporary Mary Ann Shadd Cary was a noted speaker in her own right. Daughter of a Chester County Underground Railroad operative and Philadelphia abolitionist, Cary had relocated to Canada in 1851 and encouraged other Black people to do the same. When she crossed paths with Harper while on a fundraising tour of the Old Northwest, she disclosed to her husband, Thomas Cary, her plan to give Harper some space so as to avoid direct comparisons. Although capable of reaching even those audiences who opposed her emigrationist politics, Cary admitted that she was not in Harper's league: "Why the white & colored people here are just crazy with excitement about her. She is the greatest female speaker ever was here, so wisdom obliges me to keep out of the way as with her prepared lectures there would just be no chance of a favorable comparison."[118]

Sarah Parker Remond joined the chorus of Black abolitionists to speak frankly about the particular plight of enslaved women. Remond had come up through the ranks of the American Anti-Slavery Society to become one of its national agents along with her brother Charles. By 1856, she was giving lectures in New York State along with Abby Kelley, Kelley's husband, Stephen Foster, Garrison, and Wendell Phillips. Her successes as a speaker led to trips to Ohio and Pennsylvania in 1857. She and her brother Charles filled the prestigious speakers' roles at the Philadelphia Anti-Slavery Fair of December 1857. The following year, she spoke at the National Women's Rights Convention in 1858. In a letter to Abby Kelley in December 1858, she credited Kelley's mentorship but reminded her of the obstacles a woman of color needed to surmount to take on the work of the speaker's circuit. "I feel almost sure I never should have made the attempt but for the words of encouragement I received from you," she acknowledged graciously, adding, "Although my heart was in the work, I felt that I was in need of a good English education . . . the only reason why I did not obtain what I so much desired was because I was the possessor of an unpopular complexion."[119]

Remond was only the second African American woman to embark on a lecture tour in the British Isles. She reached out to the well-networked Maria Weston Chapman to get help with introductions and to set up her lectures. Her 1859–1861 lecture tour through the working-class districts of Scotland, Ireland, and northern England, areas dominated by the textile industry and subject to the harshest effects of the 1834 Poor Law, came at a time of hardship for working women and their families. Remond built on the successes of her predecessor Ellen Craft, but reframed Craft's encouragement of white working women's identification with the plight of enslaved women by emphasizing the uniqueness of enslaved women's suffering.

Picking up on themes she had broached in her earlier speaking tour in England, Remond emphasized that women were slavery's greatest victims owing to the "fearful licentiousness" of the white South, and for that reason deserved special attention from English women. Her goal was to stir British antislavery sentiment so that it could be weaponized like "hot lead" to be poured on the heads of the Americans. She began her speaking tour in Warrington, England, in January 1859, addressing an overflow crowd for well over an hour. Of the southern slave market, she divulged, "in the open market place women are exposed for sale—their persons not always covered." Worse still, Remond added, they were "subjected to the most shameful indignities. The more Anglo-Saxon blood that mingles with the blood of a slave, the more gold is poured out when the auctioneer has a woman for sale, because they are sold to be concubines for white Americans." Addressing an audience in Bedford Square, London, in 1859, about the unparalleled vulnerability of enslaved women, Remond compared their situation unfavorably to that of the oppressed needlewomen of English factories. "The slavewoman was the victim of the heartless lust of her master, and the children whom she bore were his property," she observed, citing the enslaved woman's lack of embodied self-sovereignty and inability to confer birthright to her child as the reasons for her greater vulnerability. As Remond herself emphasized often to audiences, it was impossible to convey the suffering of a slave: "No one can describe the slave's life, it cannot be told," she declared at a speech in 1859 at the Athenaeum in Manchester, England.[120]

Despite her remove to a welcoming England, Remond soon confronted her own vulnerability as a person of color in the post–*Dred Scott* United States. When she sought a visa to travel to France in December 1859, the secretary of the U.S. legation refused to issue it, claiming that her passport was no longer valid in the aftermath of the *Dred Scott* decision. Remond wrote a series of candid letters to British newspapers, exposing the outrage. When she received no remedy for the wrong, Remond traveled to France without a visa.[121]

Remond's brother Charles, a longtime activist and speaker on the circuit, had already responded to the *Dred Scott* ruling with new militance. At a series of meetings during the summer of 1858, Charles Remond reframed the "one blood" claims of abolitionists to give voice to the frustrations of many Black people. Rather than pursue legal or political means to the equality suggested by "one blood" universalism, Remond posited the "slave's right to shed blood and take life" to obtain his liberty. Kelley's husband, Stephen Foster, concurred with the turn to political and physical means to oppose slavery. All means, including violent resistance, were needed in this dire moment.[122]

Abolitionists of the 1850s knew that they were in the midst of a political cataclysm rooted in the struggle over Black bodies. All around them, racist science defined blood as a signifier of distinct racial ancestry rather than of universalism. The refugees who moved their bodies into what they hoped would be spaces of liberty found that these spaces were highly contested. Their movement across jurisdictional lines brought conflicts between state and federal laws to a head. The notion that, if ultraists got their wish, state borders might become national boundaries forced proslavery southerners to reckon with their own dependence on the federal government to protect slavery. Ultimately, the steady flow into Pennsylvania of people who had escaped slavery provided the strongest refutation of racist medical arguments about African-descended people's suitability for slavery and the best evidence for their entitlement to the same birthright liberties as white people.[123]

Conclusion

Frances Ellen Watkins Harper had been lecturing and traveling relentlessly up and down the Eastern Seaboard from Maine to Ohio. The urgent pace had taken its toll. Her lungs were irritated, her voice feeble, and her body exhausted. Back in Philadelphia, in the apartment she shared with the Underground Railroad activists and historians William and Letitia Still, she penned a poem that reflected her low spirits. "Bury Me in a Free Land" appeared in the *Anti-slavery Bugle* in 1858:

Make me a grave where'er you will,
In a lowly plain, or a lofty hill;
Make it among earth's humblest graves,
But not in a land where men are slaves.
I could not rest if around my grave
I heard the steps of a trembling slave;
His shadow above my silent tomb
Would make it a place of fearful gloom.
I could not rest if I heard the tread
Of a coffle gang to the shambles led,
And the mother's shriek of wild despair
Rise like a curse on the trembling air.
I could not sleep if I saw the lash
Drinking her blood at each fearful gash,
And I saw her babes torn from her breast,
Like trembling doves from their parent nest.
I'd shudder and start if I heard the bay
Of bloodhounds seizing their human prey,
And I heard the captive plead in vain
As they bound afresh his galling chain.
If I saw young girls from their mother's arms
Bartered and sold for their youthful charms,
My eye would flash with a mournful flame,

My death-paled cheek grow red with shame.
I would sleep, dear friends, where bloated might
Can rob no man of his dearest right;
My rest shall be calm in any grave
Where none can call his brother a slave.
I ask no monument, proud and high,
To arrest the gaze of the passers-by;
All that my yearning spirit craves,
Is bury me not in a land of slaves.

Harper's poem depicted the violence of slavery as so powerful it could keep the dead from their well-earned rest. No sleep, no calm, were possible as long as men and women were beaten, separated, hunted, and sold. The disruption of the dead was no mere metaphor; it was all too real for enslaved and free people of color who had for much of the antebellum period experienced the theft of their loved ones' bodies from cemeteries.[1]

Abolitionists were both the architects of and the witnesses to a period of profound change in contemporary understandings of the human body. Their vision of an unfettered, uncolonized body connected the libertarian protests of seventeenth-century English prisoners with those of nineteenth-century African-descended slaves and triggered shifts in legal and medical thinking. Abolitionists identified a minimal threshold of rights to protection—what I have termed "embodied self-sovereignty"—needed by enslaved people if they were to claim the privileges of full adult personhood. First, human beings had the right not to have their blood spilled by another. Second, as articulated by Richard Allen, they had a right not to expend their bodies in agricultural labor that would serve only to enrich and secure the national belonging of another. Third, women had a right not to have their own blood and milk appropriated to produce property for the master instead of to nurture their own networks of family and kin. The children of enslaved women, moreover, like all other children, were entitled to a birthright rather than a life sentence of slavery. And finally, they had a right to move at will to spaces of liberty. Robert Pleasants's complex litigation against his white family members to free enslaved people still trapped in the Pleasants estate was a powerful example of a white enslaver-turned abolitionist joining forces with an enslaved person, Ned, to confront the tangle of blood, birthright, and maternal inheritance. But we also saw it in his efforts to rein in the aggressive behavior of white neighbors, his own family, and the state of Virginia by leaving a legacy of land and funds for schooling for the descendants of the people he had freed.

In the visceral language of abolitionists, blood signified the vitality of enslaved people, expended for the sake of the market in commodities like cotton, sugar, and tobacco.[2] This equation of blood with life hearkened to older notions of *spiritus vitalis* but was increasingly at odds with nineteenth-century medical scholarship in which the interpretation and evaluation of the body was being reduced to a study of its parts: skulls of different shapes and allegedly different cranial capacities, cadavers that could be appropriated without the consent of loved ones and dismembered on the dissection table. These foundations of racist science anchored concepts of biological race and strengthened the exclusive meanings of blood as signifying race rather than universal humanity. To those abolitionists dedicated to free produce purchases, activism followed from the politics of "one blood." Free labor advocates were aware of the movement of goods from the producer's to the consumer's body. Moral consumer activity, as they defined it, was not an abstract transaction but reflective of morality, intention, and the refusal to benefit from the products of exploited enslaved labor. The free produce movement rebuked consumers who failed to consider where their goods came from.

Using the language of blood, abolitionists denounced coercion and offered a vision of universal humanity with radical potential to refashion markets, labor, family hierarchies, and the nation. As with all universals, however, "one blood" could not encompass the ways that different personal histories and social locations had different consequences for people's bodies. Human beings may have been of one blood, but historical experiences left divergent imprints on bodies, even those with shared political commitments. For Black activists, references to "African blood" or the ties of "consanguinity" with the enslaved expressed a special connection forged by the common experience of racism as well as shared African ancestry. In addition, there was much that could not be communicated in the language of blood, especially by female activists. Both African-American and white poets depicted enslaved mothers as bleeding from grief and loss rather than from rape and childbirth. Any allusion to menstrual blood needed to be avoided if women were to be spurred to greater consumer vigilance and morality. Popular notions of blood as family connection, moreover, were not easily reconciled with the conflicting legal standards of maternal lineage to determine slave or free status and the paternal lineage that in other contexts defined the legal standing of children. These examples of dissonance hinted at some of the issues around race, gender, marriage, and family not resolved by abolitionist campaigns. By the 1850s, even abolitionists who insisted on "one blood" occasionally defaulted to the language appropriated by scientific racism and white nationalism, expressed in references to "Anglo Saxon blood" and "Negro blood."

For enslaved people, the main question was not whether, in the abstract, enslaved people had the right to act as agents in the world. It was also not simply whether enslaved people had the right to acquire and dispose of property. In their efforts to escape slavery—to remove their bodies from the scenes of exploitation—enslaved people evinced their desire to withdraw from all dealings with slaveholders and the intimate, daily, and brutal violations they perpetrated. The stance of ultraist abolitionists to have no union with slaveholders, an example of radicalism that initially appeared to have been driven more by white northerners' desires for moral purity than by concern for the liberation of enslaved people, actually leveraged an enormous sanction: it threatened to transform enslaved people's escapes into Pennsylvania into national border crossings that would have stripped enslavers of the federal support they depended on to extend their reach into free jurisdictions. The threat of disunion, in other words, gave enslaved people's movements as refugees new meaning. A few white abolitionists and many Black activists engaged their own bodies to provide direct bodily care and support to these refugees, whose escapes had such political, legal, and medical significance.[3]

* * *

Abolitionists had expended their bodies to end slavery, but as of 1859 slavery was still not defeated. If anything, aggressive enforcement of the Fugitive Slave Law and the *Dred Scott* decision reinforced slavery's power to efface the most rudimentary forms of enslaved people's embodied self-sovereignty, leaving individuals, families, and communities unprotected from bodily domination by enslavers. Enslaved people endured engineered disabilities that seeped into their intimate lives and persons and stymied their self-direction: to stay put or move at will, to labor by choice and in exchange for wages, to raise their own children, and to have the ties of marriage and kinship acknowledged and respected by others. The lack of embodied self-sovereignty took its toll in innumerable ways, but ultimately it also eroded health, well-being, and survival.

Despite their considerable vulnerabilities, the steady stream of enslaved people who put their bodies on the line to escape slavery had tremendous political impact. Persistent efforts to escape across state lines, even after the 1850 Fugitive Slave Law mobilized the federal government, helped to trigger South Carolina's secession and the Civil War. By increasing the pressure on the federal government to deliver on the promise of the Fugitive Slave Law, refugees broke open the conflict and prompted medical as well as legal and political responses. The physician A. P. Merrill warned in 1856 of the dire medical consequences of emancipation for African-descended people in North America based on proslavery "positive good" arguments that they not only tolerated slavery physically but actually required it to survive. The physician H. L. Byrd responded to the crisis with calls in 1858 and 1859 for reopening the transatlantic slave trade on the specious medical grounds of the need for "fresh African blood." That same year, James McCune Smith published two essays in the *Anglo-African*, one written years earlier, to dispute Josiah Nott's race-science arguments for white supremacy and to argue for the need to end racial caste in the United States for the sake of the nation's future progress.[4]

Harper's poem came on the brink of this escalating conflict in the United States over the future of slave labor. Within a year of its publication, John Brown gathered his followers to do something that white abolitionists had not attempted previously: the staging of a military coup in the countryside surrounding the Harpers Ferry Federal Arsenal. This militant collaboration between white and Black abolitionists brought the sectional crisis to a head. Harper's cousins George Watkins and William Watkins Jr. decided not to participate in the October 1859 raid. After the event, Frederick Douglass carefully managed the fact that he had met frequently with his fiery friend Brown and passed along donations to support the raid.[5]

White northerners' responses varied from shock to exuberant support. Some denounced Brown as a madman. Although feelings ran high among Quaker abolitionists that the turn to violence was regrettable, the *Anti-Slavery Reporter* put the raid in the context of familiar abolitionist language: "John Brown went not as an insurgent against peaceable men, but against an armed band of insurgents. Blood was there already—blood, drop by drop wrung from the hearts of poor defenseless people, deprived of every means of freedom. He interfered; he saw a strong man in the act of beating out the brains of a weak man, and he interposed himself between." PFAS described Brown as a "martyr in the glorious cause of human liberty." In a far cry from their 1837 disavowal of Elijah Lovejoy's use of a gun to defend himself, PFAS members declared the violence at Harpers Ferry to be "one of the natural fruits of the system of American slavery." The raid came as a solemn warning to end slavery peacefully "lest that system should be overthrown in blood." Almost as an afterthought, the PFAS statement mentioned that they still rejected "weapons of physical warfare."[6]

The capture, trial, and execution of Brown and his men put all of his sympathizers at risk, including the Watkins cousins and Frederick Douglass. William Watkins Jr. penned his own defense based on the *Dred Scott* decision, but he nonetheless took steps to flee to Toronto. Frederick Douglass quietly crossed the border into Canada. Dispirited as well as ill, Frances Watkins Harper joined the group of abolitionists who sent money to Brown's widow, Mary Day Brown, and helped her to lay him to rest in North Elba, New York, where African Americans had settled on land donated by Gerrit Smith. She sent a copy of "Bury Me in a Free Land" to one of Brown's young followers awaiting execution.[7]

Following Brown's execution, the militant abolitionist developed a cultlike following in the North that spread not only through his sanctification by fellow activists, but popularly by means of a military march sung and extemporized by groups of men in formation: "John Brown's body lies a mouldering in the grave / His soul's marching on!" Union soldiers approaching their own mortal trials in battle extemporized verses that emphasized the need for soldiers to sacrifice their lives to free enslaved people. These types of verses emerged more powerfully later in the war, once war aims were more squarely focused on ending slavery rather than preserving the Union.[8]

Soon after the war broke out, PFAS members expressed the hope that there would no longer need to be an annual antislavery fair to raise money to support abolition and the work with fugitives. Members made resolutions that reflected optimism but still expressed a sharp political edge. Mary Grew recorded in the June 12, 1862, meeting minutes praise for Lincoln's antislavery acts but condemnation of his repudiation of his generals' early emancipation proclamations and the reenslavement of people who had escaped to the District of Columbia. As activists soon discovered, moreover, the work of petitioning, fundraising, and providing supplies for refugees from slavery (known as "contraband") only intensified.[9]

African American abolitionists found new ways to put Black bodies squarely in the center of their activism during the war. In December 1861, Frederick Douglass began a series of lectures about the power of pictures to provoke political change. Although Douglass knew well that race scientists like Agassiz and others had used daguerreotypes to create degrading images that allegedly provided objective visual evidence of racial distinctions, he wondered optimistically about the possibilities of using the medium for other goals. Likening the impact of a visual image to the power of song, Douglass imagined that the picture of a dignified Black person would trigger physical impulses to travel through the viewer's sensory circuitry to make an impression on the mind. If these types of images circulated throughout the country, Douglass mused, racism could be combatted.[10]

Despite Douglass's approach, in the hands of some abolitionists, the work of undoing slavery still took the form of sensationalist displays like that in the *Scourged Back*, the first abolitionist use of photographic technology to exhibit the damaged body of an enslaved person. The 1863 image depicted the scarred back of an enslaved man named Peter or Gordon who came to the attention of Union troops in Baton Rouge after his escape from Mississippi. Union surgeons and physicians circulated the image to their northern correspondents, where it became the subject of newspaper accounts celebrating the man's sturdy resolve, evident in his profile, in the face of exquisite, Christlike suffering. As the *Liberator* noted, even though the wounds had healed, "as long as the flesh lasts will this fearful impress remain." Slavery left permanent traces, though not always taking the form of scars, on the bodies of the enslaved.[11]

William Wells Brown, in contrast with Douglass, stuck with the conventional approach of producing biographies of leading African Americans. In *The Black Man and His Antecedents*, published in 1863, Brown revealed his pan-African Atlanticism and his militancy. He included several leaders of the rebellions at Saint Domingue, including Toussaint L'Ouverture, Jean Pierre Boyer, Henri Christophe, and Jean-Jacques Dessalines. Only a handful of Black women made the grade, including Phillis Wheatley, Charlotte Forten, and Frances Ellen Watkins Harper. He presented Denmark Vesey and Nat Turner as heroic leaders and quoted at length from Turner's confessions, emphasizing that his experience with slavery turned him from "kind and docile feeling to the most intense hatred of the white race." Brown also dealt candidly with Turner's killing of women and children. For Brown, the killings were best understood in the context of wrongs done to Turner and Will, the man responsible for most of the deaths (as he was at pains to point out). Paraphrasing Frederick Douglass's 1848 observation that Black men were ready to claim "rights to liberty, if you would take your feet from their necks," Brown insisted that his goal for African Americans was much closer to the embodied self-sovereignty of Richard Allen and not unlike Sarah Grimké's demand for equality for all women: "All I demand for the black man is, that the white people shall take their heels off his neck, and let him rise by his own efforts."[12]

The *New York Daily Tribune* celebrated bravery and risk-taking as among Black men's qualifications for the privilege of liberty. Of Robert Smalls, an enslaved stevedore, ship rigger, deckhand, and pilot who scored a blow for the Union early in the Civil War, the paper asked rhetorically, "Is he not also a man—and is he not fit for freedom, since he made such a hazardous dash to gain it? Is he not a man and a hero—whose pluck as not been questioned by even *The Charleston Courier* or *The New York Herald?* What white man has made a bolder dash, or won a richer prize in the teeth of such perils during the war?" Public citations of Smalls's heroism reveal how, for Black men, achieving recognition as men in the eyes of their white counterparts required carefully skirting the physicality of manhood, which white people found so threatening in Black men, without actually effacing it. Contemporaries also recognized Harriet Tubman for bravely risking her own safety and security to bring enslaved people across state lines into freedom. Tubman's activism had always consisted of direct action rather than words. As soon as war broke out, she began forays into Confederate territory to shepherd enslaved people to freedom. As a Union spy, moreover, she exploited gender conventions, playing her age, her small size, and her female appearance to her advantage. It was only after the publication of her life story in 1869, however, that there was widespread public knowledge of the permanent disabling effects she suffered from an enslaver's violence.[13]

White fears of Black male militance continued to inform Union military policy. As Douglass observed in 1861, criticizing the whites-only Union military policy, "we are striking with our white hand while our black hand is chained behind us." After winning the fight to allow Black men to enlist in the military, Douglass, Mary Ann Shadd Cary, Henry Highland Garnet, and Martin Delany recruited vigorously among African Americans in the North while Tubman recruited among enslaved people in the South. Nearly two hundred thousand Black men answered the call to serve with Union forces in the fight to end slavery. Among them were Delany himself, who as a major became one of a handful of Black Union officers; Robert Bridges Forten, who served despite being in his forties; and two of Douglass's sons. In addition to these Black participants, the cause of undoing slavery stirred many white abolitionists to put their bodies on the line. Despite his advanced age, the abolitionist and physician Dr. Abraham Liddon Cox, husband of conservative New York abolitionist Abby Cox, served as the surgeon-in-chief of the First Division of the Twentieth Corps of the Army of the Cumberland. He met his death at the hospital at Lookout Mountain, Tennessee, in 1864 at the age of sixty-four.

Garnet, Gerrit Smith, and Garrison had correctly predicted that it would take bloodshed to undo slavery. Four years of war, over 750,000 deaths including those of 40,000 Black soldiers, and the suspension of habeas corpus in the North finally undid slavery for nearly four million people. Even this obvious evidence of the deep embedding of the political economy of slavery in the bodies, psyches, and wallets of white southerners fails to capture fully the stakes for Black people. White southerners were willing to die and to send their neighbors and kinsmen to their deaths to keep Black people enslaved. Enslaved people, meanwhile, were willing to risk unknown dangers, including death, to escape slavery.[14]

* * *

The fight for embodied self-sovereignty was already lost even before the debates over the Reconstruction Amendments began. Insufficient federal support for emancipation had predictable outcomes in white southern efforts to roll back emancipation with Black codes, target Black people deemed "out of place" in public venues, and move seamlessly from racist medical justifications of slavery to racist medical "evidence" of white supremacy. The Thirteenth Amendment abolished slavery but left many of the bodily relations of white supremacy untouched. As Hannah Rosen has shown, the insistent testimony of newly freed women subjected to home invasions and rape by white terrorists in Memphis in 1866 reflected a view of freedom as including bodily integrity and security. This was embodied self-sovereignty by another name, and it was at odds with the political promises of the Reconstruction Amendments—legal measures that would have required a diligent military presence and substantial material reparations to make them meaningful for Black people's daily lives.[15]

The work of countless abolitionists who took up healing, care work, and teaching after emancipation represented yet another refusal to disaggregate the body from the politically or economically recognized person. Abolitionists were never just concerned with their own health and their own bodies. Far from being a tangential issue, the health of African Americans became a central priority. African American abolitionists, in particular, imagined freedom as necessarily including physical health and well-being. Their advocacy for the health of newly-freed African American people was always connected politically to efforts to secure their rights.[16] A sizable cohort of Black women, including Elizabeth Keckley, Frances Harper, Charlotte Forten, and Rebecca Primus threw themselves into providing aid to freed people suffering from disease, hunger, and poverty. White reformer Josephine Griffing joined their efforts in response to reports of free people starving. In this respect, antebellum Vigilance Committees created the prototypes for the community provision of care for individuals in need. As the work of the Vigilance Committees revealed, health was of crucial importance not only for comfort, well-being, and longevity but for economic survival and the actualization of new political and legal rights.[17]

Significant numbers of African Americans pursued medical education or careers as an outgrowth of their commitment to equality. The physical and psychic demands of abolitionist activism often placed them at odds with conventional medical wisdom in ways that increased their skepticism, not only of medical remedies but of the science supporting theories positing the biological foundations of race and gender. The careers of Sarah Remond, James J. G. Bias, David Ruggles, James McCune Smith, Martin Delany, Sarah Mapps Douglass, and Maria W. Stewart illustrate how the pursuit of Black health was integral to African American humanitarian and human rights activism. Two relatives of William Still, moreover, his brother James and his eldest child, Caroline, trained to be medical practitioners.

African American and white abolitionist physicians and healers found emancipatory potential in healing African American bodies and using anti-racist medicine to protect the rights of the newly freed. As professor and dean of Philadelphia Women's Medical College, Ann Preston, abolitionist and Progressive Friend, created an institutional path for women of color to receive medical educations. As we have seen, Sarah Mapps Douglass attended classes taught by Preston in 1852–1853, becoming the first African American woman to attend medical school. She subsequently taught anatomy to the girls enrolled in the Girls Preparatory Department of the Institute for Colored Youth, presented lectures to mothers on female health and hygiene, and gave public talks on the workings of the human body like the one with which this book opens. Preston herself conducted the examinations of Douglass's pupils at the Institute for Colored Youth. Sarah Remond, who had taken courses in nursing at London's Bedford College for Ladies during her time in England, left the abolitionist speakers' circuit to attend medical school in Italy during the late 1860s, eventually becoming an obstetrician. After emancipation, Rebecca Lee Crumpler and Rebecca Cole, the latter a student of Douglass, graduated from medical school to become the first academically credentialed African American female doctors. Crumpler attended medical school in New England while Cole attended the Women's Medical College under Preston's deanship.[18]

Those who volunteered to teach freed people often discovered that, before they could instruct, they needed first to feed, clothe, shelter, and heal. Charlotte Forten (1837–1914), the granddaughter of James Forten and daughter of the abolitionist and Union soldier Robert Bridges Forten, volunteered as a nurse during the summer of 1863 to care for wounded soldiers of the Massachusetts Fifty-Fourth Colored Infantry. Sponsored by the Port Royal Relief Association of Philadelphia organized by abolitionist James Miller McKim, Forten found that she had to combine the skills of housekeeper and physician with those of teacher in order to care for the health and well-being of her students. Even without formal medical training, dedicated abolitionists turned to healing or the domestic arts as ways of improving the health of former slaves. Sojourner Truth tutored newly freed people in basic housekeeping skills, including cleanliness, in the Freedman's Village near Arlington Heights, Virginia. In the language of embodied rights that echoed Richard Allen and Hosea Easton, she opposed Black migration to Liberia but looked favorably on relocation to Kansas, observing, "our nerves and sinews, our tears and blood, have been sacrificed on the altar of this nation's avarice. Our unpaid labor has been a stepping stone to its financial success. Some of its dividends must surely be ours."[19]

Harriet Tubman, who had served as a nurse during the war, provided care for wounded Black soldiers as the matron of the Colored Hospital at Fortress Monroe, Virginia. Harriet Jacobs worked among freed people in Washington, D.C., for two years before returning to Edenton, North Carolina, to provide assistance to those she had known under slavery. Charles Burleigh Purvis, son of Robert and Harriet Purvis, volunteered as a nurse at the Freedman's Hospital during his training as a medical student and became a surgeon at the Freedman's

Hospital after he graduated from Wooster Medical College. Following her career as a teacher in Baltimore, the abolitionist Maria Stewart became a matron at the Freedman's Hospital.[20]

"One blood" arguments for universal humanity drawn from the Bible became less potent as discourses about raced blood, propped up by nineteenth-century scientific racism, found new political purpose in excluding Black people from the embodied rights of citizens. Long a signifier of both familial and national belonging, blood emerged as a totem of racial purity in postwar concerns about race mixing as a threat to white supremacy. As the historian Joseph Reidy observes, Samuel Gridley Howe, a commissioner of the American Freedman's Inquiry Commission (est. 1863) became fixed on the condition and fate of "mulatto" people and their impact on the American population. In correspondence with Louis Agassiz, Howe confirmed his suspicions that mulatto people, though constitutionally "feeble," represented a population capable of dragging down the entire nation. Agassiz affirmed that mulattoes, themselves degenerated, "impaired the purity and lowered the quality of national blood." In several efforts to collect data to investigate Agassiz's contention, Howe pursued information that compared Black and mulatto health, intelligence, and work habits.[21]

After the Civil War, and particularly after the Morant Bay uprising in Jamaica in 1865, "blood" and biological concepts of race became more powerful expressions of white nationalism. Sarah Remond responded with indignation to the shift in British public opinion following Morant Bay, especially the ugly racist denunciations of Black protestors and defenses of Governor Eyre's bloody reprisals. Blood continued to signify identity and belonging even as the reasons for transfusion failures revealed a more complex story. With research in 1900 documenting the existence of blood types based on the presence of antigens and antibodies, eugenically minded scientists tried unsuccessfully to correlate the geographic patterns of blood type distribution with race. Never able to muster evidence of raced blood, racist scientists persisted in trying to align newly discovered blood types with racial categories. Meanwhile, in the United States, references to blood purity and the distinct blood of white people figured prominently in the policing of interracial marriage, leading to the codification of the so-called "one drop" rule. Nowhere was the policy of racial purity pursued with more bureaucratic zeal than in Virginia, where, under the leadership of the state registrar Walter Plecker and the mandate of the state's 1924 Racial Integrity Act, officials policed the divide between Native Americans and African Americans nearly as strenuously as they did the line between white and Black.[22]

Embodied self-sovereignty was the path not taken to ensure the citizenship rights of Black people during Reconstruction, but it is difficult to see how it could have been achieved in the face of violent white reaction. The underfunded

Freedman's Bureau failed to protect freed people from terror, illness, and poverty and could do little to undo ubiquitous racism.[23] Technically no longer enslaved, many freed people, in the North and South, feared for their lives. Even those not subjected to imminent physical threat might well have found some truth in the sentiments expressed three decades earlier by Hosea Easton, who denounced the white use of racial slurs as "infest[ing] the feelings of colored travelers like the pestiferous breath of young devils," and Sarah Forten's lament that even free Black people

> feel the air they breathe
> Is tainted with oppression: and it comes
> Across their spirits with a sick'ning weight.[24]

The effort to undo slavery had technically liberated four million people but it did not undo the pattern of violations of Black people's embodied self-sovereignty. Perhaps the most pointed failure was the complicity of the United States government in new forms of exploitation and labor extraction that repurposed plantation management and slave patrols to control Black laborers and that, in other contexts, systematically destroyed the bodies of Irish and Chinese workers, the latter brought into the United States under specious contracts during the 1860s. After emancipation, bodily suffering became a private matter of the individual's health. Free laborers enjoyed few protections from pain, injury, and debility. As Frederick Douglass observed, no matter their status, people still found their bodies "carve[d] out" by their labor.[25]

Abolitionists who had spent decades seeking an end to slavery redirected their activism after emancipation to advocate for the rights of wage laborers and to argue for Black suffrage and access to public education. The abolitionist minister Theodore Parker had articulated the struggle in 1854 as one between labor and capital that "threatened the rights of man in America." Wendell Phillips, Abby Kelley, Stephen Foster, Henry Blackwell, and Parker Pillsbury pushed for workers' rights by denouncing capitalism's lethal extraction of labor from men and women as a new form of slavery, with some calling for the eight-hour day. One Massachusetts abolitionist, Henry Ingersoll Bowditch, worked with colleagues to create state-sponsored public health and tenement reform. Looking back on his activist commitments on the occasion of the fiftieth anniversary of the founding of the American Anti-Slavery Society, Phillips urged on his colleagues to the work at hand: "Let it not be said that the old abolitionist stopped with the Negro, and was never able to see that the same principles he had advocated at such cost claimed his utmost effort to protect all labor, white and black, and to further the discussion of every claim of down-trodden humanity." But for others, as Clare Midgely notes for the Edinburgh Ladies' Emancipation Society, freedom after slavery meant bringing newly freed populations into line with the demands of wage labor so that, with an understanding of "contracts, regulations of wages, and other arrangements which materially affect them," they could protect themselves from white exploitation.[26]

As so many abolitionists understood ahead of their time, racism and poverty can make a person sick—so sick that they cannot fully inhabit their political persons as rights bearers. Thwarted educational opportunity, poverty, and racism contribute systemically to ill health. Ill health, in turn, undermines educational attainment, exacerbates wealth disparities, and limits the full exercise of legal personhood. In a nation that historically produced wealth by exploiting Black women's reproductive capacity, Black maternal and infant mortality remain key markers of present-day health disparities in the United States while Black women continue to bear the physical as well as psychic costs of racial inequality.[27]

Yet as Sarah Mapps Douglass observed to her friend Rebecca White during the late 1850s about her own career as an abolitionist, teacher, and public lecturer on women's health, "I am greatly encouraged to believe that a good work has begun. I seem to see that after a while [a] way will open for us." Douglass herself felt connected to the fate of other African Americans, but she was clear that the blood in all human veins was the same and circulated according to the same principles. Sizing up her own contributions to that work, Douglass might have looked with pride at her student Rebecca Cole, who graduated from the Institute for Colored Youth under Douglass's tutelage in 1863 and the Women's Medical College of Pennsylvania under Ann Preston's tutelage in 1867. After working in New York, Cole returned to Philadelphia, where she created a Women's Directory Center to provide legal and medical services to destitute women and children. By 1899, she was running a home for Black women and their children in Washington, D.C., sponsored by the National Association for the Relief of Destitute Colored Women and Children.[28] In these and other projects, including the National Negro Health Week begun in 1915, the Black Panthers' health project of the 1960s, and the recent identification of the social determinants of health (the health impacts of the environments in which people live), activists, educators, and medical professionals build on the hard-won knowledge of the abolition movement. A fair chance to enjoy good health along with legal protections from the physical violations of self-sovereignty need to be embodied rights for the project of undoing slavery to yield its promise.[29]

Abbreviations

BL	Bodleian Library, Oxford University, U.K.
CL	William L. Clements Library, University of Michigan
HCQSC	Haverford College Quaker and Special Collections
HSP	Historical Society of Pennsylvania
JAH	*Journal of American History*
LV	Library of Virginia
MCP	Micajah Crew Papers, R. A. Brock Collection and Papers, Huntington Library, Library of Virginia Microfilm
MHS	Massachusetts Historical Society
MPCP	*Minutes of the Provincial Council of Pennsylvania* 9 vols. (Philadelphia: Jo. Severns & Company, 1852)
PFP	Pleasants Family Papers, R. A. Brock Collection and Papers, Huntington Library, Library of Virginia Microfilm
PJMPS	*Philadelphia Journal of the Medical and Physical Sciences*
PMHB	*Pennsylvania Magazine of History and Biography*
SAL (Hening, ed.)	William W. Hening, ed., *The Statutes at Large: Being a collection of all the laws of Virginia* (New York, 1823), 13 vols.
SAL (Shepherd, ed.)	Samuel Shepherd, ed., *The Statutes at Large of Virginia, from October 1792, to December session 1806* (Richmond, Va., 1836), 3 vols.
Swem	Earl Gregg Swem Library, College of William and Mary
Valentine Papers	*Edward Pleasants Valentine Papers*, 4 vols. (Richmond, Va.: Valentine Museum, 1927)
VMHB	*Virginia Magazine of History and Biography*
WMQ	*William and Mary Quarterly*

Notes

Introduction

My thanks to Jessie Regunberg, Arielle Alterwaite, Madhavi Kale, Dan Richter, Bob Lockhart, Jim Downs, Angus Corbett, and Ted Pearson for their guidance on this introduction.

1. Sarah Mapps Douglass to Rebecca White, November 28, 1855 or 1858; Douglass to White, n.d., reporting attendance of thirty-eight "deeply interested women"; Douglass to White, December 19, 1858, on a small audience; Douglass to White, October 29, 1860, on her upcoming trip to New York to lecture; Douglass to White, February 9, 1862, on her care not to provoke Mrs. R. by using big words, and a washerwoman's confidences; all in Josiah White Papers, HCQSC.

2. *The Christian Recorder*, March 30, 1861; Sarah Mapps Douglass to Rebecca White, May 30, 1855, concerning her improved health as a consequence of hydropathy, Josiah White Papers, HCQSC.

3. For Douglass's lectures on anatomy, physiology, and hygiene, see Banneker Institute Minutes, October 23, 1855, Leon Gardiner Collection, HSP; and *Weekly Anglo-African*, July 23, 1859, and November 24, 1860.

4. Hosea Easton, *A Treatise on the Intellectual Character, and Civil and Political Condition of the Colored People of the U. States; and the Prejudice Exercised Towards Them: with a Sermon on the Duty of the Church to Them* (Boston, 1837).

5. Frederick Douglass, "Oration Delivered in Corinthian Hall, Rochester, by Frederick Douglass, July 5, 1852" (Rochester, 1852). My use of "refugee" here and throughout acknowledges the desires of fugitives to escape slavery and reach what they hoped would be a safe haven, if not a space of liberty.

6. Paul Gilroy, "Declaration of Rights," in *Darker than Blue: On the Moral Economies of Black Atlantic Culture* (Cambridge, Mass.: Belknap Press of Harvard University Press, 2010), 55–119. See also Lynn Hunt, *Inventing Human Rights: A History* (New York: W. W. Norton, 2007); Jenny S. Martinez, *The Slave Trade and the Origins of International Human Rights Law* (New York: Oxford University Press, 2012); Samuel Moyn, *The Last Utopia: Human Rights in History* (Cambridge, Mass.: Belknap Press of Harvard University Press, 2010).

7. I engage concepts of biosocial and epigenetic harms broadly to invoke environmental and historical circumstances rather than theories of maternal responsibility or genetic degradation; see Sarah Richardson, *The Maternal Imprint: The Contested Science of Maternal Fetal Effects* (Chicago: University of Chicago Press, 2021).

8. Mia Bay, *The White Image in the Black Mind: African American Ideas about White People, 1830–1925* (New York: Oxford University Press, 2000); Mia Bay, Farah Griffin, Martha Jones, and Barbara Savage eds., *Towards an Intellectual History of Black Women* (Chapel Hill: University of North Carolina Press, 2015); Robin Kelley, *Freedom Dreams: The Black Radical Imagination* (Boston: Beacon, 2002); Paul Gilroy, *The Black Atlantic: Modernity and Double Consciousness* (Cambridge, Mass.: Harvard University Press, 1993); W.E.B. Dubois, *The Souls of Black Folk: Essays and Sketches* (Chicago, 1903); Dorothy Roberts, *Killing the Black Body: Race, Reproduction and the Meaning of Liberty* (New York: Vintage Books, 1997); Ibram Kendi, *Stamped from the Beginning: The Definitive History of Racist Ideas in America* (New York: Penguin Books, 2016); Rana Hogarth, *Medicalizing*

Blackness: Making Racial Difference in the Atlantic World, 1780–1840 (Chapel Hill: University of North Carolina Press, 2017); Britt Rusert, *Fugitive Science: Empiricism and Freedom in Early African American Culture* (New York: New York University Press, 2017). See also Daina Ramey Berry, *The Price for Their Pound of Flesh: The Value of the Enslaved, from Womb to Grave, in the Building of a Nation* (Boston: Beacon, 2017), for "soul values" as the counterpoint to market values of commodified enslaved bodies.

9. Dorothy Ko, *Cinderella's Sisters: A Revisionist History of Footbinding* (Berkeley: University of California Press, 2007). As Ko notes, a bound foot liberated from its wrapping did not spring back into the shape of a so-called natural foot. See also Thomas Laqueur, *The Work of the Dead: A Cultural History of Mortal Remains* (Princeton, N.J.: Princeton University Press, 2016), 237–238. Teresa Zackodnik, *Press, Platform, Pulpit: Black Feminist Publics in the Era of Reform* (Knoxville: University of Tennessee Press, 2011). For discussions of Black scientific counterdiscourses and counterpractices to white racism, see Rusert, *Fugitive Science*, esp. 95–102, for Hosea Easton, and 185–218, for Sarah Mapps Douglass. Laurent Dubois raises a similar question: "How can slavery and racism be made to disappear?" Dubois, "Inscribing Race in the Revolutionary French Antilles," in Sue Peabody and Tyler Stovall, eds., *The Color of Liberty: Histories of Race in France* (Durham, N.C.: Duke University Press, 2003), 97.

10. For the body's reality-conferring capacity and differential degrees of embodiment, see Elaine Scarry, *The Body in Pain: The Making and Unmaking of the World* (New York: Oxford University Press, 1985), esp. 124–127, 243–284; Bessel van der Kolk, *The Body Keeps the Score: Brain, Mind, and Body in the Healing of Trauma* (New York: Penguin Books, 2014). Clyde Hertzman, "Putting the Concept of Biological Embedding in Historical Perspective," *Proceedings of the National Academy of Science USA*, 2012, Oct 16; 109 (Suppl 2): 17160–17167. Nancy Krieger, *Epidemiology and the People's Health: Theory and Context* (New York: Oxford University Press, 2011); Pratik Chakrabarti, *Materials and Medicine: Trade, Conquest and Therapeutics in the Eighteenth Century* (Manchester, U.K.: Manchester University Press, 2010), for the colonial nature of eighteenth-century medicine; Brooke Newman, *A Dark Inheritance: Blood, Race, and Sex in Colonial Jamaica* (New Haven, Conn.: Yale University Press, 2018); Keechang Kim, *Aliens in Medieval Law: The Origins of Modern Citizenship* (Cambridge, U.K.: Cambridge University Press, 2000); Christopher Tomlins, *Freedom Bound: Law, Labor, and Civic Identity in Colonizing English America, 1580–1865* (New York: Cambridge University Press, 2010), 90–92; Nancy Isenberg, *Sex and Citizenship in Antebellum America* (Chapel Hill: University of North Carolina Press, 1998).

11. Robyn Wiegman, *American Anatomies: Theorizing Race and Gender* (Durham, N.C.: Duke University Press, 1995), especially 1–78.

12. Adriana Cavarero, *Stately Bodies: Literature, Philosophy, and the Question of Gender*, trans. Robert de Lucca and Deanna Shemek (Ann Arbor: University of Michigan Press, 2002). Abolitionists relied on the seemingly self-evident nature of a universal humanity with reference to the bodies of enslaved people. For historical approaches to the body, see Ko, *Cinderella's Sisters*; Mark Smith, *How Race Is Made: Slavery, Segregation and the Senses* (Chapel Hill: University of North Carolina, 2007); Joyce Chaplin, *Subject Matter: Technology, the Body, and Science on the Anglo-American Frontier, 1500–1676* (Cambridge, Mass.: Harvard University Press, 2006); and Kathleen Brown, *Foul Bodies: Cleanliness in Early America* (New Haven, Conn.: Yale University Press, 2009). See also Maurice Merleau-Ponty, *The Phenomenology of Perception*, trans. Donald A. Landes (New York: Routledge, 2012); Michel Foucault, *Discipline and Punish: The Birth of the Prison*, trans. Alan Sheridan (New York: Random House, 1979); Giorgio Agamben, *Homo Sacer: Sovereign Power and Bare Life*, trans. Daniel Heller-Roazen (Stanford, Calif.: Stanford University Press, 1998). For embodied cognition, see George Lakoff and Mark Johnson, *Metaphors We Live By*, new afterword (Chicago: University of Chicago Press, 2003), esp. 14, 40, 50, 179–183; and Roberts, *Killing the Black Body*. For transatlantic contexts, see Edward B. Rugemer, *The Problem of Emancipation: The Caribbean Roots of the American Civil War* (Baton Rouge: Louisiana State University Press, 2008). See also Samantha Seeley, *Race, Removal, and the Right to Remain* (Chapel Hill: University of North Carolina Press, 2021).

13. George Lakoff and Mark Johnson, *Philosophy in the Flesh: The Embodied Mind and Its Challenge to Western Thought* (New York: Basic Books, 1999). Edward E. Baptist, *The Half Has Never Been Told: Slavery and the Making of American Capitalism* (New York: Basic Books, 2014), speaks to slavery's extraction of profit from enslaved bodies. James Poskett, *Materials of the Mind: Phrenology, Race, and the Global History of Science, 1815–1920* (Chicago: University of Chicago Press, 2019). Melissa Stein, *Measuring Manhood: Race and the Science of Masculinity, 1830–1934* (Minneapolis: University of Minnesota Press, 2015), esp. 1–88. Edlie L. Wong, *Neither Fugitive nor Free: Atlantic Slavery, Freedom Suits, and the Legal Culture of Travel* (New York: New York University Press, 2009). For restrictions on free Black mobility that rested on models of disease quarantine, see Michael A. Schoeppner, *Moral Contagion: Black Atlantic Sailors, Citizenship, and Diplomacy in Antebellum America* (New York: Cambridge University Press, 2019). The Negro Seamen Acts would later serve as the precedent for subsequent public health measures; see Michael Willrich, *Pox: An American History* (New York: Penguin Books, 2011).

14. On *jus sanguinis* and *jus soli*, see James Brown Scott, "Nationality: *Jus Soli* or *Jus Sanguinis*," *American Journal of International Law* 24, no. 1 (January 1930): 58–64; Kristin A. Collins, "Illegitimate Borders: *Jus Sanguinis* Citizenship and the Legal Construction of Family, Race, and Nation," *Yale Law Journal* 123, no. 7 (2014): 2134–2573; Carlos Amunátegui Perelló, "Race and Nation: On *Ius Sanguinis* and the Origins of a Racist National Perspective," *Fundamina* 24, no. 2 (2018); Ed Cohen, "A Body Worth Having? Or, a System of Natural Governance," *Theory, Culture and Society* 25, no. 3 (2008): 103–129; Justin E. H. Smith, *Nature, Human Nature, and Human Difference: Race in Early Modern Philosophy* (Princeton, N.J.: Princeton University Press, 2015). See also Hunt, *Inventing Human Rights*; Martinez, *The Slave Trade and the Origins of International Human Rights.*

15. C. B. Macpherson, *Political Theory of Possessive Individualism: Hobbes to Locke* (Oxford, U.K.: Clarendon Press, 1962). See also Paul D. Halliday, *Habeas Corpus: From England to Empire* (Cambridge, Mass.: Harvard University Press, 2010), 197–201, on liberty as a place as well as an embodied condition; Banu Bargu, "Sovereignty as Erasure: Rethinking Enforced Disappearances," *Qui Parle: Critical Humanities and Social Sciences* 23, no. 1 (Fall/Winter 2014): 35–75; Mary Hawkesworth, *Embodied Power: Demystifying Disembodied Politics* (New York: Routledge, 2016).

16. Martha S. Jones, *Birthright Citizens: A History of Race and Rights in Antebellum America* (New York: Cambridge University Press, 2018), focuses on important legal challenges and acts of rights-bearing but does not address birth as the gateway to rights. See also Jennifer Spear and Kathleen Brown, "Rethinking Maternal Inheritance in Atlantic Slave Law," unpublished manuscript; Newman, *A Dark Inheritance*, 11–13; Keechang Kim, "*Calvin's Case* (1608) and the Law of Alien Status," *Journal of Legal History* 17, no. 2 (August 1996): 155–171; Polly J. Price, "Natural Law and Birthright Citizenship in Calvin's Case (1608)," *Yale Journal of Law and the Humanities* 9, no. 1 (1997): 73–145; Kim, *Aliens in Medieval Law.* See James Olney, "I Was Born: Slave Narratives, Their Status as Autobiography and as Literature," *Callaloo*, no. 20 (1984): 46–73. Nora Doyle, *Maternal Bodies: Redefining Motherhood in Early America* (Chapel Hill: University of North Carolina Press, 2018), 175–202.

17. For Locke's second thoughts about slavery as an unjust expression of the monarch's authority and planter wealth, see Holly Brewer, "Slavery, Sovereignty, and 'Inheritable Blood': Reconsidering John Locke and the Origins of American Slavery," *American Historical Review* 122, no. 4 (October 2017): 1038–1078; Berry, *Price for Their Pound of Flesh*; David Brion Davis, *The Problem of Slavery in an Age of Emancipation* (New York: Vintage, 2014); Bay, *White Image in the Black Mind*; Sven Beckert, *Empire of Cotton: A Global History* (New York: Vintage Books, 2015), 222–227.

18. Richard Tuck, *The Rights of War and Peace: Political Thought and the International Order from Grotius to Kant* (New York: Oxford University Press, 2001), cited in Tomlins, *Freedom Bound*, 98–100. For restrictions on Black mobility, see Schoeppner, *Moral Contagion.* For maternal bodies producing freedom in Spanish and Lusophone American contexts, see Camillia Cowling, *Conceiving Freedom: Women of Color, Gender, and the Abolition of Slavery in Havana and Rio de Janeiro* (Chapel Hill: University of North Carolina Press, 2013). See also Kellie Carter Jackson, *Force and Freedom: Black Abolitionists and the Politics of Violence* (Philadelphia: University of Pennsylvania Press, 2019); William J. Novak, "The Legal Transformation of Citizenship in Nineteenth-Century

America," in Meg Jacobs, William J. Novak, and Julian Zelizer, eds., *The Democratic Experiment: New Directions in American Political History* (Princeton, N.J.: Princeton University Press, 2004), 85–119. See also Steven Hahn, *A Nation Under Our Feet: Black Political Struggles in the Rural South From Slavery to the Great Migration* (Cambridge, Mass.: Harvard University Press, 2003); Michele Speitz, "Blood Sugar and Salt Licks: Corroding Bodies and Preserving Nations in *The History of Mary Prince, a West Indian Slave, Related by Herself*," in Paul Youngquist and Frances Botkin, eds., *Circulations: Romanticism and the Black Atlantic* (October 2011), https://romantic-circles.org/praxis/circulations/index.html. Hannah Arendt, "The Freedom to Be Free: The Conditions and Meaning of Revolution," in *Thinking Without a Bannister: Essays in Understanding*, ed. Jerome Kohn (New York: Schocken Books, 2018), 383, for birth as "the ontological condition sine qua non of all politics," and revolutions as analogous to actual birth.

19. On "soundness," see Dea H. Boster, *African American Slavery and Disability: Bodies, Property and Power in the Antebellum South* (New York: Routledge, 2013); Sharla M. Fett, *Working Cures: Healing, Health, and Power on Southern Slave Plantations* (Chapel Hill: University of North Carolina Press, 2002), 15–35; Douglas Baynton, "Disability and the Justification of Inequality in American History," in Paul Longmore and Lauri Umansky, eds., *The New Disability History: American Perspectives* (New York: New York University Press, 2001), 34–41; Berry, *Price for Their Pound of Flesh*, 70–72; Ariela Gross, *Double Character: Slavery and Mastery in the Antebellum Southern Courtroom* (Princeton, N.J.: Princeton University Press, 2000), 125. See also Marli Weiner with Mazie Hough, *Sex, Sickness, and Slavery: Illness in the Antebellum South* (Urbana: University of Illinois Press, 2012); Hogarth, *Medicalizing Blackness*; Ikuko Asaka, *Tropical Freedom: Climate, Settler Colonialism, and Black Exclusion in the Age of Emancipation* (Durham, N.C.: Duke University Press, 2017); Carolyn Sorisio, *Fleshing Out America: Race, Gender, and the Politics of the Body in American Literature, 1833–1879* (Athens: University of Georgia Press, 2002), 1–78; Nancy Stepan, *The Idea of Race in Science: Great Britain, 1800–1960* (London: Macmillan, 1982); James C. Mohr, *Doctors and the Law: Medical Jurisprudence in Nineteenth-Century America* (Baltimore: Johns Hopkins University Press, 1993); Poskett, *Materials of the Mind*; Christopher Willoughby, "His Native, Hot Country: Racial Science and Environment in Antebellum American Medical Thought," *Journal of the History of Medicine and Allied Sciences* 72, no. 3 (July 2017): 328–351; Suman Seth, *Difference and Disease: Medicine, Race, and the Eighteenth-Century British Empire* (New York: Cambridge University Press, 2018), 270, 276, for the interdependence of polygenist and medical arguments in the work of Alexander Wilson (1780): "Racial difference, whether rooted in a nominally changeable set of dietetic or cultural practices, or bred in the skin, bone, and nerves increasingly shaped the interactions between medical men and their patients. In turn, forms of medical knowledge increasingly shaped the course of colonialism and abolition"; and 283, for the protective function of black skin and the alleged lesser sensitivity of black bodies to pain. See also Mark Harrison, *Medicine in an Age of Commerce and Empire: Britain and Its Tropical Colonies, 1660–1830* (New York: Oxford University Press, 2010).

20. Lois Horton, "From Class to Race in Early America: Northern Post-emancipation Racial Reconstruction," in Michael A. Morrison and James Brewer Stewart, eds., *Race and the Early Republic: Racial Consciousness and Nation-Building in the Early Republic* (Lanham, Md.: Rowman and Littlefield, 2002), 55–74. John Wood Sweet, *Bodies Politic: Negotiating Race in the Early American North, 1730–1830* (Baltimore: Johns Hopkins University Press, 2003). Jen Manion, *Liberty's Prisoners: Carceral Culture in Early America* (Philadelphia: University of Pennsylvania Press, 2015).

21. Wong, *Neither Fugitive nor Free*, 1–18. Dana Elizabeth Weiner, *Race and Rights: Fighting Slavery and Prejudice in the Old Northwest, 1830–1870* (DeKalb: Northern Illinois University Press, 2013), on abolitionist free speech; Christopher Tomlins, *In the Matter of Nat Turner: A Speculative History* (Princeton, N.J.: Princeton University Press, 2020), 118–119, for the law's affirmation of its authority to control enslaved people. Edward B. Rugemer, *Slave Law and the Politics of Resistance in the Early Atlantic World* (Cambridge, Mass.: Harvard University Press, 2018); Sorisio, *Fleshing Out America*; Jesse Olsavsky, "Runaway Slaves, Vigilance Committees, and the Pedagogy of Revolutionary Abolitionism, 1835–1863," in Marcus Rediker, Titas Chakraborty, and Matthias van Rossum, eds, *A Global History of Runaways: Workers, Mobility, and Capitalism, 1600–1850* (Oakland: University

of California Press, 2019), 216–233; Jesse Olsavsky, "Women, Vigilance Committees, and the Rise of Militant Abolitionism, 1835–1859," *Slavery and Abolition* 39, no. 2 (2018): 357–382, for refugees moving out of the zone of slave extraction to produce testifying selves.

22. See Leslie A. Falk, "Black Abolitionist Doctors and Healers, 1810–1885," *Bulletin of the History of Medicine* 54 (1980): 258–272. Gretchen Long, *Doctoring Freedom: The Politics of African American Medical Care in Slavery and Emancipation* (Chapel Hill: University of North Carolina Press, 2012). Walter Johnson, "On Agency," *Journal of Social History* 37, no. 1 (Fall 2003): 113–124: Juliette Singh, *Unthinking Mastery: Dehumanism and Colonial Entanglements* (Durham, N.C.: Duke University Press, 2018); Alexander G. Weheliye, *Habeas Viscus: Racializing Assemblages, Biopolitics, and Black Feminist Theories of the Human* (Durham, N.C.: Duke University Press, 2017); Saidiya Hartman, *Scenes of Subjection: Terror, Slavery, and Self-Making in Nineteenth-Century America* (New York: Oxford University Press, 1997), 6, for the limits of approaches focused on rights and the notion of self-possession. On concepts of liberty ostensibly at odds with the categories of positive and negative liberty, see Quentin Skinner, *Thinking About Liberty: An Historian's Approach* (Firenze: Leo Olschki, 2016); Hawkesworth, *Embodied Power*; Terri L. Snyder, *The Power to Die: Slavery and Suicide in British North America* (Chicago: University of Chicago Press, 2015), 82–100. Snyder notes that "in legal terms, slave suicide was not just willful or intentional, it was, ironically, a powerful claim to personhood" (100). For Black women's activism on behalf of families and communities during the nineteenth century as "self-protective violence," see Kellie Carter Jackson, "'Dare You Meet a Woman': Black Women, Abolitionism, and Protective Violence, 1850–1859," *Slavery and Abolition* 42, no. 2 (2021): 269–292, DOI: 10.1080/0144039x.2020.1816100. See also Amy Dru Stanley, *From Bondage to Contract: Wage Labor, Marriage, and the Market in the Age of Slave Emancipation* (Cambridge: Cambridge University Press, 1998); Amy Dru Stanley, "Slave Emancipation and the Revolutionizing of Human Rights," in Gregory Downs and Kate Masur, eds., *The World the Civil War Made* (Chapel Hill: University of North Carolina Press, 2015); Sarah L. H. Gronningsater, "Born Free in the Master's House: Children and Gradual Emancipation in the Early American North," in Anna Mae Duane, ed., *Child Slavery Before and After Emancipation: An Argument for Child-Centered Slavery Studies* (New York: Cambridge University Press, 2017), 123–149, esp.140, for a definition of freedom similar to my own concept of embodied self-sovereignty. See Charles Taylor, "To Follow a Rule," *Philosophical Arguments* (Cambridge, Mass.: Harvard University Press, 1995), 165–180, and Hubert Dreyfuss and Charles Taylor, *Retrieiving Realism* (Cambridge, Mass.: Harvard University Press, 2015); van der Kolk, *The Body Keeps the Score*; Lewis R. Gordon, ed., *Existence in Black: An Anthology of Black Existential Philosophy* (New York: Routledge, 1997), esp. the introduction, with reference to "self-agency"; Lewis R. Gordon, *An Introduction to Africana Philosophy* (Cambridge, U.K.: Cambridge University Press, 2008); David McBride, *Caring for Equality: A History of African American Health and Healthcare* (New York: Rowman and Littlefield, 2018), xi, for the "health equity ideal"; Hertzman, "Putting the Concept of Biological Embedding in Historical Perspective"; Weiner and Hough, *Sex, Sickness, and Slavery*, 123; Roy Porter, *Flesh in the Age of Reason: How the Enlightenment Transformed the Way We See Our Bodies and Souls* (New York: W. W. Norton, 2003); Krieger, *Epidemiology and the People's Health*; Daniel E. Dawes, *The Political Determinants of Health* (Baltimore: Johns Hopkins University Press, 2020).

23. David Brion Davis, "The Perils of Doing History by Ahistorical Abstraction," in Thomas Bender, ed., *The Antislavery Debate: Capitalism and Abolitionism as a Problem in Historical Interpretation* (Berkeley: University of California Press, 1992), 290–309. See also Caitlin Rosenthal, *Accounting for Slavery: Masters and Management* (Cambridge, Mass.: Harvard University Press, 2018), xv, for abolition as a triumph of market regulation. Berry, *Price for Their Pound of Flesh*. For female sexual self-sovereignty, see April Haynes, *Riotous Flesh: Women, Physiology, and the Solitary Vice in Nineteenth-Century America* (Chicago: University of Chicago Press, 2015). See also Seeley, *Race, Removal, and the Right to Remain*, 271, for the community-based right to remain.

24. For enslaved people as economic assets and commodified "hands," see Rosenthal, *Accounting for Slavery*, 134–135, 143–148; Baptist, *The Half Has Never Been Told*, 100–105, 246–248; Calvin Schermerhorn, *The Business of Slavery and the Rise of American Capitalism, 1815–1860* (New Haven, Conn:

Yale University Press, 2015), 95–123. Sara Ahmed, *Willful Subjects* (Durham, N.C.: Duke University Press, 2014), 106–109; Berry, *Price for Their Pound of Flesh*, 68–72, 91–92. "Hands" are figured in assessments of able-bodiedness in Boster, *African American Slavery and Disability*, 55–58; Hartman, *Scenes of Subjection*, 134–135; Cindy Weinstein, *The Literature of Labor and the Labors of Literature: Allegory in Nineteenth-Century American Fiction* (New York: Cambridge University Press, 1995), 39. "Hands" were also commonly used to describe workers in maritime industries, agricultural contexts other than plantations, and textile factories. See Robert Steinfeld, *The Invention of Free Labor: The Employment Relations in English and American Law and Culture, 1350–1870* (Chapel Hill: University of North Carolina Press, 1991), 8, for Blackstone's theory of property growing out of the practice and habit of exploiting labor through perpetual service and captivity.

25. Eric Williams, *Capitalism and Slavery* (Chapel Hill: University of North Carolina Press, 1944); Eric Foner, *Free Soil, Free Labor, Free Men: The Ideology of the Republican Party Before the Civil War* (New York: Oxford University Press, 1970, 1995); John Ashworth, *Slavery, Capitalism, and Politics*, vol. 1, *Commerce and Compromise, 1820–1850* (New York: Cambridge University Press, 1996), 125–191; Joshua Rothman, *Flush Times and Fever Dreams: A Story of Capitalism and Slavery in the Age of Jackson* (Athens: University of Georgia Press, 2021); Beckert, *Empire of Cotton*; Walter Johnson, *River of Dark Dreams: Slavery and Empire in the Cotton Kingdom* (Cambridge, Mass.: Harvard University Press, 2013); Sven Beckert and Seth Rockman, eds., *Slavery's Capitalism: A New History of American Economic Development* (Philadelphia: University of Pennsylvania Press, 2016). See also Claire Priest, *Credit Nation: Property Laws and Institutions in Early America* (Princeton, N.J.: Princeton University Press, 2021), for the fungibility of British North American property in land and enslaved laborers to satisfy creditors. Although I disagree with many of Baptist's conclusions about the nature of southern plantations, his study is an important exception to my critique of the blind spots of the "new" histories of capitalism; Baptist, *The Half Has Never Been Told*.

26. Jeanne Boydston, *Home and Work: Housework, Wages, and the Ideology of Labor in the Early Republic* (New York: Oxford University Press, 1990); Xiomara Santamarina, *Belabored Professions: Narratives of African American Working Womanhood* (Chapel Hill: University of North Carolina Press, 2005); Jennifer L. Morgan, *Laboring Women: Reproduction and Gender in New World Slavery* (Philadelphia: University of Pennsylvania Press, 2004); Amy Dru Stanley, "Slave Breeding and Free Love: An Antebellum Argument over Slavery, Capitalism, and Personhood," in Michael Zakim and Gary J. Kornblith, eds., *Capitalism Takes Command: The Social Transformation of Nineteenth-Century America* (Chicago: University of Chicago Press, 2012), 119–144; Berry, *Price for Their Pound of Flesh*. Deirdre Cooper Owens, *Medical Bondage: Race, Gender, and the Origins of American Gynecology* (Athens: University of Georgia Press, 2017); Sasha Turner, *Contested Bodies: Pregnancy, Childrearing, and Slavery in Jamaica* (Philadelphia: University of Pennsylvania Press, 2017); Jessica Marie Johnson, *Wicked Flesh: Black Women, Intimacy, and Freedom in the Atlantic World* (Philadelphia: University of Pennsylvania Press, 2020); Katherine Paugh, *Politics of Reproduction: Race, Medicine, and Fertility in the Age of Abolition* (New York: Oxford University Press, 2017); Doyle, *Maternal Bodies*, for the poetic and visual depictions of enslaved mothers' suffering as disordered corporeality, 175–202. Gregory Smithers, *Slave Breeding: Sex, Violence, and Memory in African American History* (Gainesville: University Press of Florida, 2013), 20–43. See also Thomas Foster, *Rethinking Rufus: Sexual Violations of Enslaved Men* (Athens: University of Georgia Press, 2019), for the sexual exploitation of enslaved men. Jennifer L. Morgan, *Reckoning with Slavery: Gender, Kinship, and Capitalism in the Early Black Atlantic* (Durham, N.C.: Duke University Press, 2021).

27. Stanley, *From Bondage to Contract*; Madhavi Kale, *Fragments of Empire: Capital, Slavery, and Indian Indentured Labor in the British Caribbean* (Philadelphia: University of Pennsylvania Press, 1998); Martinez, *The Slave Trade and the Origins of International Human Rights*; Aileen Moreton-Robinson, *White Possessive: Property, Power, and Indigenous Sovereignty* (Minneapolis: University of Minnesota Press, 2015).

28. For the embodied authority of the eyewitness, see Anthony Pagden, *European Encounters with the New World: From Renaissance to Romanticism* (New Haven, Conn.: Yale University Press, 1993). See also Srinivas Aravamudan, *Tropicopolitans: Colonialism and Agency, 1688–1804* (Durham,

N.C.: Duke University Press, 1999). For beliefs in blood's spiritual potency by the Gold Coast Coromantee rebel leaders of Tacky's Revolt, see Vincent Brown, *Tacky's Revolt: the Story of an Atlantic Slave War* (Cambridge, Mass.: Belknap Press of Harvard University Press, 2020), 133.

29. Patricia Crawford, introduction to Crawford, *Blood, Bodies, and Families in Early Modern England* (New York: Taylor and Francis, 2004), 2, for blood as metaphor linking paternity, families, and nation; Maria Elena Martinez, *Genealogical Fictions: Limpieza de Sangre, Religion, and Gender in Colonial Mexico* (Stanford, Calif.: Stanford University Press, 2008); Rebecca Earle, *The Body of the Conquistador: Food, Race, and the Colonial Experience in Spanish America, 1492–1700* (Cambridge, U.K.: Cambridge University Press, 2012); Newman, *A Dark Inheritance*, 1–24, for English blood purity concerns.

30. Orlando Patterson, *Slavery and Social Death: A Comparative Study* (Cambridge, Mass.: Harvard University Press, 1982); Kathleen Brown, *Good Wives, Nasty Wenches, and Anxious Patriarchs: Gender, Race, and Power in Colonial Virginia* (Chapel Hill: University of North Carolina Press, 1996); Morgan, *Laboring Women*; Spear and Brown, "Rethinking Maternal Inheritance."

31. Pierre H. Boulle, "La construction du concept de race dans la France d'Ancien Régime" (2002); Jean-François Niort, *Le Code Noir. Idées reçues sur un texte symbolique* (Paris: Le Cavalier Bleu, 2015); Nicholas Hudson, "From 'Nation' to 'Race': The Origin of Racial Classification in Eighteenth-Century Thought," *Eighteenth-Century Studies* 29, no. 3 (1996): 246–264. Jennifer L. Palmer, *Intimate Bonds: Family and Slavery in the French Atlantic* (Philadelphia: University of Pennsylvania Press, 2106), 41–43.

32. Hogarth, *Medicalizing Blackness*, 27, 42–43, 187–189, 231. Christopher Willoughby, "Running away from Drapetomania: Samuel A. Cartwright, Medicine, and Race in the Antebellum South," *Journal of Southern History* 84, no. 3 (July 2018): 579–614; Ariela Gross, *What Blood Won't Tell: A History of Race on Trial in America* (Cambridge, Mass.: Harvard University Press, 2008); Crawford, *Blood, Bodies, and Families*, 113–139; Eva Saks, "Representing Miscegenation Law," *Raritan* 8, no. 2 (1988): 39–69.

33. Elizabeth B. Clark, "The Sacred Rights of the Weak: Pain, Sympathy, and the Culture of Individual Rights in Antebellum America," *JAH* 82, no. 2 (1995): 463–493, esp. 487–488, for a valuable framework for understanding abolition's investment in the body and cultivation of sympathy. Seth, *Difference and Disease*, 272–275, for Benjamin Moseley's *Treatise on Tropical Diseases* (1787); Hunt, *Inventing Human Rights*.

34. Ana Stevenson, *The Woman as Slave in Nineteenth-Century American Social Movements* (New York: Palgrave Macmillan, 2019), 3, 18, 49, 66–67, considers how the "woman as slave" analogy linked human rights agendas. For white appropriations, see Karen Sanchez-Eppler, *Touching Liberty: Abolition, Feminism, and the Politics of the Body* (Berkeley: University of California Press, 1993); Hartman, *Scenes of Subjection*, 17–25, for the now foundational criticism of the perils of white abolitionist empathy; Zackodnik, *Press, Platform, Pulpit*; and Carol Lasser, "Voyeuristic Abolitionism: Sex, Gender, and the Transformation of Antislavery Rhetoric," *Journal of the Early Republic*, 28, no. 1 (Spring 2008): 83–114. See also Brycchan Carey, *British Abolitionism and the Rhetoric of Sensibility: Writing, Sentiment, and Slavery, 1760–1807* (New York: Palgrave Macmillan, 2005), esp. 73–143; Marcus Wood, *Slavery, Empathy, and Pornography* (Oxford, U.K.: Oxford University Press, 2002); Markman Ellis, *The Politics of Sensibility: Race, Gender, and Commerce in the Sentimental Novel* (Cambridge, U.K.: Cambridge University Press, 1996). Kyla Schuller, *The Biopolitics of Feeling: Race, Sex, and Science in the Nineteenth Century* (Durham, N.C.: Duke University Press, 2018), 14–17, 48–49, 53, 66, analyzes post–Civil War U.S. Lamarckians who linked physical and affective capacities to support racial and sexual biopower.

35. Hartman, *Scenes of Subjection*; Sanchez-Eppler, *Touching Liberty*; Gay Gibson Cima, *Performing Anti-slavery: Activist Women on Antebellum Stages* (New York: Cambridge University Press, 2014).

36. Clark, "Sacred Rights of the Weak," notes that by the mid-nineteenth century, "legal standards came to incorporate (albeit imperfectly) the idea that to be freed of physical coercion and deliberately inflicted pain was an essential human right" (468). She also notes the liberal religious

demotion of physical suffering as an ingredient of spiritual growth (471) and abolition as the origin of rights arguments by analogy (492). Hunt, *Inventing Human Rights*; Carolyn Dean, "Empathy, Pornography, and Suffering," *differences: A Journal of Feminist Cultural Studies* 14, no. 1 (Spring 2003): 88–124. Carey, *British Abolitionism*; Wood, *Slavery, Empathy, and Pornography*; Karen Halttunen, "Humanitarianism and the Pornography of Pain in Anglo-American Culture," *American Historical Review* 100, no. 2 (1995): 303–334. Lauren Berlant, *The Female Complaint: The Unfinished Business of Sentimentality in American Culture* (Durham, N.C.: Duke University Press, 2008). For the widespread transformation in humanitarian values that accompanied the abolition movement's focus on the infliction of pain, see Margaret Abruzzo, *Polemical Pain: Slavery, Cruelty, and the Rise of Humanitarianism* (Baltimore: Johns Hopkins University Press, 2011), esp. 134–135, 198–199. Contra Abruzzo, I interpret many depictions of physical suffering as an engagement with medical arguments about race. See also Isenberg, *Sex and Citizenship in Antebellum America*; and Sanchez-Eppler, *Touching Liberty*, esp. 1–49.

37. Hortense Spillers, "Mama's Baby, Papa's Maybe: An American Grammar Book," *Diacritics* 17, no. 2 (Summer 1987): 65–81; Cheryl Harris, "Whiteness as Property," *Harvard Law Review* 106, no. 8 (1993): 1709–1791; Hartman, *Scenes of Subjection*. For the significance of Spillers's notion of "flesh" and the insufficiency of habeas corpus to remedy the subjugation of enslaved African American bodies, see Weheliye, *Habeas Viscus*, 1–88, 136–137. For nineteenth-century sentimentalism as a form of biopolitics that created taxonomies of feeling and "impressibility," see Schuller, *Biopolitics of Feeling*, 12–13, 33, 93–99. Spillers, Hartman, Weheliye, and Schuller point to the significance of bodies for Black liberation politics.

38. Matthew Fox-Amato, *Exposing Slavery: Photography, Human Bondage, and the Birth of Modern Visual Politics in America* (New York, Oxford University Press, 2019), 11, 103–105, 119–122; John Stauffer, Zoe Trodd, and Celete-Marie Bernier, eds., *Picturing Frederick Douglass: An Illustrated Biography of the Nineteenth Century's Most Photographed American* (New York: Liveright, 2015); Ginger Hill, "'Rightly Viewed': Theorizations of Self in Frederick Douglass's Lectures on Pictures," in Maurice O. Wallace and Shawn Michelle Smith, eds., *Pictures and Progress: Early Photography and the Making of African American Identity* (Durham, N.C.: Duke University Press, 2012), 42. Molly Rogers, *Delia's Tears: Race, Science, and Photography in Nineteenth-Century America* (New Haven, Conn.: Yale University Press, 2010). Jessie Morgan-Owens, *Girl in Black and White: The Story of Mary Mildred Williams and the Abolition Movement* (New York: W. W. Norton, 2019).

39. "Humanity," copied from the *Virginia Independent Chronicle*, July 7, 1790, Robert Pleasants Letterbook, HCQSC; John Coffey, "'Tremble, Britannia!': Fear, Providence and the Abolition of the Slave Trade, 1758–1807," *English Historical Review* 127, no. 527 (August 2012): 844–881.

40. Influential studies include Gerda Lerner, *The Grimké Sisters from South Carolina: Pioneers for Woman's Rights and Abolition* (New York: Schocken Books, 1971; orig. 1967); David Brion Davis, *The Problem of Slavery in the Age of Revolution, 1770–1823* (Ithaca, N.Y.: Cornell University Press, 1975); Dorothy Sterling, ed., *We Are Your Sisters: Black Women in the Nineteenth Century* (New York: W. W. Norton, 1984, 1997); James Brewer Stewart, *Holy Warriors: The Abolitionists and American Slavery* (New York: Hill and Wang, 1996); Julie Roy Jeffrey, *The Great Silent Army of Abolitionism: Ordinary Women in the Antislavery Movement* (Chapel Hill: University of North Carolina Press, 1998); Bruce Dain, *A Hideous Monster of the Mind: American Race Theory in the Early Republic* (Cambridge, Mass.: Harvard University Press, 2002); Barbara Young Welke, *Law and the Borders of Belonging in the Long Nineteenth Century United States* (New York: Cambridge University Press, 2010); Manisha Sinha, *The Slave's Cause: A History of Abolition* (New Haven, Conn.: Yale University Press, 2016); Berry, *Price for Their Pound of Flesh*; Hogarth, *Medicalizing Blackness*; Hendrik Hartog, *The Trouble with Minna: A Case of Slavery and Emancipation in the Antebellum North* (Chapel Hill: University of North Carolina Press, 2018); For persistent African American performances of citizenship, see Jones, *Birthright Citizens*. For "second slavery," see Dale Tomich, *Through the Prism of Slavery: Labor, Capital, and World Economy* (Lanham, Md.: Rowman and Littlefield, 2003); Dale Tomich, "Civilizing America's Shore: British World-Economic Hegemony and the Abolition of the International Slave Trade (1814–1867)," in Tomich, ed., *The Politics of the Second Slavery* (Albany: State University of New York Press, 2016),

1–24; Anthony Kaye, "The Second Slavery: Modernity in the Nineteenth-Century South and the Atlantic World," *Journal of Southern History* 75, no. 3 (August 2009): 627–650; Erik Mathisen, "The Second Slavery, Capitalism, and Emancipation in Civil War America," *Journal of the Civil War Era* 8, no. 4 (December 2018): 677–699; Daniel Rood, *The Reinvention of Atlantic Slavery: Technology, Labor, Race, and Capitalism in the Greater Caribbean* (New York: Oxford University Press, 2017), esp. 94–173. See also James Kettner, *The Development of American Citizenship, 1608–1870* (Chapel Hill: University of North Carolina Press, 1978); Smithers, *Slave Breeding*; Ned Sublette and Constance Sublette, *The American Slave Coast: A History of the Slave-Breeding Industry* (Chicago: Lawrence Hill Books, 2016); Walter Johnson, "Racial Capitalism and Human Rights," *Boston Review* 1 (Winter 2017): 105–110. Patrick Rael, *Eighty-Eight Years: The Long Death of Slavery in the United States, 1777–1865* (Athens: University of Georgia Press, 2015), 131–135.

41. Stevenson, *Woman as Slave*, 18, 66. Carla L. Peterson, *Doers of the Word: African American Women Speakers and Writers in the North (1830–1880)* (New York: Oxford University Press, 1995), 20–23, notes that racist representations of Black female bodies created a special dilemma for Black women's public speaking. Mary Nyquist, *Arbitrary Rule: Slavery, Tyranny, and the Power of Life and Death* (Chicago: University of Chicago Press, 2013).

42. Crawford, *Blood, Bodies, and Families*. For the significance of maternity to slavery and abolition specifically, see Paugh, *Politics of Reproduction*; Turner, *Contested Bodies*; Berry, *Price for Their Pound of Flesh*; Doyle, *Maternal Bodies*; Molly Farrell, *Counting Bodies: Population in Colonial American Writing* (New York: Oxford University Press, 2016). David Brion Davis, *The Problem of Slavery in Western Culture* (Ithaca, N. Y.: Cornell University Press, 1966), 299–301, for Quaker bodily dissidence. For the New World context for Malthusian theory, see Alison Bashford and Joyce Chaplin, *The New Worlds of Thomas Robert Malthus: Rereading the Principle of Population* (Princeton, N.J.: Princeton University Press, 2016).

43. Frederick B. Tolles, *Quakers and the Atlantic Culture* (New York: Macmillan, 1960), esp. 1–72. Kirsten Sword, "Remembering Dinah Nevil: Strategic Deceptions in Eighteenth-Century Antislavery," *JAH* 97, no. 2 (September 2010): 315–343. See also John Harley Warner, "The Idea of Southern Medical Distinctiveness: Medical Knowledge and Practice in the Old South," in Ronald Numbers and Todd Savitt, eds., *Science and Medicine in the Old South* (Baton Rouge: Louisiana State University Press, 1989), 179–205; Berry, *Price for Their Pound of Flesh*; Daniel Kilbride, "Southern Medical Students in Philadelphia, 1800–1861: Science and Sociability in the 'Republic of Medicine,'" *Journal of Southern History* 65, no. 4 (November 1999): 697–732, and 708, for Bonner, who was not a southerner by birth but later became a wealthy physician slaveholder in Holly Springs, Mississippi; W. Caleb McDaniel, *The Problem of Democracy in the Age of Slavery: Garrisonian Abolitionists and Transatlantic Reform* (Baton Rouge: Louisiana State University Press, 2013); Julie Winch, "Self-Help and Self-Determination: Black Philadelphians and the Dimensions of Freedom," and W. Caleb McDaniel, "Philadelphia Abolitionists and Antislavery Cosmopolitanism," both in Richard Newman and James Mueller, eds., *Antislavery and Abolition in Philadelphia: Emancipation and the Long Struggle for Racial Justice in the City of Brotherly Love* (Baton Rouge: Louisiana State University Press, 2011), 67–89, 149–173; Bruce Dorsey, *Reforming Men and Women: Gender in the Antebellum City* (Ithaca, N.Y.: Cornell University Press, 2002), esp. 136–194. Emma J. Lapsansky, "'Since They Got Those Separate Churches': Afro-Americans and Racism in Jacksonian Philadelphia," *American Quarterly* 32, no.1 (Spring 1980): 54–78; Gary Nash, *Forging Freedom: The Formation of Philadelphia's Black Community, 1720–1840* (Cambridge, Mass.: Harvard University Press, 1991); Rael, *Eighty-Eight Years*, 131–135. Nicholas P. Wood, "A 'Class of Citizens': The Earliest Black Petitioners to Congress and Their Quaker Allies," *WMQ*, 3rd ser., 74, no. 1 (January 2017): 109–144.

Chapter 1

1. Information on the petitioners, their connection to German Mennonites, and the writing table accessed from "1688 Petition Against Slavery," Germantown Mennonite Historic Trust, http://www

.meetinghouse.info/1688-petition-against-slavery.html. See also David Brion Davis, *The Problem of Slavery in Western Culture* (Ithaca, N.Y.: Cornell University Press, 1966), 308–309.

2. Davis, *Western Culture*, 184, 308–309; Katharine Gerbner, "'We Are Against the Traffik of Men-Body': The Germantown Quaker Protest of 1688 and the Origins of American Abolitionism," *PH* 74, no. 2 (Spring 2007): 149–172. See also Srinivas Aravamudan, *Tropicopolitans: Colonialism and Agency, 1688–1804* (Durham, N.C.: Duke University Press, 1999), especially 242–264, for the emergent anticolonial discourse in eighteenth-century literature.

3. Aravamudan, *Tropicopolitans*; Ian Baucom, *Specters of the Atlantic: Finance Capital, Slavery, and the Philosophy of History* (Durham, N.C.: Duke University Press, 2005).

4. Lauren Benton, *A Search for Sovereignty: Law and Geography in European Empires, 1400–1900* (Cambridge: Cambridge University Press, 2010), 111, 120–122, 149–161.

5. Jennifer Spear and Kathleen Brown, "Rethinking Maternal Inheritance in Atlantic Slave Law," unpublished manuscript.

6. See Antony Anghie, *Imperialism, Sovereignty, and the Making of International Law* (New York: Cambridge University Press, 2005), 13–31; for a more nuanced analysis of Vitoria and Gentili, see Christopher L. Tomlins, *Freedom Bound: Law, Labor, and Civic Identity in Colonizing English America, 1580–1865* (New York: Cambridge University Press, 2010), 122–132; Baucom, *Specters of the Atlantic*, 189–191; Benedict Anderson, *Imagined Communities: Reflections on the Origin and Spread of Nationalism* (London: Verso, 1983).

7. Jean Bodin, *Six Bookes of the Commonweal*, trans. Richard Knolles (London, 1606; orig. French edition, 1576), 408–409.

8. Bodin, *Six Bookes*, 212.

9. Bodin, *Six Bookes*, 215.

10. Bodin, *Six Bookes*. For Bodin's antislavery views, see Mary Nyquist, *Arbitrary Rule: Slavery, Tyranny, and the Power of Life and Death* (Chicago: University of Chicago Press, 2013), 180–192, esp. 183; Henry Heller, "Bodinian Slavery and Primitive Accumulation," *Sixteenth Century Journal* 25, no. 1 (Spring 1974): 53–65.

11. Bodin, *Six Bookes*, 49. For Bodin's comparison of slaves to the genitalia of the body politic (shameful to display yet still part of the whole), see Davis, *Western Culture*, 112.

12. Grotius, *Right of War and Peace* (1625), Online Library of Liberty, https://oll.libertyfund.org/title/grotius-the-rights-of-war-and-peace-2005-ed-vol-1-book-i, 190–207, 246. Nyquist, *Arbitrary Rule*, 223–226.

13. Grotius, *Rights*, 288.

14. Grotius, *Rights*, 526–538, 557, 584–629, 1375.

15. Grotius, *Rights*, 1496.

16. Paul D. Halliday, *Habeas Corpus: From England to Empire* (Cambridge, Mass.: Harvard University Press, 2010), 70–71, 202; Tomlins, *Freedom Bound*, 82–89. Polly J. Price, "Natural Law and Birthright Citizenship in Calvin's Case (1608)," *Yale Journal of Law and the Humanities* 9, no. 1 (1997): 73–145; Keechang Kim, "Calvin's Case (1608) and the Law of Alien Status," *Journal of Legal History* 17, no. 2 (August 1996): 155–171.

17. Halliday, *Habeas Corpus*, 15–16, quote on 70.

18. Ed Cohen, "A Body Worth Having? Or, a System of Natural Governance," *Theory, Culture and Society* 25, no. 3 (2008): 103–129; Halliday, *Habeas Corpus*, 65, 181–183, and 197–198, for his discussion of "to be at liberty," for liberty as a place one chooses to occupy with the body.

19. Henry Burton, *Conformitie's Deformity: In a Dialogue Between Conformity, and Conscience* (1646). David Cressy, "Puritan Martyrs in Island Prisons," *Journal of British Studies* 57, no. 4 (2018): 736–754. Kevin Sharpe, *The Personal Rule of Charles I* (New Haven, Conn.: Yale University Press, 1992). Jerome de Groot, "Prison Writing, Writing Prison During the 1640s and 1650s," *Huntington Library Quarterly* 72, no. 2 (June 2009): 147–167. See also Margaret Abruzzo, *Polemical Pain: Slavery, Cruelty, and the Rise of Humanitarianism* (Baltimore: Johns Hopkins University Press, 2011); Halliday, *Habeas Corpus*, 225–226, for Parliament's 1641 challenge to the Star Chamber's prerogative.

20. John Lilburne, *England's Birth-Right Justified against all Arbitrary Usurpation, whether Regall or Parliamentary* (London, 1646), 11–12. Rachel Foxley, "John Lilburne and the Citizenship of 'Free-Borne Englishmen,'" *Historical Journal* 47, no. 4 (December 2004): 849–874.

21. Halliday, *Habeas Corpus*, 179, 184–185, 193–197; Foxley, "John Lilburne."

22. John Lilburne, *A Declaration to the Free-borne People of England, Concerning the Government of the Commonwealth* (London, 1684), 4, 5, 6–8. As Halliday, *Habeas Corpus*, 179, notes, Lilburne sought English law protections against slavery resulting from tyranny but also invoked natural law to protest legal "enslavement." See also Kevin P. Siena, *Venereal Disease, Hospitals, and the Urban Poor: London's "Foul Wards," 1600–1800* (Rochester, N.Y.: University of Rochester Press, 2004), on disease in English jails.

23. Susan Amussen, *Caribbean Exchanges: Slavery and the Transformation of English Society, 1640–1700* (Chapel Hill: University of North Carolina Press, 2007), 127–128.

24. Carla Pestana, *The English Atlantic in an Age of Revolution, 1640–1661* (Cambridge, Mass.: Harvard University Press, 2004), 210–212, for the transportation of Rivers and Foyle, which brought this issue to a head. See also Alan Atkinson, "The Free-Born Englishman Transported: Convict Rights as a Measure of Eighteenth-Century Empire," *Past and Present* 144, no. 1 (August 1994): 88–115, for changes in convict transport, with the fiction of the convict's consent to be transported gradually replaced with a notion of mandatory penalty. Cynthia Herrup, "Punishing Pardon: Some Thoughts on the Origins of Penal Transportation," in Simon Devereaux and Paul Griffiths, eds., *Penal Practice and Culture, 1500–1900: Punishing the English* (New York: Palgrave Macmillan, 2004), 121–137.

25. Halliday, *Habeas Corpus*, 229–231, 237–246, 156–258, 266. Nyquist, *Arbitrary Rule*.

26. R. J. Sharpe, Judith Farbey, and Simon Atrill, *The Law of Habeas Corpus*, 3rd ed., (Cambridge, U.K.: Oxford University Press, 2011), 14–17. Cohen, "A Body Worth Having?"

27. Pestana, *The English Atlantic*; Carla Gardina Pestana, *The English Conquest of Jamaica: Oliver Cromwell's Bid for Empire* (Cambridge, Mass.: Harvard University Press, 2017).

28. Cohen, "A Body Worth Having?"; Halliday, *Habeas Corpus*, 197, 274.

29. Nancy Shoemaker, *A Strange Likeness: Becoming Red and White in Eighteenth-Century North America* (New York: Oxford University Press, 2006), 125; Speech of the Indians from Upper Part of the River to Governor Fletcher (1693), *MPCP* 1:373.

30. James O'Neil Spady, "Colonialism and the Discursive Antecedents of Penn's Treaty with the Indians," in Daniel Richter and William Pencak, eds., *Friends and Enemies in Penn's Woods: Colonists, Indians, and the Racial Construction of Pennsylvania* (State College: Pennsylvania State University Press, 2010), 18–40.

31. Shoemaker, *Strange Likeness*, 128; Articles of Agreement, April 23, 1701, *MPCP* 2:15.

32. Governer William Keith, Philadelphia, May 11, 1722, *MPCP* 3:169.

33. Lt. Governer Patrick Gordon to the Chiefs of the Five Nations, July 3, 1727, *MPCP* 3:273–274.

34. Proprietor Thomas Penn, Philadelphia, August 23, 1732, *MPCP* 3:436.

35. Shoemaker, *Strange Likeness*, 125; unnamed Susquehannock speaker, Council at Conestoga, July 1720, *MPCP* 3:87.

36. Tagodrancy and others, July 23, 1712, *MPCP* 2:553.

37. Speech of Whiwhinjac read by Governor Keith, May 20, 1723, *MPCP* 3:217.

38. Tawenna, Council at Conestoga, May 27, 1728, *MPCP* 3:314.

39. Shoemaker, *Strange Likeness*, 128; Teedyuscung, Council at Philadelphia, 1755, *MPCP* 6:363.

40. Shoemaker, *Strange Likeness*, 128; unnamed speaker, Council at Philadelphia, August 28, 1732, *MPCP* 3:444.

41. Shoemaker, *Strange Likeness*, 128; Bruce White, "'Give Us a Little Milk': The Social and Cultural Meaning of Gift Giving in the Lake Superior Fur Trade," *Minnesota History* 48, no. 2 (1982): 60–71. Shoemaker notes the likely influence of French metaphoric references on Haudenosaunee rhetoric and its source in Christian iconography. She claims that Indians normally did not position themselves as maternal sucklers, but as siblings who had a common mother with Europeans. See also Gunlög Fur, *A Nation of Women: Gender and Colonial Encounters Among the Delaware Indians* (Philadelphia: University of Pennsylvania Press, 2009).

42. Speeches of an Indian Council (1732), in Sylvester K. Stevens and Donald H. Kent, eds., *Wilderness Chronicles of Northwestern Pennsylvania* (Harrisburg: Pennsylvania Historical Commission, 1941), 7; see also Sassoonan, Council at Philadelphia, June 5, 1728, *MPCP* 3:319; Shickallamy conference at Philadelphia, 1733, *MPCP* 3:501; Speech of the Nanticokes, Council at Philadelphia, August 16, 1751, *MPCP* 5:544; Cayugalluef, Tokoain, Council at Easton, October 21, 1758, *MPCP* 8:212; John Curtis, Nanticoke, Council at Philadelphia, September 17, 1763, *MPCP* 9:46.

43. George Fox, *Gospel Family-Order: Being a Short Discourse Concerning the Ordering of Families, Both of Whites, Blacks, and Indians* (London, 1676), 13–14; Kenneth L. Carroll, "George Fox and Slavery," *Quaker History* 86, no. 2 (Fall 1997): 16–25; Brycchan Carey, *From Peace to Freedom: Quaker Rhetoric and Birth of American Antislavery, 1658–1761* (New Haven, Conn.: Yale University Press, 2012), 186–187, 41.

44. *The Journal of George Fox*, ed. Norman Penney (Cambridge, U.K.: Cambridge University Press, 1911); J. William Frost, "George Fox's Ambiguous Anti-slavery Legacy," Quakers and Slavery Website, https://web.tricolib.brynmawr.edu/speccoll/quakersandslavery/commentary/people/fox.php for the discrepancy between the term of years Fox recommended.

45. *An Exhortation and Caution to Friends, Concerning buying or keeping of Negroes* (New York: Thomas Bradford, 1693), reprinted in J. W. Frost, *The Keithian Controversy in Early Pennsylvania* (Norwood, Pa.: Norwood Editions, 1980), 213–218. See also Davis, *Western Culture*, 306–311; John Smolenski, *Friends and Strangers: The Making of a Creole Culture in Colonial Pennsylvania* (Philadelphia: University of Pennsylvania Press, 2011), 150–173; Madeleine Ward, *The Christian Quaker: George Keith and the Keithian Controversy* (London: Brill, 2019).

46. Benjamin Lay, *All Slavekeepers that Keep the Innocent in Bondage, Apostates* (Philadelphia, 1737); Marcus Rediker, *The Fearless Benjamin Lay: The Quaker Dwarf Who Became the First Revolutionary Abolitionist* (Boston: Beacon, 2017).

47. John Woolman, *Some Considerations on the Keeping of Negroes* (Philadelphia, 1754), discussed in Carey, *From Peace to Freedom*. Carey cites Genesis 3:20, which acknowledges Eve as the mother of all living as Woolman's inspiration, but the actual reference in Woolman is to Fox's letter and to Acts 17:26. Woolman, *The Journal of John Woolman* (Boston: Houghton and Mifflin, 1909), 99–110, includes descriptions of his distress over the nakedness of slaves, the disregard of slave marriages, and the use of the whip. See Geoffrey Plank, *John Woolman's Path to the Peaceable Kingdom: A Quaker in the British Empire* (Philadelphia: University of Pennsylvania Press, 2012), esp. 97–120; Thomas Slaughter, *The Beautiful Soul of John Woolman, Apostle of Abolition* (New York: Hill and Wang, 2008), 130–132; and Jack Marietta, *The Reformation of American Quakerism, 1748–1783* (Philadelphia: University of Pennsylvania Press, 1984), 97–128.

48. Samuel Sewell, *The Selling of Joseph: A Memorial* (Boston, 1700), 2. The OED references for "extravasat" begin in the 1660s and include commentary on veins of precious metals, plant juices, and blood. For Sewall's context for writing this pamphlet, see Wendy Warren, *New England Bound: Slavery and Colonization in Early America* (New York: W. W. Norton, 2016), 225–245.

49. Maurice Jackson, *Let This Voice Be Heard: Anthony Benezet, Father of Atlantic Abolitionism* (Philadelphia: University of Pennsylvania Press, 2010); Anthony Benezet, *A Short Account of That Part of Africa Inhabited by the Negroes* (Philadelphia, 1762).

50. Victoria Sweet, *God's Hotel: A Doctor, a Hospital, and a Pilgrimage to the Heart of Medicine* (New York: Penguin, 2012), 1–2.

51. Catrien Santing, "'For the Life of the Creature Is in the Blood' (Leviticus 17:11): Some Considerations on Blood as the Source of Life in Sixteenth-Century Religion and Medicine and Their Interconnections," and Barbara Orland, "White Blood and Red Milk: Analogical Reasoning in Medical Practice and Experimental Physiology, 1560–1730," both in Manfred Horstmanshoff, Helen King, and Claus Zittel, eds., *Blood, Sweat, and Tears: The Changing Concepts of Physiology from Antiquity into Early Modern Europe* (Leiden: Brill, 2012), 415–441, 443–478.

52. Santing, "Life of the Creature."

53. Holly Tucker, *Blood Work: A Tale of Medicine and Murder in the Scientific Revolution* (New York: W. W. Norton, 2011).

54. Andrew S. Curran, *The Anatomy of Blackness: Science and Slavery in the Age of Enlightenment* (Baltimore: Johns Hopkins University Press, 2011), 121.

55. Thomas Towns to Martin Lister, Barbados, March 26, 1675, in Anna Marie Roos, ed., *The Correspondence of Dr. Martin Lister (1639–1712)*, vol. 1, *1662–1677* (London: Brill, 2015), 782–783; Mark Harrison, *Medicine in an Age of Commerce and Empire: Britain and Its Tropical Colonies, 1660–1830* (New York: Oxford University Press, 2010), 45.

56. François Bernier, "Nouvelle division de la terre, par les differentes Especes ou races d'hommes qui l'habitent, envoyer par un fameux Voyageur a M. l'Abbe de la *** a peu pres en ces termes," *Journal des scavans*, April 1684 (Paris). Siep Stuurman, "François Bernier and the Invention of Racial Classification," *History Workshop Journal* 50, no. 1 (Autumn 2000): 1–21; Pierre Boulle, "Francois Bernier and the Origins of the Modern Concept of Race," in Sue Peabody and Tyler Stovall, eds., *The Color of Liberty: Histories of Race in France* (Durham, N.C.: Duke University Press, 2003), 11–27. But see Justin E. H. Smith, *Nature, Human Nature, and Human Difference: Race in Early Modern Philosophy* (Princeton, N.J.: Princeton University Press, 2015), especially 140–159, for important distinctions between Bernier's biogeographic concept of lineages and later nineteenth-century concepts of biological or polygenetic race.

57. Cited in Cristina Malcolmson, *Studies of Skin Color in the Early Royal Society: Boyle, Cavendish, Swift* (London: Routledge, 2013), 89.

58. Malcolmson, *Studies of Skin Color*, 69–70.

59. Malcolmson, *Studies of Skin Color*, 69.

60. Charles Leslie, *A New History of Jamaica* (London, 1739).

61. Philippe Rosenberg, "Thomas Tryon and the Seventeenth-Century Dimensions of Antislavery," *WMQ*, 3rd ser., 61, no. 4 (October 2004): 609–642, esp. 616 for the link between Tryon's intellectual and geographic movements. For the 1661 Barbardian slave code, see An Act for the Better Ordering and Governing of Negroes, September 27, 1661, reprinted in Stanley Engerman, Seymour Drescher, and Robert Paquette, eds., *Slavery* (New York: Oxford University Press, 2001), 105; Russell R. Menard, *Sweet Negotiations: Sugar, Slavery, and Plantation Agriculture in Early Barbados* (Charlottesville: University of Virginia Press, 2006), esp. 112–113; Demetri D. Debe and Russell R. Menard, "The Transition to African Slavery in Maryland: A Note on the Barbados Connection," *Slavery and Abolition* 32, no. 1 (2011): 133–136. April Lee Hatfield, *Atlantic Virginia: Intercolonial Relations in the Seventeenth Century* (Philadelphia: University of Pennsylvania Press, 2004), 92–95, 141–145, 167, 279–280n32; Tomlins, *Freedom Bound*, 466; Amussen, *Caribbean Exchanges*, 166–169. Davis, *Western Culture*, 371–374. For Tryon's influence on Benjamin Franklin and other early opponents of slavery in Pennsylvania, see David Waldstreicher, "The Origins of Antislavery in Pennsylvania: Early Abolitionists and Benjamin Franklin's Road Not Taken," in Richard Newman and James Mueller, eds., *Antislavery and Abolition in Philadelphia: Emancipation and the Long Struggle for Racial Justice in the City of Brotherly Love* (Baton Rouge: Louisiana State University Press, 2011), 45–65.

62. William Pettigrew, *Freedom's Debt: The Royal African Company and the Politics of the Atlantic Slave Trade, 1672–1752* (Chapel Hill: University of North Carolina Press, 2013).

63. Rosenberg, "Thomas Tryon."

64. "Bestiary." In *The Oxford Dictionary of Christian Art and Architecture*, eds. Devonshire Jones, Tom, Linda Murray, and Peter Murray, Oxford University Press, 2013 https://www-oxfordreference-com.proxy.library.upenn.edu/view/10.1093/acref/9780199680276.001.0001/acref-9780199680276-e-214. Rosenberg, "Thomas Tryon."

65. Thomas Tryon, *Friendly Advice to the Gentleman-Planters of the East and West Indies* (London, 1684), 49.

66. Tryon, *Friendly Advice*, 2, 22, 62, 30, 39, 62. See also Karen Kupperman, "Fear of Hot Climates in the Anglo-American Colonial Experience," *WMQ* 41, no. 2 (April 1984): 213–240.

67. Tryon, *Friendly Advice*, 45–46, 52; Colleen E. Kriger, *Cloth in West African History* (New York: Rowman and Littlefield, 2006), 121; Muhammadu Hambali Jinju, *African Traditional Medicine: A Case Study of Hausa Medical Plants and Therapy* (Zaria, Nigeria: n.p., 1990), 118, 137.

68. Tryon, "The Negro's Complaint," in Tryon, *Friendly Advice*, 82–83, 103, 105, 129.

69. Tryon, "The Negro's Complaint," in Tryon, *Friendly Advice*, 88–89, 92–93.

70. Tryon, "The Negro's Complaint," in Tryon, *Friendly Advice*, 96, 137, 109, 110. Daniel Carey, "Sugar, Colonialism and the Critique of Slavery: Thomas Tryon in Barbados," in Byron R. Wells and Philip Stewart, eds., *Interpreting Colonialism* (Oxford: Voltaire Foundation, 2004), 303–21.

71. Tryon, "Negro's Complaint," in Tryon, *Friendly Advice*, 114, 120, 109.

72. Tryon, "Negro's Complaint," in Tryon, *Friendly Advice*, 132–133, 108. See Baucom, *Specters of the Atlantic*, 261–262, for a discussion of Adam Smith's *Theory of Moral Sentiments*, especially Smith's observation that a desire for revenge arose from sympathy for the oppressed.

73. Tryon, "A discourse in way of dialogue, between an Ethiopean or negro-slave, and a Christian that was his master in America," in Tryon, *Friendly Advice*, 178, 167.

74. Tryon, "A discourse in way of dialogue," in Tryon, *Friendly Advice*, 182, 201. Baucom, *Specters of the Atlantic*, 7–8. Aravamudan, *Tropicopolitans*, 67, 347n43.

75. Tryon, "A discourse in way of dialogue," in Tryon, *Friendly Advice*, 218.

76. William D. Piersen, *Black Legacy: America's Hidden Heritage* (Amherst: University of Massachusetts Press, 1993); John Thornton, "Cannibals, Witches, and Slave Traders in the Atlantic World," *WMQ*, 3rd ser., 60, no. 2 (April 2003): 273–294; Lynn R. Johnson, "Narrating an Indigestible Trauma: The Alimentary Grammar of Boyrereau Brinch's Middle Passage," in Nicole Aljoe and Ian Finseth, eds., *Journeys of the Slave Narrative in the Early Americas* (Charlottesville: University of Virginia Press, 2014), 127–142; G. Ugo Nwokeji, *The Slave Trade and Culture in the Bight of Biafra: An African Society in the Atlantic World* (New York: Cambridge University Press, 2010), 132–133. For European accounts of Indigenous cannibalism in Africa and the Americas, see Francis Barker, Peter Hulme, and Margaret Iverson, eds., *Cannibalism and the Colonial World* (Cambridge, U.K.: Cambridge University Press, 1998).

77. Rebecca Shumway, *The Fante and the Transatlantic Slave Trade* (Rochester, N.Y.: University of Rochester Press, 2011).

78. Shumway, *Fante and the Transatlantic Slave Trade*, 34. See also Nwokeji, *Slave Trade and Culture in the Bight of Biafra*; Sylviane A. Diouf, ed., *Fighting the Slave Trade: West African Strategies* (Athens: Ohio University Press, 2004), esp. Joseph E. Inikori, "The Struggle Against the Transatlantic Slave Trade: The Role of the State," in Joseph E. Inikori and Stanley L. Engerman, eds., *The Atlantic Slave Trade: Effects on Economies, Societies, and Peoples in Africa, the Americas, and Europe* (Durham, N.C.: Duke University Press, 1992), 170–198; John Thornton, *Africa and Africans in the Making of the Atlantic World, 1400–1680* (New York: Cambridge University Press, 1992), 110–112. See also Ndubueze L. Mbah, *Emergent Masculinities: Gendered Power and Social Change in the Biafran Atlantic Age* (Athens: Ohio University Press, 2019).

79. Lauren Benton and Lisa Ford, *Rage for Order: The British Empire and the Origins of International Law, 1800–1850* (Cambridge, Mass.: Harvard University Press, 2016).

80. Emer de Vattel, *The Law of Nations* (London, 1758). See also David Armitage, *Foundations of Modern International Thought* (New York: Cambridge University Press, 2013).

81. Marianne Johnson, "'More Native Than French': American Physiocrats and Their Political Economy," *History of Economic Ideas* 10, no. 1 (2002): 15–31.

82. Vattel, *Law of Nations*, 222–225, on the subject's right to mobility; Armitage, *Foundations of Modern International Thought*; Emma Christopher, *A Merciless Place: The Fate of Britain's Convicts After the American Revolution* (New York: Oxford University Press, 2010).

83. Vattel, *Law of Nations*, 476.

84. Anghie, *Imperialism, Sovereignty, and the Making of International Law*, 13–31.

85. James Merrell, ed., *The Lancaster Treaty of 1744: With Related Documents* (Boston: Bedford St. Martins, 2008): "What is one hundred years in comparison to the length of Time since our Claim began?—Since we came out of this ground? For we must tell you that long before One hundred years Our ancestors came out of this very Ground, and Our Children have remained here ever since." "You came out of the ground in a country that lyes beyond Seas," 53.

86. Suman Seth, *Difference and Disease: Medicine, Race, and the Eighteenth-Century British Empire* (New York: Cambridge University Press, 2018), differentiates between race science and race

medicine, with the latter emerging during the abolition movement of the 1780s–1790s and into the nineteenth century.

87. Curran, *Anatomy of Blackness.*

88. Miriam Claude Meijer, *Race and Aesthetics in the Anthropology of Petrus Camper (1722–1789)* (London: Brill, 1999), 71–72; Curran, *Anatomy of Blackness*, 2, 239n25–26, notes that submission five in the 1739 contest sponsored by the Academie Royale des Sciences de Bordeaux was a manuscript version of Barrère's 1741 dissertation.

89. Alexandra Gomes, "Le Chevalier de Jaucourt: Philosophie, idées politiques et ampleur de l'implication dans L'Encyclopédie de Diderot et d'Alembert" (University of Paris Nanterre, master's thesis, 2017); Philipp Blom, *Enlightening the World: Encyclopédie, the Book That Changed the Course of History* (New York: Palgrave Macmillan, 2005), 102–109. John Mitchell, "Essay upon Different Colours of People," *Philosophical Transactions of the Royal Society* 43 (1744–1745), cited in Winthrop Jordan, *White over Black: American Attitudes Toward the Negro, 1550–1812* (Chapel Hill: University of North Carolina Press, 1968), 246–247. Curran, *Anatomy of Blackness*, 127. On Mitchell, see Gordon W. Jones, "The Library of Dr. John Mitchell of Urbanna," *VMHB* 76, no. 4 (October 1968): 441–443. A well-known collector of botanical specimens, Mitchell corresponded with both Benjamin Rush and Linnaeus.

90. Meijer, *Race and Aesthetics*, Meckel quoted on p. 73. See also Curran, *Anatomy of Blackness*, 124–125.

91. Curran, *Anatomy of Blackness*, 125.

92. Jordan, *White over Black*, 246–247; Cornelius de Pauw, *Recherches philosophiques sur les Américains* (London, 1771). Curran, *Anatomy of Blackness*, 127.

93. Curran, *Anatomy of Blackness*, 74–76; Thomas Jefferson, *Notes on the State of Virginia* (Paris, 1785; London, 1787; Philadelphia, 1788); Bruce Dain, *A Hideous Monster of the Mind: American Race Theory in the Early Republic* (Cambridge, Mass.: Harvard University Press, 2002). Well before Jefferson's *Notes*, Edward Long expressed difference in terms of racial purity; Edward Long, *History of Jamaica* 3 vols. (London, 1774), 1:327–328.

94. Aaron Fogelman, *Hopeful Journeys: German Immigration, Settlement, and Political Culture in Colonial America, 1717–1775* (Philadelphia: University of Pennsylvania Press, 1996); Christopher, *Merciless Place*; David Eltis, *The Rise of African Slavery in the Americas* (New York: Cambridge University Press, 1999).

95. Vincent Carretta, *Phillis Wheatley: Biography of a Genius in Bondage* (Athens: University of Georgia Press, 2011), 13.

96. Adam Smith, *Theory of Moral Sentiments* (Glasgow, 1759); Baucom, *Specters of the Atlantic*, 243–263.

97. Carretta, *Phillis Wheatley*, 133–135.

98. Ruth Paley, "Imperial Politics and English Law: The Many Contexts of *Somerset*," *Law and History Review* 24, no. 3 (Fall 2006): 659–664; Edlie L. Wong, *Neither Fugitive nor Free: Atlantic Slavery, Freedom Suits, and the Legal Culture of Travel* (New York: New York University Press, 2009), 19–67; Kirsten Sword, "Remembering Dinah Nevil: Strategic Deceptions in Eighteenth-Century Antislavery," *JAH* 97, no. 2 (September 2010): 315–343.

99. Granville Sharp, *A Representation of the Injustice and Dangerous Tendency of Tolerating Slavery; or of Admitting the Least Claim of Private Property in the Persons of men, in England* (London, 1769).

100. David Beck Ryden, *West Indian Slavery and British Abolition, 1783–1807* (Cambridge, U.K.: Cambridge University Press, 2009); Travis Glasson, "'Baptism Doth Not Bestow Freedom': Missionary Anglicanism, Slavery, and the Yorke-Talbot Opinion, 1701–30," *WMQ*, 3rd ser., 67, no. 2 (April 2010): 279–318; Sword, "Remembering Dinah Nevil," 317, 321–322.

101. Carretta, *Phillis Wheatley*, 120–129; Wong, *Neither Fugitive nor Free*, 28–29.

102. Benjamin Rush, *An Address to the Inhabitants of the British Settlements in America, upon Slave-Keeping* (Boston, 1773); [Richard Nisbet], *Slavery not forbidden by Scripture, or, A defence of the West-India planters, from the aspersions thrown out against them, by the author of a pamphlet,*

entitled, "An address to the inhabitants of the British settlements in America, upon slave-keeping" (Philadelphia, 1773); Rush, *An Address to the Inhabitants of the British Settlements in America, upon Slave-Keeping: To Which Are Added, Observations on a Pamphlet, Entitled, "Slavery Not Forbidden by Scripture, or a Defense of the West-India Planters"* (Philadelphia, 1773).

103. Sword, "Remembering Dinah Nevil"; Phillis Wheatley to David Wooster, October 18, 1773, https://www.masshist.org/database/771 MHS Collections Online. See also Carretta, *Phillis Wheatley*, 610n15.

104. Phillis Wheatley to David Wooster, October 18, 1773, https://www.masshist.org/database/771 MHS Collections Online.

105. Phillis Wheatley to Obour Tanner, October 30, 1773, https://www.masshist.org/database/viewer.php?item_id=774 MHS Collections Online.

Chapter 2

1. Joanna Brooks, "'This Indian World': An Introduction to the Writings of Samson Occom," in Joanna Brooks, ed., *The Collected Writings of Samson Occom, Mohegan* (New York: Oxford University Press, 2004).

2. Phillis Wheatley to Samson Occom, February 11, 1774, reprinted in the *Connecticut Gazette*, March 11, 1774. "Modern Egyptians" has been interpreted to mean Africans, but I side with those who read it as a reference to modern slave owners; see *The Broadview Anthology of Romantic Poetry*, Joseph Black, et al., eds. (Toronto: Broadview Press, 2016), 103n7. See also Elizabeth Ann Beaulieu, "Christianity," in *Writing African American Women: An Encyclopedia of Literature by and About Women of Color*, 2 vols. (Westport, Conn.: Greenwood, 2006), 1:174. For Samson Occom, see David Silverman, *Red Brethren: The Brothertown and Stockbridge Indians and the Problem of Race in Early America* (Ithaca, N.Y.: Cornell University Press, 2016); Eileen Razzari Elrod, *Piety and Dissent: Race, Gender, and Biblical Rhetoric in Early American Autobiography* (Amherst: University of Massachusetts Press, 2008), 21–37. See also Peter A. Dorsey, *Common Bondage: Slavery as Metaphor in Revolutionary America* (Knoxville: University of Tennessee Press, 2009); John Shuler, *Calling Out Liberty: Human Rights Discourse and Early American Literature* (Jackson: University Press of Mississippi, 2010). On the use of "slavery" to refer to the political consequences of tyranny, see Mary Nyquist, *Arbitrary Rule: Slavery, Tyranny, and the Power of Life and Death* (Chicago: University of Chicago Press, 2013).

3. David Hollinger, "The Circle of We," cited in Thomas Laqueur, "Mourning, Pity, and the Work of Narrative," in R. D. Brown, ed., *Humanitarianism and Suffering: The Mobilization of Empathy* (New York: Cambridge University Press, 2009).

4. "The Petition of a Grate Number of Blackes of this Province," Jeremy Belknap Papers, MHS Collections online; Joanne Pope Melish, *Disowning Slavery: Gradual Emancipation and "Race" in New England, 1780–1860* (Ithaca, N.Y.: Cornell University Press, 1998); Jared Ross Hardesty, *Unfreedom: Slavery and Dependence in Eighteenth-Century Boston* (New York: New York University Press, 2016).

5. "To the Tradesmen, Mechanics, &c. of the Province of Pennsylvania," *Boston Post Boy*, December 13–20, 1773. For alarm in the colonies over the East India Company's atrocities, see Jonathan Eacott, *Selling Empire: India in the Making of Britain and America, 1600-1830* (Chapel Hill: University of North Carolina Press, 2016), 204–226.

6. Susan Amussen, *An Ordered Society: Gender and Class in Early Modern England* (New York: Columbia University Press, 1988); David Underdown, *Revel, Riot, and Rebellion: Popular Culture and Politics in England, 1603–1660* (New York: Oxford University Press, 1985). Philip Joseph Deloria, *Playing Indian* (New Haven, Conn.: Yale University Press, 1998).

7. Brendan McConville, *The King's Three Faces: The Rise and Fall of Royal America, 1688–1776* (Chapel Hill: University of North Carolina Press, 2006).

8. Jane Calvert, *Quaker Constitutionalism and the Political Thought of John Dickinson* (New York: Cambridge University Press, 2008).

9. T. H. Breen, *American Insurgents, American Patriots: The Revolution of the People* (New York: Hill and Wang, 2010).

10. Benjamin Franklin Papers: Series I, 1772–1783; Petition of the Continental Congress to the King, Philadelphia, Pa., Oct. 26, 1774 (vol. 10), Library of Congress, https://www.loc.gov/item/mss21451011/

11. Wendy Warren, *New England Bound: Slavery and Colonization in Early America* (New York: W. W. Norton, 2017).

12. "1774 Petition to the King," Library of Congress.

13. Ibid.

14. Andrew O'Shaughnessy, *An Empire Divided: The American Revolution and the British Caribbean* (Philadelphia: University of Pennsylvania Press, 2000).

15. Eric Foner, *Tom Paine and Revolutionary America*, 2nd ed. (New York: Oxford University Press, 2005), 6–7. Jason Sharples, *The World That Fear Made: Slave Revolts and Conspiracy Scares in Early America* (Philadelphia: University of Pennsylvania Press, 2020).

16. Sophia Rosenfeld, *Common Sense: A Political History* (Cambridge: Harvard University Press, 2011); Bruce Kuklick, *A History of Philosophy in America, 1720–2000* (New York: Oxford University Press, 2001).

17. For doubts about Paine's authorship of "African Slavery in America," see James V. Lynch, "The Limits of Revolutionary Radicalism: Tom Paine and Slavery," *PMHB* 123, no. 3 (July 1999): 177–199.

18. Thomas Paine, "A Serious Thought," *Pennsylvania Magazine*, October 18, 1775.

19. Simon Newman and Peter S. Onuf, *Paine and Jefferson in the Age of Revolutions* (Charlottesville: University of Virginia Press, 2013).

20. Lynch, "Limits of Revolutionary Radicalism."

21. Nell Irvin Painter, "Why White People Are Called 'Caucasian,'" Proceedings of the Fifth Annual Gilder Lehrman Center International Conference, Yale University, November 7–8, 2003, https://glc.yale.edu/sites/default/files/files/events/race/Painter.pdf; Raj Bopal, "The Beautiful Skull and Blumenbach's Errors: The Birth of the Scientific Concept of Race," *British Medical Journal* 335, no. 7633 (December 2007), 1308–1309, http://www.bmj.com/content/335/7633/1308; Stephen Jay Gould, "The Geometer of Race," *Discover Magazine*, November 1, 1994.

22. Ruth Bodin, "'Liberty Further Extended': A 1776 Antislavery Manuscript by Lemuel Haynes," *WMQ* 40, no. 1 (1983): 85–105. See also Richard Newman, ed., *Black Preacher to White America: The Collected Writings of Lemuel Haynes, 1774–1833* (Brooklyn, N.Y.: Carlson Publishing, 1989); John Saillant, *Black Puritan, Black Republican: The Life and Thought of Lemuel Haynes, 1753–1833* (New York: Oxford University Press, 2003).

23. Alan Taylor, *The Civil War of 1812: American Citizens, British Subjects, Irish Rebels, and Indian Allies* (New York: Knopf, 2010).

24. Gary Nash, *Forging Freedom: The Formation of Philadelphia's Black Community, 1720–1840* (Cambridge, Mass.: Harvard University Press, 1988); Sarah L. H. Gronningsater, "Born Free in the Master's House: Children and Gradual Emancipation in the Early American North," in Anna Mae Duane, ed., *Child Slavery Before and After Emancipation: An Argument for Child-Centered Slavery Studies* (New York: Cambridge University Press, 2017), 123–149.

25. Christopher Brown, *Moral Capital: Foundations of British Abolitionism* (Chapel Hill: University of North Carolina Press, 2006); Eliga H. Gould, *Among the Powers of the Earth: The American Revolution and the Making of a New World Empire* (Cambridge, Mass.: Harvard University Press, 2012).

26. James Walvin, *The Zong: A Massacre, the Law, and the End of Slavery* (New Haven, Conn.: Yale University Press, 2011), esp. 140, 153–155. See also Vincent Carretta, *Equiano, the African: Biography of a Self-Made Man* (New York: Penguin, 2005), 237–238.

27. Ian Baucom, *Specters of the Atlantic: Finance Capital, Slavery, and the Philosophy of History* (Durham, N.C.: Duke University Press, 2005).

28. "Mr. Burke's speech on the 1st December 1783 upon the question for the Speaker's leaving the chair, in order for the House to resolve itself into a committee on Mr. Fox's East India Bill," (London,

1784) Oxford Text Archive, http://hdl.handle.net/20.500.12024/K040908.000; see Frederick Whelan, *Edmund Burke and India: Political Morality and Empires* (Pittsburgh: University of Pittsburgh Press, 1996), 279–303; Sudipta Sen, *Distant Sovereignty: National Imperialism and the Origins of British India* (New York: Routledge, 2002), 5, 11–12, 38.

29. Brown, *Moral Capital*, 371.

30. The pamphlet, often misattributed to Benezet, was coauthored by Dillwyn, by then living in England, and Lloyd, and published by the Quaker printer James Phillips. Brown, *Moral Capital*, 366; Seymour Drescher, *Capitalism and Antislavery: British Mobilization in Comparative Perspective* (New York: Oxford University Press, 1987), 62–65; Judith Jennings, *The Business of Abolishing the British Slave Trade, 1783–1807* (New York: Routledge, 1997), 32n20. See also Patrick C. Lipscomb III and Edward C. Milligan, "A Note on the Authorship of *The Case of Our Fellow Creatures*," *Quaker History* 55, no. 1 (Spring 1966): 47–51. They dispute the attribution of *Case of Our Fellow Creatures* to Benezet, a judgment affirmed by Jennings.

31. *The Case of Our Fellow Creatures, The Oppressed Africans, Respectfully Recommended to the Serious Consideration of the Legislature of Great-Britain, by the people Called Quakers* (London, 1783).

32. Quaker Anti-Slavery Petition, 1783, Bill of Rights Institute, https://billofrightsinstitute.org/activities/quaker-anti-slavery-petition-1783; David Brion Davis, *The Problem of Slavery in the Age of Revolution, 1770–1823* (Ithaca, N.Y.: Cornell University Press, 1975), 218–219.

33. Brown, *Moral Capital*, 366–370, 375–376. Suman Seth, *Difference and Disease: Medicine, Race, and the Eighteenth-Century British Empire* (New York: Cambridge University Press, 2018), 259.

34. Ramsay, *Essay on the Treatment and Conversion of African Slaves* (London, 1784); Ramsay, *Inquiry into the Effects of putting a stop to the African Slave Trade* (London, 1784); *London Times*, March 8, 1788, quoted in Brown, *Moral Capital*, 371.

35. Katherine Paugh, *The Politics of Reproduction: Race, Medicine, and Fertility in the Age of Abolition* (Oxford, U.K.: Oxford University Press, 2017); Seth, *Difference and Disease*, 251; Trevor G. Burnard and John D. Garrigus, *The Plantation Machine: Atlantic Capitalism in French Saint-Domingue and British Jamaica* (Philadelphia: University of Pennsylvania Press, 2016); Richard Sheridan, *Doctors and Slaves: A Medical and Demographic History of the British West Indies, 1680–1834* (New York: Cambridge University Press, 1985).

36. Brown, *Moral Capital*, 328, 386.

37. David Waldstreicher, *Slavery's Constitution: From Revolution to Ratification* (New York: Hill and Wang, 2010), 103; Molly Farrell, *Counting Bodies: Population in Colonial American Writing* (New York: Oxford University Press, 2016), 70–71, 73.

38. Walvin, *Zong*, 189–190; Jennings, *Business of Abolishing the British Slave Trade.*

39. Manisha Sinha, *The Slave's Cause: A History of Abolition* (New Haven, Conn.: Yale University Press, 2016), 98–99; Jacqueline Francis, "The *Brooks* Slave Ship Icon: A 'Universal Symbol'?," *Slavery and Abolition* 30, no. 2 (2009): 327–338. Eric Herschthal, *The Science of Abolition: How Slaveholders Became the Enemies of Progress* (New Haven, Conn.: Yale University Press), 76–80.

40. Sasha Turner, "Home-Grown Slaves: Women, Reproduction, and the Abolition of the Slave Trade, Jamaica, 1788–1807," *Journal of Women's History* 23, no. 3 (2011): 39–62. Anthony Page, "Rational Dissent, Enlightenment, and Abolition of the British Slave Trade," *Historical Journal* 54, no. 3 (2011): 741–772; Laura Brace, "Fallacies of Hope: Contesting Narratives of Slavery in Turner's *Slave Ship*," *Atlantic Studies* 17, no. 4 (October 2020): 441–461; Stephanie Smallwood, *Saltwater Slavery: A Middle Passage from Africa to American Diaspora* (Cambridge, Mass.: Harvard University Press, 2008).

41. "Description of a slave ship" (London, 1786), Beinecke Rare Book and Manuscript Library, http://brbl-dl.library.yale.edu/vufind/Record/3439779; Marcus Wood, *Blind Memory: Visual Representations of Slavery in England and America, 1780–1865* (Manchester: Manchester University Press, 2000), esp. 16–17. Francis, "The *Brooks* Slave Ship Icon."

42. Davis, *Age of Revolution*, 95–100, 138–140; Marcel Dorigny and Bernard Gainot, *La Société des Amis des Noirs* (Paris: Editions UNESCO, 1998); David Geggus, "Racial Equality, Slavery, and Colonial Secession During the Constituent Assembly," *American Historical Review* 94, no. 5

(December 1989): 1290–1308. Robin Blackburn, *Overthrow of Colonial Slavery, 1776–1848* (London: Verso, 1988),169–172; J. R. Oldfield, *Transatlantic Abolitionism in the Age of Revolution: An International History of Anti-slavery, c. 1787–1820* (New York: Cambridge University Press, 2013), 89–93. Lawrence C. Jennings, *French Anti-slavery: The Movement for the Abolition of Slavery in France, 1802–1848* (New York: Cambridge University Press, 2000).

43. The most persuasive case for Equiano's birth in South Carolina is Carretta, *Equiano, the African*, 1–16. But see "Questioning Equiano" in *Equiano's World*, http://equianosworld.org.

44. Kirsten Sword, "Remembering Dinah Nevil: Strategic Deceptions in Eighteenth-Century Antislavery," *JAH* 97, no. 2 (September 2010): 315–343.

45. George Boulukos, "Capitalism and Slavery, Once Again with Feeling," in Stephen Ahern, ed., *Affect and Abolition in the Anglo-Atlantic, 1770–1830* (Surrey, England: Ashgate, 2013), 23–44. For two versions of Wilberforce's 1789 speech, see Brycchan Carey, "Wilberforce's 1789 Abolition Speech," https://brycchancarey.com/abolition/wilberforce2.htm

46. William H. Sewell Jr., "Historical Events as Transformations of Structure: Inventing Revolution at the Bastille," *Theory and Society* 25, no. 6 (December 1996): 841–881. Micah Alpaugh, "A Self-Defining '*Bourgeoisie*' in the Early French Revolution: The *Milice Bourgeoise*, the Bastille Days of 1789, and Their Aftermath," *Journal of Social History* 47, no. 3 (Spring 2014): 696–720.

47. Susan Dunn, *Sister Revolutions: American Light, French Lightening* (New York: Faber and Faber, 1999); Jefferson, *Notes on the State of Virginia* (Paris, 1785; London, 1787; Philadelphia, 1788); Winthrop Jordan, *White over Black: American Attitudes Toward the Negro, 1550–1812* (Chapel Hill: University of North Carolina Press, 1968); Bruce Dain, *A Hideous Monster of the Mind: American Race Theory in the Early Republic* (Cambridge, Mass.: Harvard University Press, 2002). David Walker, *Appeal to the Coloured Citizens of the United States* (Boston, 1829).

48. "Declaration of the Rights of Man and Citizen," in Lynn Hunt, ed., *The French Revolution and Human Rights: A Brief Documentary History* (New York: Bedford, 1996).

49. Edmund Burke, *Reflections on the Revolution in France* (London, 1790), 55–56.

50. For the uses of "common sense" in English, Scottish, French, and North American political arguments, see Rosenfeld, *Common Sense*. See also Mary Wollstonecraft, *A Vindication of the Rights of Men* (London, 1790), 9–13.

51. Wollstonecraft, *Vindication of the Rights of Men*, 19–20.

52. Wollstonecraft, *Vindication of the Rights of Men*, 15, 30.

53. Denver Brunsman, *The Evil Necessity: British Naval Impressment in the Eighteenth-Century Atlantic World* (Charlottesville: University of Virginia, 2013), esp. 1–10.

54. Alan Atkinson, "The Free-Born Englishman Transported: Convict Rights as a Measure of Eighteenth-Century Empire," *Past and Present* 144, no. 1 (August 1994): 88–115.

55. A. Roger Ekirch, *Bound for America: The Transportation of British Convicts to the Colonies, 1718–1775* (New York: Oxford University Press, 1987); Gwenda Morgan and Peter Rushton, *Eighteenth-Century Criminal Transportation: The Formation of the Criminal Atlantic* (New York: Palgrave Macmillan, 2004); Emma Christopher, *A Merciless Place: The Fate of Britain's Convicts After the American Revolution* (New York: Oxford University Press, 2010); Cassandra Pybus, "Bound for Botany Bay: John Martin's Voyage to Australia," in Emma Christopher, Cassandra Pybus, and Marcus Rediker, eds., *Many Middle Passages: Forced Migration and the Making of the Atlantic World* (Berkeley: University of California Press, 2007), 92–108; Emma Christopher, "'The Slave Trade Is Merciful Compared to [This]': Slave Traders, Convict Transportation, and the Abolitionists," in Christopher, Pybus, and Rediker, *Many Middle Passages*, 109–128. Robert Hughes, *The Fatal Shore: The Epic of Australia's Founding* (New York: Random House, 1988).

56. Moira Ferguson, "Mary Wollstonecraft and the Problematic of Slavery," *Feminist Review* 42, no. 1 (Autumn 1992): 82–102.

57. Mary Wollstonecraft, review of Gustavus Vassa, *Analytical Review*, May 1789.

58. Wollstonecraft, *Vindication of the Rights of Men*, 31, 51–52, 21.

59. Linda Colley, *Captives: Britain, Empire, and the World, 1600–1850* (New York: Random House, 2002).

60. Wollstonecraft, *Vindication of the Rights of Men*, 22.

61. Wollstonecraft, *Vindication of the Rights of Men*, 16, 18.

62. Wollstonecraft, *Vindication of the Rights of Men*, 30, 40, 46.

63. G. C. Parsons, *Reflections of the Slave Trade with Remarks on its Policy of Abolition* (London: 1791), "Appendix," 56.

64. Seymour Drescher, "Public Opinion and Parliament in the Abolition of the British Slave Trade," *Parliamentary History* 26, no. S1 (June 2010): 42–65.

65. Charlotte Sussman, *Consuming Anxieties: Consumer Protest, Gender, and British Slavery, 1713–1833* (Stanford, Calif.: Stanford University Press, 2000), 110–129; Clare Midgley, *Women Against Slavery: The British Campaigns, 1780–1870* (New York: Routledge, 1992); Clare Midgley, "The Dissenting Voice of Elizabeth Heyrick," and Timothy Whelan, "Martha Gurney and the Anti-Slave Trade Movement, 1788–94," both in Elizabeth J. Clapp and Julie Roy Jeffrey, eds., *Women, Dissent, and Antislavery in Britain and America, 1790–1865* (New York: Oxford University Press, 2011), 44–65, 88–110. Whelan (46) notes that Gurney's family was distantly related to the Quaker Gurneys of Norwich, who would subsequently play a prominent role in British abolitionism. See also Anna Vaughan Kett, "'Without the Consumers of Slave Produce There Would Be No Slaves,'" in Brycchan Carey and Geoffrey Plank, eds., *Quakers and Abolition* (Urbana: University of Illinois Press, 2014), 56–72; Carol Faulkner, "The Root of the Evil: Free Produce and Radical Antislavery, 1820–1860," *Journal of the Early Republic* 27, no. 3 (Fall 2007): 377–405. For the special resonance of sugar and sugar work with women, see Kim Hall, "Culinary Spaces, Colonial Spaces: The Gendering of Sugar in the Seventeenth Century," in Valerie Traub, ed., *Feminist Readings of Early Modern Culture: Emerging Subjects* (New York: Cambridge University Press, 1996), 168–190.

66. Sussman, *Consuming Anxieties*, 114–115.

67. Christopher, "'The Slave Trade Is Merciful'"; Michael Flynn, *The Second Fleet: Britain's Grim Convict Armada of 1790* (Sydney: Library of Australian History, 1993).

68. Mary Wollstonecraft, *Vindication of the Rights of Woman*, ed. Miriam Kramnick (New York: Penguin, 1978), 123–124, 109.

69. Wollstonecraft introduced a notion of women's essential nature to Enlightenment thought by focusing on the condition of women in the socioeconomically "natural" state of the middle class. *Vindication of the Rights of Woman*, 81.

70. Wollstonecraft, *Vindication of the Rights of Woman*, 80, 188. Ruth Bernard Yeazell, *Harems of the Mind: Passages of Western Art and Literature* (New Haven, Conn.: Yale University Press, 2000), 74–83; Kellie Holzer, "Lady Montagu's Smokers' Pastils and *The Graphic*: Advertising the Harem in the Home," in Deirdre H. McMahon and Janet C. Myers, eds., *The Objects and Textures of Everyday Life in Imperial Britain* (New York: Routledge, 2016), 207–232; Midgley, *Women Against Slavery*, 26–27; Clare Midgley, *Feminism and Empire: Women Activists in Imperial Britain, 1790–1865* (London: Routledge, 2007), 17–28.

71. Wollstonecraft's most common use of the woman-slave analogy presumed a domestic context in which the slavery was based on a subordinate's need to please another (195), a focus reflected in her dedication's warning against women's domestic confinement and exclusion from civil and political rights (87–88).

72. Ferguson, "Mary Wollstonecraft and the Problematic of Slavery." Ferguson's insightful analysis of Wollstonecraft's antislavery politics emphasizes the novelty of Wollstonecraft's inclusion of African (what Ferguson calls "colonial") slavery in her use of the woman-slave analogy in the *Vindication of the Rights of Woman*. Ferguson counts eighty references to slavery in the second *Vindication* compared to only five in the first. Less than a dozen of the eighty, however, clearly refer to African slavery. Clare Midgley, "British Abolition and Feminism in Transatlantic Perspective," in Kathryn Kish Sklar and James Brewer Stewart, eds., *Women's Rights and Transatlantic Antislavery in the Era of Emancipation* (New Haven, Conn.: Yale University Press, 2007), 121–141.

73. Wollstonecraft, *Vindication of the Rights of Woman*, 311, 257. Midgley, *Women Against Slavery*, 26–27; Midgley, *Feminism and Empire*, 17–28.

74. Wollstonecraft, *Vindication of the Rights of Woman*, 144–145.

75. Wollstonecraft, *Vindication of the Rights of Woman*, 310–311.

76. Mary Wollstonecraft, review of Gustavus Vassa, *Analytical Review*, May 1789; Wollstonecraft, *A Vindication of the Rights of Woman*, chapter 4. Jennifer L. Morgan, *Laboring Women: Reproduction and Gender in New World Slavery* (Philadelphia: University of Pennsylvania Press, 2004); Barbara Bush, *Slave Women in Caribbean Society, 1650–1838* (Bloomington: Indiana University Press, 1990); Trevor G. Burnard, *Mastery, Tyranny, and Desire: Thomas Thistlewood and His Slaves in the Anglo-Jamaican World* (Chapel Hill: University of North Carolina Press, 2004).

Chapter 3

1. David Brion Davis, *The Problem of Slavery in the Age of Revolution, 1770–1823* (Ithaca, N.Y.: Cornell University Press, 1975), esp. 196–197; James H. Kettner, "Persons or Property? The Pleasants Slaves in the Virginia Courts, 1792–1799," in Ronald Hoffman and Peter J. Albert, eds., *Launching the "Extended Republic": The Federalist Era* (Charlottesville: University of Virginia Press, 1996), 136–155; John Sassi, "Communications," *WMQ*, 3rd ser., 69, no. 1 (January 2012): 196–201; Kenneth Carroll, "Robert Pleasants on Quakerism: "Some Account of the First Settlement of Friends in Virginia," *VMHB* 86, no. 1 (1978): 14; Eva Sheppard Wolf, *Race and Liberty in the New Nation: Emancipation in Virginia from the Revolution to Nat Turner's Rebellion* (Baton Rouge: Louisiana State University Press, 2006); William Fernandez Hardin, "Litigating the Lash: Quaker Emancipator Robert Pleasants, the Law of Slavery, and the Meaning of Manumission in Early and Revolutionary Virginia" (PhD diss., Vanderbilt University, 2013); and William Fernandez Hardin, "'This Unpleasant Business': Slavery, Law, and the Pleasants Family in Post-revolutionary Virginia," *VMHB* 125, no. 3 (2017): 211–245. See also Andrew Levy, *The First Emancipator: The Forgotten Story of Robert Carter, the Founding Father Who Freed His Slaves* (New York: Random House, 2005); Paul Finkelman, *Slavery and the Founders: Race and Liberty in the Age of Jefferson*, 3rd ed (New York: Routledge, 2014); Richard R. Beeman, *The Old Dominion and the New Nation, 1788–1801* (Lexington: University Press of Kentucky, 1972); Robert McColley, *Slavery and Jeffersonian Virginia* (Urbana: University of Illinois Press, 1964); Winthrop Jordan, *White over Black: American Attitudes Toward the Negro, 1550–1812* (Chapel Hill: University of North Carolina Press, 1968); Jennifer L. Morgan, *Reckoning with Slavery: Gender, Kinship, and Capitalism in the Early Modern Black Atlantic* (Durham, N.C.: Duke University Press, 2021).

2. Lynn Hunt, *Inventing Human Rights: A History* (New York: W. W. Norton, 2007); Patricia Grimshaw, Katie Holmes, and Marilyn Lake, eds., *Women's Rights and Human Rights: International Historical Perspectives* (New York: Palgrave, 2001); Thomas Laqueur, "Mourning, Pity, and the Work of the Narrative," in R. A. Wilson and R. D. Brown, eds., *Humanitarianism and Suffering: The Mobilization of Empathy* (New York: Cambridge University Press, 2009); Samuel Moyn, *The Last Utopia: Human Rights and History* (Cambridge, Mass.: Harvard University Press, 2010); Manisha Sinha, *The Slave's Cause: A History of Abolition* (New Haven, Conn.: Yale University Press, 2016); Keith Ewing, "Human Rights," in Peter Cane and Mark Tushnet, eds., *The Oxford Handbook of Legal Studies* (Oxford, U.K.: Oxford University Press, 2003), 298–324. See also David Brion Davis, "The Perils of Doing History by Ahistorical Abstraction," in Thomas Bender, ed., *The Antislavery Debate: Capitalism and Abolitionism as a Problem in Historical Interpretation* (Berkeley: University of California Press, 1992), 290–309. Elizabeth B. Clark, "'Sacred Rights of the Weak': Pain, Sympathy, and the Culture of Individual Rights in Antebellum America," *JAH* 82, no. 2 (1995): 463–493, especially 471, 492.

3. Edmund Morgan, *American Slavery, American Freedom: The Ordeal of Colonial Virginia* (New York: W. W. Norton, 1975), 215–217. For the legal action taken against John I for being a Quaker, see *Valentine Papers*, 2:1069; Stephen Beauregard Weeks, *Southern Quakers and Slavery: A Study in Institutional History* (Baltimore: Johns Hopkins Press, 1896). Official persecution of Quakers did not end until James II's 1687 Liberty of Conscience Act and William and Mary's 1689 Act of Toleration. Lorena S. Walsh, *Motives of Honor, Pleasure, and Profit: Plantation Management in the Colonial*

Chesapeake, 1607–1763 (Chapel Hill: University of North Carolina Press, 2010), for strategic diversification of Quaker household economies.

4. *Valentine Papers*, 2:1069.

5. *Valentine Papers*, 2:1069; Jacob M. Price and Paul G. E. Clemens, "A Revolution of Scale in Overseas Trade: British Firms in the Chesapeake Trade, 1675–1775," *Journal of Economic History* 47, no. 1 (1987): 14–37. Paggen was one of the leaders of the separate trader movement opposed to the Royal African Company's monopoly; see William A. Pettigrew, *Freedom's Debt: The Royal African Company and the Politics of the Atlantic Slave Trade, 1672–1752* (Chapel Hill: University of North Carolina Press, 2013), 62–73. See also Walsh, *Motives of Honor*, 217–222, 549–551.

6. Anthony S. Parent Jr., *Foul Means: The Formation of a Slave Society in Virginia, 1660–1740* (Chapel Hill: University of North Carolina Press, 2003), 43–45; C. Ray Keim, "Primogeniture and Entail in Colonial Virginia," *WMQ*, 3rd ser., 25, no. 4 (1968): 545–586; Allan Kulikoff, *Tobacco and Slaves: The Development of Southern Cultures in the Chesapeake, 1680–1800* (Chapel Hill: University of North Carolina Press, 1986), 45–54.

7. Lois Carr, Lorena Walsh, and Russell Menard, *Robert Cole's World: Agriculture and Society in Early Maryland* (Chapel Hill: University of North Carolina Press, 1991); Walsh, *Motives of Honor*, 468–469, 549–551; Joseph Galloway, clerk of the West River, Maryland Meeting, March 17, 1749, to John Pleasants III, PFP.

8. Will of Jane Larcome Tucker Pleasants, *Valentine Papers*, 2:1074–1077.

9. David Brion Davis, *The Problem of Slavery in Western Culture* (Ithaca, N.Y.: Cornell University Press, 1966); Thomas Drake, *Quakers and Slavery in America* (New Haven, Conn.: Yale University Press, 1965); Jack D. Marietta, *The Reformation of American Quakerism, 1748–1783* (Philadelphia: University of Pennsylvania Press, 1984); Jean Soderlund, *Quakers and Slavery: A Divided Spirit* (Princeton, N.J.: Princeton University Press, 1985); Richard S. Newman, *The Transformation of American Abolitionism: Fighting Slavery in the Early Republic* (Chapel Hill: University of North Carolina Press, 2002).

10. Ian Baucom, *Specters of the Atlantic: Finance Capital, Slavery, and the Philosophy of History* (Durham, N.C.: Duke University Press, 2005); Thomas L. Haskell, "Capitalism and the Origins of Humanitarian Sensibility, Parts 1 and 2," in Bender, *The Antislavery Debate*.

11. John II listed as consignee of Paggan and Company, *Valentine Papers*, 2:1081.

12. Walsh, *Motives of Honor*, 549–551; Will of Jane Larcome Tucker Pleasants, *Valentine Papers*, 2:1077; John Pleasants II estate inventory, *Valentine Papers*, 2: 1089.

13. John Pleasants II estate inventory, *Valentine Papers*, 2:1087–1091; Walsh, *Motives of Honor*, 412–413, 422–423.

14. John Pleasants III to Robert Pleasants, December 9, 1745, PFP. See J. William Frost, *The Quaker Family in Colonial America* (New York: St. Martin's Press, 1973), 143–144, 204; and Frederick B. Tolles, *Meeting House and Counting House: The Quaker Merchants of Colonial Philadelphia, 1682–1763* (Chapel Hill: University of North Carolina Press, 1948).

15. Ann Smart Martin, *Buying into the World of Goods: Early Consumers in Backcountry Virginia* (Baltimore: Johns Hopkins University Press, 2008).

16. Will of John Pleasants III, 1771; the original in PFP is missing the first two pages; transcript of the entire will in *Valentine Papers*, 2:1116–1128.

17. In 1765, Langley mortgaged slaves and 375 acres of land to his agent John Hunt, who was Isaac Pemberton's insurance agent and Robert Pleasants's creditor. Hunt's agent in Virginia, Samuel Gordon, subsequently devised these slaves to John III and another man, where they remained at the time of John III's death; Hunt and Langley bond, October 21, 1765. See also Micajah Crew and Robert Crew, executors of Robert Pleasants, July 8, 1811; all in MCP. For Hunt's role in Quaker financial networks, see Theodore Thayer, *Israel Pemberton, King of the Quakers* (Philadelphia: Historical Society of Pennsylvania, 1943), 19, 39, for Robert's debt to Hunt of twenty thousand pounds sterling.

18. Kettner, "Persons or Property?"

19. Walsh, *Motives of Honor*, notes the decline in West Africans purchased by the largest Chesapeake planters along the Rappahannock River (474–475) and Tidewater (402–403) and the reliance

on births to fill labor and inheritance needs. See also Philip D. Morgan, *Slave Counterpoint: Black Culture in the Eighteenth-Century Chesapeake and Lowcountry* (Chapel Hill: University of North Carolina Press, 1998), 498–515.

20. Kathleen Brown, *Good Wives, Nasty Wenches, and Anxious Patriarchs: Gender, Race, and Power in Colonial Virginia* (Chapel Hill: University of North Carolina Press, 1996).

21. Will of John Pleasants III, 1771, original in PFP; transcript in *Valentine Papers*, 2:1116–1128.

22. Morgan, *Slave Counterpoint*, 515–518.

23. Extracts from Philadelphia Yearly Meeting Minutes, held in Philadelphia, July 20, 1735, HC-QSC. See Frost, *Quaker Family*, 143–144, 204.

24. Henrico Meeting Minutes, *Valentine Papers*, 2:1200. Many wealthy Quaker merchants assisted their sons' entrance into business by sending them to England, Philadelphia, and the Caribbean, where they were encouraged to connect with Quaker merchants, many of whom were involved in the slave trade. See Frost, *Quaker Family*, 134, 143–144, 204.

25. Thayer, *Israel Pemberton*, 1–21, 39; Thomas Doerflinger, *A Vigorous Spirit of Enterprise: Merchants and Economic Development in Revolutionary Philadelphia* (Chapel Hill: University of North Carolina Press, 1986), 57. Mary Pemberton to Robert Pleasants, Philadelphia, June 14, 1754, PFP. Israel Pleasants to Robert Pleasants, June 19, 1756, PFP. Robert's brother Samuel, who moved to Philadelphia in 1762, later married Mary Pemberton, Israel Jr.'s daughter. Robert sent his son Robert Jr. to Philadelphia in 1771 for education. Robert Pleasants to son, November 16, 1771, *WMQ* 1, no. 2 (April 1921): 109; March 8, 1772, *WMQ* 2, no. 4 (October 1922): 259.

26. "List of the members of the APS, held at Philadelphia, for Promoting Useful Knowledge," *American Philosophical Society* (January 17, 1890); John Smith of Philadelphia to Robert Pleasants; February 30?, 1750, November 26, 1752, PFP. See also Tolles, *Meeting House and Counting House*, 223.

27. Josiah Webster to Robert Pleasants, May 10, 1749; Josiah Webster to Robert Pleasants, May 15, 1759, both in PFP.

28. John Woolman, *The Journal of John Woolman* (Cambridge, Mass.: Harvard Classics, 1909), 99–110; Thomas Slaughter, *The Beautiful Soul of John Woolman, Apostle of Abolition* (New York: Hill and Wang, 2008), 130–132; Marietta, *Reformation of American Quakerism*, 97–128.

29. Philadelphia Yearly Meeting, extracts from 1758 meeting, Mss. Coll. 970, HCQSC. See also Soderlund, *Quakers and Slavery*, 87.

30. Ellen Ross, "'Liberation Is Coming Soon': The Radical Reformation of Joshua Evans (1731–1798)," in Brycchan Carey and Geoffrey Plank, eds., *Quakers and Abolition* (Urbana: University of Illinois Press, 2014), 15–28; Marietta, *Reformation of American Quakerism*, 110.

31. See, for example, October 21, 1765, slaves made over to John Pleasants, mortgaged by Robert Langley to John Hunt, PFP.

32. Stephanie Smallwood, *Saltwater Slavery: A Middle Passage from Africa to American Diaspora* (Cambridge, Mass.: Harvard University Press, 2008); Morgan, *Slave Counterpoint*; Kulikoff, *Tobacco and Slaves*, 72–75. Doug Chambers, *Murder at Montpelier: Igbo Africans in Virginia* (Jackson: University Press of Mississippi, 2005).

33. Anthony Benezet, Philadelphia, to Robert Pleasants, March 14, 1762, Robert Pleasants Letterbook, HCQSC. Weeks, *Southern Quakers and Slavery*.

34. Virginia Yearly Meeting minutes, Curles, June 17, 1766, *Valentine Papers*, 2:1235; Wolf, *Race and Liberty*, 8. Richard K. MacMaster, "Arthur Lee's 'Address on Slavery': An Aspect of Virginia's Struggle to End the Slave Trade, 1765–1774," *VMHB* 80, no. 2 (April 1972): 149.

35. His sister-in-law Mary Pemberton Pleasants wrote to console him; Samuel Pleasants, Philadelphia, to Robert Pleasants, July 20, 1763, Robert Pleasants Letterbook, HCQSC.

36. Obituary for Mary Pleasants, Robert Pleasants Letterbook, HCQSC.

37. Robert Pleasants to John Pleasants Jr. concerning marriage choice; obituary for brother John Pleasants, listed as deceased in his thirty-fourth year on July 12, 1764, both in Robert Pleasants Letterbook, HCQSC. The John Pleasants Jr. recorded as dying in June 1765 (*Valentine Papers*, 1198, 1235) was the son of Thomas Pleasants of Curles, not the son of John III. John III's son, John Pleasants Jr.,

appeared in the Virginia Quarterly Meeting records until mid-1763. He was the father of Samuel, a major legatee in his grandfather John III's will and also named in his uncle Jonathan's will as the son of John; *Valentine Papers*, 2:116–1124, 1126. See also John Pleasants Sr. and John Pleasants Jr. in Cumberland County, *Valentine Papers*, 2:960; Robert Carter Sr. and Robert Carter Jr., 1762 mortgage of 313 acres in Cumberland County, to John Pleasants Sr. and John Pleasants Jr., Robert Pleasants Letterbook, Swem; Robert Pleasants to Samuel Pleasants, March 23, 1772, debt due to our Brother's estate, in reference to Cumberland County, *WMQ* 2, no. 4 (October 1922): 261.

38. MacMaster, "Arthur Lee's 'Address on Slavery.'"

39. Wolf, *Race and Liberty*, 12. MacMaster, "Arthur Lee's 'Address on Slavery,'" 144.

40. MacMaster, "Arthur Lee's 'Address on Slavery,'" 154.

41. MacMaster, "Arthur Lee's 'Address on Slavery,'" 153–156. Lee's public declarations on human equality (which there are reasons to interpret as politically strategic and expedient), did little to improve the reputations of white southern enslavers, who became the topic of lampoon for northern abolitionists. See *Pennsylvania Chronicle*, March 6–13, 1769, 3, no. 7, p. 52.

42. MacMaster, "Arthur Lee's 'Address on Slavery,'" 149; T. H. Breen, *Tobacco and Slavery: The Mentality of the Great Tidewater Planters on the Eve of Revolution* (Princeton, N.J.: Princeton University Press, 1985).

43. MacMaster, "Arthur Lee's 'Address on Slavery,'" 148–149; Woody Holton, *Forced Founders: Indians, Debtors, Slaves, and the Making of the American Revolution in Virginia* (Chapel Hill: University of North Carolina Press, 1999), 70–72, 104–105. Robert Pleasants to Colonel Richard Bland, March 15, 1770, Robert Pleasants Letterbook, HCQSC.

44. Will of John Pleasants III, 1771, original missing first two pages in PFP, transcript in *Valentine Papers*, 2:1116–1128.

45. Sarah L. H. Gronningsater, "Born Free in the Master's House: Children and Gradual Emancipation in the Early American North," in Anna Mae Duane, ed., *Child Slavery Before and After Emancipation: An Argument for Child-Centered Slavery Studies* (New York: Cambridge University Press, 2017), 123–149. There is no evidence from the Pleasants family that John III drew on Quaker uses of child apprenticeship in stipulating a term of service before emancipation.

46. Will of John Pleasants III, 1771, original missing first two pages in PFP, transcript in *Valentine Papers*, 2:1116–1128.

47. Kettner, "Persons or Property?," 141.

48. "1772–1773 Accts of Robert Pleasants Mills at Fine Creek Included to Samuel Pleasants for the hire of Frank"; 1773 Benjamin Russell & Co to the estate of John Pleasants; hire of Saunders and Sal; all in PFP.

49. Robert Pleasants Ledger Book, Swem. The British mercantile firms included Mean and Coldwell, Tredway and Bailey, James David, Benjamin Horrocks, Farrell and Jones, Joseph Wharton, and John and Robert Barclay. Robert shipped bulk wheat and barley flour, hams, hominy, rum, and other goods to his brother Samuel. See Robert Pleasants to Samuel Pleasants, November 16, 1771, *WMQ* 1, no. 2 (April 1921): 111; November 27, 1771, *WMQ* 2, no. 4 (October 1922): 257–258; March 8, 1772, *WMQ* 2, no. 4 (October 1922), 260; May 10, 1772, *WMQ* 2, no. 4 (October 1922): 265; and August 3, 1772, *WMQ* 2, no. 4 (October 1922): 268–270.

50. Robert Pleasants to Anthony Benezet, February 22, 1774, *WMQ* 1, no. 2 (April 1921): 108. MacMaster, "Arthur Lee's 'Address on Slavery,'" 150–152; Bruce A. Ragsdale, *A Planter's Republic: The Search for Economic Independence in Revolutionary Virginia* (Madison: University of Wisconsin Press, 1996), 129–135; see Holton, *Forced Founders*, 71–73, for the Lee brothers' communication about slave consignments, and 104–105, for Richard Lee's effort to purchase enslaved people for his brother. During this moment of increasing tensions with Britain, the prolific nature of Robert's family prompted him to biopolitical reflections. In correspondence with Charles Pleasants, an Irish cousin, in 1774, Pleasants noted that the Virginia Pleasants family, by which term he meant only his white kin, vastly outnumbered their Irish counterparts. Robert Pleasants to Charles Pleasants, 1774, Robert Pleasants Letterbook, HCQSC.

51. Petition and copy from Anthony Benezet, 1773, urging testimony to Parliament, PFP Brock.

52. Robert Pleasants to friend, February 22, 1774, PFP; Robert Pleasants to Anthony Benezet, August 20, 1774; Robert Pleasants to William Fisher, August 20, 1774; both in *WMQ* 1, no. 2 (April 1921): 107–108.

53. James Pemberton to Robert Pleasants, 1775, PFP.

54. Robert Bolling to Robert Pleasants November 29, 1774, and February 26, 1775, PFP. Robert Pleasants to Robert Bolling, Buckingham, England, January 10, 1775, Robert Pleasants Letterbook, HCQSC.

55. Benjamin Quarles, *The Negro in the American Revolution* (Chapel Hill: University of North Carolina Press, 1961); Sylvia Frey, *Water from the Rock: Black Resistance in a Revolutionary Age* (Princeton, N.J.: Princeton University Press, 1991); Holton, *Forced Founders*; Alan Taylor, *The Internal Enemy: Slavery and War in Virginia* (New York: W. W. Norton, 2013); Wolf, *Race and Liberty*, 15.

56. *Valentine Papers*, 2:1126, and will of Jonathan Pleasants, 1130–1133; Robert Pleasants to Samuel Pleasants, July 8, 1776, Robert Pleasants Letterbook, HCQSC; Samuel Pleasants to Robert Pleasants, August 15, 1776, PFP.

57. Wolf, *Race and Liberty*, 1.

58. William Blakey to Robert Pleasants, December 14, 1776, PFP.

59. The Memorial of Robert Pleasants, n.d., PFP; Davis, *Age of Revolution*, 197, for "terrorists." "To the Printer," in Augustine Davies, ed., *Virginia Independent Chronicle*, July 7, 1790, and Robert Pleasants to Joseph Lewis, churchwarden, July 29, 1778, both in Robert Pleasants Letterbook, HCQSC.

60. The Memorial of Robert Pleasants, n.d., PFP.

61. Israel Pemberton to Robert Pleasants, January 13, 1777, Robert Pleasants Letterbook, HCQSC.

62. Carroll, "Robert Pleasants on Quakerism," 14; Wolf, *Race and Liberty*, 32; Hardin, "Litigating the Lash," 91; Robert Pleasants to Patrick Henry, March 28, 1777, Robert Pleasants Letterbook, Swem; Kettner, "Persons or Property?," 141.

63. Robert Pleasants to Israel Pemberton, April 21, 1777, Robert Pleasants Letterbook, HCQSC.

64. "To George Washington from Mary Pemberton, 31 March 1778," *Founders Online*, National Archives, http://founders.archives.gov/documents/Washington/03-14-02-0347. (Original source: *The Papers of George Washington, Revolutionary War Series*, vol. 14, *1 March 1778–30 April 1778*, ed. David R. Hoth (Charlottesville: University of Virginia Press, 2004) 371–372.)

65. See Thomas Nicholson to Robert Pleasants, North Carolina, November 1778, Robert Pleasants Letterbook, HCQSC.

66. Thomas D. Morris, *Free Men All: The Personal Liberty Laws of the North, 1780–1861* (Baltimore: Johns Hopkins University Press, 1974), 5–6; Holton, *Forced Founders*, 215; Wolf, *Race and Liberty*; Thomas Pleasants to Thomas Jefferson, Raleigh, October 24, 1785, on the need to protect tobacco production and Virginia merchants from Britain and France, *Founders Online*, National Archives. In 1781 Thomas Pleasants Jr. (1737–1804) planter and merchant of Goochland County, served as the state's commercial representative to the national government. January 17, 1793, and with Zachariah Alvis, accounts 1783–1792, PFP Brock.

67. Robert Pleasants to General Arnold, January 30, 1781, Robert Pleasants Letterbook, Swem; Robert Pleasants to Samuel and Mary Pleasants, February 15, 1781, and Robert Pleasants Memorandum, August 14, 1781, both in Robert Pleasants Letterbook, HCQSC; Loss of slaves already manumitted, Henrico Monthly Meeting, May 15, 1782, PFP; Hardin, "Litigating the Lash," 115, 119–120.

68. For Robert's seventy-eight manumissions on August 31, 1782, see Henrico Deed Book 1, 42–43, and 37 for his manumission of three additional people from another estate. Robert might well have been behind the publication of an essay in the *Virginia Gazette and Weekly Advertiser*, May 25, 1782, Number 22, "A Friend to Liberty," by the New Jersey Quaker John Cooper. The text is identical to John Cooper's September 20, 1780, essay in the *New Jersey Gazette*. Robert made references to blood and treasure in letters to Joseph Lewis, churchwarden, and George Washington in 1785.

69. Petition, June 8, 1782, Henrico County records, VSL microfilm, a month after the passage of the Manumission Act and responding specifically to the pretense of "putting slaves free"; Wolf,

Race and Liberty, 112. Signatory Robert Baine had petitioned for recompense for goods requisitioned during the war and to allege theft by slaves who were subsequently executed; John Mayo, John Mayo Jr., Thomas Prosser, whose enslaved laborer Gabriel later planned a rebellion, and [?] Foushee, presumably P. Foushee, and others had previously petitioned; 1779 petition to General Assembly Henrico County Records, VSL microfilm. A separate group of Henrico petitioners urged a narrow interpretation of state citizenship to exclude traitors and those who had not fought in the war, an attack on Quaker abolitionists but perhaps also a reference to freedmen; Henrico County petition, June 1783, Henrico County Records LV microfilm.

70. Pleasants family manumissions, July 4, 1781; November 9, 1781, both in PFP.

71. Robert Pleasants to Miriam Pleasants, January 14, 1784, PFP.

72. Robert Pleasants to Francis Irby, November 22, 1784, Robert Pleasants Letterbook, HCQSC. By 1786, Robert's leadership on abolition had clearly become known across the Atlantic in English Quaker circles; see Robert Pleasants, August 15, 1786, PFP.

73. James Pemberton to James Phillips, November 18, 1784, Gilder Lehrman Collection #GLC04237.

74. Robert Pleasants to George Washington, December 11, 1785, and Robert Pleasants to John Michie, December 4, 1787, challenging the idea that a benevolent master keeps his laborers enslaved so that he can serve as their protector and guardian; both in Robert Pleasants Letterbook, HCQSC. John Dickinson, "Sentiments on What is Freedom, and what is Slavery," in Robert Bell, *Illuminations for Legislators, and for Sentimentalists* (Philadelphia, 1784).

75. Robert Pleasants to Jacob Shoemaker, April 12, 1788, Robert Pleasants Letterbook, HCQSC.

76. James Pemberton to Robert Pleasants, August 14, 1788; November 16, 1789; February 28, 1790; April 20, 1790; and May 9, 1790, all in PFP. The petitions to Congress in 1790 called for an end to the slave trade and the abolition of slavery. Pemberton feared that concerns over the new nation's finances were impeding attention to slavery. See David Waldstreicher, *Runaway America: Benjamin Franklin, Slavery, and the American Revolution* (New York: Hill and Wang, 2004), 234–239; Newman, *Transformation of American Abolitionism*, 39–49. Robert G. Parkinson, "Manifest Signs of Passion? The First Federal Congress, Antislavery, and the Legacy of the Revolutionary War," in John Craig Hammond and Matthew Mason, eds., *Contesting Slavery: The Politics of Bondage and Freedom in the New American Nation* (Charlottesville: University of Virginia Press, 2011), 49–68; Gary B. Nash, *Warner Mifflin: Unflinching Quaker Abolitionist* (Philadelphia: University of Pennsylvania Press, 2017).

77. Robert Pleasants to Job Scott, March 9, 1790; Robert Pleasants to James Pemberton, June 19, 1790; Robert Pleasants to Samuel Bailey, July 23, 1790; all in Robert Pleasants Letterbook, HCQSC.

78. James Pemberton to Robert Pleasants, August 25, 1790; James Pemberton to Robert Pleasants, October 5, 1790, both in PFP.

79. 1783 Zachariah Alvis accounts with Thomas Pleasants for rum, corn, wheat, double soled "negro" shoes, mowing wheat and oats; see also October 7, 1790, Robert Pleasants sends tobacco to Robert Crew, London, to offset balance; 1799 Robert Pleasants accounts with Robert Pleasants and Co., wheat, sundries, flour, salt; all in PFP. See also Doerflinger, *Vigorous Spirit of Enterprise*, 290, for Robert's 1787 accounts with John Grove of Richmond and Daniel Tyson, merchant, of Philadelphia, who was involved in the James River tobacco trade.

80. Robert Pleasants to Patrick Henry, January 1790; many thanks to Jon Kukla for this reference. Robert Pleasants to Patrick Henry, September 1, 1790, Robert Pleasants Letterbook and Collected Papers, HCQSC.

81. Robert Pleasants, July 7, 1790, Robert Pleasants Letterbook, HCQSC; the long piece in the *Virginia Independent Chronicle*, signed "Humanity," includes material from Robert's letterbook identified as appearing in the *Virginia Gazette* on June 17 but with no year listed. I have not found it in any extant issues of the *Virginia Gazette*.

82. Robert Pleasants to Samuel Bailey, July 23, 1790; Robert Pleasants to Charles Carter, August 17, 1790, both in Robert Pleasants Letterbook, HCQSC.

83. Robert Pleasants to James Madison, June 6, 1791, Robert Pleasants Letterbook, HCQSC.

84. Robert Pleasants to Robert Carter, October 8, 1791, Robert Pleasants Letterbook, HCQSC. Levy, *First Emancipator.*

85. "Benevolence," in the *Virginia Gazette and General Abolition*, October 19, 1791, and in Robert Pleasants Letterbook, HCQSC.

86. Laurent Dubois, *Avengers of the New World: The Story of the Haitian Revolution*, (Cambridge, Mass.: Harvard University Press, 2004), 60–90. Edward B. Rugemer, *The Problem of Emancipation: The Caribbean Roots of the American Civil War* (Baton Rouge: Louisiana State University Press, 2008), 42–53.

87. Julius Scott, *The Common Wind: Afro-American Currents in the Age of the Haitian Revolution* (London: Verso, 2018); Wolf, *Race and Liberty*, 5–6. James Sidbury, "Saint Domingue in Virginia: Ideology, Local Meanings, and Resistance to Slavery, 1790–1800," *Journal of Southern History* 63, no. 3 (1997): 531–552; Robert Pleasants to James Madison, June 6, 1791, Robert Pleasants Letterbook, HCQSC; James Madison to Robert Pleasants, October 30, 1791, Robert Pleasants Letterbook, Swem; John Elliot to Robert Pleasants, June 20, 1791, PFP.

88. *An Inquiry into the Cause of the Insurrection at St. Domingue, added observations by M. Garran-Coulon, read in his absence by M. Guadet before the National Assembly, 29th Feb. 1792* (Philadelphia: Joseph Cruikshank, 1792). The Philadelphia edition is paginated differently but otherwise identical in content. Robert Pleasants to Patrick Henry, July 21, 1792, Robert Pleasants Letterbook, HCQSC. Davis, *Age of Revolution*, 380–381, lists William Roscoe as the author although digitized sources do not acknowledge him. J. R. Oldfield, *Transatlantic Abolitionism in the Age of Revolution: An International History of Anti-slavery, 1787–1820* (Cambridge, U.K.: Cambridge University Press, 2013), 96–97, attributes the pamphlet to SEAST and Clarkson as part of his effort to manage the reaction to the rebellion in Saint Domingue to minimize its damage to British abolition.

89. James Pemberton to Robert Pleasants, July 23, 1792, and February 28, 1793, both in PFP Brock. Rugemer, *Problem of Emancipation*, 42–53, for the influence of Bryan Edwards's historical survey of the French Colony of Saint Domingue (1797); but Pleasants's correspondence reveals that this argument appeared immediately after the rebellion began.

90. Zachariah Nixon to Robert Pleasants, January 28, 1793, Robert Pleasants Letterbook, HCQSC.

91. John Hough to Robert Pleasants, September 21, 1792, and January 9, 1793, Robert Pleasants Letterbook, HCQSC.

92. Thomas Ott, *The Haitian Revolution, 1789–1804* (Knoxville: University of Tennessee Press, 1973), 61–62; Jordan, *White over Black*, 381; Wolf, *Race and Liberty*, 116. Ashli White, *Encountering Revolution: Haiti and the Making of the Early Republic* (Baltimore: Johns Hopkins University Press, 2010).

93. Sidbury, "Saint Domingue in Virginia," 537.

94. "Citizen of the World," *Richmond and Manchester Advertiser*, November 25, 1793; also in Robert Pleasants Letterbook, HCQSC.

95. Other possible works by Robert copied into his letterbook include "Serious Reflections," *Richmond and Manchester Advertiser*, November 10, 1794, and signed "A Professed Christian," November 13, 1794; Robert Pleasants Letterbook, HCQSC.

96. Robert Pleasants to James Pemberton, November 15, 1793, Robert Pleasants Letterbook, HCQSC.

97. Robert Pleasants, 1795 agreement to rent Cedar Point but not to interfere with Benjamin and Titus, PFP.

98. Christopher Johnson accounts and suits for slaves in Albemarle, N.C., PFP.

99. Robert Pleasants to John Webster, July 1, 1794, Robert Pleasants Letterbook, HCQSC.

100. James Binford, Northampton County, Va., to Robert Pleasants, November 4, 1794, Robert Pleasants Letterbook, HCQSC.

101. Robert Pleasants to John Elliot, June 9, 1794 Robert Pleasants Letterbook, HCQSC. James Phillips to Robert Pleasants, May 5, 1795, PFP.

102. Virginia Slaves Freed after 1782, Goochland County Personal Property Tax List 1782–1809, p. 28, LV microfilm no. 136.

103. St. George Tucker, *Dissertation on Slavery—With a Proposal for the Gradual Abolition of it, in the State of Virginia* (Philadelphia, 1796); Robert Pleasants to St. George Tucker, May 30, 1797, Robert Pleasants Letterbook, HCQSC.

104. Robert Pleasants to Thomas Jefferson, June 1, 1796, on the need to educate Black children; Robert Pleasants to Thomas Jefferson, February 8, 1797, on schools for children of color; both in Robert Pleasants Letterbook, HCQSC.

105. Wolf, *Race and Liberty*, 117; *SAL* (Shepherd, ed.), 1:128.

106. *SAL* (Shepherd, ed.), 1:122–130.

107. Henrico Personal Property Tax Lists 1783, 1784, 3rd precinct. Thanks to Scott Wilds for locating these records.

108. "Virginia in the High Court of Chancery," (Richmond, Va., 1798), March 16, 1798, Evans Early American Imprint.

109. Robert Cover, *Justice Accused: Antislavery and the Judicial Process* (New Haven, Conn.: Yale University Press, 1975), 69–70.

110. *Pleasants v. Pleasants* 6 Va 319 in Daniel Call, *Reports of Cases argued and adjudged in the Court of Appeals of Virginia* (Richmond, Va., 1802), 2: 350 (Justice Pendleton, President).

111. Timothy Sandefur, "Why the Rule Against Perpetuities Mattered in *Pleasants v Pleasants*," *Real Property, Probate and Trust Journal* 40, no. 4 (2006): 667–677. Alfred L. Brophy, *University, Court, and Slave: Pro-slavery Thought in Southern Colleges and Courts and the Coming of the Civil War* (New York: Oxford University Press, 2016), 257.

112. *Pleasants v. Pleasants* 6 Va.319 in Call, *Reports of Cases argued*, at 344–345.

113. *Pleasants v, Pleasants* 6 Va 319 in Call, *Reports of Cases argued* 2: 348, opinions of Carrington, Judge; 2: 354–357, Pendleton, President; 334, Roane, Judge, Dissenting. Thomas Morris, *Southern Slavery and the Law, 1619–1860* (Chapel Hill: University of North Carolina Press, 1996), 404–406.

114. Hardin, "'This Unpleasant Business'," 228. Morris, *Southern Slavery and the Law*, 405–406.

115. In the High Court of Chancery, September 12, 1798, Evans Early American Imprints.

116. *Pleasants v. Pleasants* 6 Va.319 in Call, *Reports of Cases argued* 2: 343 (Justice Roane), 256 (Justice Pendleton), and 349 (Justice Carrington).

117. *Pleasants v. Pleasants* 6 Va.319 in Call, *Reports of Cases argued*, 2: 343 (Justice Roane), and 348 (Justice Carrington).

118. Hardin, "'This Unpleasant Business,'" 225–228.

119. *Pleasants v. Pleasants* 6 Va.319 in Call, *Reports of Cases argued*, 2: 343, 349; Wolf, *Race and Liberty*, 150, 154.

120. *Pleasants v. Pleasants* 6 Va.319 in Call, *Reports of Cases argued*, 2: 343, 349; Wolf, *Race and Liberty*, 150, 154.

121. *Pleasants v. Pleasants* 6 Va.319 in Call, *Reports of Cases argued*, 2: 343 (Justice Roane).

122. *Pleasants v. Pleasants* 6 Va.319 in Call, *Reports of Cases argued*, 2: 343 (Justice Roane), and 349 (Justice Carrington).

123. *Journal of Negro History* 2., no. 4 (October 1917): 429–430.

124. Henrico County Personal Property Tax Lists, 1782–1814, LV film 171, and Land tax, reel 143, include the following: 1811 A Upper District Personal Property Tax List, Ned Pleasants free negro, 1 tithe; 1813 A Upper District Personal Property Tax List, Ned Pleasants & wife; 1820 U.S. federal census, Alexandria, District of Columbia [now Virginia], p. 156; National Archives and Records Administration (NARA) M33, roll 5, lists Ned Pleasants as head of a household with three tithables: 1 free colored male over 45, 1 free colored female over 45, and 1 free female slave under 14 [b. 1806–1820]. See also Dorothy S. Provine, abstractor and indexer, *Alexandria County, Virginia Free Negro Registers, 1797–1861* (Bowie, Md.: Heritage Books, 1990), 34, citing volume 1, p. 137, registration #219, September 11, 1827: "Edward Pleasants is about 60 years old [b. 1767], has a dark complexion, and is about 5 feet 4¼ inches tall. He is a free man, as appears by affidavit of Edward A. Mayfield." 1830 U.S. federal census, Alexandria, Washington, District of Columbia, p. 251; NARA, M19, roll 14: Edward Pleasants, 1 free colored male 55–99, 1 free colored female 55–99. My thanks to Scott Wilds for this information.

125. 1801 Barrell of corn for Old Dick; 1802 support of Old Dick by Ladd; 1803 accounts of Mary Pleasants, fees for maintaining ex slaves; all in PFP. Will of Thomas Pleasants honoring the court order that slaves would become free after serving a term of service; Diana goes to Mary Younghusband, other children to be taught, 100 pounds provided for this service; in *Valentine Papers*, 2:976. 1805 to Ladd for provision supplied to Old Gloster, in Micajah Crew, "Statement relating to Black People Put under my care by Robert Pleasants," MCP.

126. Slaves of Mr. Samuel Pleasants, Powhatan County, have been set free, June 22, 1816, *Valentine Papers*, 2:1286.

127. 1800 Samuel Pleasants, Argus editor, allows advertisements for slaves; PFP; James Pleasants Jr. elected 1st Vice President of Richmond auxiliary of American Colonization Society, November 11, 1823, *Valentine Papers*, 2:1292; John H. Pleasants as manager of ACS, James Pleasants a vice president again, January 19, 1832, and in 1836; all in *Valentine Papers*, 2:1294, 1295.

128. Wm. Davis to Micajah Crew, May 15, 1804, about Sam Flathead and Wapping; Wm. Pope to Micajah Crew, July 30, 1809, action against Francis Saunders and John Morton over Phillis, daughter of Mourning, and her children to show why they retain them in slavery contrary to decree of the High court. They belonged to Charles Logan and Robert Pleasants and had been sold two years earlier to Sanders and Morton; all in MCP.

129. July 8, 1811, suits connected to the Langley mortgage; John Mosby to Micajah Crew, February 6, 1811, names of Agy's family; August 3, 1805, Eliza Pleasants's maid Esther trying to hire herself out; all in MCP.

Chapter 4

1. Richard S. Newman, *Freedom's Prophet: Bishop Richard Allen, the AME Church, and the Black Founding Fathers* (New York: New York University Press, 2008), 238–263. Julie Winch, *Philadelphia's Black Elite: Activism, Accommodation, and the Struggle for Autonomy, 1787–1848* (Philadelphia: Temple University Press, 1988), 35–61.

2. Claude Clegg, *The Price of Liberty: African Americans and the Making of Liberia* (Chapel Hill: University of North Carolina Press, 2004), 90–91. Paul Goodman, *Of One Blood: Abolitionism and the Origins of Racial Equality* (Berkeley: University of California Press, 1998), 30. Antonio McDaniel, *Swing Low, Sweet Chariot: The Mortality Cost of Colonizing Liberia in the Nineteenth Century* (Chicago: University of Chicago, 1994).

3. Jenny S. Martinez, *The Slave Trade and the Origins of International Human Rights Law* (New York: Oxford University Press, 2012), 13.

4. Elizabeth B. Clark, "'The Sacred Rights of the Weak': Pain, Sympathy, and the Culture of Individual Rights in Antebellum America," *JAH* 82, No. 2 (Sept 1995): 463–493, esp. 487–488; Nancy Isenberg, *Sex and Citizenship in Antebellum America* (Chapel Hill: University of North Carolina Press, 1998); Karen Sanchez-Eppler, *Touching Liberty: Abolition, Feminism, and the Politics of the Body* (Berkeley: University of California Press, 1993), esp. 1–49. For political debates about colonization and rights to land in temperate and tropical climates, see Ikuko Asaka, *Tropical Freedom: Climate, Settler Colonialism, and Black Exclusion in the Age of Emancipation* (Durham, N.C.: Duke University Press, 2017).

5. Caitlin Rosenthal, *Accounting for Slavery: Masters and Management* (Cambridge, Mass.: Harvard University Press, 2018), 143–149. Note the body references in *Constitution of the American Society of Free Persons of Colour, for Improving Their Condition in the United States* (Philadelphia, 1831).

6. Andrew Shankman, "Neither Infinite Wretchedness nor Positive Good: Mathew Carey and Henry Clay on Political Economy and Slavery During the Long 1820s," in John Craig Hammond and Matthew Mason, eds., *Contesting Slavery: The Politics of Bondage and Freedom in the New American* Nation (Charlottesville: University of Virginia Press, 2011), 247–266. Julie Winch, "Self-Help and Self-Determination: Black Philadelphians and the Dimensions of Freedom," in Richard Newman and James Mueller, eds., *Antislavery and Abolition in Philadelphia: Emancipation and the Long Struggle*

for Racial Justice in the City of Brotherly Love (Baton Rouge: Louisiana State University Press, 2011), 78.

7. John Wood Sweet, *Bodies Politic: Negotiating Race in the American North, 1730–1830* (Baltimore: Johns Hopkins University Press, 2003); Patrick Rael, *Eighty-Eight Years: The Long Death of Slavery in the United States, 1777–1865* (Athens: University of Georgia Press, 2015), 131–135, for race science emerging out of white popular culture in the postslavery North.

8. See the Penn and Slavery Project, http://pennandslaveryproject.org, especially research by Carson Eckhard and Archana Upadhyay, on the William Horner specimen collection, the Samuel Morton crania collection, and the Penn Medical School. Carolyn Sorisio, *Fleshing Out America: Race, Gender, and the Politics of the Body in American Literature, 1833–1879* (Athens: University of Georgia Press, 2002). For the use of phrenology and craniology to solidify sex differences, see Cynthia Eagle Russett, *Sexual Science: The Victorian Construction of Womanhood* (Cambridge, Mass.: Harvard University Press, 1989). James Poskett, *Materials of the Mind: Phrenology, Race, and the Global History of Science, 1815–1920* (Chicago: University of Chicago Press, 2019).

9. John Harley Warner, *The Therapeutic Perspective: Medical Practice, Knowledge, and Identity in America, 1820–1885* (Cambridge, Mass.: Harvard University Press, 1986), 71; John Harley Warner, "The Idea of Southern Medical Distinctiveness: Medical Knowledge and Practice in the Old South," in Ronald Numbers and Todd Savitt, eds., *Science and Medicine in the Old South* (Baton Rouge: Louisiana State University Press, 1989), 179–205; James O. Breeden, "States Rights Medicine in the Old South," *Bulletin of the New York Academy of Medicine* 52, no. 3 (March–April 1976): 348–372; Mark Harrison, *Medicine in an Age of Commerce and Empire: Britain and Its Tropical Colonies, 1660–1830* (New York: Oxford University Press, 2010), esp. 47–120. Conevery Bolton Valencius, *The Health of the Country: How American Settlers Understood Themselves and Their Land* (New York: Basic Books, 2002); Etienne Benson, *Surroundings: A History of Environments and Environmentalisms* (Chicago: University of Chicago Press, 2020), chapter 2, "Environments of Empire: Disease, Race, and Statistics in the British Caribbean," 51–52. Asaka, *Tropical Freedom*; Christopher D. Willoughby, "'His Native, Hot Country': Racial Science and Environment in Antebellum American Medical Thought," *Journal of the History of Medicine and Allied Sciences* 72, no. 3 (July 1, 2017): 328–351, esp. 336, 342. Marli Weiner with Mazie Hough, *Sex, Sickness, and Slavery: Illness in the Antebellum South* (Urbana: University of Illinois Press, 2012), 64–92. Patrick Rael, "A Common Nature, A United Destiny: African-American Responses to Racial Science from the Revolution to the Civil War," in Timothy Patrick McCarthy and John Stauffer, eds., *Prophets of Protest: Reconsidering the History of American Abolitionism* (New York: New Press, 2006), 183–199.

10. Samantha Seeley, *Race, Removal, and the Right to Remain* (Chapel Hill: University of North Carolina Press, 2021).

11. Denver Brunsman, *The Evil Necessity: British Naval Impressment in the Eighteenth-Century Atlantic World* (Charlottesville: University of Virginia Press, 2013), 245–246.

12. Brunsman, *Evil Necessity*, 246–249; Alan Taylor, *The Civil War of 1812: American Citizens, British Subjects, Irish Rebels, and Indian Allies* (New York: Random House, 2010); Edlie L. Wong, *Neither Fugitive nor Free: Atlantic Slavery, Freedom Suits, and the Legal Culture of Travel* (New York: New York University Press, 2009).

13. Emma Christopher, *A Merciless Place: The Fate of Britain's Convicts After the American Revolution* (New York: Oxford University Press, 2010).

14. Madhavi Kale, *Fragments of Empire: Capital, Slavery, and Indian Indentured Labor in the British Caribbean* (Philadelphia: University of Pennsylvania Press, 1998).

15. Elizabeth Maddock Dillon and Michael Drexler, eds., *The Haitian Revolution and the Early United States: Histories, Textualities, Geographies* (Philadelphia: University of Pennsylvania Press, 2016); Ashli White, *Encountering Revolution: Haiti and the Making of the Early Republic* (Baltimore: Johns Hopkins University Press, 2010), 5; Julia Gaffield, *Haitian Connections in the Atlantic World: Recognition After Revolution* (Chapel Hill: University of North Carolina, 2016); David Geggus, ed., *The Impact of the Haitian Revolution in the Atlantic World* (Columbia: University of South Carolina Press, 2001); and especially Elizabeth Colwill, "'Fêtes de l'hymen, fêtes de la liberté': Matrimony,

Emancipation, and the Creation of New Men," in David Geggus and Norman Fiering, eds., *The World of the Haitian Revolution* (Bloomington: Indiana University Press, 2009), 125–155. For the shift from a law of nations grounded in natural rights to positivist international law, see Antony Anghie, *Imperialism, Sovereignty, and the Making of International Law* (New York: Cambridge University Press, 2005). Laurent Dubois, "Atlantic Freedoms," *Aeon*, November 7, 2016, https://aeon.co/essays/why-haiti-should-be-at-the-centre-of-the-age-of-revolution, for his claim that the Haitian Revolution "was the most radical (and therefore one of the most important) assertions of the *right to have rights* in human history." See also Carolyn Fick, "The Haitian Revolution and the Limits of Freedom: Defining Citizenship in the Revolutionary Era," *Social History* 32, no. 4 (November 2007): 394–414; Franklin W. Knight, "The Haitian Revolution and the Notion of Human Rights," *Journal of the Historical Society* 5, no. 3 (2005): 391–416.

16. White, *Encountering Revolution*, 79–80, 130–131.

17. James Sidbury, *Ploughshares to Swords: Race, Rebellion, and Identity in Gabriel's Virginia, 1730–1810* (New York: Cambridge University Press, 1997); Michael L. Nicholls, *Whispers of Rebellion: Narrating Gabriel's Conspiracy* (Charlottesville: University of Virginia Press, 2012).

18. Sidbury, *Ploughshares to Swords*; Nicholls, *Whispers of Rebellion*.

19. Petition of December 2, 1800, L.P., King and Queen County, LV Digital Collections; among the petitioners was Carter Braxton II, son of the signer of the declaration; see also Eva Sheppard Wolf, *Race and Liberty in the New Nation: Emancipation in Virginia from the Revolution to Nat Turner's Rebellion* (Baton Rouge: Louisiana State University Press, 2006), 121.

20. Daniel Call, *Reports of Cases argued and adjudged in the Court of Appeals of Virginia*, 2 vols. (Richmond, 1802) 2: 319–357, and for opinions by Carrington, Judge, 348, Pendleton, President, 356, Roane, Judge, Dissenting, 334; Thomas Morris, *Southern Slavery and the Law, 1619–1860* (Chapel Hill: University of North Carolina Press, 1996), 405–406. "An Act for regulating the police of towns in this commonwealth, and to restrain the practice of negroes going at large," December 10, 1793, in *SAL* (Shepherd, ed.) 1:238, and reinforced in "An Act more effectually to restrain the practice of negroes going at large," January 13, 1803, in *SAL* (Shepherd, ed.) 2:417–418. Wolf, *Race and Liberty*, 120.

21. *Valentine Papers*, 2:1282.

22. Patrick Wolfe, *Settler Colonialism and the Transformation of Anthropology: The Politics and Poetics of an Ethnographic Event* (London: Cassell, 1999); Lisa Ford, *Settler Sovereignty: Jurisdiction and Indigenous People in America and Australia, 1788–1836* (Cambridge, Mass.: Harvard University Press, 2010); John Bowes, *Land Too Good for Indians: Northern Indian Removal* (Norman: University of Oklahoma Press, 2016); Claudio Saunt, *Unworthy Republic: The Dispossession of Native Americans and the Road to Indian Territory* (New York: W. W. Norton, 2020); Adam Pratt, *Toward Cherokee Removal: Land, Violence, and the White Man's Chance* (Athens: University of Georgia Press, 2020).

23. Walter Johnson, *Soul by Soul; Life Inside the Antebellum Slave Market* (Cambridge, Mass.: Harvard University Press, 1999); Michael Tadman, *Speculators and Slaves: Masters, Traders, and Slaves in the Old South* (Madison: University of Wisconsin Press, 1989); Jeffrey Kerr-Ritchie, *Rebellious Passage: Revolt and America's Coastal Trade* (New York: Cambridge University Press, 2019), chapter 2, "The Coastal Passage," 37–65. Steven Deyle, *Carry Me Back: The Domestic Slave Trade in American Life* (New York: Oxford University Press, 2005), Appendix A, 283–290. For New Jersey, see James J. Gigantino II, *The Ragged Road to Abolition: Slavery and Freedom in New Jersey, 1775–1865* (Philadelphia: University of Pennsylvania Press, 2015), 149–173. Gwendolyn Midlo Hall, *Afro-Louisiana History and Genealogy*, 2009 Web Archive. https://www.loc.gov/item/lcwaN0004248/ for the repurposing of skilled Chesapeake slaves as cotton field hands, cited in Edward E. Baptist, *The Half Has Never Been Told: Slavery and the Making of American Capitalism* (New York: Basic Books, 2014), 444n17.

24. Robert H. Gudmestad, "Slave Resistance, Coffles, and the Debates over Slavery in the Nation's Capital," in Walter Johnson, ed., *The Chattel Principle: Internal Slave Trades in the Americas* (New Haven, Conn.: Yale University Press, 2004); Calvin Schermerhorn, *The Business of Slavery and*

the Rise of American Capitalism, 1815–1860 (New Haven, Conn.: Yale University Press, 2015), 6, 10–32, 35–37. Gregory Smithers, *Slave Breeding: Sex, Violence, and Memory in African American History* (Gainesville: University Press of Florida, 2012); Ned Sublette and Constance Sublette, *The American Slave Coast: A History of the Slave-Breeding Industry* (Chicago: Lawrence Hill Books, 2016); Saidiya Hartman, *Scenes of Subjection: Terror, Slavery and Self-Making in Nineteenth-Century America* (New York: Oxford University Press, 1997), for the coffle as the quintessential staging of slave subjection; Charles Ball, *Slavery in the United State: A Narrative of the Life and Adventures of Charles Ball* (1837); James Kirke Paulding, *Letters from the South, Written During an Excursion in the Summer of 1816* (New York: James Eastburn, 1817), 128; WPA Narrative of W. L. Bost, 1937, National Humanities Center, http://nationalhumanitiescenter.org/pds/maai/enslavement/text1/wlbost.pdf.

25. Levi Coffin, *Reminiscences of Levi Coffin, the Reputed President of the Underground Railroad* [. . .], 2nd ed. (Cincinnati, 1880), 12–13. Clegg, *Price of Liberty*, 9; Stephen Beauregard Weeks, *Southern Quakers and Slavery: A Study in Institutional History* (Baltimore: Johns Hopkins Press, 1896), 105–109. Deyle, *Carry Me Back*, 174–205.

26. Reginald Horsman, *Race and Manifest Destiny: The Origins of American Racial Anglo-Saxonism* (Cambridge, Mass.: Harvard University Press, 1981).

27. Eric Hinderaker and Peter Mancall, *At the Edge of Empire: The Backcountry in British North America* (Baltimore: Johns Hopkins University Press, 2003), 98–160; Philip J. Schwarz, *Migrants Against Slavery: Virginians and the Nation* (Charlottesville: University of Virginia Press, 2001); Andrew Cayton, *The Frontier Republic: Ideology and Politics in the Ohio Country, 1780–1825* (Kent, Ohio: Kent State University Press, 1986), 76–95; Stephen Middleton, *The Black Laws: Race and the Legal Process in Early Ohio* (Athens: Ohio University Press, 2005), 46–53. See also John Craig Hammond, *Slavery, Freedom, and Expansion in the Early American West* (Charlottesville: University of Virginia Press, 2007), 127–149; Matthew Salafia, *Slavery's Borderland: Freedom and Bondage Along the Ohio River* (Philadelphia: University of Pennsylvania Press, 2015); M. Scott Heerman, *The Alchemy of Slavery: Human Bondage and Emancipation in the Illinois Country, 1730–1865* (Philadelphia: University of Pennsylvania Press, 2018); Andrew Cayton, "Land, Power, and Reputation: The Cultural Dimension of Politics in the Ohio Country," *WMQ* 47, no. 2 (April 1990): 266–286; Peter S. Onuf, *Statehood and Union: A History of the Northwest Ordinance* (Notre Dame, In.: University of Notre Dame Press, new ed. 2019).

28. Paul Finkelman, "The Strange Career of Race Discrimination in Antebellum Ohio," *Case Western Reserve Law Review* 55, no. 2 (2004): 373–408, https://scholarlycommons.law.case.edu/caselrev/vol55/iss2/5. Middleton, *The Black Laws*, 46–53; Kate Masur, *Until Justice Be Done: America's First Civil Rights Movement, from the Revolution to Reconstruction* (New York: W. W. Norton, 2021), 1–41; Seeley, *Race, Removal, and the Right to Remain*.

29. Wolf, *Race and Liberty*, 120.

30. Greg Ablavsky, "Making Indians 'White': The Judicial Abolition of Native Slavery in Revolutionary Virginia and Its Racial Legacy," *University of Pennsylvania Law Review* 159 (2011): 1457. For interpretations of this important case, see Adrienne D. Davis, "Identity Notes Part One: Playing in the Light," *American University Law Review* 45 (1996): 695–720, esp. 702–711; Daniel Sharfstein, "Crossing the Color Line: Racial Migration and the One-Drop Rule, 1600–1860," 91 *Minnesota Law Review* 592 (2007): esp. 621–626; Ariela Gross, "Litigating Whiteness: Trials of Racial Determination in the Nineteenth-Century South," *Yale Law Journal* 108, no. 1 (1998): 109–188. For complexion consciousness among white British North American colonials, see Sharon Block, *Colonial Complexions: Race and Bodies in Eighteenth Century America* (Philadelphia: University of Pennsylvania Press, 2018).

31. *Hudgins v. Wrights* 11 Va. 134 (Va. 1806) in William W. Hening and William Munford, *Reports of Cases Argued and Determined in the Supreme Court of Appeals of Virginia* (Philadelphia: Smith and Maxwell, 1808), 1: 134. Wolf, *Race and Liberty*, 146–156; Kirt von Daacke, *Freedom Has a Face: Race, Identity, and Community in Jefferson's Virginia* (Charlottesville: University of Virginia Press, 2012). Ohio lawmakers' efforts to prohibit African American testimony soon sent the state on a similar path of trying to parse racial identity. The 1807 prohibition forbade the use of the legal testimony of Black or mulatto witnesses to prosecute white people, but the state's definition of whiteness

proved expansive enough to include people described in the court record as "quadroon" and "octoroon"; see Middleton, *The Black Laws*, 52, 57. For judicial recourse to the guiding principle of appearance reflecting blood as a consequence of ancestry, see *Hook v Pagee* Va 16 Va. 379 (1811) in William Munford, *Reports of Cases Argued and Determined in the Supreme Court of Appeals of Virginia* (New York, 1814), 2: 379–387, for the determination of Nanny Pagee's freedom based on her appearance of whiteness "upon inspection"; *State v. Mary Hayes* 11 SCL (1 Bail.) 275 (1829), in Henry Bailey, *Reports of the Cases Argued and Determined in the Court of Appeals of South Carolina* (Charleston, S.C., 1833), 1: 275–277, in which Hayes's mulatto appearance "upon inspection" trumped her birth to a white woman; *Peavey v. Robbins* 48 N.C. 339 (N.C. 1856), in Hamilton C. Jones, *Reports of Cases at Law Argued and Determined in the Supreme Court of North Carolina* (Salisbury, N.C., 1856), 3: 339–342, in which Peavey claimed white identity and wrongful exclusion from voting based on his descent from a white mother and grandmother, but was found to be properly excluded on the basis of "mixed blood" and the election official not at fault for failing to investigate his ancestry. Later cases turning on assessments of appearance, estimations of blood, and performance of race include *Daniel v. Guy*, 19 Ark. 121 (1857) in L.E. Barber, *Reports of Cases at Law and in Equity Argued and Determined in the Supreme Court of Arkansas* (Little Rock, Ark., 1889), 19: 121–122; *Gary v. Stevenson*, 19 Ark. 580 (1858) in Barber, *Reports of Cases* 19: 580–587; *Van Camp v. Board of Education in the Incorporated Village of Logan*, 9 Ohio St. 406 (1859) in Leander J. Critchfield, *Reports of Cases Argued and Determined in the Supreme Court of Ohio* (Columbus, Oh., 1860), 9: 406–425.

32. Ellen Katz, "African American Freedom in Antebellum Cumberland County, Virginia: Personal Liberty and Private Law," *Chicago-Kent Law Review* 70, no. 3 (1995): 927; von Daacke, *Freedom Has a Face*; Melvin Patrick Ely, *Israel on the Appomattox: A Southern Experiment in Black Freedom from the 1790s Through the Civil War* (New York: Vintage Books, 2005); Seeley, *Race, Removal, and the Right to Remain*, 251–271.

33. Finkelman, "The Strange Career of Race Discrimination," 377. Wolf, *Race and Liberty*, 120. "An Act to Prevent further the practice of slaves going at large or hiring out themselves," *SAL* (Shepherd, ed.) 1807 3:372.

34. Emer de Vattel, *The Law of Nations* (London, 1758), 222–225, on the subject's right to mobility; David Armitage, *Foundations of Modern International Thought* (New York: Cambridge University Press, 2013); Christopher, *A Merciless Place*; Ian Baucom, *Specters of the Atlantic: Finance Capital, Slavery, and the Philosophy of History* (Durham, N.C.: Duke University Press, 2005), esp. 189–191, for the consequences of state-sponsored human rights on noncitizens.

35. Heerman, *Alchemy of Slavery*, 183–187.

36. General Assembly of Pennsylvania, "An Act for the Gradual Abolition of Slavery," March 1, 1780, Pennsylvania Historical and Museum Commission, http://www.phmc.state.pa.us/portal/communities/documents/1776-1865/abolition-slavery.html; "An Act Respecting Fugitives from Justice, and Persons Escaping from the Service of their Masters," February 12, 1793, Second Congress, Second Session, National Archives and Records Administration, https://catalog.archives.gov/id/124068301.

37. H. Robert Baker, "The Fugitive Slave Clause and the Antebellum Constitution," *Law and History Review* 30, no. 4 (2012): 1143; Nicholas P. Wood, "A 'Class of Citizens': The Earliest Black Petitioners to Congress and Their Quaker Allies," *WMQ*, 3rd ser., 74, no. 1 (January 2017): 109–144. Thomas Morris, *Free Men All: The Personal Liberty Laws of the North, 1780–1861* (Baltimore: Johns Hopkins University Press, 1974), 32. William R. Leslie, "The Pennsylvania Fugitive Slave Act of 1826," *Journal of Southern History* 18, no. 4 (1952): 429–445.

38. Baker, "The Fugitive Slave Clause," esp. 1140.

39. *Commonwealth v. Holloway* (Penn. SC) July 1816 in Thomas Sergeant and William Rawle, Jun., *Reports of Cases Adjudged in the Supreme Court of Pennsylvania* (Philadelphia, 1820) 2: 305–309.

40. Baker, "The Fugitive Slave Clause," 1146, notes that the Pennsylvania Abolition Society habeas corpus hearings did not always have the intended outcome. See also Morris, *Free Men All*, 42. For Kitty's case, see Richard S. Newman, *The Transformation of American Abolitionism: Fighting Slavery in the Early Republic* (Chapel Hill: University of North Carolina Press, 2002), 78–79.

41. Newman, *Transformation of American Abolitionism*; Morris, *Free Men All*, 45.

42. John Noonan Jr., *The* Antelope: *The Ordeal of the Recaptured Africans in the Administration of James Monroe and John Quincy Adams* (Berkeley: University of California Press, 1990); Jonathan Bryant, *Dark Places of the Earth: The Voyage of the Slave Ship* Antelope (New York: Liveright, 2015).

43. Richard Bell, *Stolen: Five Free Boys Kidnapped into Slavery and Their Astonishing Odyssey Home* (New York: Simon and Schuster, 2019).

44. "An Act to Give Effect to the Provisions of the Constitution of the United States, Relative to Fugitives from Labor, for the Protection of Free People of Color, and to Prevent Kidnapping," ch. 50, 1825 Pa Laws, March 25, 1826, in *Acts of the General Assembly of the Commonwealth of Pennsylvania* (Harrisburg, Pa., 1826), 150–155; Baker, "The Fugitive Slave Clause," 1150. H. Robert Baker, *Prigg v Pennsylvania: Slavery, the Supreme Court, and the Ambivalent Constitution* (Lawrence: University Press of Kansas, 2012), 78.

45. Newman, *Freedom's Prophet*, 202–207. Clegg, *Price of Liberty*, 35; Winch, *Philadelphia's Black Elite*, 34–39.

46. "Meeting of a respectable portion of the free people of color of the city of Richmond, January 24, 1817," in William Lloyd Garrison, *Thoughts on African Colonization* (Boston, 1832), Part II, Sentiments of the People of Color, 62–63. See also Marie Tyler McGraw, "Richmond Free Blacks and African Colonization, 1816–1832." *Journal of American Studies* 21, no. 2 (1987): 207–24. http://www.jstor.org/stable/27554832.

47. Clegg, *Price of Liberty*, 17–52, esp. 38–44; Goodman, *Of One Blood*, 16–35; Bruce Dain, *A Hideous Monster of the Mind: American Race Theory in the Early Republic* (Cambridge, Mass.: Harvard University Press, 2002), 93–111. Coffin, *Reminiscences*, 75.

48. See, for example, "The Sixth Annual Report of the American Society for Colonizing the Free People of Colour of the United States with an Appendix" (Washington City, 1823).

49. Winch, *Philadelphia's Black Elite*, 52–55, 59–60.

50. Clegg, *Price of Liberty*, 43–46, 48; Dain, *Hideous Monster*, 93–111; Leslie M. Alexander, "Black Republic: The Influence of the Haitian Revolution on Northern Black Political Consciousness, 1816–1862," in Maurice Jackson and Jacqueline Bacon, eds., *African Americans and the Haitian Revolution* (New York: Routledge, 2010), 57–79; Goodman, *Of One Blood*, 31–35; Thomas Taylor to George Washington Taylor, January 1828, Taylor Family Papers, unprocessed material, HCQSC. Schermerhorn, *Business of Slavery*, 62. Lundy began his newspaper in 1821 in Ohio before moving to Maryland in 1824; Merton L. Dillon, *Benjamin Lundy and the Struggle for Negro Freedom* (Urbana: University of Illinois Press, 1966).

51. Thomas Eddy to Thomas Cope, New York, July 29, 1824, Cope Family Papers, HCQSC; Goodman, *Of One Blood*, 31–35; Asaka, *Tropical Freedom*.

52. J. H. Gibbon to Thomas Cope, February 7, 1825, Port au Prince, Haiti, Cope Family Papers, HCQSC.

53. Sara Fanning, *Caribbean Crossing: African Americans and the Haitian Emigration Movement* (New York: New York University Press, 2015), 102–103.

54. Fanning, *Caribbean Crossing*, 108–109.

55. Clegg, *Price of Liberty*, 63–64, 68–69, 139–140; Goodman, *Of One Blood*, 30.

56. Newman, *Freedom's Prophet*, 171, notes Allen's admission to the Philadelphia Dispensary, founded in 1786 by Benjamin Rush to provide medical care to the poor, which may have been where he learned how to bleed patients. Seen also Daina Ramey Berry, *The Price for Their Pound of Flesh: The Value of the Enslaved, from Womb to Grave, in the Building of a Nation* (Boston: Beacon, 2017).

57. Suzanne M. Shultz, *Body Snatching: The Robbing of Graves for the Education of Physicians in Early Nineteenth Century America* (Jefferson, N.C.: McFarland, 1992); Michael Sappol, *A Traffic of Dead Bodies: Anatomy and Embodied Social Identity in Nineteenth-Century America* (Princeton, N.J.: Princeton University Press, 2002), 51–54; Kariann Yokota, *Unbecoming British: How Revolutionary America Became a Postcolonial Nation* (New York: Oxford University Press, 2011), 192–225.

58. Samuel Stanhope Smith, *Essay on the Causes of the Variety of Complexion and Figure in the Human Species* (Philadelphia, 1787); Mia Bay, *The White Image in the Black Mind: African-American Ideas About White People, 1830–1925* (New York: Oxford University Press, 2000); Dain, *Hideous Monster*; Nicholas Guyatt, "Samuel Stanhope Smith," *Princeton Alumni Weekly,* May 11, 2016, https://paw.princeton.edu/article/samuel-stanhope-smith

59. Absalom Jones and Richard Allen, *A Narrative of the proceedings of the black people, during the late awful calamity in Philadelphia, in the year 1793* (Philadelphia, 1794). See Newman, *Freedom's Prophet* (91) for white fears of being bled by black attendants. See also Rana Hogarth, *Medicalizing Blackness: Making Racial Difference in the Atlantic World, 1780–1840* (Chapel Hill: University of North Carolina Press, 2017), 25–47, for Rush's ambivalence as a form of scientific racism.

60. Sappol, *Traffic of Dead Bodies*, 44–45, mentions raids on a Black burial ground in New York in 1788 and a poem about white doctors cannibalizing African American bodies in 1789. Penn medical students relied on the almshouse for both patients and cadavers.

61. Johann Blumenbach, *Elements of Physiology* trans. Charles Caldwell, (Philadelphia, 1795); *Transactions of the College of Physicians of Philadelphia* 9 (1887): Appendix, cccxxv.

62. Charles Caldwell, "Sameness of Certain Diseases," Medical Dissertation, University of Pennsylvania, 1796, reflected the still dominant unitary theory of disease. Christopher Booth, *John Haygarth, FRS (1740–1827): Physician of the Enlightenment* (Philadelphia: American Philosophical Society, 2005), 120–124; Harriet Warner, *The Autobiography of Charles Caldwell* (Philadelphia: Lippincott, 1855). Charles Caldwell, "An Experimental Inquiry Respecting the Vitality of Blood," in *Medical Theses Selected Among the Inaugural Dissertations, Published and Defended by the Graduates in Medicine*, ed. Charles Caldwell (Philadelphia, 1805).

63. Holly Tucker, *Blood Work: A Tale of Medicine and Murder in the Scientific Revolution* (New York: W. W. Norton, 2011). Warner, *Therapeutic Perspective*; Winthrop Jordan, *White over Black: American Attitudes Toward the Negro, 1550–1812* (Chapel Hill: University of North Carolina Press, 1968), 249. See also Cornelius De Pauw, *Recherches philosophiques sur les Américains* (Berlin, 1768); Andrew Curran, *The Anatomy of Blackness: Science and Slavery in the Age of Enlightenment* (Baltimore: Johns Hopkins University Press, 2011).

64. Charles Caldwell, "Critical Review of Samuel Stanhope Smith's 'An Essay on the Causes of the Variety of Complexion and Figure in the Human Species,'" *Port Folio* 4, no. 2 (1814): 150. I was drawn to Caldwell's early publications by the research of Grace Cho, Penn and Slavery Project, http://pennandslaveryproject.org.

65. Charles Caldwell, "Critical Review of Samuel Stanhope Smith's 'An Essay on the Causes of the Variety of Complexion and Figure in the Human Species,'" *Port Folio* 4, no. 1 (1814): 21, 23.

66. Charles Caldwell, "Critical Review of Samuel Stanhope Smith's 'An Essay on the Causes of the Variety of Complexion and Figure in the Human Species,'" *American Review of History and Politics and General Repository of Literature and State Papers* 2 (1811); Caldwell, *Port Folio,* (1814): 256.

67. Ibram F. Kendi, *Stamped from the Beginning: The Definitive History of Racist Ideas in America* (New York: Bold Type Books, 2016), 132–134. Caldwell, "Critical Review" (1811): 141. Caldwell, "Critical Review" (1814): 452.

68. Sappol, *Traffic of Dead Bodies*, 51–54; Yokota, *Unbecoming British*, 192–225.

69. There were limits, however, as the student James Kello argued; blood's vitality could not regenerate damaged blood vessels. James Kello, "An Inaugural Dissertation Against the Vitality of the Blood," Medical Dissertation, University of Pennsylvania, 1807. Throughout this study, I draw on the remnant of medical dissertations written by University of Pennsylvania medical students and preserved in the Kislak Center archives as evidence of the medical training of southern students.

70. Adam Seybert, "An Inaugural Dissertation: Being an Attempt to Disprove the Doctrine of the Putrefaction of the Blood of Living Animals," Medical Dissertation, University of Pennsylvania, 1793.

71. N. Chapman, "Elements of Therapeutics and Materia Medica, to Which Are Prefixed Two Discourses on the History and Improvement of the Materia Medica, Originally Delivered as

Introductory Lectures" (Philadelphia, 1825), 68–78. Chapman, who married into the wealthy Biddle family, became an influential faculty member at Penn and in 1847 founded the American Medical Association.

72. Hutchinson benefited from his Quaker father's membership on the medical faculty and trusteeship of the university and his mother's Biddle family connections. James Hutchinson, "An Experimental Essay on the Conversion of Chyle into Blood," Medical Dissertation, University of Pennsylvania, 1803.

73. Hutchinson, "Experimental Essay on the Conversion of Chyle into Blood," 946–947.

74. Charles Jones, *A Candid Examination of the Origin of the Difference of Colour in the Human Family* (Philadelphia, 1812).

75. Matthew Rowlinson, "On the First Medical Blood Transfusion Between Human Subjects, 1818," *BRANCH: Britain, Representation, and Nineteenth Century History*, ed. Dino Franco Felluga, August 2012, https://www.branchcollective.org/?ps_articles=matthew-rowlinson-on-the-first-medical-blood-transfusion-between-human-subjects-1818; Harold W. Jones and Gulden Mackmull, "The Influence of James Blundell on the Development of Blood Transfusion," *Annals of Medical History* 10, no. 3 (1928): 242–248. J. H. Young, "James Blundell (1790–1878): Experimental Physiologist and Obstetrician," *Medical History* 8, no. 2 (1964): 159–169.

76. "Transfusion of Blood," *PJMPS* (1825) 11: 205–207.

77. "Examination of the Blood, and its Actions in the different Phenomena of Life," *PJMPS* (1822) 4: 414; *The Annual Register, or a view of the History, Politics, and Literature of the Year 1822* (London, 1823), 677–678.

78. Chapman review of Dyckman, "Inaugural Dissertation on the Pathology of the Fluids," *PJMPS*, 1822, 345–365. Sappol, *Traffic of Dead Bodies*, 48, 59, citing Simon Baatz, "'A Very Diffused Disposition," *PMHB* 108 (1984); William Barlow and David O. Powell, "A Dedicated Medical Student: Solomon Mordecai, 1819–1822," *Journal of the Early Republic* 7 (1987): 377–397.

79. Sappol, *Traffic of Dead Bodies*, 48. Caldwell left Philadelphia in 1819 to found the new medical school at Transylvania.

80. Shultz, *Body Snatching*; Sappol, *Traffic of Dead Bodies*, 51–54, 110–116; Yokota, *Unbecoming British*, 192–225. See also Berry, *Price for Their Pound of Flesh*, 154–165, esp. 156 for her discussion of cadaver bags. Horner quoted in Sappol, *Traffic of Dead Bodies*, 114; F. S. Beattie to W. E. Horner, quoted in James Webster, *Facts Concerning Anatomical Instruction in Philadelphia* (Philadelphia, 1832), 11. Thomas Laqueur, *The Work of the Dead: A Cultural History of Mortal Remains* (Princeton, N.J.: Princeton University Press, 2015); Paul Wolff Mitchell, "Black Philadelphians in the Samuel George Morton Cranial Collection," Penn Program on Race, Science, and Society, February 15, 2021, https://prss.sas.upenn.edu/penn-medicines-role/black-philadelphians-samuel-george-morton-cranial-collection.

81. "An Easy Way to Secure Dead Bodies in Their Graves," *Freedom's Journal*, March 30, 1827. For the security of buried loved ones among enslaved African Americans, see Jamie Warren, "To Claim One's Own: Death and the Body in Antebellum Slavery," in Craig Thompson Friend and Lori S. Glover, eds., *Death in the American South* (New York: Cambridge University Press, 2015). Sappol, *Traffic of Dead Bodies*, 110–117, discusses the trade in dead bodies during the 1810s and 1820s with a focus on New York.

82. Josiah White, "Inaugural Essay on the Circulation of the Blood," Medical Dissertation, University of Pennsylvania, 1829.

83. Benjamin Sandford, "Inaugural Essay on the Circulation of the Blood," Medical Dissertation, University of Pennsylvania, 1822. Joshua Rhoads, "Inaugural Essay on the Circulation of the Blood," Medical Dissertation, University of Pennsylvania, 1828, discusses red oxygenated blood versus black blood, but not in racial terms. Samuel Stones, "An Inaugural Essay on the Nature and Properties of the Blood," Medical Dissertation, University of Pennsylvania, 1828. Thomas Ingram, "Inaugural Essay on the Sanguiferous Circulation," Medical Dissertation, University of Pennsylvania, 1829. John P. Goodwyn, "An Essay on the Circulation of the Blood," Medical Dissertation, University of Pennsylvnia, 1848.

84. Isaac Jones, "The Blood," Medical Dissertation, University of Pennsylvania, 1860, 9.

85. John Crawford Spear, "The Blood," Medical Dissertation, University of Pennsylvania, 1861.

86. Blencove Fryer, "Constituents of the Blood," Medical Dissertation, University of Pennsylvania, 1859.

87. Melson Rowland, "The Tranfusion of Blood," Medical Dissertation, University of Pennsylvania, 1859.

88. Sappol, *Traffic of Dead Bodies*, esp. 168–189, for William Alcott's notion of anatomical citizenship. John Redman Coxe, *Inquiry into Claims of Dr. Wm. Harvey on the Circulation of Blood* (1834).

89. See Clark, "Sacred Rights of the Weak," 474, for an abolitionist woman's description of an enslaved man's blood as "orthodox."

90. George Gliddon and Josiah Nott, *Types of Mankind* (Philadelphia: Lippincott and Grambo, 1854). James Meigs, "Indigenous Races of the Earth," in Gliddon and Nott, *Types of Mankind* (1857); Ann Fabian, *The Skull Collectors: Race, Science, and America's Unburied Dead* (Chicago: University of Chicago Press, 2010).

91. William Horner Papers, inventory by Joseph Leidy, Kislak Center, University of Pennsylvania; research by Archana Upadhyay, Penn and Slavery Project. Timothy Kent Holliday, "Morbid Sensations: Intimacy, Coercion, and Epidemic Disease in Philadelphia, 1793–1854" (PhD diss., University of Pennsylvania, 2020). Daniel Kilbride, "Southern Medical Students in Philadelphia, 1800–1861: Science and Sociability in the 'Republic of Medicine,'" *Journal of Southern History* 65, no. 4 (November 1999): 697–732. J. O. Breeden, "States Rights Medicine in the Old South," *Bulletin of the New York Academy of Medicine* 52, no. 3 (March–April 1976): 348–372.

92. Horner, *Lessons in Practical Anatomy for the Use of Dissectors* (1823), 211.

93. William E. Horner, *Special Anatomy and Histology with Numerous Illustrations*, 2 vols., 7th ed. (Philadelphia, 1846), 1:378–379. Henry Smith and William Horner, *Anatomical Atlas, Illustrative of the Structure of the Human Body* (1843), proved similarly long-lived as a standard textbook in the field. Christopher Willoughby, "Running away from Drapetomania: Samuel A. Cartwright, Medicine, and Race in the Antebellum South," *Journal of Southern History* 84, no. 3 (July 2018): 579–614.

94. Stephen Tomlinson, *Head Masters: Phrenology, Secular Education, and Nineteenth-Century Social Thought* (Tuscaloosa: University of Alabama Press, 2005), 50–96.

95. James Poskett, "Phrenology, Correspondence, and the Global Politics of Reform, 1815–1848," *Historical Journal* 63, no. 2 (November 5, 2018): 409–442.

96. George Combe, *Elements of Phrenology*, 1st American ed. (Philadelphia, 1826).

97. John Bell, "On Phrenology, or the Study of the Intellectual and Moral Nature of Man," read before the Central Phrenological Society in Philadelphia, March 1822, in *PJMPS*, (1822), 4: 72–113, quotes on 107, 113. Officers of the Phrenological Society of Philadelphia included Philip Syng Physick, MD, William E. Horner, MD, Clement Biddle, William P. C. Barton, MD, Aaron B. Tucker, MD, John Bell, MD, Benjamin Coates, MD, and Joseph Cabot; see *PJMPS* 4: 204. Fabian, *Skull Collectors*; John van Whye, *Phrenology and the Origins of Victorian Scientific Naturalism* (Burlington, Vt.: Ashgate, 2004); Tomlinson, *Head Masters*; Poskett, *Materials of the Mind*.

98. Charles Caldwell, *Elements of Phrenology* (1827).

99. Charles Caldwell, *Thoughts on the Original Unity of the Human Race* (New York, 1830), 15, 134.

100. Caldwell, *Thoughts on the Original Unity of the Human Race*, 109.

101. Julien-Joseph Virey, *Histoire naturelle du genre humain; cinquieme race: de negres ou noirs*, 4 vols. (Paris, revised ed.1824), 2: 4, 23, 50, 80. *The Natural History of the Negro Race* trans. J. H. Guenebault (Charleston, S.C., 1837).

102. Caldwell, *Thoughts on the Original Unity of the Human Race*, 177.

103. Caldwell, *Thoughts on the Original Unity of the Human Race*, 177, 129–130, 121.

104. Caldwell, *Thoughts on the Original Unity of the Human Race*, 177, 123–120, 121; Samuel Morton, *Crania Americana* (Philadelphia, 1839). See Willoughby, "Running away from Drapetomania," 604, for Cartwright at Caldwell's Transylvania University. Morton's racism can be attributed to both weaknesses in his methods for cranial measurement and his racist interpretive frame. See Paul Wolff Mitchell, "The Fault in His Seeds: Lost Notes to the Case of Bias in Samuel George Morton's

Cranial Race Science," *PLoS Biology* 16, no. 10 (2018); Michael Weisberg, "Remeasuring Man," *Evolution and Development* 16, no. 3 (2014): 166–178; J. Lewis, D. DeGusta, M. Meyer, J. Monge, A. Mann, and R. Holloway, (2011) "The Mismeasure of Science: Stephen Jay Gould versus Samuel George Morton on Skulls and Bias," PLoS Biol 9(6): e1001071. https://doi.org/10.1371/journal.pbio.1001071; Stephen Jay Gould, *The Mismeasure of Man* (New York: W. W. Norton, 1981).

105. Lucretia Mott to George Combe, June 13, 1839, 50–54; Lucretia Mott to George and Cecilia Combe, September 10, 1848, 168–172, both in Beverly Wilson Palmer, ed., *Selected Letters of Lucretia Coffin Mott* (Urbana: University of Illinois Press, 2002). Emily Renschler and Janet Monge, "The Samuel George Morton Cranial Collection," *Expedition Magazine* 50, no. 3 (2008), https://www.penn.museum/sites/expedition/the-samuel-george-morton-cranial-collection/. But see Mitchell, "The Fault in His Seeds." See also Cynthia S. Hamilton, "'Am I Not a Man and Brother?' Phrenology and Anti-slavery," *Slavery and Abolition* 29, no. 2 (2008): 173–187, for phrenology's environmentalist strain; Thomas Morgan, "The Education and Medical Practice of Dr. James McCune Smith (1813–1865), the First Black American to Hold a Medical Degree," *Journal of the National Medical Association* 95, no. 7 (2003): 603–614; John Stauffer, "Introduction," in John Stauffer, ed., *The Works of James McCune Smith: Black Intellectual and Abolitionist* (New York: Oxford University Press, 2006), xxiii; Britt Rusert, *Fugitive Science: Empiricism and Freedom in Early African American Culture* (New York: New York University Press, 2017), 122–126.

106. Willoughby, "Running away from Drapetomania." J.-J. Virey, *Natural History of the Negro Race*, trans. J. H. Guenebault (Charleston, S.C., 1837), i. Guenebault's translation was widely distributed throughout the South.

107. Hogarth, *Medicalizing Blackness*, 58–77; Willoughby, "His Native, Hot Country"; Harrison, *Medicine in an Age of Commerce and Empire*, 47–120.

108. William McCaa, "The Manner of Living and Disease of the Slaves on the Wateree River," Medical Dissertation, University of Pennsylvania, 1822. I am indebted to Calvary Jones, Penn and Slavery Project, for calling my attention to McCaa's thesis. See also Berry, *Price for Their Pound of Flesh*; Hogarth, *Medicalizing Blackness*, 117–118, 125.

109. James H. Gregory, "Inaugural Essay on Bilious Fever, as It Prevailed in Mecklenberg County, Virginia," Medical Dissertation, University of Pennsylvania, 1827. M. T. Lynch, "An Account of the Epidemic Fever as It Occurred in Botetourt County Virginia During the Summer of the Year 1821," Medical Dissertation, University of Pennsylvania, 1823. Elisha Embree, "The Summer and Autumnal Diseases of the Western Country," Medical Dissertation, University of Pennsylvania, 1823.

110. John Parham, "An Inaugural Dissertation on the Autumnal Fever of Greensville County, Virginia," Medical Dissertation, University of Pennsylvania, 1824.

111. Samuel Jones, "A Dissertation on the Causes, Nature, Symptoms, and the Treatment of the Endemic Fever, Which Prevailed in the City of Philadelphia During the Summer of 1820 [. . .]," Medical Dissertation, University of Pennsylvania,1822. Jones identified a micro-outbreak in the "Negro alleys," which a professional acquaintance claimed was similar to yellow fever in New Orleans. Jones noted that people of African descent suffered greater mortality than white people and that many victims were employed on the wharves.

112. Peter H. Anderson, "Inaugural Dissertation on the Typhoid Fever of Amelia City, Virginia, in the Years 1827–1828," Medical Dissertation, University of Pennsylvania, 1829. Like his classmate Anderson, John W. Potts noted similarities between Washington, D.C., North Carolina, and other subtropical places. John W. Potts, "An Essay on the Medical Topography and Autumnal Fever of Washington, North Carolina," Medical Dissertation, University of Pennsylvania, 1829. Suman Seth, *Difference and Disease: Medicine, Race, and the Eighteenth-Century British Empire* (New York: Cambridge University Press, 2018), 261.

113. John D. Porter, "Inaugural Essay on the Bilious Diseases Which Prevailed on the Rappahannock River," Medical Dissertation, University of Pennsylvania, 1829.

114. William W. Waddell, "An Inaugural Essay on the State of the Biliary Secretion in Fever," Medical Dissertation, University of Pennsylvania, 1828.

115. Jeremiah F. X. McCredy, "An Inaugural Essay on Miasmata," Medical Dissertation, University of Pennsylvania, 1828.

116. James E. Gayley, "An Essay on the Etiology of Intermittent and Remittent Fevers," Medical Dissertation, University of Pennsylvania, 1848.

117. Seth, *Difference and Disease*, 265.

118. *Liberator* 2, no. 29 (July 21, 1832).

119. Hosea Easton, *A Treatise on the Intellectual Character and Civil and Political Condition of the Colored People of the U. States; and the Prejudice Exercised Towards Them; with a Sermon on the Duty of the Church to Them* (Boston, 1837), in George R. Price and James Brewer Stewart, *To Heal the Scourge of Prejudice: The Life and Writings of Hosea Easton* (Amherst: University of Massachusetts Press, 1999), 67–68, 85–89, quote on 113–114; Dain, *Hideous Monster*, 170–196; Rusert, *Fugitive Science*, 97–102.

120. Leslie M. Alexander, "Black Republic: The Influence of the Haitian Revolution on Northern Black Political Consciousness, 1816–1862," in Jackson and Bacon, *African Americans and the Haitian Revolution*, 57–79. See also Charlotte Sussman, *Consuming Anxieties: Consumer Protest, Gender, and British Slavery, 1713–1833* (Stanford, Calif.: Stanford University Press, 2000), 117, for abolitionist body language.

Chapter 5

1. "Free" or "remunerated" labor signified work in which the laborer benefited directly in the form of wages or through the ownership of the cultivated land and its products. Free labor was presumptively male, as activists imagined it, and relied on the unpaid domestic labor of women and other household members to support the body of the male wage earner. Free or remunerated agricultural labor yielded "free produce."

2. See Bronwyn Everill, *Not Made by Slaves: Ethical Capitalism in the Age of Abolition* (Cambridge, Mass.: Harvard University Press, 2020), for her distinction between ethical sourcing and consumption; Michelle McDonald, "Consuming with a Conscience: The Free Produce Movement in Early America," in Louis Hyman and Joseph Tohill, eds., *Shopping for Change: Consumer Activism and the Possibilities of Purchasing Power* (Ithaca, N.Y.: Cornell University Press, 2017), 17–28; Julie Holcomb, *Moral Commerce: Quakers and the Transatlantic Boycott of the Slave Labor Economy* (Ithaca, N.Y.: Cornell University Press, 2016); Anna Vaughan Kett, "'Without the Consumers of Slave Produce There Would Be No Slaves,'" in Brycchan Carey and Geoffrey Plank, eds., *Quakers and Abolition* (Urbana: University of Illinois Press, 2014), 56–72; Charlotte Sussman, *Consuming Anxieties: Consumer Protest, Gender, and British Slavery, 1713–1833* (Stanford, Calif.: Stanford University Press, 2000), esp. 110–114; Carol Faulkner, "The Root of the Evil: Free Produce and Radical Antislavery, 1820–1860," *Journal of the Early Republic* 27, no. 3 (Fall 2007): 377–405; Lawrence Glickman, *Buying Power: A History of Consumer Activism in America* (Chicago: University of Chicago Press, 2009), 61–89. Mimi Sheller, "Bleeding Humanity and Gendered Embodiments: From Antislavery Sugar Boycotts to Ethical Consumers," *Humanity* (Fall 2011): 171–192; Chris Dixon, *Perfecting the Family: Antislavery Marriages in Nineteenth-Century America* (Amherst: University of Massachusetts Press, 1997), 97–101. An older generation of scholars emphasized the movement's failures: Ruth Ketring Nuermberger, *The Free Produce Movement: A Quaker Protest Against Slavery* (Durham, N.C.: Duke University Press, 1942); Norman B. Wilkinson, "The Philadelphia Free Produce Attack upon Slavery," *PMHB* 66, no. 3 (July 1942): 294–313. For early expressions of free labor as a positive demographic alternative to slavery, see Benjamin Franklin, *Observations Concerning the Increase of Mankind* (London, 1751), and Eva Sheppard Wolf, "Early Free Labor Thought and the Contest over Slavery in the Early Republic," in John Craig Hammond and Matthew Mason, eds., *Contesting Slavery: The Politics of Bondage and Freedom in the New American Nation* (Charlottesville: University of Virginia Press, 2011), 32–48. See also Amy Dru Stanley, *From Bondage to Contract: Wage Labor,*

Marriage, and the Market in the Age of Slave Emancipation (New York: Cambridge University Press, 1998).

3. Global histories of abolition and cotton usually privilege supply-side circuitry over domestic consumption. See Sven Beckert, *Empire of Cotton: A Global History* (New York: Knopf, 2014),122–128, 226, 268–269. Beckert's account of the creation of a mercantile and industrial empire of cotton represents consumer desire for cotton as an almost natural (and universal) attraction to bright colors and soft textures. Christopher Brown, *Moral Capital: Foundations of British Abolitionism* (Chapel Hill: University of North Carolina Press, 2006); Seymour Drescher, *Abolition: A History of Slavery and Antislavery* (New York: Cambridge University Press, 2009); Robin Blackburn, *The American Crucible: Slavery, Emancipation, and Human Rights* (London: Verso, 2013); W. Caleb McDaniel, *The Problem of Democracy in the Age of Slavery: Garrisonian Abolitionists and Transatlantic Reform* (Baton Rouge: Louisiana State University Press, 2013); Manisha Sinha, *The Slave's Cause: A History of Abolition* (New Haven, Conn.: Yale University Press, 2016).

4. McDaniel, *Problem of Democracy*, 76–78, for Garrisonian transatlantic networks.

5. Sussman, *Consuming Anxieties*, 110–129; Clare Midgley, *Women Against Slavery: The British Campaigns, 1780–1870* (New York: Routledge, 1992); Clare Midgley, "The Dissenting Voice of Elizabeth Heyrick," and Timothy Whelan, "Martha Gurney and the Anti-Slave Trade Movement, 1788–94," both in Elizabeth Clapp and Julie Roy Jeffrey, eds., *Women, Dissent, and Anti-slavery in Britain and America, 1790–1865* (New York: Oxford University Press, 2011), 44–65, 88–110; Kett, "Without the Consumers"; Faulkner, "Root of the Evil." For women's special relationship with sugar and sugar work, see Kim Hall, "Culinary Spaces, Colonial Spaces: The Gendering of Sugar in the Seventeenth Century," in Valerie Traub, ed., *Feminist Readings of Early Modern Culture: Emerging Subjects* (New York: Cambridge University Press, 1996), 168–190. Erin Pearson, "A Person Perverted into a Thing: Cannibalistic Metaphors and Dehumanizing Physicality in Late Eighteenth-Century British Abolitionism," *ELH* 83, no. 3 (2016): 741–769. For Rush's interest in maple sugar, see Benjamin Rush, "Memorable Facts, Events, Opinions, Thoughts . . . ," in George W. Corner, ed., *The Autobiography of Benjamin Rush* (Princeton, N.J.: Princeton University Press, 1948); Alan Taylor, *William Cooper's Town: Power and Persuasion on the Frontier of the Early American Republic* (New York: Knopf, 1995), 117–138; Holcomb, *Moral Commerce*, 65–68; Wolf, "Early Free Labor Thought."

6. "Dissidence," from the Latin for "sitting apart," suggests the physicality of expressing political opposition.

7. Elias Hicks, *Observations on the Slavery of the Africans and Their Descendants* (New York: Samuel Wood, 1811).

8. Elizabeth Heyrick, *Immediate, Not Gradual Abolition; or, An Inquiry into the Shortest, Safest, and Most Effectual Means of Getting Rid of West Indian Slavery* (Philadelphia, 1824); Elizabeth Heyrick, *Instructive Hints in Easy Lessons for Children* (London, 1816). See also Carol Lasser, "Immediatism, Dissent, and Gender: Women and the Sentimentalization of Transatlantic Anti-slavery Appeals," in Clapp and Jeffrey, eds, *Women, Dissent, and Anti-slavery*, 111–131; Wilkinson, "Philadelphia Free Produce Attack," 297; and Nuermberger, *Free Produce Movement*, 7.

9. "Speech of J. J. Gurney, Esq., on the Abolition of Negro Slavery, Delivered at a Public Meeting, Held in the Guildhall in the City of Norwich, Wednesday, 28 January 1824" (Liverpool, 1824). James Cropper's initiative in 1825 to source free sugar and cotton for his Irish factories was the first of many such plans; see *The Injurious Effects of Slave Labour: An Appeal to the Reason, Justice, and Patriotism of the People of Illinois* (London, 1824); Alex Tyrrell, *Joseph Sturge and the Moral Radical Party in Early Victorian Britain* (London: Christopher Helm, 1987), 48.

10. Tyrrell, *Joseph Sturge*, 48, 141, for the difficulties of dating the Sturges' exclusion of slave produce from their household. Sophia, a founding member of the Ladies Society of Birmingham for the Relief of Negro Slaves, is reputed to have visited as many as three thousand homes to distribute pamphlets and sell abolitionist paraphernalia. R. J. Ellis, "Joseph Sturge, Harriet Beecher Stowe, and the Free-Labor Movement," in Beth L. Lueck, Sirpa Salenius, and Nancy Lusignan Schultz, eds., *Transatlantic Conversations: Nineteenth-Century American Women's Encounters with Italy and the*

Atlantic World (Durham, N.H.: University of New Hampshire Press, 2017), 179. Midgley, *Women Against Slavery.*

11. [John Sturge], *Short Review of the Slave Trade and Slavery, with Considerations on the Benefits That Would Arise from Cultivating Tropical Productions with Free Labour* (Birmingham, 1827). In his report to the World Anti-Slavery Convention of 1840, John Sturge took credit for this pamphlet.

12. Richard Allen, letter to *Freedom's Journal*, November 2, 1827; Leslie M. Alexander, "Black Republic: The Influence of the Haitian Revolution on Northern Black Political Consciousness, 1816–1862," in Maurice Jackson and Jacqueline Bacon, eds., *African Americans and the Haitian Revolution* (New York: Routledge, 2010), 57–79.

13. Holcomb, *Moral Commerce*, 75–76; Paul Goodman, *Of One Blood: Abolitionism and the Origins of Racial Equality* (Berkeley: University of California Press, 1998); Margaret Hope Bacon, *But One Race: The Life of Robert Purvis* (Albany: State University of New York Press, 1997).

14. *Constitution of the Free Produce Society* (Philadelphia, 1827); Lucretia Mott to Adam Mott and Anne Mott, Philadelphia, April 23, 1826, in Beverly Wilson Palmer, ed., *Selected Letters of Lucretia Coffin Mott* (Urbana: University of Illinois Press, 2002), 15; Carol Faulkner, *Lucretia Mott's Heresy: Abolition and Women's Rights in Nineteenth-Century America* (Philadelphia: University of Pennsylvania Press, 2011), 55; Richard S. Newman, *Freedom's Prophet: Bishop Richard Allen, the AME Church, and the Black Founding Fathers* (New York: New York University Press, 2008), 264–268.

15. Elizabeth Margaret Chandler, *An Appeal to the Ladies of the United States* (1829), reprinted in *Poetical Works of Elizabeth Margaret Chandler: With a Memoir of Her Life and Character by Benjamin Lundy* (Philadelphia: Lemuel Howell, 1836), 20. Civis, "To the Public," *Genius of Universal Emancipation*, April 1830. Marcia J. Heninga Mason, ed., *Remember the Distance That Divides Us: The Family Letters of Philadelphia Quaker Abolitionist and Michigan Pioneer Elizabeth Margaret Chandler, 1830–1842* (East Lansing: Michigan State University Press, 2014).

16. Nuermberger, *Free Produce Movement*, 119. "Free Dry Goods' Store," *Genius of Universal Emancipation*, May 1830. White's store at 86 N. Fifth Street later moved to 42 N. Fourth Street.

17. Howard Bell, ed., *Minutes of the National Negro Conventions* (New York: Arno Press, 1969), 30; Goodman, *Of One Blood*, 32–35; Bacon, *But One Race*, 97.

18. Philadelphia Female Anti-Slavery Society Meeting Minutes, HSP (hereafter PFAS Minutes), December 9, 1833; March 9, 1837; August 10, 1837.

19. *The Journal: A Paper Devoted to the Interests of the Society of Friends*, April 18, 1883.

20. R. C. Smedley, *History of the Underground Railroad, in Chester and the Neighboring Counties of Pennsylvania* (Mechanicsburg, Pa.: Stackpole Books, 2005), 167, 312. McKim's daughter subsequently married W. L. Garrison's son. See also Elizabeth K. Barnard, *Friend's Intelligencer*, January 7, 1911; Everill, *Not Made by Slaves*, 77, 123, 225.

21. Levi Coffin to Samuel Rhoads, February 16, 1846, Newport, Indiana, Taylor Family Papers, HCQSC. Before they relocated to Elkton, Ohio, Coffin and his wife, Catherine, were disowned by the Indiana Yearly Meeting in 1843 and, along with fellow abolitionists, formed a separate Yearly Meeting of Anti-Slavery Friends.

22. Benjamin Lundy, "Memoir," in *Poetical Works of Elizabeth Margaret Chandler*, 21.

23. Faulkner, *Lucretia Mott's Heresy*, 54. Faulkner, "Root of the Evil."

24. Faulkner, "Root of the Evil"; Everill, *Not Made by Slaves*, 91, 94, for price discrepancies in George Washington Taylor's marketing of goods.

25. David Brion Davis, *The Problem of Slavery in Western Culture* (Ithaca, N.Y.: Cornell University Press, 1966), 294; Faulkner, "Root of the Evil," 398.

26. Chandler, *Poetical Works*, 108–109. See also Lasser, "Immediatism, Dissent, and Gender"; Sussman, *Consuming Anxieties*, 116–119; Pearson, "A Person Perverted into a Thing."

27. Chandler, *Poetical Works*, 111.

28. Mason, *Remember the Distance*, 129, 143; Stanley Stein, *Vassouras: A Brazilian Coffee County, 1850–1900* (Princeton, N.J.: Princeton University Press, 1986); Holcomb, *Moral Commerce*, 120, identifies Townsend as the creator of the alphabet.

29. Joseph Sturge and Thomas Harvey, *The West Indies in 1837; Being the Journal of a Visit to Antigua, Montserrat, Dominica, St. Lucia, Barbadoes, and Jamaica; Undertaken for the Purpose of Ascertaining the Actual Condition of the Negro Population of These Islands* (London, 1838). For Harvey, see "Thomas Harvey (1812–1884): Anti-slavery Campaigner and Philanthropist," Thoresby Society, https://www.thoresby.org.uk/content/people/harvey.php. See also Edward Rugemer, *The Problem of Emancipation: The Caribbean Roots of the American Civil War* (Baton Rouge: Louisiana State University Press, 2008), 165–170.

30. Sturge and Harvey, *The West Indies in 1837*, 18.

31. Sturge and Harvey, *The West Indies in 1837*, 14–16.

32. Sturge, *The West Indies in 1837*, 7–8, 40–41, for men and women in jail in Barbados and the beating of women sentenced to the treadmill.

33. Sturge and Harvey, *The West Indies in 1837*, 81–82, 84–85, 87, 88.

34. Sturge and Harvey, *The West Indies in 1837*, 52, 56, 61. See also Katherine Paugh, *The Politics of Reproduction: Race, Medicine, and Fertility in the Age of Abolition* (Oxford, U.K.: Oxford University Press, 2017).

35. Sturge and Harvey, *The West Indies in 1837*, 77.

36. Sturge and Harvey, *The West Indies in 1837*, 56, 61, 69–70.

37. Sophia Sturge to "Friend," July 31, 1837, Sturge Papers, BL. Henry Sterne, *A Statement of Facts, Submitted to the Right Hon. Lord Glenelg, His Majesty's Principal Secretary of State for the Colonies . . . with an Exposure of the Present System of Jamaica Apprenticeship by Henry Sterne* (London, 1837); Sturge had likely requested "Interior View of a Jamaican House of Correction,"1837.

38. James Thome and J. Horace Kimball, *Emancipation in the West Indies* (New York: American Anti-Slavery Society, 1838). Thome, the son of a Kentucky slave owner, was one of the Lane Seminary abolitionist "rebels" who, along with Theodore Weld, left the seminary for Oberlin College. Kimball, the editor of the *Herald of Freedom* (Concord, N.H.), died before he was able to do much writing. The Amherst College professor Sylvester Hovey published his own account of emancipation, *Letters from the West Indies: Relating Especially to the Danish Islands of St. Croix, and to the British Islands Antigua, Barbadoes, and Jamaica* (New York, 1838).

39. PFAS Minutes, February 8, 1838; March 8, 1838; April 12, 1838; May 10, 1838; June 14, 1838, HSP. Among the delegates was Elizabeth Clark Bunting, who later defended medical lecturer Frederick Hollick's right to speak to a female audience about women's sexual anatomy. See PFAS Minutes, April 12, 1838; *Pennsylvania Freeman*, March 12, 1846, p. 3, col. 4; April Haynes, *Riotous Flesh: Women, Physiology, and the Solitary Vice in Nineteenth-Century America* (Chicago: University of Chicago Press, 2015).

40. *Minutes of the Proceedings of the Requited Labor Convention Held in Philadelphia* (Philadelphia: Merrihew and Gunn, 1838); "Destruction of the Hall [graphic] / Drawn from the spot and engraved by J. Sartrain," Library Company of Philadelphia, 1838, https://digital.librarycompany.org/islandora/object/digitool%3A129971; Beverly Tomek, *Pennsylvania Hall: a "legal lynching" in the Shadows of the Liberty Bell* (New York: Oxford University Press, 2014); Daniel Kilbride, "Southern Medical Students in Philadelphia, 1800–1861: Science and Sociability in the 'Republic of Medicine,'" *Journal of Southern History* 65, no. 4 (November 1999): 697–732. Mott quote from PFAS Minutes, June 14, 1838, HSP.

41. PFAS Minutes, August 10, 1837, HSP. *Proceedings of the Requited Labor Convention Held in Philadelphia.*

42. *Proceedings of the Requited Labor Convention Held in Philadelphia*; Sussman, *Consuming Anxieties*, 116–119.

43. *Proceedings of the Requited Labor Convention Held in Philadelphia.*

44. PFAS Minutes, 1838, 1839–1844, HSP. Jean R. Soderlund, "Priorities and Power: The Philadelphia Female Anti-Slavery Society," in Jean Fagan Yellin and John C. Van Horne, *The Abolitionist Sisterhood: Women's Political Culture in Antebellum America* (Ithaca, N.Y.: Cornell University Press, 1994); Julie Roy Jeffrey, *The Great Silent Army of Abolitionism: Ordinary Women in the Antislavery Movement* (Chapel Hill: University of North Carolina Press, 1998), 108–126. See also Susan Zaeske,

Signatures of Citizenship: Petitioning, Antislavery, and Women's Political Identity (Chapel Hill: University of North Carolina Press, 2003). For the politics of the Boston Anti-Slavery Fairs, see Debra Gold Hansen, *Strained Sisterhood: Gender and Class in the Boston Female Anti-Slavery Society* (Amherst: University of Massachusetts Press, 1993), 124–139. The PFAS Minutes included condemnation of the annexation of Texas (November 13, 1845), a declaration in favor of disunion with slaveholders (October 14, 1847), and petitions against the Nebraska Bill (February 9, 1854), HSP.

45. Joseph Sturge to "Friend," January 6, 1839, transport of Madagascar slaves to Mauritius, Sturge Papers, BL; Joseph Sturge, "To the Members of the British Association for the Advancement of Science," July 1839, and quote from Daniel O'Connell, Sturge Papers, BL; Joseph Sturge to "Friend," February 6, 1840, concerning Lord Russell's sanction of the traffic in South Asian labor to Mauritius, BL; Palmer, *Letters of Lucretia Mott*, 141; Joseph Sturge to "Friend" May 7, 1840, Sturge Papers, BL. See Madhavi Kale, *Fragments of Empire: Capital, Slavery, and Indian Indentured Labor in the British Caribbean* (Philadelphia: University of Pennsylvania Press, 1998); James Heartfield, *The British and Foreign Anti-Slavery Society, 1838–1956: A History* (New York: Oxford University Press, 2016). Richard Huzzey, *Freedom Burning: Anti-slavery and Empire in Victorian Britain* (Ithaca, N.Y.: Cornell University Press, 2012), 10–14.

46. L. E. Sturge to unknown correspondent, April 1840, Sturge Papers, BL. Andrea Major, "'Hill Coolies': Indian Indentured Labour and the Colonial Imagination, 1836–38," *South Asian Studies* 33, no. 1 (2017): 23–36. Andrea Major, *Slavery, Abolitionism and Empire in India, 1772–1843* (Liverpool: Liverpool University Press, 2012), 326.

47. Howard Temperly, "The O'Connell-Stevenson Contretemps," *Journal of Negro History* 47, no. 4 (1962): 217–233; Betty Fladeland, *Men and Brothers: Anglo-American Antislavery Cooperation* (Urbana: University of Illinois Press, 1972), 241–242; John F. Quinn, "Expecting the Impossible? Abolitionist Appeals to the Irish in Antebellum America," *New England Quarterly* 82, no. 4 (2009).

48. Joseph Sturge to "Friend," February 6, 1840; Joseph Sturge to "Friend," May 7, 1840; all in Sturge Papers, BL. Palmer, *Letters of Lucretia Mott*, 141. See also Kale, *Fragments of Empire*.

49. Joseph Sturge to "Friend," January 6, 1840, Sturge Papers, BL.

50. Bertram Wyatt-Brown, *Lewis Tappan and the Evangelical War Against Slavery* (Cleveland, Ohio: Case Western Reserve University Press, 1969); Lawrence J. Friedman, "Confidence and Pertinacity in Evangelical Abolitionism: Lewis Tappan's Circle," in John R. McKivigan, ed., *Abolitionism and American Religion* (New York: Routledge, 2000). The British delegation had already traveled to Paris to "tighten the bond that existed already between the two societies" [BFAS and the Société Française pour l'abolition de l'esclavage]; see Lawrence C. Jennings, *French Anti-slavery: The Movement for the Abolition of Slavery in France, 1802–1848* (New York: Cambridge University Press, 2000), 144.

51. Palmer, *Letters of Lucretia Mott*, 78n2.

52. Lucretia Mott to Maria Weston Chapman, Dublin, July 29, 1840, in Palmer, *Letters of Lucretia Mott*, 78–81.

53. Lucretia Mott to Daniel O'Connell, MP, June 17, 1840, in Palmer, *Letters of Lucretia Mott*, 77.

54. Palmer, *Letters of Lucretia Mott*, 81n7. Sophia Sturge to unknown correspondent, November 28, 1840, Sturge Papers, BL; Faulkner, *Lucretia Mott's Heresy*, 91–97.

55. John Sturge, "Report on Free Labour given to the General Anti-Slavery Convention," Sturge Papers, BL. Douglas H. Maynard, "The World's Anti-Slavery Convention of 1840," *Mississippi Valley Historical Review* 47, no. 3 (December 1960): 452–471, esp. 461–462; Faulkner, *Lucretia Mott's Heresy*, 98–99.

56. Maynard, "The World's Anti-Slavery Convention of 1840," 452–471; Kale, *Fragments of Empire*; Ellis, "Joseph Sturge, Harriet Beecher Stowe, and the Free Labor Movement," 182; Faulkner, *Lucretia Mott's Heresy*, 107–108.

57. Joseph Sturge to John Soul, November 4, 1840, Sturge Papers, BL.

58. Sturge, *A Visit to the United States in 1841* (Boston: Dexter and King, 1842), 50.

59. Sturge, *Visit to the United States*, 45–46; letter from Robert Purvis to Sturge, reprinted in Bacon, *But One Race*, 71–72.

60. Betty Fladeland, *Abolitionists and Working-Class Problems in the Age of Industrialization* (London: Macmillan, 1984), 64.

61. Sturge, *Visit to the United States*, 116, 136, 165; PFAS Minutes, October 10, 1841, HSP, for Angelina Grimké's letter explaining the importance of abstinence from slave-produced goods. Nuermberger, *Free Produce Movement*; Wilkinson, "Philadelphia Free Produce Attack." Sara Fanning, *Caribbean Crossing: African Americans and the Haitian Emigration Movement* (New York: New York University Press, 2015), 70.

62. Lucretia Mott to Richard D. Webb and Hannah Webb, Philadelphia, February 25, 1842, in Palmer, *Letters of Lucretia Mott*, 110. McDaniel, *Problem of Democracy*, 163–166, for the influence of the Corn Law League's tactics on U.S. abolitionists; Paul A. Pickering and Alex Tyrrell, *The People's Bread: A History of the Anti-Corn Law League* (New York: Leicester University Press, 2000).

63. Sturge, *Visit to the United States*, 156. Ellis, "Joseph Sturge, Harriet Beecher Stowe, and the Free Labor Movement," 177–194, esp. 182.

64. Joseph Sturge to "Friend," March 20, 1841; Sophia Sturge to "Friend," May 21, 1841; both in Sturge Papers, BL.

65. Sophia Sturge to Richard Allen, April 8, 1841, Sturge Papers, BL. Charles Remond arrived in the United States with O'Connell's statement in January 1842, at a tumultuous political moment discussed in Chapter 7; see McDaniel, *Problem of Democracy*, 170.

66. Joseph Sturge to John Soul, September 7, 1841. See also Joseph Sturge to John Soul, November 17, 1841, about armed police, and Joseph Sturge to John Soul, March 23, 1844, on his efforts to stop an execution; all in Sturge Papers, BL.

67. Sophia Sturge to John Soul, 1843, Sturge Papers, BL.

68. In 1844, Joseph Sturge joined protests against the practice of British ships transporting exploited South Asian labor to Caribbean and American ports. Sturge also spoke out against the use of armed police in Birmingham. Kale, *Fragments of Empire*, 128–132.

69. *British and Foreign Anti-Slavery Reporter*, vol. 5, Wednesday, April 3, 1844, 54–55. "Extracts from letters in reply to Joseph Sturge's circular," March 1844, Sturge Papers, BL. See also Joseph Sturge to John Soul, August 9, 1844, and August 12, 1844, Sturge Papers, BL. Maynard, "World's Anti-Slavery Convention of 1840," 452–471.

70. Joseph Sturge to John Soul, April 9, 1844, Sturge Papers, BL. The end of West Indian protections came in 1846; see Huzzey, *Freedom Burning*, 98–113.

71. For the PFAS commitment to free produce, see PFAS Minutes, December 14, 1833; March 9, 1837; August 10, 1837; June 3, 1839; October 10, 1841; October 13, 1842; December 8, 1842; April 13, 1843; May 18, 1843; all in HSP. For PFAS efforts to spread free produce commitments, see Sidney Ann Lewis's instruction to the new British Anti-Slavery League to adopt free produce consumption, PFAS Minutes, October 20, 1846; Mott's encouragement of free produce principles, April 11, 1848; and her joy at the Philadelphia Clarkson Society's adoption of free produce principles, September 11, 1851; all in HSP. See also Erica Armstrong Dunbar, *Fragile Freedom: African American Women and Emancipation in the Antebellum City* (New Haven, Conn.: Yale University Press, 2011), 93–95.

72. S. A. Calder, Belfast, to Samuel Rhoads, December 1, 1845, Taylor Family Papers, HCQSC. On abolitionist providentialism see John Coffey, "'Tremble, Britannia!': Fear, Providence and the Abolition of the Slave Trade, 1758—1807," *English Historical Review* 127, no. 527 (August 2012): 844–881.

73. S. A. Calder to Samuel Rhoads, Belfast, December 1, 1845, Taylor Family Papers, HCQSC.

74. Joseph Kent Farm Ledger, Chester County Historical Society, Chester, Pa.; Lucy Simler and Paul Clemens, "Rural Labor and the Farm Household in Chester County, Pennsylvania, 1750–1820," in Stephen Innes, ed., *Work and Labor in Early America* (Chapel Hill: University of North Carolina Press, 1988), 106–143; Christopher Densmore, introduction to Smedley, *Underground Railroad*; Joan Jensen, *Loosening the Bonds: Mid-Atlantic Farm Women 1750–1850* (New Haven, Conn.: Yale University Press, 1986); Eric Foner, *Gateway to Freedom: The Hidden History of the Underground Railroad* (Oxford, U.K.: Oxford University Press, 2015). For George W. Taylor's early personal aversion to close contact between Black people and white people, see Sarah M. Grimke and Theodore Weld to

Elizabeth Pease, November 14, 1840, in Dwight L. Dumond and Gilbert H. Barnes, eds., *The Letters of Theodore Dwight Weld, Angelina Grimké Weld, and Sarah Grimké*, 2 vols. (New York: D. Appleton-Century Company, 1934) 1: 855, cited in Ryan P. Jordan, *Slavery and the Meetinghouse: The Quakers and the Abolitionist Dilemma, 1820–1865* (Bloomington: Indiana University Press, 2007), 37.

75. *Anti-slavery Reporter*, August 6, 1845, 150–151, for the meeting in Philadelphia on March 23, 1845.

76. Thomas Clarkson to Samuel Rhoads, two versions of letter, April 18, 1846, and May 1, 1846, Rhoads Family Papers, HCQSC.

77. Joseph Sturge to Samuel Rhoads, April 3, 1846, Rhoads Family Papers, HCQSC.

78. For examples of Taylor's correspondence, see Thistlewaite to George W. Taylor, November 30, 1846, Millville, N.Y.; B. Parsons, August 5, 1847, Flushing, N.Y.; Elias Coleman to George W. Taylor, July 18, 1848, Jonesborough, Tenn., all in Taylor Family Papers, HCQSC.

79. Beckert, *Empire of Cotton*, 199–241.

80. E. Tucker, *History of Randolph County, Indiana, with Illustrations and Biographical Sketches* (Chicago, 1882), 171–172. Jordan, *Slavery and the Meetinghouse*, 49; John Michael Vlach, "Above Ground on the Underground Railroad: Places of Flight and Refuge," in David Blight, ed., *Passages to Freedom: The Underground Railroad in History and Memory* (Washington, D.C.: Smithsonian, 2004), 95–115. See also William Still, *The Underground Railroad*, rev. ed. (Philadelphia, 1878), 16–17, for Coffin's work to help free Still's brother. See also Nathan Thomas, Find A Grave, New Garden Indiana Friends Cemetery, https://www.findagrave.com/memorial/90538088/nathan-thomas

81. "The cotton is not all of the quality we wanted, were a little too late in the season for the first picking"; Nathan Thomas to George W. Taylor, January 14, 1846, Taylor Family Papers, HCQSC.

82. Levi Coffin to Samuel Rhoads, November 14, 1845; Nathan Thomas to Samuel Rhoads, Memphis, January 14, 1846; both in Taylor Family Papers, HCQSC.

83. Committee of Manufactures Report, March 4, 1847, Taylor Family Papers, HCQSC.

84. Joseph Sturge to Samuel Rhoads, Birmingham, April 3, 1846, Rhoads Family Papers, HCQSC.

85. Israel Johnson and Edward Garrett on behalf of the Committee, "To the Board of Managers of Free Produce of Friends of the Philadelphia Yearly Meeting," March 16, 1847, Taylor Family Papers, HCQSC.

86. George W. Taylor to Nathan Thomas, November 30, 1847; J. Krafft to George W. Taylor, January 17, 1848, urges them to identify free gins rather than make purchases of cotton; both in Taylor Family Papers, HCQSC.

87. Thomas Clarkson to Samuel Rhoads, April 18, 1846, Rhoads Family Papers, HSQSC. See also Beckert, *Empire of Cotton*, 122–131; R. J. M. Blackett, *Building an Antislavery Wall: Black Americans in the Atlantic Abolition Movement, 1830–1860* (Baton Rouge: Louisiana State University Press, 1983), 121, 141, 184.

88. Levi Coffin to Samuel Rhoads, Newport, Indiana, March 4, 1846, Taylor Family Papers, HCQSC.

89. The 1850 census, Memphis Ward 4, Shelby County, Tennessee, lists John H. Krafft, cotton broker, aged fifty-one and born in Pennsylvania, along with his wife, M. S. Krafft, aged forty-two, and his daughter Clara Krafft, aged nineteen. Krafft had done business with John B. Budd, Philadelphia merchant. See also *Reports of Cases Argued and Determined in the Supreme Court of Tennessee, 1846–1847*, West H. Humphreys, state reporter (Nashville, Tenn.: 1847), 553–558, for Krafft's role as an agent for a road-grading firm in *Levering and Carncross v. The Mayor et als.* Beckert, *Empire of Cotton*, 220–222, for cotton factors.

90. J. Krafft to Messrs Brown and Bowen, Memphis, December 6, 1845, Taylor Family Papers, HCQSC.

91. J. Krafft to Messrs Brown and Bowen, Memphis, December 6, 1845; Certificate, Insurance Company of the State of Pennsylvania, January 8, 1846; both in Taylor Family Papers, HCQSC. See also Beckert, *Empire of Cotton*, 203–213.

92. J. Krafft to George W. Taylor, Memphis, January 20, 1846; Nathan Thomas to Samuel Rhoads, January 16, 1847, and M. C. Cope to Nathan Thomas, October 9, 1847, concerning his desire for fifty bales of free cotton and payment for a cotton gin; all in Taylor Family Papers, HCQSC.

93. J. Krafft to George W. Taylor, Memphis, January 20, 1846; Taylor Family Papers, HCQSC.

94. J. Krafft to Samuel Rhoads, October 26, 1846; Taylor Family Papers, HCQSC.

95. J. Krafft to Samuel Rhoads, December 8, 1846, Taylor Family Papers, HCQSC.

96. J. Krafft to Samuel Rhoads, December 9, 1846, Taylor Family Papers, HCQSC.

97. Samuel Rhoads to J. Krafft, February 15, 1847, Taylor Family Papers, HCQSC. Liverpool cotton brokers Reginald Hodgson and Arthur Ryley were known abolitionists; see C. Peter Ripley, ed., *Black Abolitionist Papers*, 3 vols. (Chapel Hill: University of North Carolina Press, 1985), 1:102, for Charles Remond's references to the abolitionist wives of the two British merchants; see *Liverpool Commercial List* (1866), for Hodgson and Ryley.

98. J. Krafft to Samuel Rhoads, October 26, 1846, Taylor Family Papers, HCQSC.

99. J. Krafft to Samuel Rhoads, January 17, 1848. Taylor Family Papers, HCQSC.

100. J. Krafft to Samuel Rhoads, October 26, 1846; Samuel Rhoads to J. Krafft, November 27, 1846; both in Taylor Family Papers, HCQSC. Rhoads wanted twenty more to go New Orleans to Liverpool marked JS/B c/o [Reginald] Hodgson [Hodgston] and [Arthur] Ryley, cotton brokers.

101. J. Krafft to Samuel Rhoads, February 16, 1847; J. Krafft to Samuel Rhoads, March 19, 1847, Taylor Family Papers, HCQSC.

102. Carson and Newbold were Philadelphia merchants in the credit business, specializing in the New Orleans trade; see *Pennsylvania State Reports*, vol. 15, for business in 1844 and on appeal, in *Howland & Aspinall v. Carson & Newbold*, in *Supreme Court of Pennsylvania*, vol. 15 (Philadelphia, 1851), December 1850, 453–456.

103. In 1841, Byrne was listed as a Liverpool calico printer; *Spectator* 14 (1841): 1219. He was listed as a failed banker and merchant in the *Merchants Magazine and Commercial Review* 18 (November–December 1848): 191.

104. J. Krafft to Samuel Rhoads, January 17, 1848; February 4, 1848; Taylor Family Papers, HCQSC. Rhoads requested that Krafft notify him when he subsequently sent cotton to the Liverpool firm Thompson and Midgely.

105. Levi Coffin to Samuel Rhoads, March 5, 1847, Taylor Family Papers, HCQSC. Coffin would test this claim by purchasing $7,000 of free cotton for manufacturing cloth, for which he was reimbursed only $3,000. Levi Coffin, *Reminiscences of Levi Coffin, the Reputed President of the Underground Railroad* [. . .], 2nd ed. (Cincinnati, 1880), 277. The manufacturers, Pearce and Brothers, were listed in *The Ohio Cultivator*, vol. 6 (1850).

106. See Walter L. Wheeler to Abram L. Pennock, West Elkton, Preble County, Ohio, November 14, 1845; Levi Coffin to Samuel Rhoads, Newport, March 16, 1846; Wheeler to George W. Taylor, May 28, 1847; all in Taylor Family Papers, HCQSC.

107. Joseph Sturge to John Soul, April 9, 1844, Sturge Papers, BL.

108. Tyrrell, *Joseph Sturge*, 141.

109. Merle Curti, ed., *The Learned Blacksmith: The Letters and Journals of Elihu Burritt* (New York: Wilson-Erickson, 1937); Peter Tolis, *Elihu Burritt: Crusader for Brotherhood* (Hamden, Conn.: Archon Books, 1968); Glenn M. McNair, "The Elijah Burritt Affair: David Walker's *Appeal* and Partisan Journalism in Antebellum Milledgeville," *Georgia Historical Quarterly* 83, no. 3 (1999): 448–478.

110. Lewis Tappan to John Scoble, January 19, 1845, BL.

111. Soderlund, "Priorities and Power"; Faulkner, "Root of the Evil."

112. Elizabeth Allen to Anne Rhoads, Samuel Rhoads, May 29, 1848, Rhoads Family Papers, HCQSC.

113. Hannah Sturge to Anne Rhoads, September 23, 1847, Rhoads Family Papers, HCQSC.

114. Anna Richardson, "To the Friends of the Slave in Great Britain," *British Friend* (April 1848): 103–105.

115. Richardson, "To the Friends of the Slave in Great Britain." See also PFAS Minutes, May 10, 1849; March 1, 1850; and March 13, 1851, HSP.

116. John Dunmore Lang, "Prospectus of a Company for the Encouragement and Promotion of the Cultivation of Cotton and Other Tropical Produce by Means of European Free Labor in the Territory of Cooksland in North Eastern Australia," and Appendix, "To Gentlemen in the Cotton Trade, and to the Friends of the Abolition of Negro Slavery," Manchester, August 28, 1847, David Scott Mitchell Library, State Library of New South Wales, Sydney, Australia. Lang's detailed plan for the Cooksland Cotton Cultivation Company included using shareholder money to transport suitable farmers and laborers to Queensland, where they would labor on model farms, superintended by persons from the southern cotton growing states. Company shareholders were to be reimbursed from the surplus generated by land sales. Books by Lang include *Cooksland in Northeastern Australia: The Future Cotton Field of Great Britain* (London, 1847); *Phillipsland, or the Country Hitherto Designated Port Phillip* (London, 1847); *Queensland, Australia: A Highly Eligible Field for Emigration and the Future Cotton-Field of Great Britain* (London, 1861).

117. Elihu Burritt to George W. Taylor, Exeter, England, September 29, 1846, Taylor Family Papers, HCQSC. Burritt lobbied to reduce the cost of transatlantic postage from twenty-five cents to a penny ("ocean penny postage"), a campaign that succeeded by 1872 and became a boon to transatlantic reformers. See Holcomb, *Moral Commerce*, 181, who dates Burritt's London depot to 1853.

118. Elihu Burritt to George W. Taylor, September 29, 1846, Taylor Family Papers, HCQSC.

119. Elihu Burritt to George W. Taylor, October 19, 1846, Taylor Family Papers, HCQSC.

120. After being supplied with cotton seed by Taylor, in 1855 Downman reported that he was finally growing cotton and other crops in Utoy, Georgia, where he noted that most planters cared little about seed variety and simply planted the same cotton species; Downman to George W. Taylor, May 30, 1855, Taylor Family Papers, HCQSC. For Burritt's subsequent free produce exploits, see Everill, *Not Made by Slaves*, 220–221.

121. Nathan Thomas to Samuel Rhoads, March 20, 1850, Taylor Family Papers, HCQSC.

122. Nathan Thomas to Samuel Rhoads on January 16, 1847; Taylor Family Papers, HCQSC.

123. Nathan Thomas to George W. Taylor, December 14, 1849, Taylor Family Papers, HCQSC.

124. Nathan Thomas to George W. Taylor, December 14, 1849, Taylor Family Papers, HCQSC.

125. Nathan Thomas to George W. Taylor, December 14, 1849. Taylor Family Papers, HCQSC.

126. Nathan Thomas to Samuel Rhoads, November 28, 1849; Nathan Thomas to Samuel Rhoads, December 20, 1849, both in Taylor Family Papers, HCQSC. Edward E. Baptist, *The Half Has Never Been Told: Slavery and the Making of American Capitalism* (New York: Basic Books, 2014).

127. Nathan Thomas to Samuel Rhoads, New Orleans, January 2, 1850, Taylor Family Papers, HCQSC.

128. Nathan Thomas to Samuel Rhoads, June 12, 1848. Taylor Family Papers, HCQSC.

129. J. Krafft to George W. Taylor, Memphis, January 20, 1846, Taylor Family Papers, HCQSC.

130. J. Krafft to Samuel Rhoads, December 8, 1846. Taylor Family Papers, HCQSC.

131. J. Krafft to George W. Taylor, January 20, 1846; Nathan Thomas to Samuel Rhoads, Memphis, January 14, 1846; J. Krafft to Samuel Rhoads, October 26, 1846, and December 9, 1849; Nathan Thomas to Samuel Rhoads, Holly Springs, December 8, 1849; all in Taylor Family Papers, HCQSC. Nuermberger, *Free Produce Movement*, 69–70.

132. J. Krafft to George W. Taylor, Memphis, January 20, 1846, Taylor Family Papers, HCQSC.

133. J. Krafft to Samuel Rhoads, January 17, 1848; Nathan Thomas to George W. Taylor, December 9, 1849, Taylor Family Papers, HCQSC.

134. Nathan Thomas to Samuel Rhoads, Memphis, January 14, 1846, Taylor Family Papers, HCQSC.

135. Nathan Thomas to George W. Taylor, November 18, 1849, Taylor Family Papers, HCQSC.

136. L. E. Sturge, May 1, 1849, Sturge Papers, BL; *Anti-slavery Reporter*, September 3, 1849, December 26, 1849. Midgley, *Women Against Slavery*.

137. Douglass attended a Birmingham Temperance Society meeting in December with Sturge, who greeted him warmly and invited him to dine at his home. Sturge subsequently arranged for

Douglass's Reception Speech at Finsbury Chapel in May 1846; see John McKivigan, ed., *Frederick Douglass Papers* (New Haven, Conn.: Yale University Press, 2009). L. E. Sturge wrote in 1855 enquiring about the publication of Frederick Douglass's autobiography.

138. W. C. Taber to George W. Taylor, February 24, 1849, Taylor Family Papers, HCQSC.

139. Mary Blewett, *Constant Turmoil: The Politics of Industrial Life in Nineteenth-Century New England* (Amherst: University of Massachusetts Press, 2000), 27. The elder Robeson had been a Pennsylvania flour miller.

140. Nathan Thomas to Samuel Rhoads, December 20, 1849, Taylor Family Papers, HCQSC.

141. Nathan Thomas to Samuel Rhoads, New Orleans, January 2, 1850, Taylor Family Papers, HCQSC.

142. Nathan Thomas to Samuel Rhoads, January 22, 1850. Taylor Family Papers, HCQSC.

143. Nathan Thomas to Samuel Rhoads, February 17, 1850; and March 13, 1850, Taylor Family Papers, HCQSC.

144. Samuel Rhoads to Margaret Collins, March 6, 1847, Taylor Family Papers, HCQSC.

145. Boston Refining Company to George W. Taylor, April 28, 1847; agents Josiah Stuckney and Js. Schofield to George W. Taylor, May 25, 1847, both in Taylor Family Papers, HCQSC.

146. George W. Taylor, November 1848, Taylor Family Papers, HCQSC; Everill, *Not Made by Slaves*, 91–92, 123–124, 182, 216–218.

147. George W. Taylor Correspondence, Taylor Family Papers, HCQSC. Nuermberger, *Free Produce Movement*, 79.

148. David White to George W. Taylor, April 1849, Taylor Family Papers, HCQSC.

149. [?], Burlington, to George W. Taylor, September 10, 1849, Taylor Family Papers, HCQSC.

150. *Friends' Intelligencer*, vol. 68 (January 7, 1911).

151. Webster had also experimented successfully with a new technique for the manufacture of spool cotton, a grade of cotton thread suitable for sewing and wound on a wooden spool; see Wilkinson, "Philadelphia Free Produce Attack." George W. Taylor to William M. Hayes, December 28, 1872, Chester County Historical Society.

152. *Anti-slavery Reporter*, August 6, 1845.

153. Wilkinson, "Philadelphia Free Produce Attack," concludes, following Garrison, that the lack of reaction by southern slaveholders suggests that the free produce movement was an empty gesture. Ellis, "Joseph Sturge, Harriet Beecher Stowe, and the Free Labor Movement," "Sketches of the Sayings and Doings at the New England Anti-Slavery Convention," *Liberator*, June 4, 1847; and McDonald, "Consuming with a Conscience," 26.

154. *National Era*, June 9, 1853.

155. Joseph Sturge to Samuel Rhoads, Birmingham, England, January 21, 1859, Rhoads Family Papers, HCQSC. For Sturge's donation in 1847, see Nuermberger, *Free Produce Movement*, 71.

156. Faulkner, "Root of the Evil," 396. "Free Produce" and "The Free Produce Question," *Liberator*, March 1, 1850; Jacob C. White Jr., "The Inconsistency of Colored People Using Slave Produce," December 30, 1852, Leon Gardiner Collection of American Negro Historical Society Records, HSP. Eric Herschthal, *The Science of Abolition: How Slaveholders Became the Enemies of Progress* (New Haven, Conn.: Yale University Press), 231–240.

157. Douglass, quoted in the *Anti-slavery Reporter* (London), November 1, 1855.

158. Winthrop Jordan, *White over Black: American Attitudes Toward the Negro, 1550–1812* (Chapel Hill: University of North Carolina Press, 1968); Kim Hall, *Things of Darkness: Economies of Race and Gender in Early Modern England* (Ithaca, N.Y.: Cornell University Press, 1995).

159. See "Free Labor," in Frances Ellen Watkins, *Poems on Miscellaneous Subjects* (Boston, 1854); Margaret Washington, "Frances Ellen Watkins: Family Legacy and Antebellum Activism," *Journal of African American History* 100, no. 1 (2015): 59–86.

160. F. E. W. Harper to William Still, Temple, Maine, October 20, 1854, in Still, *Underground Railroad*, 759. Faulkner, "Root of the Evil," 399. Pearson, "A Person Perverted into a Thing."

161. Douglass in *Anti-slavery Reporter*, November 1, 1855.

Chapter 6

1. *Liberator*, October 15, 1858. Strain and his wife, Jane, both born in Ohio, resided in Boone County, Indiana, in 1850 and Kosciusko County, Indiana, in 1860. Married at the age of nineteen and unlikely to have had much formal medical training, Strain was later appointed postmaster by the Democratic president James Buchanan and removed by the Republican Abraham Lincoln. Thanks to Scott Wilds for this information. See also Nell Irvin Painter, *Sojourner Truth: A Life, A Symbol* (New York: Norton, 1996), 138–142; Margaret Washington, *Sojourner Truth's America* (Urbana: University of Illinois Press, 2009), 285–286; Teresa Zackodnik, *Press, Platform, Pulpit: Black Feminist Publics in the Era of Reform* (Knoxville: University of Tennessee Press, 2011), xiii–xvii, 96–111; Xiomara Santamarina, *Belabored Professions: Narratives of African American Working Womanhood* (Chapel Hill: University of North Carolina Press, 2005); Karen Sanchez-Eppler, *Touching Liberty: Abolition, Feminism, and the Politics of the Body* (Berkeley: University of California Press,1993); Robyn Wiegman, *American Anatomies: Theorizing Race and Gender* (Durham, N.C.: Duke University Press, 1995). For the gender valence of nineteenth-century female activism, see Jen Manion, *Female Husbands: A Trans History* (New York: Cambridge University Press, 2020), 165–197. See also Ariela Gross, *What Blood Won't Tell: A History of Race on Trial in America* (Cambridge, Mass.: Harvard University Press, 2008); Ariela Gross, *Double Character: Slavery and Mastery in the Antebellum Southern Courtroom* (Princeton, N.J.: Princeton University Press, 2000), 122–152. Dana Elizabeth Weiner, *Race and Rights: Fighting Slavery and Prejudice in the Old Northwest, 1830–1870* (Dekalb: Northern Illinois University Press, 2013), 177–179, 184–187, notes similar questions raised in 1861 against the white activist Josephine S. Griffing in Warsaw, Indiana.

2. Underground Railroad records suggest that enslaved people who disguised their gender were overwhelmingly women dressed as men, not men dressed as women.

3. Emily West and R. J. Knight, "Mothers' Milk: Slavery, Wet Nursing, and Black and White Women in the Antebellum South," *Journal of Southern History* 83, no. 1 (February 2017): 37–68.

4. For an important disentanglement of gender and sexed bodies, see Manion, *Female Husbands*. Jeanne Boydston, *Home and Work: Housework, Wages, and the Ideology of Labor in the Early Republic* (New York: Oxford University Press, 1990). Nora Doyle, *Maternal Bodies: Redefining Motherhood in Early America* (Chapel Hill: University of North Carolina Press, 2018), charts the growing divide between sentimental depictions of white women's maternal labor as disembodied, and representations of enslaved women's corporeality as disordered. I am indebted to her argument but I interpret this disorder differently, especially in the poems written by Black women, as part of the larger abolitionist effort to reveal slavery's violence by representing its capacity to unmoor human beings and harm their bodies. See also Robyn Wiegman, *American Anatomies: Theorizing Race and Gender* (Durham, N.C.: Duke University Press, 1995).

5. Nicole Eustace, *1812: War and the Passions of Patriotism* (Philadelphia: University of Pennsylvania Press, 2012), esp. 1–35; Gillian Skinner, *Sensibility and Economics in the Novel: The Price of a Tear* (New York: St. Martin's, 1999), for sentimental arguments implicated in economic and political debates. See also Marie Jenkins Schwartz, *Birthing a Slave: Motherhood and Medicine in the Antebellum South* (Cambridge, Mass.: Harvard University Press, 2006). Marlie F. Weiner with Mazie Hough, *Sex, Sickness, and Slavery: Illness in the Antebellum South* (Urbana: University of Illinois Press, 2012), 61–63, for the racial medicalization of female bodies: organs of generation (ovaries, uterus) for white women, and genitals (vulva, clitoris, vagina, buttocks) for Black women.

6. Linda Kerber, *No Constitutional Right to be Ladies: Women and the Obligations of Citizenship* (New York: Hill and Wang, 1998), 36. Kathleen Brown, *Good Wives, Nasty Wenches, and Anxious Patriarchs: Gender, Race, and Power in Colonial Virginia* (Chapel Hill: University of North Carolina Press, 1996); Jennifer L. Morgan, *Laboring Women: Reproduction and Gender in New World Slavery* (Philadelphia: University of Pennsylvania Press, 2000); Jennifer L. Morgan, *Reckoning with Slavery: Gender, Kinship, and Capitalism in the Early Black Atlantic* (Durham, N.C.: Duke University Press, 2021). The literature on colonialism points to patterns of severing Indigenous children's familial ties and subverting Native identities. Margaret Jacobs, *White Mothers to a Dark Race: Settler*

Colonialism, Maternalism, and the Removal of Indigenous Children in the American West and Australia, 1880–1940 (Lincoln: University of Nebraska Press, 2009). For the racial as well as gendered adjudication of citizenship after the Civil War, see Kristin A. Collins, "Illegitimate Borders: *Jus Sanguinis* Citizenship and the Legal Construction of Family, Race, and Nation," *Yale Law Journal* 123, no. 7 (2014): 2134–2573.

7. Daina Ramey Berry, *The Price for Their Pound of Flesh: The Value of the Enslaved, from Womb to Grave, in the Building of a Nation* (Boston: Beacon, 2017), 19–21. Amy Dru Stanley, "Slave Breeding and Free Love: An Antebellum Argument over Slavery, Capitalism, and Personhood," in Michael Zakim and Gary J. Kornblith, eds., *Capitalism Takes Command: The Social Transformation of Nineteenth-Century America* (Chicago: University of Chicago Press, 2012), 119–144; Adrienne Davis, "'Don't Let Nobody Bother Yo' Principle': The Sexual Economy of American Slavery," in Sharon Harley, ed., *Sister Circle: Black Women and Work* (New Brunswick, N.J.: Rutgers University Press, 2002), 103–127; Gregory Smithers, *Slave Breeding: Sex, Violence, and Memory in African American History* (Gainesville: University Press of Florida, 2013), 20–43; Ned Sublette and Constance Sublette, *The American Slave Coast: A History of the Slave-Breeding Industry* (Chicago: Lawrence Hill Books, 2016). See also Thomas A. Foster, *Rethinking Rufus: Sexual Violations of Enslaved Men* (Athens: University of Georgia Press, 2019), for the sexual exploitation of enslaved men. Katherine Paugh, *The Politics of Reproduction: Race, Medicine, and Fertility in the Age of Abolition* (Oxford, U.K.: Oxford University Press, 2017). Suman Seth, *Difference and Disease: Medicine, Race, and the Eighteenth-Century British Empire* (New York: Cambridge University Press, 2018), 251. Edward Baptist, "Cuffy, Fancy Maids," in Walter Johnson, ed., *The Chattel Principle: Internal Slave Trades in the Americas* (New Haven, Conn.: Yale University Press, 2005), 165–202; Caitlin Rosenthal, *Accounting for Slavery: Masters and Management* (Cambridge, Mass.: Harvard University Press, 2018), 121–156, esp. 130, 252n19.

8. Sanchez-Eppler, *Touching Liberty*. For gendered forms of antislavery activism, see Bruce Dorsey, *Reforming Men and Women: Gender in the Antebellum City* (Ithaca, N.Y.: Cornell University Press, 2002), 136–194; Elizabeth B. Clark, "'The Sacred Rights of the Weak': Pain, Sympathy, and the Culture of Individual Rights in Antebellum America," *JAH* 82, no. 2 (1995): 463–493, esp. 478, 486; Karen Halttunen, "Humanitarianism and the Pornography of Pain in Anglo-American Culture," *American Historical Review* 100, no. 2 (1995): 303–334. See also Margaret Abruzzo, *Polemical Pain: Slavery, Cruelty, and the Rise of Humanitarianism* (Baltimore: Johns Hopkins University Press, 2011); Gay Gibson Cima, *Performing Anti-slavery: Activist Women on Antebellum Stages* (New York: Cambridge University Press, 2014); Martha J. Cutter, *The Illustrated Slave: Empathy, Graphic Narrative, and the Visual Culture of the Transatlantic Abolition Movement, 1800–1852* (Athens: University of Georgia Press, 2017), xii–xvii.

9. Buxton quoted in Frank J. Klingberg, *The Anti-slavery Movement in England: A Study in English Humanitarianism* (New Haven, Conn.: Yale University Press, 1926).

10. Kathleen Brown, "The Life Cycle: Motherhood During the Enlightenment," in Ellen Pollack, ed., *A Cultural History of Women in the Age of Enlightenment*, 4 vols. (London: Bloomsbury, 2013), 4:30–43. Thomas Laqueur, *Making Sex: Body and Gender from the Greeks to Freud* (Cambridge, Mass.: Harvard University Press, 1992); G. J. Barker-Benfield, *The Culture of Sensibility: Sex and Society in Eighteenth-Century Britain* (Chicago: University of Chicago Press, 1992); Sarah Knott, *Sensibility and the American Revolution* (Chapel Hill: University of North Carolina Press, 2009).

11. Harriet Taylor Mill, *Enfranchisement of Women* (New York, 1852), 13, Women's Rights Tracts, New York Historical Society.

12. Hannah More, *Slavery* (London, 1788).

13. *Report of the Agency Committee of the Anti-Slavery Society, established in June 1831 for the purpose of disseminating information by lectures on colonial slavery* (London, 1832), 3. Dickson D. Bruce Jr., "Print Culture and the Antislavery Community: The Poetry of Abolitionism, 1831–1860," in Timothy Patrick McCarthy and John Stauffer, eds., *Prophets of Protest: Reconsidering the History of American Abolitionism* (New York: New Press, 2006), 220–234.

14. *The First Report of the Female Society for Birmingham, West-Bromwich, Wednesbury, Walsall, and Their Respective Neighbourhoods, for the Relief of British Negro Slaves* (Birmingham, 1826). This society went by several different names during its early years.

15. Nancy Isenberg, *Sex and Citizenship in Antebellum America* (Chapel Hill: University of North Carolina Press, 1998), xviii, 11, 118–119. Abruzzo, *Polemical Pain*; Sarah N. Roth, *Gender and Race in Antebellum Popular Culture* (New York: Cambridge University Press, 2014).

16. Judith Butler, *Undoing Gender* (New York: Routledge, 2004); Erica Armstrong Dunbar, *A Fragile Freedom: African American Women and Emancipation in the Antebellum City* (New Haven, Conn.: Yale University Press, 2011), 51, 61.

17. Elizabeth Margaret Chandler, *Genius of Universal Emancipation*, February 1, 1831; Jean Fagan Yellin, *Women and Sisters: The Antislavery Feminists in American Culture* (New Haven, Conn.: Yale University Press, 1992), 12–14; Cima, *Performing Anti-slavery*, 39–90. Saidiya Hartman, *Scenes of Subjection: Terror, Slavery, and Self-Making in Nineteenth-Century America* (New York: Oxford University Press, 1997), 17–23, provides a compelling critique of white empathy aroused only by replacing the slave's person imaginatively with one's own. Ana Stevenson, *The Woman as Slave in Nineteenth-Century American Social Movements* (New York: Palgrave Macmillan, 2019), 43–45, concedes Chandler's appropriation and misuse of the Hindu concept but notes that the exercise she recommended was also employed by free African American women. Despite its narcissistic dynamic, metempsychosis appears to have enabled Black as well as white abolitionists to become effective activists.

18. "The Slave Mother's Farewell," in *The Poetical Works of Elizabeth Margaret Chandler* (Philadelphia: Lemuel Howell, 1836), 122.

19. Chandler, "Declaration of Independence," in *Poetical Works*, 14–16; "for the Afric's tears of blood atone" refers to Luke 44:22.

20. Chandler, *Poetical Works*, 59; Susan Zaeske, *Signatures of Citizenship: Petitioning, Antislavery, and Women's Political Identity* (Chapel Hill: University of North Carolina Press, 2003), 62–63. Cima, *Performing Anti-slavery*, 107.

21. Chandler, "Think of Our Country's Glory," in *Poetical Works*, 64.

22. Cima, *Performing Anti-slavery*; Julie Winch, "Sarah Forten's Anti-slavery Networks," in Kathryn Kish Sklar and James Brewer Stewart, eds., *Women's Rights and Transatlantic Slavery in the Era of Emancipation* (New Haven, Conn.: Yale University Press, 2007), 143–157.

23. "The Slave Girl's Address to Her Mother," *Liberator*, January 29, 1831.

24. Ada, "An Appeal to Women," *Liberator*, February 1, 1834.

25. Janet Gray, *Race and Time: American Women's Poetics from Antislavery to Racial Modernity* (Iowa City: University of Iowa Press, 2004), 78–79.

26. *Proceedings of the Antislavery Convention, Assembled at Philadelphia, December 4, 5, and 6, 1833* (New York, 1833).

27. PFAS Minutes, December 14, 1833, HSP.

28. Amy Swerdlow, "Abolition's Conservative Sisters: The Ladies' New York City Anti-Slavery Societies, 1834–1840," in Jean Fagan Yellin and John C. Van Horne, eds., *The Abolitionist Sisterhood: Women's Political Culture in Antebellum America* (Ithaca, N.Y.: Cornell University Press, 1994), 31–65, esp. 40n31, for Cox's racism.

29. Sklar and Stewart, *Women's Rights and Transatlantic Antislavery.*

30. *A Memoir of the Life and Ministry of Ann Freeman, a Faithful Servant of Jesus Christ* (Exeter, N.H., 1831), 89. The language "no stranger may intermeddle" began during the late 1830s and 1840s to appear in pamphlets and tracts that attempted to reconcile dissonance between different types of authority, usually civic and moral. See also Deborah M. Valenze, *Prophetic Sons and Daughters: Female Preaching and Popular Religion in Industrial England* (Princeton, N.J.: Princeton University Press, 1985), 140–158.

31. Clark, "Sacred Rights of the Weak," 484, for Maria Weston Chapman's observation that woman's work was to breathe sympathy into men's hearts.

32. Carol Faulkner, *Lucretia Mott's Heresy: Abolition and Women's Rights in Nineteenth-Century America* (Philadelphia: University of Pennsylvania Press, 2013), 78–79.

33. Angelina Grimké, *An Appeal to the Women of the Nominally Free States*, 1837.

34. Gerda Lerner, ed., *The Feminist Thought of Sarah Grimké* (New York: Oxford University Press, 1998); Pamela Durso, *The Power of Woman: The Life and Writings of Sarah Moore Grimké* (Macon, Ga.: Mercer University Press, 2003).

35. Angelina Grimké, *Appeal to the Christian Women of the South* (New York, 1836).

36. Sarah Moore Grimké to Harriot Hunt, August 22, 1848?, reporting on Angelina's hydropathic treatments; Theodore Weld to Angelina Grimké Weld, September 1848, about the doctor's prediction of a miscarriage, and the return of her prolapsed uterus; Angelina Grimké Weld to Theodore Weld, September 5, 1849, reports a hernia diagnosis and the doctor's prescription of a sitz bath; Angelina Grimké Weld to Sarah Mapps Douglass, 1849, claiming that Douglass's hernia, like her own conditions, could be cured with hydropathic treatments; Sarah Moore Grimké to Harriot Hunt, June 10, 1850, about Angelina's recurrence of spasms; Sarah Moore Grimké to Harriot Hunt, October 1849?, reporting that Angelina's uterus "does not come entirely out"; all in Weld-Grimké Papers, box 9, CL; Gerda Lerner, *The Grimké Sisters from South Carolina: Pioneers for Woman's Rights and Abolition* (1967; repr., New York: Schocken Books, 1971), 288–292.

37. Dorothy Sterling, *Ahead of Her Time: Abby Kelley and the Politics of Anti-slavery* (New York: W. W. Norton, 1991), 87–89.

38. Sterling, *Ahead of Her Time*, 92, 142. James Lindsey Smith, *Autobiography of James L. Smith, Including, Also, Reminiscences of Slave Life, Recollections of the War, Education of Freedmen, Causes of the Exodus, Etc.* (Norwich, Conn.: Press of the Bulletin Company, 1881).

39. Sterling, *Ahead of Her Time*, 108–109; Swerdlow, "Abolition's Conservative Sisters." Ludlow was an ally of the abolitionist Tappan brothers and an Underground Railroad operative.

40. Abby Kelley to Erasmus Darwin Hudson, August 6, 1840, Abigail Kelley Foster Papers, digitized collections, American Antiquarian Society; Sterling, *Ahead of Her Time*, 116–117.

41. Sterling, *Ahead of Her Time*, 141, 148.

42. Abby Kelley to Nathaniel Rogers, July 8, 1841, quoted in Sterling, *Ahead of Her Time*, 132–133. Kelley attended the June 10, 1841, meeting of PFAS, whose members had begun donating to the Philadelphia Vigilance Committee as early as 1839. See Joseph Boromé, Jacob C. White, Robert B. Ayres, and J. M. McKim, "The Vigilant Committee of Philadelphia," *PMHB* 92, no. 3 (July 1968): 320–351, esp. 339, 341, for donations to the Female Vigilance Committee from Mother Bethel Church and from Clementine Green, Elizabeth Earle, Sarah Pearson, Lucretia Mott, Ester Justice, and Elizabeth Bunting.

43. Abby Kelley to Nathaniel Rogers, July 8, 1841, quoted in Sterling, *Ahead of Her Time*, 132–133.

44. Sterling, *Ahead of Her Time*, 117–118.

45. For evangelical and reform tactics, see Ronald G. Walters, *American Reformers, 1815–1860* (New York: Hill and Wang, 1978), 23–24, 32–33, 37; Richard Newman, *The Transformation of American Abolitionism* (Chapel Hill: University of North Carolina Press, 2002), 157. See also John R. McKivigan, *The War Against Proslavery Religion: Abolitionism and the Northern Churches, 1830–1865* (Ithaca, N.Y.: Cornell University Press, 1984), 67.

46. Matthew Fox-Amato, *Exposing Slavery: Photography, Human Bondage, and the Birth of Modern Visual Politics in America* (New York: Oxford University Press, 2019), 103–106; Aston Gonzalez, "The Art of Racial Politics: The Work of Robert Douglass, Jr., 1833–46," *PMHB* 138, no. 1 (January 2014): 5–37.

47. Abby Kelley to Alla, September 7, 1847, Abby Kelley Foster Papers, photocopies at HCQSC.

48. Quoted in Sterling, *Ahead of Her Time*, 251. For Maria Weston Chapman's travel for reasons of her husband's illness while her child was still an infant, see Lee V. Chambers, *The Weston Sisters: An American Abolitionist Family* (Chapel Hill: University of North Carolina Press, 2014), 125–126.

49. Abby Kelley to Alla, April 17, 1852, Abby Kelley Foster Papers, photocopies at HCQSC.

50. *Liberty Chimes* (Providence, R.I., 1845), 82–83.

51. April Haynes, *Riotous Flesh: Women, Physiology, and the Solitary Vice in Nineteenth-Century America* (Chicago: University of Chicago Press, 2015); Roth, *Gender and Race in Antebellum Popular Culture*. See also the poem in the same collection by SLL featuring an enslaved mother and child spared the pain of separation by mercifully timed deaths in their sleep; *Liberty Chimes*, 108–110.

52. Whittier, "Farewell of a Virginia Slave Mother," *Signal of Liberty*, August 14, 1843; John Collins, *The Slave Mother* (Philadelphia: Pennsylvania Anti-Slavery Fair, 1855), which Collins claimed had been inspired by a report in Elihu Burritt's *Bonds of Brotherhood*. Thanks to Paul Wolff Mitchell for calling my attention to Collins.

53. Martha S. Jones, *All Bound Up Together: The Woman Question in African American Public Culture, 1830–1900* (Chapel Hill: University of North Carolina Press, 2007).

54. Jones, *All Bound Up Together*, 84, 87–117, 125–126.

55. Sarah John Dymond to Anne Rhoads, 1851, Rhoads Family Papers, HCQSC.

56. Zillah, "Moonlight," *Liberator*, April 7, 1832; Sarah Mapps Douglass, "Mental Feast," *Liberator*, July 21, 1832; Cima, *Performing Anti-slavery*, 107, 132n44.

57. Cima, *Performing Anti-slavery*, 118.

58. Julie Roy Jeffrey, *The Great Silent Army of Abolitionism: Ordinary Women in the Antislavery Movement* (Chapel Hill: University of North Carolina Press, 1998), 41–42.

59. PFAS Minutes, December 14, 1833, for list of PFAS signatories and officers; December 8, 1836, lists Sarah Douglass as one of the nominated PFAS officers; March 8, 1838, for PFAS taking charge of the school; April 9, 1840, for Douglass's call to regain control of her school; March 8, 1849, and May 10, 1849, all in HSP. Margaret Hope Bacon, "New Light on Sarah Mapps Douglass and Her Reconciliation with Friends," *Quaker History* 90, no. 1 (Spring 2001): 28–49, esp. 29. Douglass described an enslaved mother's suffering at the hands of a female enslaver in "A Mother's Love," *Liberator*, July 28, 1832. Sarah Mapps Douglass to Rebecca White, n.d., "I feel unabated interest in my school," Josiah White Papers, HCQSC.

60. Sarah Mapps Douglass to Rebecca White, February 9, 1863, HCQSC; Britt Rusert, *Fugitive Science: Empiricism and Freedom in Early African American Culture* (New York: New York University Press, 2017), 198–203.

61. Jones, *All Bound Up Together*, 125–126.

62. Haynes, *Riotous Flesh*, 132–177; Dorothy Sterling, ed., *We Are Your Sisters: Black Women in the Nineteenth Century* (New York: W. W. Norton, 1984), 175–180. Willi Coleman, "'Like Hot Lead to Pour on the Americans . . .': Sarah Parker Remond—From Salem, Mass., to the British Isles," in Sklar and Stewart, eds., *Women's Rights and Transatlantic Antislavery*, 173–188.

63. *A Brighter Coming Day: A Frances Ellen Watkins Harper Reader*, ed. Frances Smith Foster (New York: Feminist Press, 1990), 58, 72; Jesse Olsavsky, "Runaway Slaves, Vigilance Committees, and the Pedagogy of Revolutionary Abolitionism, 1835–1863," in Marcus Rediker, Titas Chakraborty, and Matthias van Rossum, eds., *A Global History of Runaways: Workers, Mobility, and Capitalism, 1600–1850* (Oakland: University of California Press, 2019), 223. Margaret Washington, "Frances Ellen Watkins: Family Legacy and Antebellum Activism," *Journal of African American History* 100, no. 1 (2015): 59–86; Dunbar, *A Fragile Freedom*; Shirley Yee, *Black Women Abolitionists: A Study in Activism, 1828–1860* (Knoxville: University of Tennessee Press, 1992).

64. Sanchez-Eppler, *Touching Liberty*.

65. Deirdre Cooper Owens, *Medical Bondage: Race, Gender, and the Origins of American Gynecology* (Athens: University of Georgia Press, 2017), for white immigrant and working-class women who were also subjected to experimental gynecological surgeries.

66. E. Brooks Holifield, "The Wealth of Nineteenth-Century Physicians," *Bulletin of the History of Medicine* 64, no. 1 (Spring 1990): 79–85. James C. Mohr, *Doctors and the Law: Medical Jurisprudence in Nineteenth-Century America* (Baltimore: Johns Hopkins University Press, 1993). See also Owens, *Medical Bondage*; and Rana Hogarth, *Medicalizing Blackness: Making Racial Difference in the Atlantic World, 1780–1840* (Chapel Hill: University of North Carolina Press, 2017). For cases in southern courts calling on medical experts but ultimately relying on the "common sense of race,"

see Gross, *What Blood Won't Tell*, 1–72; Gross, *Double Character*, 122–152; Weiner and Hough, *Sex, Sickness, and Slavery*, 93–153. Dea H. Boster, *African American Slavery and Disability: Bodies, Property, and Power in the Antebellum South, 1800–1860* (New York: Routledge, 2013), esp. 34–54. Steven M. Stowe, "Seeing Themselves at Work: Physicians and the Case Narrative in the Mid-Nineteenth-Century American South," *American Historical Review* 101, no. 1 (February 1996): 41–79, quotation on 43; John Harley Warner, "Science, Healing, and the Physician's Identity: A Problem of Professional Character in Nineteenth-Century America," in W. F. Bynum and V. Nutton, eds., *Essays in the History of Therapeutics* (Amsterdam: Rodopi, 1991), 65–88.

67. Doyle, *Maternal Bodies*, 35–51; J. M. Boisnot, "Women Physiologically," Medical Dissertation, University of Pennsylvania, 1858. For Sims, see Deborah Kuhn McGregor, *From Midwives to Medicine: The Birth of American Gynecology* (New Brunswick, N.J.: Rutgers University Press, 1998), esp. 47–54; Owens, *Medical Bondage*; research by Archana Upadhyay, Penn and Slavery Project, http://pennandslaveryproject.org/. Penn medical theses from the 1810s refer to the treatment of almshouse patients as part of their practical training. See also William Horner Papers, 1834, for transporting medical students to the almshouse, Kislak Center, University of Pennsylvania.

68. W. Tyler Smith, "Tyler Smith's Lectures on Obstetrics," *New Orleans Medical News and Hospital Gazette* 3 (May 1856). Robert E. Campbell, "Observations upon Menstruation, Its Causes, Character, and Effects upon Female Economy," *Atlanta Medical and Surgical Journal* 2 (September 1856). Doyle, *Maternal Bodies*; Hogarth, *Medicalizing Blackness*; Weiner and Hough, *Sex, Sickness, and Slavery*. See especially McGregor, *From Midwives to Medicine*, 49. Christopher D. E. Willoughby, "Running away from Drapetomania: Samuel A. Cartwright, Medicine, and Race in the Antebellum South," *Journal of Southern History* 84, no. 3 (August 2018): 579–614.

69. Thanks to Owen Pearson for attempting this tabulation of thesis titles, and to Alexis Broderick Neumann and Archana Upadhyay for sharing their research with me.

70. Lucretia Mott, *A Sermon to the Medical Students delivered to Lucretia Mott at Cherry Street Meeting House, Philadelphia* (Philadelphia, 1849), quotes on 12, 13, 14. Lucretia Mott to Joseph Dugdale and Ruth Dugdale, March 28, 1849, in Beverly Wilson Palmer, ed., *Selected Letters of Lucretia Coffin Mott* (Urbana: University of Illinois Press, 2002), 178–183. Daniel Kilbride, "Southern Medical Students in Philadelphia, 1800–1861: Science and Sociability in the 'Republic of Medicine,'" *Journal of Southern History* 65, no. 4 (November 1999): 697–732.

71. Berry, *Price for Their Pound of Flesh*, 50–52.

72. Ruth Perry, "Colonizing the Breast: Sexuality and Maternity in Eighteenth-Century England," *Journal of the History of Sexuality* 2, no. 2 (1991): 204–234. Adrian Davis, *The Making of Man-Midwifery: Childbirth in England, 1660–1770* (London: University College London Press, 1995). Mark Harrison, *Medicine in an Age of Commerce and Empire: Britain and Its Tropical Colonies, 1660–1830* (New York: Oxford University Press, 2010), for the influence of military medicine.

73. Thomas Denman, *An Introduction to the Practice of Midwifery* (London, 1788), 310–316. For previous guides, see William Smellie, *A Treatise on the Theory and Practice of Midwifery* (London, 1752); Alexander Hamilton, *A Treatise of Midwifery* (London, 1781).

74. Denman, *Introduction to the Practice of Midwifery*, 310–316. The first New York edition appeared in 1802. See McGregor, *Midwives to Medicine*, 47, for the contrast between Denman's recommendations and Sims's gynecological "breakthrough" in the examination of the white "Mrs. Merrill."

75. Patricia Crawford, "Attitudes to Menstruation in Seventeenth-Century England," *Past and Present*, no. 91 (May 1981): 47–73. H. O. McCall (Kentucky), "A Dissertation on Menstruation," Medical Dissertation, University of Pennsylvania, 1818. All of the theses discussed in this paragraph, except for Hill's, came well before John Robertson's study, *On the Period of Puberty in Negro Women*, (Edinburgh, 1841), drawn from data on Afro-Caribbean women. See also Campbell, *Observations Upon Menstruation* (1856). For a case revolving around an enslaved woman's menstruation, see Gross, *Double Character*, 136–137, Adams County Circuit Court, Mississippi, 1853.

76. Elias Willis Napier, "Dissertation on the Causes, Symptoms, and Treatment of Amenorrhea," Medical Dissertation, University of Pennsylvania, 1811; Richard Mason, "Essay on Menstruation," Medical Dissertation, University of Pennsylvania, 1816; Robert Moseley, "On Amenorrhea," Medi-

cal Dissertation, University of Pennsylvania, 1816. For the debate over the impact of labor on fertility, see Philip Gibbes, *Instructions for the Treatment of Negroes* (London, 1786); Robert Thomas, *Medical Advice to the Inhabitants of Warm Climates, on the Domestic Treatment of All the Diseases Incidental Therein: With a Few Useful Hints to New Settlers, for the Preservation of Health, and the Prevention of Sickness* (London, 1790); Paugh, *Politics of Reproduction*; Seth, *Difference and Disease*, 256. Hubbard Taylor Minor (Virginia), "On Amenorrhea," Medical Dissertation, University of Pennsylvania, 1817; J. M. Hill, "Menstruation," Medical Dissertation, University of Pennsylvania, 1855.

77. Napier, "Dissertation on the Causes, Symptoms, and Treatment of Amenorrhea"; Mason, "Essay on Menstruation"; Moseley, "On Amenorrhea."

78. William McCaa (Camden, South Carolina), "The Manner of Living and Diseases of the Slaves on the Wateree River," Medical Dissertation, University of Pennsylvania, 1822, 12.

79. Lafayette Leecraft (North Carolina), "An Essay on the Influence of Intermarriage over Generation," Medical Dissertation, University of Pennsylvania, 1858.

80. See, for example, Minor, "Amenorrhea," on these remedies; Israel Bailey Bradley (Maine), Medical Dissertation, University of Pennsylvania, 1829, on the lifesaving potential of cesarean sections.

81. J. M. Hill, "Menstruation," Medical Dissertation, University of Pennsylvania, 1855; Isaac N. Jones (Fayette, Tennessee), "The Blood," Medical Dissertation, University of Pennsylvania, 1860.

82. Thomas Denman, *Aphorisms on the Application and Use of the Forceps* (London, 1783); a Philadelphia edition was circulating as early as 1803. Denman, *Essays on the Puerperal Fever* (London, 1768); Thomas Denman, *An Introduction to the Practice of Midwifery in 2 volumes* (1762), 6th ed. 1824, 7th ed. 1832; see theses by Napier, Mason, and Hill cited above. Charles E. Rosenberg, "The Therapeutic Revolution: Medicine, Meaning, and Social Change in Nineteenth-Century America," in Morris J. Vogel and Charles E. Rosenberg, eds., *The Therapeutic Revolution: Essays in the Social History of American Medicine* (Philadelphia: University of Pennsylvania Press, 1979), 3–25, notes the lingering influence of humoral theory even as new theories gained a following.

83. William Freeman (Norfolk, Virginia), "Depletion by Bloodletting," Medical Dissertation, University of Pennsylvania, 1861.

84. Daniel C. Malone (Pennsylvania), "Hemorrhagia Uterina," Medical Dissertation, University of Pennsylvania, 1869.

85. Blencove Fryer (Philadelphia), "The Constituents of the Blood," Medical Dissertation, University of Pennsylvania, 1859.

86. Melson L. Rowland, "Transfusion of Blood," Medical Dissertation, University of Pennsylvania, 1859.

87. Robert Woodhull Clark, "Signs of Pregnancy," Medical Dissertation, University of Pennsylvania, 1860.

88. Clark noted, "the signs of pregnancy during the first three months, both rational and physical, are, as we have seen, quite equivocal . . . no prudent practitioner would commit himself positively, during this period at least, as to its existence or non-existence." See also Weiner and Hough, *Sex, Sickness,and Slavery*, 109–112.

89. Clark, "Signs of Pregnancy."

90. Clark, "Signs of Pregnancy"; Mohr, *Doctors and the Law*, 56, for the use of the stethoscope by the 1820s to detect fetal heartbeat and the administration of urine tests by the 1840s, the latter of which Clark did not discuss in his thesis.

91. James Mohr, *Abortion in America: the Origins and Evolution of National Policy* (New York: Oxford University Press, 1978), 23, and 270n7, 270n10; John P. Batchelder, *On the Causes Which Degrade the Profession of Physick* (Bellows Falls, Vt., 1818).

92. For Batchelder, see Mohr, *Doctors and the Law*, 32. John W. Reese (Philadelphia), "Inaugural Essay on Amenorrhea," Medical Dissertation, University of Pennsylvania, 1827; Jehu Peters, "Inaugural Dissertation on Amenorrhoea," Medical Dissertation, University of Pennsylvania, 1828. See also Monica E. Eppinger, "The Health Exception," *Georgetown Journal of Gender and Law* 17, no. 3 (2016): 665–744, esp. 706–707.

93. William A. McClure, "Essay on the Signs of Pregnancy and Delivery," Medical Dissertation, University of Pennsylvania, 1846.

94. Reva B. Siegel, "Reasoning from the Body," *Stanford Law Review* 44, no. 2 (January 1992): 261–381. Eppinger, "The Health Exception," 31–32; Mohr, *Abortion in America*, 147–170.

95. Charles McCall, "Criminal Abortion," Medical Dissertation, University of Pennsylvania, 1858; William Savery, "On Abortion," Medical Dissertation, University of Pennsylvania, 1861. For the diminishing clout of physicians in courtrooms by the 1840s, see Mohr, *Doctors and the Law*.

96. Schwartz, *Birthing a Slave*, 67–106, esp. 98, on the use of cotton root; Emily West and Erin Shearer, "Fertility Control, Shared Nurturing, and Dual Exploitation: The Lives of Enslaved Mothers in the Antebellum United States," in Camillia Cowling, Maria Helena Pereira Toledo Machado, Diana Paton, and Emily West, eds., *Motherhood, Childlessness, and the Care of Children in Atlantic Slave Societies* (New York: Routledge, 2020). Smithers, *Slave Breeding*; Sharla M. Fett, *Working Cures: Healing, Health, and Power on Southern Slave Plantations* (Chapel Hill: University of North Carolina Press, 2002), 176–177; Hogarth, *Medicalizing Blackness*, 98–100; Deborah Gray White, *Ar'n't I a Woman: Female Slaves in the Plantation South* (New York: W. W. Norton, 1985).

97. Richard Sheridan, *Doctors and Slaves: A Medical and Demographic History of the British West Indies, 1680–1834* (New York: Cambridge University Press, 1985), 224, for Jamaican governor Edward Trelawney's claim that low population growth among the enslaved could be attributed to enslaved women procuring abortions. E. M. Pendleton, "On the Comparative Fecundity of the Caucasian and African Races," *Charleston Medical Journal and Review* 6 (1851): 351–356; E. M. Pendleton, "On the Susceptibility of the Caucasian and African Races to Different Classes of Disease," *Southern Medical Reprints* (1849): 336–343. Pendleton had likely read the English translation of J.-J. Virey, *Natural History of the Negro Race* (Charleston, S.C., 1837). Thanks to Paul Wolff Mitchell for this citation. See also John H. Morgan, "An Essay on the Causes of the Production of Abortion Among Our Negro Population," *Nashville Journal of Medicine and Surgery* 19, no. 2 (August 1, 1860): 117–123. Jenifer L. Barclay, "Bad Breeders and Monstrosities: Racializing Childlessness and Congenital Disabilities in Slavery and Freedom," *Slavery and Abolition* 38, no. 2 (2017): 287–302; Nancy Krieger, "Shades of Difference: Theoretical Underpinnings of the Medical Controversy on Black/White Difference in the United States, 1830–1870," *International Journal of Health Services* 17, no. 2 (1987): 259–278.

98. Doyle, *Maternal Bodies*, 82–83; Jacqueline H. Wood, *Deliver Me from Pain: Anesthesia and Birth in America* (Baltimore: Johns Hopkins University Press, 2009), 13–43; Martin S. Pernick, *A Calculus of Suffering: Pain, Professionalism, and Anesthesia in Nineteenth-Century America* (New York: Columbia University Press, 1985); T. J. Reid (Fayette, Tennessee), "Essay on Anaesthesia in Parturation," Medical Dissertation, University of Pennsylvania, 1861.

99. *Daniel v. Guy*, 19 Ark. 121 (1857) in L. E. Barber, *Reports of Cases at Law and in Equity Argued and Determined in the Supreme Court of Arkansas* (Little Rock, Ark., 1889), 19:121–122; *Gary v. Stevenson*, 19 Ark. 580 (1858) in Barber, *Reports of Cases* 19: 580–587; *Van Camp v. Board of Education in the Incorporated Village of Logan*, 9 Ohio St. 406 (1859) in Leander J. Critchfield, *Reports of Cases Argued and Determined in the Supreme Court of Ohio* (Columbus, Oh., 1860), 9: 406–425; *State v. Jacobs*, 51 N.C. 284 (1859) in Hamilton C. Jones, *Cases at Law Argued and Determined in the Supreme Court of North Carolina* (reprinted 1905), 51: 284–289.

100. Painter, *Sojourner Truth*.

101. PFAS Minutes, January 12, 1853; May 12, 1853; both in HSP.

102. *The Anti-slavery Harp: A Collection of Songs for Anti-slavery Meetings* (Boston: Bela Marsh, 1848).

103. Edward Hayes, ed., *Ballads of Ireland*, vol. 2 (London, 1856), 301–302. "Thomas Moore," Oxford Dictionary of National Biography, https://www.oxforddnb.com/view/10.1093/ref:odnb/9780198614128.001.0001/odnb-9780198614128-e-19150?docPos=4. Linda Kelly, *Ireland's Minstrel: A Life of Tom Moore, Poet, Patriot, and Byron's Friend* (London, I. B. Tauris, 2006)).

104. Kelly, *Ireland's Minstrel*; *Araby's Daughter: from Lalla Rookh, Written by Thomas Moore Esq., Composed by George Kiallmark* (Philadelphia, 1824).

105. Washington, *Sojourner Truth's America*; Painter, *Sojourner Truth*.

106. Sarah Grimké to Harriot Hunt, December 16, 1849, Belleville, N.J., Weld-Grimké Papers, CL. For Angelina's grappling with the resistance from human institutions to the continual change that was the rule of the natural world, see Angelina Grimké Weld, "Letter from Angelina Grimké Weld to the Women's Rights Convention, Held at Syracuse, Sept. 1852," Women's Rights Tracts, no. 8, New York Historical Society.

107. *Proceedings of the Pennsylvania Yearly Meeting of Progressive Friends, Held at Old Kennett, Chester County, May 1853* (New York, 1853), 1–9, Swarthmore College; Painter, *Sojourner Truth*, 145–148.

108. Washington, *Sojourner Truth's America*, 146–147. William Still, *The Underground Railroad*, rev. ed. (Philadelphia, 1878).

Chapter 7

Note to epigraph: Henry Highland Garnet, "Address to the Slaves" (Troy, N.Y., 1848), originally delivered 1843, Colored Conventions Project, https://coloredconventions.org/garnet-address-1843/introduction/; Earl Ofari Hutchinson, *Let Your Motto Be Resistance: The Life and Thought of Henry Highland Garnet* (Boston: Beacon Press, 1972).

1. James Horton, "Freedom's Yoke: Gender Conventions Among Antebellum Free Blacks," *Feminist Studies* 12 no. 1 (Spring 1986): 51–76. James Oakes, "The Political Significance of Slave Resistance," *History Workshop Journal* 22, no. 1 (1986): 89–107. Leon F. Litwack, "The Emancipation of the Negro Abolitionist," in Martin Duberman, ed., *The Antislavery Vanguard: New Essays On The Abolitionists* (Princeton, N.J.: Princeton University Press, 1965); Jane H. Pease and William H. Pease, "Black Power—The Debate in 1840," *Phylon* 29, no. 1 (1968): 19–26. Donald Jacobs, ed., *Courage and Conscience: Black and White Abolitionists in Boston* (Bloomington: Indiana University Press, 1993); James Horton and Lois Horton, "The Affirmation of Manhood: Black Garrisonians in Antebellum Boston," in Jacobs, *Courage and Conscience*, 127–154; Saidiya Hartman, *Scenes of Subjection: Terror, Slavery, and Self-Making in Nineteenth-Century America* (New York: Oxford University Press, 1997), 153, 163; Stanley Harrold, *The Rise of Aggressive Abolitionism: Addresses to the Slaves* (Lexington: University Press of Kentucky, 2004), esp. 3, 13, 122; John R. McGivigan and Stanley Harrold, eds., *Antislavery Violence: Sectional, Racial, and Cultural Conflict in Antebellum America* (Knoxville: University of Tennessee Press, 1999); Joel Schor, *Henry Highland Garnet: A Voice of Black Radicalism in the Nineteenth Century* (Westport, Conn.: Praeger, 1977). James Jasinski, "Constituting Antebellum African American Identity: Resistance, Violence, and Masculinity in Henry Highland Garnet's (1843) 'Address to the Slaves,'" *Quarterly Journal of Speech* 93, no. 1 (2007): 27–57; Thavolia Glymph, *Out of the House of Bondage: The Transformation of the Plantation Household* (New York: Cambridge University Press, 2008); Kathleen Brown, "'Strength of a Lion . . . and Arms like Polished Iron': Embodying Black Masculinity in an Age of Slavery and Propertied Manhood," in Thomas Foster, ed., *New Men: Manliness in Early America* (New York: New York University Press, 2011), 172–192; Martin B. Pasternak, *Rise Now and Fly to Arms: The Life of Henry Highland Garnet* (New York: Routledge, 1994); James Oliver Horton, *Free People of Color: Inside the African American Community* (Washington, D.C.: Smithsonian, 1993); John Stauffer, *Black Hearts of Men: Radical Abolitionists and the Transformation of Race* (Cambridge, Mass.: Harvard University Press, 2001); Kellie Carter Jackson, *Force and Freedom: Black Abolitionists and the Politics of Violence* (Philadelphia: University of Pennsylvania Press, 2019). On Black manhood, see Libra R. Hilde, *Slavery, Fatherhood, and Paternal Duty in African American Communities over the Long Nineteenth Century* (Chapel Hill: University of North Carolina Press, 2020); Craig Steven Wilder, *In the Company of Black Men: The African Influence on African American Culture in New York City* (New York: New York University Press, 2001), esp. 120–141. Melissa Stein, *Measuring Manhood: Race and the Science of Masculinity, 1830–1934* (Minneapolis: University of Minnesota Press, 2015), esp. 1–88.

2. Stephanie Camp, *Closer to Freedom: Enslaved Women and Everyday Resistance in the Plantation South* (Chapel Hill: University of North Carolina Press, 2004); Thomas A. Foster, *Rethinking Rufus: Sexual Violations of Enslaved Men* (Athens: University of Georgia Press, 2019).

3. Hilde, *Slavery, Fatherhood, and Paternal Duty*; Sophie White, *Voices of the Enslaved: Love, Labor, and Longing in French Louisiana* (Chapel Hill: University of North Carolina Press, 2019); Tera W. Hunter, *Bound in Wedlock: Slave and Free Black Marriage in the Nineteenth Century* (Cambridge, Mass.: Harvard University Press, 2017); Frances Smith Foster, *'Til Death or Distance Do Us Part: Love and Marriage in African America* (New York: Oxford University Press, 2010); Emily West, *Chains of Love: Slave Couples in Antebellum South Carolina* (Urbana: University of Illinois Press, 2004); Heather Williams, *Help Me to Find My People: The African American Search for Family Lost in Slavery* (Chapel Hill: University of North Carolina Press, 2012); Herbert Gutman, *The Black Family in Slavery and Freedom, 1750–1925* (New York: Vintage, 1976).

4. Jen Manion, *Female Husbands: A Trans History* (New York: Cambridge University Press, 2020); Emily Skidmore, *True Sex: The Lives of Trans Men at the Turn of the Twentieth Century* (New York: New York University Press, 2017).

5. Steve Hahn, *A Nation Under Our Feet: Black Political Struggles in the Rural South from Slavery to the Great Migration* (Cambridge, Mass.: Harvard University Press, 2003); Vincent Brown, *Reaper's Garden: Death and Power in the World of Atlantic Slavery* (Cambridge, Mass.: Harvard University Press, 2010); Shane White and Graham White, *Sounds of Slavery: Discovering African American History Through Songs, Sermons, and Speech* (Boston: Beacon, 2005).

6. Kim Hall, *Things of Darkness: Economies of Race and Gender in Early Modern England* (Ithaca, N.Y.: Cornell University Press, 1995); Foster, *Rethinking Rufus*, 9–15; Gregory Smithers, *Slave Breeding: Sex, Violence, and Memory in African American History* (Gainesville: University Press of Florida, 2013).

7. Nicole Eustace, *Passion Is the Gale: Emotion, Power, and the Coming of the American Revolution* (Chapel Hill: University of North Carolina Press, 2008); G. Barker Benfield, *The Culture of Sensibility: Sex and Society in Eighteenth-Century Britain* (Chicago: University of Chicago Press, 1992); Sarah Knott, *Sensibility and the American Revolution* (Chapel Hill: University of North Carolina Press, 2009).

8. Jeffrey Bolster, *Black Jacks: African American Seamen in the Age of Sail* (Cambridge, Mass.: Harvard University Press, 1997), 158–170, 180, 187–188; Ifeoma Kiddoe Nwankwo, *Black Cosmopolitanism: Racial Consciousness and Transnational Identity in the Nineteenth-Century Americas* (Philadelphia: University of Pennsylvania Press, 2005).

9. Bolster, *Black Jacks*, 206. See Michael Schoeppner, "Peculiar Quarantines: The Seamen Acts and Regulatory Authority in the Antebellum South," *Law and History Review* 31, no. 3 (August 2013): 559–586; Michael A. Schoeppner, *Moral Contagion: Black Atlantic Sailors, Citizenship, and Diplomacy in Antebellum America* (New York: Cambridge University Press, 2019), 154. For affirmations of sailors' national citizenship, see Nathan Perl-Rosenthal, *Citizen Sailors: Becoming American in the Age of Revolution* (Cambridge, Mass.: Harvard University Press, 2015); and Kate Masur, *Until Justice Be Done: America's First Civil Rights Movement, from the Revolution to Reconstruction* (New York: W. W. Norton, 2021), 122–127. See also Michael D. Thompson, *Working on the Dock of the Bay: Labor and Enterprise in an Antebellum Southern Port* (Columbia: University of South Carolina Press, 2016); Julius S. Scott, *The Common Wind: Afro-American Currents in the Age of the Haitian Revolution* (London: Verso, 2018); Edlie L. Wong, *Neither Fugitive nor Free: Atlantic Slavery, Freedom Suits, and the Legal Culture of Travel* (New York: New York University Press, 2009). Shane White, *Somewhat More Independent: The End of Slavery in New York City, 1770–1810* (Athens: University of Georgia Press, 1991), 195–197, 201–202. Graham White and Shane White, *Stylin': African American Expressive Culture from Its Beginnings to the Zoot Suit* (Ithaca, N.Y.: Cornell University Press, 1998); Ayana D. Byrd and Lori L. Tharps, *Hair Story: Untangling the Roots of Black Hair in America* (New York: St. Martin's, 2002).

10. Sharla M. Fett, *Working Cures: Healing, Health, and Power on Southern Slave Plantations* (Chapel Hill: University of North Carolina Press, 2002); Camp, *Closer to Freedom*; Catherine Clinton, *Harriet Tubman: The Road to Freedom* (New York: Little, Brown, 2004).

11. Wilder, *In the Company of Black Men*; Stephen Kantrowitz, *More Than Freedom: Fighting for Black Citizenship in a White Republic, 1829–1889* (New York: Penguin, 2012); Albert J. Raboteau,

Slave Religion: The "Invisible Institution" in the Antebellum South (New York: Oxford University Press, 1978).

12. Camp, *Closer to Freedom*; White and White, *Stylin'*; Hilde, *Slavery, Fatherhood, and Paternal Duty.*

13. Benjamin Quarles, "Black History's Antebellum Origins," *Proceedings of the American Antiquarian Society* 89 (1979): 89–122.

14. Anonymous manuscript, African American History Collection, CL. For Russwurm's authorship of this manuscript, see Winston James, *The Struggles of John Brown Russwurm: The Life and Writings of a Pan-Africanist Pioneer, 1799–1851* (New York: New York University Press, 2010), 261n63. Russwurm to John Summer Russwurm, January 9, 1826, quoted in Sandra Sandiford Young, "John Brown Russwurm's Dilemma: Citizenship or Emigration?," in Timothy Patrick McCarthy and John Stauffer, eds., *Prophets of Protest: Reconsidering the History of American Abolitionism* (New York: New Press, 2006), 97.

15. Russwurm, *Freedom's Journal*, March 14, 1829, in James, *Struggles of John Brown Russwurm*, 208.

16. James, *Struggles of John Brown Russwurm*, 208.

17. James, *Struggles of John Brown Russwurm.*

18. Darryl Scriven, *A Dealer of Old Clothes: Philosophical Conversations with David Walker* (Washington, D.C.: Lexington Books, 2007).

19. David Walker, *Appeal to the Coloured Citizens of the United States* (Boston, 1829); Bolster, *Black Jacks*, 197; Peter P. Hinks, *To Awaken My Afflicted Brethren: David Walker and the Problem of Antebellum Slave Resistance* (University Park: Pennsylvania State University Press, 1997), xv, 119, 171, 239.

20. Glenn M. McNair, "The Elijah Burritt Affair: David Walker's *Appeal* and Partisan Journalism in Antebellum Milledgeville," *Georgia Historical Quarterly* 83, no. 3 (1999): 448–478, for the political infighting that led to Burritt's flight. Burritt was the older brother of the abolitionist Elihu Burritt and opposed the Cherokee removals from Georgia but might not have been an abolitionist himself; Hinks, *To Awaken My Afflicted Brethren*, 123–126.

21. Paul A. Gilje, *Rioting in America* (Bloomington: University of Indiana Press, 1996); David Grimsted, *American Mobbing, 1828–1861: Toward Civil War* (New York: Oxford University Press, 1998); Janet Moore Lindman, *Bodies of Belief: Baptist Community in Early America* (Philadelphia: University of Pennsylvania Press, 2008); Christine Leigh Heyrman, *Southern Cross: The Beginnings of the Bible Belt* (Chapel Hill: University of North Carolina Press, 1998); Amy S. Greenberg, *Manifest Manhood and the Antebellum American Empire* (New York: Cambridge University Press, 2005); Bruce Dorsey, *Reforming Men and Women: Gender in the Antebellum City* (Ithaca, N.Y.: Cornell University Press, 2002).

22. Vincent Carretta, *Equiano, the African: Biography of a Self-Made Man* (New York: Penguin, 2005); Silvia R. Frey and Betty Wood, *Come Shouting to Zion: African American Protestantism in the American South and British Caribbean to 1830* (Chapel Hill: University of North Carolina Press, 1998), 63–83.

23. Philip S. Foner and Robert James Branham, introduction to Foner and Branham, eds., *Lift Every Voice: African American Oratory, 1787–1900* (Tuscaloosa: University of Alabama, 1948); Frey and Wood, *Come Shouting to Zion*, 98–103, 114–117, 118–125, 143–148; White and White, *Sounds of Slavery*; Hahn, *A Nation Under Our Feet*; Michael A. Gomez, *Exchanging Our Country Marks: The Transformation of African Identities in the Colonial and Antebellum South* (Chapel Hill: University of North Carolina Press, 1998); Raboteau, *Slave Religion.*

24. Graham Hodges, ed., *Robert Roberts, A House Servant's Directory* (1828) (New York: Routledge, 1998); Kathleen M. Brown, *Foul Bodies: Cleanliness in Early America* (New Haven, Conn.: Yale University Press, 2009), 251–259. For Roberts's subsequent testimony against the kidnapping of free Black people and his connection to Hosea Easton, see George R. Price and James Brewer Stewart, "The Roberts Case, the Easton Family, and the Dynamics of the Abolitionist Movement in Massachusetts, 1776–1870," *Massachusetts Historical Review* 4 (2004): 89–115.

25. At the 1848 Colored National Convention, Martin Delaney and J. D. Patterson debated the inherent dignity of manual labor and service work after Frederick Douglass pushed for a compromise, that all work was inherently honorable. *Report of the Proceedings of the Colored National Convention, Held at Cleveland, Ohio, Wednesday September 6, 1848* (Rochester, 1848), 5–6.

26. Sally Greene, "State v. Mann Exhumed," *North Carolina Law Review* 87, no. 3 (2009): 701.

27. Christopher Tomlins, *In the Matter of Nat Turner: A Speculative History* (Princeton, N.J.: Princeton University Press, 2020).

28. Kenneth S. Greenberg, ed., *Nat Turner: A Slave Rebellion in History and Memory* (New York: Oxford University Press, 2003), especially Patrick Breen, "A Prophet in His Own Land," 103. But see also Vincent Harding, "Symptoms of Liberty and Blackhead Signposts: David Walker and Nat Turner," in Greenberg, *Nat Turner*, 79–102; Hinks, *To Awaken My Afflicted Brethren*, 160.

29. David F. Allmendinger, *Nat Turner and the Rising in Southampton County* (Baltimore: Johns Hopkins University Press, 2014); Patrick H. Breen, *The Land Shall Be Deluged in Blood: A New History of the Nat Turner Revolt* (New York: Oxford University Press, 2015); Kenneth S. Greenberg, "Name, Face, Body," in Greenberg, *Nat Turner*, 3–23. Tomlins, *In the Matter of Nat Turner*, 114, 122–124, on the dissection and interpretation of Turner's body, and 130–131. The Virginia native Orris A. Browne graduated from Penn's Medical School in 1825 after completing a medical thesis, "Rubeola." See also Vincent Woodard, *The Delectable Negro: Human Consumption and Homoeroticism Within U.S. Slave Culture* (New York: New York University Press, 2014).

30. Marie Jenkins Schwartz, *Birthing a Slave: Motherhood and Medicine in the Antebellum South* (Cambridge, Mass.: Harvard University Press, 2006).

31. Sarah N. Roth, *Gender and Race in Antebellum Popular Culture* (New York: Cambridge University Press, 2014); Louis P. Masur, *1831: Year of the Eclipse* (New York: Hill and Wang, 2001); Greenberg, "Name, Face, Body"; and Mary Kemp Davis, "'What Happened in This Place?': In Search of the Female Slave in the Nat Turner Slave Insurrection," in Greenberg, *Nat Turner*, 162–178.

32. Ira Berlin, "After Nat Turner: A Letter from the North," *Journal of Negro History* 55, no. 2 (April 1970): 144–151. Hinks, *To Awaken My Afflicted Brethren*, 131–134; Kay Wright Lewis, *A Curse upon the Nation: Race, Freedom, and Extermination in America and the Atlantic World* (Athens: University of Georgia Press, 2017), 107–108.

33. John Runcie, "'Hunting the Nigs' in Philadelphia: The Race Riot of August 1834," *Pennsylvania History* 39, no. 2 (April 1972): 187–218. John C. McWilliams, "'Men of Colour': Race, Riots, and Black Firefighters' Struggle for Equality from the Afa to the Valiants," *Journal of Social History* 41, no. 1 (Fall 2007): 105–125.

34. Dana Elizabeth Weiner, *Race and Rights: Fighting Slavery and Prejudice in the Old Northwest, 1830–1870* (DeKalb: Northern Illinois University Press, 2013), 104–107; PFAS Minutes, December 14, 1837, and January 4, 1838, HSP.

35. Howard Jones, *Mutiny on the* Amistad*: The Saga of a Slave Revolt and Its Impact on American Abolition, Law, And Diplomacy* (New York: Oxford University Press, 1987); Marcus Rediker, *The* Amistad *Rebellion: An Atlantic Odyssey of Slavery and Freedom*, rev. ed. (New York: Penguin, 2013).

36. Plea to the Jurisdiction of Cinque and Others, August 21, 1839, *Thomas R. Gedney v. Schooner Amistad*, Case Files, 1790–1911, Records of District Courts of the United States, Record Group 21, National Archives at Boston, Waltham, Mass. (Online version, https://www.docsteach.org/documents/document/plea-jurisdiction-cinque). Warrant for Habeas Corpus, September 21, 1839, *United States v. Cinque and the Africans*, Case Files, 1790–1911, Records of District Courts of the United States, Record Group 21, National Archives at Boston, Waltham, Mass. (Online version, https://www.docsteach.org/documents/document/warrant-for-habeas-corpus).

37. PFAS Minutes, March 11, 1841, HSP. Susan Branson, "Phrenology and the Science of Race in Antebellum America," *Early American Studies* 15, no. 1(Winter 2017): 164–193.

38. For the slave South after Nat Turner, see Edward B. Rugemer, *The Problem of Emancipation: The Caribbean Roots of the American Civil War* (Baton Rouge: Louisiana State University Press, 2008), 108–110, who notes the persistence of Bryan Edwards's proslavery interpretation of insurrection

in Saint Domingue. Thomas Morgan, "The Education and Medical Practice of Dr. James McCune Smith (1813–1865), the First Black American to Hold a Medical Degree," *Journal of the National Medical Association* 95, no. 7(July 2003): 603–614, esp. 608, 610. Smith's data from his work at Lock Hospital appeared in "On the Influence of Opium upon the Catamenial Functions," *New York Journal of Medicine* 2 (1844): 57–58. Joseph Sturge, *A Visit to the United States in 1841* (Boston, 1842), 7.

39. *Colored American*, September 23, 30, 1837, and October 28, 1837; Morgan, "Education and Medical Practice of Dr. James McCune"; John Stauffer, introduction to *The Works of James McCune Smith: Black Intellectual and Activist* (New York: Oxford University Press, 2006), xxi, xxiii; Leslie A. Falk, "Black Abolitionist Doctors and Healers, 1810–1885," *Bulletin of the History of Medicine* 54, no. 2 (1980): 258–272; James McCune Smith, introduction to Frederick Douglass, *My Bondage, My Freedom* (New York, 1855).

40. James McCune Smith, "The Abolition of Slavery and the Slave Trade in the British and French Colonies," *Colored American*, 1838.

41. James McCune Smith, "A Lecture on the Haytien Revolutions: with a Sketch of the Character of Toussaint L'Ouverture" (New York, 1841).

42. Smith, "Lecture on the Haytien Revolutions."

43. Smith, "Lecture on the Haytien Revolutions."

44. Leslie M. Harris, *In the Shadow of Slavery: Africans Americans in New York City, 1626–1863* (Chicago: University of Chicago Press, 2003), esp. 187. James McCune Smith, "The Destiny of the People of Color" (New York, 1843). See also Mia Bay, *The White Image in the Black Mind: African-American Ideas About White People, 1830–1925* (New York: Oxford University Press, 2000), 58–63; Bruce Dain, *A Hideous Monster of the Mind: American Race Theory in the Early Republic* (Cambridge, Mass.: Harvard University Press, 2002).

45. William Still, *The Underground Railroad*, rev. ed. (Philadelphia, 1878); "Underground Railroad in Guilford College Woods," https://library.guilford.edu/undergroundrr. Thomas D. Hamm, "Addison Coffin, Quaker Visionary," *Southern Friend: Journal of the North Carolina Friends Historical Society* 18, no. 1 (Spring 1996): 51–66. Keith P. Griffler, *Front Line of Freedom: African Americans and the Forging of the Underground Railroad in the Ohio Valley* (Lexington: University Press of Kentucky, 2004); David M. Blight, ed., *Passages to Freedom: The Underground Railroad in History and Memory* (Washington, D.C.: Smithsonian, 2004); William C. Kashatus, *Just Over the Line: Chester County and the Underground Railroad* (University Park: Pennsylvania State University Press, 2001). Christopher Densmore, "Quakers and the Underground Railroad: Myths and Realities," https://web.tricolib.brynmawr.edu/speccoll/quakersandslavery/commentary/organizations/underground_railroad.pdf (accessed May 28, 2021). See also Robert Churchill, *The Underground Railroad and the Geography of Violence in Antebellum America* (New York: Cambridge University Press, 2020).

46. Cheryl Janifer LaRoche, *Free Black Communities and the Underground Railroad: The Geography of Resistance* (Urbana: University of Illinois Press, 2014). See also John Michael Vlach, "Above Ground on the Underground Railroad," in Blight, *Passages to Freedom*, 95–115.

47. Eric Foner, *Gateway to Freedom: The Hidden History of America's Fugitive Slaves* (New York: Oxford University Press, 2015); Richard P. McCormick, "William Whipper: Moral Reformer," *Pennsylvania History* 43, no. 3 (1976): 23–46; Thomas M. Lessl, "William Whipper (c. 1804–1876), Businessman, Abolitionist, Reform Activist," in Richard W. Leeman, ed., *African-American Orators: A Bio-critical Sourcebook* (Westport, Conn.: Greenwood, 1996).

48. Joseph Boromé, Jacob C. White, Robert B. Ayres, and J. M. McKim, "The Vigilant Committee of Philadelphia," *PMHB* 92, no. 3 (July 1968), 320–351, and 331 for Whipper's involvement on June 27, 1839.

49. William Whipper, "Non Resistance to Offensive Aggression," *Colored American*, September 9, 16, 23, and 30, 1837.

50. Graham Russell Gao Hodges, *David Ruggles: A Radical Black Abolitionist and the Underground Railroad in New York City* (Chapel Hill: University of North Carolina Press, 2010), 113, 120–132, 144–153; *Liberator*, August 13, 1841.

51. The Female Vigilance Committee raised ten dollars for an escaped woman at Willow Grove, September 10, 1839; see Boromé, "The Vigilant Committee of Philadelphia," especially 333, 339, 341, for women listed among the donors for the final quarter of 1839 and January 1840; and 344, for the collection of money taken by Hetty Reckless. Lucretia Mott's donation of ten dollars was listed in the PFAS Minutes, April 25, 1841, HSP. *Liberator*, June 2, 1843. Harrold, *Rise of Aggressive Abolitionism*; Caitlin Rosenthal, *Accounting for Slavery: Masters and Management* (Cambridge, Mass.: Harvard University Press, 2018), 135–136; *Narrative of the Life and Adventures of Henry Bibb, an American Slave, Written by Himself* (New York, 1849).

52. *Liberator*, April 29, 1842; W. Caleb McDaniel, *The Problem of Democracy in the Age of Slavery: Garrisonian Abolitionists and Transatlantic Reform* (Baton Rouge: Louisiana State University Press, 2013), 168. *Congressional Globe*, 27th Congress, 2nd session, 168, 170–174, 181.

53. *Liberator*, June 27, 1845; PFAS Minutes, September 12, 1844, and October 14, 1847, both in HSP; Elizabeth R. Varon, *Disunion! The Coming of the American Civil War, 1789–1859* (Chapel Hill: University of North Carolina Press, 2008); Martha S. Jones, *Birthright Citizens: A History of Race and Rights in Antebellum America* (New York: Cambridge University Press, 2018), 97, for the right to travel across state lines; William Yates, *Rights of Colored Men to Suffrage, Citizenship and Trial by Jury: Being a Book of Facts, Arguments and Authorities, Historical Notices and Sketches of Debates—With Notes* (Philadelphia, 1838).

54. David E. Swift, *Black Prophets of Justice: Activist Clergy Before the Civil War* (Baton Rouge: Louisiana State University Press, 1999), 62; Schor, *Henry Highland Garnet*; Sterling Stuckey, "A Last Stern Struggle: Henry Highland Garnet and Liberation Theory," in Leon Litwack and August Meier, eds., *Black Leaders of the Nineteenth Century* (Urbana: University of Illinois Press, 1988), 129–147.

55. Peter Paul Simons, "Lecture Delivered Before the African Clarkson Association, New York, New York," April 23, 1839, reprinted in C. Peter Ripley, ed., *The Black Abolitionist Papers*, 5 vols. (Chapel Hill: University of North Carolina Press, 1991): 3:288–292; *Colored American*, June 1, 1839. See Jasinski, "Constituting Antebellum African American Identity," 29–30, 48–49n9.

56. Harris, *In the Shadow of Slavery*, 173, 202, 216, 222.

57. *Liberator*, August 13, 1841.

58. Garnet, "Address to the Slaves," 1843.

59. Harrold, *Rise of Aggressive Abolitionism* 33–36; See Jasinski, "Constituting Antebellum African American Identity," for a nuanced interpretation of Garnet's position. Garnet's address was not included in the minutes and was defeated as a resolution to the convention; *Liberator*, September 22, 1843; *Liberator*, December 8, 1843. See also Leigh Fought, *Women in the World of Frederick Douglass* (New York: Oxford University Press, 2017), 81.

60. Harrold, *Rise of Aggressive Abolitionism*.

61. Robert S. Levine, *Martin Delany, Frederick Douglass, and the Politics of Representative Identity* (Chapel Hill: University of North Carolina Press, 1997); Robert S. Levine, *Martin R. Delany: A Documentary Reader* (Chapel Hill: University of North Carolina Press, 2003), 26, for his training with Drs. Andrew M. McDowell and William Elder.

62. Dorothy Sterling, *The Making of an Afro-American: Martin Robison Delany, 1812–1885* (New York: Da Capo, 1971, repr. 1996); Dorsey, *Reforming Men and Women*; Levine, *Martin Delany, Frederick Douglass*.

63. "Peace Congress at Paris," *Bathurst Free Press* (NSW), December 29, 1849, 2.

64. Paula Garrett and Hollis Robbins, eds., *The Works of William Wells Brown: Using His "Strong, Manly Voice"* (New York: Oxford University Press, 2006); William Wells Brown, *St. Domingo: Its Revolutions and Its Patriots* (Boston, 1855).

65. Emma Jones Lapsansky, "'Since They Got Those Separate Churches': Afro-Americans and Racism in Jacksonian Philadelphia," *American Quarterly* 32, no. 1 (1980): 54–78; Julie Winch, "Self-Help and Self-Determination: Black Philadelphians and the Dimensions of Freedom," in Richard Newman and James Mueller, eds., *Antislavery and Abolition in Philadelphia: Emancipation and the Long Struggle for Racial Justice in the City of Brotherly Love* (Baton Rouge: Louisiana State University Press, 2011), 82. Boromé, "The Vigilant Committee of Philadelphia"; Thomas D. Morris, *Free Men*

All: The Personal Liberty Laws of the North, 1780–1861 (Baltimore: Johns Hopkins University Press, 1974), 42–70.

66. Beverley C. Tomek, "Vigilance Committees," The Encyclopedia of Greater Philadelphia, 2015, https://philadelphiaencyclopedia.org/archive/vigilance-committees/.

67. Margaret Hope Bacon, *But One Race: The Life of Robert Purvis* (Albany: State University of New York Press, 2007), 29–57.

68. Bacon, *But One Race*, 44–47.

69. PFAS Minutes, April 19, 1835, HSP; Boromé, "The Vigilant Committee of Philadelphia," 321–323. Bacon, *But One Race*, 76–78.

70. Robert Purvis, *Appeal of Forty Thousand Citizens* (Philadelphia, 1838), quote on 15.

71. Boromé, "The Vigilant Committee of Philadelphia," 331, 333.

72. For Mary Gilmore's adoptive parents and the false claim that she was a slave, see "Elizabeth and Jacob Gilmore, https://coloredconventions.org/women-economic-power/bakeries/elizabeth-jacob-gilmore/. For the silver pitcher given to David Paul Brown, see https://philadelphiaencyclopedia.org/archive/artifact-presentation-pitcher/ accessed August 2, 2020. See also the *Liberator*, August 18, 1837. For Brown's vice presidency of the American Anti-Slavery Society, see *First Annual Report of the American Anti-Slavery Society*, vol. 1, May 6, 1834, 35.

73. Boromé, "The Vigilant Committee of Philadelphia," 339, 345. The list of donors to the PVC for 1839–1840 included individual women, Bethel Church, and the Female Vigilance Committee, 10. The peak of PVC activity was 1840–1841. See *Anti-slavery Standard*, November 19, 1840, notice of public meeting; PFAS Minutes, March 11, 1841; November 11, 1841; January 13, 1842 ($50 contribution); September 8, 1842; October 13, 1842; January 12, 1832 ($100 contribution); all in HSP. Jesse Olsavsky, "Women, Vigilance Committees, and the Rise of Militant Abolitionism, 1835–1859," *Slavery and Abolition* 39, no. 2 (2018): 357–382. Julie Roy Jeffrey, *The Great Silent Army of Abolitionism: Ordinary Women in the Antislavery Movement* (Chapel Hill: University of North Carolina Press, 1998), 181–190. For "body work," see Brown, *Foul Bodies*, 5.

74. H. Robert Baker, *Prigg v. Pennsylvania: Slavery, The Supreme Court, and the Ambivalent Constitution* (Lawrence: University of Kansas Press, 2012), 102–105.

75. Baker, *Prigg v. Pennsylvania*, 109.

76. The issue was deferred to the next session of the Pennsylvania Assembly; then a "voluntary submission" law in April 1839 allowed Prigg to remain free and the matter to go first to the Pennsylvania Supreme Court and then to the U.S. Supreme Court. Pennsylvania's position was that the requirements of the Pennsylvania liberty law had not been followed (procurement of a certificate of removal); Maryland's was that the Pennsylvania liberty law violated the Constitution.

77. See Baker, *Prigg v. Pennsylvania*, 130, for Justice Marshall's 1825 opinion in the *Antelope* case that the slave trade was not contrary to law of nations.

78. Barbara Holden-Smith, "Lords of Lash, Loom, and Law: Justice Story, Slavery, and *Prigg v. Pennsylvania*," *Cornell Law Review* 78 (1993): 1086–1151. Baker, *Prigg v. Pennsylvania*, 101–126. Paul Finkelman, "Story Telling on the Supreme Court: *Prigg v. Pennsylvania* and Justice Joseph Story's Judicial Nationalism," *Supreme Court Review* 1994 (1994): 247–294.

79. "Lombard Street Riots Site," http://www.philaplace.org/story/62/; Boromé, "The Vigilant Committee of Philadelphia," 327; Rugemer, *Problem of Emancipation*, 228–257, for the violent reprisals in Philadelphia in 1842; Mitch Kachun, *Festivals of Freedom: Memory and Meaning in African American Emancipation Celebrations, 1808–1915* (Amherst: University of Massachusetts Press, 2003); Bacon, *But One Race*; Julie Roy Jeffrey, "'No Occurrence in Human History Is More Deserving of Commemoration Than This': Abolitionist Celebrations of Freedom," in McCarthy and Stauffer, *Prophets of Protest*, 200–219, esp. 208–210. Geneviève Fabre, "African American Commemoration Celebrations in the Nineteenth Century," in Geneviève Fabre and Robert O'Meally, eds., *History and Memory in African American Culture* (New York: Oxford University Press, 1994), 72–91.

80. Baker, *Prigg v. Pennsylvania*, 101–126; Boromé, "The Vigilant Committee of Philadelphia," 324.

81. Jean Fagan Yellin, *Harriet Jacobs: A Life* (New York: Perseus Books, 2004), 65–67.

82. Boromé, "The Vigilant Committee of Philadelphia." Elizabeth Varon, '"Beautiful Providences': William Still, the Vigilance Committee, and Abolitionists in the Age of Sectionalism," in Newman and Mueller, *Antislavery and Abolition in Philadelphia*, 229–245, esp. 231.

83. Foner, *Gateway to Freedom.*

84. *Laws of the General Assembly of the Commonwealth of Pennsylvania Passed at the Session of 1847* (Harrisburg, Pa., 1847), law 159; R. J. M. Blackett, *Making Freedom: The Underground Railroad and the Politics of Slavery* (Chapel Hill: University of North Carolina Press, 2013), 32–67. See also Junius P. Rodriguez, *Encyclopedia of Slave Resistance and Rebellion*, 2 vols. (Westport, Conn.: Greenwood, 2007), 2:373, for similarity of the Pennsylvania 1847 law to the Massachusetts Latimer law asserting the state's right to extend the writ of habeas corpus to free Blacks claimed under the 1793 Fugitive Slave Law.

85. Fought, *Women in the World of Frederick Douglass*; Janet Kemper Beck, *Creating the John Brown Legend: Emerson, Thoreau, Douglass, Child, and Higginson in Defense of the Raid on Harpers Ferry* (Jefferson, N.C.: McFarland, 2009), 54.

86. Weiner, *Race and Rights*, 158, quoting Rebecca Fussell; David W. Blight, *Frederick Douglass: Prophet of Freedom* (New York: Simon and Schuster, 2018), 133–134.

87. *Frederick Douglass Papers*, ed. John McKivigan (New Haven, Conn.: Yale University Press, 2009).

88. McDaniel, *Problem of Democracy*, 173.

89. Douglass, "Reception Speech," Finsbury Chapel, May 12, 1846 (London, 1846), 6.

90. Douglass, "Reception Speech," 7.

91. Douglass, "Reception Speech," 8.

92. Douglass, "Reception Speech," 9.

93. Sturge forwarded ten copies of Weld's text to John Soul in 1840; Sturge to Soul, October 21, 1840, Sturge Papers, BL.

94. Douglass, "Reception Speech," 14–15.

95. Douglass, "Reception Speech," 17.

96. Douglass, "Reception Speech," 17–18.

97. Douglass, "Reception Speech," 18–19.

98. Douglass, "Reception Speech," 20–21. When Douglass and two "fair Quakeresses" carved into the church green the words "Send back the money," he was informed that he was committing a felony, but Campbell mused that dealing with Baillie Gray might not be so scary to a man who had "braved the fury of the slave holder."

99. Stauffer, *Black Hearts of Men.*

100. Laura Wexler, "'A More Perfect Likeness': Frederick Douglass and the Image of the Nation," in Maurice O. Wallace and Shawn Michelle Smith, eds., *Pictures and Progress: Early Photography and the Making of African American Identity* (Durham, N.C.: Duke University Press, 2012), 32; Ginger Hall, "'Rightly Viewed': Theorizations of Self in Frederick Douglass's Lectures on Pictures," in Wallace and Smith, *Pictures and Progress*, 49, 53, 54.

101. Jeffrey R. Kerr-Ritchie, *Rebellious Passage: The Creole Revolt and America's Coastal Slave Trade* (New York: Cambridge University Press, 2019).

Chapter 8

1. On African American efforts to distinguish phrenology from craniology, see Britt Rusert, *Fugitive Science: Empiricism and Freedom in Early African American Culture* (New York: New York University Press, 2017), 121–127; Cynthia S. Hamilton, "'Am I Not a Man and Brother?' Phrenology and Anti-slavery," *Slavery and Abolition* 29, no. 2 (2008): 173–187; James Poskett, "Phrenology, Correspondence, and the Global Politics of Reform, 1815–1848," *Historical Journal* 63, no. 2 (November 5, 2018): 409–442; Frederick Douglass, *The Claims of the Negro, Ethnologically Considered: An Address Before the Literary Societies of Western Reserve College* (Rochester, 1854), quotes on 12–13.

See also Ann Fabian, *The Skull Collectors: Race, Science, and America's Unburied Dead* (Chicago: University of Chicago Press, 2010), 116–119.

2. William Parker, "The Freedmen's Story," *Atlantic Monthly*, February 1866, 159–162; R. J. M. Blackett, *The Captive's Quest for Freedom: Fugitive Slaves, the 1850 Fugitive Slave Law, and the Politics of Slavery* (New York: Cambridge University Press, 2018), 80–81, 359. Thomas P. Slaughter, *Bloody Dawn: the Christiana Riot and Racial Violence in the Antebellum North* (New York: Oxford University Press, 1991).

3. Douglass, *Address Before the Literary Societies of Western Reserve College*, 29–30. See also Patrick Rael, "A Common Nature, A United Destiny: African-American Responses to Racial Science from the Revolution to the Civil War," in Timothy Patrick McCarthy and John Stauffer, eds., *Prophets of Protest: Reconsidering the History of American Abolitionism* (New York: New Press, 2006), 183–199.

4. Kellie Carter Jackson, *Force and Freedom: Black Abolitionists and the Politics of Violence* (Philadelphia: University of Pennsylvania Press, 2019), 33; Robert Churchill, *The Underground Railroad and the Geography of Violence in Antebellum America* (New York: Cambridge University Press, 2020); Andrew Delbanco, *The War Before the War: Fugitive Slaves and the Struggle for America's Soul from the Revolution to the Civil War* (New York: Penguin, 2018); Steven Lubet, *Fugitive Justice: Runaways, Rescuers, and Slavery on Trial* (Cambridge, Mass.: Belknap Press of Harvard University Press, 2010); Thomas D. Morris, *Free Men All: The Personal Liberty Laws of the North, 1780–1861* (Baltimore: Johns Hopkins University Press, 1974), 130–147.

5. "Remedy for Slavery," *Signal of Liberty*, October 31, 1846.

6. Drew Gilpin Faust, ed., *The Ideology of Slavery: Proslavery Thought in the Antebellum Thought, 1830–1860* (Baton Rouge: Louisiana State University Press, 1981); Larry E. Tise, *Proslavery: A History of the Defense of Slavery in America, 1701–1840* (Athens: University of Georgia Press, 1987).

7. Edward E. Baptist, *The Half Has Never Been Told: Slavery and the Making of American Capitalism* (New York: Basic Books, 2014); Manisha Sinha, *The Slave's Cause: A History of Abolition* (New Haven, Conn.: Yale University Press, 2016); Ana Stevenson, The *Woman as Slave in Nineteenth-Century American Social Movements* (New York: Palgrave Macmillan, 2019).

8. Graham Russell Gao Hodges, *David Ruggles: A Radical Black Abolitionist and the Underground Railroad in New York City* (Chapel Hill: University of North Carolina Press, 2010), 109–110; Bessel van der Kolk, *The Body Keeps the Score: Brain, Mind, and Body in the Healing of Trauma* (New York: Penguin, 2014); Dorothy B. Porter, "David M. Ruggles, an Apostle of Human Rights," *Journal of Negro History* 28: 23–50.

9. *Liberator*, July 7, 1837. Julie Roy Jeffrey, *The Great Silent Army of Abolitionism: Ordinary Women in the Antislavery Movement* (Chapel Hill: University of North Carolina Press, 1998), 202–203. For self- and communal care as a politics of resistance, see Johanna Hedva, "Sick Woman Theory," *Mask Magazine*, 2016.

10. *Green Mountain Spring* 1 no. 5, May 1846; *Water Cure Journal and Teacher of Health*, November 15, 1846; Hodges, *David Ruggles*, 188. For the significance of physical intimacy for medical science, see Timothy Holliday, "Morbid Sensations: Intimacy, Coercion and Epidemic Disease in Philadelphia, 1793–1854" (PhD dissertation, University of Pennsylvania, 2020).

11. Hodges, *David Ruggles*, 190–191. Nell Irvin Painter, *Sojourner Truth: A Life, A Symbol* (New York: W. W. Norton, 1996), 138–142. Margaret Washington, *Sojourner Truth's America* (Urbana: University of Illinois Press, 2009). Bonnie Laughlin-Schultz, *The Tie That Bound Us: The Women of John Brown's Family and the Legacy of Radical Abolitionism* (Ithaca, N.Y.: Cornell University Press, 2013), 26–28.

12. David Blight, *Frederick Douglass: Prophet of Freedom* (New York: Simon and Schuster, 2018), 187–188.

13. Angelina Grimke Weld (AGW) to Theodore Weld (TW), May 22, 1846; Sarah Grimke (SG) to Harriet Hunt (HH), August 22, 1848; AGW to TW, September 7, 1848; TW to AGW, September 1848; AGW and SG to TW, 1849; AGW to Sarah Mapps Douglass (SMD), 1849; AGW to TW, May 20, 1849; AGW to TW, September 5, 1849; AGW to SMD, 1849; SG to AGW, December 16, 1849;

SG to HH, June 10, 1850, all in Weld-Grimké Papers, CL. SMD to Rebecca White, May 30, 1855, on her return to hydropathy to treat her palpitations, HCQSC.

14. Stephen Nissenbaum, *Sex, Diet, and Debility in Jacksonian America: Sylvester Graham and Health Reform* (Westport, Conn.: Greenwood, 1980); Dorothy Sterling, *Ahead of Her Time: Abby Kelley and the Politics of Anti-slavery* (New York: W. W. Norton, 1991), 29–31.

15. Andrew Combe, *The Principles of Physiology* (Edinburgh, 1834).

16. Abby Kelley to Stephen Foster, Duxbury, Massachusetts, written from West Brookfield, February 26, 1844, Abby Kelley Foster Papers, photocopies, HCQSC. Kelley mentioned a field agent named "James" whose "cough has become worse and is constantly increased by speaking—He decided therefore to go to studying and I believe has fixed on Oberlin." See also Kelley to Foster, November 1844, "Have had some slight cold which has kept my throat about as it was—but I think it is beginning to heal—or rather to grow thinner."

17. Kelley to Foster, Utica, January 3, 1844, Abby Kelley Foster Papers, photocopies, HCQSC.

18. Kelley to Foster, January 30, 1843, Abby Kelley Foster Papers, photocopies, HCQSC.

19. Kelley to Foster, Canterbury, N.H., January 30, January 3, 1844, Abby Kelley Foster Papers, photocopies, HCQSC.

20. Kelley to Foster, April 1847, Abby Kelley Foster Papers, photocopies, HCQSC.

21. Davis's previous husband, Francis Wright, died in 1845 despite hydropathic treatments. See Kelley to Foster, January 3, 1845; Sterling, *Ahead of Her Time*, 202.

22. Kelley to Foster, August 18, 1847, and September 28, 1847, both in Abby Kelley Foster Papers, photocopies, HCQSC. The latter letter noted that she was weighing the baby and had pumped and moved the bath water herself. "I can't plunge her now, as it hurts me to pump so much water, but I wash her in cold water."

23. Kelley to Foster, August 1850, Abby Kelley Foster Papers, photocopies, HCQSC.

24. Kelley to Foster, December 2, 1851, Abby Kelley Foster Papers, photocopies, HCQSC.

25. April Haynes, *Riotous Flesh: Women, Physiology, and the Solitary Vice in Nineteenth-Century America* (Chicago: University of Chicago Press, 2015), 142–143.

26. Kelley to Foster, September 28, 1847, Abby Kelley Foster Papers, photocopies, HCQSC.

27. Kelley to Foster, July 21, 1850, Abby Kelley Foster Papers, photocopies, HCQSC. Anna M. Speicher, *The Religious World of Antislavery Women: Spirituality in the Lives of Five Abolitionist Lecturers* (Syracuse, N.Y.: Syracuse University Press, 2000), 177. Elizabeth Jones, *Young Abolitionists; or, Conversations on Slavery* (Boston, 1848); Deborah C. De Rosa, *Into the Mouths of Babes: An Anthology of Children's Abolitionist Literature* (Westport, Conn.: Praeger, 2005); *Ohio Women's Convention, Held at Salem, April 19th and 20th, 1850, with an Address by J. Elizabeth Jones* (Cleveland, 1850), 52–62.

28. Haynes, *Riotous Flesh*, 121–126, 144, and 127–131 for Hollick's endorsement of scientific racism. Harriot Hunt and Sarah Grimke turned against Mary Gove Nichols when she criticized marriage and urged voluntary spiritual unions. Thanks to Scott Wilds for information on Bunting's involvement; see *Pennsylvania Freeman*, March 12, 1846, p. 3, col. 4; accessed through GenealogyBank.com.

29. Sarah Mapps Douglass to Rebecca White, n.d., Josiah White Papers, HCQSC; Haynes, *Riotous Flesh*, 142; Susan H. Brandt, *Women Healers: Gender, Authority, and Medicine in Early Philadelphia* (Philadelphia: University of Pennsylvania Press, 2022).

30. Sarah Mapps Douglass to Rebecca White, November 28, 1855 or 1858; Douglass to White, n.d., reporting attendance of thirty-eight "deeply interested women"; Douglass to White, December 19, 1858, on a small audience; Douglass to White, October 29, 1860, on her upcoming trip to New York to lecture; Douglass to White, February 9, 1862, on her care not to provoke Mrs. R. by using big words, and a washerwoman's confidences; all in Josiah White Papers, HCQSC. Rusert, *Fugitive Science*, 198–203; Haynes, *Riotous Flesh*, 152–162.

31. Belleville, February 19, 1845 (written on Office of AAS communication signed by Arthur Tappan), Weld-Grimké Papers, CL.

32. Samuel George Morton, "On the Question of Hybridity in Animals, Considered in Reference to the Unity of the Human Species," *American Journal of Science and Arts*, 2nd ser., 3 (1847):

37–50, 203–212, quote on 212, from a lecture Morton delivered in November 1846 at Philadelphia's Academy of Natural Sciences. Caldwell had already made this point on the basis of natural history.

33. Samuel George Morton, *Crania Americana; or, a Comparative View of the Skulls of Various Aboriginal Nations of North and South America: to Which Is Prefixed an Essay on the Varieties of the Human Species* (Philadelphia, 1839). Beverly Wilson Palmer, ed., *Selected Letters of Lucretia Coffin Mott* (Urbana: University of Illinois Press, 2002): Lucretia Mott to George Combe, Philadelphia, June 13, 1839, 50–53; Lucretia Mott to George and Cecelia Combe, September 10, 1848, 168–172. PFAS Minutes, November 1848, HSP, for Mott's reading of Andrew and George Combe's letters. Poskett, "Phrenology, Correspondence, and the Global Politics of Reform"; Stephen Tomlinson, *Head Masters: Phrenology, Secular Education, and Nineteenth-Century Social Thought* (Tuscaloosa: University of Alabama Press, 2005), 231–234.

34. Hamilton, "'Am I Not a Man and Brother?'" For a craniological study that found little racial difference, see Frederick Tiedemann, "On the Brain of the Negro, Compared with That of the European and the Orang-outang," *Philosophical Transactions of the Royal Society of London* 23 (1836): 497–528.

35. Matthew Fox-Amato, *Exposing Slavery: Photography, Human Bondage, and the Birth of Modern Visual Politics in* America (New York: Oxford University Press, 2019), 36–37, for the unusual staging of the Agassiz daguerreotypes. Suzanne Schneider, "Louis Agassiz and the American School of Ethnoeroticism: Polygenesis, Pornography, and other 'Perfidious Influences,'" in Maurice O. Wallace and Shawn Michelle Smith, eds., *Pictures and Progress: Early Photography and the Making of African American Identity* (Durham, N.C.: Duke University Press, 2012), 211–243; Molly Rogers, *Delia's Tears: Race, Science, and Photography in Nineteenth-Century America* (New Haven, Conn.: Yale University Press, 2010). For abolitionists' capitalization on public sentiment around the white appearance of some slaves, see Jessie Morgan-Owens, *Girl in Black and White: The Story of Mary Mildred Williams and the Abolition Movement* (New York: Norton, 2019).

36. Thomas M. Morgan, "The Education and Medical Practice of Dr. James McCune Smith (1813–1865), First Black American to Hold a Medical Degree," *Journal of the National Medical Association* 95, no. 7 (July 2003): 603–614; John Stauffer, introduction to *The Works of James McCune Smith: Black Intellectual and Abolitionist*, ed. John Stauffer (New York: Oxford University Press, 2006), xxi, xxiii; Leslie A. Falk, "Black Abolitionist Doctors and Healers, 1810–1885," *Bulletin of the History of Medicine* 54 (1980): 258–272; James McCune Smith, introduction to Frederick Douglass, *My Bondage, My Freedom* (New York, 1855).

37. James McCune Smith, "Dissertation on the Influence of Climate on Longevity" (New York, 1846). Bruce Dain, *A Hideous Monster of the Mind: American Race Theory in the Early Republic* (Cambridge, Mass.: Harvard University Press, 2002), 238–239.

38. Smith, "Lay Puffery of Homeopathy" (1847), in Morgan, "Education and Medical Practice of Dr. James McCune Smith," 611, and Stauffer, ed., *Works of James McCune Smith*; Thomas C. Patterson, "An Archaeology of the History of Nineteenth-Century U.S. Anthropology: James McCune Smith, Radical Abolitionist and Anthropologist," *Journal of Anthropological Research* 69, no. 4 (Winter 2013): 459–484.

39. "Heads of the Colored People," *Frederick Douglass's Paper* (1852), in Stauffer, ed., *Works of James McCune Smith*; Rachel Banner, "Thinking Through Things: Labors of Freedom in James McCune Smith's 'The Washerwoman,'" *ESQ: Journal of the American Renaissance* 59, no. 2 (2013): 291–328.

40. Patterson, "James McCune Smith, Radical Abolitionist and Anthropologist."

41. Hamilton, "'Am I Not a Man and Brother?'" Notice of 1848 Rochester lectures of Dr. Henry E. Lewis, in Dorothy Porter Wesley and Constance Porter Uzelac, eds., *William Cooper Nell: Selected Writings, 1832–1874* (Baltimore: Black Classic Press, 2002), 209, document 134. Banneker Institute Records, undated, Leon Gardiner of American Negro Historical Society Records, HSP. Harry C. Silcox, "Philadelphia Negro Educator, Jacob C. White, Jr., 1837–1902," *PMHB* 97, no. 1 (1973): 75–98; Rusert, *Fugitive Science*, 190, 269n24.

42. Julietta Singh, *Unthinking Mastery: Dehumanism and Decolonial Entanglements* (Durham, N.C.: Duke University Press, 2018).

43. Douglass, *The Claims of the Negro, Ethnologically Considered*, 8.

44. Douglass, *The Claims of the Negro, Ethnologically Considered*, 8, 10.

45. Douglass, *The Claims of the Negro, Ethnologically Considered*, 15–16.

46. Douglass, *The Claims of the Negro, Ethnologically Considered*, 20. For Wendell Phillips's use of similar language by the 1850s, see James Brewer Stewart, "Comfortable in His Own Skin: Wendell Phillips and Racial Egalitarianism," in A. J. Aiséirithe and Donald Yacovone, eds., *Wendell Phillips, Social Justice, and the Power of the Past* (Baton Rouge: Louisiana State University Press, 2016), 111–132, esp. 131n28.

47. Douglass, *The Claims of the Negro, Ethnologically Considered*, 30, 35. Douglass's comment reflected Agassiz's concession that diverse origins might not necessarily mean a lack of unity in the human race; see Eric Herschthal, *The Science of Abolition: How Slaveholders Became the Enemies of Progress* (New Haven, Conn.: Yale University Press, 2021), 216–217.

48. Douglass, *The Claims of the Negro, Ethnologically Considered*, 34, 36.

49. Barbara Holden-Smith, "Lords of the Lash, Loom, and Law: Justice Story, Slavery, and *Prigg v. Pennsylvania*," *Cornell Law Review* 78 (1993): 1086–1151.

50. "A Letter to the American Slaves from Those Who Have Fled from American Slavery," *North Star*, September 5, 1850, 3. Fox-Amato, *Exposing Slavery*, 136–137. Stanley Harrold, "The Cazenovia Convention," Historians Against Slavery, https://www.historiansagainstslavery.org/main/the-cazenovia-convention/ (accessed January 26, 2021). Elder spoke at the December 1850 Pennsylvania Anti-Slavery Meeting and is quoted in Stanley Harrold, *Border War: Fighting over Slavery Before the Civil War* (Chapel Hill: University of North Carolina Press, 2010), 138–158. See also John Brooke, *"There is a North": Fugitive Slaves, Political Crisis, and Cultural Transformation in the Coming of the Civil War* (Amherst: University of Massachusetts Press, 2019).

51. History of Manchester Township, Dearborn County, Indiana, in Archibald Shaw, ed., *History of Dearborn County, Indiana: Her People, Industries, and Institutions* (Indianapolis: B. F. Bowen & Co., 1915), cited in Blackett, *Captive's Quest*, 75. See also R. J. M. Blackett, *Making Freedom: The Underground Railroad and the Politics of Slavery* (Chapel Hill: University of North Carolina Press, 2013), 53.

52. Josiah Clark Nott, "Nature and Destiny of the Negro," *DeBow's Review* 10 (1851): 329–332; James O. Breeden, "States-Rights Medicine in the Old South," *Bulletin of the New York Academy of Medicine* 52, no. 3 (March–April 1976): 348–372, esp. 350–354. Josiah Nott and George Gliddon, *Types of Mankind* (Philadelphia, 1854). Hedva, "Sick Woman Theory."

53. Samuel Cartwright, "Report on the Diseases and Physical Peculiarities of the Negro Race" *New Orleans Medical and Surgical Journal* (1851); Christopher Willoughby, "Running away from Drapetomania: Samuel A. Cartwright, Medicine, and Race in the Antebellum South," *Journal of Southern History* 84, no. 3 (July 2018): 579–614; Marli F. Weiner with Mazie Hough, *Sex, Sickness, and Slavery: Illness in the Antebellum South* (Urbana: University of Illinois Press, 2012), 21–22, 225nn31–32.

54. John K. Kane, letter, 1854, Hugenschmidt Autograph Collection, Kislak Center, University of Pennsylvania.

55. Simon A. Cole, *Suspect Identities: A History of Fingerprinting and Criminal Identification* (Cambridge, Mass.: Harvard University Press, 2001). Jesse Olsavsky, "Runaway Slaves, Vigilance Committees, and the Pedagogy of Revolutionary Abolitionism, 1835–1863," in Marcus Rediker, Titas Chakraborty, and Matthias van Rossum, eds., *A Global History of Runaways: Workers, Mobility, and Capitalism, 1600–1850* (Oakland: University of California Press, 2019), 216–233; Olsavsky notes Jonathan Walker's belief that American empire required slaves to be immobilized, 233. Jackson, *Force and Freedom*, 48–79. For the use of "expert" testimony to determine racial identity, see *Daniel v. Guy*, 19 Ark. 121 (1857) in L. E. Barber, *Reports of Cases at Law and in Equity Argued and Determined in the Supreme Court of Arkansas* (Little Rock, Ark., 1889), 19: 121–122; *Gary v. Stevenson*, 19 Ark. 580 (1858) in Barber, *Reports of Cases* 19: 580–587; *State v. Jacobs*, 51 N.C. 284 (1859) in Hamilton C. Jones, *Cases at Law Argued and Determined in the Supreme Court of North Carolina* (reprinted 1905), 51: 284–289.

56. William Still, *The Underground Railroad*, rev. ed. (Philadelphia, 1878), 562–575. *Philadelphia Public Ledger*, February 7–8, 1851, and February 10, 1851; Ashley Council, "Ringing Liberty's Bell: African American Women, Gender, and the Underground Railroad in Philadelphia," *Pennsylvania History* 87, no. 3 (Summer 2020): 494–531. Blackett, *Captive's Quest*, 63, 346–348.

57. Euphemia Williams case, reported in *Philadelphia Public Ledger*, February 7, 8, 10, 1851; *Philadelphia Evening Bulletin*, February 10, 1851; *Pennsylvania Freeman*, February 13, 1851, all in Independence Hall in American Memory, companion site, http://www.independencehall-americanmemory.com/slavery-and-freedom/fugitive-slave-hearings-of-the-1850s/euphemia-williams. Still, *Underground Railroad*, 562–575.

58. Still, *Underground Railroad*, 565–566, 571–572.

59. The turban that hid the scar on her forehead was the brainchild of Lt. Gouldy of the mayor's police; Still, *Underground Railroad*, 574. Published in the *Pennsylvania Freeman*, January 13, 1857. For a fugitive slave case turning on racial classification and involving a phrenologist, see James Poskett, *Materials of the Mind: Phrenology, Race, and the Global History of Science, 1815–1920* (Chicago: University of Chicago Press, 2019), 75–76. Kane became prominent in Philadelphia's Democratic Party and worked on Andrew Jackson's presidential campaign. He was rewarded with appointment as attorney general of Pennsylvania in 1845 and judge on the United States District Court for the Eastern District of Pennsylvania in 1846.

60. Slaughter, *Bloody Dawn*; Jackson, *Force and Freedom*, 54–57. Kellie Carter Jackson, "'Dare You Meet a Woman': Black Women, Abolitionism, and Protective Violence, 1850–1859," *Slavery and Abolition* 42, no. 2 (2021): 269–292.

61. Joseph Boromé, "The Vigilant Committee of Philadelphia," *PMHB* 92 (July 1968): 328; Blackett, *Making Freedom*, 54–64, for the kidnapping of two sisters, Elizabeth and Rachel Parker, from Chester County in December 1851.

62. Still, *Underground Railroad*, 605.

63. *Provincial Freeman*, May 5, 1855. William Kashatus, *William Still: The Underground Railroad and the Angel at Philadelphia* (Notre Dame, Ind.: University of Notre Dame Press, 2021).

64. Report of J. McKim, PFAS Minutes, January 15, 1855, HSP. James J. Gigantino II, *The Ragged Road to Abolition: Slavery and Freedom in New Jersey, 1775–1865* (Philadelphia: University of Pennsylvania Press, 2015), 168–169.

65. Charles L. Blockson Collection, Temple University, accessed online; James Oliver Horton, "A Crusade for Freedom: William Still and the Real Underground Railroad," in David Blight, ed., *Passages to Freedom: The Underground Railroad in History and Memory* (Washington, D.C.: Smithsonian, 2004), 175–193. Blackett, *Making Freedom*, 15. Still first published his extensive notes on the Underground Railroad in 1872, after he had reunited with one of his lost brothers and learned of the other's death, to testify to the stream of refugees leaving the South during the 1840s and 1850s.

66. Still, *Underground Railroad*, 3, 82, 491, 58.

67. Elizabeth Varon, '"Beautiful Providences': William Still, the Vigilance Committee, and Abolitionists in the Age of Sectionalism," in Richard Newman and James Mueller, eds., *Antislavery and Abolition in Philadelphia: Emancipation and the Long Struggle for Racial Justice in the City of Brotherly Love* (Baton Rouge: Louisiana State University Press, 2011), 229–245, esp. 233–234; *Pennsylvania Freeman*, December 1853; *National Anti-slavery Standard*, November 4, 1854.

68. Varon, '"Beautiful Providences,'" 232. Still, *Underground Railroad*, for list of goods sent to the PVC, 1860, 584–586; 1855 correspondence with Graceanna Lewis, 529; and November 1857 correspondence with E. H. Pennypacker, 30.

69. Still *Underground Railroad*, 24–25.

70. Still, *Underground Railroad*, 183, 199, 208, and 65, for Mary Epps/Emma Brown, Petersburg, Virginia, who appeared before the PVC on March 1, 1855, and wrote to Still to give respect to "his lady."

71. Jeffrey, *Great Silent Army*, 181–190; Jesse Olsavsky, "Women, Vigilance Committees, and the Rise of Militant Abolitionism, 1835–1859," *Slavery and Abolition* 39, no. 2 (2018): 357–382, for details of Black female PVC agents working in the field. Stanley Harrold, *Subversives: Antislavery Community in Washington, D.C., 1828–1865* (Baton Rouge: Louisiana State University Press, 2002),

for the free Black washerwoman in Washington, D.C., who worked with Thomas Smallwood and Charles Torrey to ferry wagons of fugitives to Philadelphia and Canada.

72. PFAS Minutes, April 10, 1845, for Hetty Reckless seeking funds for new fugitives. Women were among the earliest donors listed in PVC accounts in 1839–1840; Boromé, "Vigilant Committee of Philadelphia," 341.

73. PFAS Minutes, June 10, 1847, and April 10, 1856.

74. "Resurrectionist" was also used to describe procurers of cadavers. For a similar process in the post-emancipation French Caribbean, see Laurent Dubois, "Inscribing Race in the Revolutionary French Antilles," in Sue Peabody and Tyler Stovall, eds., *The Color of Liberty: Histories of Race in France* (Durham, N.C.: Duke University Press, 2003), 100–102.

75. Still, *Underground Railroad*, 43–146.

76. Still, *Underground Railroad*, 37–40.

77. Still, *Underground Railroad*, 40–43.

78. "An Act Providing Additional Protection for the Slave Property of Citizens of This Commonwealth," *Acts of the General Assembly of Virginia, Passed in 1855–6, in the Eightieth Year of the Commonwealth* (Richmond, Va.: William F. Ritchie, 1856), 38–41. Still, *Underground Railroad*, 276, 56. The law authorized inspections on water travel to prevent the escape of slaves; Cassandra L. Newby-Alexander, *Virginia Waterways and the Underground Railroad* (Charleston, S.C.: History Press, 2017), 52–93, esp. 59.

79. Still, *Underground Railroad*, 71–74, 36. The man who boxed Brown, Samuel A. Smith, was arrested and imprisoned. Lucretia Mott to Joseph Dugdale and Ruth Dugdale, March 28, 1849, in Palmer, *Letters of Lucretia Mott*, 179–180.

80. Still, *Underground Railroad*, 602–603; Olsavsky, "Women, Vigilance Committees," 360. I am indebted to Scott Wilds for information about Rachel Myers drawn from the 1850 census and her death certificate in 1861.

81. Still, *Underground Railroad*, 280–281.

82. Still, *Underground Railroad*, 178–182, 556.

83. Olsavsky, "Women, Vigilance Committees," 359, for data on 364 women gathered from Vigilance Committees in Philadelphia, New York, and Boston. Still, *Underground Railroad*, 360.

84. Olsavsky, "Women, Vigilance Committees," 360, 364, 372. PFAS Minutes, January 12, 1853, and May 12, 1853 (Sojourner Truth); September 13, 1855 (Julietta Sargent); February 11, 1856 (refugee Hannah Moore); December 10, 1857 (Sarah Remond). Frances Smith Foster, ed., *A Brighter Coming Day: A Frances Ellen Watkins Harper Reader* (New York: Feminist Press, 1990); Jane Rhodes, *Mary Ann Shadd Cary: The Black Press and Protest in the Nineteenth Century* (Bloomington: Indiana University Press, 1998).

85. Still, *Underground Railroad*, 66.

86. Still, *Underground Railroad*, 119.

87. Still, *Underground Railroad*, 166–167, for Matilda Mahoney.

88. Still, *Underground Railroad*, 114.

89. Still, *Underground Railroad*, 149, Mary Ennis testimony; 491, Caroline Gassway had "keen insight into the system under which she had been oppressed."

90. Blackett, *Captive's Quest*, 238–239.

91. Still, *Underground Railroad*, 105–109. On the limits of habeas corpus rights for Black people, see Alexander G. Weheliye, *Habeas Viscus: Racializing Assemblages, Biopolitics, and Black Feminist Theories of the Human* (Durham, N.C.: Duke University Press, 2017), 132–133.

92. Chris Walker, "The Fugitive Slave Case of John Freeman and Its Influence on Indiana Politics," *Indiana Magazine of History* 114, no. 1 (March 2018): 1–38. Blackett, *Captive's Quest*, 211–213.

93. Varon, "'Beautiful Providences,'" 239; Blackett, *Captive's Quest*, 347–351.

94. Blackett, *Captive's Quest*, 351–352. PFAS Minutes, April 12, 1860, HSP.

95. *New York Herald*, July 24, 1855. Blackett, *Captive's Quest*, 334, citing *New York Tribune*, July 27, 1855. *Provincial Freeman*, August 22, 1855, Library Company website; Still, *Underground Railroad*, 77–88; Blackett, *Captive's Quest*, 332–334; Varon, "'Beautiful Providences,'" 234–235;

Daniel S. Farbman, "Resistance Lawyering," *California Law Review* 107, no. 6 (2019): 1877–1953, who notes, "No thoughtful lawyer could imagine that by rescuing a single alleged fugitive they could undermine the system of slavery embedded in the fabric of American law" (1932).

96. Blackett, *Captive's Quest*, 282; *Pennsylvania Freeman*, May 1, 1851; Gerald G. Eggert, "The Impact of the Fugitive Slave Law on Harrisburg: A Case Study," *Pennsylvania Magazine of History and Biography* 109, no. 4 (1985): 537–556. Richard McAllister was the most tenacious of the Fugitive Slave Law commissioners in the country; see "Richard McAllister, Class of 1840: Fugitive Slave Commissioner," Dickinson and Slavery, https://richardmcallister.weebly.com.

97. Blackett, *Captive's Quest*, 346–347. PFAS Minutes, March 13, 1851, for its denunciation of the claimant lawyers and commissioners enforcing the Fugitive Slave Law.

98. George Fitzhugh, *Sociology for the South* (Richmond, Va., 1854); George Fitzhugh, *Cannibals All! or, Slaves without Masters*, ed. C. Vann Woodward (Cambridge, Mass.: Belknap Press of Harvard University Press, 1960, 1988). See also Edward B. Rugemer, *The Problem of Emancipation: The Caribbean Roots of the American Civil War* (Baton Rouge: Louisiana State University Press, 2008), 265–268, for the proslavery verdict that West Indian emancipation had been a failure.

99. Abolitionist rejoinders to Fitzhugh, in contrast, offered graphic evidence of injured bodies and effaced family ties; see Charles Whipple, *The Family Relation as Affected by Slavery* (Cincinnati: American Reform Tract and Book Society, 1858); Lydia Maria Child, *The Patriarchal Institution, as Described by Members of Its Own Family* (New York: American Anti-Slavery Society, 1860).

100. Fitzhugh, *Cannibals All!*

101. Karl Marx, *Capital*, 2 vols. (New York: Penguin Classics, 1992), 1:1031–1034; Amy Dru Stanley, *From Bondage to Contract: Wage Labor, Marriage, and the Market in the Age of Slave Emancipation* (New York: Cambridge University Press, 1998).

102. Angelina Grimké Weld to Sarah Moore Grimké and Theodore Weld, May 27, 1846, Weld-Grimké Papers, CL.

103. Ann Rhoads diary, 1847, Rhoads Family Papers, HCQSC.

104. Sinha, *Slave's Cause*, 339–380. Stanley, *From Bondage to Contract.*

105. Joseph Sturge to Samuel Rhoads, Birmingham, January 21, 1859, Rhoads Family Papers, HCQSC.

106. Alex Tyrrell, *Joseph Sturge and the Moral Radical Party in Early Victorian Britain* (London: Christopher Helm, 1988), 232. Howard Fergus, *Gallery Montserrat: Some Prominent People in Our History* (Kingston, Barbados: Canoe Press, 1996), 65–67. Sturge died within months of communicating news about free sugar production in Montserrat. His brother Edmund and sister-in-law Lydia traveled to Montserrat in 1862 and stayed for a year to oversee the transition of the estate to lime production. Montserrat's lime industry became the island's main industry after Sturge family members made use of the Encumbered Estates Court (1865) to buy up half of the island's bankrupt plantation properties. Eventually, the Sturge brothers supplied citric acid to their chemical works in Birmingham and lime juice to Crosse and Blackwell and Schweppes of Australia and New Zealand.

107. "Enthusiastic Meeting of the Colored Citizens of Boston," *Weekly Anglo-African*, September 10, 1859; Garnet, "African Civilization Society" (1858); Howard H. Bell, "Negro Nationalism: A Factor in Emigration Projects, 1858–1861," *Journal of Negro History* 47, no. 1 (January 1962): 42–53; Levine, *Martin R. Delany: A Documentary Reader* (Chapel Hill: University of North Carolina Press, 2003), 316–318.

108. Don E. Fehrenbacher, *The Dred Scott Case: Its Significance in American Law and Politics* (New York: Oxford University Press, 1978); Paul Finkelman, *Dred Scott v. Sandford: A Brief History with Documents*, 2nd ed. (New York: Bedford Books, 2017), 1–54; Kate Masur, *Until Justice Be Done: America's First Civil Rights Movement, from the Revolution to Reconstruction* (New York: W. W. Norton, 2021), 255–260, for Taney's distinction between state citizenship, which he acknowledged, and the higher bar for national citizenship, from which he excluded Scott and all other Black people. Martha S. Jones, *Birthright Citizens: A History of Race and Rights in Antebellum America* (New York: Cambridge University Press, 2018), for African Americans in Baltimore exercising several of these rights de facto, including possessing firearms and traveling across state lines.

109. Douglass, "The Dred Scott Decision," May 14, 1857, Frederick Douglass Papers, Library of Congress.

110. PFAS Minutes, Mott quoting from William Cullen Bryant, May 13, 1858; November 11, 1858, both in HSP.

111. PFAS Minutes, October 12, 1854; June 11, 1857; November 12, 1857; April 8, 1858; April 14, 1859; February 9, 1860; April 12, 1860; all in HSP.

112. PFAS Minutes, January 13, 1859; February 10, 1859; February 9, 1860, all in HSP; Jeffrey, *Great Silent Army*, 108–126.

113. Martin Delany, *The Condition, Elevation, Emigration, and Destiny of the Colored People of the United States, Politically Considered* (1852); Martin Delany, *Blake: or the Huts of America, Anglo-African Magazine* (1859), *Weekly Anglo-African* (1860, 1861); Rhodes, *Mary Ann Shadd Cary.*

114. J. Harlan Buzby, *John Stewart Rock: Teacher, Healer, Counselor* (Salem, N.J.: Salem County Historical Society, 2002). Willi Coleman, "'Like Hot Lead to Pour on the Americans,'" in Kathryn Kish Sklar and James Brewer Stewart, eds., *Women's Rights and Transatlantic Slavery in the Era of Emancipation* (New Haven, Conn.: Yale University Press, 2007), 173–188; Brandt, *Women Healers.*

115. T. R. Davis, "Lectures by Miss Watkins," *Liberator*, February 24, 1860. Foster, *A Brighter Coming Day*, 13, 15. Dana Elizabeth Weiner, *Race and Rights: Fighting Slavery and Prejudice in the Old Northwest, 1830–1870* (DeKalb: Northern Illinois University Press, 2013), 183–185. PFAS Minutes, April 9, 1857; June 11, 1857; March 11, 1858; October 13, 1859; all in HSP. Rhodes, *Mary Ann Shadd Cary*, 109, 131.

116. T. R. Davis, "Lectures by Miss Watkins," *Liberator*, February 24, 1860. Foster, *A Brighter Coming Day*, 13, 15. Weiner, *Race and Rights*, 183–185. PFAS Minutes, April 9, 1857; June 11, 1857; March 11, 1858, all in HSP. Carla L. Peterson, *Doers of the Word: African-American Women Speakers and Writers in the North (1830–1880)* (New York: Oxford University Press, 1995), 21–22, 120–124.

117. *National Anti-slavery Standard*, May 23, 1857.

118. Rhodes, *Mary Ann Shadd Cary*, 109, 131.

119. Sarah Parker Remond to Abby Kelley, December 21, 1858, in Dorothy Sterling, ed., *We Are Your Sisters: Black Women in the Nineteenth Century* (New York: W. W. Norton, 1997 ed.), 176–177. PFAS Minutes, December 10, 1857, January 14, 1858, both in HSP.

120. "Miss Remond on Slavery," *Liberator*, July 8, 1859; Peterson, *Doers of the Word*, 135–145; Coleman, "'Like Hot Lead to Pour on the Americans'"; C. Peter Ripley, ed., *The Black Abolitionist Papers*, 5 vols. (Chapel Hill: University of North Carolina Press, 1991): 1:435–444, 457–461; Teresa Zackodnik, *Press, Platform, Pulpit: Black Feminist Publics in the Era of Reform* (Knoxville: University of Tennessee Press, 2011), 79–92.

121. Ripley, *Black Abolitionist Papers*, 1:469–471. Among Remond's correspondents was George Mifflin Dallas, the U.S. ambassador to Britain, a former vice president of the United States, and a former mayor of Philadelphia.

122. "Annual Meeting of the Massachusetts Anti-Slavery Society," *Liberator*, February 5, 1858; *Liberator*, March 12, 1858; "Anniversary of British West India Emancipation," "The Negroes in Council," *New York Herald*, August 5, 1858; Palmer, *Letters of Lucretia Mott*, 277n5. Stephen Kantrowitz, *More Than Freedom: Fighting for Black Citizenship in a White Republic, 1829–1889* (New York: Penguin, 2012), 237.

123. Lubet, *Fugitive Justice*, 3–8.

Conclusion

1. "Bury Me in a Free Land" was first published in the *Anti-slavery Bugle*, November 20, 1858, 3; see also Frances Smith Foster, ed., *A Brighter Coming Day: A Frances Ellen Watkins Harper Reader* (New York: Feminist Press, 1990), 17; William Still, *The Underground Railroad* rev. ed. (Philadelphia, 1878), 757. Donald Yacavone, "Sacred Land Regained: Frances Ellen Watkins Harper and the

'Massachusetts Fifty-Fourth,' a Lost Poem," *PH* 62, no. 1 (Winter 1995): 90–110. Margaret Hope Bacon, "'One Great Bundle of Humanity': Frances Ellen Watkins Harper (1825–1918)," *PMHB* 113, no. 1 (January 1989): 21–43, for the correct publication date and context for Harper's poem.

2. Karl Marx, *Capital*, 2 vols. (New York: Penguin Classics, 1992), 1:377.

3. W. Caleb McDaniel, *The Problem of Democracy in the Age of Slavery: Garrisonian Abolitionists and Transatlantic Reform* (Baton Rouge: Louisiana State University Press, 2013); Elizabeth R. Varon, *Disunion! The Coming of the American Civil War, 1789–1859* (Chapel Hill: University of North Carolina Press, 2008).

4. A. P. Merrill, "An Essay on Some of the Distinction Peculiarities of the Negro Race, No. III," *Southern Medical and Surgical Journal* 12 (March 1856); H. L. Byrd, "African Race—Reopening of the Slave Trade," *Oglethorpe Medical and Surgical Journal* 10 (August 1858); "African Slave Trade," *Oglethorpe Medical and Surgical Journal* (February 1859); Rana Hogarth, *Medicalizing Blackness: Making Racial Difference in the Atlantic World, 1780–1840* (Chapel Hill: University of North Carolina Press, 2017); Bruce Dain, *A Hideous Monster of the Mind: American Race Theory in the Early* Republic (Cambridge, Mass.: Harvard University Press, 2002), 256–263.

5. Janet Kemper Beck, *Creating the John Brown Legend: Emerson, Thoreau, Douglass, Child, and Higginson in Defense of the Raid on Harpers Ferry* (Jefferson, N.C.: McFarland, 2009), 19–28, 52–52. David W. Blight, *Frederick Douglass: Prophet of Freedom* (New York, Simon and Schuster, 2018), 294–305.

6. PFAS Minutes, November 16, 1859, HSP.

7. Sharon Hartman Strom, *Fortune, Fame, and Desire: Promoting the Self in the Long Nineteenth* Century (Lanham, Md.: Rowman and Littlefield, 2016), 86–87. Blight, *Frederick Douglass*, 305–309.

8. Beck, *Creating the John Brown Legend.*

9. PFAS Minutes, June 12, 1862, HSP; Julie Roy Jeffrey, *The Great Silent Army of Abolitionism: Ordinary Women in the Antislavery Movement* (Chapel Hill: University of North Carolina Press, 1998), 210–232.

10. Matthew Fox-Amato, *Exposing Slavery: Photography, Human Bondage, and the Birth of Modern Visual Politics in America* (New York: Oxford University Press, 2019), 176–177, on *cartes de visites* revealing the transformation of enslaved children once emancipated. Maurice O. Wallace and Shawn Michelle Smith, eds., *Pictures and Progress: Early Photography and the Making of African American Identity* (Durham, N.C.: Duke University Press, 2012), especially articles by Laura Wexler and Ginger Hall; Henry Louis Gates, epilogue to *Picturing Frederick Douglass: An Illustrated Biography of the Nineteenth Century's Most Photographed American*, by John Stauffer, Zoe Tradd, and Celeste-Marie Bernier (New York: Liveright, 2015), 189–208, esp. 202, 208.

11. Fox-Amato, *Exposing Slavery*, 171–176. "The Dumb Witness," *Liberator*, June 12, 1863.

12. "Great Anti-colonization Mass Meeting of the Colored Citizens of the State of New York," April 22, 1849, in *National Anti-slavery Standard*, May 3, 1849. William Wells Brown, *The Black Man and His Antecedents* (New York, 1863), 47–48, 59.

13. Sarah H. Bradford, *Scenes from the Life of Harriet Tubman* (Auburn, N.Y., 1869), 13; Jean M. Humez, *Harriet Tubman, The Life and Life Stories* (Madison: University of Wisconsin Press, 2003); Catherine Clinton, *Harriet Tubman: The Road to Freedom* (New York: Little, Brown, 2004); Carla L. Peterson, *Doers of the Word: African-American Women Speakers and Writers in the North (1830–1880)* (New York: Oxford University Press, 1995), 186–206; Janell Hobson, "Of 'Sound' and 'Unsound' Body and Mind: Reconfiguring the Heroic Portrait of Harriet Tubman," *Frontiers* 40, no. 2 (2019): 193–218.

14. James M. McPherson, "Who Freed the Slaves?," *Proceedings of the American Philosophical Society* 139, no. 1 (March 1995): 4–10; Stanley Harrold, *The Rise of Aggressive Abolitionism: Addresses to the Slaves* (Lexington: University Press of Kentucky, 2004), 145; Martha S. Jones, *All Bound Up Together: The Woman Question in African American Public Culture, 1830–1900* (Chapel Hill: University of North Carolina Press, 2007), 121–126.

15. Hogarth, *Medicalizing Blackness*. Hannah Rosen, *Terror in the Heart of Freedom: Citizenship, Sexual Violence, and the Meaning of Race in the Postemancipation South* (Chapel Hill: University

of North Carolina Press, 2009). For Abby Kelley Foster's and Stephen Foster's persistent criticisms of the Union war effort, Lincoln, and the abolitionist acceptance of emancipation as achieving their goals of racial equality, see Frank J. Cirillo, "Waiting for the Perfect Moment: Abby Kelley Foster and Stephen Foster's Union War," in Gary W. Gallagher and Elizabeth R. Varon, eds., New Perspectives on the Union War (New York: Fordham University Press, 2019), 9–38.

16. Jim Downs, *Sick from Freedom: African American Illness and Suffering During the Civil War and Reconstruction* (New York: Oxford University Press, 2009); Margaret Humphreys, *Marrow of Tragedy: The Health Crisis of the American Civil War* (Baltimore: Johns Hopkins University Press, 2013); Margaret Humphreys, *Intensely Human: The Health of the Black Soldier in the American Civil War* (Baltimore: Johns Hopkins University Press, 2008); Gretchen Long, *Doctoring Freedom: The Politics of African American Medical Care in Slavery and Emancipation* (Chapel Hill: University of North Carolina Press, 2012).

17. Jeffrey, *Great Silent Army*, 220, on similarities between work with "contraband" and the care of refugees before the war; Erica Armstrong Dunbar, A *Fragile Freedom: African American Women and Emancipation in the Antebellum City* (New Haven, Conn.: Yale University Press, 2008), 3, for the Philadelphia Vigilance Committee's care for refugees as a preview of what Willie Lee Rose dubbed the "Rehearsal for Reconstruction," General Sherman's experiment in the South Carolina Sea Islands. See also Carol Faulkner, *Women's Radical Reconstruction: The Freedmen's Aid Movement* (Philadelphia: University of Pennsylvania Press, 2004), 67, 79, for legal, material, and educational assistance.

18. Willi Coleman, "'Like Hot Lead to Pour on the Americans,'" in Kathryn Kish Sklar and James Brewer Stewart, eds., *Women's Rights and Transatlantic Slavery in the Era of Emancipation* (New Haven, Conn.: Yale University Press, 2007), 173–188; Dorothy B. Porter, "Sarah Parker Remond, Abolitionist and Physician," *Journal of Negro History* 20, no. 3 (July 1935): 287–293. Dorothy Sterling, ed., *We Are Your Sisters: Black Women in the Nineteenth Century* (New York: W. W. Norton, 1997), 175–180.

19. Sterling, *We Are Your Sisters*, 252–256; Joseph H. Reidy, *Illusions of Emancipation: The Pursuit of Freedom and Equality in the Twilight of Slavery* (Chapel Hill: University of North Carolina Press, 2019), 286–293, 305–306; Brenda Stevenson, ed., *The Journals of Charlotte Forten Grimké* (New York: Oxford University Press, 1988), 37–42; Sojourner Truth, *The Narrative of Sojourner Truth, A Bondswoman of Olden Time*, eds. Olive Gilbert and Francis Titus (Battle Creek, Mich., 1884), 197, https://docsouth.unc.edu/neh/truth84/truth84.html; Peterson, *Doers of the Word*, 205. Faulkner, *Women's Radical Reconstruction*, 67, and 77, for Truth's interest in a land grant for freed people.

20. Jean Fagan Yellin, *Harriet Jacobs: A Life* (New York: Perseus Books, 2004); Peterson, *Doers of the Word*; Faulkner, *Women's Radical Reconstruction*, 73–74. Margaret Hope Bacon, *But One Race: The Life of Robert Purvis* (Albany: State University of New York Press, 2007), 161, 168–169.

21. Reidy, *Illusions of Emancipation*, 259–260; Melissa Stein, *Measuring Manhood: Race and the Science of Masculinity, 1830–1934* (Minneapolis: University of Minnesota Press, 2015), 91–92, for the shift of scientific interest to questions of hybridity.

22. Clare Midgley, *Women Against Slavery: The British Campaigns, 1780–1870* (New York: Routledge, 1992), 190–197; Sarah Remond to the editor, *Daily News*, November 22, 1868, in C. Peter Ripley, *The Black Abolitionist Papers*, vol. 1 (Chapel Hill: University of North Carolina Press, 1985), doc. 102; Eva Saks, "Representing Miscegenation Law," *Raritan* 8, no. 2 (1988): 39–69; Christine B. Hickman, "The Devil and the One Drop Rule: Racial Categories, African Americans, and the U.S. Census," *Michigan Law Review* 95 (1997):1161–1265; Daniel Sharfstein, "Crossing the Color Line,: Racial Migration and the One Drop Rule, 1600–1860," *Minnesota Law Review* 91(2007): 592–656; Michael Eliot, "Telling the Difference: Nineteenth-Century Legal Narratives of Racial Taxonomy," *Law and Social Inquiry* 24 (1999): 611–636; Peter Wallenstein, "Race, Marriage, and the Law of Freedom: Alabama and Virginia 1860s–1960s," *Chicago-Kent Law Review* 70 no. 2 (1994): 371–438; Winthrop Jordan, "The Historical Origins of the One Drop Racial Rule in the United States," ed. Paul Spickard, (2014) https://escholarship.org/content/qt91g761b3/qt91g761b3_noSplash_0a796cdb2405 9058c5fcd734be4d73b3.pdf; Peggy Pascoe, *What Comes Naturally: Miscegenation Law and the Making of Race in America* (New York: Oxford University Press, 2009); Paul Schor, *Counting Americans:*

How the U.S. Census Classified the Nation trans. Lys Ann Weiss (New York, Oxford University Press, 2017; orig. 2009); Arica L. Coleman, *That the Blood Stay Pure: African Americans, Native Americans, and the Predicament of Race and Identity in Virginia* (Bloomington: Indiana University Press, 2013), esp. 89–148.

23. Rosen, *Terror in the Heart of Freedom;* Downs, *Sick from Freedom*; Humphreys, *Health Crisis of the American Civil War.*

24. Sarah Forten [Ella], *The Colored American*, January 20, 1838.

25. Scott Reynolds Nelson, "After Slavery: Forced Drafts of Irish and Chinese Labor in the American Civil War, or the Search for Liquid Labor," in Emma Christopher, Cassandra Pybus, and Marcus Rediker, eds., *Many Middle Passages: Forced Migration and the Making of the Modern World* (Berkeley: University of California Press, 2007), 150–165; Gunther Peck, *Reinventing Free Labor: Padrones and Immigrant Laborers in the North American West, 1880–1930* (New York: Cambridge University Press, 2000).

26. Parker quoted in John Cumbler, *From Abolition to Rights for All: The Making of a Reform Community in the Nineteenth Century* (Philadelphia: University of Pennsylvania Press, 2008), 142; Phillips quoted in ibid., 136. For Bowditch's plan for state medicine, see ibid., 12–13. For Phillips's retrospective, see *Commemoration of the Fiftieth Anniversary of the Organization of the American Anti-Slavery Society in Philadelphia* (Philadelphia: T. S. Dando, 1884), 15. On Phillips's career as a labor reformer and radical Republican politician, see David Montgomery, *Beyond Equality: Labor and the Radical Republicans, 1862–1872* (New York: Knopf, 1967). For the legal battles of Black Americans in the North, see Hugh Davis, "*'We Will Be Satisfied with Nothing Less': The African American Struggle for Equal Rights in the North During Reconstruction* (Ithaca, N.Y.: Cornell University Press, 2011). Midgley, *Women Against Slavery*, 193.

27. D. M. Ely and A. K. Driscoll, "Infant Mortality in the United States, 2018: Data from the Period Linked Birth/Infant Death File," *National Vital Statistics Reports* 69, no 7 (Hyattsville, MD: National Center for Health Statistics, 2020); Gopal Singh and Stella Yu, "Infant Mortality in the United States, 1915–2017: Large Social Inequalities Have Persisted for Over a Century," *International Journal of Maternal and Child Health and AIDS* 8, no. 1 (2019): 19–31; Myra J. Tucker, Cynthia J. Berg, William M. Callaghan, and Jason Hsia, "The Black-White Disparity in Pregnancy-Related Mortality from Five Conditions: Differences in Prevalence and Case-Fatality Rates," *American Journal of Public Health* 97, no. 2 (February 2007): 247–251; Gopal K. Singh, *Maternal Mortality in the United States, 1935–2007: Substantial Racial/Ethnic, Socioeconomic, and Geographic Disparities Persist* (Rockville, Md.: U.S. Department of Health and Human Services, 2010), http://www.mchb.hrsa.gov/. Elizabeth A. Howell, Natalia N. Egorova, Amy Balbierz, Jennifer Zeitlin, and Paul L. Hebert, "Site of Delivery Contribution to Black-White Severe Maternal Morbidity Disparity," *American Journal of Obstetrics and Gynecology* 215, no. 2 (August 2016): 143–152; D. L. Hoyert, "Maternal Mortality Rates in the United States, 2019," *NCHS Health E-Stats*, April 2021, DOI: https://doi.org/10.15620/cdc:103855.

28. See "Dr. Rebecca Cole," https://cfmedicine.nlm.nih.gov/physicians/biography_66.html.

29. Sarah Mapps Douglass to Rebecca White, n.d., Josiah White Papers, HCQSC; Susan L. Smith, *Sick and Tired of Being Sick and Tired: Black Women's Health Activism in America, 1890–1950* (Philadelphia: University of Pennsylvania Press, 1995); Alondra Nelson, *Body and Soul: The Black Panther Party and the Fight Against Medical Discrimination* (Minneapolis: University of Minnesota Press, 2013); Nancy Krieger, *Epidemiology and the People's Health: Theory and Context* (New York: Oxford University Press, 2011).

Index

The Able Doctor, or America Swallowing the Bitter Draught (1774), *58*
Abolition: body politics, defined, 1–20, 32, 56, 84, 158, 164–166, 314, 337; ideal of embodied self-sovereignty, 10–11, 109, 136, 218, 296–302, 305, 310, 327, 336, 338, 341–343, 345–347; intellectual and legal roots of, 21–87; early calls for, 21–87; and "one blood," 88–122; gradual, 19, 101, 107, 108, 112, 113, 115, 116, 136, 137; and maternal inheritance, 3, 9, 14, 18, 87–89, 118–122, 134, 208–211, 336; and scientific racism, 3, 5, 10, 11, 13, 125–126, 142, 161–163; and African American national belonging, 123–135, 142, 161–163; and free labor produce activism, 164–206; and the focus on motherhood, 207–251; and diasporic manhood, 252–291; and the political impact of refugees, 274, 334, 338; and health reform, 223, 233, 343, 296–302
Abortion, 236, 239–244
Activism: and focus on violated motherhood, 230–235; and respectability, 230–231, 233; militant, 253–261, 271–291; bodily toll of, 296–302; medical care as, 304; particular stresses of for Black abolitionists, 296–298, 302. *See also* abolition; body politics; metempsychosis
Advertisement for Lydia White's store, *171*
Africa: Biafra, Bight of, 37, 42; Guinea, residents of, 36, 39; Hausa, 39, 41; Benin, 37, 76; Fante, 42; Igbo, 98; Gold Coast, 27, 80, 98, 357n28
African Americans: as intellectual producers, 5; labor of as qualification for citizenship, 123, 125, 142; and exclusion from birthright, 133–134; vulnerability to body-snatching, 151, 154, 236–236; and sense of solidarity with the enslaved, 204
Africans, 22, 23, 34, 37–42, 54, 61, 66–67; as informants, 39, 41; alleged to be racial type, 146–147; as victims of the slave trade, 135, 267–268; as born free, 268; as earning a homeland in the U.S. through labor, 123–126; and exclusion from birthright, 133–134
Agassiz, Louis, 157, 303–304, 306, 340, 345. *See also* photography; scientific racism
Agricultural labor: Irish, 307, 324, 325; British, 195. *See also* free labor
Agriculture, plantation, 42–43: and enslaved labor, 4, 11–12, 38–41, 86, 94, 126, 139, 142, 336; and wealth creation, 37–41, 93–96; and disease, 158–160; and free labor, 295. *See also* coffee; cotton; rice; sugar; tobacco
Air: as manifestation of bodily liberty, 8, 50, 289; and health, 47–53; as reflective of racism, 346. *See also* climate
Allen, Richard, 123–126, 130, 131, 139, 140, 142, 159, 162, 163, 169, 170, 336, 341; medical expertise of, 144–145; *Narrative of the Proceedings of the Black People*, 144. *See also* emigration; nation, belonging to
Almshouse, Philadelphia, patients in, 151, 154, 160, 236, 240. *See also* scientific racism; University of Pennsylvania Medical School
An Amalgamation Waltz (1839), *221*
American and Foreign Anti-Slavery Society, 182, 224
American Anti-Slavery Society (AAS), 178, 182, 213, 218, 219, 224, 267, 276, 279, 280, 332, 346
American Colonization Society (ACS), 122–125, 138–142, 157, 169. *See also* emigration; migration, forced
American Free Produce Association (AFPA), 172–173, 179, 183
American Revolution, 54–69, 133, 135
Amistad, 184, 267–268

Anatomy: turn to, 45–47, 141–143, 145, 147, 151–158; racist theories drawn from, 4, 14, 36, 45–47, 65, 125, 145–148, 153–158, 163, 310; Sarah Mapps Douglass's knowledge of, 1, 233, 269, 301–302, 344; James McCune Smith's training in, 269. *See also* dissection; scientific racism
Ancestry, 8, 13, 14, 24, 110, 134, 147, 245, 253, 294, 306, 307, 314, 334, 337
Anglo-Saxon: uses of term, 17, 246, 293–294, 306, 307; blood identified as, 314, 333, 337. *See also* race; racism
Animals, 6, 9, 21, 38, 39, 311; treatment of, likened to that of enslaved people, 75, 114, 287; human superiority to, 273, 305–306; humans derogatorily compared to, 207, 218, 250
Antislavery Convention of American Women (NYC), 179–181, 218–219, 224. *See also* motherhood
Antislavery fairs, 166, 181, 329–330, 340. *See also* Philadelphia Female Anti-Slavery Society; Vigilance Committees
Apprenticeship, British, 176–178, 181
Arson, 179–181, 267

Banneker Institute (Pa.), 302, 305
Barbados, 22, 28, 29, 33, 36–41, 97, 102, 177, 201. *See also* Tryon, Thomas
Beauty: geopolitics of, 65–66; female, 225, 238; and blackness, 330
Benezet, Anthony, 34, 49, 50, 66, 98, 99, 103, 104. *See also* Quakers
Bernier, François, 36, 143, 156. *See also* race; scientific racism
Bias, Elizabeth, 315
Bias, James J. G., 280, 315, 343; *Synopsis of Phrenology*, 305
Bibb, Henry, 195, 203
Bile, black, as source of African blackness, 36, 45–46, 148, 157
Birth, 4, 8–9, 16, 18, 19, 23–24, 26, 28, 67, 69, 99, 283; as beginning of new political relationship, 8–9, 25, 29, 56, 64–65; and relationship with place, 162, 209–210; and reproduction of slavery, 19, 89, 95–96, 98, 101, 119–120, 122, 209–210, 222, 250, 316, 372–373n19; and jurisdictional conflicts, 136–137, 283, 321–322. *See also* birthplace; birthright; children; enslaved women; jurisdiction; motherhood
Birthplace, 8, 24, 25, 26, 29, 209–210, 222, 321–322. *See also* birth; jurisdiction; *jus soli*
Birthright, 11, 14, 23–30, 54–87, 88, 89, 105, 110, 116, 118, 133, 135, 139, 222, 281; forfeiture of, for crime, 24, 80; relationship to actual birth, 8–9, 29, 56, 64–65, 86–87; enslaved child's forfeiture of at birth, 2, 87, 88–89, 107, 110, 114–115, 265, 333, 336; as key to undoing slavery, 9, 87, 88–91. *See also* birth; children; natural rights; rights, of Englishmen
Blackness, 13, 14, 36–37, 45–57, 132–133, 154, 156–157; of blood, 13, 110–111; of skin, 2, 21, 34, 36–37, 45–47, 110, 133–134, 142, 146–148, 154; of bile, 157; as bodily pigment, 154, 156–157; understood as a fundamental characteristic, 21, 110–111; and presumption of enslavement, 133–134, 138; white perceptions of, 177
Blackwell, Henry B., 319, 346. *See also* Underground Railroad
Blood: meanings of, 6, 13–14, 88–122, 142–143, 331, 336–337; and ancestry, 13, 14, 88, 122, 125, 134, 143, 146–148, 294, 314, 334, 337; as source of life, 6, 13, 143, 145, 148; vitality of, 145, 148, 149, 152, 158, 163, 336–337; and identity, 6, 13–14, 134, 146–148, 152, 337; transfusions of, 35–36, 38, 149–150, 241; and free African American solidarity with the enslaved, 204; maternal, 207–251; *jus sanguinis*, 8, 24; and national belonging, 23–24, 43–45, 123–126, 135, 139, 142, 161–163, 252, 260, 345; as source of nation's vitality, 43, 345; universal nature of, 1, 143, 150, 153, 163, 337; and claims to "one blood," 8, 13–14, 17, 30–34, 67, 88–122, 142–145, 150, 153, 158, 163, 177, 217, 218, 292, 294, 328, 331, 333, 337, 345; violent shedding of, 3, 13, 24, 64, 68, 71, 203–205, 287–288, 333, 336, 339–340; Christ's, 33, 106; sacrifice of, 27, 43, 124–125, 142, 204, 277, 318, 344; consumption of, 40–41, 68, 84, 175, 179–180; appropriated, 9, 86, 289, 336; black, 14, 34–37, 45–47, 110–111, 142, 156–157, 158; scientific study of, 14, 45–47, 142–153, 240–241, 345; and chyle, 35, 148, 156; menstrual, 175, 240–241, 337; shared by mother and child, 13, 134, 220, 233–235; letting of, as medical therapy, 15, 37, 124, 142, 144, 149, 160, 239, 241; transfusion of, 35–36, 38, 149–150, 241; African, 230, 293, 314, 337, 339; Anglo-Saxon, 333, 337, 293; white, 314; purity of, 281, 345; "negro," 293, 307, 337; "one-drop" rule, 345; types, 345.

See also ancestry; families; nation; scientific racism
Blumenbach, Johann Friederich, 65–66; *Varieties of Humankind* 65–66; *Elements of Physiology*, 145. *See also* race; scientific racism
Bodies: materiality of, 2, 5, 6, 11–12, 23–24, 32, 81–82, 84; as constraining to spirit and intellect, 6–7; humoral, 34–41, 45–47, 148; impressionability of, 2, 5–6, 9–10, 22, 293, 305, 307, 337, 341; influence of climate on, 2, 3, 6, 38–41, 47–53, 144, 158–162; impact of conditions on, 6, 293, 296, 307; historical changes in, 241; and personal histories, 5, 6, 311, 314, 337; and disability, 5, 9–11, 17, 55, 108, 223, 338, 342, 307; physical punishment of, 2–3, 5–7, 12, 26, 177, 287–288; suffering of as evidence of violated rights, 2–4, 7, 15, 22, 26, 82, 323, 325–327, 346; imagined freedom of, 20, 47–53, 297; care of, 3, 5–6, 10, 11, 48–53, 296–302; health of, 15, 22, 38–41, 175, 177, 296–302, 343–344; and illness, 4, 5, 22, 38–41, 48–53, 163, 296–302; and brain, 6, 7, 153–158; dissection of, 19, 36–37, 45–46, 143, 246–248, 151, 154, 162; skeletal structure of, 10, 144, 147; sexed, 7, 207–208, 212; female, deceptive appearances of, 242, 245; maternal, 2–4, 39–40, 56, 64–65; as legal evidence, 133–134, 320; biopolitical interest in, 88, 89, 177–178, 209; political value of, 3, 5, 23–25, 74; metaphorical meanings of, 17, 30–32. *See also individual listings of bodily fluids and parts of the body*; birth; blood; medicine; race; scientific racism
Body politics, defined, 1–20, 32, 56, 84, 158, 164–166, 314, 337
Body snatching, 145, 151–152, 336, 337. *See also* African Americans; almshouse; anatomy; dissection
Borders: state, 132, 137–138, 271, 274, 293–295, 319, 328, 334, 338; national, 69, 127, 316, 339; potential impact of disunion on, 274, 334, 338. *See also* escape; Fugitive Slave Law, 1793; Fugitive Slave Law, 1850; refugees; Underground Railroad
Boston Sugar Refining Company, 199, 200. *See also* free labor produce
Boycotts, 4, 10, 11, 75, 165–170, 186–188; during American revolution, 59, 60, 167; British, of sugar, 83–84, 86, 167–169, 175, 179–180, 185; of cotton, 169–170, 186–188, 190, 194, 195, 203; African American support for, 171–172, 203–206. *See also* consumers; free labor produce; free labor
Boyer, Jean Pierre, 124, 125, 140–141, 163, 341
Brazil, 103, 176, 186, 195, 203. *See also* coffee; sugar
Breast, 207–208, 246, 250. *See also* enslaved women; milk; motherhood
Breeding of enslaved people, 210, 288
Brooks ("Description of a Slave Ship"), 75, 76
Brown, Christopher, 72, 127
Brown, David Paul, 282, 311, 322. *See also* Philadelphia Vigilance Committee; refugees
Brown, Mary Ann Day, 297, 339
Brown, William Wells, 200, 206, 228, 229, 246, 253, 279, 329, 341; *Clotel*, 279; *The Black Man and His Antecedents*, 341
Burke, Edmund, 50, 70–71, 79–82; *Reflections on the Revolution in France*, 79–82
Burritt, Elihu, 194–196, 205, 325; *League of Universal Brotherhood*, 195. *See also* boycotts; free labor produce; Sturge, Joseph
Burritt, Elijah, 185, 260–261, 266. *See also* Walker, David

Cadwalader, John, 320, 329
Calder, Francis Anderson, 187, 188
Caldwell, Charles, 145–148, 151, 155–158, 303; *Thoughts on the Original Unity of the Human Race*, 156. *See also* blood; craniology; polygenesis; scientific racism
Calvin's Case, 25–26
Canada, 315, 316, 320, 332, 339. *See also* borders
Cannibalism, slavery as, 40–41, 68, 84, 113, 175–176. *See also* blood
Capitalism, 11–12, 295, 323, 325–326, 346, 353n13; separation of wage labor from the care of the body, 12, 346; extraction of laborers from enslaved women's bodies, 12, 207–251; connected to natural order through marriage, 325–326; and agency of liberal subject, 17; and suffering of wage laborers, 323; and industrial manufacture, 324. *See also* consent; contract; free labor; marriage
Care, Henry, 28–29
Cartwright, Samuel, 157, 310–311; "Report on the Diseases and Physical Peculiarities of the Negro Race," 310; critical reviews of, 310–311. *See also* scientific racism
Cary, Mary Ann Shadd, 318, 332
Caucasian, 65, 156, 157, 294. *See also* Anglo-Saxon; race; racism

Chandler, Elizabeth, 16, 170, 173–176, 215–216, 232; "The Slave Mother's Farewell," 215; "The Kneeling Slave," 216
Chapman, Maria Weston, 183, 278, 332
Chapman, Nathaniel, 149–151, 161, 243, 385–386n71. *See also* medicine; scientific racism; University of Pennsylvania Medical School
Chester County, Pa., 170, 172–173, 187–188, 199, 201, 203, 206, 310, 328, 332. *See also* Cary, Mary Ann Shadd; Preston, Ann; Taylor, George Washington; Underground Railroad
Child, David Lee, 179–180, 296
Child, Lydia Maria, 179, 219, 296
Childbirth: occlusions of, 45, 64–65, 67, 86; medical risks of, 149, 223, 237–245, 299–300; alleged racial differences in, 239–240, 244; representations of, 208–235, 337; study of, 209, 237–245; use of anesthesia during, 244–245; and white women's complicity in slavery, 265. *See also* birth; birthright; enslaved women; motherhood
Children, 2–4, 6, 8, 39–40, 44, 46, 69; violations of, 55, 106–107; unborn, 25, 27, 115; birthright of, 2, 23, 56, 110, 114; blood shared with mother, 13; status inherited from mother, 3, 4, 6, 24; enslaved women's nurture of, 39, 89, 101; slaves depicted as figurative, 31–33, 60. *See also* birth; birthright; motherhood
Cinque, 267, 268, 277, 290. See also *Amistad*
Citizenship, 4, 17, 18, 19, 43, 79, 127, 135, 140, 287, 310, 358n40, 383n34; determinations of, 24, 123–125, 162, 169, 209–210, 253, 255; of women, 85–87, 209–210, 222, 301; Haitian, 124, 128, 163; restrictions on Black, 132, 133, 137, 138, 141, 259–261, 281, 290, 308, 319, 327–331, 376n69, 421n108; and national belonging, U.S., 123–125, 160–163, 326, 345–346, 399–400n6, 408n9. *See also* motherhood; nation; rights of Englishmen
Civil War, U.S., 328, 340–342, 345
Clarkson, Thomas, 73–74, 83, 128, 186, 188; *Essay on the Slavery and Commerce of the Human Species*, 73–74
Clay, Henry, 139, 200, 202
Climate, 2, 3, 6, 38–41, 47–53, 144, 158–162, 176; as a source of disease, 126, 158–163; tropical, 38–41, 158, 239; debunked as the reason for human difference, 146–148; as cause of physical adaptations, 162. *See also* agriculture; disease
Coffee, 164, 180–181. *See also* boycotts; free labor produce
Coffin, Levi, 131, 139, 173, 189, 190, 193–194, 198, 205, 271. *See also* free labor produce; Underground Railroad
Coker, Daniel, 123, 141. *See also* emigration
College of Physicians, 144–146. *See also* medicine; scientific racism
Collins, Charles, 169, 185. *See also* free labor produce
Collins, John: "The Slave Mother," 230; and Morton's *Crania Americana*, 230
Combe, Andrew, 298–299, 302. *See also* health, reforms of
Combe, George, 155–157, 298–299, 302–303; *The Constitution of Man Considered in Relation to External Objects*, 299. *See also* phrenology
Commodification: of enslaved people's bodies, 11–12, 23, 37–41, 65, 75, 77, 98, 119, 130, 179, 215, 218, 355n24; of enslaved women's maternity, 208; of enslaved men's bodies, 254, 256; and slave-produced goods, 11, 18–19, 84, 164–165, 167, 172–176, 179, 181, 183, 187, 204–206, 323, 336–337. *See also* consumers; cotton; maternal inheritance; sugar; tobacco
Consent, 99, 127, 294, 324–325. *See also* capitalism; contract; free labor
Constitution, U.S., 11, 74, 135, 138, 218, 274, 275, 284, 299, 321, 327, 328, 331–332. *See also* Fugitive Slave Law, 1793; Fugitive Slave Law, 1850; rights
Consumers, 4, 11, 18, 83–84, 164–175, 183. *See also* boycotts; cotton; sugar
Contract, 294, 295, 321–325, 346–347. *See also* capitalism; consent; free labor; marriage; South Asia
Convicts, transported, 28–30, 80–81, 84, 126–127. *See also* transportation, coerced
Cope, Thomas P., 141, 192. *See also* Quakers
Cornish, Samuel, 141–142, 170, 259, 274, 276. *See also Freedom's Journal*
Cotton, 4, 75, 130, 164–206, 336–337; as commodity, 164–165, 191–193, 205, 288; planting of, 165, 196; picking of, 165, 189, 191–192; ginning of, 165, 189, 192, 196; manufactures, 174, 188, 190–191, 194, 325; calicoes, 174, 190, 194, 200; whiteness of, 173; marketing of, 197; British market for, 184; special interest of women in, 170; boycotts of, 164–165, 175–176, 180–181; difficulties

sourcing free labor product, 187–194, 196–200, 205; flax as substitute for, 203, 325; South Asian sourcing of, 188, 190, 193. *See also* boycotts; free labor produce; gins
Cox, Abby Ann Newbold, 219–21. *See also* motherhood
Cox, Abraham Liddon, 219, 342
Craft, Ellen and William, 231, 332. *See also* gender; refugees
Crania: comparisons of, 153–158, 245, 293–294, 337; as evidence of race, 10, 14, 157, 294; and brain's capacity, 155, 294. *See also* craniology; phrenology; scientific racism
Craniology, 10, 155, 157, 294, 303, 305, 327; vs. phrenology, 303. *See also* crania; Morton, Samuel; phrenology; scientific racism
Cromwell, Oliver, 27–29, 37
Crummell, Alexander, 169, 275, 284. *See also* Garnet, Henry Highland; Philadelphia Vigilance Committee
Cuba, 186, 200, 203, 257, 267, 268, 275
Cuffee, Paul, 123, 140, 141. *See also* emigration

Declaration of Independence, 64–66, 77, 104, 105
Delany, Martin, 278–279, 342, 343; medical training of, 278; *Mystery*, 279; *Blake: Huts of America*, 279, 330; and free labor cotton in Liberia and Nigeria, 326; *The Condition, Elevation, Emigration, and Destiny of the Colored People of the United States*, 330. *See also* emigration
Dickinson, John, 58–59; *Sentiments on What is Freedom and What is Slavery, By a Farmer*, 111
Disability, 1, 10, 307, 342. *See also* bodies, impressionability; disease; health; race; slavery
Disease, 7, 22, 127, 141, 144–145, 158–163, 241; intemperance and, 38–41; climate and, 38, 126, 127, 145, 158–161; insects and, 145; and blood, 148–150; study of, 209, 236, 269; labor and, 160–161; distinctive Southern, 126, 158–161; and race, 148, 240, 310; women as suffering from, 236, 239; immorality of slavery likened to, 203, 289; and justifications of slavery, 159, 240, 310. *See also* agriculture; climate; settler colonialism
Dissection, 36, 45–46, 125, 142–146, 151, 154, 157, 160, 162, 209, 264, 269, 337. *See also* almshouse; anatomy; bodysnatching; medicine
"Do as we would be done by" ("do unto others"), 40, 71, 99–100; Golden Rule, 111, 223
Domestic life, white, 84, 164, 166; labor of, 178, 181, 294; as innocent, 253–254, 266; as camouflage for slavery's violence, 253–254, 286; as constraint on abolitionist militance, 254. *See also* enslaved men; manhood; settler colonialism
Douglass, Frederick, 2–3, 200, 228, 253, 257, 274, 278, 279, 286–291, 297–298, 307–309, 313, 325, 328, 329, 340, 342; and photography, 17, 290; July 4th speech of, 2; Reception Speech of, 286–290; Western Reserve speech of, 292–293, 305–307; support of free labor produce, 203–206; on the speaker's circuit with Abby Kelley, 225; exile in Britain, 286–290; *The Narrative of the Life of Frederick Douglass*, 289, 291; *The Heroic Slave*, 290–291; *North Star*, 279, 308
Douglass, Grace Bustill, 161, 231–233
Douglass, Robert Jr., 227. *See also* photography
Douglass, Sarah Mapps, 1, 3, 6, 14, 16, 161–162, 174, 220, 227, 302, 343, 344; and national belonging, 162; scientific lectures of, 1, 233, 301–302; "Moonlight," 232; relationship of with mother, 231–233; health of, 223, 233, 298, 301–302; marriage of, 233; as educator, 6, 233, 347; as PFAS member, 233, 331
Dred Scott v. Sanford, 19, 295–296, 327–334, 338, 339. *See also* citizenship; habeas corpus; jurisdiction; nation, belonging to; polygenesis; rights
Dymond, Sarah, 194, 231

East India Company, 57, 70–71, 79
East-West opposition, 64, 82, 85–87, 180, 202–203, 212, 214, 215, 224, 235, 247–249, 265, 281, 324, 331–332
Easton, Hosea, 2, 3, 162, 344, 346; *A Treatise on the Intellectual Character and Civil and Political Condition of the Colored People of the United States*, 2; and the adaptation of African bodies, 2, 304; and maternal impressions; 2, 5
Education: of free Black people, 1–2, 10, 132, 230, 233, 258, 259, 269, 272, 279, 301–302, 330, 332, 343–344, 346, 347; of formerly enslaved people, 105, 121; of children of enslaved mothers, 114, 116; opportunities for, in Haiti, 156; as privilege, 211, 276, 305; obstacles to, 267, 277, 278, 287. *See also* education, medical

Education, medical, 1, 19, 235–245, 249, 269, 343–344; and phrenology, 156
Emancipation, 5, 8–10, 18, 69, 112, 116, 121, 122, 129, 237, 250, 277, 289, 338, 421n98; as political birth, 9; and Quakers, 3, 88, 101, 104, 106–108, 111, 115; in Saint Domingue, 56, 259; cost of for enslavers, 105, 118; in the British empire, 50, 176, 184, 194, 347; self-, 135, 136, 310; celebrations of, West Indian, 284; during Civil War, 201, 340, 342–344, 346, 424n15. *See also* escape; *Pleasants v. Pleasants*; refugees
Embodied self-sovereignty, 10–11, 109, 136, 139, 218, 296–302, 305, 310, 327, 336, 338, 341–343, 345–347; and motherhood, 207–251; and anatomical knowledge, 233; incompatible with slavery, 314; and male demeanor, 258
Emigration, of free Black people, 123–126, 138–142, 169, 232, 278, 326, 330, 332. *See also* American Colonization Society; Haiti
Emotion, 6, 7, 15–16; as evidence of humanity, 51, 210–213, 306; alleged difference in enslaved people, 159; bodily nature of, 211–215, 233–235; maternal, 210–220, 228–235, 245–251. *See also* grief
Empathy, white, 14–17, 77, 208, 210–211, 213, 220–221, 224, 253, 357n34, 401n17
Enslaved men: 252–262, 264, 268, 274, 277, 289–290, 330; manhood of, strengthened by ordeal of enslavement, 289–290, 414n98. *See also* fatherhood; manhood; Turner, Nat
Enslaved people: damage to bodies of, 5–6, 9, 38–41, 226, 255, 272–273, 287–288, 314, 316, 318–319, 341; unprotected condition of, 9; bodily evaluations of, 119; alleged suitability for plantation labor, 10, 50, 294–295, 310, 323, 334; extraction of labor from, 20, 37–41, 88–122; financial uses of as collateral, 9, 11–12, 94–95, 97, 102, 122, 372n17, 273n31; analogized to status of women, 85–87; as happy and well cared for, 323. *See also* children; enslaved men; enslaved women; refugees; slavery
Enslaved people, of Pleasants estate; Woodson, Beck (children Mourning, Fanny, Sam, Joseph), 88, 120; Dick and Joseph, 91; Neddy, 92; Judy (children Lucy, Delphia, Letty, Mourning, Tabb), 91; Caeser and Betty, 92, 93; Pendah, 93; Mariah and Will (children Rose, Kate, Jacob), 93, 102; Pindar (five children), 95; Phillis (child Sylvia), 95; Tabb (children Ned, Nick, Sythax), 90, 95–96, 105, 117, 122; Grace (children Biddy, Jack, Milly, Sally), 100; Joe Cooper, Old Sukey, Old Robin, Carpenter Will, Old Nat, Old Cesar, Aggy, 101; Charles White (two sons), 101; Phil, 101, Sharper and Biddy, 101, 105; Jenny, 101; Fanny (four children), 101–102; Sam, 102; Cuffy, 102; Gabe, 102; Rachel (and child), 102; Patt (four children), 102; Rachel (children Sally, Gaby, Winny), 104; Phillis and Caesar, 105; Judy, 105; Steven (wife and child), 105; Carter Jack and London, 108; Benjamin and Titus, 115, Daphne Cooper (children Nancy, Diana, Becky), 115; Roger Cooper and Clarissa Cooper (children Agnes, John, Royall, Benjamin), 115; Chloe (daughters Clarissa, Nancy, Bridget), 115; Averilla Cooper (daughters Sally, Catherine), 115; Nancy Copper (children Sally, Sam, Peggy, Allen), 115; Sylvia (sons John, Joe), 115; Sukey and Cuffee (children Mourning, Hampton, Jerry, Aggy), 117; Mourning, 122; Phillis and children, 122; Fanny, 129. *See also* Ned; Ned Sr.; Tabb
Enslaved women: as mothers, 2, 4–6, 9, 12, 19, 73, 95–96, 208–210, 212–215, 218; as producers of planter wealth, 88–91, 118–119; sexual abuse of, 2, 3, 113, 252, 301, 219, 333; as transmitters of enslaved status, 5, 18, 117–118, 208–209, 333; obscured in arguments by analogy, 85–87; multiple labors of, 12, 175, 239, 244, 319; as reproducers of enslaved labor, 4, 9, 12, 18, 19, 86, 88–91, 95–96, 135, 208–209, 222, 319; alleged ease of during childbirth, 159, 240. *See also* agriculture; children; enslaved men; enslaved people; maternal inheritance; motherhood
Equiano, Olaudah, 7, 49, 70, 76, 81, 86, 87, 257; *Interesting Narrative of the Life of Olaudah Equiano*, 81, 86
Escape, 7–9, 294, 338; as rebirth, 9, 316, 322; as militant resistance, 253–254, 271–291, 311; tendency to figure as disease, 310; as triggering jurisdictional conflicts, 311, 334. *See also* Fugitive Slave Law, 1793, Fugitive Slave Law, 1850; refugees; Vigilance Committees

Families, of enslaved, 6, 7; mothers at the center of, 85, 95, 208–209; duties of, 55–56, 85; separation of as violation, 3, 4, 7, 21–22, 47, 51, 52, 55–56, 67–68, 72, 177, 218, 319;

threats to integrity of, 4, 282–284, 287; reclamations of, 10, 313–314; and materiality of belonging, 220; erasure of enslaved fathers from, 253–254. *See also* enslaved men; enslaved women; fatherhood; manhood; maternal inheritance; motherhood
Family list (children born to enslaved women in the Pleasants estate), *120*
Family trees: of Ned's family, *90*; of Pleasants family, *90*
Fatherhood, 252–261, 289–290: exclusions of under slavery, 253–254; disregard of free Black men's, 282–284; as epitome of male personhood, 289–290; diasporic search for meaning of, 252–291. *See also* enslaved men; manhood
Fitzhugh, George, 322–327; *Cannibals All! Or, Slaves without Masters*, 322–327; and suffering bodies of wage workers, 323; links between Virginia and Pennsylvania, 323–324
Forten family: Charlotte, 341, 343, 344; Harriet Davy (Purvis), 171, 184, 249, 280, 331; James, 123, 139–141, 170, 184, 216, 272; Sarah Louisa, "The Slave Girl's Address to Her Mother," and "An Appeal to Women," 216–217; Robert Bridges, 342, 344
Foster, Stephen (husband of Abby Kelley), 202, 227–229, 299–301, 332, 333, 346. *See also* Kelley, Abby
Fox, George, 33, 34, 101. *See also* Quakers
Franklin, Benjamin, 50, 61, 73, 143
Free labor, 13, 164–206, 324–326; as expression of natural law, 169; in Haiti, 141; questions about the nature of, 166; changing nomenclature for, 179–180; investigations of, 166, 174–178; gender politics of, 165, 177–178, 183–184; benefits of, 169, 176–178; political economy of, 165, 176–178; and well-being of wage earners, 165, 183, 184, 295, 324; plans to establish colony, 196; and small producers, 165, 189, 197–198, 324; free Black men's suitability for, 290; and South Asian and Chinese labor, 202. *See also* contract, free labor produce; wage labor
Free labor produce, 19, 164–206, 218, 323, 326; local vs. global strategies, 166; problems of authentication, 173, 188–190; problems with quality, 173–174, 188, 189; shops dedicated to, 166, 170–171, 189, 190, 193; high cost of, 174, 190; politicizing impact of, 174; African American support for, 166, 276, 278, 280, 305. *See also* boycotts; consumers
Freedom, imagined, 17, 106; as birthright, 99; benefits of, 177–178. *See also* liberty
Freedom's Journal, 123, 124, 141–142, 151–152, 170, 259–260. *See also* Cornish, Samuel; Russwurm, John Brown
French Revolution, 56, 77–79. *See also* Haiti; Saint Domingue
Fugitive Slave Law, 1793, 132, 136–138, 274; free Black petition against in Philadelphia, 135; and protection of slave property, 287. *See also* Fugitive Slave Law, 1850; personal liberty laws; refugees
Fugitive Slave Law, 1850, 2, 18, 292–295, 308–323, 329, 338; and authority of federal commissioners, 310–311, 319–321. *See also* refugees; Vigilance Committees
Fugitive Slave Law Convention, *309*

Gall, Franz Joseph, 155, 156. *See also* phrenology
Garnet, Henry Highland, 200, 252–254, 258, 269, 275–278, 290, 308, 342; "Call to Rebellion," 252–254, 275–278; African Civilization Society, 326
Garrett, Thomas, 275, 315
Garrison, William Lloyd, 166, 169, 174, 182, 184–186, 202, 203, 274, 297, 298, 329, 332, 342
Gender, 5, 7, 207–208; and antislavery medallions, 74–76, 213; conformity, as evidence of university humanity, 207–208; and antislavery activism, 213–214; disguise of by refugees, 318. *See also* bodies; enslaved women; enslaved men; motherhood
Germantown petitioners (Pa.), 21–22, 32, 61
Gins, cotton, 165, 173, 189, 192, 197–199
Gliddon, George, 293, 306. *See also Types of Mankind*
Gould, Hannah Flagg, 217–218; "The Slave Mother's Prayer," 217–218
Gove, Mary (Nichols), 223, 300, 301
Graham, Sylvester, 185, 298–299; principles of, 223, 300
Grew, Mary, 301, 315–316, 321, 340
Grief: depictions of as reflecting sexual violations of slavery, 210, 212–213, 235, 246–247; of enslaved mother, 233–235, 249
Grimké, Angelina (Weld), 185, 206, 219, 220, 222–224, 228; *Appeal to the Christian Women of the South*, 222–223; disability of, 223; impressions of textile factory, 325

Grimké, Sarah Moore, 180, 185, 222, 223, 249, 298, 301, 302; *Letters on the Equality of the Sexes*, 222

Grotius, Hugo, 24–25, 66, 124–125, 142; *Rights of War and Peace*, 24–25, 43. *See also* law of nations; mercantilism

Gunn, Lewis, 179–181

Habeas corpus, 19, 25–30, 49, 59, 133–134, 136, 137, 257, 268, 281, 285, 311, 319–322, 327–329, 358n37, 414n84, 420n91; Habeas Corpus Act, 28; as natural rights entitlement, 27; suspension of during U.S. Civil War, 342. *See also* rights, of Englishmen; Vigilance Committees

Haiti: independence of, 124–125, 127–128, 134–135, 140–141, 259–260, 270, 341; antislavery society in, 172; and African lineage as criteria for citizenship, 125, 163; conditions of African American migrants to, 141; international refusal to recognize, 126; and international abandonment of natural rights, 128; as source of free labor produce, 201. *See also* emigration; Saint Domingue; Toussaint L'Ouverture

Halliday, Paul, 26, 28, 29

Hartman, Saidiya, 16, 355n22, 357n34

Haynes, Lemuel, 66–69; "Liberty Further Extended: or Free Thoughts on the Illegality of Slave Keeping," 66. *See also* liberty; rights

Health, 15, 17, 22, 24, 28, 38–41, 48, 142, 145, 148, 151, 175, 304, 338, 343–344; impact of climate on, 46, 49, 51, 52, 75, 159, 162, 197, 239; threats to, 124, 162–163; and agriculture, 160–161; and free labor, 164, 177, 326; reforms, 223, 233, 343; of activists, 223, 274, 296–302, 343; of enslaved people, 236, 237; of wage workers, 323, 324; of African-Anglo-American people, 345. *See also* bodies; disease

Henrico County, Va., 91–96, 106, 108–109, 129; as home of Robert Pleasants, 88–122; as site of Gabriel Prosser's conspiracy, 128

Henry, Patrick, 104, 107, 111–113

Heyrick, Elizabeth, 168, 223

Horner, William, 151, 153–155; *Special Anatomy and Histology*, 154; *Treatise on Special Anatomy*, 154. *See also* dissections; medicine; scientific racism; University of Pennsylvania Medical School; Virginia

Horrid Massacre in Virginia (1831), *266*

Hudgins v. Wrights, 133–134, 145. *See also* bodies; race

Humanity: universal, 23; racist scientific divisions of, 45–47, 65–66, 145–148, 151, 155–158, 303; exclusions from, 23; gendered nature of, 84–87; reason as an attribute of, 84–87; soul as component of, 84; full adult, 44, 65, 85–87. *See also* bodies; personhood; rights

Hunt, Harriot, 223, 249, 298, 301. *See also* health

Identity, 129; based on blood, 6, 13–14, 134, 146–148, 152, 337; based on birth and birthplace, 209–210; legal determinations of, 311–322

Impressment, of sailors, 29–30, 69, 80–82, 126–127, 134–135

Innocence: of enslaved women and children, 254, 264–265, 295; of children born to enslaved mothers, 107, 114, 210; of white women and children, 264–265, 295, 323; and proximity to white domestic life, 253–254; of consumers, 167

Institute for Colored Youth (ICY), 203, 301–302, 344, 347

Intellect, 1; of enslaved Africans, 2, 5, 47, 78; and theories of white superiority, 156; and theories of African-Anglo-American superiority, 307; environmental influences on, 157; Africans and Native Americans compared, 303. *See also* body; mind

Intimacy: as human right, 3, 4, 6, 7, 208, 211; as bodily, 162, 223, 302; of mother and child, 209, 214; of gynecological examinations, 236, 238, 241; of care, 315; obstructions to, 55, 254; of food and clothing consumption, 84, 164–165, 167, 205; as basis for mother's religious authority, 219; of bodily violation, 214, 338, 415n10. *See also* body; domestic life

Islam, 64, 82, 85, 331. *See also* East-West opposition

Jacobs, Harriet, 233, 284, 318, 344. *See also* refugees

Jamaica, 37, 49, 69, 73, 178, 201, 203, 245, 259–260

Java (Dutch), 176, 179. *See also* coffee; free labor produce

Jefferson, Thomas, 4, 46–47, 77–78, 113, 130–131, 134–135, 279, 305; *Notes on the State of Virginia*, 46–47, 78, 111, 116, 305; Declara-

tion of Independence, 64–66; 1806 State of the Union message, 134–135, 163. *See also* Pleasants, Robert; race; scientific racism
Jews: and context for "one blood," 17; blood of as the source of brown complexion, 146–147; and persistence of racial traits, 157; and biblical precedent for slavery, 71, 223; and allusions to greed, 331. *See also* scientific racism
Johnson, Jane, 314, 320–321
Jones, Jane Elizabeth Hitchcock, 228, 300–301
Jurisdiction: and determination of slave status, 4, 9–10, 135–139, 210, 283–284, 294, 319–322; crossing of boundaries of, 19, 49–51, 283–284, 311–322, 334, 338; federal, 135, 138, 222, 291, 295–296, 319–320, 334. *See also* birth; birthright; Fugitive Slave Law 1793; Fugitive Slave Law 1850
Jus sanguinis, 8, 24
Jus soli, 8, 24
Just war, concept of, 42, 43, 99

Kane, John K., Judge, 312, 321, 322, 329
Kelley, Abby (Foster), 16, 18, 180, 182, 202, 220, 223–229, 318, 332, 346; effectiveness as speaker, 224–225; attacks upon, 224, 225–226, 227; pregnancy of, 299–300; health regimen of, 298–301
Kidnapping, 4, 51, 68, 76, 136–138, 232, 268, 280, 284, 285, 292, 310, 313, 319, 321, 328, 409n24, 419n61
Krafft, John, 190, 191–193, 198–200. *See also* cotton; free labor produce

Labor: of enslaved people, 2, 5–7, 10, 94–96, 123–126; agricultural, 10, 94, 140, 176–178; domestic and reproductive, 12, 88–122, 201, 239, 244, 319, 336; imprint of on bodies, 293, 297. *See also* enslaved women; free labor; motherhood
Land: as tilled soil, 123, 129, 135; as property, 29, 82, 92, 94, 102, 121, 140, 254, 256, 336; as agricultural resource, 43, 106, 107, 117, 129, 131, 139, 169, 196, 198, 339
Lang, J.D., 195
Law, 3, 5; of maternal inheritance of slavery, 3, 9; of nature, 22, 39, 40, 56–62, 66–69, 110; of nations, 22–23, 32, 41–45, 60, 66, 99, 128; and limitations on free Black rights, 8, 128–129, 131–135, 141, 293; international, 126, 128. *See also* Fugitive Slave Law, 1793; Fugitive Slave Law, 1850; habeas corpus; jurisdiction; *jus soli*; *jus sanguinis*, maternal inheritance, natural law; personal liberty laws
Lay, Benjamin, 33–34
Le Cat, Claude-Nicolas, 46, 143, 148, 156
Leclerc, Georges-Louis (Comte de Buffon), 46, 78, 143, 156. *See also* scientific racism
Lee, Arthur, 103; "Address on Slavery," 99; "Philanthropos," 99–100. *See also* American Revolution
Leeuwenhoek, Antonie, 36
Liberator, 162, 203, 207, 217, 227, 232, 274–276, 278, 340
Liberia, 123–126, 139, 140, 200–201, 259
Liberty, 18; as belonging to Englishmen, 8, 23, 26, 59–60; conceived of as a place, 26, 28, 334, 336; imagined, 3, 8, 121; defined in terms of futures, 101; defined in terms of the body, 3, 8, 21–23, 25–30, 50, 52–53, 136; universalism of, 7, 110, 268; diasporic African claims to, 55–56, 66–69; Pennsylvania legal protections of free Black people, 135–138, 279, 281, 283–284, 285, 308; alleged unsuitability for enslaved people, 295. *See also* birthright; freedom; natural rights; personal liberty laws
Lilburne, John, 27–28
Linnaeus, Carl, 45, 65
Liverpool, merchants, 69, 76–77, 102, 188, 191–193
L'Ouverture, Toussaint, 259–260, 270, 277, 279, 341
Lovejoy, Elijah, 267, 308, 339
Lundy, Benjamin, 140, 169–170, 174, 179; *Genius of Universal Emancipation*, 170

Madison, James, 112, 113
Magna Carta, 26, 29
Manhood, Black, 19, 205, 252–264, 289–291, 341; relationship to personhood, 255–256, 289–291, 306; depictions of, 256; evangelical, 261–263; and perils of bodily assertions, 262, 286; as based on protective care over others, 282–284, 290; white efforts to demean, 262; white fears of, 341–342; African American criticisms of, 276. *See also* enslaved men; fatherhood
Mansfield, Lord, 50, 70; and Somerset case, 70
Markets, 18; for free labor produce, 164–206. *See also* capitalism; free labor; wage labor
Marriage: of newly emancipated people, 177–178; contract, 324–336. *See also* free labor

Maryland, 34, 96, 130, 274, 288, 331; coffles from, 130–131; enslaved people's escapes from, 135–137, 275, 280–285, 294–295, 313, 317, 319, 321, 322; enslavers, 136, 137, 311–312, 321, 322, 327. *See also* borders; Fugitive Slave Law, 1793; Fugitive Slave Law, 1850; refugees

Maternal inheritance, 3, 9, 14, 18, 87–89, 118–122, 134, 208–211, 336; of intellect, 307; and the link between race and slavery, 328. *See also* birth; birthright; law; motherhood; race; slavery

McKim, J. Miller, 172, 284, 285, 311, 315, 317, 322, 328, 344

Medicine: and professional aspirations of practitioners, 1, 3, 5, 10, 14, 236, 243–245; training in, 126, 235–245; and examinations of patients, 235–245; and experiments, 148–150; racist, 2, 3, 4, 8, 10, 14, 18, 19, 237–245, 334, 337. *See also* racism; scientific racism

Menstruation: avoidance of public allusions to, 176; disordered, 235, 236; and disease, 239; and medical management of women, 209, 236–245; as secretion distinct from circulating blood, 240–241; emmenagogues to provoke, 239, 243

Mercantilism, 22–23, 29–30, 32, 41–45, 48, 56–60, 80–83, 92–94, 96–97, 102–103. *See also* capitalism; law of nations; property

Metempsychosis, 215, 226, 232, 401n27. *See also* activism

Migration: forced, 7, 126–135; consensual, 140–141. *See also* emigration; trafficking; transatlantic slave trade; transportation

Milk, 9, 35, 148, 150, 220, 242, 336

Mind, 2; as part of body, 6, 7; and Western mind-body dichotomy, 7; universality of, 224. *See also* body; emotion; intellect

Mississippi, 196; free cotton production in, 188, 191; Holly Springs, 189, 197; Fulton, 197. *See also* cotton; Philadelphia Free Labor Produce Society of Friends; Thomas, Nathan

Mob violence, white, 267, 275, 277, 284, 286, 293, 345–346. *See also* racism, popular; white hostility; white supremacy

Montserrat, 177, 203

Moore, Thomas, 247–248; "Lalla Rookh," 247–248

Morgan, Jerry, 282–284

Morgan, Margaret, 282–284

Mortality, of African-descended people, 123–124, 139, 142; infant, 177. *See also* Smith, James McCune

Morton, Samuel George, 155, 157, 306–307, 310; *Crania Americana*, 230, 302–303. *See also* crania; craniology; scientific racism

Mother Bethel African Methodist Episcopal Church, 1, 145, 170, 171, 258, 272, 280, 282

Motherhood, 2–4, 6, 8, 9, 84–87, 118–122, 207–251; as necessary for birthright, 9; as defining women's relationship to the state, 85; and determinations of a child's status, 3, 9; and responsible adulthood, 85; and rights, 86–87, 211, 219–220, 235; representations of by abolitionists, 208, 235; medicalization of, 209, 235–245, 250–251; as condition of being one flesh with a child, 214; and white middle-class cultural capital, 211; political coalitions build on, 218–223. *See also* birth; birthright; enslaved women; maternal inheritance

Mott, James, 170, 184

Mott, Lucretia Coffin, 155, 157, 170, 174, 179, 180, 182–185, 206, 237, 245, 303, 315–318, 320–322, 328–329

Nation: belonging to, 23, 123–135, 142, 161–163; exclusions from, 123, 131–135; as place of birth conferring identity, 14; citizens of shaped by climate, 23; as political formation, 23, 62, 66; wealth of, 43; and international protections, 44. *See also* birthright; law of nations

Native Americans, 23, 131, 139; bodies of, 78, 147; one body tropes of, 18, 22, 30–32; rights concepts of, 44–45; presumed freedom of, 133–134; exclusions of, from rights frameworks, 62; dispossessions of, 22, 29, 44–45, 126, 161; removals of, 124, 129–130, 236; as subjects of scientific racism, 154, 237; Indian Harry, 31; Conoys, 31 (Whiwhinjac), 32; Haudenosaunees, 31–32, 44–45 (Gachadow); Delawares, 32 (Teedyuscung); Lenapes, 30, 31, 32; Mingos, 30 (Tammanend, Tyoninhongaro), 32; Potomacs, 31, Susquehannocks, 31 (Knawonhut, Soachkoat, Tagedrancey, Tanyahtickanungh), 32

Natural rights. *See* rights, natural

Ned (co-litigant in *Pleasants v. Pleasants*), 88–90, 95–96, 100, 105, 117–122

Ned Sr., 117, 122. *See also* enslaved people, Pleasants estate; Tabb

New Garden, Indiana, 189, 192, 200. *See also* free labor produce; Underground Railroad
North Carolina, 320, 344; wrongful sale of freed people in, 107, 115; Quaker presence in, 91, 97, 131, 166, 172, 173, 189, 264, 271; free produce sourced from, 171, 172; *North Carolina v. Mann*, 263–264; escape from, 316–317
Nott, Josiah, 293, 306, 310, 339. *See also* Gliddon, George; *Types of Mankind*

Occum, Samson, 54, 56
O'Connell, Daniel, 182, 185
Ohio, 131–132, 134–135, 189, 193–194, 203, 228, 248, 260, 271, 292, 300, 331, 335

Paine, Thomas, 60–64; "Justice and Humanity," 61–62; "A Serious Thought," 62; *Common Sense*, 62–63
Parker, William, 292–293, 312–313
Pemberton family; Israel, Jr., 96–98, 107; James, 96, 98, 103, 104, 107, 110, 111
Pennsylvania, as border state, 274–275, 282, 284; gradual abolition act, 69, 101, 108, 136, 137; personal liberty laws, 137, 138, 279–281, 283–285, 329; "Act to Prevent Kidnapping," 1820, 137; "Act to give effect to the Provisions of the Constitution . . . for the protections of free people of colour," 1826, 138; 1847 personal liberty law, 285. *See also* border states; Underground Railroad
Pennsylvania Hall, 178–181, 184, 186, 220, 224
Personal liberty laws (Pa.), 135–138, 279, 281, 283–285, 308
Personhood: legal, 3, 8, 109; male body as prototype for, 255; bodily foundation for, 8–9, 343, 347; full adult, 22, 23, 44, 53, 124, 336; and womanhood, 211, 238–240, 245; and manhood, 252–291. *See also* human rights
Philadelphia, 19, 50, 76; medical education in, 142–161; free produce activism in, 168, 170–174, 179–181, 184, 186–188, 190, 193, 201; merchants in, 193; refugees to, 135–138, 271–275, 280–285, 311–322. *See also* Underground Railroad
Philadelphia Female Anti-Slavery Society (PFAS), 171–172, 179–181, 186, 218, 233, 246, 267, 268, 274, 280, 282, 301, 316, 318, 321, 328, 329, 339, 340; and care of refugees, 226
Philadelphia Free Produce Society of Friends (PFPSF); 172, 186–203, 205–206, 298. *See also* boycotts; cotton; free labor produce
Philadelphia Vigilance Committee (PVC), 268, 273, 280–285, 311–322; Female Vigilance Committee, 282, 284, 312, 315–316, 318, 321; "resurrection," 316–318. *See also* Vigilance Committees
Phillips, Wendell, 166, 202, 332, 346–347
Photography, 303–304, 340–341. *See also* Douglass, Frederick
Phrenology, 6, 7, 155–158, 229–230, 304–305, 314; as progressive, 7, 155–157, 268, 305; as supporting concepts of biological race, 7, 155–157, 303; as insufficiently scientific, 269, 304; vs. craniology, 303; *See also* Combe, George; Smith, James McCune
Physicians, 10, 13, 14, 19, 35, 46, 125, 143, 148, 150, 151, 156, 158, 235–245, 293, 299, 304, 305, 340, 343, 344
Pleasants family, 88–122; family tree, 90; Pleasants, John III, 89, 94–98; will of John III, 100–102, 108, 117, 129; Pleasants, Jonathan, 95–96, 105; Pleasants, Samuel, 91, 93, 107, 117, 119, 129; Pleasants, Thomas (kinsman of Robert), 109, 115; Pleasants, Elizabeth, 95–96, 117. *See also* Quakers; Pleasants, Robert; Virginia
Pleasants, Robert, 88–122, 128, 168, 210, 265; "A Virginian," 100; "Benevolence," 112; "Humanity," 112; "Citizen of the World," 114; emancipation of enslaved people, 106, 108, 117; manumission plan of, 107–115; and interracial marriage, 116; will of, 121–122, 132. *See also* American Revolution; Quakers; Saint Domingue
Pleasants v. Pleasants, 88, 89, 102, 116–122, 125, 211; account of profits remedy, 117–121. *See also* enslaved people, Pleasants estate; Ned; Pleasants, Robert; Virginia
Political economy, 5, 10, 48, 50, 79, 126, 141, 158, 169, 175–178, 197–198, 209, 331; and white southerners, 342. *See also* capitalism, free labor, slavery
Polygenesis, 36, 37, 126, 155, 156, 292–296, 303, 306, 310–311, 327–328. *See also* craniology; scientific racism
Population: enslaved, growth of by birth, 12; newly emancipated, West Indian, 177–178; increase, as evidence of mortality and well-being, 177; as evidence of free Black resilience, 270, 304. *See also* Smith, James McCune; Sturge, Joseph
Portraiture, racial dynamics of, 74–75, 256. *See also* photography

Power: manifested in control over bodies, 3, 4, 136, 263, 338; of enslaver, 9, 11, 24, 263, 294, 338; private, 24; inequities of, in the U.S., 11
Pregnancy, 236–245; quickening as evidence of, 242–244. *See also* abortion; motherhood
Preston, Ann, 172; membership in Progressive Friends, 249; medical training of, 301, as dean of Women's Medical College of Pennsylvania, 343–344, 347
Prigg v. Pennsylvania, 282–284, 308, 321. *See also* Fugitive Slave Law, 1793; jurisdiction; refugees
Property: as white colonial right, 60; in arguments against slavery, 61; enslaved people claimed as, 3, 9, 11, 40–41, 116–122, 236, 294; of enslavers, 65, 139; materialized through punishment of enslaved people, 12, 287; legal protections of, 3, 13, 18, 29–30, 133–134, 136; as self-ownership, 168; impediments to free Black people's ownership of, 256; relationship of to manhood and personhood, 255–256; as foundation for social order, 322. *See also* rights
Proslavery: evaluations of enslaved bodies, 12; depictions of enslaved people as happy and healthy, 16, 323; arguments about the cruelty of wage labor, 295; dangers of free labor for white women, 295, 323–324. *See also* Fitzhugh, George
Prosser, Gabriel, 131, 330; conspiracy of 128–129. *See also* Virginia
Puerto Rico, as source for free sugar, 200, 201. *See also* free labor produce
Purity: of consumers, 173, 175, 204; of free labor produce, 164–168, 173; as white female attribute, 233; of fictional enslaved woman, 230
Purvis, Robert, 169–170, 174, 184, 249, 268, 272, 280–281, 284–285, 290, 330; *Appeal of Forty Thousand Citizens*, 281. *See also* Forten, Harriet; Philadelphia Vigilance Committee; Underground Railroad

Quaker meetings: Abington, Pa., 21; Arch St. Weekly (Phila.), 231–232; Cedar Creek, Va., 96, 97, 99; Haddonfield, N.J., 97; Henrico, Va., 108; Jericho, N.Y., 168; New Garden, In., 189; Philadelphia Yearly, 34, 96, 97, 111; Virginia Yearly, 98, 99, 103
Quakers, 13, 21–23, 28, 30–34, 38, 71–72, 93; slave ownership of, 21, 88–122; and "one blood," 30–34, 71–72, 88–122; activism of, 32–34, 71–72, 74, 75, 97–122; Hicksite, 168, 170, 221, 248–249; "The Case of Our Fellow Creatures," 71–72; and free Black migration to Haiti, 140–141; and ethical consumption, 164–174; Progressive Friends, 245–250

Race: and ancestry, 132–134, 294, 306, 337; and inherited maternal status, 4, 13–14, 122, 134; and blackness, 13, 14, 36–37, 45–47, 132–133, 154, 156–157; as inheritable, 6, 36, 155; alleged hierarchy of, 3, 5, 126, 145, 303; figured as a type of disability, 10, 310; alleged bodily characteristics of, 2, 7, 10, 133–134, 162, 245; and complexion, 2, 34, 36–37, 45–47, 133–134, 142, 146, 148, 156, 162, 311, 314; and hair, 2, 10, 14, 34, 133–134, 162; and facial features, 2, 133–134, 293–294; alleged biological basis for, 3–7, 10, 14, 345; alleged to be innate, 3, 10, 125, 303, 310–311; and blood, 14, 34–37, 50, 293, 314, 337; and anatomy, 10, 14, 145–148, 151, 153–158; as the basis for legal exclusions, 8, 10, 128–129, 131–135, 141, 293; as a rationale for slavery, 36, 37, 126, 145–148, 151, 155, 156–158, 292–295, 296, 303, 306, 310–311, 327–328, 338–339; reality of, debunked, 304–305. *See also* birth, blackness; bodies; craniology; families; maternal inheritance; phrenology; polygenesis; scientific racism
Racism: legal, 8, 18, 19, 131–135, 295–296, 312, 327–334; medical, 2–4, 8, 10, 14, 18, 19, 237–245, 334, 337; popular, of white people, 2, 18, 153, 250; and harm to Black people, 139, 162, 168, 293. *See also* mob violence, white; scientific racism; white hostility
Rape, 71, 208, 273–274, 306, 343; as trope symbolizing rights violation, 58, 64; constraints on discussing publicly, 230–231
Reckless, Hetty, 282, 284, 315–316
Refugees, 2, 9, 10, 18, 19, 125, 131, 135–136, 139, 203, 224, 226, 234, 244, 250, 257, 258, 271–272, 275, 277, 279–290, 296, 308, 311–322, 328, 334, 338, 340; care of, 315–318, 338, 340, 351n5, 355n21, 419n65; white, from Haiti, 128. *See also* escape; Vigilance Committees
Registrations: of free Black people in Virginia, 129, 132–133; of enslaved people in Pennsylvania, 136
Remond, Charles, 228, 297, 329, 330, 333
Remond, Sarah, 233, 329, 332–333, 343–345

Residency, constraints on for free Black people; 125, 129, 131–135
Rhoads, Anne Gibbons, 186, 194, 195, 231, 325
Rhoads, Samuel, 173, 186–188, 190–193, 203, 205, 326; travel to Britain, 194–196. *See also* cotton; Philadelphia Free Produce Society of Friends; Sturge, Joseph; Taylor, George Washington
Rice, 4, 164, 180–181, 201, 205
Rights: birthright, 2, 8–9, 11, 14, 20–30, 54–87, 222, 294; divine source of, 8, 9, 17, 218, 293; of Englishmen, 8, 18, 25–30, 50, 60, 65, 66, 81; natural, 7–9, 11, 14, 29–30, 44, 55–56, 64, 66, 67, 71–72, 80, 86–89, 99, 101, 105, 110, 128, 137, 209, 214; human, 3–5, 7, 9, 13, 17, 50, 64–65, 72, 124, 126, 134–135, 210, 222, 307, 327; Native American concepts of, 44–45; embodied nature of, 8, 9, 17, 218, 293; and embodied self-sovereignty, 10–11, 109, 136, 139, 218, 296–302, 305, 310, 327, 336, 338, 341–343, 345–347; universal nature of, 3, 7, 29, 64, 66, 80, 292; and natural law, 8, 9, 22, 155; and liberties, 3, 25–30; inalienable, 9, 64, 218; protections afforded by, 3, 4, 6, 8, 9, 11, 18, 22–24, 27–30, 41–45, 47, 53, 60, 62, 65, 69, 79, 81, 84, 89, 99, 106, 109, 116, 117, 124–125, 128, 131–138, 218, 222, 268, 274, 279, 285, 321, 331–338, 346; gendering of, 84–87, 207–211; and family integrity, 4, 11, 218, 338; and mobility, 4, 7, 29–30, 44–45, 47–53, 80–81, 125, 127, 134, 139–140, 279, 291, 294, 310, 328, 336, 338; to remain, 7, 29, 338; to resist enslavement, 268; to bear arms, 328; of unborn, 243–244; of children, 55–56, 86–87, 137; women's, 84–87, 207–251; and international law, 41–45, 53, 128; federal protections of, 133, 135; state protections of, 135; racial exclusions from, 8, 10, 18, 64, 128–129, 131–135, 141, 293; mothers' position in relation to, 56, 65, 67, 86–87; violations of, 9, 26, 63, 71, 85, 100; property 3, 9, 13, 18, 29–30, 89, 133–134, 136, 284–285, 287, 288. *See also* birthright; embodied self-sovereignty; law, of nations
Roane, Justice, 118, 119, 121, 134
Royal African Company, 22, 36, 37. *See also* trafficking; transatlantic slave trade
Ruggles, David, 273–276, 280, 296–297, 302, 343; *Mirror of Liberty*, 273–274; *Abrogation of the Seventh Commandment*, 273–274
Rush, Benjamin, 14, 50, 73, 103–104, 143–145, 159, 282; *Address to the Inhabitants of the British Settlement in America. See also* scientific racism; University of Pennsylvania Medical School
Russwurm, John Brown, 141–142, 170, 258–260, 269

Saint Domingue, 56, 83, 84, 112–114, 128, 341. *See also* Haiti
Scars, 16, 311, 320
Scientific racism, 3, 5, 10, 11, 13, 45–47, 65–66, 125–126, 142–148, 153–158, 209, 212, 250, 253, 293–295, 302, 306–308, 310–311, 314, 322, 333–334, 345
Self-ownership, 9, 11, 168. *See also* embodied self-sovereignty; property
Semen, 9, 35, 235; as "seed," 40; raced, 46–47. *See also* bodies; race
Settler colonialism, 8, 12, 32, 44–45, 65–66, 125, 126, 129–130, 158–161, 236; and white female fertility, 236
Sharp, Granville, 49–51, 74, 76, 83; *A Representation of the Injustice and Dangerous Tendency of Tolerating Slavery*, 49
Sims, J. Marion, 239, 244; and surgeries on Betsy, Anarcha, and Lucy, 244. *See also* medicine, racist
Skin, as evidence of race, 2, 10, 14; color of, 21, 34, 36–37, 41, 45–47, 110–111, 142, 146–148, 154; structure of, 36–37, 147–148, 154. *See also* bodies; race
Skulls. *See* crania
Slave catchers, 19, 138, 280, 281, 285, 310, 319, 321–322. *See also* Fugitive Slave Law 1793; Fugitive Slave Law, 1850; kidnapping
Slavery: and transatlantic traffic, 2, 4, 8, 18, 23, 135; as mutual exchange of labor for sustenance, 24–25; inheritable, 4, 10, 118; reproduction of, 9, 135; political economy of, 4, 165; profitability of captives vs. slaves by birth, 118; agricultural productivity of vs. free labor, 165; as theft, 18, 174, 287; as state of war, 308; as "traffic in blood," 182; as prison, 274; likened to disease, 289; as unrepresentable, 226–227, 333; defenders of, 5, 10, 322–327
Smalls, Robert, 257, 341. *See also* manhood
Smith, Gerrit, 182, 185, 186, 274, 308–309, 342; "Letter to the American Slaves from those who have fled from American Slavery," 308
Smith, James McCune, 157, 184, 253, 269–271, 273, 275, 278, 304–305, 339, 343; medical training of, 269; demographic arguments of

Smith, James McCune (continued)
for free labor, 270, 304; "The Fallacy of Phrenology," 269, 304; "Abolition of Slavery and the Slave Trade," 269; "A Lecture on the Haytien Revolutions," 270; "Circulation of the Blood," 270–271; "The Destiny of the People of Color," 271; "Dissertation on the Influence of Climate on Longevity," 304; "Heads of the Colored People: Done with a Whitewash Brush," 305; "On the Fourteenth Query of Thomas Jefferson's Notes on Virginia," 305. *See also* scientific racism
Société des Amis des Noirs, 75–76, 113, 114, 128
Society for Effecting the Abolition of the Slave Trade (SEAST), 74–77, 83, 213
Somerset, James, 47, 49–50
Soul: 6, 27, 40, 41, 48, 49, 51, 82, 84, 98, 106, 204, 226, 258, 262, 263, 287, 302, 340
South Asia: British destruction of lives in, 57, 62, 70; as alternative source of labor, 202–203; and contract labor, 127, 182, 185, 203, 325; cotton produced in, 188, 190, 193, 195
Southampton Rebellion (Nat Turner's Rebellion), 232, 252, 253, 264–267; depictions of, 265–266; as trigger for non-resistant white abolitionism, 267. *See also* Turner, Nat
Species: and blood transfusion, 150, 152–152; and fertility, 157
Speech, public, 1, 2, 10, 285–290, 297–298; health consequences of, 299. *See also* activism
Spillers, Hortense, 16, 358n37
Spurzheim, Johann Gaspar, 155, 156
Stanley, Amy Dru, 324–326
Stewart, Maria W., 231, 343, 345
Still, Letitia, 314, 315, 317, 318, 331, 335. *See also* refugees; Underground Railroad
Still, William, 204, 245, 250, 253, 285, 313–321, 335; family of, 313–314, 343. *See also* refugees; Underground Railroad
Story, Joseph, Justice, 268, 284
Strain, Theodore W., 207–208, 235, 250–251. *See also* physicians; racism, popular; scientific racism
Sturge, John, *Short Review of the Slave Trade and Slavery*, 169, 183. *See also* free labor
Sturge, Joseph, 168–169, 176–178, 181–186, 188, 192, 194–196, 199–200, 203, 205, 279, 286, 288–290; "The Equalization of the Duties on the Tropical Productions by Free Labourers," 182; free labor sugar in Monserrat, 326. *See also* cotton; free labor produce; World Antislavery Convention, 1840
Sturge, Lydia Albright, 182, 186, 200
Sturge, Sophia, 169, 178, 183, 185–186
Sugar: produced by slave labor, 4, 37–41, 86, 164, 203–205, 336–337; maple, 167; produced by free labor, 173, 193, 200–201, 326; boycotts of, 83–84, 180–181, 194, 212, 218, 223. *See also* boycotts; consumers
Sweat, 9, 13, 24, 25, 40, 41, 50, 78, 82, 111, 123, 139, 142, 163, 175, 205, 215, 273, 299, 302, 318

Tabb (mother of co-litigant in *Pleasants v. Pleasants*), 90, 95–96, 105, 117, 122
Taney, Roger, Justice, 268, 284, 327–328. *See also Dred Scott v. Sanford*
Tappan, Lewis, 182, 186, 188, 224
Taylor, George Washington, 186, 187–202, 205–206. *See also* Chester County, Pa.; cotton; Philadelphia Free Produce Society of Friends; Rhoads, Samuel; sugar
Tears, 13, 123, 124, 135, 142, 148, 163, 175, 204, 205, 207, 210, 215–217, 220, 233–235, 252, 260, 306, 308
Thomas, Nathan, 189–192, 196–200, 205, 298; wife of, 196–197. *See also* Coffin, Levi; cotton; Philadelphia Free Produce Society of Friends
Tobacco, 4, 164, 205, 337
Trafficking: of enslaved Africans, 22, 29–30, 47, 72, 92, 98, 108, 111, 114, 135, 138; of cadavers, 145, 151, 153; U.S. internal, of enslaved African Americans, 130, 161, 288. *See also* transatlantic slave trade
Transatlantic slave trade, 22, 29–30, 41–44, 47, 66; as evidence of British cruelty, 62, 65; political efforts to end, 72; abolished by Britain, 127; abolished by the United States, 135. *See also* trafficking
Transportation: coerced, 65, 125, 127, 162–163; as punishment, 26, 28–30, 80–81, 134; fictive consent to, 49, 80; of convicts, 80–81, 126–127. *See also* American Colonization Society; Botany Bay; Liberia
Truth, Sojourner, 207–209, 220, 235–236, 245–251, 297, 330–331, 344; and "The Slave Mother," 246–249. *See also* enslaved women; motherhood
Tryon, Thomas, 37–41, 53, 128; *Friendly Advice to the Gentlemen-Planters of the East and West Indies*; 38–41

Tubman, Harriet, 258, 315, 341–342, 344
Tucker, St. George, 116, 133–134
Turner, Nat, 262, 264, 266, 268, 277, 330; body of, 264, 341. *See also* Southampton Rebellion
Types of Mankind, 293, 310. *See also* Douglass, Frederick; Gliddon, George; Nott, Josiah
Tyranny, 55, 57, 65, 71, 73; and subject's body, 23–24, 26–27

Underground Railroad, 19, 135, 172, 173, 180, 184, 189, 245, 249, 250, 255, 271–275; free Black support of, 271–277, 279–285, 293, 311–322, 335. *See also* Fugitive Slave Law, 1793; Fugitive Slave Law, 1850; refugees
United States: and end of transatlantic slave trade, 134–135; as homeland for people of African descent, 123–125, 139, 142, 161–162; and internal trafficking of enslaved people, 120–131,161, 288; and repurposing of settler colonialism, 129–130; and jurisdictional conflicts over refugees, 4, 9–10, 135–139, 210, 283–284, 294, 319–322; and repudiation of citizenship rights for African-descended people, 19, 295–296, 327–334, 338, 339
University of Pennsylvania Medical School, 143, 145, 146, 148–149, 151–157, 235–245; medical theses: 148–149, 152, 158–161, 235–245; southern student enrollment, 154–155, 237. *See also* Horner, William; Pennsylvania Hall; scientific racism

Vattel, Emer de, 43–45, 47, 60, 66, 124–125, 142; *Law of Nations*, 43–44. *See also* law of nations; mercantilism; natural rights
Vesey, Denmark, 158–159, 257, 262, 277, 330, 341
Vigilance Committees, 2, 181, 279–280, 343; New York Vigilance Committee, 273–274, 280. *See also* Philadelphia Vigilance Committee; Purvis, Robert; refugees; Ruggles, David; Underground Railroad
Virginia, 12, 13, 19, 34, 46, 88–122, 128–135, 139, 144, 149, 153–155, 158–161, 168, 182, 184, 224, 230, 239, 241, 247, 259, 264, 266, 267, 274, 278, 282, 285, 290, 295, 305, 308, 317–320, 322, 323, 327, 331, 336, 344, 345; codification of maternal inheritance, 13, 19, 89; 1782 Manumission Act, 108–109; internal slave trafficking from, 120–131; restrictions on free Black people, 132–134; escapes of enslaved people from, 135–136, 278, 290, 294–295, 317–328; Racial Integrity Act of 1929, 345
Virginia Abolition Society (VAS), 111–113. *See also* Pleasants, Robert

Wage labor, 295, 324–325, 346–347. *See also* free labor
Walker, David, 254, 260–261, 263, 277; *Appeal to the Colored Citizens of the United States*, 260–261, 264, 266
Washington, George, 111, 164, 186. *See also* Pleasants, Robert
Washington, Madison, 277, 290–291. *See also* Douglass, Frederick
Watkins, Frances Ellen (Harper), 204, 206, 220, 233–235, 297, 339, 343; "The Slave Mother," 233–235, 331–332; "Bury Me in a Free Land," 335–337, 339, 341
Webster, Daniel, 319, 320. *See also* refugees; Underground Railroad
Wedgwood, Joseph, 74–76
Weld, Theodore, 185, 223, 288, 298; *American Slavery as It Is*, 288. *See also* Grimké, Angelina; Grimké, Sarah
West Indies, planters, 73, 176; political lobby of, 50, 60, 83
Wheatley, John and Susannah, 47, 49, 52
Wheatley, Phillis, 7, 47–55, 56, 341; "On Imagination," 48; *Poems on Various Subjects, Religious and Moral*, 51
Whipper, William, 253, 272–273, 275, 278; and nonviolent resistance, 272–273; and slavery's toll on the body, 272–273
White hostility: towards Black people, 91, 106, 108–109, 115, 279, 336; triggered by enslaved men's expressions of manhood, 255–256. *See also* mob violence; racism; white supremacy
White, Jacob C., Jr., 203, 206, 305. *See also* Institute for Colored Youth
White, Jacob C., Sr., 280, 282, 285; medical practice of, 280; as proprietor of Lebanon Cemetery, 203, 285, 317; as founder of Gilbert Lyceum, 302
White, Lydia, 170–171, 174, 180, 186. *See also* free labor produce
White supremacy, 5, 10, 18, 20, 128, 157, 258, 262–264, 273, 323, 329, 342. *See also* mob violence; racism; white hostility
Whiteness, and commodification of slave-produced goods, 173, 204–206. *See also* free labor produce
Whittier, John Greenleaf, 185, 202, 230, 288; "Farewell of a Virginia Slave Mother," 230. *See also* Sturge, Joseph

Wilberforce, William, 76–77, 128, 168, 212; speech to Parliament on transatlantic slave trade, 76–77
Will: bodily incarnation of, 5, 291; subordination of, 23, 53, 310; domination of by others, 24; expressions of, 109; violations of, 131. *See also* embodied self-sovereignty
Williamson, Passmore, 285, 311, 320–322
Wollstonecraft, Mary, 7, 79–87, 212, 219, 222, 249; *Vindication of the Rights of Men*, 79–83; *Vindication of the Rights of Woman*, 84–87
Wombs: status of, defined by law, 4, 119, 122; claims on, 101; as spaces of liberty, 220. *See also* birth; maternal inheritance
Women's Medical College of Pennsylvania (WMCP), 1, 301, 343–344, 347
Woolman, John, 34, 49, 97, 362n.47; *Some Considerations on the Keeping of Negroes*, 34; *Epistle of Caution and Advice*, 34; visit to New Garden, N.C., 131
World Anti-Slavery Convention: 1840 (London), 182–184, 186; 1843 (London), 186
Wright, Paulina (Davis), 299–300, 302; medical education of, 300. *See also* health

Zong massacre, 69–70, 76

Acknowledgments

It is a privilege to live a life devoted to teaching and learning. I have been blessed with opportunities beyond my wildest imaginings. Gerda Lerner's work on the abolitionist Grimké sisters and Dorothy Sterling's impeccably researched biographies and primary source compendium on African American women have provided a strong foundation for my own work. I have learned much from the recent historical literature on abolition, a topic that has seen a resurgence of interest since 2008. Works by Britt Rusert, Rana Hogarth, Daina Ramey Berry, and April Haynes have inspired me to rethink what I thought I knew about nineteenth-century gender, race, and the body, and encouraged me to think about abolition in relation to the history of medicine, labor history, and the history of the body. I have also learned a great deal from the works of Elizabeth Varon, Christopher Willoughby, William Fernandez Hardin, and Jesse Olsavsky. Being a series coeditor at Penn Press has given me the opportunity to learn from the authors with whom I have been privileged to work, including Jen Manion, Sasha Turner, Marisa Fuentes, Jennifer Morgan, Sophie White, Jessica Johnson, Bethel Saler, Randy Browne, Sharon Block, Mairin Odle, and Laurel Clark Shire. I am grateful to all of these scholars and hope that they can see the significance of their work for my own.

Funding for research and time to think are privileges. My thanks to the University of Pennsylvania Department of History and the deans of the School of Arts and Sciences for supporting academic leaves that made it possible for me to work on my book. I am deeply grateful for the David Boies Chair of History, which has supported my research. A Guggenheim Fellowship in 2015 enabled me to complete a large portion of the research and writing. Without the support from Ellen Dubois, Nancy Hewitt, David Barnes, and Bruce Dorsey, I could not have gained this funding.

My research was made pleasant and rewarding by librarians at many institutions. Special thanks to Sandy Treadway and the staff at the Library of Virginia; the staff at the Earl Gregg Swem Library Special Collections; the staff at the Alderman Library at the University of Virginia; Christopher Densmore at Friends Historical Library of Swarthmore College; Sarah Horowitz and the staff at the

Quaker and Special Collections at Haverford College; the Historical Society of Pennsylvania; the College of Physicians; John Pollack and the staff at the Kislak Center of Van Pelt Library at the University of Pennsylvania; Mark Lloyd and Jim Duffin at Penn's University Archives; the staff at the Bodleian Library Manuscript Room; and the staff at the Library of the Society of Friends, London. I am grateful to Stephanie Arias at the Huntington Library, and Jordan Landes at Friends Historical Library for timely assistance with illustration permissions.

Several individuals assisted with the research for this book. Agnès Trouillet helped me identify French race theorists; Paul Wolff Mitchell offered feedback on phrenology, craniology, and racist science; and Dani Holtz helped me find my way through the works of Bodin and Grotius. Scott Wilds, genealogist extraordinaire, saved me from many errors and provided crucial assistance with the genealogical tangle of the Pleasants family.

I am always a bit reticent about asking people to read my drafts, so I am especially grateful to those who do. Bruce Dorsey and the anonymous reader for Penn Press offered encouragement and important criticism. Bruce Kuklick read an early version of the manuscript and offered steady friendship throughout the many years it has taken me to finish it. My wonderful former student Cassie Good generously slogged through several early drafts. At a late stage in the manuscript, Dan Richter gave me honest feedback about its shortcomings. Jim Downs provided a tough response to the introduction and modeled a better approach. My clear-thinking former student Jessie Regunberg helped me out of an intellectual cul-de-sac. Madhavi Kale read a version of the Introduction and listened to my endless ramblings about bodies. Sally Gordon and Sarah Gronningsater patiently answered my last-minute questions about legal citation, motherhood, and citizenship and put me on to Kris Collins, who responded generously and thoughtfully to my queries.

Pandemic closures and isolation affected how and what I could consult as I finished this work. This is not an excuse for the book's shortcomings, but a fact of its production that made me more than ordinarily reliant on the kindness of friends and colleagues. I don't know what I would have done without the wit, wisdom, and friendship of Madhavi, Lynn Lees, Barbara Savage, Bruce K., Carrie Cohen, Kristen Stromberg Childers, Ann Farnsworth-Alvear, Gwendolyn Beetham, Maria Murphy, Shana Bahemat, Jonathan Katz, Ann Itzkowitz, Tracey Weis, and Jackie and Stu Cohen. I am also grateful for the collegiality and intellectual rigor of Sarah, Sally, Dan, Beth Wenger, Eve Troutt Powell, Amy Offner, Emma Hart, Walter Licht, Ben Nathans, and Nancy Hirschmann.

Learning from one's own students is an amazing experience. I have been inspired by the wonderful students who made the Penn and Slavery Project into a vital research endeavor. VanJessica Gladney, Matthew Palczynski, Dillon

Kersh, Caitlin Doolittle, and Brooke Krancer pioneered the project and set a high bar for research excellence. Carson Eckhard, Archana Upadhyay, Sam Orloff, Ashley Waiters, Bryan Anderson-Wooten, Anna Lowenstein, Grace Cho, Breanna Moore, and Dallas Taylor took it to new topics and places. Arielle Julia Brown and Alexis Broderick Neuman helped to guide the project and taught me much. Thanks to Department Chair Beth Wenger, Provost Wendell Pritchett, and Vice President Joanne Mitchell for supporting the project. The students, with help from faculty and staff, created an augmented reality tour of Penn's campus (accessed through the Penn and Slavery Project website http://pennandslaveryproject.org) that enhanced my understanding of the body's engagement with landscape and environment and expanded my view of what it meant to produce and share knowledge. I am grateful to Tim Holliday, Archana, Carson, Arielle Alterwaite, and Anders Bright, for reading my manuscript and offering helpful feedback.

I learned a great deal from the questions and comments of participants at several seminars and public lectures. My thanks to engaged audiences at the McNeil Center for Early American Studies, Steve Hahn's U.S. Nineteenth Century Seminar, the University of Virginia, the University of Connecticut, the Australia-New Zealand American Studies Association conferences in 2010 and 2019, Rutgers University Center for Historical Analysis, New York University, Yale University, Marquette University, Davidson College, Loyola New Orleans, Carleton College, University of Paris VIII, the Delaware Valley British Studies Association run by Lynn and Seth Koven, and Mike Zuckerman's salon. Being in residence as Cambridge University's Pitt Professor of American History and Institutions during 2021–2022 made it possible for me to benefit from the wisdom of the Cambridge American History Seminar. I am especially grateful for Nick Guyatt's probing comment and the questions of Gary Gerstle, Theresa Singleton, and Bobby Lee.

Publishing with Penn Press has been a wonderful decision. Peter Agree's early encouragement about the project was sustaining. Having collaborated with Bob Lockhart as a series editor at Penn Press for nearly twenty years, I knew him to be smart, diligent, and generous; working with him on *Undoing Slavery* has only deepened my respect. His editorial guidance has been superb and he has been very generous in reading portions of the manuscript several times. Noreen O'Connor-Abel and Sara Lickey have made the copyediting a useful learning experience; I appreciate their time and effort.

I am grateful for my family's support. My mother, Sheila Brown, has always encouraged my research and writing. Ted Pearson has gamely co-parented our three children, cared for our daughter's dog, and read my long-winded chapter drafts. William, Owen, and Emily crossed the divide between childhood and young adulthood while I worked on this book. Thanks to them, I occasionally cleared off the dining room table so that we could have a family meal together. William generously shared his talents as a graphic designer to create art for the book that ultimately did not become the book's cover, but that nonetheless crystallized my own thinking about the book's larger argument. During the process of writing this book, I had the unexpected joy of getting to know my half-sister, Anne Trotter.

My husband, Angus Corbett, has brought a generous spirit, a sharp intellect, and many valuable practical skills to our family. He has been my rock for these last thirteen years through crises, big and small, and patiently waded through many manuscript drafts. Being a stepparent is never easy, but he has persisted and brought out the best in all of us. I am grateful for the Corbett family's warm welcome to new family members: thank you to all, but especially to Charm and David. This book is dedicated to Angus and to the memory of his father, David Corbett, whose interest in me and my work touched me deeply. He is greatly missed.